*Permanent Observer Mission
of the Holy See to the United Nations*

*Path to Peace Foundation
New York City*

SERVING THE HUMAN FAMILY
*The Holy See at the Major
United Nations Conferences*

FOREWORDS BY

His Eminence Angelo Cardinal Sodano
Secretary of State

His Excellency Archbishop Jean-Louis Tauran
Secretary for Relations with States

His Excellency Archbishop Renato R. Martino
*Apostolic Nuncio, Permanent Observer of the Holy See
to the United Nations*

Monsignor Carl J. Marucci, *Editor*

The Path to Peace Foundation
New York City
1997

Serving the Human Family: The Holy See at the Major United Nations Conferences / Forewords by Angelo Sodano, Jean-Louis Tauran, Renato R. Martino; Carl J. Marucci, editor.

At head of title: Permanent Observer Mission of the Holy See to the United Nations; Path to Peace Foundation.
Includes index.

Copyright © 1997, The Path to Peace Foundation, New York City
All Rights Reserved. No part of this book may be reproduced without written permission from the publisher. The Path to Peace Foundation, 25 East 39th Street, New York, New York 10016-0903; (212) 370-7885.

ISBN 0-9651613-2-3

1. Church and social problems — Catholic Church. 2. Church and international organization — Catholic Church. I. Marucci, Carl J., 1958-- II. Catholic Church. Permanent Observer Mission of the Holy See to the United Nations. III. Path to Peace Foundation.
HN37.C3S455 1997
261.8'3 — dc21

97-40759
CIP

Cover Photography
United Nations Headquarters-U.N. Photo 185522/A. Brizzi 1063L
Saint Peter's Basilica, Vatican City-Arturo Mari/L'Osservatore Romano

"... Fifty years after its founding, the need for such an Organization *(the United Nations)* is even more obvious, but we also have a better understanding, on the basis of experience, that the effectiveness of this great instrument for harmonizing and coordinating international life depends on the international culture and ethic which it supports and expresses. . . The United Nations Organization needs to rise more and more above the cold status of an administrative institution and to become a moral centre where all the nations of the world feel at home and develop a shared awareness of being, as it were a "family of nations." The idea of "family" immediately evokes something more than simple functional relations or a mere convergence of interests. The family is by nature a community based on mutual trust, mutual support and sincere respect. In an authentic family the strong do not dominate; instead, the weaker members, because of their very weakness, are all the more welcomed and served."

— Address of His Holiness Pope John Paul II to the Fiftieth General Assembly of the United Nations Organization, New York, 5 October 1995, no. 14.

FOREWORD BY
HIS EMINENCE ANGELO CARDINAL SODANO
SECRETARY OF STATE

Over a half century ago in San Francisco, the Charter of the United Nations was signed by representatives of nations who came together for a distinct purpose: to create an international organization dedicated:

> *"to save generations from the scourge of war . . . and to reaffirm faith in fundamental human rights, in the dignity and worth of the human person, in the equal rights of men and women and of nations large and small, and to establish conditions under which justice and respect for the obligations arising from treaties and other sources of international law can be maintained, and to promote social progress and better standards of life in larger freedom."*
> *(Preamble)*

As we approach the new millennium, we reflect on how well or how poorly the nations of the world have fared in living out the hopes and dreams enumerated in the Charter. This era continues to demonstrate the existence of wars and conflicts not just *among* nations, but *within* them. And yet, modern times have offered us moments of great promise as we witnessed the successful dismantling of concrete walls and iron curtains which separated one people from another.

In his celebrated speech before the United Nations General Assembly on 4 October 1965, Pope Paul VI stressed the important role played by the United Nations, when he said that it *"represents the obligatory path of modern civilization and of world peace."* And at the United Nations the Holy See willingly takes its place among the community of nations in order to combat effectively the *reasons of force* with the *force of reason.* The Holy See's activity at the United Nations has as its focus the *human person* — every person — regardless of race, religion, sex or nationality. It seeks to uphold the dignity of the human person both by enunciating principles of a general nature and by materially serving the needs of the human family, particularly the poorest and most oppressed. The Church considers herself, in the words of Pope Paul VI, an *"expert in humanity,"* and able to speak in the international forum on behalf of the human person.

Unlike secular nations which understandably must be concerned about their Gross National Product, about the political and military balance of power, about balances of trade and national prestige, the Holy See is a *"disinterested"* State, in the sense that the usual aims of national politics are not part of its international agenda. At the United Nations the Holy See can thus speak about international matters from a very different and far less self-interested perspective. Given the Church's universal nature and the worldwide Pastorate of the Roman Pontiff, the Holy See speaks with a deep, universal concern for all nations and peoples in all regions of the world, without aligning itself with any particular region or geographic group within the family of nations.

"Serving the Human Family: The Holy See at the Major United Nations Conferences," presents the Holy See's efforts to defend and promote the human person, individually and collectively, at United Nations-sponsored meetings dealing with important topics affecting the human family. The Holy See's interventions at these Conferences echo the sentiments of His Holiness Pope John Paul II in his 1995 Address to the members of the Diplomatic Corps accredited to the Holy See, where he stated:

> *"What is at stake is the transcendent dimension of man: this can never be made subject to the whims of statesmen or ideologies. . . There is a morality of service to the earthly city which excludes not only corruption but, even more, ambiguity and the surrender of principles. The Holy See considers itself at the service of this reawakening of conscience."*

The entire human family groans from within as it awaits a rebirth in solidarity, and it yearns for the day when every nation — developed and developing, large and small — is enabled and encouraged to offer the contribution of its humanity and culture to the building of the common good. It is my wish that this publication will be a witness to the service of the Holy See to the human family.

✠ **ANGELO CARDINAL SODANO**
Secretary of State

Foreword by
His Excellency Archbishop Jean-Louis Tauran
Secretary for Relations with States

The Holy See possesses a diplomatic service whose origins date back to the beginnings of the permanent Diplomatic Missions, which were initiated with the rise of the modern States in the fifteenth century. A natural outflow of the Holy See's concept of active participation in the life of the international community has been its firm support of the activity of the United Nations. Certainly the Popes, since the time of Pope Pius XII, have expressed words of appreciation and affirmation — and at times words of challenge and exhortation — as the U.N. strives to make its mission of peace a reality.

The Holy See has supported the United Nations Organization not only in its words but in its actions. Prior to its official establishment as a Permanent Observer Mission in 1964, the Holy See had already come into contact with the United Nations system. From 1946-47 to 1952, the Holy See participated in the activities of the IOR *(International Organization for Refugees)*, which was instituted and charged by the U.N. to deal with the problem of refugees. And in 1951 when the IOR became the UNHCR *(United Nations High Commissioner for Refugees)*, the Holy See was one of the first members of its Executive Committee.

On 23 November 1948, the Holy See appointed an Observer to the FAO *(Food and Agriculture Organization)*. Since the transfer of FAO from Washington to Rome in 1951, relations between the Holy See and this organization have been even closer. Rarely has there been a session of the FAO without its participants having been received by the Holy Father.

One might not be aware that the Holy See was one of the founding members of the IAEA *(International Atomic Energy Agency)*, participating in the process which brought about the Conference of Plenipotentiaries which, begun on 26 October 1956, established the said agency. The Secretary General of the United Nations, Dag Hammarskjöld, attached great importance to the Holy See's participation at this Conference, since he was convinced that its presence was a signal of irrefutable proof of the peaceful intentions and purposes of that endeavor. Likewise, since the summer of that same year the Holy See has been represented at the meetings of ECOSOC *(Economic and Social Council of the United Nations)*.

Since the establishment of the ILO *(International Labor*

Organization) in 1919, Mr. Albert Thomas, the organization's founder, often stressed the importance of the Holy See's collaboration, about which he spoke openly in the plenary sessions of the organization. It was this same individual who deemed necessary the presence of an Advisor for Socio-Religious Affairs on the staff of the ILO office. Since 1967 the activities of the ILO have been officially followed by a representative of the Holy See.

In May 1951, during the 26th Session of UNESCO *(United Nations Educational, Scientific and Cultural Organization)*, which established rules for non-member States wishing to send a Permanent Observer to this body, the Holy See immediately expressed its great interest. Utilizing these new provisions, the Holy See appointed its first Observer in the person of then Apostolic Nuncio to France, Archbishop Angelo Roncalli, who later became Pope John XXIII. Later, in 1953, the Holy See appointed a full time Observer to UNESCO.

Since 1952, the Holy See has also been represented at the World Health Assemblies and, beginning in 1967, the Holy See Observer in Geneva has served also as Observer at WHO *(World Health Organization)*.

In a 21 March 1964 letter to Mr. U Thant, then Secretary-General of the United Nations, the Secretary of State expressed the desire of the Holy See to establish more stable relations with the United Nations. In that same year, the Holy See sent its first Permanent Observer to the United Nations. U Thant responded that this decision of the Holy See demonstrated, once again, its interest in the activities of the United Nations Organization, and that this was cause for rejoicing. And on 1 February 1967 an Observer Mission was likewise established at the Office of the United Nations in Geneva.

This publication, *"Serving the Human Family: The Holy See at the Major United Nations Conferences,"* is a compilation of the official statements made by representatives of the Holy See at major United Nations Summits and Conferences, beginning with the World Summit for Children in 1990. The work also contains an extensive appendix of important documents related to the themes of the conferences. The Holy See is pleased to place this edition at the disposal of the diplomatic community. It is also intended for those wishing to learn more about the official positions of the Holy See on these topics. As such, it is an important resource which should be included in all seminary, university or personal libraries.

✠ **ARCHBISHOP JEAN-LOUIS TAURAN**
Secretary for Relations with States

Foreword by
His Excellency Archbishop Renato R. Martino
Apostolic Nuncio, Permanent Observer of the
Holy See to the United Nations

In 1995, the United Nations celebrated its Fiftieth Anniversary, and for more than thirty years, the Holy See has participated officially in the work of the Organization as an Observer Mission.

Beginning in 1990, the United Nations sponsored a series of International Summits, Conferences and Meetings, dealing with important issues such as human rights, environment and development, population, social development, women, children, natural disaster reduction, small island developing States, human settlements, and food resources and distribution. The discussions and deliberations were of great importance, particularly in view of their vision, plans of action, and their impact upon individuals, families and nations around the world.

As the Holy See is an active participant in international diplomacy, it is my desire at the outset of this publication, to offer the reader some brief reflections on Vatican diplomacy, with particular emphasis on the Holy See's representation at the United Nations.

Since the fourth century, the Holy See has sent and received diplomatic missions. For many centuries, the Vicar of Christ held temporal control over the Papal States, which initially included a broad band of territory across central Italy, as well as the city of Rome. In 1861, at the time of the general unification of Italy, almost all of the lands under Papal sovereignty were occupied by the Kingdom of Italy. However, the Holy See continued to regard itself as a separate entity in international law, having already been recognized as such by numerous States with which it retained normal diplomatic relations. On 11 February 1929 the Holy See and Italy resolved the *"Questione Romana"* by signing the Lateran Treaty *(which was ratified on 7 June 1929)*. By means of the Treaty Vatican City State came into existence. Article 12 of the Treaty notes that diplomatic relations with the Holy See are governed by the rules of International Law. Years later, the Vienna Convention on Diplomatic Relations (1961), convened for the purpose of codifying diplomatic law, went even further by formally recognizing the practice accepted by any receiving State regarding the precedence of the representative of the Holy See within the Diplomatic Corps (Art. 16, §3).

In my travels I have come to learn that many confuse two related, albeit not identical, terms — *"Holy See"* and *"Vatican City."* For clarification purposes, I would like to note that Vatican City is the physical or territorial base of the Holy See, almost a pedestal upon which is posed a much larger and unique independent and sovereign power: that of the Universal Church, respected and esteemed by many, suspected and combated by others, yet always present by its stature, its history and its influence in the international forum. The State of Vatican City itself also possesses a personality under international law and, because of such, enters into international agreements. However, it is the ***Holy See*** which internationally represents Vatican City State. In fact, when the Holy See enters into agreements for Vatican City State, it uses the formula: *"acting on behalf and in the interest of the State of Vatican City."* In October 1957, in order to avoid uncertainty in its relations with the United Nations, it was affirmed that relations are established between the United Nations and the Holy See. And it is the Holy See which is represented by the Delegations accredited by the Secretariat of State to international organizations.

In the *Listing of Country Names*, published annually by the United Nations, a note is added to the Holy See's entry, stating that — in United Nations documents — the term *"Holy See"* is to be used except in texts concerning the International Telecommunications Union and the Universal Postal Union, where the term *"Vatican City State"* is to be used. States, then, do not entertain diplomatic relations with Vatican City State, but with the Holy See.

Basically, the term *"Holy See"* refers to the supreme authority of the Church, that is the Pope as Bishop of Rome and head of the college of Bishops. It is the central government of the Roman Catholic Church. As such, the Holy See is an institution which, under international law and in practice, has a legal personality that allows it to enter into treaties as the juridical equal of a State and to send and receive diplomatic representatives. As noted above, it is the *"Holy See"* that is present at United Nations Headquarters in New York and at U.N. centers abroad, as well as at other international organizations such as the European Community, the Organization of American States, etc. At the time of this publication, the Holy See maintains full diplomatic relations with one-hundred sixty-eight (168) countries, many of which are not of Catholic tradition and belong to non-Western and non-Christian cultures.

A question often asked is: "Why does the Holy See take such an active part in the international forum?" And why do so many countries seek official contacts with the Holy See? Political support or material aid they will certainly not expect. What they do seek is what the Holy See, by its very nature and tradition, can offer: orientation and spiritual inspiration that should animate the life of nations and their mutual relationships.

The Holy See enjoys by its own choice the status of *Permanent Observer* at the United Nations, rather than of a full Member. This is due primarily to the desire of the Holy See to maintain absolute neutrality in specific political problems. Full membership would involve the Holy See too directly in political, military, economic and commercial matters. As a full Member the Holy See would be obliged to abstain too often in these areas, due to the fact that it would go beyond the scope of its own specific mission.

The representatives of the Holy See at the United Nations and most of its agencies are Observers and participate in their activities as such. This being said, when the United Nations organizes world conferences on matters of universal interest, the invitation is sent to all States or States Members of the United Nations and States Members of U.N. agencies. As the Holy See fills both of these categories it has participated, within the past decade, in the many conferences and meetings on important topics discussed in this book.

The Holy See has actively participated in the work of the United Nations, both formally and informally, since the Organization's beginnings, and shall continue to do so in the future. For more than ten years I have had the opportunity to serve as Permanent Observer of the Holy See to the United Nations. In that time, I have seen firsthand how important is the participation of the Holy See in international dialogue, since it is a voice that both transcends geographical boundaries, while at the same time embraces all cultures. Through mutual dialogue and exchange, may the nations of the world move more and more away from the selfishness of individual agendas, and toward the goals of true freedom and lasting peace based upon the overarching truth of what really fulfills man — individually and as a world community.

At this point I would like to offer an expression of deep gratitude — in my own name as well as on behalf of those in whose hands this book will fall — to my associate, Monsignor Carl J. Marucci, for his tireless good work in coordinating and editing this important publication.

✠ **ARCHBISHOP RENATO R. MARTINO**
Apostolic Nuncio, Permanent Observer of the
Holy See to the United Nations

PRELIMINARY NOTE BY
MONSIGNOR CARL J. MARUCCI, EDITOR
ATTACHÉ, PERMANENT OBSERVER MISSION OF THE HOLY SEE
TO THE UNITED NATIONS

"Serving the Human Family: The Holy See at the Major United Conferences" is a publication of the **PATH TO PEACE FOUNDATION**, which was established in 1991 for the purpose of spreading the message of peace by which the Catholic Church, through the words and activities of the Holy Father and of the Holy See, strives to "guide our steps into the path of peace" *(Luke 1:79)*.

The Foundation, independent from but in collaboration with the Holy See Mission, directs its activities primarily, albeit not exclusively, to the international stage of the United Nations. It disseminates information and documentation on statements and initiatives of the Holy Father, of the Holy See and of Catholic Organizations. By doing so it helps them in their work of building a world of justice, charity and peace; of initiating programs, such as conferences, seminars, and lectures to study the Church's social teaching; and in promoting cultural initiatives which touch on the Christian heritage of art, music and the humanities. Additionally, the Foundation fosters projects of a religious, conciliatory, humanitarian and charitable nature with a view to promoting fundamental human rights by calling attention to specific emergency needs arising in different parts of the world.

This publication has already enjoyed significant interest and support from individuals and organizations around the world, since it is a single compilation of the many valuable statements which the Holy See has pronounced at United Nations meetings on such vital topics as the family, children, women, the environment, population, development and human rights.

It would be practical at the outset of this endeavor to offer the reader a note of explanation on the outline of the edition. Each of the chapters are organized according to the following format:

- *Messages and Addresses of the Holy Father*, i.e. Messages to Heads of Conferences, Addresses at the General Audiences and on the occasions of the weekly Angelus or Regina Coeli;

- *National Reports of the Holy See* on Conference themes;

- *Statements by the Secretary of State*;

- *Statements offered by Heads of the Pontifical Councils* on particular Conference themes;

- *Interventions offered by Members of the Holy See Delegation*, in date order;

- *Interviews and Press Releases*.

The reader will also note an extensive Appendix containing related documents which are not directly connected to an actual Conference itself, i.e. Letters of the Holy Father to Children, Women, etc.; Pontifical Council documents related to Conference themes, i.e. *"World Hunger, A Challenge For All,"* (issued by the Pontifical Council *"Cor Unum"*); Interventions of the Holy See Delegation during the United Nations General Assembly and other Meetings; Statements issued by Episcopal Conferences and Organizations around the world.

A detailed Index has also been added at the end of the publication to offer the reader greater access to particular topics.

Finally, the reader will notice that *"Serving the Human Family: The Holy See at the Major United Nations Conferences,"* while thorough, is not exhaustive. Certainly there exist numerous other statements issued by Episcopal Conferences, Catholic Organizations and individuals. This book aims primarily to present official statements made by the Holy Father and the Holy See Delegation in connection with these important United Nations meetings, and to offer relevant documents and interventions not immediately connected with a particular Conference.

I am very pleased to have the task of coordinating and editing this important edition, for which our offices have received countless requests. It is my hope that it will serve as an instrument of Truth that will help man to more fully realize that which will truly fulfill him as he journeys, both individually and collectively, toward the God who has created him and who calls him to Himself.

MONSIGNOR CARL J. MARUCCI
Editor
Attaché, Permanent Observer Mission of the
Holy See to the United Nations

TABLE OF CONTENTS

Foreword by His Eminence Angelo Cardinal Sodano
Secretary of State of His Holiness 7

Foreword by His Excellency Archbishop Jean-Louis Tauran
Secretary for Relations with States 9

Foreword by His Excellency Archbishop Renato R. Martino
Apostolic Nuncio, Permanent Observer of the Holy See
to the United Nations 11

Preliminary Note by Monsignor Carl J. Marucci, *Editor*
Attaché, Permanent Observer Mission of the Holy See
to the United Nations 15

Table of Contents 17
List of Abbreviations/Acronyms/Scripture Text Abbreviations 37

Chapter 1: The World Summit for Children
United Nations Headquarters, New York; 29 - 30 September 1990 39

    Introduction by His Excellency Archbishop Renato R. Martino
    Apostolic Nuncio, Permanent Observer of the Holy See
    to the United Nations 43

    Message of His Holiness Pope John Paul II
    to His Excellency Javier Pérez de Cuéllar, Secretary-General
    of the United Nations; 22 September 1990 47

    Address of His Holiness Pope John Paul II
    at the General Audience, St. Peter's Square
    26 September 1990 51

    Homily of His Eminence Agostino Cardinal Casaroli,
    Secretary of State, at a Mass in the presence of Heads of
    State or Government and their Delegations to the
    World Summit for Children; New York, 29 September 1990 ... 52

    Intervention of His Eminence Agostino Cardinal Casaroli
    Secretary of State, at the World Summit for Children
    New York, 30 September 1990 56

Contribution of Monsignor Henri Bodet,
    Secretary-General of the Pontifical Mission Aid Society
    of the Holy Childhood 58

Statement by His Excellency Archbishop Renato R. Martino,
    Apostolic Nuncio, Permanent Observer of the Holy See
    to the U.N., before the Third Committee of the U.N.
    General Assembly on Item 108: "Adoption of a Convention
    on the Rights of the Child"
    New York, 13 November 1989 61

Statement by His Excellency Archbishop Renato R. Martino,
    Apostolic Nuncio, Permanent Observer of the Holy See
    to the U.N., at the Meeting of the Executive Board
    of UNICEF; New York, 17 April 1990 64

Statement by His Excellency Archbishop Renato R. Martino,
    Apostolic Nuncio, Permanent Observer of the Holy See
    to the U.N., on the Occasion of the Accession of the Holy See
    to the Convention on the Rights of the Child
    New York, 20 April 1990 67

    and Declaration and Reservations on the Occasion of the
    Accession of the Holy See to the Convention on the Rights
    of the Child; New York, 20 April 1990 69

Statement by His Excellency Archbishop Renato R. Martino,
    Apostolic Nuncio, Permanent Observer of the Holy See
    to the U.N., before the Third Committee of the U.N.
    General Assembly on Item 97: "Implementation of the
    Convention on the Rights of the Child"
    New York, 14 November 1990 71

Statement by Mr. John M. Klink to the Regular Session of the
    Executive Board of UNICEF
    New York, 24 April 1991 73

The Holy See's Initial Report to the Committee on the Rights
    of the Child in Application of Article 44 of the Convention
    2 March 1994 76

Summary Note on the Holy See's Participation at the
    World Summit for Children
    by Mr. John Klink 100

Serving the Human Family: The Holy See at the Major U.N. Conferences 19

Chapter 2: The United Nations Conference on Environment and Development
Rio de Janeiro, Brazil; 1 - 13 June 1992 . . . . **105**

    Address of His Holiness Pope John Paul II
        before the Angelus, St. Peter's Square; 31 May 1992 109

    Memorandum on the Holy See's Position on Environment
        and Development *(published in L'Osservatore Romano,*
        English edition, N. 23, 10 June 1992) 111

    Statement by His Eminence Angelo Cardinal Sodano,
        Secretary of State of His Holiness, at the Summit of the
        U.N. Conference on Environment and Development
        Rio de Janeiro, Brazil, 13 June 1992 115

    Statement by His Excellency Archbishop Renato R. Martino,
        Apostolic Nuncio, Permanent Observer of the Holy See
        to the U.N., before the Second Committee on Item 77:
        "Development and International Cooperation
        — e) Environment"; New York, 20 November 1991 118

    Statement by His Excellency Archbishop Renato R. Martino,
        Apostolic Nuncio, Permanent Observer of the Holy See
        to the U.N., Head of the Holy See Delegation to the
        U.N. Conference on Environment and Development
        Rio de Janeiro, Brazil, 4 June 1992 122

    Statement by His Excellency Archbishop Renato R. Martino,
        Apostolic Nuncio, Permanent Observer of the Holy See
        to the U.N., before the Plenary Session of the General
        Assembly, on Item 79: "Report of the U.N. Conference
        on Environment and Development"
        New York, 6 November 1992 129

    Statement by His Excellency Archbishop Renato R. Martino,
        Apostolic Nuncio, Permanent Observer of the Holy See
        to the U.N., before the Second Committee of the General
        Assembly, on Item 99: "Implementation of Decisions and
        Recommendations of the U.N. Conference on Environment
        and Development"; New York, 23 November 1993 133

Chapter 3: The World Conference on Human Rights
Vienna, Austria; 14 - 25 June 1993 135

    Recommendations submitted by the Holy See regarding the
        World Conference on Human Rights, contained in
        United Nations Document A/Conf.157/PC/6
        22 August 1991 139

    Intervention of the Holy See Delegation at the Regional
        Meeting (Latin America and the Caribbean),
        in preparation for the World Conference on Human Rights
        Costa Rica; 20 January 1993 144

    Intervention of His Eminence Roger Cardinal Etchegaray,
        President, Pontifical Council for Justice and Peace, at a Panel
        during the World Conference on Human Rights:
        "Human Rights, Democracy and Development"
        Vienna, 17 June 1993 147

    Intervention of His Excellency Archbishop Jean-Louis Tauran,
        Secretary for Relations with States, at the World Conference
        on Human Rights; Vienna, 21 June 1993 151

    Statement of Interpretation of the Holy See's Consensus to the
        Final Document adopted by the World Conference on
        Human Rights; Vienna, 25 June 1993 155

    Statement by His Excellency Archbishop Jean-Louis Tauran,
        Secretary for Relations with States, before the
        Third Committee of the U.N. General Assembly,
        on Item 114: "Human Rights Questions"
        New York, 17 November 1993 156

    Interview of His Excellency Archbishop Donato Squicciarini,
        Apostolic Nuncio to Austria, Head of the Holy See Delegation
        to the World Conference on Human Rights, to the
        Radio Programme "Christ in Time"
        20 June 1993 161

    Interview of His Excellency Archbishop Donato Squicciarini,
        Apostolic Nuncio to Austria, Head of the Holy See Delegation
        to the World Conference on Human Rights,
        Catholic Press News Story; 22 June 1993 163

**Chapter 4: The World Conference on the Sustainable Development
of Small Island Developing States**
Bridgetown, Barbados; 25 April - 6 May 1994 .... **165**

    Statement by His Excellency Archbishop Renato R. Martino,
        Apostolic Nuncio, Permanent Observer of the Holy See
        to the U.N., at the World Conference on the
        Sustainable Development of Small Island Developing States
        Bridgetown, Barbados, 29 April 1994 169

Chapter 5: The World Conference on Natural Disaster Reduction
Yokohama, Japan; 23 - 27 May 1994 .... **173**

    Intervention of Monsignor Iván Marín,
        Secretary of the Pontifical Council "Cor Unum" and
        Head of the Delegation of the Holy See to the
        World Conference on Natural Disaster Reduction
        Yokohama, Japan, 23-27 May 1994 177

Chapter 6: The International Conference on Population and Development
Cairo, Egypt; 5 - 13 September 1994 .... **179**

    Introduction by His Excellency Archbishop Renato R. Martino
        Apostolic Nuncio, Permanent Observer of the Holy See
        to the U.N. and Head of the Holy See Delegation to the
        United Nations Conference on Population and Development ... 189

    Message of His Holiness Pope John Paul II
        to Mrs. Nafis Sadik, Secretary General of the
        1994 International Conference on Population and Development
        and Executive Director of the United Nations Population Fund
        Vatican, 18 March 1994 191

    Letter of His Holiness Pope John Paul II
        to the World's Heads of State
        Vatican, 19 March 1994 199

    Addresses of His Holiness Pope John Paul II
        at the General Audience and before the Angelus 203
        General Audience, 6 April 1994 203
        Angelus, St. Peter's Square, 17 April 1994 203
        Angelus, St. Peter's Square, 12 June 1994 205
        Angelus, St. Peter's Square, 19 June 1994 206
        Angelus, St. Peter's Square, 26 June 1994 208

Angelus, St. Peter's Square, 3 July 1994 209
Angelus, St. Peter's Square, 10 July 1994 210
Angelus, Castel Gandolfo, 17 July 1994 211
Angelus, Castel Gandolfo, 24 July 1994 212
Angelus, Castel Gandolfo, 31 July 1994 214
Angelus, Castel Gandolfo, 7 August 1994 215
Angelus, Castel Gandolfo, 14 August 1994 216
Angelus, Castel Gandolfo, 28 August 1994 218

National Report of the Holy See
   in preparation for the
   International Conference on Population and Development
   23 March 1993 221

Address of His Eminence Angelo Cardinal Sodano,
   Secretary of State, on the position of the Holy See regarding the
   International Conference on Population and Development,
   at the Special Assembly for Africa of the Synod of Bishops
   Vatican, 21 April 1994 229

Statement by His Eminence Alfonso Cardinal López Trujillo,
   President of the Pontifical Council for the Family, at a Meeting for
   Ambassadors Accredited to the Holy See
   Vatican, 25 March 1994 238

Statement by His Eminence Roger Cardinal Etchegaray,
   President of the Pontifical Council for Justice and Peace, at a
   Meeting for Ambassadors Accredited to the Holy See
   Vatican, 25 March 1994 246

Statement by His Excellency Archbishop Jean-Louis Tauran,
   Secretary for Relations with States, at a Meeting for
   Ambassadors Accredited to the Holy See
   Vatican, 25 March 1994 251

Statement by the College of Cardinals, meeting in Extraordinary
   Consistory, proposed by His Eminence John Cardinal O'Connor,
   Archbishop of New York; Vatican, 14 June 1994 261

Intervention of His Excellency Bishop James T. McHugh, STD,
   Bishop of Camden, New Jersey, Member of the Holy See Delegation
   to the 26th Session of the United Nations Population Commission
   - Session I of the Preparatory Committee for the
   International Conference on Population and Development
   New York, 28 February 1991 263

Intervention of His Excellency Bishop Elio Sgreccia,
    Secretary of the Pontifical Council for the Family,
    at the Meeting of the European Population Conference,
    in preparation for the International Conference on Population
    and Development; Geneva, 23-26 March 1993 265

Statement by Monsignor Diarmuid Martin,
    Under-Secretary of the Pontifical Council for Justice and Peace,
    Head of the Holy See Delegation to the Latin American and
    Caribbean Regional Conference on Population and
    Development, Ministerial Planning Meeting
    Mexico City, 3 May 1993 269

Statement by His Excellency Archbishop Renato R. Martino,
    Apostolic Nuncio, Permanent Observer of the Holy See
    to the U.N., Head of the Delegation of the Holy See to the
    II Session of the Preparatory Committee for the
    International Conference on Population and Development
    New York, 17 May 1993 273

Statement by Monsignor Frank J. Dewane,
    Member of Delegation of the Holy See to the II Session
    of the Preparatory Committee for the International Conference
    on Population and Development; New York, 18 May 1993 279

Statement by Mr. John M. Klink,
    Member of Delegation of the Holy See to the II Session
    of the Preparatory Committee for the International Conference
    on Population and Development; New York, 19 May 1993 281

Statement by Monsignor Joseph A. DeAndrea,
    Member of Delegation of the Holy See,
    before the Second Committee of the General Assembly,
    on Item 96: "International Conference on Population and
    Development"; New York, 5 November 1993 284

Statement by Monsignor Diarmuid Martin,
    Under-Secretary of the Pontifical Council for Justice and Peace,
    and Head of the Delegation of the Holy See to the III Session
    of the Preparatory Committee for the International Conference
    on Population and Development, New York, 5 April 1994 287

Report of Monsignor Diarmuid Martin,
    Secretary of the Pontifical Council for Justice and Peace, at the
    Special Assembly for Africa of the Synod of Bishops, on the work
    of the III Session of the Preparatory Committee for the

International Conference on Population and Development
Vatican, 28 April 1994 291

Remarks of His Excellency Bishop Elio Sgreccia,
Secretary of the Pontifical Council for the Family, on a
Report of the Pontifical Academy of Sciences
Vatican, 19 June 1994 297

Briefing by Dr. Joaquín Navarro-Valls,
Director of the Holy See Press Office, on the Draft Program
of the International Conference on Population and Development
Vatican, 8 August 1994 302

Briefing by Dr. Joaquín Navarro-Valls,
Director of the Holy See Press Office, in view of the
International Conference on Population and Development
Vatican, 31 August 1994 306

Statement by His Excellency Archbishop Renato R. Martino,
Apostolic Nuncio, Permanent Observer of the Holy See
to the U.N. and Head of the Delegation of the Holy See, at the
International Conference on Population and Development
Cairo, 7 September 1994 311

Statement by His Excellency Archbishop Renato R. Martino,
Apostolic Nuncio, Permanent Observer of the Holy See
to the U.N. and Head of the Delegation of the Holy See,
at the Concluding Session of the International Conference
on Population and Development
Cairo, 13 September 1994 318

Reservations of the Holy See to the Programme of Action adopted
at the International Conference on Population and Development
Cairo, 13 September 1994 321

Statement by His Excellency Archbishop Renato R. Martino,
Apostolic Nuncio, Permanent Observer of the Holy See
to the U.N., before the Plenary Session of the General Assembly,
on Item 158: "Report on the International Conference on
Population and Development"
New York, 18 November 1994 323

Interviews given to Vatican Radio by
His Excellency Archbishop Renato R. Martino,
Apostolic Nuncio, Permanent Observer of the Holy See
to the U.N. and Head of the Delegation of the Holy See to the

International Conference on Population and Development 328
    30 August 1994 328
    2 September 1994 331
    3 September 1994 333
    4 September 1994 335
    16 September 1994 337

Press Releases issued by the Delegation of the Holy See during the
    International Conference on Population and Development 339
    Cairo, 5 September 1994 339
    Cairo, 6 September 1994 341
    Cairo, 8 September 1994 344

Message of Mother Teresa of Calcutta to the
    United Nations International Conference on Population
    and Development; 7 September 1994 345

Intervention of Mr. John M. Klink,
    Member of the Holy See Delegation to the UNICEF
    Executive Board, on Document E/ICEF/1995/12:
    "UNICEF Follow-up to the International Conference on
    Population and Development"
    New York, 23 March 1995 352

Intervention of Mr. John M. Klink,
    Member of the Holy See Delegation to the UNICEF
    Executive Board, on Document E/ICEF/1995/12/Rev.1:
    "UNICEF Follow-up to the International Conference on
    Population and Development"
    New York, 20 September 1995 356

Chapter 7: The World Summit for Social Development
Copenhagen, Denmark; 6 - 12 March 1995 359

Addresses of His Holiness Pope John Paul II before the Angelus . . . 365
    St. Peter's Square, 26 February 1995 365
    St. Peter's Square, 5 March 1995 366
    St. Peter's Square, 12 March 1995 367

Statement by His Eminence Angelo Cardinal Sodano,
    Secretary of State of His Holiness, at the
    World Summit for Social Development
    Copenhagen, 12 March 1995 369

Statement of Interpretation and Reservations of the Holy See
    to the Declaration and Programme of Action of the
    World Summit for Social Development
    Copenhagen, 12 March 1995 374

Statement by His Eminence Roger Cardinal Etchegaray,
    President of the Pontifical Council for Justice and Peace,
    to the Annual Session of the United Nations Economic and
    Social Council (ECOSOC), on the topic of the
    World Summit for Social Development
    Geneva, 30 June 1993 375

Statement by Monsignor Diarmuid Martin,
    Under-Secretary of the Pontifical Council for Justice and Peace,
    Head of the Holy See Delegation to the First Session of the
    Preparatory Committee for the World Summit for Social
    Development; New York, 3 February 1994 378

Statement by Monsignor Diarmuid Martin,
    Under-Secretary of the Pontifical Council for Justice and Peace,
    Head of the Holy See Delegation to the First Session of the
    Preparatory Committee for the World Summit for Social
    Development; New York, 7 February 1994 383

Comments by Monsignor Diarmuid Martin,
    Secretary of the Pontifical Council for Justice and Peace,
    Head of the Holy See Delegation to the Preparatory Committee
    for the World Summit for Social Development
    New York, 22 August 1994 386

Comments by Monsignor Diarmuid Martin,
    Secretary of the Pontifical Council for Justice and Peace,
    Head of the Holy See Delegation to the Preparatory Committee
    for the World Summit for Social Development, on the Section:
    "Reduction and Elimination of Widespread Poverty"
    New York, 23 August 1994 388

Comments by Monsignor Frank J. Dewane,
    Member of the Holy See Delegation to the Preparatory Committee
    for the World Summit for Social Development, on the Section:
    "Social Integration"; New York, 24 August 1994 390

Comments by Monsignor Frank J. Dewane,
    Member of the Holy See Delegation to the Preparatory Committee
    for the World Summit for Social Development, on the Section:
    "The Declaration"; New York, 25 August 1994 391

Serving the Human Family: The Holy See at the Major U.N. Conferences 27

Statement by Dr. Joaquín Navarro-Valls,
    Director of the Press Office of the Holy See, on the
    World Summit for Social Development
    Vatican, 28 February 1995 393

Statement by Monsignor Diarmuid Martin,
    Secretary of the Pontifical Council for Justice and Peace,
    Head of the Holy See Delegation to the
    World Summit for Social Development
    Copenhagen, 7 March 1995 397

Interview of Dr. Joaquín Navarro-Valls,
    Director of the Press Office of the Holy See, after the
    Inauguration of the World Summit for Social Development
    Copenhagen, 8 March 1995 401

Holy See Press Conference by Dr. Joaquín Navarro-Valls,
    Msgr. Diarmuid Martin and Mrs. Patricia Donahoe,
    during the World Summit for Social Development
    Copenhagen, 9 March 1995 402

Intervention of Monsignor Diarmuid Martin,
    Secretary of the Pontifical Council for Justice and Peace,
    at the 34th Session of the Commission for Social Development, on
    Item 5: "Priority Subject: World Summit for Social Development"
    New York, 18 April 1995 405

Intervention of His Excellency Archbishop Renato R. Martino,
    Apostolic Nuncio, Permanent Observer of the Holy See
    to the U.N., before the Plenary Session of the U.N. General
    Assembly, on Item 161: "World Summit for Social Development"
    New York, 8 December 1995 408

Chapter 8: The Fourth World Conference on Women
Beijing, China; 4 - 15 September 1995 . . . . **413**

Message of His Holiness Pope John Paul II
    to Mrs. Gertrude Mongella, Secretary General of the
    Fourth World Conference on Women
    Vatican, 26 May 1995 419

Message of His Holiness Pope John Paul II
    to the Delegation of the Holy See to the Fourth World Conference
    on Women; Vatican, 29 August 1995 425

Addresses of His Holiness Pope John Paul II at the General Audience
and before the Angelus 429
    Angelus, St. Peter's Square, 1 January 1995 429
    Angelus, St. Peter's Square, 5 February 1995 430
    Angelus, St. Peter's Square, 12 February 1995 431
    Angelus, St. Peter's Square, 19 February 1995 433
    Angelus, St. Peter's Square, 26 February 1995 434
    Angelus, St. Peter's Square, 18 June 1995 435
    Angelus, St. Peter's Square, 25 June 1995 436
    Angelus, St. Peter's Square, 9 July 1995 437
    Angelus, Les Combes - Valle d'Aosta, 16 July 1995 439
    Angelus, Castel Gandolfo, 23 July 1995 440
    Angelus, Castel Gandolfo, 30 July 1995 441
    Angelus, Castel Gandolfo, 6 August 1995 442
    Angelus, Castel Gandolfo, 13 August 1995 443
    Angelus, Castel Gandolfo, 15 August 1995 444
    Angelus, Castel Gandolfo, 20 August 1995 446
    Angelus, St. Peter's Square, 27 August 1995 447
    Angelus, St. Peter's Square, 3 September 1995 448
    General Audience, 6 December 1995 449

National Report of the Holy See in Preparation for the
Fourth World Conference on Women
30 May 1994 453

Statement by Ms. Sheri Rickert,
Member of the Holy See Delegation, at the 38th Session
of the Commission on the Status of Women, on Preparations
for the Fourth World Conference on Women
New York, 9 March 1994 467

Statement by Monsignor Frank J. Dewane,
Member of the Holy See Delegation, at the Second Asian and
Pacific Ministerial Conference on Women in Development
Jakarta, Indonesia, 9 June 1994 471

Statement by Monsignor Candido Rubiolo,
Member of the Delegation to the Sixth Regional Conference
on the Integration of Women in the Economic and Social
Development of Latin America and the Caribbean
Mar del Plato, Argentina; 25-29 September 1994 475

Statement by Bishop Paul Josef Cordes,
Secretary, Pontifical Council for the Laity, at the High-Level
Regional Preparatory Meeting for the Fourth World Conference
on Women; Vienna, 18 October 1994 479

Statement by Ms. Sheri Rickert,
  Member of the Holy See Delegation, at the Fifth African
  Regional Conference on Women (Preparatory Meeting
  to the Fourth World Conference on Women)
  Dakar, Senegal, 19 November 1994 483

Statement by His Excellency Archbishop Renato R. Martino,
  Apostolic Nuncio, Permanent Observer of the Holy See
  to the U.N., before the Third Committee of the General Assembly,
  on Item 97: "Advancement of Women"
  New York, 5 December 1994 487

Statement by Ms. Sheri Rickert,
  Member of the Holy See Delegation at the 39th Session of the
  Commission on the Status of Women, on Preparations for the
  Fourth World Conference on Women
  New York, 15 March 1995 491

Statement by His Excellency Archbishop Renato R. Martino,
  Apostolic Nuncio, Permanent Observer of the Holy See
  to the U.N., at the 39th Session of the Commission on the
  Status of Women, on Preparations for the Fourth World
  Conference on Women
  New York, 16 March 1995 493

Statement by His Excellency Archbishop Jean-Louis Tauran,
  Secretary for Relations with States, on the Holy See's Position
  on the Draft Platform for Action for the Fourth World
  Conference on Women; Vatican, 26 May 1995 497

Briefing by Dr. Joaquín Navarro-Valls,
  Director of the Holy See Press Office, on the topic of the
  Fourth World Conference on Women
  Vatican, 20 June 1995 505

Second Briefing by Dr. Joaquín Navarro-Valls,
  Director of the Holy See Press Office, on the topic of the
  Fourth World Conference on Women
  Vatican City, 25 August 1995 514

Statement by Professor Mary Ann Glendon,
  Head of the Delegation of the Holy See to the
  Fourth World Conference on Women
  Beijing, China, 5 September 1995 523

Statement by Professor Mary Ann Glendon,
>	Head of the Delegation of the Holy See, at the Concluding
>	Session of the Fourth World Conference on Women
>	Beijing, China, 15 September 1995 531
>>	*and* Reservations and Statements of Interpretation of the
>>		Holy See 533
>>	*and* Statement of Interpretation of the Term "Gender" 536
>>	Beijing, China, 15 September 1995

Press Release issued by the Delegation of the Holy See during the
>	Fourth World Conference on Women
>	Beijing, 9 September 1995 537

Press Release issued by the Delegation of the Holy See during the
>	Fourth World Conference on Women
>	Beijing, 15 September 1995
>	"Holy See Challenge: Real Commitment, not Paper Promises" . 539

Statement by His Excellency Archbishop Renato R. Martino,
>	Apostolic Nuncio, Permanent Observer of the Holy See
>	to the U.N., before the Third Committee of the General Assembly,
>	on Item 107: "Advancement of Women: Report of the
>	Fourth World Conference on Women"
>	New York, 16 November 1995 541

Intervention of Mr. John Klink,
>	Member of the Holy See Delegation to the UNICEF
>	Executive Board, on Document E/ICEF/1996/3:
>	"UNICEF Follow-up to the Fourth World Conference on Women"
>	New York, 25 January 1996 545

Chapter 9: The Second United Nations Conference on Human Settlements (Habitat II)
Istanbul, Turkey; 3 - 14 June 1996 .... **549**

Address of His Holiness Pope John Paul II
>	to Participants at a Meeting sponsored by the
>	European Bureau for the Environment
>	*(Non-Governmental Organizations of Europe and the
>	Mediterranean Basin)*; 7 June 1996 553

Addresses of His Holiness Pope John Paul II in conjunction with the
>	Angelus and Regina Coeli Prayers 555
>	Regina Coeli, St. Peter's Square, 26 May 1996 555
>	Angelus, St. Peter's Square, 2 June 1996 555

Angelus, St. Peter's Square, 9 June 1996 556
Angelus, St. Peter's Square, 16 June 1996 557

Address of His Excellency Archbishop Paul Josef Cordes,
President of the Pontifical Council "Cor Unum", at the
International Colloquium organized by the
International Catholic Centre for UNESCO
Venice, Italy, 28 March 1996 559

Intervention of His Excellency Archbishop Renato R. Martino,
Apostolic Nuncio, Permanent Observer of the Holy See
to the U.N. and Head of the Holy See Delegation to the
U.N. Conference on Human Settlements (Habitat II)
Istanbul, 4 June 1996 567

Intervention of Monsignor Diarmuid Martin,
Secretary of the Pontifical Council for Justice and Peace,
at the High Level Segment of the U.N. Conference
on Human Settlements, Istanbul, 13 June 1996 572

Statement by His Excellency Archbishop Renato R. Martino,
Apostolic Nuncio, Permanent Observer of the Holy See
to the U.N. and Head of the Holy See Delegation to the
U.N. Conference on Human Settlements (Habitat II)
Istanbul, 14 June 1996 575

and Reservations and Statements of Interpretation 575

Statement by Mother Teresa of Calcutta, Missionaries of Charity,
to the U.N. Conference on Human Settlements (Habitat II)
28 May 1996 577

Address to His Holiness Pope John Paul II
by His Excellency Archbishop Renato R. Martino,
Apostolic Nuncio, Permanent Observer of the Holy See
to the U.N., on the occasion of the Papal Audience to the
Members of the Holy See Delegation to the U.N. Conference
on Human Settlements (Habitat II)
Vatican, 17 June 1996 579

Address of His Holiness Pope John Paul II
to the Members of the Holy See Delegation to the
U.N. Conference on Human Settlements (Habitat II)
Vatican, 17 June 1996 581

Statement by His Excellency Archbishop Renato R. Martino,
 Apostolic Nuncio, Permanent Observer of the Holy See
 to the U.N., before the Second Committee of the General Assembly,
 on Item 96: "Sustainable Development and International
 Economic Cooperation: (e) Human Settlements and
 (f) Eradication of Poverty"; New York, 30 October 1996 582

Chapter 10: The World Food Summit
Rome, Italy; 13 - 17 November 1996 .... **587**

Address of His Holiness Pope John Paul II
 at the World Food Summit
 Rome, 13 November 1996 591

Intervention of His Eminence Angelo Cardinal Sodano
 Secretary of State of His Holiness,
 to the World Food Summit, FAO Headquarters
 Rome, Italy, 16 November 1996 595

and Reservations and Statement of Interpretation of the Holy See
 to the Final Document adopted by the World Food Summit 598

Statement by His Excellency Archbishop Renato R. Martino,
 Apostolic Nuncio, Permanent Observer of the Holy See
 to the U.N., before the Second Committee of the General Assembly,
 on Item 97: "Sectoral Policy Questions, Food and
 Sustainable Agricultural Development"
 New York, 25 October 1996 599

Appendix **603**

World Summit for Children; New York, USA
 Letter of His Holiness Pope John Paul II to Children
 in the Year of the Family, 13 December 1994 609

U.N. Conference on Environment and Development; Rio de Janeiro, Brazil
 "Ecology and Population: Birth rate does not create
 greatest drain on resources," by
 His Excellency Bishop James T. McHugh, STD,
 Bishop of Camden (from *L'Osservatore Romano*, English ed.,
 n.35, 2 September 1992, p.2) 617

Intervention of His Excellency Archbishop Jean-Louis Tauran
Secretary for Relations with States, at the 19th Special Session
of the General Assembly of the United Nations; "Rio+5"
New York, 27 June 1997 621

International Conference on Population and Development; Cairo, Egypt
Letter of His Holiness Pope John Paul II to Families
"1994-Year of the Family"
Vatican, 2 February 1994 623

Address of His Holiness Pope John Paul II
to a Gathering of Families from Around the World
Attending the World Meeting with Families
St. Peter's Square, 8 October 1994 687

Address *(excerpts)* of His Holiness Pope John Paul II to
Members of the Diplomatic Corps Accredited
to the Holy See; Vatican, 9 January 1995 693

"Charter of the Rights of the Family"
presented by the Holy See to all Persons,
Institutions and Authorities concerned with the
Mission of the Family in Today's World
Vatican, 22 October 1983 697

"Ethical and Pastoral Dimensions of Population Trends"
issued by the Pontifical Council for the Family
Vatican, 25 March 1994 711

Declaration of the Pontifical Academy for Life
issued by the Executive Board at their First Meeting
Vatican, 19 June 1994 755

Address of His Eminence Alfonso Cardinal López Trujillo,
President of the Pontifical Council for the Family, at the
Press Conference presenting the Proceedings of a
Study Conference on Natural Family Planning Methods
Vatican, 7 July 1994 757

Statement by His Eminence Alfonso Cardinal López Trujillo,
President of the Pontifical Council for the Family,
to the United Nations General Assembly, on the Occasion of
the International Conference on Families
New York, 19 October 1994 764

34 Contents

Report of His Eminence Alfonso Cardinal López Trujillo,
    President of the Pontifical Council for the Family, to the
    Twenty-Seventh General Congregation of the Synod
    of Bishops, on the Year of the Family and the
    Cairo Conference; Vatican, 28 October 1994 768

Selected Statements by Bishops' Conferences, Pro-Life Leaders
    and Organizations regarding the International Conference on
    Population and Development: 780

    - Letter of the Latin American Episcopal Council (CELAM)
        to Mrs. Nafis Sadik; 14 March 1994 780

    - Letter on behalf of the African Bishops, to Secretary-General
        Boutros Boutros-Ghali; Rome, 23 April 1994 785

    - United States Cardinals and Conference President's
        Letter to President William Clinton
        29 May 1994 787

    - Statement by the United States Bishops at their
        June 1994 Meeting 790

    - European Bishops Declaration (President and Vice-
        Presidents of the Council of European
        Episcopal Conferences); 4 June 1994 793

    - Message of the Presidents of the Latin American Bishops'
        Conferences to the Leaders of the Region, Santo
        Domingo; 18 June 1994 795

    - European Bishops Issue Final Declaration
        4-5 July 1994 802

    - Canadian Bishops' Conference on Cairo Conference
        Letter to Prime Minister Jean Chrétien
        18 July 1994 805

    - German Bishops' Statement, 4 August 1994 806

    - European Pro-Life Leaders Issue Declaration
        8-9 July 1994 807

    - Knights of Columbus Statement, 13 September 1994 809

Speech by Mr. John M. Klink,
    Advisor, Permanent Observer Mission of the Holy See
    to the United Nations, to the organization "Women
    Affirming Life"; Washington, D.C., 24 September 1994 811

Serving the Human Family: The Holy See at the Major U.N. Conferences   35

<u>Fourth World Conference on Women; Beijing, China</u>
    Message of His Holiness Pope John Paul II
        for the celebration of the World Day of Peace,
        "Women: Teachers of Peace"; Vatican, 1 January 1995 821

    Letter of His Holiness Pope John Paul II to Women
        Vatican, 29 June 1995 829

    Message of His Holiness Pope John Paul II for
        World Migration Day
        Vatican, 10 August 1995 839

    Message of Pope John Paul II for the 30th World
        Communications Day — "The Media: Modern Forum
        for Promoting the Role of Women in Society"
        24 January 1996 845

    Statements regarding "Catholic for a Free Choice" 849
        - United States Catholic Conference Press Release
            Washington, D.C., 16 March 1995, ... 849
            (two attachments):

            a) Statement by His Eminence William Cardinal Keeler
                NCCB/USCC President, Washington, D.C.
                16 March 1995 850
            b) Statement by the Administrative Committee of the
                National Conference of Catholic Bishops,
                Washington, D.C., 4 November 1993 851

        - Holy See Mission Press Release
            "Holy See Delegation Questions Accreditation of
            'Catholics for a Free Choice'"
            New York, 17 March 1995 853

        - Holy See Mission Press Release
            "Holy See Delegation Challenges NGO Accreditation
            of 'Catholics for a Free Choice' to United Nations
            Women's Conference"
            New York, 21 March 1995 854

<u>World Food Summit; Rome, Italy</u>
    Address of His Holiness Pope John Paul II
        at the Opening Session of the International Conference
        on Nutrition, sponsored by the Food and Agriculture
        Organization (FAO) and the World Health Organization
        (WHO); FAO Headquarters, Rome; 5 December 1992 855

36 Contents

Address of His Holiness Pope John Paul II
    to Participants in the 28th Conference of the
    United Nations Food and Agriculture Organization (FAO)
    Vatican, 23 October 1995 861

Message of His Holiness Pope John Paul II
    to Mr. Jacques Diouf, Director-General of the Food
    and Agriculture Organization (FAO), for the
    Annual Observance of World Food Day
    12 October 1996 867

"World Hunger, A Challenge for All: Development in Solidarity",
    issued by the Pontifical Council "Cor Unum"
    Vatican, 4 October 1996 869

Statement by His Excellency Archbishop Renato R. Martino,
    Apostolic Nuncio, Permanent Observer of the Holy See
    to the U.N., before the Second Committee of the
    U.N. General Assembly, on Item 97:
    "Sectoral Policy Questions, Food and Sustainable
    Agricultural Development"
    New York, 25 October 1996 943

Statement by His Excellency Archbishop Renato R. Martino,
    Apostolic Nuncio, Permanent Observer of the Holy See
    to the U.N., at the UN/FAO Pledging Conference for the
    World Food Programme
    New York, 4 November 1996 946

Index **947-960**

LIST OF ABBREVIATIONS/ACRONYMS

AAS	Acta Apostolicae Sedis
ADD	Addendum
CCC	Catechism of the Catholic Church
CCL or **CIC**	Code of Canon Law/Codex Iuris Canonici
CELAM	Latin American Episcopal Council
ECOSOC	Economic and Social Council of the United Nations
FAO	Food and Agriculture Organization of the United Nations
IAEA	International Atomic Energy Agency
ICCB	International Catholic Child Bureau
ICO	International Catholic Organizations
ICPD	International Conference on Population and Development
ILO	International Labour Organization
NCCB/USCC	National Conference of Catholic Bishops (U.S.A.)/United States Catholic Conference
NGO	Non-Governmental Organization
PrepCom	Preparatory Committee Meeting
UNCED	United Nations Conference on Environment and Development
UNCHS	United Nations Centre for Human Settlements
UNCTAD	United Nations Conference on Trade and Development
UNDP	United Nations Development Programme
UNFP/UNFPA	United Nations Population Fund
UNEP	United Nations Environment Programme
UNESCO	United Nations Educational, Scientific and Cultural Organization
UNHCR	Office of the United Nations High Commissioner for Refugees
UNICEF	United Nations Children's Fund
WFP	World Food Programme
WHO	World Health Organization

SCRIPTURE TEXT ABBREVIATIONS

1 Cor	1 Corinthians		**Lk**	Luke
Dt	Deuteronomy		**Mk**	Mark
Eph	Ephesians		**Mt**	Matthew
Gen	Genesis		**Num**	Numbers
Ex	Exodus		**Ps**	Psalms
Ezek	Ezekiel		**Rom**	Romans
Hag	Hagar		**Ru**	Ruth
Is	Isaiah		**Rv**	Revelations
Jer	Jeremiah		**Sir**	Sirach
Jn	John		**2 Tim**	2 Timothy
Lev	Leviticus			

Chapter One

THE WORLD SUMMIT FOR CHILDREN

United Nations Headquarters
New York

29 - 30 September 1990

Chapter Contents

The World Summit for Children
United Nations Headquarters, New York;
29 - 30 September 1990

Introduction by His Excellency Archbishop Renato R. Martino
Apostolic Nuncio, Permanent Observer of the Holy See
to the United Nations 43

Message of His Holiness Pope John Paul II
to His Excellency Javier Pérez de Cuéllar, Secretary-General
of the United Nations; 22 September 1990 47

Address of His Holiness Pope John Paul II
at the General Audience, St. Peter's Square
26 September 1990 51

Homily of His Eminence Agostino Cardinal Casaroli,
Secretary of State, at a Mass in the presence of Heads of
State or Government and their Delegations to the
World Summit for Children; New York, 29 September 1990 . . . 52

Intervention of His Eminence Agostino Cardinal Casaroli
Secretary of State, at the World Summit for Children
New York, 30 September 1990 56

Contribution of Monsignor Henri Bodet,
Secretary-General of the Pontifical Mission Aid Society
of the Holy Childhood 58

Statement by His Excellency Archbishop Renato R. Martino,
Apostolic Nuncio, Permanent Observer of the Holy See
to the U.N., before the Third Committee of the U.N.
General Assembly on Item 108: "Adoption of a Convention
on the Rights of the Child"
New York, 13 November 1989 61

Statement by His Excellency Archbishop Renato R. Martino,
Apostolic Nuncio, Permanent Observer of the Holy See
to the U.N., at the Meeting of the Executive Board
of UNICEF; New York, 17 April 1990 64

Statement by His Excellency Archbishop Renato R. Martino,
Apostolic Nuncio, Permanent Observer of the Holy See
to the U.N., on the Occasion of the Accession of the Holy See

Chapter One

    to the Convention on the Rights of the Child
        New York, 20 April 1990 67

    and Declaration and Reservations on the Occasion of the
        Accession of the Holy See to the Convention on the Rights
        of the Child; New York, 20 April 1990 69

Statement by His Excellency Archbishop Renato R. Martino,
    Apostolic Nuncio, Permanent Observer of the Holy See
    to the U.N., before the Third Committee of the U.N.
    General Assembly on Item 97: "Implementation of the
    Convention on the Rights of the Child"
    New York, 14 November 1990 71

Statement by Mr. John M. Klink to the Regular Session of the
    Executive Board of UNICEF
    New York, 24 April 1991 73

The Holy See's Initial Report on the Committee on the Rights
    of the Child in Application of Article 44 of the Convention
    2 March 1994 76

Summary Note on the Holy See's Participation at the
    World Summit for Children by Mr. John Klink 100

See Appendix for the following related document:

    Letter of His Holiness Pope John Paul II to Children
        in the Year of the Family, 13 December 1994 609

INTRODUCTION BY
HIS EXCELLENCY ARCHBISHOP RENATO R. MARTINO
APOSTOLIC NUNCIO, PERMANENT OBSERVER OF THE HOLY SEE
TO THE UNITED NATIONS

At the United Nations the Holy See has the privilege of serving the Universal Church and the entire human family in a unique way. Its membership in the community of nations entitles the Holy See to take part in the pivotal meeting place of all of the nations of the world: the United Nations. In this forum the Holy See has the status of an "Observer," along with other nations who opt to fully participate in the United Nations Organization, but who do not wish to become politically involved *per se* by voting on issues which come before the General Assembly. Such a role is particularly appropriate for the Holy See whose Apostolic mandate as teacher and guardian of eternal moral principles necessitates its presence in international fora as an ethical counselor and as an advocate for those whose voices are oppressed and who otherwise could not be heard.

Thus, what this means for the Holy See and its Mission in New York, in practical terms, is a permanent presence in the various centers of discussion within the United Nations. These consist of the General Assembly and its six standing Committees. Their role is to discuss the issues which pertain to their respective mandates, to formulate and negotiate draft resolutions, and to present them to the General Assembly for its final vote.

Thus, while not voting on actual resolutions, through its Mission's active presence in these many United Nations fora, the Holy See is kept fully informed on the evolving international issues at hand. From time to time, through both spoken and written interventions in the Committees and in the General Assembly itself, as well as in the various institutions and agencies, an important opportunity is provided for a vital global representation of the Church's moral guidance and teachings.

The vast array of changes in the political structure of the world at large over the course of the last several years has been, and continues to be, most keenly felt in the United Nations. At long last, the original mandate of the United Nations is beginning to be fulfilled: to be the global center for all governments to resolve their differences, to work toward a binding set of international law to protect the basic rights of all the world's citizens, and to commonly work towards the implementation of this international code of law.

One of the most prominent activities of the United Nations over the course of recent years has been in favor of the greatest resource of, and all too often heretofore the least protected resource of, mankind: the world's children. Thus, the Holy See has been particularly gratified to have been at the forefront of the United Nations' concrete, interrelated and historic efforts for children: the *Convention on the Rights of the Child*, and the World Summit for Children.

The Convention on the Rights of the Child is a world treaty negotiated by the various countries of the world. On November 20, 1989, the 10th Anniversary of the passage by the General Assembly of the *Declaration on the Rights of the Child, the Convention on the Rights of the Child* was adopted by the General Assembly of the United Nations. Subsequent to the passage of such a treaty document, the individual nations of the world are invited to become signatories of the Convention, and to "ratify" it following its formal acceptance by the legislative and executive branches of their respective governments. Such ratification signifies the assurance given by each country that its own national laws are in full conformance with — *or exceed* — the minimum standards called for in the Convention itself.

The Holy See was thus particularly proud to have been the fourth of all nations to ratify the Convention. This action on the part of the Holy See gives both concrete and symbolic support for this historic initiative on behalf of the children of the world. By so doing, the Holy See is urging all nations of the world to prioritize the needs of its children for themselves by the meaningful endorsement of the Convention's minimum standards of protection for their most vital resource. Further, the Holy See would seek to emphasize as it did with the Reservations which it formally took at the time of its ratification of the Convention, that such standards are indeed minimum, and that each country should seek to further extend the protection of children to the greatest extent possible.

The Holy See's Reservations which follow its signature on the Convention document itself seek to emphasize the moral concepts which it holds to be of paramount importance. It is to these Reservations which His Holiness Pope John Paul II made reference in his *Letter to Secretary General Javier Pérez de Cuéllar on the Occasion of the World Summit for Children:*

> "The International *Convention on the Rights of the Child* constitutes a statement of priorities and obligations which can serve as a reference point and stimulus for action on behalf of children everywhere. The Holy See gladly acceded to and endorses the *Convention* on the understanding that goals, programmes and actions stemming from it will respect the moral and religious convictions of

those to whom they are directed, in particular the moral convictions of parents regarding the transmission of life, with no urging to resort to means which are morally unacceptable, as well as their freedom in relation to the religious life and education of their children. Children who are to learn to be supportive of their fellow man must learn the reality of mutually supportive relationships in the family itself, where there is profound respect for all human life, unborn as well as born, and where both *mother and father jointly make responsible decisions regarding the exercise of their parenthood.*" (Letter to Secretary General Javier Pérez de Cuéllar on the Occasion of the World Summit for Children, 22 September 1990).

Laws are, by their very nature, expressions of what an individual society considers to be the minimum standards of acceptable behavior and the Holy See again emphasizes by means of its early ratification of the Convention that the attainment of such minimum standards is laudable. Further, however, all nations should seek to expand such minimums to reach out in every way possible to protect the innocence and vulnerability of, to develop the natural talents of, and, most importantly, to provide an opportunity for the spiritual fulfillment of its youngest citizens — from the first moment of conception.

The main stated scope of the second major activity of the United Nations in this extremely active year in favor of children, the World Summit for Children, was: "to undertake a joint commitment and to make an urgent universal appeal: to give every child a better future." It is no accident that the first "Commitment" of the *Declaration* of the World Summit for Children is towards the Convention:

> "(1) We will work to promote earliest possible ratification and implementation of the *Convention on the Rights of the Child...*" (para. 20).

Thus, again in keeping with the high priority it gives to the rights of children, the Holy See actively negotiated in the drafting sessions for the two documents of the World Summit for Children: the *World Declaration on the Survival, Protection and Development of Children*; and the *Plan of Action for Implementing the World Declaration on the Survival, Protection and Development of Children in the 1990's.* While in agreement with the documents' general advocacy for children, the original drafts contained language which did not adequately promote the rights of spouses in their own planning for their family, including the spacing of births. Further, not enough emphasis was given to the need for pre-natal care and the implicit recognition thereby not only to the right-to-life of the fetus, but of the importance of proper care and nutrition to the mother in the future health of the child after birth.

Following months of intensive, successful negotiations on the part of representatives of all the governments involved, His Eminence Agostino Cardinal Casaroli, the Secretary of State of the Holy See, joined 70 other Heads of State/Government in active participation at the World Summit for Children — the largest gathering to date of Heads of State/Government in the history of the world.

Cardinal Casaroli's signature on the *World Declaration on the Survival, Protection and Development of Children* gives further witness to the Catholic Church's "bi-millenary tradition of service to those in material or spiritual need, especially the weaker members of the human family, among whom children have always received special attention." (*Letter of Pope John Paul II to Secretary General Pérez de Cuéllar*, 22 September 1990). The universality of the Church's mandate is thus given appropriate voice in this historic document which itself symbolizes a global recognition of mankind's call toward unity and concern for "the least" of our fellow-men.

We who have had the privilege of working on the documents contained in this publication's chapter and who were Official Delegates of the Holy See to the World Summit for Children invite all readers to utilize them not only for informational purposes, but rather to support their final goal: their effective translation into appropriate national legislation in order that — in the words of the Declaration itself — every child may be given "a better future." The important "minimum" which they represent for the rights of children can be an historic base from which far greater inroads will be made for the coming generations whose future ancestors are our own daughters and sons — both born and unborn.

MESSAGE OF
HIS HOLINESS POPE JOHN PAUL II
TO HIS EXCELLENCY JAVIER PÉREZ DE CUÉLLAR
SECRETARY-GENERAL OF THE UNITED NATIONS

TO HIS EXCELLENCY JAVIER PÉREZ DE CUÉLLAR
SECRETARY-GENERAL OF THE UNITED NATIONS ORGANIZATION
ON THE OCCASION OF THE
WORLD SUMMIT FOR CHILDREN

"Your children will be like olive shoots around your table." (Ps 128:3)

These simple words of the Psalmist speak of children as a great blessing from God and a source of intense joy for the family.

Inspired by this positive view of human life, the Holy See applauds the *World Summit for Children* as an important expression and consolidation of the increased awareness which has been shown by public opinion and States regarding the need to do much more to safeguard the well-being of the world's children, to enunciate the rights of the child and to protect those rights through cultural and legislative actions imbued with respect for human life as a value in itself, independently of sex, ethnic origin, social or cultural status, or political or religious conviction. Not being able personally to take part in the Summit, I extend warmest greetings to you, Mr. Secretary-General, and to the distinguished Heads of State and of Government present. Confident that the achievements of the human race are a sign of God's greatness and the fulfillment of his mysterious design, I ardently invoke divine light and wisdom upon your deliberations.

I am pleased to express the appreciation of the Catholic Church for all that has been and is being done under the auspices of the United Nations and its Specialized Agencies to guarantee the survival, health, protection and integral development of children, the most defenceless of our brothers and sisters, the most innocent and deserving sons and daughters of our common

Father in heaven. The Holy See's prompt accession to the *Convention on the Rights of the Child* adopted by the United Nations General Assembly on 20 November 1989, accords with the Catholic Church's bi-millenary tradition of service to those in material or spiritual need, especially the weaker members of the human family, among whom children have always received special attention. In the Child of Bethlehem, Christians contemplate the uniqueness, the dignity and the need for love of every child. In the example and teaching of her Founder, the Church perceives a mandate to devote special care to the needs of children *(cf. Mk 10:14)*; indeed, in the Christian view, our treatment of children becomes a measure of our fidelity to the Lord himself *(cf. Mt 18:5)*.

The Church has a vivid perception of the immense burden of suffering and injustice borne by the children of the world. In my own ministry and pastoral journeys, I am a witness of the heartbreaking plight of millions of children in every continent. They are most vulnerable, because they are least able to make their voice heard. My contribution to this *Summit,* Mr. Secretary-General, is meant to reinforce before this powerful Assembly the often wordless but no less legitimate and insistent appeal which the children of the world address to those who have the means and the responsibility to make better provision for them.

The children of the world cry out for love. In this case love stands for the real concern of one human being for another, for the good that each owes to the other in the bond of our common humanity. A child cannot survive physically, psychologically and spiritually without the solidarity which makes us all responsible for all, a responsibility which assumes particular intensity in the self-giving love of parents for their offspring. The Holy See attributes particular significance to the fact that the *Convention* recognizes *the irreplaceable role of the family* in fostering the growth and well-being of its members. The family is the first and vital cell of society because of its service to life and because it is the first school of the social virtues that are the animating principle of the existence and development of society itself. The well-being of the world's children therefore depends greatly on the measures taken by States to support and help families to fulfill their natural life-giving and formative functions.

The children of the world cry out for greater respect for their inalienable individual dignity and for their right to life from the first moment of conception, even in the face of difficult circumstances or personal handicap. Every individual, no matter how small or how seemingly unimportant in utilitarian terms, bears the imprint of the Creator's image and likeness *(cf. Gen 1:26)*. Policies and actions which do not recognize that unique condition of innate dignity cannot lead to a more just and humane world, for they go against the very values which determine objective moral categories and which form the basis of rational moral judgments and right actions.

The International Convention on the Rights of the Child constitutes a statement of priorities and obligations which can serve as a reference point and stimulus for action on behalf of children everywhere. The Holy See gladly acceded to and endorses the *Convention* on the understanding that goals, programmes and actions stemming from it will respect the moral and religious convictions of those to whom they are directed, in particular the moral convictions of parents regarding the transmission of life, with no urging to resort to means which are morally unacceptable, as well as their freedom in relation to the religious life and education of their children. Children who are to learn to be supportive of their fellow man must learn the reality of mutually supportive relationships in the family itself, where there is profound respect for all human life, unborn as well as born, and where both *mother and father jointly make responsible decisions* regarding the exercise of their parenthood.

During the International Year of the Child in 1979 I had the opportunity of addressing the UN General Assembly. I repeat today, with increased emphasis, the conviction and hope I manifested at that time:

> "No country on earth, no political system can think of its own future otherwise than through the image of these new generations that will receive from their parents the manifold heritage of values, duties and aspirations of the nation to which they belong and of the whole human family. Concern for the child, even before birth, from the first moment of conception and then throughout the years of infancy and youth, is the primary and fundamental test of the relationship of one human being to another. And so, what better wish can I express for every nation and for the whole of mankind, and for all the children of the world than *a better future* in which respect for human rights will become a complete reality" (*Address to the United Nations*, 2 October 1979, no. 21).

May Almighty God lead this Summit to lay a solid juridical foundation for the achievement of such a reality!

From the Vatican, 22 September 1990

Address of
His Holiness Pope John Paul II
at the General Audience
St. Peter's Square
26 September 1990

Next Sunday, 30 September, a World Summit of Heads of State and Governments will be held at United Nations Headquarters in New York; it is devoted, for the first time exclusively, to children; its goal is to guarantee their inalienable rights, to face the numerous and serious problems which concern them and to assure in the most effective way possible their integral development in conformity with the dignity of all human persons.

The Church has always followed with great concern issues relating to children; they are closely connected to those of the family and of mothers in their humanitarian and moral aspects; she has ceaselessly worked especially on behalf of the poorest and most neglected among the little ones who were the Saviour's special favorites.

I was asked to participate personally, but I am unable to; the Holy See will be represented by an official Delegation, led by the Cardinal Secretary of State.

Today I wish to invite you — and through you, all the faithful in the Church, especially parents and teachers — to take this opportunity to examine your attitudes towards children and to pay increasing attention to their moral, spiritual and religious needs.

HOMILY OF
HIS EMINENCE AGOSTINO CARDINAL CASAROLI, SECRETARY OF STATE OF HIS HOLINESS DURING THE CELEBRATION OF HOLY MASS AT HOLY FAMILY CHURCH IN THE PRESENCE OF HEADS OF STATE OR GOVERNMENT AND THEIR DELEGATIONS TO THE WORLD SUMMIT FOR CHILDREN
NEW YORK, 29 SEPTEMBER 1990

Your Majesties, Your Excellencies, Ladies and Gentlemen, beloved in Christ.

In the name of God, Father, Son and Holy Spirit, on behalf of His Holiness Pope John Paul II and the Church Universal, on behalf of His Eminence Cardinal O'Connor and the Church that lives in New York, I extend to each of you a most respectful salute and cordial welcome.

I would like to look upon this August assembly as if it were an extension of the scene we just heard described in the Gospel of Saint Mark. Immediately before the solemn opening of the World Summit for Children, each one of you, all of us assembled here in prayer, have come to bring to the Lord Jesus the children of your own countries and of all the countries of the world, for him to place his hands on them, to embrace and bless them.

The very laudable initiative of gathering such an impressive assembly of Heads of State and of Government to celebrate the children of the world and to devote to them pre-eminent attention, declares to the whole world the paramount concern which the national and international communities must have for that large portion of the human family which is the most beautiful, the most promising, but also the most vulnerable and the most defenseless: the children of the world.

The words of His Holiness Pope John Paul II to the General Assembly of the United Nations on 2 October 1979, remain timely indeed. "In the presence of the representatives of so many nations of the world gathered here, I wish to express the joy that we all find in children, the springtime of life, the anticipation of the future history of each of our present earthly homelands. No country on earth, no political system can think of its own future otherwise than through the image of these new generations that will receive from their parents the manifold heritage of values, duties and aspirations of the nations to which they belong and of the whole human family. Concern for the child, even before birth, from the first moment of conception and then throughout the years of infancy and youth, is the primary fundamental test of the relationship of one human being to another." And addressing the Executive Council of the United Nations Children's Fund in April 1984, the Holy Father said: "What is at stake in childhood and in concern for the child is the fate and the destiny of the person, of human life and existence. The child is a sign of the mystery of life and a testing-ground of the authenticity of our respect for the mystery of life. Every child is in some way a sign of the hope posited and expressed by the love of parents: a sign of the hopes of a nation and a people."

In recent years the concern about children has led to worldwide discussion of children's rights and we have rejoiced in the final adoption by the United Nations of the *International Convention on the Rights of the Child*. Such fundamental rights, that is the right to life, the rights to security and social advancement, the right to means necessary for proper development, must be not only universally recognized, but effectively protected and implemented.

While such questions are the concern of society itself, they are also and especially pertinent within the Christian community. The child represents a special sign for the Church. Concern for the child is linked, in fact, with the Church's fundamental mission. As Pope John Paul II recalled in his Apostolic Exhortation *Familiaris consortio,* the Church "is called upon to reveal and put forward anew in history the example and the commandment of Christ the Lord, who placed a child at the heart of the Kingdom of God: 'Let the children come to me, and do not hinder them; for to such belongs the kingdom of heaven' (Lk 18:16)." Indeed Christ goes so far as to identify himself with the children: "Whoever receives one such child in my name receives me" (Mt 18:5). Every single child in this world is a living sign of that mystery of life and hope that has been revealed in Jesus Christ. (cf. 1984 *Address to UNICEF*).

We thus learn that the child is not only the child of his or her parents. Every child is a child of God. God's creative love, his providential care and his eternal plan fully enter into the story of every infant and child.

We learn to celebrate life, to regard parenthood as an exalted mission of responsibility. At the very root of all the rights of the child we learn to discover his or her vocation to life and love, his or her primary need to love and to be loved. A family environment molded in love not only contributes to the stability of society, but it ensures that children receive a joyful welcome and a well-rounded personal development. The Church considers it her duty to inspire and assist families in meeting their obligations toward children, as well as to defend parents' rights with regard to procreation and the education of their children against attempts to limit those rights and against undue pressures on the part of the State or of international organizations. At the same time she reminds parents of their responsibilities toward society, subject always to the superior demands of morality in the exercise of those responsibilities.

Each period of human history has brought to the fore specific needs and problems in regard to children. In our own century, many sufferings have been visited upon innocent and defenseless children by the atrocities of wars, by economic and political crises, by the breakdown of family values and stability, by epidemics, famines and natural calamities. The international community, especially through the United Nations and its agencies, first among them the United Nations Children's Fund, has worked at the formulation and execution of national and regional programs of assistance to children all over the world.

In her long history, the Church has been the initiator of innumerable activities, projects and institutions aimed at the protection and advancement of children, especially in the fields of health and education, without neglecting their spiritual and religious development. Whenever and wherever her presence has been allowed, the Church has been in the front line, ready to offer her services through the selfless dedication of legions of her members and consistently with her irrevocable moral principles. Thus millions of orphaned or abandoned children, whether in refugee camps or in the squalor of urban slums, have been, and are today, touched and healed in body and soul by the love of Christians. This task of compassion is never ending, since the plight of many children in today's world is indeed critical.

In his most recent pastoral visit to Africa, His Holiness Pope John Paul II again called the attention of the world to the unspeakable tragedy of a special group of children whose number increases at a frightening rate, those who are victims of the plague of AIDS. In their innocence, they suffer physically and morally, sometimes deprived of the love of their parents and often rejected by the communities in which they have been born, almost certainly doomed to an early death. It is all the more heartbreaking because these children have done nothing to contract the disease, but it has been passed on to them by adults. The Pope's appeal transcends all geographic boundaries, when he calls upon all to "help those who are sick and surround them with care and affection." We must continue giving them the witness of our full compassion, in the style of Christ who shows us how to overcome the barriers of sickness.

The Church must forcefully remind one and all of her members, in the words of the Holy Father, "to overcome the barriers of sickness or even moral failure" in order to give credible witness to her mission of love. The same appeal the Church must address to national and international organizations: these children have an inalienable right to care and love.

Nor can we neglect the many young victims of various conflicts which have stolen from them the security of their homes, the warmth of their families, the innocent joy of their childhood. To emphasize the love and concern of the Holy Father and of the Church for such children everywhere, but especially in the Middle East, the Holy See Delegation to the Summit counts among its members a very young person, daughter of the nation of Lebanon, Rita Hage-Boutros, who is with us here this evening.

Now we shall return to the altar, carrying in our hearts, as it were, the joys and the sufferings of all the children of the world. We shall present them to the Lord Jesus and ask him to embrace each one of them, to place his healing hands on them and bless them. And, with them, to bless each one of us.

AMEN.

Intervention of
His Eminence Agostino Cardinal Casaroli
Secretary of State of His Holiness
at the World Summit for Children
United Nations Headquarters
New York, 30 September 1990

It is a great honor for me to convey the greetings and best wishes of His Holiness Pope John Paul II to the distinguished Heads of State and of Government who are participating in the World Summit for Children.

On this occasion, the Holy See would like to solemnly restate its continuing commitment to work for the benefit of those who have so rightly been called "The Springtime of Life."

Children bring to us the benefit of their love, of their trust, of their acceptance of our attempts to respond to their needs as truly human persons whose well-being brings with it the promise of the well-being of society as a whole.

Although with some reservations stemming from serious concerns of an ethical nature which it has always honestly made present, the Holy See's prompt accession to the *International Convention on the Rights of the Child* shows the Church's firm resolve to continue its two-thousand year history of unstinting efforts and to collaborate with the whole of mankind — independently of differences in race, culture, faith or conviction — for the true and complete welfare of all the children of the world. In each child the Church, in effect, sees the dignity of a child of God, made in his own image and likeness, endowed from the beginning of his or her existence, already in the mother's womb, with innate and inalienable rights.

In various quarters concern has been expressed about the large increase of population in some parts of the world, while in other regions a considerable fall in the number of births points to a continuing ageing of the population, with a growing lack of creative energies and a foreseeable decline of ancient, noble civilizations.

In the face of one and the other of these situations, which need to be considered in a broad and serious global and historical vision, the Holy See reaffirms its absolute conviction that these very grave problems can be solved only on the basis of clear and solid moral principles. These principles, it is convinced, are valid both for those responsible for national and international life, as well as for individual families, whose role and freedom must be acknowledged and respected, in order to avoid the danger of open or veiled intrusions of the State which might threaten the freedom or moral character of peoples.

Much has been done on behalf of the child. But the Holy See hopes and fervently wishes that all Governments and the appropriate International Organizations — especially UNICEF — as well as religious agencies and voluntary bodies, will work with renewed commitment to promote programs aimed at offsetting infant mortality and improving the life prospects of children and mothers around the world, particularly where needs are greatest.

May God bless all the children of the world! May he give us hearts large enough to embrace children everywhere and hands strong enough to protect and help them!

Contribution of Monsignor Henri Bodet
Secretary-General of the Pontifical Mission Aid Society of the Holy Childhood

"Children are capable of cooperating in the work of justice, solidarity and peace"

The Holy See eagerly welcomed the *International Convention on the Rights of the Child* and fully participated in the World Summit on Children through its Delegation led by the Cardinal Secretary of State. The Holy Father's messages on this occasion, as well as the declarations of the Cardinal Secretary of State and of the Permanent Observer of the Holy See to the United Nations in New York, demonstrated the importance the Holy See attaches to these United Nations efforts to safeguard and promote children. Furthermore, these masterful declarations were the means by which the entire Catholic Church could salute this historic moment when governments manifested their growing recognition of the supreme value of the human person, especially in its most innocent expression — the child.

Beyond just being a political and moral position, the attitude of the Holy See must be seen as a kind of maternal and spiritual stirring when this project of the nations was announced to recognize and restore to children their dignity. The Church knows She is the depository of God's plan of love for all people and keeps in Her heart and living memory the Lord and Master's privileged care for these little ones, whom He set as an example for entering the Kingdom of God. From Jesus, the Church learned that to welcome a child is to welcome God Himself. It is in light of this revelation that the Catholic Church, through the voice of the Holy See, discerned that the efforts of the United Nations certainly converge with an evangelical love for children.

Over the centuries, this same inspiration has led God's people, communities of men and women, religious or lay, to welcome, protect and educate children — especially those most deprived. In each generation millions of children have thus been introduced and re-introduced into society by nurseries, schools, residences or orphanages founded by these communities.

With the emergence of a responsible Christian laity, especially in recent decades, new forms of lay associations have developed which not only assure the protection of children, but also encourage them to play an active role in the Church and in the world. The Church recognizes and encourages these International Catholic Organizations such as the International Catholic

Bureau for Children, the International Movement for the Apostolate of Children and the Pontifical Mission Aid Society of the Holy Child for their efforts worldwide. These associations solidly support the United Nations *Convention on the Rights of the Child*. They see in it, officially recognized at the intergovernmental level, most of the aims they pursue. Like the Holy See, they have declared themselves active partners in the campaign to obtain worldwide governmental ratification of the Convention and of the Plan of Action.

All the articles in the Convention have met with their approval. But no one will be surprised that being Catholic Associations they are particularly sensitive to the articles calling for the rights of children to freedom of thought, convictions and religion (Art. 14-1), and to practice one's religion and faith (Art. 14-3), including those States where religious minorities exist (Art.30). Also they feel in harmony with articles 23, 27 and 32 which, recalling the situation of children handicapped by threats, both by an insufficient standard of living or by exploitation, demand the right of these children to their "personal development in both the cultural and spiritual domain," and to "their physical, mental, spiritual, moral and social development." It is the conviction of these Catholic Associations that religious freedom and spiritual growth constitute the base and vehicle of a child's overall development.

In their cooperation in projects and programs of the United Nations regarding children, the Church and her Associations, nonetheless, do not expect everything from favorable legislation of States. They also aim even for the participation of children to their own promotion as well as that of their younger brothers and sisters throughout the world. The Second Vatican Council emphasized in several sections of its decrees the capacity of children to lead "their own apostolic life, to become living vital members of the People of God", "to share in the sufferings of their brothers and sisters and to generously provide for their needs." Within the framework of the works of these associations, thousands of children throughout the world have witnessed, without fanfare, their solidarity and fraternal love. If it is necessary for governments to legislate on behalf of children, it is no less important and in harmony with the fundamental rights of children, to construct a better world along with them.

From His position of authority Pope John Paul II had already affirmed this conviction in his message to the Pontifical Mission Aid Society of the Holy Child, at the occasion of the International Year of the Child in 1979, when He wrote:

"Today still, very young Christians, formed to knowledge

and evangelical love of children of their age deprived of the goods necessary for their complete development, are capable of cooperating in this work of justice, solidarity, peace and advance of the Kingdom of God. And doing so, not only does their baptismal and human life develop and become personalized, but such children question and evangelize the world of adults who are sometimes hardened and skeptical about the necessity and the efficacy of solidarity and the gift of oneself."

This view was not absent during the World Summit for Children held at the United Nations in New York in September 1990. Following the discussions of 71 Heads of State or Government, children from around the world expressed in their own words their personal appeals to the Assembly of Delegations present. Let us hope that the voice of the world's children continues to be expressed and heard, that they may be associated with their own development and with that of their peers. As a successful educator of street children stated in a residence for children, "if the project succeeded, it is because children themselves elaborated it. No developmental initiative can work without the input of the interested party and without that party's principal involvement."

STATEMENT BY
HIS EXCELLENCY ARCHBISHOP RENATO R. MARTINO
APOSTOLIC NUNCIO, PERMANENT OBSERVER OF THE HOLY SEE
TO THE UNITED NATIONS
BEFORE THE THIRD COMMITTEE, ON ITEM 108:
"ADOPTION OF A CONVENTION ON THE RIGHTS OF THE CHILD"
NEW YORK, 13 NOVEMBER 1989

In this statement I will address agenda item 108: Adoption of a *Convention on the Rights of the Child*.

During the ten years of the drafting process of this convention, the Holy See has been an active participant. Indeed, the Holy See felt it a moral duty to actively join the international community in such a vital and praiseworthy endeavor as the drafting of a convention to protect the rights of the child.

My Delegation pays tribute to the Government of Poland for its initial efforts and continued support in regard to this Convention. Special recognition should also be given to Professor Adam Lopatka of Poland, who served with distinction as Chairman of the Working Group established to draft the Convention.

Defense of the child's rights is a central obligation for the Church, and one she gladly accepts. As Pope John Paul II has pointed out, Jesus goes so far as to identify himself with children when he says in Scripture (Mt. 18:5), "Whoever receives one such child in my name receives me" (*Address to Mr. James Grant, UNICEF Director*, 26 April 1984).

In one of the last private audiences before his death in 1978, Pope Paul VI mentioned the Church's contemporary concerns regarding children to Mr. Henry R. Labuisse, then the Executive Director of UNICEF. He said: "Despite the technological progress, children still suffer and die from basic lack of nourishment, or as victims of violence and armed conflicts that they do not even understand. Others are victims of emotional neglect. There are people who poison the minds of the young by passing on to them prejudices and empty ideologies. And today, children are exploited even to the point of being used to satisfy the lowest depravities of adults" (*Paths to Peace*, n. 2345, 28 June 1978).

In the current draft before us, the fruit of ten years of dedicated work by advocates of the rights of the child, many of these concerns have been addressed; the draft, if approved, would mark important advances in several areas, including adoption, the rights of children to health care and the right of children to be heard in judicial proceedings affecting their future.

The draft is also significant for the recognition it gives to a child's ethnic, religious and linguistic heritage in cases when alternative family care must be provided. Also praiseworthy is the protection the document would afford to children against economic and sexual exploitation, and the special attention paid to children who have been victimized by abuse, neglect, torture, or exploitation.

While conscious of the progress which adoption of the convention would signify for the international community, and especially for its smallest and youngest members, the Holy See must also make several observations on the draft as submitted:

1. The first regards the protection which the draft affords to the unborn child's right to life. The Church's defense of the right to life from the moment of conception is well known. In the speech quote above, Pope John Paul II stated that: "The Church's concern for children emerges also from the fact that the Church is on the side of life. The Church considers it a priority aspect of her mission in today's world to proclaim the value of each and every human person, especially those who are least able to defend themselves. For this reason the Church will never cease to raise her prophetic voice proclaiming that human life must be respected and protected from the moment of conception" (*Paths to Peace*, n.2360).

My Delegation is pleased that preambular paragraph nine of the draft before us now reads: "Bearing in mind that, as indicated in the Declaration of the Rights of the Child adopted by the General Assembly of the United Nations on 20 November 1959, "the child, by reason of his physical and mental immaturity, needs special safeguards and care, including appropriate legal protection, before as well as after birth."

Some have said that, if the current draft of the convention is adopted, it will mark the first time in an international convention that the right to life of the unborn child has been recognized so clearly. We view this as very significant.

Still, the Holy See would like to have seen further defense of the life of the unborn child in certain articles of the convention. We realize, however, that the current wording is the fruit of laborious dialogue and difficult compromise. We also are confident that the preambular paragraph cited above will serve as the perspective through which the rest of the Convention will be interpreted, in conformity with article 31 of the Vienna

Convention on the Law of Treaties of 23 May 1969.

2. As for the issue of recruitment for military service, my Delegation agrees with other Delegations which proposed age 18 as the minimum age for recruitment to military service. As the Holy See Delegate, Miss Mary Reiner, said here at headquarters during the conference for the International Youth Year in 1985: "Youth long to live, and yet they are the first to be forced to take up arms, the first to be indoctrinated and manipulated in favor of violence and war" (*Paths to Peace*, n. 2468).

3. Finally, the Holy See feels that more specific mention should have been made of the right of parents to provide for the religious and moral education of their children. Pope John Paul II said in a message to Heads of State of Countries which signed the Helsinki Final Act that States must guarantee "freedom for parents to educate their children in the religious convictions that inspire their own life, and to have them attend catechetical and religious instruction as provided by their faith community" (1 Sept. 1980).

In stating these points, the Holy See is well aware that each of them has been the object of extensive debate in the Working Group over the past ten years. And, while not changing its position on any of them, my Delegation considers nevertheless, that, if adopted, this text would mark significant gains for the world's children and the cause of human rights. Therefore, the Delegation of the Holy See urges that the Third Committee adopt the draft text as presented by the Working Group.

Thank you, Mr. Chairman.

STATEMENT BY
HIS EXCELLENCY ARCHBISHOP RENATO R. MARTINO
APOSTOLIC NUNCIO, PERMANENT OBSERVER OF THE HOLY SEE
TO THE UNITED NATIONS
AT THE MEETING OF THE EXECUTIVE BOARD OF UNICEF
NEW YORK, 17 APRIL 1990

Madam Chairman,

I am pleased to announce to you and to the Executive Board of UNICEF that the Holy See has decided to accede to the *Convention on the Rights of the Child* and that in the next few days I will have the honour to deposit the instruments of accession with the Secretary-General of the United Nations.

The Holy See has always maintained that children are, in the words of His Holiness Pope John Paul II, "that precious treasure given to each generation as a challenge to its wisdom and humanity." Responding to such challenge, the United Nations has concluded the laborious work of drafting and adopting a Universal Convention to enounce and defend the rights of children. One could have wished that the rights of the child should have been formally codified much sooner than now, even before the adoption of other specific human rights instruments, for the child represents the primordial subject of human rights and, in his total state of dependency, needs and merits absolute protection. The key to the correct understanding and respect of the rights of children is rooted in the unambiguous recognition of their human nature. It is not governments or adult individuals that choose to grant the child his rights. It is the human nature of the child that constitutes the infrangible and indivisible foundation of the child's rights, without regard to the levels of development of his precious existence or to the convenience or inconvenience caused by his presence. The violation or neglect of these rights — first among them the very right to life itself — represent crimes of a most hideous nature.

As I had the opportunity to state on 13 November 1989, before the Third Committee of the General Assembly, the Holy See recognizes the long and laborious work that has produced the *Convention on the Rights of the Child* and takes note of the positive contributions that such an instrument can make to many aspects of the well-being of children. The text of the Convention, however, represents the minimum grounds upon which agreement could be achieved and, therefore, presents areas where the consensus of the parties does not indicate their complete satisfaction.

The Holy See has held and continues to maintain definite positions on several items which were the object of the extensive debate that led to the formulation of the text of the Convention. With a view to avoiding further delaying the long process and considering that the adopted text would contribute to the safeguard of the rights of children, the Holy See accepted, albeit with reservations, the final text.

By choosing now to be among the first in acceding to the *Convention on the Rights of the Child*, the Holy See would like to encourage all countries and peoples to join in assuring legal protection and effective support to the well-being of all the children of the world.

The accession of the Holy See to the *Convention on the Rights of the Child* is accompanied by a declaration and some reservations.

The Holy See insists that, in keeping with the ninth preambular paragraph of the Convention and with the express affirmation of the previous United Nations "Declaration of the Rights of the Child," the rights of children be safeguarded before as well as after birth.

In its reservations, the Holy See upholds the primary and inalienable rights of parents, especially in regard to education, religion, association with others and privacy, and interprets the phrase "Family planning education and services" in Article 24.2, to mean only those methods of family planning which it considers morally acceptable.

With reference to the current debate during this meeting of the Executive Board of UNICEF, the Holy See has noted with satisfaction the benefits obtained by millions of children in various parts of the world, not infrequently with the direct cooperation of the local Catholic Church.

At the same time, the Holy See views with great alarm some repeated proposals to the effect that this United Nations agency, established for the well-being of children, become involved in the destruction of existing human life, even to the point of suggesting that UNICEF become an advocate for abortion in countries whose sovereign legislation does not allow it. The Holy See firmly opposes such proposals not only on moral grounds, but also because they would bring a totally unacceptable deviation from the stated purpose of UNICEF in favour of children. Moreover, such proposals appear to reveal a dangerous form of neo-colonialism — to which the developing countries are justifiably sensitive — where the mighty will try to impose on the less powerful the adoption of practices contrary to those cultural, social, moral and religious values which have historically formed their heritage and have sustained them in their difficult path to independence and development.

The Holy See maintains that the interests of children will be promoted and assured by the real development of their countries, that will provide them with the educational, economic and social rights to which their right to life entails them.

In conclusion, I am pleased to announce that the Holy See, through the Pontifical Society of the Holy Childhood — an agency which aims at forming in children and adolescents awareness of and solidarity for the resources and needs of their fellow children throughout the world — is making a symbolic contribution of US$3,000, earmarked for the budget for Mobilization Activities related to the forthcoming World Summit for Children.

Thank you, Madam Chairman.

STATEMENT BY
HIS EXCELLENCY ARCHBISHOP RENATO R. MARTINO
APOSTOLIC NUNCIO, PERMANENT OBSERVER OF THE HOLY SEE TO THE UNITED NATIONS AT A PRESS CONFERENCE ON THE OCCASION OF THE ACCESSION OF THE HOLY SEE TO THE CONVENTION ON THE RIGHTS OF THE CHILD
NEW YORK, 20 APRIL 1990

I am pleased to announce that this morning, 20 April 1990, I have deposited with the Secretary-General of the United Nations the instruments of accession of the Holy See to the *Convention on the Rights of the Child*.

By choosing to be among the first in acceding to the *Convention on the Rights of the Child*, the Holy See would like to encourage all countries and peoples to join in assuring legal protection and effective support to the well-being of all the children of the world.

The Holy See has always maintained that children are, in the words of His Holiness Pope John Paul II, "that precious treasure given to each generation as a challenge to its wisdom and humanity." Responding to such challenge, the United Nations concluded on 20 November 1989, the laborious work of drafting and adopting a Convention to enounce and defend the rights of children. The United Nations, since its inception, has considered human rights one of its fundamental concerns; the *Convention on the Rights of the Child*, once ratified, will have its rightful place among the major International Instruments on Human Rights which the Organization has produced.

One could have wished that the rights of the child should have been formally codified much sooner than now, even before the adoption of other specific human rights instruments, for the child represents the primordial subject of human rights and, in his total state of dependency, needs and merits absolute protection.

The key to the correct understanding and respect of the rights of children is rooted in the unambiguous recognition of their human nature. It is not governments or adult individuals that choose to grant the child his rights. It is the human nature of the child that constitutes the infrangible and indivisible foundation of the child's rights, without regard to the levels of development of his precious existence or to the convenience or inconvenience caused by his presence. The violation or neglect of these rights — first among them the very right to life itself — represent crimes of a most hideous nature.

As I had the opportunity to state on 13 November 1989, before the Third Committee of the General Assembly, the Holy See has recognized the long and laborious work that has produced the *Convention on the Rights of the Child* and has taken note of the positive contributions that such an instrument can make to many aspects of the well-being of children. The text of the Convention, however, represents the minimum grounds upon which agreement could be achieved and, therefore, presents areas where the consensus of the parties does not indicate their complete satisfaction.

The Holy See has held and continues to maintain definite positions on several items which were the object of the extensive debate that led to the formulation of the text of the Convention. With a view to avoiding further delay in the long process and considering that the adopted text would contribute to the safeguard of the rights of children, the Holy See accepted, albeit with reservations, the final text.

The accession of the Holy See to the *Convention on the Rights of the Child* is accompanied by the following declaration and reservations:

(Declaration and Reservations follow.)

DECLARATION AND RESERVATIONS
ON THE OCCASION OF THE
ACCESSION OF THE HOLY SEE TO THE
CONVENTION ON THE RIGHTS OF THE CHILD
20 APRIL 1990

Declaration

The Holy See regards the present Convention as a proper and laudable instrument aimed at protecting the rights and interests of children, who are "that precious treasure given to each generation as a challenge to its wisdom and humanity" (Pope John Paul II, 26 April 1984).

The Holy See recognizes that the Convention represents the enactment of principles previously adopted by the United Nations, and, once effective as a ratified instrument, will safeguard the rights of the child before as well as after birth, as expressly affirmed in the "Declaration of the Rights of the Child" [Res.136 (XIV)] and restated in the ninth preambular paragraph of the Convention. The Holy See remains confident that the ninth preambular paragraph will serve as the perspective through which the rest of the Convention will be interpreted, in conformity with Article 31 of the Vienna Convention on the Law of Treaties of 23 May 1969.

By acceding to the *Convention on the Rights of the Child*, the Holy See intends to give renewed expression to its constant concern for the well-being of children and families. In consideration of its singular nature and position, the Holy See, in acceding to this Convention, does not intend to prescind in any way from its mission which is of a religious and moral character.

Reservations

The Holy See, in conformity with the dispositions of Article 51, accedes to the *Convention on the Rights of the Child* with the following reservations:

a) that it interprets the phrase "family planning education and services" in Article 24.2, to mean only those methods of family planning which it considers morally acceptable, that is, the natural methods of family planning.

b) that it interprets the Articles of the Convention in a way that safeguards the primary and inalienable rights of parents, in particular insofar as these rights concern education (Articles 13 and 28), religion (Article 14), association with others (Article 15) and privacy (Article 16).

c) that the application of the Convention be compatible in practice with the particular nature of the Vatican City State and of the sources of its objective law (Article 1, Law of 7 June 1929, n. 11), and, in consideration of its limited extent, with its legislation in the matters of citizenship, access and residence.

STATEMENT BY
HIS EXCELLENCY ARCHBISHOP RENATO R. MARTINO
APOSTOLIC NUNCIO, PERMANENT OBSERVER OF THE HOLY SEE
TO THE UNITED NATIONS
ON AGENDA ITEM 97 OF THE
FORTY-FIFTH SESSION OF THE GENERAL ASSEMBLY
"IMPLEMENTATION OF THE CONVENTION ON THE
RIGHTS OF THE CHILD"
NEW YORK, 14 NOVEMBER 1990

The Holy See would like to express its particular satisfaction in regard to two historic events which have taken place during these last twelve months in favour of children: the adoption of the *Convention on the Rights of the Child* on 20 November 1989, and the World Summit for Children on 29-30 September 1990. The nations of the world have given clear signs about their commitment to the most cherished of their resources — their children — who must be carefully protected, nurtured and educated.

By its prompt ratification of the *Convention on the Rights of the Child*, the Holy See not only has given new evidence of its millenary interest and efforts on behalf of children, but it has intended to give broad encouragement to all nations in their commitment to give renewed attention to their precious little ones.

On the occasion of the celebration of the *World Summit for Children*, His Holiness Pope John Paul II sent a personal message to H.E. Mr. Javier Pérez de Cuéllar, Secretary-General of the United Nations, in which he restated the endorsement of the *Convention on the Rights of the Child* and clearly formulated the concerns expressed by the Holy See in the form of reservations at the time of the ratification.

"The *International Convention on the Rights of the Child* constitutes a statement of priorities and obligations which can serve as a reference point and stimulus for action on behalf of children everywhere. The Holy See gladly acceded to and endorses the *Convention* on the understanding that goals, programmes and actions stemming from it will respect the moral and religious convictions of those to whom they are directed, in particular the moral convictions of parents regarding the transmission of life, with no urging to resort to means which are morally unacceptable, as well as their freedom in relation to the religious life and education of their children. Children who are to learn to be supportive of their fellow man must learn the reality of mutually supportive relationships in the family itself, where there is profound respect for all human life, unborn as well as born, and where both mother and father jointly make responsible decisions regarding the exercise of their parenthood." (*Letter to H.E. Javier Pérez de Cuéllar,* 22 September 1990.)

In his statement at the *World Summit for Children*, His Eminence Cardinal Casaroli, Secretary of State and Head of Government of the Holy See, while expressing profound pleasure at the significance of the unprecedented event, also touched upon the grave problem of high birth rates in some countries and of extremely low birth rates in others, which, he said, "can be solved only on the basis of clear and solid moral principles, valid both for national and international leaders, as well as for each family, whose responsible role and freedom must be acknowledged and respected in order to avoid the danger of open or veiled excessive State influence which could threaten the moral strength and liberty of peoples."

Mr. Chairman, the Holy See's Delegation wishes to express once more its earnest hope that the two milestone events — the *Convention on the Rights of the Child* and the World Summit for Children — will produce solid results corresponding both to the solemn undertaking of the highest leaders of the Nations and to the justified expectations of all people and in particular of children.

STATEMENT BY
MR. JOHN M. KLINK
MEMBER OF THE HOLY SEE DELEGATION
TO THE REGULAR SESSION OF THE EXECUTIVE BOARD OF UNICEF
NEW YORK, 24 APRIL 1991

Madame Chairperson,

The Holy See would like to take this opportunity to underline the importance it attaches to the events of the past year, and most particularly, the landmark Summit of world leaders which gathered to focus the world's attention on the plight and the needs of its most vital resource: its children.

The most recent update, given by the Executive Director in his opening statement, that 77 countries have already adopted the *Convention on the Rights of the Child* gives the most eloquent testimony of the importance of the Summit and its creative molding of world opinion into action. The Holy See continues to urge all nations who have not yet ratified the Convention to proceed to do so with all dispatch. It is important that the text of the Convention and the Declaration and Plan of Action of the World Summit for Children be widely disseminated in order that each family know the rights which its children should enjoy and its responsibility to act as the advocate for these rights.

Madame Chairperson,

My Delegation has noted the Executive Board's firm support for UNICEF's promise of a "first call" on the resources of society for the needs of children. It has also noted the Board's focus on the need to always further integrate UNICEF programmes into each recipient nation's long-term development efforts.

Once could also not help but notice several interventions on the need for UNICEF to focus on its already existent programmes, given a perceived limitation of resources, rather than embark on new priorities. In the words of Mr. Grant, "the Secretariat seeks no new goals, no new programmes, no new areas of activity beyond those identified by the Board last year." My Delegation will not comment on the fiscal questions before the Board except to further encourage the world's growing generosity towards all effective programmes aimed at the protection of children and mothers. This is the heart of UNICEF, and what it does best.

Madame Chairperson,

Despite such calls for fiscal rigor, my Delegation cannot help but notice several requests for UNICEF to involve itself further and further in family planning activities. For this reason, our Delegation would like to draw attention to the "Joint letter to staff of WHO, UNICEF, UNDP and UNFPA on maternal and child health and family planning," signed by the respective heads of these agencies. This document clearly outlines what has been UNICEF's policy from the outset. UNICEF continues to offer its collaboration with those agencies mandated by the United Nations with carrying out health and family planning programmes, but most importantly, only within the terms of its own mandate.

While noting that "there is a fair degree of similarity and complementarity in the goals of the organization" insomuch as all four organizations "seek to improve maternal health and safe motherhood, reduce maternal mortality and raise the status of women," the joint letter notes that nevertheless, "this does not mean ... that our goals and approaches are identical." It further states that while "UNFPA goals in turn are more specific as to family planning ... WHO-UNICEF goals are more detailed in terms of child health." The letter further notes that "while UNICEF recognizes the importance of family planning," it "prefers in its advocacy to emphasize birth spacing."

Madame Chairperson,

The strong encouragement towards this sort of collaboration to avoid duplication of efforts has been at the heart of so many discussions within these chambers, not only of the UNICEF Executive Board, but of the United Nations in general. No person nor entity can be "all things to all people," and it is the opinion of this Delegation that UNICEF cannot and should not be an exception to this rule — particularly as it is a rule more and more clearly enunciated in these times of considerable financial uncertainty.

Thus, rather than come under criticism for clearly providing its collaboration within its own mandate, UNICEF should be praised for not wasting its limited resources to duplicate the actions and activities of other agencies. If you will pardon the analogy, Madame Chairperson, UNICEF is clearly practicing what has been "preached" by a fiscally concerned Board.

UNICEF is, among all the United Nations agencies, the one most widely known and loved by millions of people, especially by children themselves. It is correctly perceived to be an agency for life in its most precious and innocent stages. This is in keeping with the solemn statement from the "Declaration on the Rights of the Child" which the Convention has recently repeated, that "the child, by reason of his physical and mental immaturity, needs special safeguards and care, including appropriate legal protection, before as well as after birth."

In closing, Madame Chairperson, the Holy See would like to return for a moment to the admonishment by some Delegations to ensure that its programmes are not peripheral to, nor even parallel to, those of the individual host country. My Delegation would concur that the most effective programmes in the long-term are those which are not UNICEF programmes *per se*, but host country/indigenous programmes which UNICEF itself may or may not have helped to start, but which UNICEF continues to nurture. This, simply put, makes good development sense.

In this regard, the Holy See would like to draw emphasis to the preambular paragraph of "Goals for children and development in the 1990s" which stresses that they "are recommended for implementation by all countries where they are applicable, with appropriate adaptation to the specific situation of each country in terms of phasing, standards, priorities and availability of resources." And most importantly, as the preambular paragraph goes on to imply, it is vital to note, that with precariously limited resources, UNICEF programmes should continue to be implemented through indigenous host country programmes and projects which have as their hallmark "respect for cultural, religious and social traditions."

Madame Chairperson,

This Board, the United Nations itself, and the world in general can be justifiably proud of UNICEF's work. Recent UNICEF policy statements indicate its sensitivity to the need to fully respect not only its own mandate, but to respect cultural, religious and social traditions of its counterparts. By so doing UNICEF will continue to ensure that its work is not only noteworthy, but non-duplicative, cost-effective and developmentally successful in the long-term.

Thank you, Madame Chairperson.

The Holy See's Initial Report to the Committee on the Rights of the Child, in Application of Article 44 of the Convention on the Rights of the Child
2 March 1994
(translation from the original French)

CONTENTS

I. Affirmation of the rights of the child in the teachings of the Holy See
- A. Dignity of the child
- B. The Church places the rights and well-being of the child in the context of the family
- C. Right to life
- D. Right to education
- E. Right to freedom of religion
- F. The Holy See and the Convention
- G. Statements by the Holy See in favour of the Convention on the Rights of the Child

II. Activity of the Holy See on behalf of children
- A. Holy See and Church structures dealing with children
- B. Implementation of the Convention

III. Activities of the Pontifical Council for the Family for the protection of the rights of the child
- A. Meeting on the rights of the child
- B. International meeting on the sexual exploitation of children through prostitution and pornography
- C. International meeting on the family and child labour
- D. Meeting of experts on drug abuse as it affects children
- E. Meeting on natural methods of regulating fertility

IV. Conclusion

List of annexed documents

INTRODUCTION

1.   The Holy See wishes to draw the attention of the Committee on the Rights of the Child to its singular nature within the international community. As the highest organ of government of the Catholic Church, the Holy See is recognized as a sovereign subject of international law. It is nevertheless distinguished by its particular nature, which is essentially of a universal religious and moral character. Similarly, its jurisdiction over a territory, known as the Vatican City State, serves solely to provide a basis for its autonomy and to guarantee the free exercise of its spiritual mission. The presence of the Holy See in the international organizations, beginning with the United Nations, and its accession to international conventions such as the *Convention on the Rights of the Child*, which it was among the first to ratify, are prompted by the same reasons.

2.   In this connection, we would like to refer to the words of Pope John Paul II before the United Nations General Assembly on 2 October 1979, concerning the bond that exists between the Holy See and the United Nations: "The existence of this bond, which is held in high esteem by the Holy See, rests on the sovereignty with which the Apostolic See has been endowed for many centuries. The territorial extent of that sovereignty is limited to the small State of Vatican City, but the sovereignty itself is warranted by the need of the papacy to exercise its mission in full freedom, and to be able to deal with any interlocutor, whether a government or an international organization, without dependence on other sovereignties. Of course the nature and aims of the spiritual mission of the Apostolic See and the Church make their participation in the tasks and activities of the United Nations Organization very different from that of the States, which are communities in the political and temporal sense."

3.   For this reason, the report submitted by the Holy See cannot be structured in the way established by the Committee on the Rights of the Child in document CRC/C/5 of 30 October 1991. We shall, however, attempt to follow its general lines, in particular in part III of this report.

I.   AFFIRMATION OF THE RIGHTS OF THE CHILD IN THE TEACHINGS OF THE HOLY SEE

A.   **Dignity of the child** (art. 3 of the Convention)

4.   The Holy See and the Catholic Church have never ceased to affirm the importance they attach to recognizing the inherent dignity of the child, in

his or her capacity as a human being, which is the source of children's rights and society's duties towards children. The following two texts illustrate this:

> "In the family, which is a community of persons, special attention must be devoted to the children, by developing a profound esteem for their personal dignity, and a great respect and generous concern for their rights. This is true for every child, but it becomes all the more urgent the smaller the child is and the more it is in need of everything, when it is sick, suffering or handicapped.
>
> "By fostering and exercising a tender and strong concern for every child that comes into this world, the Church fulfills a fundamental mission: for she is called upon to reveal and put forward anew in history the example and the commandment of Christ the Lord, who placed the child at the heart of the Kingdom of God: 'Let the children come to me, and do not hinder them; for to such belongs the kingdom of heaven'. (Pope John Paul II, Apostolic Exhortation *Familiaris consortio,* 22 November 1981, N.26,).
>
> "... I wish to express the joy that we all find in children, the springtime of life, the anticipation of the future history of each of our present earthly homelands. No country on earth, no political system can think of its own future otherwise than through the image of these new generations that will receive from their parents the manifold heritage of values, duties and aspirations of the nation to which they belong and of the whole human family. Concern for the child, even before birth, from the first moment of conception and then throughout the years of infancy and youth, is the primary and fundamental test of the relationship of one human being to another.
>
> "And so, what better wish can I express for every nation and the whole of mankind, and for all the children of the world than *a better future* in which respect for human rights will become a complete reality throughout the third millennium, which is drawing near" (Pope John Paul II, *Address to the General Assembly of the United Nations*, 2 October 1979).

B. **The Church places the rights and well-being of the child in the context of the family** (Preambular paras. 5 and 6; arts. 5, 9, 10, 11, 16, 18 (1-2), 19, 20, 21, 25, 27 (4), 39).

5. As the Apostolic Exhortation "*Familiaris consortio*" explains, the Church believes that children's rights cannot be seen outside of the context of the family, the first and most vital unit of society. For that reason, protection of children's rights cannot become fully effective unless the family and its rights are fully respected by the legal systems of States and the international community.

6. In order to enable the family fully to play its role in society, particularly with regard to children, the Bishop's Synod, meeting in Rome in 1980 to discuss the topic, "The Role of the Christian Family in the Modern World," asked the Pope to promulgate a *Charter of the Rights of the Family*. The *Charter*, dated 22 October 1983, states in preambular paragraph A: "The rights of the person, even though they are expressed as rights of the individual, have a fundamental social dimension which finds an innate and vital expression in the family"; and in preambular paragraph D: "The family, a natural society, exists prior to the State or any other community, and possesses inherent rights which are inalienable." Preambular paragraph F adds that "The family is the place where different generations come together and help one another to grow in human wisdom and to harmonize the rights of individuals with other demands of social life."

C. **Right to life** (preambular para. 7; arts. 6, 23, 24, 26, 27 (1-3).

7. The Church's teaching on the right to life is widely known and has remained unchanged throughout history: "Human life is sacred, since from its very inception it reveals the creating hand of God" (Pope John XXIII, Encyclical *Mater et magistra*, 15 May 1961, part III). "The human being is entitled to such rights in every phase of development, from conception until natural death; and in every condition, whether healthy or sick, whole or disabled, rich or poor" (Apostolic Exhortation *Christifideles laici*, 30 December 1988, N.38).

8. Article 4 of *Charter of the Rights of the Family* spells out the different dimensions of the right to life, as it relates to children.

"Human life must be respected and protected absolutely from the moment of conception.

   a)   Abortion is a direct violation of the fundamental right to life of the human being.

 b) Respect of the dignity of the human being excludes all experimental manipulation or exploitation of the human embryo.

 c) All interventions on the genetic heritage of the human person that are not aimed at correcting anomalies constitute a violation of the right to bodily integrity and contradict the good of the family.

 d) Children, both before and after birth, have the right to special protection and assistance, as do their mothers during pregnancy and for a reasonable period of time after childbirth.

 e) All children, whether born in or out of wedlock, enjoy the same right to social protection, with a view to their integral personal development.

 f) Orphans or children who are deprived of the assistance of their parents or guardians must receive particular protection on the part of society. The State, with regard to foster-care or adoption, must provide legislation which assists suitable families to welcome into their home children who are in need of permanent or temporary care. This legislation must, at the same time, respect the natural rights of the parents.

 g) Children who are handicapped have the right to find in the home and the school an environment suitable to their human development."

D. **Right to education** (arts. 28, 29 and 31 of the Convention).

9. The Catholic Church's conception of education has been set forth in numerous Holy See documents, which state that education cannot be decided *a priori* and imposed on children, but must be based on the child's own situation, the result of his specific personal characteristics, inclinations and potentialities. In this connection, the Vatican II Declaration on Christian Education, of 28 October 1965, states:

> "All men of whatever race, condition or age, in virtue of their dignity as human persons, have an inalienable right to education. This education should be suitable to the particular destiny of the individuals, adapted to their ability, sex and national cultural traditions, and should be conducive to fraternal relations with other nations in order to promote true unity and peace in the world. True education is directed

towards the formation of the human person in view of his final end and the good of that society to which he belongs and in the duties of which he will, as an adult, have a share" (N.1).

10. Article 5 of the *Charter on the Rights of the Family* states that parents have the original, primary and inalienable right to educate their children. This article develops the different dimensions of this right/duty of parents:

> "a) Parents have the right to educate their children in conformity with their moral and religious convictions, taking into account the cultural traditions of the family which favour the good and the dignity of the child; they should also receive from society the necessary aid and assistance to perform their education role properly.
>
> b) Parents have the right to choose freely schools or other means necessary to educate their children in keeping with their convictions. Public authorities must ensure that public subsidies are so allocated that parents are truly free to exercise this right without incurring unjust burdens. Parents should not have to sustain, directly or indirectly, extra charges which would deny or unjustly limit the exercise of this freedom.
>
> c) Parents have the right to ensure that their children are not compelled to attend classes which are not in agreement with their own moral and religious convictions. In particular, sex education is a basic right of the parents and must always be carried out under their close supervision, whether at home or in educational centres chosen and controlled by them.
>
> d) The rights of parents are violated when a compulsory system of education is imposed by the State from which all religious formation is excluded.
>
> e) The primary right of parents to educate their children must be upheld in all forms of collaboration between parents, teachers and school authorities, and particularly in forms of participation designed to give citizens a voice in the functioning of schools and in the formulation and implementation of educational policies.

f) The family has the right to expect that the means of social communication will be positive instruments for the building up of society, and will reinforce the fundamental values of the family. At the same time the family has the right to be adequately protected, especially with regard to its youngest members, from the negative effects and misuse of the mass media."

E. **Right to freedom of religion** (arts. 14 and 15 of the Convention).

11. Church doctrine on freedom of religion was proclaimed in the *Declaration on Religious Liberty* adopted by Vatican II on 7 December 1965. It states that "religious freedom is based on the very dignity of the human person as known through the revealed word of God and by reason itself. This right of the human person to religious freedom must be given such recognition in the constitutional order of society as will make it a civil right" (N.2). "This freedom is the foundation for all other freedoms" and "is the condition and basis for the genuine dignity of the human being" (N.13). "Violation of this freedom is a blatant injustice that undermines what is authentically human" (N.14).

Naturally, this freedom concerns children as well as adults, but for children the role of the parents becomes crucial, for they "have the right to decide in accordance with their own religious beliefs the form of religious upbringing which is to be given to their children" (N. 5). Therefore, "The civil authority must ... recognize the right of parents to choose with genuine freedom schools or other means of education. Parents should not be subjected directly or indirectly to unjust burdens because of this freedom of choice. Furthermore, the rights of parents are violated if their children are compelled to attend classes which are not in agreement with the religious beliefs of the parents or if there is but a single compulsory system of education from which all religious instruction is excluded" (N.5).

F. **The Holy See and the Convention**

12. The Holy See has supported the international community's efforts better to define the rights of the child, and before acceding to the *Convention on the Rights of the Child* on 20 April 1990, it participated actively in the travaux preparatoires for that instrument.

13. In the words of H.E. Archbishop Renato R. Martino, Permanent Observer for the Holy See to the United Nations, spoken at a press

conference given on the occasion of the Holy See's deposit of its instrument of accession, in New York:

> "The Holy See appreciates the long and arduous efforts that led to the *Convention on the Rights of the Child* and has noted the positive contributions that the Convention can provide for many aspects of children's well-being. However, the text of this Convention is a minimal basis for reaching an agreement, and therefore contains areas with which the parties are not completely satisfied (...) In order to avoid any further delay in this long process, and in view of the fact that the text adopted will help protect children's rights, the Holy See has approved the final text, although with reservations" (*L'Osservatore Romano*, weekly French-language edition, No. 20, 15 May 1990, p.4).

14. For that reason, the Holy See, in accordance with the provisions of article 51 of the Convention, submitted a declaration and three reservations when it acceded to the Convention.

15. The declaration reaffirms a position maintained by the Holy See throughout the drafting of the Convention, i.e. that the Convention "represents an enactment of principles previously adopted by the United Nations and, once effective as a ratified instrument, will safeguard the rights of the child before as well as after birth, as expressly affirmed in the Declaration of the Rights of the Child (General Assembly resolution 1386 (XIV) of 20 November 1959) and restated in the ninth preambular paragraph of the Convention" (*ibid*). In addition, "the Holy See, in acceding to this Convention, does not intend to prescind in any way from its specific mission which is of a religious and moral character" (*ibid*).

16. The meaning of the Holy See's reservations to the Convention can easily be understood in the light of the foregoing:

Reservations: "The Holy See, in conformity with the dispositions of article 51, [ratifies] the *Convention on the Rights of the Child* with the following reservations:

(a) Reservation a): "That it interprets the phrase 'family planning, education and services' in article 24 (2) to mean only those methods of family planning which it considers morally acceptable, that is, the natural methods of family planning." The position of the Holy See on "family planning, education and services" (art. 24 (2) (f)) is guided by the Catholic Church's conception of the transmission of human life, as explained in the Encyclical

Humanae vitae (1968) and the Apostolic Exhortation *Familiaris consortio* (1981). The Church recommends responsible planning of family size, when parents take decisions relating to procreation for sound reasons and when they use natural methods of fertility regulation. It also would like this point of view to be transmitted through education, and it is opposed to contraception, sterilization and abortion;

(b) Reservation b): "That it interprets the articles of the Convention in a way which safeguards the primary and inalienable rights of parents, in particular in so far as these rights concern education (arts. 13 and 28), religion (art. 14), association with others (art. 15) and privacy (art. 16)." It is obvious that children's rights must be protected in cases where it is proved that abuses have been committed within the family. However, under normal circumstances, the civilian authorities must not intervene, because of the "primary and inalienable rights of parents," in particular in all matters relating to education, religion, association with others and privacy:

i) Some parents are concerned at the fact that articles 13 and 28 of the Convention, which deal with education, do not sufficiently protect parents' rights against State control, despite the clarifications contained in article 29 (2). More specifically, some parents wish to educate their children according to their own religion, in religious schools or at home;

ii) Some parents have expressed concern at the implementation of articles 14, on religion, 15, on association with others and 16, on privacy. They might imply, in some cases, that children would have the right to make certain choices that might be against their own interests and the integrity of family life and values. In order for articles 14, 15 and 16 not to be used to enable children to join certain religious sects, to associate with corrupt individuals and to live a life of vice, they must be interpreted in the light of the rights/duties of parents and the family. This interpretation is in conformity with that of the Human Rights Committee in its General Comment No. 22 (48) on article 18 of the International Covenant on Civil and Political Rights (CCPR/C/21/Rev.1/Add.4);

iii) A serious study should be conducted of the problem of implementing specific articles of the Convention in certain social and political situations. It is true that some safeguards of the rights of parents and the family have been included in the Convention, but they need to be explained and clarified, in order to guarantee the rights and well-being of children without undermining the rights of their parents and the well-being of their families;

(c) Reservation c): concerns the implementation of the Convention in the specific context of the Vatican City State: "That the application of the Convention be compatible in practice with the particular nature of the Vatican City State and of the sources of its objective law (art. 1, Law of 7 June 1929, N. 11) and, in consideration of its limited extent, with its legislation in matters of citizenship, access and residence."

G. **Statements by the Holy See in favour of the Convention**

17. The Holy See has repeatedly made statements for the defense and promotion of the *Convention on the Rights of the Child*. Particular mention should be made of the following as the most specific positions taken:

a) Message by Pope John Paul II on the occasion of the World Summit for Children, on 29 September 1990;

b) Address by Pope John Paul II at the conclusion of the International Conference on the Problems of the Child, sponsored by the Pontifical Council for Pastoral Assistance to Health Care Workers, on 20 November 1993: the Pope made a solemn appeal for universal ratification of the Convention;

c) Message of Pope John Paul II for the celebration of the World Day of Peace on 1 January 1994, "The Family Creates the Peace of the Human Family";

d) Statement by H.E. Cardinal Agostino Casaroli, representative of the Holy See to the World Summit for Children, on 30 September 1990;

e) Statement by H.E. Cardinal Alfonso Lopez Trujillo, President of the Pontifical Council for the Family, to the First World Congress on Family Law and Children's Rights, Sydney, 4 to 9 July 1993;

f) H.E. Archbishop Renato R. Martino, Permanent Observer of the Holy See to the United Nations, has made several statements on the Convention, in particular at the meeting on the rights of the child organized by the Pontifical Council for the Family, in Rome, from 18 to 20 June 1992.

These statements indicate the importance the Church attaches to the promotion of the Convention for improving the observance of the rights it proclaims. They emphasize in particular the right to life and the role of the family.

II. ACTIVITY OF THE HOLY SEE ON BEHALF OF CHILDREN

18. The Church's activity on behalf of children has been a constant in the history of mankind. In adapting to the circumstances of each period, the Church has endeavoured to meet the religious, spiritual, moral, cultural and material needs of children. It is impossible to give an exhaustive account of these activities, they are carried out by persons desirous of imitating Jesus Christ's special predilection for children. The Holy See still today encourages and supports a very extensive network of institutions dedicated to the welfare of children.

A. Holy See and Church structures dealing with children

19. First, mention should be made of the *Pope's personal actions* during encounters, pastoral journeys, audiences, etc. In addition, the Pope habitually entrusts the coordination and direction of the Church's action on behalf of children to a number of bodies in the Holy See:

a) *Pontifical Council for the Family*, under Cardinal Alfonso Lopez Trujillo, is responsible for dealing with all questions concerning children;

b) *Congregation for Catholic Education*, under Cardinal Pio Laghi, is concerned with education issues;

c) *Pontifical Council for Lay Persons*, under Cardinal Eduardo Pironio, deals with relations with the International Catholic Organizations (ICO), some of which are concerned exclusively with children;

d) *Pontifical Council for Pastoral Assistance to Health Care Workers*, under Cardinal Fiorenzo Angelini, is devoted to health issues. The health of children is one of its main concerns, as may be seen from the theme selected for its Eighth Annual Conference, held in November 1993: "The Child and the Future of society." The various aspects of children's problems were discussed: medical and paramedical problems, problems with regard to pastoral assistance and social and health problems, as well as their philosophical, anthropological, legal, moral and religious implications.

Although the records have not yet been published, the list of statements and their speakers is available; they include eminent specialists, several Nobel Prizewinners and the Directors-General of WHO and UNICEF.

20. *Pontifical Missionary Society of the Holy Childhood*, founded 150 years ago, is concerned with rallying Catholic children to come to the aid of poor children throughout the world, without distinction as to race, religion or sex. This international organization is unique in so far as it mobilizes children themselves to help other children. Millions of young Catholics thus become aware of the needs of their less fortunate brothers and sisters and also help them materially. In 1991, they were able with US$ 13,210,000 to implement projects for the survival, protection and development of other children. The Pontifical Society was honoured by UNESCO in May 1993, on the occasion of International Literacy Day.

21. Certain *International Catholic Organizations* devote their efforts exclusively to the service of children:

a) Particular mention may be made of the *International Catholic Child Bureau* (ICCB) which has its headquarters at Geneva and is in consultative status with ECOSOC and UNICEF. As stated in its triennial report for 1990-1992, ICCB promotes a large number of initiatives (assistance, training, research and development and communications to help children, particularly the most deprived). It has embarked on a major consciousness-raising effort *vis-à-vis*, international and national bodies, in particular to promote the implementation of the *Convention on the Rights of the Child*;

b) *International Movement of Apostolate of Children* (IMAC), which has its headquarters in Paris and is in consultative status with ECOSOC, UNICEF and ILO, was set up 30 years ago for the purpose of coordinating the numerous movements for the evangelization of children. Its aim is to support the training, human development and Christian faith of all children.

22. *Various bodies within the structure of the Catholic Church* are actively involved in meeting the needs of children:

a) The Episcopal Conferences are grouped regionally, enabling them to coordinate some of their activities at continent level. They generally have a specialized children's branch, as is the case, for example, of the children's and young people's department of the Latin American Episcopal Council (CELAM), which recently launched a children's pastoral programme for Latin America;

b) The Episcopal Conferences, which coordinate the Church's action at country level, have children's departments and episcopal commissions which work with the evangelization and religious teaching, health assistance and education movements and with the organs of the Catholic children's press. These diversified activities at diocese and parish level involve thousands of professionals and volunteers. Particular mention should be made of the numerous religious congregations which specialize in a specific aspect of assistance to and promotion of children and young people — education, health, handicapped children, etc.

23. This activity on behalf of children by the Holy See and the Church is a contribution to the observance and implementation of the rights of the child as defined in the Convention. In order to illustrate this activity, this report will follow the guidelines adopted by the Committee on the Rights of the Child in document CRC/C/5.

B. Implementation of the Convention

General principles

24. In its teaching and in its action, the Church stresses the inherent dignity of the child, from which derive the absolute right to life, survival and development, non-discrimination and respect. These principles are clearly asserted in the pontifical documents already mentioned, and serve as guidelines for the programmes implemented by the Catholic organizations. It would be superfluous to mention the Holy See's action *on behalf of life* from the moment of conception. It may be noted that many children's movements have as their aim *the overall development of the child including the religious, spiritual and moral dimensions, and the implementation of his rights;* this may be illustrated by the guidelines which serve as a basis for the International Movement of Apostolate of Children (IMAC), namely, that (a) the child is an individual; (b) the child is capable of acting, transforming and evangelizing; (c) the Movement's teaching methods and methodology should be based on these capabilities inherent in children.

25. The method used by the Pontifical Missionary Society of the Holy Childhood is based on the conviction that children themselves should take part in their own development and manifest solidarity with their fellows.

The family

26. This report has already illustrated the importance given to the family by the Church and the link between the rights of the child and those of the

family; this explains why its action is directed at the protection and promotion of the family and its values. This is particularly relevant in the preparation for marriage which young people receive. In addition, in order to palliate family shortcomings, the Church has set up a large number of institutions which provide children with the family environment they need for their development.

27. It should also be remembered that the *civil rights and freedoms of children* as set out in the Convention cannot be considered in isolation from the family. Cardinal Angelo Sodano, Secretary of State, recalled this in his message to the World Forum of Non-Governmental Organizations held in preparation for the International Year of the Family on the subject of "promoting the family for the well-being of individuals and society" (Valetta, Malta, 28 November - 2 December 1993).

Health and welfare

28. It is impossible to depict the scope of the Church's activities on behalf of children's health, which are conducted largely through a network of 21,757 health institutions, mainly in developing countries, as a contribution to State efforts in this area. The Church provides special care for children and mothers in 5,000 hospitals and 14,000 clinics.

29. At the Seventh International Conference of the Pontifical Council for Pastoral Assistance to Health Care Workers, on the theme of disabled persons in society, Cardinal Edouard Gagnon gave a very well documented lecture on the *role and presence of the Church in relation to the family and the handicapped child*: a great many institutions devote themselves to physically and mentally handicapped children.

30. Various initiatives have been taken in recent years by the Holy See, either directly or in cooperation with Catholic agencies, to assist child victims of the Chernobyl nuclear accident. Several hundred were admitted to the Holy See's hospitals in Italy and, on the initiative of Catholic charitable organizations, several thousand more were taken in by families in Europe.

31. The care of children who are victims of AIDS has become a priority in numerous Catholic hospitals. For example, the Nsambya Hospital in Kampala, Uganda, has launched a large-scale medical research project for mothers and children infected with the HIV virus. This project is financed by contributions from North America, through the "Path to Peace Foundation."

Education

32. The whole of the Church's action can be said to be directed at the education of the child as a person, in all his dimensions. The Church considers that its own work of religious training is an essential contribution to the proper education of children. The intention of the Church institutions (schools, bible teaching centres, various movements, marriage preparation centres, etc.), is to provide an education adapted to the real needs of the child at the various stages of his physical, intellectual and moral development, by endeavouring to apply appropriate educational methods which will, in particular, develop the child's sense of responsibility.

33. Education is primarily a family responsibility, for which the Church provides support and assistance.

34. There are numerous training centres and 160,898 Catholic schools, attended, on 1 January 1991, by 40,975,865 pupils (see the detailed statistics in annex 15). These institutions are the responsibility of the Bishops and are often run by religious congregations.

35. The male and female religious congregations which devote themselves first and foremost to education are very numerous. The best known are the Selesian brothers and sisters, the Jesuits, the Marist Brothers etc. There are, for example, the Brothers of the Christian Schools, who were received by the Pope on 14 May 1993 on the occasion of their general Chapter: 7,800 brothers, members of this Congregation, are at the service of 850,000 young people in 82 countries. They received the Noma prize, awarded by UNESCO in 1990, on the occasion of International Literacy Day (see *Bulletin de l'Institut des Fréres des Ecoles Chrétiennes,* June 1991, on literacy, and April 1993, on the Brothers of the Christian Schools in Africa).

36. The Church also makes considerable efforts in informal education and training, in the context of the parish and children's and young people's movements, particularly through recreational and cultural activities. In addition, some 10,000 centres specializing in the education or re-education of children operate under the auspices of the Church.

Special measures to protect children

37. The Holy See, the Bishops and the Catholic organizations have been mobilized with regard to particularly serious and alarming situations concerning children:

38. *Sexually-exploited children.* In a statement to the Executive Council of the World Tourism Organization, Pope John Paul II said that he wished to reiterate the words of some Asian bishops who had expressed their horror at

the degrading practices of sex tourism. Young people, both boys and girls, were lured into that industry, in which they were treated as mere objects. Like his audience he could hear the voices of thousands of children who had been abused and robbed of their physical and moral dignity asking for the protection due to them under international agreements and demanded by the conscience of mankind.

39.   The Pontifical Council for the Family organized a meeting of experts on child prostitution, in Bangkok, from 9 to 11 September 1992. This was an occasion for taking stock of the question of the sexual exploitation of minors, particularly in Asia and Latin America, and the many initiatives which the churches in those countries had taken to help them. In particular, there was the participation of the Church in the international campaign against sex tourism, led by ECPAT (End Child Prostitution in Asian Tourism). ICCB, in collaboration with Caritas Internationalis, has also set up a world programme on the sexual exploitation of children ("Children at risk, Child victims of sexual exploitation and children with AIDS").

40.   *Street children*. Many initiatives have also been taken by local churches with the encouragement of the Holy See and the support of International Catholic Organizations, such as the ICCB or Caritas Internationalis, to help *street children*. In its volume on *"Street Children, Problems or Persons?,"* published by ICCB in 1992, the author has put together a very wide-ranging experience of more than 10 years with street children. Examples of the many local experiences of assistance to street children are those of Father François Lefort in Mauritania; the Undugu Society of Kenya founded in 1973, by Father Arnold Grol; the work undertaken since 1972 by the Adorers of the Blood of Christ in Colombia in response to the challenge represented by the marginalization of young girls in their country; the Fountain of Life Centre at Pattaya (Thailand), inaugurated in 1988 by the Sisters of the Good Shepherd, to support sexually exploited children in their transition towards another lifestyle; and the "Nanban" Centre, set up at Madurai, in southern India, by the Brothers of the Congregation of Saint John the Baptist for street children and working children. The "Le Nid" Movement operates assistance teams as part of the ICAR Project (Intervention Contact auprès des Adolescents de la Rue).

41.   *Children forced to work*. The international meeting on the family and child labour, organized in Manila (Philippines) from 1 to 4 July 1993 by the Pontifical Council for the Family examined the labour situation of children and the Church's response in various parts of the world. Father Pierre Tritz, S.J., founded the Educational Research and Development Assistance (ERDA) Foundation in Manila in 1974, in order to help school rejects obtain vocational training.

42. The Church also provides special care to *children who are drug addicts, prisoners or refugees*.

43. *Children and war.* The Holy See and the local churches are particularly concerned by the situation of children who are the first victims of armed conflicts, children who are mutilated, displaced or refugees, orphans and children used as soldiers. This subject was brought up by the Pope and the Bishops in the context of the conflicts in the former Yugoslavia and in several African countries (Liberia). Initiatives taken on behalf of such children include orphanages and special schools for the reintegration of child soldiers. At the International Conference on Children on 18 November 1993, Cardinal Roger Etchegaray, President of the Pontifical Council "Cor Unum" and the Pontifical Council for Justice and Peace, gave moving accounts of what he had seen during his missions throughout the world. With reference to children forcibly enrolled in armies in conflict, he said that, according to the principles contained in article 38 of the United Nations *Convention on the Rights of the Child*, children who had not attained the age of 15 years could not take a direct part in hostilities; that was a particularly odious form of servitude. Such children were often subjected to cruel treatment or savage rites intended to harden them for fighting. He had in mind a country which did not hesitate to make use of children by dispatching them into mine fields in order to clear a path for the soldiers who were to follow them.

III. ACTIVITIES OF THE PONTIFICAL COUNCIL FOR THE FAMILY FOR THE PROTECTION OF THE RIGHTS OF THE CHILD

44. In view of the fact that the Holy See considers that the rights of the child are inseparable from the rights of the family, it is the Pontifical Council for the Family which is most directly concerned with the question of the implementation of the *Convention on the Rights of the Child*. The President of the Council, His Eminence Cardinal Alfonso Lopez Trujillo, has therefore organized five international expert meetings since 1991 to deal with special problems relating to respect for the rights of the child.

A. **Meeting on the rights of the child** (Rome, 18-20 June 1992)

45. The meeting was chaired by Cardinal Lopez Trujillo, who after reading out a message from Pope John Paul II, recalled the importance of the solidity of the family for the protection of children; the work of the meeting covered six topics each presented by a different speaker: the central position of children in the Church's social doctrine; the action of the International Catholic Child Bureau in the present international context; the history of the

rights of the child since antiquity and the role of the Church; legal aspects of the rights of the child in Europe and the specific problems encountered by the Christian view *vis-à-vis* modern positive law on the subject of the definition of the child, particularly in relation to the affirmation of the right to life from the moment of conception and the definition of the family; evangelization and children; the inception of the *Convention on the Rights of the Child* and the contribution of the Holy See (His Excellency Archbishop Renato R. Martino); the situation of children in Brazil and Austria.

46. The records of this meeting will be published and sent to the national conferences of bishops and to agencies involved in the protection of children and the promotion of their rights.

B. **International meeting on the sexual exploitation of children through prostitution and pornography** (Bangkok, 9-11 September 1992)

47. A large number of organizations concerned with these problems took part: Pontifical Council for the Pastoral Care of Migrants and Itinerant People, Pontifical Missionary Society of the Holy Childhood, UNICEF, United Nations (ESCAP), ECPAT, RAAP (Religious Alliance Against Pornography), Caritas Project (Toronto), PROVIVE (Venezuela), PROVIDA (Mexico), and representatives of Germany, India, Indonesia, the Philippines, Singapore, Spain, Thailand, etc.

48. Under the chairmanship of Cardinal Lopez Trujillo, the speakers described the situation in the various countries, initiatives to combat the phenomenon, pastoral action already carried out and what could still be achieved. His Excellency Archbishop Renato R. Martino spoke about the prostitution of children in the context of the *Convention on the Rights of the Child*.

49. A number of problems occupied the attention of participants: *sex tourism,* which degrades the tourist industry and constitutes exploitation of third world children by the developed countries; *organizations of pedophiles*: in order to comply with article 34 of the Convention, the age of consent should be established in accordance with the definition of the child in article 1 and measures should be taken to prevent corrupt persons from misusing the provisions of articles 15 and 16 concerning children's right to freedom of association and privacy; *child pornography*: the Pontifical Council for the Family is working on the question with the ecumenical association RAAP; the *effects of pornography on children:* the corruption of children ranges from pornography to abuse of the mass media, particularly by means of films

containing scenes of explicit sex and violence, thus violating article 34 of the Convention.

50.   A Final Declaration was adopted for general distribution. After defining the nature and characteristics of this "contemporary form of slavery," it sets out a number of guidelines for those who wish to combat this evil and concludes by saying: "The sexual exploitation of children is a grave crime against the truth of the human person. Each person is the image of God, the child of God. Each life is a precious gift of God. In each face shines the great dignity of the human person. Children, who are the most vulnerable members of society, must be guaranteed enjoyment of all the rights which appertain to human persons. They must be loved, protected and respected in a special way. Every abuse against their dignity is a crime against humanity and against the future of the human family. The children of the world trapped in prostitution, pornography and sexual exploitation cry for help. The Lord calls His people to action. Deliberating, resolving and acting together, we pledge to respond."

C.   **International meeting on the family and child labour** (Manila, 1-4 July 1993)

51.   Experts and members of national organizations concerned with this specific problem took part, including representatives of UNICEF, ILO, ICCB, IMAC, and World Movement of Christian Workers (WMCW).

52.   Under the chairmanship of Cardinal Lopez Trujillo, the discussions began with statements on child labour in the context of the world economic situation, on child labour and social legislation, and on ILO's work to abolish child labour, and with reports on child labour in each continent.

53.   A Final Declaration was adopted; following a description of the situation, it proposed courses of action for the gradual reduction of child labour. The Declaration called on States and international organizations to liberate children from this injustice, emphasizing that the problem would not be solved until it was confronted within the family itself, which must be given adequate means to live on.

D.   **Meeting of experts on drug abuse as it affects children** (Rome, 20-22 June 1991)

54.   Under the chairmanship of Cardinal Lopez Trujillo, experts and representatives of Catholic organizations involved in the work of drug

rehabilitation considered the phenomenon of drug abuse and its consequences for the individual, the family and society.

55.   The participants were of the opinion that the roots of the problem had to do with the rights and well-being of children. The main cause of drug abuse was to be found in the shortcomings of family upbringing, which prevented children from attaining a degree of maturity enabling them to come to terms with themselves, with God, with those around them and with their environment.

56.   The conclusions of the work of the meeting and guidelines to help to solve the problem have been compiled by the Pontifical Council for the Family in the volume *From Despair to Hope: Family and Drug Addiction*.

E.   **Meeting on natural methods of regulating fertility** (Rome, 9-11 December 1992)

57.   The well-being of children was one of the basic topics of this meeting which studied the latest developments in the natural methods of regulating fertility. WHO was represented by Doctor Earle Wilson (Task Force on Methods for the Natural Regulation of Fertility, Special Programme of Research, Development and Research Training in Human Reproduction).

58.   In the Final Declaration, the participants asserted that "the natural methods promote a positive attitude to the child and maintain reverence for human life at all stages of development."

59.   A number of questions affecting the well-being of children were discussed in the course of the meeting:

a)   *Health and human rights:* Participants asserted that "The health of mothers and infants is furthered through spacing childbirth in a natural way which harms neither the mother nor her baby." They observed that certain contraceptive methods and substances might harm the child by damaging the health of the mother or even endangering her life. Adolescents were also in danger and their rights were violated when contraceptives were supplied to them without consent and without information as to their true effects and side effects;

b)   *Breast-feeding:* Participants supported breast-feeding for the good of the family, the child and the mother and as a way of spacing childbirths and encouraged public policy which would enable mothers to breast-feed their children. The experts stressed the nutritional value of breast-feeding, in accordance with article 24.2 (e) of the Convention;

(c) *Moral problems*: Children might suffer when their morality and that of their family were affected by an attitude with regard to contraceptives and methods which might lead to promiscuity and sexual exploitation, which in turn contributed to the higher incidence of sexually-transmitted diseases and teenage pregnancies. Respect for the moral dimension was an essential aspect of the best interests of the child (art. 3) and the child's welfare (art. 36);

(d) *Family planning clinics*: Clinics, particularly when located near places where children worked or studied, represented a serious obstacle to the protection of the rights of children (and their parents) since they indiscriminately promoted contraception and provided access to abortion;

(e) *Sex education unlinked to the teaching of values*: Without the transmission of values, sex education was liable to lead children to premature and irresponsible sexual activity. In addition, this form of sexual information violated the rights of parents. Pope John Paul II expressed concern on this issue in the Apostolic Exhortation *Familiaris consortio* (N. 37).

IV. CONCLUSION

60. In his message to the World Summit on Children on 22 September 1990, Pope John Paul II said: "The Holy See's prompt accession to the *Convention on the Rights of the Child* ... accords with the Catholic Church's bi-millenary tradition of service to those in material or spiritual need, especially the weaker members of the human family, among whom children have always received special attention. In the Child of Bethlehem, Christians contemplate the uniqueness, the dignity and the need for love of every child. In the example and teaching of her Founder, the Church perceives a mandate to devote special care to the needs of children; indeed, in the Christian view, our treatment of children becomes a measure of our fidelity to the Lord himself."

61. This is why the Church's dearest wish is to create an environment to promote the integral development of children and the observance of their rights so that their psycho-social, cultural, moral, spiritual and religious needs will be taken into account along with their intellectual and physical needs. An even deeper aspiration of the Church is that the child himself should be considered and loved for what he is, in accordance with his inherent dignity, which makes him the subject of these rights.

LIST OF ANNEXED DOCUMENTS (some of the following documents are included in this publication *"Serving the Human Farmily: The Holy See at the Major United Nations Conferences"*).

- Annex 1: Apostolic exhortation "*Familiaris consortio*," 22 November 1981.

- Annex 2: *Charter of the Rights of the Family*, 22 October 1983.

- Annex 3: Message from Pope John Paul II to the World Summit for Children, 29 September 1990 to the World Summit for Children, 29 September 1990 (*L'Osservatore Romano*, French edition, N. 41, 9 October 1990).

- Annex 4: Address by Pope John Paul II to the Eighth International Conference on the Problems of the Child, organized by the Pontifical Council for Pastoral Assistance to Health Care Workers, 20 November 1993 (*L'Osservatore Romano*, French edition, N. 48, 30 November 1993).

- Annex 5: Message from Pope John Paul II in celebration of the World Day of Peace, 1 January 1994, "*The Family Creates the Peace of the Human Family.*"

- Annex 6: Statement by H.E. Cardinal Agostino Casaroli, Secretary of State, representative of the Holy See to the World Summit for Children, 30 September 1990 (*L'Osservatore Romano*, French edition, N. 41, 9 October 1990).

- Annex 7: Statement by H.E. Cardinal Alfonso Lopez Trujillo, President of the Pontifical Council for the Family, to the First World Congress on Family Law and Children's Rights, Sydney, 4-9 July 1993 (*L'Osservatore Romano,* French edition, N. 30, 27 July 1993).

- Annex 8: Statement by H.E. Archbishop Renato R. Martino, Permanent Observer of the Holy See to the United Nations, on the *Convention on the Rights of the Child*, at the Meeting on the Rights of the Child, organized by the Pontifical Council for the Family, Rome, 18-20 June 1992.

- Annex 9: Programme of the Eighth International Conference, *"Puer natus est nobis, The Child is the Future of Society,"* organized by the Pontifical Council for Pastoral Assistance to Health Care Workers, 18-20 November 1993.

- Annex 10: Pontifical Missionary Society of the Holy Childhood: *"L'Enfance Missionaire, une organisation au service de l'alphabétisation des enfants du monde depuis 150 ans,"* presentation to UNESCO, 1993.

- Annex 11: Rapport trisannuel 1990-1991-1992 of the International Catholic Child Bureau.

- Annex 12: *"Pastoral de la Infancia,"* Latin American Episcopal Council (CELAM), Bogotá, February 1993.

- Annex 13: Message from H.E. Cardinal Angelo Sodano, Secretary of State, to the World Forum of NGOs held in preparation for the International Year of the Family on the theme "Promoting the family for the well-being of the individual and society," Valetta, Malta, 28 November - 2 December 1993 (*L'Osservatore Romano*, 2 December 1993).

- Annex 14: Statement by H.E. Cardinal Edouard Gagnon to the Seventh International Conference organized in November 1992 by the Pontifical Council for Pastoral Assistance to Health Care Workers, *"Présence et rôle de l'Eglise auprès de la famille de l'enfant handicapé"* (Dolentium hominum, N. 22, Année VIII, 1993, n. 1, pp. 136-139).

- Annex 15: Some statistics on Catholic schools throughout the world.

- Annex 16: *"Alphabétisation et promotion de la culture", "Les Frères des Ecoles Chrétiennes en Afrique,"* Bulletin de l'Institut des Frères des Ecoles Chrétiennes, N. 234, June 1991 and N. 238, April 1993.

- Annex 17: *"Children at Risk - Children Victims of Sexual Exploitation and Children with AIDS,"* Report of a Think Tank organized by the International Catholic Child Bureau and Caritas Internationalis, Bangkok, 21-23 November 1992.

- Annex 18: Stefan Vanistendael, *"Street children: Problems or Persons?,"* ICCB Series, Geneva, 1992.

- Annex 19: Eyewitness accounts of experiences of assisting street children and child victims of prostitution in *"Children Worldwide,"* ICCB, Vol. 19, n. 2/1992.

- Annex 20: International meeting on the family and child labour, organized from 1-4 July 1993, in Manila, by the Pontifical Council for the Family; statements on *"Children and Work in Colombia"; "Family and Child Labour in Mexico"; "The Family and Child Labour in Peru"; "Children's Work in Africa"; "Child Labour in India"; "The Family and Child Labour in the Philippines"; "Family and Child Labour in Thailand."*

- Annex 21: Fr. Pierre Tritz, S.J., *"ERDA: A New Hope for the Underprivileged Children"* and *Report for the Pilot Project on "Child Scavengers in Metro Manila"* (International meeting on the family and child labour, Manila, 1-4 July 1993).

- Annex 22: Statement by H.E. Cardinal Roger Etchegaray, President of the Pontifical Council for Justice and Peace, at the International Conference on Children, 18 November 1993: *"Children, Culture of Peace and Culture of War."*

- Annex 23: Message from Pope John Paul II to H.E. Cardinal Alfonso Lopez Trujillo, President of the Pontifical Council for the Family, on the occasion of the Meeting on the Rights of the Child, Rome, 18-20 June 1992.

- Annex 24: Final Declaration of the International Summit on the Sexual Exploitation of Children through Prostitution and Pornography, Bangkok, 9-11 September 1992.

- Annex 25: Final Declaration of the International Meeting on the Family and Child Labour, Manila, 1-4 July 1993.

- Annex 26: Pontifical Council for the Family, *"From Despair to Hope: Family and Drug Addiction,"* Libreria Editrice Vaticana, 00120 Città del Vaticano.

- Annex 27: Final Declaration of the Summit Meeting on Natural Methods of Regulating Fertility, Rome, 9-11 December 1992.

Summary Note on the
Holy See's Participation at the
World Summit for Children, New York
by Mr. John M. Klink, Advisor of the
Permanent Observer Mission of the Holy See
to the United Nations

The agendas for Summits of world leaders are generally limited to the maintenance of economic, defense, or general regional mutual interests. Participation therein is thus, by definition, limited both in the number of sovereign nations involved, as well as in the predictability of the ultimate conclusions reached. However, as only the political events of the past two years can demonstrate, the expected can be surpassed, normal perspectives can be enormously broadened, and the bases for positive dialogue can be expanded.

In this light the event of the World Summit for Children at the end of September 1990 gives further basis for judicious optimism for a betterment of global conditions and, in particular, for the amelioration of conditions for children throughout the world. Around a table in one of the chambers of the United Nations which, significantly, was reconstructed to allow all participating Delegations to have the opportunity to view one another face-to-face, the topic on the agenda was one which in itself speaks of universality — the common desire of mankind to protect its greatest *resource:* its children.

At the UNICEF Executive Board Meeting in 1988, the probability for success of the proposal made by UNICEF Executive Director James P. Grant for the Heads of State or Government of the nations of the world to come together to jointly discuss the plight of the world's children was deemed to be virtually nil. Nevertheless, the Prime Ministers of Canada and Pakistan became convinced of the viability of Mr. Grant's proposal for a World Summit for Children and were able to convince the Heads of State/Government of Egypt, Mali, Mexico, and Sweden to commit themselves as "initiating countries." These "Initiators" agreed with Mr. Grant's evaluation that the World Summit for Children was "an idea whose time has come." Eventually, in the forum of the UNICEF Executive Board, enough support was garnered amongst the nations of the world to commence work on a Draft Declaration and Plan of Action to be signed by participating countries. Slowly, and painstakingly, draft after draft was hammered out until a consensus document was approved — finally only some two weeks before the commencement of the Summit itself. The Holy See, through its Permanent Observer Mission to the United Nations, was an active participant in these negotiations, unusual in itself given its normal status as an "Observer" at the United Nations.

The finalized documents of the World Summit for Children have as their focus the diminution and eventual eradication of the estimated 40,000 daily deaths of children from a handful of common illnesses combined with varying degrees of malnutrition. They call for the reduction of the number of infant deaths in the world by one-third by the year 2000; of the number of women who die during childbirth by one-half; and they urge the governments of the world to guarantee that children have access to clean water, adequate nourishment and basic education.

The cornerstone of these documents is the *Convention on the Rights of the Child* — an international instrument aimed at codifying into the national legal systems of participating countries the basic rights of all children to a life free from deprivation, ignorance and abuse. In an effort to lend its support to this landmark document, the Holy See was the fourth nation to ratify the *Convention* while maintaining some official reservations regarding some of the wording thereof.

The Declaration and Plan of Action were simultaneously signed by the participating 71 Heads of State/Government on 30 September 1990 at the World Summit for Children. These documents promote the further ratification of the *Convention on the Rights of the Child* by all of the nations of the world who have not yet done so. They further commit the participating world's leaders to mobilize the breadth of resources required to put today's low-cost and affordable child protection knowledge into action on the necessary scale. The importance of the ratification of the *Convention on the Rights of the Child* cannot be overemphasized as a first step in promoting the basic rights of children on a global basis.

To the unprecedented world forum of the World Summit for Children, His Eminence Agostino Cardinal Casaroli brought a message of solidarity and support from the Holy Father. His Holiness John Paul II's letter to Secretary General Javier Pérez de Cuéllar expressed to all participating countries his particular concern that "Children who are to learn to be supportive of their fellow man must learn the reality of mutually supportive relationships in the family itself, where there is a profound respect for all human life, unborn as well as born, and where both *mother and father jointly make responsible decisions regarding the exercise of their parenthood.*"

On the eve of the Summit, His Eminence Cardinal Casaroli celebrated a Mass in New York in the presence of 17 Heads of State or Government.

In his homily His Eminence called to mind Pope John Paul II's statements made during his recent pastoral visit to Africa concerning the growing tragedy of children with AIDS. Cardinal Casaroli urged the assembled dignitaries and all national and international organizations to give these children who "have an inalienable right to care and love ... the witness of our full compassion, in the style of Christ who shows us how to overcome the barriers of sickness."

The Heads of State/Government present included:

United Nations: Secretary General Javier Pérez de Cuéllar;
Barbados: Prime Minister L. Erskine Sandiford;
Belgium: His Majesty King Baudouin of the Belgians and Her Majesty Queen Fabiola of the Belgians;
Brazil: President Fernando Collor;
Central African Republic: President Andre Kolingba;
Chile: President Patricio Aylwin;
Dominica: Prime Minister Eugenia Charles;
El Salvador: President Alfredo Cristiani;
Ireland: Prime Minister Charles J. Haughey;
Italy: Prime Minister Giulio Andreotti;
Liechtenstein: Prime Minister Hans Brunhart;
Monaco: Prime Minister Jean Ausseil;
Panama: President Guillermo Endara Galimany;
Peru: Prime Minister Juan Carlos Hurtado Miller;
Rwanda: President Juvenal Habyarimana;
Senegal: Mrs. Abdou Diouf *(First Lady)*
Vanuatu: Prime Minister Walter H. Lini.

Additionally, other nations, including the *Philippines* and *Uganda*, were represented by their Foreign Ministers and several countries sent Delegations.

On 30 September 1990, Cardinal Casaroli addressed the assembled 71 Heads of State or Government participating in the Summit and reiterated the "Church's firm resolve to continue its two-thousand year history of unstinting efforts and to collaborate with the whole of mankind — independently of differences in race, culture, faith or conviction — for the true and complete welfare of all children of the world." "In each one of [these children]," the Cardinal stated, "one sees the dignity of a child of God, created in his own image and likeness, endowed from the beginning of his or her existence, already in the mother's womb, with innate and inalienable rights."

Cardinal Casaroli highlighted the paradoxical nature of the problem of increases of population in some parts of the world "while in other regions a considerable fall in the number of births points to a continuing ageing of the population, with a growing lack of creative energies and a foreseeable decline of ancient, noble civilizations." The very complexity of these problems, the Cardinal noted, demands that their solution be seen with "a broad and serious global and historical vision," which must be based on "clear and solid moral principles." In this light, the Cardinal cautioned, "in order to avoid the danger of open or veiled intrusions of the State which might threaten the freedom or moral character of people," one must at all times acknowledge the "role and freedom of individual families."

One of the members of the Official Delegation of the Holy See to the World Summit for Children was a Lebanese girl, Ms. Rita Hage-Boutros. Ms. Hage-Boutros' presence, the Cardinal stated, brought further emphasis to the Holy Father's love and concern for the many young victims of various conflicts throughout the world which have stolen from them the security of their homes and the warmth of their families.

Other members of the Holy See Delegation included Archbishop Angelo Sodano, Secretary for Relations with States; Archbishop Renato R. Martino, the Permanent Observer of the Holy See to the United Nations; Msgr. Henri Bodet, Secretary of the Pontifical Mission Aid Society of the Holy Childhood; and Mr. John Klink, Advisor to the Holy See Mission to the United Nations.

While the Summit's initiating sponsors hoped for the possible participation of 20 to 30 world leaders, their cautious optimism proved contagious. What is perhaps most important in the final turnout of 71 Heads of State/Government — nearly double the attendance record for any previous Summit — is not in the final documents which had been negotiated in advance, or in the carefully crafted texts of the participants' interventions, none of which should, however, be underestimated. At the World Summit for Children what was most noted by the participants was perhaps that which continues to surprise those generations raised on cold war rhetoric: the desire of the majority of the participants to listen to one another.

The restructuring of the conference room table of the Summit is symbolic of the restructuring of the dialogue amongst all States — and the *raison d'etre* of the Summit is symbolic of the restructuring of the priorities of the political will of all peoples: that children deserve, in the words of the Executive Director of UNICEF, "the first call" on the world's resources.

His Eminence Cardinal Casaroli's benediction to the World Summit participants that all people "be given a heart large enough to embrace all children and hands strong enough to hold them" seemed at the end of the Summit weekend like many other prayers which have been so bountifully answered in these last remarkable years of political and diplomatic change: prayers which take root in the shared bonds of mankind's fellowship as human beings — prayers which are being answered before our own disbelieving eyes.

Chapter Two

THE UNITED NATIONS CONFERENCE ON ENVIRONMENT AND DEVELOPMENT

Rio de Janeiro, Brazil

1 - 13 June 1992

Chapter Contents

The United Nations Conference on Environment and Development
Rio de Janeiro, Brazil;
1 - 13 June 1992

Address of His Holiness Pope John Paul II
    before the Angelus, St. Peter's Square; 31 May 1992 109

Memorandum on the Holy See's Position on Environment
    and Development *(published in L'Osservatore Romano,*
    English edition, N. 23, 10 June 1992) 111

Statement by His Eminence Angelo Cardinal Sodano,
    Secretary of State of His Holiness, at the Summit of the
    U.N. Conference on Environment and Development
    Rio de Janeiro, Brazil, 13 June 1992 115

Statement by His Excellency Archbishop Renato R. Martino,
    Apostolic Nuncio, Permanent Observer of the Holy See
    to the U.N., before the Second Committee, on Item 77:
    "Development and International Cooperation
    — e) Environment"; New York, 20 November 1991 118

Statement by His Excellency Archbishop Renato R. Martino,
    Apostolic Nuncio, Permanent Observer of the Holy See
    to the U.N., Head of the Holy See Delegation to the
    U.N. Conference on Environment and Development
    Rio de Janeiro, Brazil, 4 June 1992 122

Statement by His Excellency Archbishop Renato R. Martino,
    Apostolic Nuncio, Permanent Observer of the Holy See
    to the U.N., before the Plenary Session of the General
    Assembly, on Item 79: "Report of the U.N. Conference
    on Environment and Development"
    New York, 6 November 1992 129

Statement by His Excellency Archbishop Renato R. Martino,
    Apostolic Nuncio, Permanent Observer of the Holy See
    to the U.N., before the Second Committee of the General
    Assembly, on Item 99: "Implementation of Decisions and
    Recommendations of the U.N. Conference on Environment
    and Development"; New York, 23 November 1993 133

See Appendix for the following related documents:

"*Ecology and Population: Birth Rate Does Not Create Greatest Drain on Resources,*" by
His Excellency Bishop James T. McHugh, STD
Bishop of Camden, New Jersey, USA
(from *L'Osservatore Romano* English edition,
Ed. N. 35, 2 September 1992, p.2) 617

Intervention of His Excellency Archbishop Jean-Louis Tauran,
Secretary for Relations with States,
at the 19th Special Session of the
United Nations General Assembly, "Rio+5"
New York, 27 June 1997 621

**ADDRESS OF
HIS HOLINESS POPE JOHN PAUL II
BEFORE THE ANGELUS
ST. PETER'S SQUARE
31 MAY 1992**

On Wednesday next, in Rio de Janeiro, the United Nations Conference on Environment and Development will open. After two weeks of work, the Conference will conclude with the participation of many Heads of State and Government.

This important meeting sets out to examine in depth the relationship between protection of the environment and the development of peoples. These are problems which have, at their roots, a profound ethical dimension, and which involve, therefore, the human person, the centre of creation, with those rights of freedom which derive from his dignity of being made in the image of God and with the duties which every person has towards the future generations.

I invite all to pray with me that the high representatives of the various nations of the world, who will gather shortly in that beautiful Brazilian city, will be farseeing in their deliberations and will know how to orientate humanity along the path of solidarity with humankind and of responsibility in the common commitment to the protection of the earth which God has given us.

MEMORANDUM ON THE HOLY SEE'S POSITION ON ENVIRONMENT AND DEVELOPMENT

(published in L'Osservatore Romano, English edition N. 23, 10 June 1992)

The position of the Holy See regarding Environment and Development has been set out in various discourses of His Holiness Pope John Paul II and in particular in the *Message for the World Day of Peace 1990*: "Peace with God the Creator, Peace with all of Creation." The basic principles that should guide our considerations of environmental issues are the integrity of all creation and respect for life and the dignity of the human person.

1. As the title of the above message suggests, the basic inspiration of the Holy See's concern is religious in nature, but it also contains references to many fundamental moral considerations which are shared by persons of good will. The ecological crisis is essentially a moral crisis and the solution of many of the ecological problems confronting the entire human family requires strategies and motivation "based on a morally coherent world view" (Pope John Paul II, *Message for the World Day of Peace 1990*, n. 2). The international community cannot overlook this ethical dimension.

2. The human person occupies a central place within the world and the promotion of the dignity and the rights of all persons without distinction "is the ultimate guiding norm for any sound economic, industrial and scientific development ... Pollution and environmental destruction are the result of an unnatural and reductionist vision which at times leads to genuine contempt for man" (*Message for the World Day of Peace 1990*, n. 7).

3. The human person has a responsibility of stewardship in regard to all creation with which he or she lives in interdependence. When persons consciously ignore or transgress the order of any aspect of creation, they provoke a disorder which has inevitable repercussions on the rest of the created order and the well-being of future generations (cf. *Message for the World Day of Peace 1990*, n. 6).

4. The goods of the earth — including those produced by human activity — are for the benefit of all. All peoples and countries have a right to fundamental access to those goods — natural, spiritual, intellectual and technological — which are necessary for their integral development.

5. An adequate policy of development must be based on the dignity and rights of the human person and on the common good. "The Holy See notes

that the spiritual as well as the material well-being of the person must be taken into account in the development process because spiritual values give meaning to material progress, to technical advances and to the creation of political and social structures that serve the community of persons we call society" (*Holy See's Intervention at the 1984 World Population Conference*).

      Maintaining and protecting the common good requires the solidarity of all those concerned. Solidarity implies an awareness and an acceptance of co-responsibility for the causes and solutions relative to the ecological challenge. Recognizing the shared responsibility of all for the causes of the ecological crisis will make possible a dialogue, based on mutual trust and respect, in seeking solutions. Equity may, however, demand that the universal duty to foster solidarity be differentiated and complementary according to the needs and abilities of the parties.

6.   In the field of technology, States, in accord with the duty of solidarity and giving due consideration to the rights of the developers of such technology, have an obligation to ensure a just and equitable transfer of appropriate technology which is favourable to sustaining the development process and protecting the environment.

7.   Clearly defined ethical principles must prevail in the area of biotechnology, which touches closely on the dignity and integrity of the human person. The human person is much more than a composite of biochemical elements, and he or she should not be made the subject of biological or chemical experiments for the sake of biotechnological progress. All interventions on the genetic structure or heritage of the person that are not aimed at correcting anomalies constitute a violation of the right to bodily integrity (cf. Holy See, *Charter of the Rights of the Family*, 22 October 1983, 4c). Science and technology are at the service of the human person and ethical principles must prevail over any other interest, especially purely economic interests. Where possible, appropriate legal instruments must be found to ensure respect for ethical principles.

8.   The damage to the human and natural environment caused by *war* is an increasingly serious problem. Pope John Paul II noted already in 1990: "Today, any form of war on a global scale would lead to incalculable ecological damage. But even local or regional wars, however limited, not only destroy human life and social structures, but also damage the land, ruining crops and vegetation, as well as poison the soil and water. The survivors of war are forced to begin a new life in very difficult environmental conditions" (*Message for the World Day of Peace 1990*, n. 12).

9.   The relationship of development and the environment to population

growth is complex and often tenuous. In recent decades population growth rates have fallen in most areas of the world, while they still remain high in some of the least developed countries. Population growth, of and by itself, is seldom the primary cause of environmental problems. In most cases, there are no causal links between the numbers of people and the degradation of the environment. In fact, the less-populated nations of the North are directly or indirectly responsible for most of the abuse of the global environment. Therefore, policies aimed at reducing population do little to help solve urgent problems of environment and development. True solutions to these problems must involve not only sound economic planning and technology but justice for all the peoples of the earth.

The Holy See is especially concerned about strategies that make population decline the primary factor in overcoming ecological problems. Programmes for reducing population directed and financed by the developed nations of the North easily become a substitute for justice and development in the developing nations of the South. These programmes evade the question of the just distribution and development of the abundant resources of the earth. On many occasions the Holy See has expressed its opposition to the setting of quantitative population targets or goals, which involve the violation of human dignity and human rights. Systematic campaigns against birth, directed towards the poorest populations, may even lead to "a tendency towards a form of racism, or the promotion of equally racist forms of eugenics" (*Sollicitudo rei socialis,* n. 25).

10.	Policies and strategies to protect the environment must also respect the family unit, which is "the natural and fundamental group unit of society and is entitled to protection by society and the state" (cf. *U.N. Universal Declaration of Human Rights* 16,3). The Holy See emphasizes that "society, and in particular manner the State and International Organizations, must protect the family through measures of a political, economic, social and juridical character, which aim at consolidating the unity and stability of the family so that it can exercise its specific functions" (Holy See, *Charter of the Rights of the Family*, Preamble, I).

Accordingly, the Holy See opposes those strategies which in any way attempts to limit the freedom of couples in deciding about the size of the family or the spacing of births (cf. *Charter of the Rights of the Family*, 3a). In international relations, economic aid for the advancement of peoples should not be conditioned on acceptance of programmes of contraception, sterilization or abortion (cf. *Holy See's intervention at the 1984 World Population Conference*; also, *John Paul II to Rafael Salas,* 1984, n.6). In this way, the Holy See defends the human rights of women and men in developing countries who are subjected to programmes of population control which do not respect their consciences, their rights and dignity, or their ethnic and religious cultures.

Surgical or pharmaceutical methods of abortion continue to be promoted as a method of birth control in the context of policies and programmes aimed at reducing population. Such practice runs contrary to Recommendation 18 of the 1984 International Conference on Population, Mexico City: namely, that abortion should not be promoted as a method of family planning. The Holy See objects to family planning programmes which include abortion as a method of family planning or which pressure couples to use sterilization or other methods of contraception that are morally objectionable.

STATEMENT OF
HIS EMINENCE ANGELO CARDINAL SODANO
SECRETARY OF STATE OF HIS HOLINESS
AT THE SUMMIT OF THE
UNITED NATIONS CONFERENCE ON ENVIRONMENT AND DEVELOPMENT
RIO DE JANEIRO, BRAZIL; 13 JUNE 1992

In one of the books of the Bible, much cherished by millions of believers, we read that in the beginning God created the universe with all its wonders — the heavens, the earth, the sea. Last of all, God created man to be the ruler of this universe and entrusted it to his care. This is the account found in the Book of Genesis.

The view of the Catholic Church — and of the Holy See in particular — regarding the problems under discussion, is inspired by those pages of the Bible. Those pages are part of the heritage of all mankind. Allow me to briefly recall them. They tell us that the created universe has been entrusted by God to man, who has a central place in the world. He is to govern it with wisdom and responsibility, and with respect for the order which God has placed within his creation (cf. John Paul II, *Address to the Pontifical Academy of Sciences*, 22 November 1991, No. 6). In the light of this profound conviction we can make the following considerations:

1. The present ecological crisis is one disturbing aspect of a more profound moral crisis. It is the result of a mistaken concept of inordinate development, which fails to take into account the natural environment, its limits, its laws and its harmony, especially with regard to the use or abuse of scientific and technological progress. The earth is suffering because of human selfishness.

2. "God intended the earth and all that it contains for the use of every human being and people, in such a way that created goods should abound for them in a reasonable way, according to the law of justice, inseparable from charity" (Second Vatican Ecumenical Council, Pastoral Constitution *Gaudium et spes*, on the Church in the Modern World, 69). This is the basis of the duty of solidarity among all and towards all, and the basis of cooperation for a development which gives priority to the less favoured peoples (cf. John Paul II, Encyclical Letter *Sollicitudo rei socialis*, 45).

3. The words of Pope Paul VI have proved prophetic: "The peoples who suffer hunger are making a dramatic appeal to the peoples blessed with abundance" (*Populorum progressio*, 3). The increasing, morally unacceptable and unjust gap between the North of our world, which is

growing ever richer, and the South, which is growing ever poorer, is obvious. To the "undoubtedly grave instances of omission on the part of the developing nations themselves, and especially on the part of those holding economic and political power" (*Sollicitudo rei socialis*, 16) must be added the "growing forms of selfish isolation" on the part of the more developed countries and the tendency to "ignore for questionable reasons [their] duty to cooperate in the task of alleviating human misery" (*ibid*, 23).

4.   It is necessary that humanity discover its common roots and that our awareness of being brothers and sisters give rise to a great creative effort aimed at the effective exercise of solidarity. It should be considered quite normal for an advanced country to devote a part of its production to meet the needs of the developing nations (cf. *Populorum progressio*, 48). In the early centuries of the Christian era it was said: "Feed the person dying of hunger, because otherwise you are responsible for that person's death" (Gratian, *Decretum*, ch. 21 dist. 86: ed. Friedberg, I 302; cf. *Gaudium et spes*, 69). A proper ecological balance will not be found without directly addressing the structural forms of poverty that exist throughout the world (cf. John Paul II, *Message for the 1990 World Day of Peace*, 11), and unless the rich societies seriously revise their pleasure-seeking and extravagant way of life.

5.   Everyone is aware of the problems that can come from a disproportionate growth of the world population. "The Church is aware of the complexity of the problem ... (But) the urgency of the situation must not lead into error in proposing ways of intervening. To apply methods which are not in accord with the true nature of man actually ends up by causing tragic harm... placing the heaviest burden on the poorest and weakest sectors of society, thus adding injustice to injustice" *(Speech to the Pontifical Academy of Sciences*, 22 November 1991, Nos. 4 and 6). It is not possible, from the moral point of view, to justify the attitude of that part of the world which highlights human rights but attempts to deny the rights of those in less fortunate circumstances by deciding, in a "devastating tyranny" (*ibid*. 6), how many children they can have, and by threatening to link aid for development to that dictate.

6.   The association between poverty and the high rate of population growth certainly demands appropriate attention. In any case, "the poor, to whom the earth is entrusted no less than to others, must be enabled to find a way out of their poverty" (*Message for the 1990 World Day of Peace*, 11). This will require addressing the structural forms of poverty, by ensuring employment, education and primary health care for mothers and children, with special concern for overcoming child mortality.

   The earth and its resources will be sufficient if only humanity will learn to share them instead of wasting them among the few. On the other hand, it is clear that the pollution of the environment and risks to the ecosystem do not come primarily from the most densely populated parts of the planet (cf. *Speech to the Pontifical Academy of Sciences*, 22 November 1991, 4).

As the work of this great World Assembly comes to a close, we must remember that we are only stewards of the common patrimony of the planet. The dignity of the human person, who is the only creature in this world capable of concern for the other species, for the environment that surrounds us, and for our brothers and sisters, ought to lead us not only to protect the balance of nature in general but also "to safeguard the moral conditions for an authentic 'human ecology'" (John Paul II, Encyclical Letter *Centesimus annus*, 38). "Not only has God given the earth to man, who must use it with respect for the original good purpose for which it was given to him, but man too is God's gift to man. He must therefore respect the natural and moral structure with which he has been endowed" (*ibid*).

God grant that the Rio Conference will offer our contemporaries new reasons to hope, to believe and to love!

Statement of
His Excellency Archbishop Renato R. Martino
Apostolic Nuncio, Permanent Observer of the Holy See to the United Nations
Before the Second Committee, on Item 77:
"Development and International Economic Cooperation — e) Environment"
New York, 20 November 1991

Mr. Chairman,

It is my distinct honor to address the distinguished representatives of the Second Committee assembled here on the fundamentally important subject of the environment and the moral imperatives for international cooperation in protecting nature in its totality as the precious original gift of God to mankind. The Holy See speaks not on the basis of specific scientific expertise but rather in the context of its special competence to consider the role of man as steward of nature. The failure to fulfill this stewardship has caused the senseless destruction of the natural environment through arbitrary use of the earth's resources. This depredation has provoked a rebellion on the part of nature which has been more tyrannized than governed by man as its steward (*Centesimus annus*, n. 37).

The irrational depredation of the natural environment also extends to the deterioration of the human environment arising from the serious problems of modern urbanization as well as the perpetuation of adverse living conditions in the developing countries. These catastrophic conditions arise from a variety of factors attributable in large measure to inequitable usage of the world's resources and a lack of solidarity among peoples and nations in rectifying our deteriorating environment in its totality *(Sollicitudo rei socialis*, n. 26).

Mr. Chairman, His Holiness Pope John Paul II incisively formulated the precepts for remedying this morally unacceptable depredation of the world's environment in his Message of 8 December 1989 entitled *"Peace With God The Creator, Peace With All of Creation."* His Holiness stated:

"In our day, there is a growing awareness that world peace is threatened not only by the arms race, regional conflicts and continued injustices among peoples and nations, but also by a lack of due respect for nature, by the plundering of natural resources and by a progressive decline in the quality of life. The sense of precariousness and insecurity that such a situation engenders is a seed-bed for collective selfishness, disregard for others and dishonesty.

Faced with the widespread destruction of the environment, people everywhere are coming to understand that we cannot continue to use the goods of the earth as we have in the past. The public in general as well as political leaders are concerned about this problem, and experts from a wide range of disciplines are studying its causes. Moreover, a new ecological awareness is beginning to emerge which, rather than being down-played, ought to be encouraged to develop into concrete programmes and initiatives."

Pope John Paul II reaffirmed the universal applicability of these precepts in his recent encyclical *Centesimus annus* (n. 37), in which he explicates the interdependence of peoples and nations and the objective truths about man's natural rights and obligations.

Mr. Chairman,

The decision of the United Nations to convene a Conference on Environment and Development in 1992 recognizes the imperative to counteract the threat upon our environment and simultaneously to address the interrelated just demands of developing countries for industrialized development. It is now recognized that this attack on the ecology takes many forms such as spoliation and contamination of land and seas through the disposal of toxic and hazardous wastes, abusive fishing, agricultural and forestation practices, uncontrolled destruction of animal life and a reckless use of natural resources through unbridled industrial and technological exploitation. Most particularly, the entire world community must be concerned by the pollution of the atmosphere which sustains life on our planet, and also by the related depletion of the ozone which has now reached crisis proportions.

Mr. Chairman,

Many thoughtful scientists have argued that since the beginning of the industrial revolution, humanity has been conducting a gigantic, and yet uncontrolled, experiment with our atmosphere. Only recently have we come to realize that we may have irretrievably changed the future course of our planet which, since it does not belong to us, we ought to pass along, if not improved, at the very least in the same state of health as we received it. Since that minimum requirement has probably already been violated, it is our immediate duty to make sure that the deterioration does not continue.

The enormity of this threat is manifested in the release of the so-called "greenhouse gases", i.e., carbon dioxide, methane, nitrous oxides and the well-known chlorofluoro-carbons, the CFCs. These gases, by trapping the otherwise outgoing heat from the earth, may increase the earth's temperature up to two to six degrees centigrade by the middle of the next century. The prediction acquires a clearer significance when we recall that the temperature difference between glacial and interglacial periods is of the same order, three to six degrees centigrade. To that sobering prediction, we must add the unique fact that while the transition from glacial to interglacial took typically tens of thousands of years, the possible anthropogenic warming is predicted to occur in less than one hundred years, an unprecedented compression of time that may catch humanity unprepared even to believe what is happening, let alone to set up effective counter-measures. Perhaps the most severe difficulty in countering the impending anthropogenic changes to our atmosphere is that they are not an event, like the eruption of a volcano, but rather a trend diluted in time that we may tend to ignore, a process that while admittedly dictated more by inertia than ill intentions, is nevertheless equally dangerous.

The burning of fossil fuel has spurred the industrial revolution that has brought so much economic relief to millions of people. However, the technical civilization which is enjoyed by only privileged nations and peoples, poses a danger on a worldwide basis. Scientists now acknowledge that the uncontrolled burning of fossil fuel injects into the atmosphere gases that can increase the earth's temperature which in turn adversely affects agricultural production, as for example, the yield of rice, a staple food for literally hundreds of millions of people. By the same token, the predicted warming might induce a significant sea-level rise that will affect tens of millions of people today and generations of their descendants. Similarly, the reduction in the Antarctic ozone layer, a finding considerably more severe than predicted by scientists, is another eloquent example of the threat to our environment. The chlorofluoro-carbons released by industrialized enterprises travel worldwide, rise into the earth's stratosphere and destroy the ozone layer over the Antarctic. The flood of ultraviolet radiation that is let through the hole damages not only neighboring countries but also the marine life that absorbs part of the carbon dioxide we emit into the atmosphere. The more carbon dioxide remains aloft, the higher will be the global warming everywhere in the world. These examples are far from exhaustive but they illustrate the deleterious effect of anthropogenic activities. The realization of the phenomenon is already a significant achievement but man must act with solidarity to mitigate the impact of this potentially devastating phenomenon.

Mr. Chairman,

Since no one nation, nor one particular generation has created the threats to our environment, it is not the time to postulate that any one entity or nation should or can rectify the impending predicament. The phenomenon is truly transnational and intergenerational, the first of such kind ever to face humanity as a whole. Any condition that will happen will be global in scale and will affect every living creature on earth. There will be no winners — all stand to lose.

The set of environmental phenomena is totally new, the implications are global, and mankind must use new ways of thinking — radically new ways — if we are to fulfill our stewardship of creation. Regional and even national considerations become outmoded notions in our interdependent environment. In the words of Pope John Paul II: "It is necessary however, that the entire human community — individuals, States and international bodies — take seriously the responsibility that is theirs" (*Peace with God the Creator, Peace with All of Creation*, n. 6).

Mr. Chairman,

The Holy See will not attempt to add to the significant technical discourse that is underway under the auspices of UNEP but we feel it is our duty to contribute some considerations of the moral imperatives for intergenerational equity. We have inherited a habitable blue planet, and we must see to it that we do not leave behind a scorched planet. Otherwise, we are literally abusing God's precious gifts and denying to future generations their common heritage (*Peace With God The Creator, Peace With All of Creation*, n. 8).

The present environmental crisis reveals the urgent need for a new solidarity between the industrialized nations and developing nations for the rational use of resources to promote a peaceful and healthy environment for all mankind. Truly, the words of Pope Paul VI that "the new name of peace is development" apply to the interrelationship of environmental health, development and the cooperative and peaceful relations among States and peoples. Real equity and peace depends upon the solidarity of men as stewards of God's gifts to this world.

Thank you, Mr. Chairman.

STATEMENT BY
HIS EXCELLENCY ARCHBISHOP RENATO R. MARTINO
APOSTOLIC NUNCIO, PERMANENT OBSERVER OF THE HOLY SEE
TO THE UNITED NATIONS AND
HEAD OF THE HOLY SEE DELEGATION
TO THE UNITED NATIONS CONFERENCE ON
ENVIRONMENT AND DEVELOPMENT
RIO DE JANEIRO, BRAZIL; 4 JUNE 1992

The people of the whole world look with keen interest and great expectation to this United Nations Conference on Environment and Development. The challenge facing the international community is how to reconcile the imperative duty of the protection of the environment with the basic right of all people to development.

I. The centrality of the human person

The Catholic Church approaches both the care and protection of the environment and all questions regarding development from the point of view of the human person. It is the conviction of the Holy See, therefore, that all ecological programmes and all developmental initiatives must respect the full dignity and freedom of whomever might be affected by such programmes. They must be seen in relation to the needs of actual men and women, their families, their values, their unique social and cultural heritage, their responsibility toward future generations. For the ultimate purpose of environmental and developmental programmes is to enhance the quality of human life, to place creation in the fullest way possible at the service of the human family.

The ultimate determining factor is the human person. It is not simply science and technology, nor the increasing means of economic and material development, but the human person, and especially groups of persons, communities and nations, freely choosing to face the problems together, who will, under God, determine the future.[1]

The word "environment" itself means "that which surrounds." This very definition postulates the existence of a centre around which the environment exists. That centre is the human being, the only creature in this

---

[1] Cf. *Address of Pope John Paul II to the United Nations Centre for the Environment*, Nairobi, 18 August 1985.

world who is not only capable of being conscious of itself and of its surroundings, but is gifted with the intelligence to explore, the sagacity to utilize, and is ultimately responsible for its choices and the consequences of those choices. The praiseworthy heightened awareness of the present generation for all components of the environment, and the consequent efforts at preserving and protecting them, rather than weakening the central position of the human being, accentuate its role and responsibilities.

Likewise, it cannot be forgotten that the true purpose of every economic, social and political system and of every model of development is the integral advancement of the human person. Development is clearly something much more extensive than merely economic progress measured in terms of gross national product. True development takes as its criterion the human person with all the needs, just expectations and fundamental rights that are his or hers.[2]

Complementing respect for the human person and human life is the responsibility to respect all creation. God is creator and planner of the entire universe. The universe and life in all its forms are a testimony to God's creative power, His Love, His enduring presence. All creation reminds us of the mystery and love of God. As the Book of Genesis tells us: "And God saw everything that He had made, and behold, it was very good." (Gen. 1:31)

II. The moral dimension

In the very early stages that led to the convening of this Conference, the General Assembly emphasized that "in view of the global character of major environmental problems, there is a common interest of all countries in pursuing policies aimed at achieving a sustainable and environmentally sound development within a sound ecological balance."[3]

The Holy See has been and continues to be keenly interested in the issues which this Conference is addressing. During the laborious preparatory phases, the Holy See Delegation carefully and respectfully examined the many proposals of technological, scientific and political nature put forth and appreciates the contributions made by so many participants in the process. Faithful to its nature and its mission, the Holy See has continued to

---

[2] Cf. *Address of Pope John Paul II to the 21st Session of the Conference of the Food and Agricultural Organization*, Vatican, 13 November 1981.

[3] Resolution 43/196 of the General Assembly, 20 December 1988.

emphasize the rights and the duties, the well-being and the responsibilities of individuals and of societies. For the Holy See the problems of environment and development are, at their root, issues of a moral, ethical nature, from which derive two obligations: the urgent imperative to find solutions and the inescapable demand that every proposed solution meet the criteria of truth and justice.

"Theology, philosophy and science all speak of a harmonious universe, of a 'cosmos' endowed with its own integrity, its own internal, dynamic balance. This order must be respected. The human race is called to explore this order, to examine it with due care and to make use of it while safeguarding its integrity."[4] The Creator has placed human beings at the centre of creation, making them the responsible stewards, not the exploiting despots, of the world around them. "On the other hand, the earth is ultimately a common heritage, the fruits of which are for the benefits of all. This has direct consequences for the problem at hand. It is manifestly unjust that a privileged few should continue to accumulate excess goods, squandering available resources, while masses of people are living in conditions of misery at the very lowest level of subsistence. Today, the dramatic threat of ecological breakdown is teaching us the extent to which greed and selfishness — both individual and collective — are contrary to the order of creation, an order which is characterized by mutual interdependence."[5]

III. The resulting obligations: stewardship and solidarity

The concepts of an ordered universe and a common heritage both point to the necessity of developing in the heart of every individual and in the activities of every society a true sense of stewardship and of solidarity.

It is the obligation of a responsible steward to be one who cares for the goods entrusted to him and not one who plunders, to be one who conserves and enhances and not one who destroys and dissipates. Humility, and not arrogance, must be the proper attitude of humankind vis-a-vis the environment. The exciting scientific discoveries of our century have enabled the human mind to pierce with equal success into the infinitesimally small, as well as into the immeasurably large. The results have been ambivalent, for we have witnessed that, without ethics, science and technology can be

---

[4] Message of Pope John Paul II for the 1990 World Day of Peace on the theme *"Peace with God the Creator, Peace with All of Creation,"* 8 December 1989. n. 8.

[5] *Ibid.*

employed to kill as well as to save lives, to manipulate as well as to nurture, to destroy as well as to build.

Responsible stewardship demands a consideration for the common good: no one person, no one group of people in isolation are allowed to determine their relationship with the universe. The universal common good transcends all private interests, all national boundaries, and reaches, beyond the present moment, to the future generations.

Hence, solidarity becomes an urgent moral imperative. We are all part of God's creation — we live as a human family. The whole of creation is everyone's heritage. All equally created by God, called to share the goods and the beauty of the one world, human beings are called to enter into a solidarity of universal dimensions, "a cosmic fraternity" animated by the very love that flows from God. Education to solidarity is an urgent necessity of our day. We must learn again to live in harmony, not only with God and with one another, but with creation itself. The "*Canticle of the Sun*" of Francis of Assisi could well become the anthem of a new generation that loves and respects in one embrace the Creator and all God's creatures.

Responsible stewardship and genuine solidarity are not only directed to the protection of the environment, but, equally so, to the inalienable right and duty of all peoples to development. The earth's resources and the means to their access and use must be wisely monitored and justly shared. The demands for the care and protection of the environment cannot be used to obstruct the right to development, nor can development be invoked in thwarting the environment. The task of achieving a just balance is today's challenge.

The scandalous patterns of consumption and waste of all kinds of resources by a few must be corrected, in order to ensure justice and sustainable development to all, everywhere in the world. Pope John Paul II has reminded that: "Simplicity, moderation and discipline, as well as a spirit of sacrifice, must become part of everyday life, lest all suffer the negative consequences of the careless habits of a few."[6] The developing countries, in their legitimate ambition to improve their status and emulate existing patterns of development, will realize and counteract the danger that can derive to their people and to the world by the adoption of highly wasteful growth strategies hitherto widely employed, that have led humanity into the present situation.

---

[6] *Message for the 1990 World Day of Peace*, n. 13.

New resources, the discovery of substitute new materials, determined efforts at conservation and recycling programmes, have assisted in the protection of known reserves; the development of new technologies has the promise of using resources more efficiently. For developing nations, at times rich in natural resources, the acquisition and use of new technologies is a clear necessity. Only an equitable global sharing of technology will make possible the process of sustainable development.

When considering the problems of environment and development one must also pay due attention to the complex issue of population. The position of the Holy See regarding procreation is frequently misinterpreted. The Catholic Church does not propose procreation at any cost. It keeps on insisting that the transmission of, and the caring for human life must be exercised with an utmost sense of responsibility. It restates its constant position that human life is sacred; that the aim of public policy is to enhance the welfare of families; that it is the right of the spouses to decide on the size of the family and spacing of births, without pressures from governments or organizations. This decision must fully respect the moral order established by God, taking into account the couple's responsibilities toward each other, the children they already have and the society to which they belong.[7] What the Church opposes is the imposition of demographic policies and the promotion of methods for limiting births which are contrary to the objective moral order and to the liberty, dignity and conscience of the human being. At the same time, the Holy See does not consider people as mere numbers, or only on economic terms.[8] It emphatically states its concern that the poor not be singled out as if, by their very existence, they were the cause, rather than the victims, of the lack of development and of environmental degradation.

Serious as the problem of interrelation among environment, development and population is, it cannot be solved in an over-simplistic manner and many of the most alarming predictions have proven false and have been discredited by a number of recent studies. "People are born not only with mouths that need to be fed, but also with hands that can produce,

---

[7] Cf. *Message of His Eminence Cardinal Maurice Roy*, President of the Pontifical Commission Justice and Peace to H.E. U Thant, Secretary-General of the United Nations, on the occasion of the launching of the Second Development Decade, Vatican, 19 November 1970.

[8] Cf. *Address of Pope John Paul II to Mr. Rafael Salas*, Secretary-General of the 1984 International Conference on Population, and Executive Director of the United Nations Fund for Population Activities (UNFPA), Vatican, 7 June 1984.

and minds that can create and innovate."[9] As for the environment, just to mention one instance, countries with as few as 5% of the world population are responsible for more than one quarter of the principal greenhouse gas, while countries with up to a quarter of the world population contribute as little as 5% of the same greenhouse gas.

A serious and concerted effort aimed at protecting the environment and at promoting development will not be possible without directly addressing the structural forms of poverty that exist throughout the world. Environment is devastated and development thwarted by the outbreak of wars, when internal conflicts destroy homes, fields and factories, when intolerable circumstances force millions of people to desperately seek refuge away from their lands, when minorities are oppressed, when the rights of the most vulnerable — women, children, the aged and the infirm — are neglected or abused.

"The poor, to whom the earth is entrusted no less than to others, must be enabled to find a way out of their poverty. This will require a courageous reform of structures, as well as new ways of relating among peoples and States."[10]

Finally, the Holy See invites the international community to discover and affirm that there is a spiritual dimension to the issues at hand. Human beings have the need for and the right to more than clean air and water, to more than economic and technological progress. Human beings are also fragile and an alarm must be sounded against the poisoning of the minds and the corruption of the hearts, both in the developed and developing worlds. The dissemination of hatred, of falsehood and vice, the traffic and use of narcotic drugs, the ruthless self-centeredness which disregards the rights of others — even the right to life — are all phenomena that cannot be gauged by technical instruments, but whose chain-effects destroy individuals and societies. Let us strive to give to every man, woman and child a safe and healthy physical environment. Let us join forces in providing them with real opportunities for development. But, in the process, let us not allow them to be robbed of their souls. On a closely related level, the aesthetic value of the environment must also be considered and protected, thus adding beauty and inspiring artistic expression to developmental activities.

---

[9] *The Wall Street Journal*, in "Review and Outlook": Prince Malthus, Tuesday, 28 April 1992.

[10] *Message for the 1990 World Day of Peace*, n. 11.

The Holy See regards this Conference as a major challenge and a unique opportunity that the people of the world are presenting to the international community. The problems facing today's world are serious indeed and even threatening. Nonetheless, the opportunity is at hand. Avoiding confrontation, and engaging in honest dialogue and sincere solidarity, all forces must be joined in a positive adventure of unprecedented magnitude and cooperation that will restore hope to the human family and renew the face of the earth.

STATEMENT BY
HIS EXCELLENCY ARCHBISHOP RENATO R. MARTINO
APOSTOLIC NUNCIO, PERMANENT OBSERVER OF THE HOLY SEE
TO THE UNITED NATIONS
BEFORE THE PLENARY SESSION OF THE GENERAL ASSEMBLY
ON ITEM 79: "REPORT OF THE UNITED NATIONS CONFERENCE
ON ENVIRONMENT AND DEVELOPMENT"
NEW YORK, 6 NOVEMBER 1992

Mr. President,

A few short months ago the eyes of the world were focused on Rio de Janeiro, where the representatives of the countries of the world solemnly stated their commitment to seek and implement ways of reconciling the imperative duty of care and protection of the environment with the fundamental right of all peoples to development.

Even before considering the results achieved in Rio, it is most important to notice that UNCED has brought about a very remarkable change of perspective. If in the past it was conceivable to speak of environment and of development separately, such is not the case anymore, for the two have now been placed in a mutually reinforcing and interactive parallelism. The pressing demands for the care and protection of the environment cannot be used to deny the right to development, nor can the urgency of development be invoked to justify damage to the environment. The interrelation of environment and development presents new and formidable challenges, requiring radical changes in the attitude and conduct of individuals and nations, but it cannot be ignored.

The documents issued by UNCED, namely the Rio Declaration, Agenda 21 and the two Conventions, do not pretend to resolve the immense problems examined at the Conference, but they provide a valid foundation for the arduous work of building a world in which environment and development will complement, rather than destroy, each other.

Principle 1 of the Rio Declaration on Environment and Development correctly identifies human beings as the central point of convergence of all the issues pertaining to environment and development. The principle of the primacy and centrality of the human person has been consistently upheld by the Holy See, insisting that all ecological programmes and all developmental initiatives must respect and enhance the dignity, the rights and the duties of all individuals affected by them.

Because they are centered on the human person, the issues of environment and development are, at their root, issues of a moral, ethical nature, and thus carrying rights and duties. The centrality of the human person means that the world of nature has its converging point in the human being and that development can only be understood by taking into account the total dimensions of the human being. There follow, as immediate consequences, the inherent obligations to exercise both responsible stewardship in regard to the environment and genuine solidarity with all other people in the process of development. Responsible stewardship and genuine solidarity, as grave moral obligations, fall on everyone, without exception, and must effectively take into consideration the rights of present as well as of future generations. Since we have inherited the environment and its resources, we have the obligation to pass it on to the next generations possibly improved, certainly not damaged.

Everyone is aware of the difficult task that lies ahead, but, hopefully, UNCED has succeeded in awakening and directing the commitment of governments, organizations and individuals, since at stake is nothing less than the well-being — even the survival — of the inhabitants of our planet.

Since there is no world government that could compel everyone to defend our planet, there is an obvious danger of inertia. This is so because, contrary to other natural threats to our lives that can be categorized as "events" localized in space and time with an immediate impact on us, the environmental threat is a "trend" slow in building. Since the true magnitude of the results can only be gauged as an integrated effect over many decades, there is a clear danger of succumbing to the inertial tendency of "wait and see," or, worse yet, of letting future generations take care of the problem.

A similar danger derives from the ambiguous position adopted by so many until now. Individuals, companies and national governments cannot continue to deplore environmental degradation on the one hand, while continuing to contribute to that process on the other, as if the deterioration of the environment were somebody else's problem. It is a common and global problem, demanding real changes in individual and collective lifestyles and productive systems.

Underlying such dangers is the common assumption that an individual's choices in protecting or in polluting the environment are too insignificant to affect society as a whole, in the face of the magnitude of the problems confronting the world. Yet, life would become unlivable in a society where the majority of the people felt that way.

What is urgently needed is a new "education in ecological

responsibility" that inculcates human values such as respect for one's neighbours, love of nature, a sense of responsibility and solidarity, so that each individual will relinquish egoistic behaviour in order that communities assume more responsible lifestyles.

At the national and international levels, the achievement of sustainable development does not take place spontaneously; society needs actions, strategies and institutions to reach this goal. The problem is most clearly perceived at a world level because of the strict ecological and economic interdependencies among different geographical areas. The Holy See does not intend to offer technical and political solutions which would go beyond its sphere of competence, but stresses the need that the ethical dimension of all national and international programmes be given due consideration. There are, in fact, important issues of justice involved in working out equitable access to the resources and technologies needed for development and in allocating the inherent costs. There are many criteria demanding consideration, such as, for instance, the historical accountability for past activities, the current status quo, or the allocation of permits on the basis of degrees of development or of population, but none of them, if taken in isolation, can provide equitable and efficient solutions. Conceptual and practical difficulties still abound, but adequate study and courageous action in this regard are an inescapable moral obligation. With specific reference to the allocation of permits, the Holy See respectfully suggests that consideration be given to devise ways to relate these problems to the crucial issue of the repayment of external indebtedness, thus enabling countries to better attain their rightful development while protecting and enhancing the environment.

At the Rio Conference, the Holy See also invited the international community to discover and affirm the spiritual dimension of the issue at hand. If the human being is at the center of concern in all matters pertaining environment and development, then the total dimensions of his being must be taken into consideration. Human beings have the need for and the right to more than clean air and water, to more than economic and technological progress. The reconciliation of environment and development will also offer to the human spirit new expressions of its artistic and aesthetic capacities.

In conclusion, may I be allowed to repeat the words of Pope John Paul II:

> "Authentic human development can hardly ignore the solidarity which binds man and his environment, nor can it exclude a universal concern for the needs of all the earth's peoples. Any attempt to assess the relationship between

environment and development which ignores these deeper realities will inevitably lead to further and perhaps more destabilizing imbalances." (*Address to the "Nova Spes" IV Nobel Prizewinners Meeting*, 14 December 1989).

Thank you, Mr. President.

STATEMENT BY
HIS EXCELLENCY ARCHBISHOP RENATO R. MARTINO
APOSTOLIC NUNCIO, PERMANENT OBSERVER OF THE HOLY SEE TO THE UNITED NATIONS
BEFORE THE SECOND COMMITTEE OF THE
48TH SESSION OF THE GENERAL ASSEMBLY ON ITEM 99:
IMPLEMENTATION OF DECISIONS AND RECOMMENDATIONS OF THE UNITED NATIONS CONFERENCE ON ENVIRONMENT AND DEVELOPMENT
NEW YORK, 23 NOVEMBER 1993

Mr. Chairman,

My Delegation wishes to express its satisfaction with regard to many initiatives that have been taken in the wake of the United Nations Conference on Environment and Development, celebrated in Rio de Janeiro in June 1992.

The establishment of the United Nations Commission on Sustainable Development has opened the mechanism for the necessary institutional arrangements to follow up the Conference. The decisions of the General Assembly at its forty-seventh session have succeeded in establishing the framework for the elaboration of an international Convention to combat desertification, the convening of two Conferences, one on Sustainable Development of Small Island Developing States, and the second on Straddling Fish Stocks and Highly Migratory Fish Stocks. Substantial progress has been made regarding these initiatives.

My Delegation has followed with special interest the preparatory process for the Global Conference on the Sustainable Development of Small Island Developing States. While the Holy See does not intend to offer technical and political solutions which would go beyond its sphere of competence, it continues to stress the need for due consideration of the ethical dimensions of problems affecting developing countries and specifically the Small Island Developing States. There are, in fact, important issues of justice in working out equitable access to the resources and technologies needed for development and in allocating the inherent costs.

Once again, the Holy See considers it a duty to respectfully but forcefully remind all States of the fundamental primacy of the human person when they consider all the issues of environment and development. Enshrined as the first principle of the Rio Declaration, this primacy of the human being must be translated in the practical decisions of every day.

The concept of sustainable development cannot be employed only in regard to developing countries. The Rio Conference has amply demonstrated that the levels of development achieved by many industrial countries have often proved to be neither morally nor economically "sustainable," and certainly cannot be replicated world-wide. This applies particularly to the patterns of consumption — and frequently of waste — of energy and natural resources. The burden of true development is to be shared, and to this end there is an urgent need for education and re-education of individuals and communities all over the world. Chapter 4 of Agenda 21, entitled "Changing consumption patterns," implies and demands a profound and widespread change of habits and attitudes.

My Delegation applauds and encourages all efforts made in such direction, but at the same time it notices with dismay that this fundamental aspect of the problem receives mostly lip service, rather than genuine and concerted action. The Rio Conference has correctly restated that everyone on earth has a right and an invitation to share at the banquet of life. But what kind of a banquet would it be if a few first comers gobble the largest portion of the food on the table and then pity the remaining fellow guests, maybe even faulting them for simply being so many or so hungry?

The call of Rio to "re-evaluate" consumption and lifestyles also questions the fashionable equation between "quality of life" and the simple increased production and consumption of non-basic material goods. Economic systems certainly need to be readjusted in order to achieve equitable development. But beyond that, if the correct emphasis has to be kept on the human person, it becomes evident that full development requires more than that. A "happy life" demands the satisfaction of the basic needs of food, shelter and health care, but it also needs an environment of peace, where people respect each other, where values take precedence over objects, where the human spirit can give expression to its artistic and aesthetic capacities.

Mr. Chairman,

I would like to conclude these remarks by quoting the words addressed yesterday morning by His Holiness Pope John Paul II on the occasion of the presentation of the letters of credence by the Ambassador of Venezuela to the Holy See. "In order to increase economic and social development, the principles of equality in the just distribution of efforts and sacrifices on the part of all must be respected. The common objective must be that of struggling against poverty, unemployment and ignorance; transforming the potential resources of nature with intelligence, industriousness, responsibility, constancy and honest management, thus reducing big inequalities."

Thank you, Mr. Chairman.

Chapter Three

THE WORLD CONFERENCE ON HUMAN RIGHTS

Vienna, Austria

14 - 25 June 1993

Chapter Contents

The World Conference on Human Rights
Vienna, Austria;
14 - 25 June 1993

Recommendations submitted by the Holy See regarding the
    World Conference on Human Rights, contained in
    United Nations Document A/Conf.157/PC/6
    22 August 1991 139

Intervention of the Holy See Delegation at the Regional
    Meeting (Latin America and the Caribbean),
    in preparation for the World Conference on Human Rights
    San Jose, Costa Rica; 20 January 1993 144

Intervention of His Eminence Roger Cardinal Etchegaray,
    President, Pontifical Council for Justice and Peace, at a Panel
    during the World Conference on Human Rights:
    "Human Rights, Democracy and Development"
    Vienna, 17 June 1993 147

Intervention of His Excellency Archbishop Jean-Louis Tauran,
    Secretary for Relations with States, at the World Conference
    on Human Rights; Vienna, 21 June 1993 151

Statement of Interpretation of the Holy See's Consensus to the
    Final Document adopted by the World Conference on
    Human Rights; Vienna, 25 June 1993 155

Statement by His Excellency Archbishop Jean-Louis Tauran,
    Secretary for Relations with States, before the
    Third Committee of the U.N. General Assembly,
    on Item 114: "Human Rights Questions"
    New York, 17 November 1993 156

Interview of His Excellency Archbishop Donato Squicciarini,
    Apostolic Nuncio to Austria, Head of the Holy See Delegation
    to the World Conference on Human Rights, to the
    Radio Programme "Christ in Time"; 20 June 1993 161

Interview of His Excellency Archbishop Donato Squicciarini,
    Apostolic Nuncio to Austria, Head of the Holy See Delegation
    to the World Conference on Human Rights,
    Catholic Press News Story; 22 June 1993 163

(The Appendix contains no related documents for this chapter.)

RECOMMENDATIONS SUBMITTED BY THE HOLY SEE REGARDING THE WORLD CONFERENCE ON HUMAN RIGHTS CONTAINED IN UNITED NATIONS DOCUMENT A/CONF.157/PC/6 22 AUGUST 1991

1. In his Address to the International Conference on Human Rights at Tehran in 1968, His Holiness Pope Paul VI said: "To speak of human rights is to affirm a common good of mankind, it means working to build a fraternal community" (15 April 1968). This statement is more valid than ever today, as the conscience of mankind is now highly sensitive to the issue of human rights and they have become fundamental to man's search for reconciliation and peace. A long distance has been covered since the Tehran Conference, but much still remains to be done for human rights to be effectively recognized and respected throughout the world.

2. The period since the adoption of the *Universal Declaration of Human Rights* can be divided into three phases. During the first phase, progress was made in work of a legislative nature by the international organizations, in an essentially institutional framework, with the aim of more clearly defining the rights proclaimed in the *Universal Declaration* and expanding them further.

3. This phase, which was characterized in particular by the activity of experts and governmental representatives, was followed by a period which began with the Tehran Conference and was marked by a greater interest in human rights, with closer attention being given to the problem of violation of those rights. This, secondly, led to progressive expansion and dissemination of the concept to increasingly wider sectors of world public opinion, at least in the Western countries. It was discovered that the topic could make an impact on foreign policy choices but, unfortunately, it was also discovered that human rights could be effectively used as a new weapon in the political and ideological confrontation taking place throughout the world, to the detriment of true respect for these rights within countries. It is indeed a paradox that the effective protection of human rights sometimes appears to be in inverse proportion to the length of the debates on the subject.

4. A third phase, which began in the early 1980s, took a more definite form at the end of that decade, during which major political changes took place in several countries. This present period could be described as a period of maturing. One section of public opinion that has been subjected by the communications media to selective condemnations of human rights or to misleading manipulation of their interpretation seems to be afflicted with a

kind of apathy. This does not mean that the cause of human rights has lost its importance. Rather it shows clearly that different priorities should be set. It is no longer enough to draw attention to human rights. What is needed is to find the root of the problems and to do this a veritable education programme must be undertaken. Here the Holy See is in a position to make a valuable contribution, through the social education and the pastoral services of the Catholic Church, to the performance of this long-term but vitally important task.

5. The context in which the forthcoming World Conference on Human Rights is being prepared offers encouraging prospects and gives rise to well-founded hopes. The time of sterile polemics over the relative importance of the various categories of human rights appears to be over. The annex to resolution 1991/30 adopted by the Commission on Human Rights at its forty-seventh session very appropriately highlights "the equal importance and indivisibility of all categories of human rights, as well as the interrelationship between human rights, democracy and development in full respect for the *Charter of the United Nations*" (para. 2). Continued reference to an order of precedence among these categories of rights is now indicative of reluctance to defend and promote human rights more effectively, as recommended in the annex referred to above (see para. 4).

6. It is, moreover, obvious that a distinction has to be made between "primordial human rights," such as the right to life, and "fundamental human rights," such as the right to work or to health care. Whereas the former must be respected always and everywhere, the latter are observed only where certain specific conditions are met. It is to be hoped that the page of ideological clashes masking more or less unacknowledgeable interests can now be turned once and for all. For those working to promote human rights this represents a goal which demands the cooperation of everyone, in a spirit of goodwill, mutual trust and genuine concern for human beings.

7. Here are a few ideas, which the Holy See would like to submit to the Preparatory Committee, on the principles that should guide the forthcoming World Conference:

a) Certain human rights are "natural" rights

If, as article 1 of the of *Universal Declaration Human Rights* solemnly proclaims "All human beings are born free and equal in dignity and rights," it follows that human rights existed prior to the formation of the State. In other words, the State is not required to grant any "recognition" of these rights, because they must necessarily derive from the dignity that is inherent in every human being, who is independent of the State structures. In the Christian doctrine, this dignity is based on the fact that man was created "in the image of God." The State, on the other hand, has a duty to promote and defend the full exercise of and effective respect for human rights.

b) Universality of human rights

There is one constantly growing criticism of the *Universal Declaration* which could be termed "relativist" and it began with the observation that the United Nations of 1948 could not genuinely claim to represent the entire world. The *Universal Declaration* is criticized for failing to reflect all the various cultural traditions. However, it cannot be said exactly how the framers of the *Declaration* specifically contradicted the value systems of civilizations that were unable to participate in the debates of 1948. This criticism has often served as the pretext for practices that show little regard for human rights. The universality of human rights should be reasserted emphatically on the basis of the unquestionable truth that all human beings are the same in nature.

c) Rights and obligations: two sides of the same coin

On the question of duties it is generally article 29 of the *Declaration* that is cited. However, it is too easily forgotten that article 1 affirms that all human beings "should act towards one another in a spirit of brotherhood." At a time when a sort of inflation of rights is sometimes to be observed, it is desirable to point out that rights will remain a dead letter if, at the same time, the obligations and responsibilities of each and everyone, in other words the moral dimension of human rights, are not more clearly perceived.

d) The collective dimension of human rights

The broadening of the concept of human rights has fortunately widened the scope of their application. One can therefore speak of a collective dimension of these rights from two viewpoints: on the one hand, there are collective subjects of rights, such as the family, minorities, peoples and nations and, on the other, there are rights which belong both to the individual and to the community, such as the right to peace, the right to development and the right to security in the environment.

e) The importance of freedom of conscience and freedom of religion

In the opinion of the Holy See, this is a "radical" right, in the sense that it is at the "root" of any edifice of human rights because it affects the primordial relationship of the human being with his Creator. The Catholic Church defends religious freedom disinterestedly for every religion, because it is the most profound expression of freedom of conscience. It is unacceptable that certain religious faiths refuse to accept the principle of changing one's religion — if the decision has been taken deliberately and freely according to the dictates of the conscience of a person seeking the truth — when article 18 of the *Universal Declaration* explicitly recognizes this right.

f) Primacy of the right to life

It is not fortuitous that this right is the first in the list of rights set forth in the *Universal Declaration* (article 3), because, in fact, it is obvious that there can be no specific reference to human rights if there is no one entitled to these rights. In the opinion of the Holy See, this right belongs to every human being from the moment of his conception. It is with this belief that the Holy See acceded to the *Convention on the Rights of the Child*, the preamble of which rightly recalls the need for the child to have "appropriate legal protection, before as well as after birth." It is also this belief that led the Holy See to reject as unacceptable any practice of euthanasia or any other similar form of aggression against life.

g) Violations of human rights

The first formulation of human rights in modern history was prompted by a reaction against the arbitrary concept that the State has absolute power and it is still often believed that these rights may be asserted only vis-à-vis the public authorities. However, we now see violations of human rights being perpetrated by groups which are not responsible to the State and which even attack the representatives of the State, notwithstanding the fact that the latter's role is to protect the rights of its citizens. These are very serious developments which take the form of terrorism or organized crime. In some countries, certain areas are completely outside the control of the legitimate authorities. This is a threat to the functioning of any State governed by the rule of law, without which there can be no security for the people and therefore no protection of their rights. It would be desirable if the forthcoming World Conference on Human Rights could discuss this tragic situation.

h) The efforts now being made to strengthen the present juridical regime in the area of human rights could include discussion of the desirability of setting up a world body to which individuals or communities could appeal against violations of human rights.

Intervention of the Holy See Delegation at the Regional Meeting (Latin America and the Caribbean) in Preparation for the World Conference on Human Rights
San Jose, Costa Rica; 20 January 1993

The Holy See Delegation wishes to make some comments regarding the main topics of this Regional Meeting of Latin America and the Caribbean, since it considers the contribution of the Latin American countries to the field of human rights to be of great importance.

In fact, in spite of the mishaps which occurred in the course of its history, this region forged its juridical institutions in the light of the ideals of equality, justice and freedom which enabled it to contribute efficiently to the institutional progress of the theme treated.

On the other hand, the Church, aware of the fact that "upon peoples rooted in Christian faith often were imposed structures of injustice" (*Puebla: Evangelizacion en el Presente y en el Futuro de America Latina*, Latin American Episcopal Council, 1979, n. 437), has always encouraged in the light of the Gospel — which is the profound root of the human person and of his rights — a positive evolution in the society of respect for the human person, of fraternity and of solidarity, irrespective of race, sex, creed or nationality.

Man, made in the image and likeness of God and redeemed by Jesus Christ, is a being imbued with rights which are constitutional to him. And States — who do not grant these rights — are to protect and develop them because they belong to the very nature of man. Pope John Paul II said recently in this regard: the heart of international life is not the States, but human beings.

For 500 years this was the nucleus of the teaching of Fray Francisco de Vitoria and Fray Bartolome de las Casas in their true interpretation of the Gospel; this nucleus was accepted in the Constitution of Cadiz thanks to, among others, the contribution of one of the most illustrious Costa Ricans, Fr. Florencio del Castillo.

These truths were also echoed in this hall in these days, where authoritative voices were repeatedly raised in defense of the centrality of man, his civil and political rights, as well as his economic, social, religious and cultural rights, which indissolubly united, form a single whole for the full realization of the human being.

In this regard the social teaching of the Church has been continuous and coherent and the great social encyclicals, since the final decade of the last century, have shed light, in an unprecedented way, on important decisive questions of our day. In this line and in his repeated defense of human rights, Pope John Paul II affirmed in his recent Message for the World Day of Peace: "The number of people living in conditions of extreme poverty is enormous ... Such a situation is not only an affront to human dignity but also represents a clear threat to peace ... The poorest countries' right to development imposes upon the developed countries a clear duty to come to their aid" (Pope John Paul II, *1993 World Day of Peace Message*, n. 3).

The problem of external debt also negatively affects the proper exercise of human rights. In this regard, the Pope asks in the same Message: "Is it not the poorest groups in these countries which often have to bear the major burden of repayment?" (*ibid*, n. 3). The time has come to thoroughly examine the problem, with due priority, in search of solutions which seriously take into consideration the grave social consequences of the programmes of an economic nature.

On the other hand, it is necessary to examine the causes of debts, produced sometimes by less responsible administrations, and to guarantee that the subsidies reach the true addressees which are the more needy groups and are — in the case of Latin America — the majority.

Madam Chairperson, with special reference to the mechanisms for the promotion and protection of human rights, the Holy See Delegation expresses its satisfaction that in this meeting several speakers have supported the creation of a High Commissioner for Human Rights. We believe that the mechanisms already existing in this field will be strengthened by the creation of an international instance of the highest level, with sufficient faculties to monitor the full observance of human rights in the world.

This proposal could be discussed as an important contribution of the Latin American and Caribbean countries in the World Conference of Vienna.

Madam Chairperson, if the international community should guarantee the full enjoyment of human rights, it should not forget that none of them can be exercised if the principal right which God has given to man — the right to life — is not respected.

This right is inseparable from the human being and no reason can ever justify its disrespect. This is a binding ethical principle not only for

Christians but also for followers of every faith. The right to life should be guaranteed from the moment of conception until the final breath. As reaffirmed last October in Santo Domingo by the IV General Conference of the Latin American Bishops, held on the occasion of the Fifth Centenary of the Evangelization of America: God alone is the Lord of life and man is not and cannot be the master or arbitrator of human life.

Madam Chairperson, the Holy See Delegation would like to wish every success to this Meeting, in the conviction that its results could contribute successfully in shaping a more just international community, in which the spirit of solidarity, properly that of the Gospel, will be practiced among all men.

INTERVENTION OF
HIS EMINENCE ROGER CARDINAL ETCHEGARAY
PRESIDENT OF THE PONTIFICAL COUNCIL FOR JUSTICE AND PEACE
GIVEN AT A PANEL DURING THE
WORLD CONFERENCE ON HUMAN RIGHTS
VIENNA, AUSTRIA, 17 JUNE 1993

Human Rights, Democracy and Development

On the occasion of the United Nations World Conference on Human Rights, which Vienna has the honour of hosting, the Austrian government had the excellent idea of organizing three panels. That of today deals directly with topics that are on the Conference agenda. Without a doubt, the question of the relationships between Human Rights, Democracy and Development will be one of the most widely debated, and our panel would like to bear witness to both the necessity and the complexity of this debate.

However, from the very beginning, we must be aware of the pitfalls underlying this debate: are there any other words today that lend themselves so well to elasticity, even inflation of meaning, than those of "human rights," "democracy," and "development"? What Paul Valéry said about the word "liberty" applies, therefore, to them: "one of those detestable words that sing more than speak, that ask more than answer, one of those words that has turned its hand to all trades ... very good words for dialectics, for eloquence, as suitable for illusory analyses as for those sentence-endings that set thunder rolling." What is at stake is too serious for us not to take the care to give these words the full substance of their meaning, the full plenitude of human aspirations. This is my intention in this opening speech.

1. Human rights

In face of the hesitations of a humanity which is losing direction and beginning to lose confidence in itself, a disorderly appeal to human rights is the instinctive cry of those who want to survive; the clenched hands with which humanity grasps human rights are hands clinging to a life buoy. Yet, what a range there is in the definition of human rights and in the choice of which rights to defend first! Yet, what a gulf separates East and West, North and South! Yet, what battering goes on over these rights between countries which allow themselves certain concessions in order to better protect their own particular interests and which treat human rights as if they were nothing more than a simple means of exchange.

Today more than ever, a person needs to be assured that he is a person, a person conscious of his most original identity, that of his origin; and of his most fundamental identity, that of his foundation. To do so, it is not sufficient to multiply nor to regionalize declarations, even though many rights still remain to be recognized and proclaimed; it is not sufficient to clothe human rights in juridical armour, although much still remains to be done as regards mechanisms for their protection. To be sure, the perception and the enjoyment of human rights will never be uniform across the world: each person, each people, each State continues to recite a longer or shorter litany of rights, with its own particular accent, in function of its culture and history, of what it has achieved and of what it still needs. But, far from resigning ourselves to reducing them to a variable geometric figure, we must do our best to focus attention on the major invariables in human rights that belong to the constant, undisputable patrimony of all persons and of all peoples. There is a truth about the human person, transcending circumstances of time and place, which demands that absolute respect be accorded to the human person. The source of this respect comes from beyond the person, from beyond any social contract: lest some shred of his humanity be stripped away, the human person must be solidly anchored in a transcendent horizon that makes it impossible for any power whatsoever, be it political or religious, to take exclusive possession of him.

2. Democracy and human rights

The exercise of democracy is perhaps the most significant, but also the most trying, test for the recognition of human rights. Taken in its simplest definition, that of Abraham Lincoln, democracy is "government of the people, by the people, and for the people." Nothing could be more captivating, to the point that even totalitarian regimes has masqueraded under the title of "people's democracy." Nothing could be more deceptive, to the point that today's liberal regimes are stricken with "democratic melancholy," according to the expression of a political economist (Pascal Bruckner). The collapse of the Marxist eschatology has brutally revealed how powerless we are to imagine a future, in that being part of a regime based on human rights, while giving a human outline to the future, does not automatically give it a recognizable face. Nothing is more exacting than the call for the responsibility, for the participation, of all and of each one. The taste for democracy is an acquired one and is constantly being refined, but it can just as easily be dulled and lost. The greatest challenge that an authentic democracy presents for human rights is to consider at one and the same time both person and society in a way which is not antagonistic.

Finally, a people cannot be free to determine its destiny if, at the same time, the human beings that form it are not, in the first place, free themselves. The recent experience of those peoples who emerged from the shadows and hastened to follow the paths of democracy, shows that one cannot become free overnight and that one only has that degree of liberty that one is capable of assuming. Still more, liberty cannot be given to people from the outside, through constitutions or by making life easier: in fact, one can actually only free persons who are already interiorly free. If a great deal of virtue is needed to live under a totalitarian regime, still more is required to live in a democratic society. As Dostoyevsky pointed out, because a natural inclination leads the human person to consider liberty a burden, he seeks to rid himself of it by placing it in the hands of those who are stronger, those who are wiser. In comparison with the Creons of this world, rare are the Antigones! Today, the human person can also reach the point of doubting his capability of intervening in the increasingly complex mechanisms of society: this is the modern version of a fatalism that undermines the exercise of human rights where democracy seems to be losing its momentum.

3. Development and human rights

Where are we after so many "development decades" called for by the international community, after so many intelligent and generous strategies? The famous gap between rich and poor, between "the peoples in hunger" and "the people blessed with abundance" (Paul VI, *Populorum progressio*, No. 3) is wider than ever. The disparities between North and South are more flagrant than ever ... and what country, what city — in whatever latitude — does not have its North and its South! Disappointed by the models of development that they themselves developed, or let down by those that were imposed on them, many countries have reached the point where they call development itself into doubt and think that the star towards which they were heading is nothing more than a dead star.

In this climate of uncertainty, and even of scepticism, we must give new impetus to development as the lever which is still capable of energizing humanity and human rights. In 1986, the United Nations drew up a very worthwhile Declaration on the right to development, but everything depends on what concept of the human person we put under the banner of development. True development, affirmed Pope John Paul II, "must be measured and oriented according to the reality and vocation of man seen in his totality, namely according to his *interior dimension*" (*Sollicitudo rei socialis*, n. 29). There is no development possible without the integral development of the human person. There is no development possible without the development in solidarity of humanity. The temptation remains to want to draw up immediately theories, models of development, with keys in hand, ready to wear, that it would suffice to hand over to nations at a time when the period of trial and error that we are going through has not yet taught us all of its lessons. Would it not be better to begin by reaching agreement on the stature of the person whom we want to promote: "the human development index," drawn up in the past four years by the United Nations Development Programme (UNDP), is a timid sign, but one which still holds promise, to the degree that it will be able to integrate all the constitutive dimensions of the human person.

For this very reason, it is among those who are the most deprived, among the poor, especially those of the "fourth world," that we must learn about and achieve human rights. We could not choose better guides, ones who will constantly lead us back to the most concrete paths, there where rights are not those of persons but of a person with flesh and bones, of a person who, at times, lacks a human face and who therefore begs simply for the right to be a person.

I shall stop here because my role as Chairman is to allow each one to speak freely. I do not think that I have gone beyond my rights in trying to bring in a breath of air, a spirit that can help each one of you to carry things to their logical conclusion, to go to the very depths of yourself, there where you can recognize yourself as a person who is at the service of your brothers and sisters.

Intervention of
His Excellency Archbishop Jean-Louis Tauran
Secretary for Relations with States
at the World Conference on Human Rights
Vienna, 21 June 1993

Mr. President,

1. I am glad to be among those who have cordially congratulated you upon your election to the presidency of this important Conference. I am also pleased to convey the heartfelt gratitude of the Holy See's Delegation to the Austrian authorities for organizing this highly significant meeting in this prestigious city of Vienna, which present and past history has made the crossroads of people and their aspirations.

2. This World Conference on Human Rights is in itself a special event. The presence of so many Delegations shows the extent to which the leaders of nations are aware that a harmonious and stable international and national life cannot exist without taking into consideration every aspect of the human being. If we are in Vienna today, it is also because each of us is convinced that, since 10 December 1948, the date when the *Universal Declaration of Human Rights* was adopted, and since the Teheran Conference in 1968, the time has come to assess the situation, and further, to establish more reliable indicators for the rights and freedoms that concern each human being.

3. By its very nature and mission, the Holy See could not miss this meeting and is glad to be able to make its contribution to the work of the Conference. It does so all the more willingly since the Catholic Church, by her Founder's wishes and since her beginning, has sought to ensure that human beings, their nature, dignity, freedom and spiritual aspirations should never be sacrificed to individual interests. In this we are also joined by other religious families who recognize God's image in the human person, who thinks and loves.

4. At the time of this assessment, it is comforting to be able to reap the harvest of the immense labour undertaken by the United Nations and other regional agencies; I am thinking in particular of the Organization of American States, of the Council of Europe, of the Organization for African Unity and of the Conference for Security and Cooperation in Europe. The codification of international legislation, the perfecting of verification procedures, declarations, debates and information are all concrete expressions of this service to humanity over the years. The Holy See is very pleased with this constant effort, which no obstacle has been able to discourage. This

perseverance is the best guarantee for the future, as the Conference's motto so aptly expresses: "We keep the flame burning."

  To this patient work, the result of the frequently hidden labour of experienced diplomats, there is added the diligent action of the non-governmental organizations, which, by their concrete approach to situations, have constantly recalled that all codification is valid to the extent that it bears on and improves the living conditions of every man and woman.

5. Unfortunately, if we look around us, we cannot but see the frightening presence of injustice, destruction and death, which torment our world today. Too many people do not yet enjoy freedom of conscience and speech. Religious freedom is far from being a reality everywhere. Underdevelopment, social injustice, dictatorships of all kinds still prevent millions of women and men from being partners in the social project of which they are a part. Right on our doorstep, in Bosnia-Herzegovina, one could say that every human right is being systematically violated in an ongoing way. Even as elementary a right as being able to live in the place where one was born, is no longer respected. What cause can possibly justify such a senseless and cruel war as that which is devastating this part of Europe? The indecision of all those who have political and moral responsibility in these fratricidal struggles will be severely judged by history. In recent days, further violence has led to bloodshed in one part of Africa, Somalia, where populations extenuated by years of oppression again risk becoming the victims of fresh violence capable of destroying the credibility of the very people who seek to rescue them. All this, alas, shows that the principles which the international community has so painstakingly worked out and enacted, are still far from being "the common heritage of humanity."

6. However, who could fail to admit — I would even say believe — that without peace, justice and development, the world cannot survive? Now at the root of these demands is the human person, the subject of rights and duties. Whenever there is an abuse of authority, corruption, exploitation of the weak, denial of people's right to participate in political life and decision-making, the deliberate choice of violence and terrorism prevail, peace is threatened. Whenever the life, physical integrity, conscience, thought, religious faith and the personal freedom of each citizen are not respected, it is man who is threatened.

7. This is why today it is necessary to repeat here in Vienna the importance of the civil and political rights which on the one hand guarantee people the exercise of their freedom, and on the other, facilitate the active participation of citizens in public affairs. And how necessary it is to recall that if they are to be productive, these individual freedoms must be

accompanied by the practical application of social, economic and cultural rights, encouraging the overall development of the person and the advent of a society based on solidarity.

8.   Indeed, the constitutional State must find its expression in the balance between these two great categories of rights. Moreover it is certainly appropriate that the entire international community unanimously agree on this point, for it has several basic underlying principles:

- *The indivisibility of human rights*, which implies that it would not be possible to invoke one right as an excuse for the violation of another. The human person consists of body and soul. These rights concern people who necessarily belong to a community, since man is social by nature.

- *The universality of the fundamental rights,* which stems from the fact that people share the same nature. There is consequently a common universal good, and this is why *Universal Declaration of Human Rights* exists. Regional experiences in safeguarding human rights contribute to the growth of universal awareness and to the drafting of laws, thus enriching the common heritage of humanity.

9.   We not only need the affirmation of universal solidarity to emerge from the Vienna Conference, but we also need commitments — with the necessary monitoring mechanisms and bodies — for a universal organization that promotes and protects basic human rights. This is all the more important since new situations are being imposed on us and require deep reflection. Let us consider for example:

- the right to *self-determination* which, with the end of the political and ideological conflicts in Europe, emerged from the colonial context that saw its birth, and which could develop into a rebirth of nationalism;

- the rights of *minorities*, which without a doubt will be the test of tomorrow's democracy;

- humanitarian laws, which appear more and more to be the expression not only of the principle of free access to victims, but also of a sense of concrete solidarity.

These are problems concerning the existence — often the survival — of millions of women and men, the solution of which cannot be left to improvisation, or even worse, to the arbitration of States. Precise and strict regulations urgently need to be drawn up. Allow me, Mr. President, to voice the hope that the present development in the practice of international law which often relegates to organizations such as the United Nations the responsibility for drafting laws and enforcing them that has until now been the prerogative of States, may continue, thus discarding an outdated way of exercising national sovereignty and thereby ensuring that the international community's solidarity and responsibility is increasingly emphasized, since the fundamental rights and freedoms of the human person are at stake!

10.   Basically, Mr. President, this meeting in Vienna should provide everyone — society's leaders and ordinary citizens alike — with the opportunity to redouble their efforts to promote real education in human rights. For if one insists quite justifiably on claiming rights, one cannot lose sight of the obligations and duties inherent in them. It is every person's duty to respect in others the rights that he claims for himself. In this task of education and sensitization religious families clearly have an important role to play. For her part, the Catholic Church is concerned, through the teaching of Pope John Paul II and the Episcopate, to remind the faithful that they "should work ceaselessly and effectively to further the dignity which each person receives from the Creator, and to join forces with those of others to defend and promote this dignity" (*Address of John Paul II at "The Church and Human Rights" Symposium*, 15 November 1988).

11.   Mr. President, in closing I should like to stress how much the Holy See hopes that the work and results of this World Conference on Human Rights may represent a sign of hope for our contemporaries. In the face of the disintegrating forces and the reappearance of the barbarism that sometimes seem to drown our world, reflecting on fundamental human rights and codifying them means approving some actions and forbidding others. It means defining what is human and what is inhuman. May I echo here the very words of Pope John Paul II: "Only upon an international order in which law and freedom are indivisible for all can the society we all hope for be founded" (*"Urbi et orbi" Message for Easter*, 1991).

STATEMENT OF INTERPRETATION OF THE HOLY SEE'S CONSENSUS TO THE FINAL DOCUMENT ADOPTED BY THE WORLD CONFERENCE ON HUMAN RIGHTS VIENNA, 25 JUNE 1993

The Holy See, in conformity with its nature and its particular mission, by joining the overall consensus of the Conference, wishes to express its understanding of certain paragraphs of the Final Document of the Conference:

1.   With reference to Part III, Section II, sub-section A, paragraph 4, the Holy See considers that the formulation "with due regard to their respective legal system" should be interpreted in the light of art. 29 of the *Universal Declaration of Human Rights*, of art. 18 of the *International Covenant on Civil and Political Rights* and of art. 1.3 of the *Declaration on Elimination of All Forms of Intolerance and of Discrimination Based on Religion or Belief*.

2.   With reference to Part III, Section II, sub-section C, paragraph 6, the Holy See's joining the consensus should in no way be interpreted as constituting a change in its well-known position concerning those family planning methods which the Catholic Church considers morally unacceptable or on family planning services which do not respect the liberty of the spouses, human dignity and the human rights of those concerned.

The Holy See requests that this statement be included in the official report of the World Conference on Human Rights.

Statement by
His Excellency Archbishop Jean-Louis Tauran
Secretary for Relations with States
before the Third Committee
of the 48th Session of the General Assembly
on Item 114: Human Rights Questions
New York, 17 November 1993

Mr. Chairman,

I am happy to speak this morning in the framework of the Third Committee of the Forty-eighth General Assembly of the United Nations Organization, all the more so because the work of this Committee has as its object many preoccupations which are shared by the Holy See.

Among the aspects of the "human dimension" of international life, in effect, we are today tending more especially towards the quality of the implementation of the international juridical instruments which ensure the safeguarding of human rights.

1. In this connection, it cannot but be recalled that in the month of June last there was held in Vienna a "World Conference on Human Rights," which had as its slogan "Let us conserve the flame." The discussions provided the occasion to verify, alas, how many of those rights-liberties remain even today in a precarious state. The information appearing each day on the teleprinters speak continually of violence, of wars, of poverty, of unemployment, of cultural underdevelopment, of disturbing genetic manipulations, even of denial of the right to be born. Now, in Vienna, there were many who forcefully declared — as I myself had the honour to do on behalf of the Holy See — that the fundamental rights of the human person are indivisible and universal. An indivisibility and a universality which can be understood only through the unity of human nature and the equality of persons, whose rights and liberties are based on their dignity, which must be respected by the various powers, whether they be political, economic or social. The fundamental rights and liberties are, therefore, inscribed in human nature, and they are not the mere expression of a culture, even if they do require it in order to be integrated in the most adequate manner into a given society.

Faced with the failures of which we are aware, and faced with the disparity between the internationally established norms and their defective application, I am reminded of the words of Pope John Paul II, just a few months after his election to the Sovereign Pontificate, in His first Message to the United Nations, on 2 December 1978: "One is bound to observe a seemingly growing divergence between the meaningful declarations of the United Nations and the sometimes massive increase of human rights violations."

The Holy See would like to repeat, once more, that respect for the rights of the human person, as they have been elaborated in the *Universal Declaration* of 1948, by the Teheran Conference of 1968, and by many subsequent international texts, are not just options among others, or a transient political programme. They pledge the international community, and those responsible within it, to ensure for each human being the requisites of his dignity and of his spiritual dimension, which belong to him by the very fact of his nature. The rights of man and his fundamental freedoms are not granted by anyone. They precede the positive law which is their expression.

It is necessary that governmental organizations, such as the United Nations, be forums which promote the expression of a common political will to implement human rights in a world ever more unified, thanks in particular to the modern means of communication which bring each one culturally and socially closer to the other. It is to be hoped that, in the course of the exchanges of these days, the available juridical instruments will serve as the basis for a continued revision of government programmes, in order that man shall never lack that of which he has need to live a truly human life.

2. Among the fundamental rights of man, there is that of freedom of religion. Very happily, it has been possible to note in recent years that progress has been made in many countries towards the effective guarantee of this for all. I think particularly of the countries of Central and Eastern Europe. And these positive results are due in large part to the thoughtful work which has been carried out here in New York, or in Geneva, and in other international gatherings, such as, for example, in the framework of the Conference on Security and Cooperation in Europe.

But, it is however regrettable for the Holy See (and, I think, for many other responsible political figures) to have to note that in too many regions, even today, believers are subjected to serious discrimination.

In certain countries of the Islamic tradition, for example, Christians are prevented not only from having places of worship in which to gather, but even from worshiping in their own homes.

In other cases, the Pope and the Holy See are prevented from maintaining with the Bishops and their faithful those normal contacts presumed by the structure of the Catholic Church and which are agreed upon in the relevant international documents.

Elsewhere, religious leaders in their communities cannot express opinions on social problems without being suspected of betraying the national interest, whereas in reality they are defending it, in its liberty and in its dignity.

Frequently, even where religious freedom is reasonably well guaranteed, it is not rare that there appears a tendency on the part of the Authorities to promulgate ever more restrictive laws and administrative dispositions, somehow as if it were desired to re-take with one hand what is given with the other.

The Holy See would wish to repeat here that what it requests, not only for Catholics, but for all communities of believers, is that everywhere, in every regime, the individual and collective rights of believing citizens be fully assured and guaranteed. Not in order to make of them separate subjects, but in order that they feel recognized and respected in that which they hold most dearly: their faith. When such is the case, then believers will participate with confidence and enthusiasm in public life and in national affairs. The deviations to be avoided are two: the first would be to place the power of the State at the service of one sole religious community; the second would be to consider religion to be destructive of the national community. When a State denies the religious dimension of man, there must be anxiety about his fate: he can very soon become an object at the mercy of the egoism of other men, or of the arbitrariness of rulers. Likewise, when a State seeks to impose the rules of a single religious system, in such a manner that other religions find themselves, in effect, excluded from national life, and that people's consciences are no longer respected, there can be anxiety about the future of national and international peace. That is why to ensure religious freedom is, in reality, to ensure social and civic peace within each nation and between nations.

3. This position of believers in the national life is all the more important in balancing the claims of other types of communities. When a citizen has confidence in a nation and in those who administer it, he is naturally inclined to cooperate in common projects.

Otherwise, there can be feared the dangerous kindling of nationalism, of tribal revendication, or of forceful conquest. We all know the dramas engendered by excesses of national sentiment, by the settled belief in the superiority of one race over another, by the subjection of peoples by the stronger. That is the reign of arbitrariness and the very negation of rights.

The Holy See is of the opinion that what must take precedence in this domain is the establishment of structures of dialogue, if necessary of negotiation, in order that collaboration and solidarity may prevail, on a footing of equality and reciprocal respect for diversity.

It is in this perspective that it would be fitting to work in order to find a solution to the problems of national minorities. If each people ought, in theory, to be able to organize itself as an independent State, we know that it is not always possible or useful for this to happen. Federal or confederal forms are then an alternative. They should be able to safeguard, on the one hand the unity of the State, and on the other hand to grant the national communities the faculty to preserve and develop their ethnic, cultural and religious identity in a larger totality which will ensure their economic and social development.

What is important is to avoid those solutions which are patched together, unjust, or the bearers of the seed of violence and of intolerance. The example of the drama that is being enacted in what was Yugoslavia, the recent disorders which have bloodied Burundi, or again the rivalries which have entangled opposing factions in Somalia, in Angola, in Sri Lanka and in many countries of the Caucasus, are there to recall to us our duties of effective solidarity with the peoples exposed to the vindictiveness of gangs and of aggressors without conscience, who pride themselves on living and acting outside the law.

Nevertheless, other achievements of the international community demonstrate that it is possible to sit around a table, to agree to listen, and to build together a better future. The steps forward in Cambodia, the abolition of apartheid in South Africa or the conversations which bring together Israelis and Palestinians are an example of this.

Nothing should be spared to put an end to these outpourings of violence and of hatred. Jurists should pursue without discouragement their efforts to define a concept such as that of "national minorities," and the international community should adopt constraining instruments in order that genocide, the forced displacements of populations and the arms trade which supports them, be prevented and punished. Accomplishments have already been achieved. In Europe, for example, there exists a Court of Arbitration. The Conference on Security and Cooperation in Europe has a High Commissioner for national minorities. But these results are insufficient. Does there always exist a political will to block the route to fragmentation, or to oppose iniquitous partitions which divide families and place them on the road to exile? It is very easy to wipe out in a short time the bonds and the achievements which generations of history have laboriously woven. In the end, there are always three exigencies to be reconciled; the rights of the person, pluralism and democracy. Because, this last does not exist unless society is founded upon respect for the innate and inalienable rights of the human person, on a sense of responsibility in the exercise of religious liberty at the service of the common good, and on structures which ensure a just equilibrium of the interests of each and of all in the context of a national community. When one of these elements is missing, arbitrariness and the desire for power take first place and tragedy is not far away.

Mr. Chairman,

I can do no more than wish that the discussions over which you will preside in these days will be more than the deliberations of specialists. The multiplication of problems of ethnicity and of nationality, the questioning of frontiers, are matters of urgent topicality, as was the case at the beginning of this century. Hopefully there can be avoided the repetition, for lack of imagination and of ambition, of the defective solutions which were applied to them, and which led to their resurgence! No advancement of civilization can be founded on indifference in the face of such deadly drift. It is time for a renewal of conscience and time for action. From the Seat of the United Nations may there come signs of hope for all men and for all peoples!

Thank you, Mr. Chairman.

INTERVIEW OF
HIS EXCELLENCY ARCHBISHOP DONATO SQUICCIARINI,
APOSTOLIC NUNCIO TO AUSTRIA,
HEAD OF THE HOLY SEE DELEGATION TO THE
WORLD CONFERENCE ON HUMAN RIGHTS
TO THE AUSTRIAN RADIO PROGRAMME (ORF) "CHRIST IN TIME"
20 JUNE 1993

(translation from the German language)

As Head of the Holy See Delegation, I am happy to offer a few words about the World Conference on Human Rights, presently in session in Vienna.

As a Member of the International Community, the Holy See works regularly with the United Nations. In that, the Holy See's concerns, above all, are questions related to the human person in all its dimensions.

Forty-five years after the *Universal Declaration of Human Rights*, this Conference wants to evaluate what has thus far been done and to give guidelines for the future. On the one hand, much has been achieved in this field, for example that which has been arrived at in the territory of the Council of Europe regarding the protection of human rights. On the other, however, as you know and as anyone could understand from the communications media, there are numerous and serious violations of the most elementary human rights: such as the right to life, the right of corporal and psychological integrity, and the right of conscience and religion.

Therefore, this Conference should appeal to all States and Societies about the general obligation to respect these human rights and at the same time it should seek means and ways to protect these rights more efficaciously in the future.

For the Church, recognition of the dignity of the human person, which for us has its foundation in the fact that God created the human being in His image, is of central importance. The highest pinnacle of this dignity is experienced in the mystery of the Incarnation of God. As Church, we are all the more called upon to engage ourselves to set human dignity as the foundation of the entire concept of human rights.

With renewed emphasis the Church, after the Second Vatican Council, has advocated for this foundation of human rights, in all International Organs and Conferences. In such a way she fulfills her mission of making effective the message of the Gospel in every sphere of human life.

This service rendered by the Church contributes to the good of every human being, believers and unbelievers alike, because God has furnished everyone with the same dignity. Such a service, in a special way, is necessary for those who need special protection in society.

Occasionally it has been assumed that human rights, or at least their concrete form, are different from culture to culture. In that way the idea of human rights will be made relative and exposed to the pressures of the State. Therefore, and in this connection, the general expansion of democratic structures is important, because they present in practice an efficacious method of control of the exercise of power. Beyond such an inner-state control there should also be an international protection of human rights so that victims of unjust Governments will have the possibility to appeal to an international forum.

Human rights are not issues of only Governments and International Organizations.

This World Conference presently being held in Vienna should be an occasion for all to take human rights seriously and to put them into practice in one's own ambient.

This appeal is addressed to families as well as to individuals in their working place or living quarters. Thus, we all could contribute a share in giving our society a more human face.

For us Christians, an encounter with any human being is an occasion to meet Christ the Lord Himself.

INTERVIEW OF
HIS EXCELLENCY ARCHBISHOP DONATO SQUICCIARINI
APOSTOLIC NUNCIO TO AUSTRIA
HEAD OF THE HOLY SEE DELEGATION TO THE
UNITED NATIONS WORLD CONFERENCE ON HUMAN RIGHTS
CATHOLIC PRESS NEWS STORY, 22 JUNE 1993

(translation from the German language)

VIENNA — 22 June 1993 (Kathpress). The Apostolic Nuncio to Austria, Archbishop Donato Squicciarini, sees in Evangelization a contribution of the Holy See for human rights. With the "good tiding," addressed to every human being, of a God who loves him, transforms him and restores him to his dignity as a human person created in His image, the Catholic Church reaches the center of the struggle for human rights, said the Head of the Vatican Delegation to the United Nations Conference in an interview to the Kathpress. Squicciarini qualified the entire teaching service of the Church as a "considerable contribution to the restructuring of society so that it could better serve human beings."

The Church and the Holy See, according to the words of the Nuncio, have "never forgotten" to engage themselves to get "the State laws to better reflect these ideals and principles." The legal, political, social and economic structures should function "according to the criteria of justice and solidarity, as concrete signs of love, whose channel and proclaimer we are."

Human rights: universally binding

Archbishop Squicciarini objected to the opinion that came up in the U.N. Conference that human rights do not have a universal binding, because they were formulated in a "typically western" context. It is true that there was only a "minimum representation" of the non-western cultures in the drafting of the *Universal Declaration of Human Rights*. But since then the same rights and freedoms were recognized in many other documents on international, regional and national levels.

For a deeper dialogue of cultures

According to Squicciarini a deeper dialogue between the different cultures could lead to a common understanding of values. "We think that these values could be found in the foundation of respect for the human person who stands at the central point," said Squicciarini. The protection of the human person as created in the image of God "should remain the prime reason for the universality of human rights." To such a task every country and every culture is bound. According to Squicciarini the "main purpose" of the U.N. Conference is to remind the States "to exercise in a better way their responsibility for the respect and application of human rights for their own citizens."

Concrete application "could fail"

According to the Archbishop, along with political and civil human rights there are also economic, social and cultural parts of a "General Concept," which should be realized in terms of the international agreements. Limiting himself, Squicciarini stated: "It does not mean that human rights cannot in its application lose as in the case of other single rights. It is enough to mention that freedom of opinion and of religion are absolute rights, whereas the right to a living or to work depend on the concrete social and economic situations of a concrete State."

How to succeed in putting human rights into practice

When asked about the success in putting human rights into practice, the Head of the Vatican Delegation spoke about the demands of Non-Governmental Organizations (NGOs) to establish an International Court and a U.N. High Commissioner for guaranteeing human rights. Squicciarini, literally: "Even though the Holy See does not consider itself competent for judging mere political or technical questions, it supports all initiatives according to which human beings are not exposed to torture or exploitation; that freedom of opinion, freedom to assemble, freedom of religion or of exercising religion are not arbitrarily curtailed and that minorities are not oppressed."

Chapter Four

THE WORLD CONFERENCE ON THE SUSTAINABLE DEVELOPMENT OF SMALL ISLAND DEVELOPING STATES

Bridgetown, Barbados

25 April - 6 May 1994

Chapter Contents

**The World Conference on the Sustainable Development
of Small Island Developing States**
*Bridgetown, Barbados;
25 April - 6 May 1994*

Statement by His Excellency Archbishop Renato R. Martino,
    Apostolic Nuncio, Permanent Observer of the Holy See
    to the U.N., at the World Conference on the
    Sustainable Development of Small Island Developing States
    Bridgetown, Barbados, 29 April 1994 169

(The Appendix contains no related documents for this chapter.)

Statement by
His Excellency Archbishop Renato R. Martino
Apostolic Nuncio, Permanent Observer of the Holy See to the United Nations at the World Conference on the Sustainable Development of Small Island Developing States
Bridgetown, Barbados; 29 April 1994

Mr. President, Excellencies, Ladies and Gentlemen,

On the road from the United Nations Conference on Environment and Development in Rio, the international community has arrived at its first intersection. These crossroads are on this beautiful island of Barbados. The journey has not always been smooth and at times the means of travel were slow and may not have functioned as the passengers might have preferred. However, this World Conference on the Sustainable Development of Small Island Developing States is one of the very first opportunities to turn the vision and guidance found in Agenda 21 into practical concrete plans and programmes aimed at achieving results.

The Holy See took an active role in UNCED and continues to take an active part in the follow-up process. Its particular nature does not place it either on the margin of or above the concrete problems on our agenda but at the center with all concerned States which participated and joined in the consensus reached at UNCED in Rio just two short years ago.

Yet the ultimate determining factor of the interest of the Holy See has been and continues to be that which is stated in the first principle of the Rio Declaration, "Human beings are at the center of concerns for sustainable development." All developmental initiatives must respect the full dignity and freedom of whomever might be affected by such programmes. They must be seen in relation to the needs of actual men and women, their families, their values, their unique social, religious and cultural heritage and traditions, their responsibility toward future generations. The enhancement of the quality of human life for the inhabitants of Small Islands must be the principal purpose of Small Island developmental programmes. But in all cases, the primary factor must remain the human person.

It is evident that the problems faced by Small Island Developing States cannot be solved by these States alone. Yet it is equally evident that to address the problems of the SIDS is in the general good of the human family as a whole. Perhaps it shall be found that the action of helping others is really helping oneself, that self-interest, provided it is sufficiently enlightened, can really promote the common good. Thus, we gather here to undertake a constructive dialogue at this World Conference to address not only the interests of the Small Island Developing States but also those of the entire human community and of each of its members, in the hope that the interests of one group of nations will truly benefit all.

The Holy See steadfastly professes the belief that all acceptable solutions must be based on human solidarity. However, this solidarity is void of meaning and doomed to failure if each and every society does not exercise a true sense of stewardship. Responsible stewardship demands a consideration for the common good; no one person, no one group of people in isolation is allowed to determine their relationship with the universe. The universal common good transcends all private interests, all national boundaries and reaches beyond the present moment to future generations.

Responsible stewardship and genuine solidarity are directed to the protection of the environment and to the inalienable right and dignity of all peoples to development. The earth's resources and the means to their access and use, whether a large or small land mass, must be wisely monitored and justly shared. The demand for the care and protection of the environment cannot be used to obstruct the right to development, nor can development be invoked in thwarting the environment. The task of achieving a just balance is today's challenge.

The fact that many inhabitants of SIDS lack the basic necessities of a decent life must not be forgotten. This is fundamentally a moral problem and it transcends the consideration of bare economic aspects. The solutions must come from a moral drive to eliminate the inequalities between developing and developed nations. There is no magic formula for solving the extremely technical and complicated problems involved in such issues as: natural and environmental disasters, management of wastes, fresh water resources, biodiversity, to list but a few examples. However, inventive wisdom and a view to interests which go beyond the particular difficulties of the moment and look to the future of humanity are a foundation for actions.

Thus, as this Conference tries honestly and realistically to re-think the pressing economic, technical, financial and — most important — human needs of the Small Island Developing States, it will re-discover and re-assert the values which will advance the lives of everyone living on this planet earth. In many ways and at diverse levels, the Holy See has participated and will continue to participate in this process with the resources it has to give, consistent with its mission.

This mission manifests itself in tasks accompanied by concrete programmes and activities to advance the people of SIDS. Along with NGOs and States, the Catholic Church has constantly been developing and promoting specific projects in the areas of health, education, cooperatives, rural development and village efforts that seek to improve human life in some of the poorest and least developed areas of Small Island Developing States.

The constant crucial problem of health and the delivery of health care, especially to rural areas, must be given high priority. Many suffer needlessly from disease simply because they live on a piece of land at a great distance from available medical supplies and care. This is then a question of justice and of rights.

Malnutrition, lack of nutrition and lack of infrastructures, especially in the overcrowded urban centers, all hinder the proper and full development of the greatest resource -- the human person.

Education, the key to the development of both the human being and of the economic level of each Small Island, is perhaps the key to the elimination of today's greatest waste of energy and resources, the waste of the human intellect and of the creativity of the human person. The promotion of education would provide an opportunity to broaden the understanding of poverty beyond its purely economic impact and could contribute to the eradication of its causes and thus lead to a development centered not only on material resources, but on "human resources" (cf. Encyclical *Centesimus annus* of Pope John Paul II, n.33).

With regard to Small Island Developing States the Holy See wishes to state once again that the giving of aid — however laudable and necessary — is not sufficient to promote the full measure of human dignity required by the solidarity of all. Nations must work towards creating new, more just, and hence more effective international structures in such spheres as economics, trade, industrial development, finance and the transfer of technology.

Despite the efforts necessarily involved in such a demanding programme, the Holy See is confident in the good will of all here present.

Chapter Five

THE WORLD CONFERENCE ON NATURAL DISASTER REDUCTION

Yokohama, Japan

23 - 27 May 1994

Chapter Contents

The World Conference on Natural Disaster Reduction
Yokohama, Japan;
23 - 27 May 1994

Intervention of Monsignor Iván Marín,
    Secretary of the Pontifical Council "Cor Unum" and
    Head of the Delegation of the Holy See to the
    World Conference on Natural Disaster Reduction
    Yokohama, Japan, 23-27 May 1994 177

(The Appendix contains no related documents for this chapter.)

Intervention of
Monsignor Iván Marín
Secretary of the Pontifical Council "Cor Unum" and Head of the Delegation of the Holy See to the World Conference on Natural Disaster Reduction
Yokohama, Japan; 23-27 May 1994

Mr. President,

Since the launching of the International Decade for Natural Disaster Reduction, the Holy See manifested its interest and support for the goals and objectives of the Decade's programme. For several years the Holy See, through the Pontifical Council "Cor Unum," has been engaged in intensifying its humanitarian action in favor of the victims of almost all natural catastrophes.

Catholic organizations have always been reaching out to populations who are victims of disasters through their humanitarian assistance. Among them it is sufficient to give, as example, the Caritas network which is active in 137 countries.

In connection with the strategies adopted for the reduction of natural disasters, I would like to highlight the action of the Holy See in three concrete aspects: the works of the "John Paul II Foundation for the Sahel"; the education programmes of the local Churches in almost all countries; and the preventive measures and preparedness programmes of Catholic NGOs.

The "John Paul II Foundation for the Sahel," established by the Holy Father in 1984, works in favor of the nine African countries of the Sahel region, with a specific aim to fight desertification and drought. The Foundation gives priority to the training of African leaders through scholarship grants in order that they help the local community in the fight against desertification after having acquired the proper technical skills. It also funds micro-projects in reforestation and conservation of water tables.

The local Churches, especially in the zones which are frequently exposed to natural disasters, promote awareness programmes and give importance to concrete contribution to rehabilitation works. To be noted are the construction of seismic-resistant houses, installation of warning devices in buildings, emergency drills, education towards responsible use of natural resources and respect for the environment.

Finally, I would like to stress the action of the NGOs, especially the

Christian organizations, which so generously commit themselves in humanitarian works in the area of natural disaster reduction and in rehabilitation. In general, there is a clear and determined awareness that it is possible to prevent, that it possible to reduce the impact of natural disasters.

It is certainly necessary to have a concerted effort and will in order to intensify the studies that will allow us to know the natural laws which govern these natural phenomena in order to advance in technological development at the service of man, while observing ethical and ecological criteria; and in order to take care of creation with a deeper sense of responsibility on behalf of future generations.

Chapter Six

THE INTERNATIONAL CONFERENCE ON POPULATION AND DEVELOPMENT

Cairo, Egypt

5 - 13 September 1994

Chapter Contents

The International Conference on Population and Development
Cairo, Egypt;
5 - 13 September 1994

Introduction by His Excellency Archbishop Renato R. Martino
    Apostolic Nuncio, Permanent Observer of the Holy See
    to the U.N. and Head of the Holy See Delegation to the
    United Nations Conference on Population and Development ... 189

Message of His Holiness Pope John Paul II
    to Mrs. Nafis Sadik, Secretary General of the
    1994 International Conference on Population and Development
    and Executive Director of the United Nations Population Fund
    Vatican, 18 March 1994 191

Letter of His Holiness Pope John Paul II
    to the World's Heads of State
    Vatican, 19 March 1994 199

Addresses of His Holiness Pope John Paul II
    at the General Audience and before the Angelus 203
    General Audience, 6 April 1994 203
    Angelus, St. Peter's Square, 17 April 1994 203
    Angelus, St. Peter's Square, 12 June 1994 205
    Angelus, St. Peter's Square, 19 June 1994 206
    Angelus, St. Peter's Square, 26 June 1994 208
    Angelus, St. Peter's Square, 3 July 1994 209
    Angelus, St. Peter's Square, 10 July 1994 210
    Angelus, Castel Gandolfo, 17 July 1994 211
    Angelus, Castel Gandolfo, 24 July 1994 212
    Angelus, Castel Gandolfo, 31 July 1994 214
    Angelus, Castel Gandolfo, 7 August 1994 215
    Angelus, Castel Gandolfo, 14 August 1994 216
    Angelus, Castel Gandolfo, 28 August 1994 218

National Report of the Holy See in preparation for
    the International Conference on Population and Development
    23 March 1993 221

Address of His Eminence Angelo Cardinal Sodano,
    Secretary of State, on the position of the Holy See regarding the
    International Conference on Population and Development,
    at the Special Assembly for Africa of the Synod of Bishops
    Vatican, 21 April 1994 229

182 Chapter Six

Statement by His Eminence Alfonso Cardinal López Trujillo,
    President of the Pontifical Council for the Family, at a Meeting for
    Ambassadors Accredited to the Holy See
    Vatican, 25 March 1994 238

Statement by His Eminence Roger Cardinal Etchegaray,
    President of the Pontifical Council for Justice and Peace, at a
    Meeting for Ambassadors Accredited to the Holy See
    Vatican, 25 March 1994 246

Statement by His Excellency Archbishop Jean-Louis Tauran,
    Secretary for Relations with States, at a Meeting for
    Ambassadors Accredited to the Holy See
    Vatican, 25 March 1994 251

Statement by the College of Cardinals, meeting in Extraordinary Consistory,
    proposed by His Eminence John Cardinal O'Connor,
    Archbishop of New York
    Vatican, 14 June 1994 261

Intervention of His Excellency Bishop James T. McHugh, STD,
    Bishop of Camden, New Jersey, Member of the Holy See Delegation
    to the 26th Session of the United Nations Population Commission
    - Session I of the Preparatory Committee for the
    International Conference on Population and Development
    New York, 28 February 1991 263

Intervention of His Excellency Bishop Elio Sgreccia,
    Secretary of the Pontifical Council for the Family,
    to the Meeting of the European Population Conference,
    in preparation for the International Conference on Population
    and Development; Geneva, 23-26 March 1993 265

Statement by Monsignor Diarmuid Martin,
    Under-Secretary of the Pontifical Council for Justice and Peace,
    Head of the Holy See Delegation to the Latin American and
    Caribbean Regional Conference on Population and
    Development, Ministerial Planning Meeting
    Mexico City, 3 May 1993 269

Statement by His Excellency Archbishop Renato R. Martino,
    Apostolic Nuncio, Permanent Observer of the Holy See
    to the U.N. and Head of the Delegation of the Holy See to the
    II Session of the Preparatory Committee for the
    International Conference on Population and Development
    New York, 17 May 1993 273

Statement by Monsignor Frank J. Dewane,
    Member of Delegation of the Holy See to the II Session
    of the Preparatory Committee for the International Conference
    on Population and Development; New York, 18 May 1993 279

Statement by Mr. John M. Klink,
    Member of Delegation of the Holy See to the II Session
    of the Preparatory Committee for the International Conference
    on Population and Development; New York, 19 May 1993 281

Statement by Monsignor Joseph A. DeAndrea,
    Member of Delegation of the Holy See,
    before the Second Committee of the General Assembly, on
    Item 96: "International Conference on Population and
    Development"; New York, 5 November 1993 284

Statement by Monsignor Diarmuid Martin,
    Under-Secretary of the Pontifical Council for Justice and Peace,
    Head of the Delegation of the Holy See to the III Session
    of the Preparatory Committee for the International Conference
    on Population and Development
    New York, 5 April 1994 287

Report of Monsignor Diarmuid Martin,
    Secretary of the Pontifical Council for Justice and Peace, at the
    Special Assembly for Africa of the Synod of Bishops, on the work
    of the III Session of the Preparatory Committee for the
    International Conference on Population and Development
    Vatican, 28 April 1994 291

Remarks of His Excellency Bishop Elio Sgreccia,
    Secretary of the Pontifical Council for the Family, on a
    Report of the Pontifical Academy of Sciences
    Vatican, 19 June 1994 297

Briefing by Dr. Joaquín Navarro-Valls,
    Director of the Holy See Press Office, on the Draft Program
    of the International Conference on Population and Development
    Vatican, 8 August 1994 302

Briefing by Dr. Joaquín Navarro-Valls,
    Director of the Holy See Press Office, in view of the
    International Conference on Population and Development
    Vatican, 31 August 1994 306

Statement by His Excellency Archbishop Renato R. Martino,
    Apostolic Nuncio, Permanent Observer of the Holy See

to the U.N. and Head of the Delegation of the Holy See, at the
International Conference on Population and Development
Cairo, 7 September 1994 311

Statement by His Excellency Archbishop Renato R. Martino,
Apostolic Nuncio, Permanent Observer of the Holy See
to the U.N. and Head of the Delegation of the Holy See,
at the Concluding Session of the International Conference
on Population and Development
Cairo, 13 September 1994 318

Reservations of the Holy See to the Programme of Action adopted
at the International Conference on Population and Development
Cairo, 13 September 1994 321

Statement by His Excellency Archbishop Renato R. Martino,
Apostolic Nuncio, Permanent Observer of the Holy See
to the U.N., before the Plenary Session of the General Assembly,
on Item 158: "Report on the International Conference on
Population and Development"
New York, 18 November 1994 323

Interviews given to Vatican Radio by
His Excellency Archbishop Renato R. Martino,
Apostolic Nuncio, Permanent Observer of the Holy See
to the U.N. and Head of the Delegation of the Holy See to the
International Conference on Population and Development 328
30 August 1994 328
2 September 1994 331
3 September 1994 333
4 September 1994 335
16 September 1994 337

Press Releases issued by Delegation of the Holy See during the
International Conference on Population and Development 339
Cairo, 5 September 1994 339
Cairo, 6 September 1994 341
Cairo, 8 September 1994 344

Message of Mother Teresa of Calcutta to the
United Nations International Conference on Population
and Development; 7 September 1994 345

Intervention of Mr. John M. Klink,
Member of the Holy See Delegation to the UNICEF
Executive Board, on Document E/ICEF/1995/12:
"UNICEF Follow-up to the International Conference on

Population and Development"
New York, 23 March 1995 352

Intervention of Mr. John M. Klink,
Member of the Holy See Delegation to the UNICEF
Executive Board, on Document E/ICEF/1995/12/Rev.1:
"UNICEF Follow-up to the International Conference on
Population and Development"
New York, 20 September 1995 356

See Appendix for the following related documents:

Letter of His Holiness Pope John Paul II to Families
"1994 – Year of the Family"
Vatican, 2 February 1994 623

Address of His Holiness Pope John Paul II
to a Gathering of Families from Around the World
attending the World Meeting with Families
St. Peter's Square, 8 October 1994 687

Address *(excerpts)* of His Holiness Pope John Paul II to
Members of the Diplomatic Corps Accredited
to the Holy See; Vatican, 9 January 1995 693

"Charter of the Rights of the Family"
presented by the Holy See to all Persons,
Institutions and Authorities concerned with the
Mission of the Family in Today's World
Vatican, 22 October 1983 697

"Ethical and Pastoral Dimensions of Population Trends"
issued by the Pontifical Council for the Family
Vatican, 25 March 1994 711

Declaration of the Pontifical Academy for Life
issued by the Executive Board at their First Meeting
Vatican, 19 June 1994 755

Address of His Eminence Alfonso Cardinal López Trujillo,
President of the Pontifical Council for the Family,
at the Press Conference presenting the
Proceedings of a Study Conference on
Natural Family Planning Methods
Vatican, 7 July 1994 757

Statement by His Eminence Alfonso Cardinal López Trujillo,
    President of the Pontifical Council for the Family,
    to the United Nations General Assembly, on the Occasion of
    the International Conference on Families
    New York, 19 October 1994 764

Report of His Eminence Alfonso Cardinal López Trujillo,
    President of the Pontifical Council for the Family, to the
    Twenty-Seventh General Congregation of the Synod
    of Bishops, on the Year of the Family and the
    Cairo Conference; Vatican, 28 October 1994 768

*Selected Statements by Bishops' Conferences, Pro-Life Leaders
and Organizations regarding the International Conference on
Population and Development:* 780

    - Letter of the Latin American Episcopal Council (CELAM)
        to Mrs. Nafis Sadik; 14 March 1994 780

    - Letter on behalf of the African Bishops, to Secretary-
        General Boutros Boutros-Ghali
        Rome, 23 April 1994 785

    - United States Cardinals and Conference President's
        Letter to President William Clinton
        29 May 1994 787

    - Statement by the United States Bishops at their
        June 1994 Meeting 790

    - European Bishops Declaration (President and Vice-
        Presidents of the Council of European
        Episcopal Conferences); 4 June 1994 793

    - Message of the Presidents of the Latin American Bishops'
        Conferences to the Leaders of the Region, Santo
        Domingo; 18 June 1994 795

    - European Bishops Issue Final Declaration
        4-5 July 1994 802

    - Canadian Bishops' Conference on Cairo Conference
        Letter to Prime Minister Jean Chrétien
        18 July 1994 805

    - German Bishops' Statement, 4 August 1994 806

    - European Pro-Life Leaders Issue Declaration
        8-9 July 1994 807

- Knights of Columbus Statement, 13 September 1994 809

Speech by Mr. John M. Klink,
　Advisor, Permanent Observer Mission of the Holy See
　to the United Nations, to the organization "Women
　Affirming Life"; Washington, D.C.
　24 September 1994 811

Introduction by
His Excellency Archbishop Renato R. Martino
Apostolic Nuncio, Permanent Observer of the Holy See to the United Nations and Head of the Holy See Delegation to the the United Nations International Conference on Population and Development

The United Nations Conference on Population and Development, held in Cairo, Egypt, from 5-13 September 1994, provided a unique opportunity for the nations of the world to reflect on a number of crucial issues facing the human family. Its topic was a controversial one, given that the earth's resources are limited, that population pressures exist in certain regions, particularly the poorest, and the lack of an agreed understanding of the term "development."

The Holy See, as is universally known, participated actively in numerous preparatory meetings for the Cairo Conference, as well as to the Conference itself. Holy See Delegates listened objectively to the testimonies offered by individuals, organizations and nations from every corner of the globe, and offered their own ideals and reflections based on the Church's grass-roots involvement in the lives of people in every part of the world and its belief in the centrality of the human person in development and in the sacredness of all human life. Thus, the Holy See approached the Conference from its own unique perspective. Its views are founded primarily upon these fundamental principles, and are not swayed by geographical boundaries or national self-interests — or financial dependence on wealthier nations — which can persuade nations, willingly or forcibly, to adopt or accept particular platforms.

Due to its unique position and its belief in the importance of every human being, the Holy See was able to serve as a voice for those without a voice: the unborn, the uneducated, the underdeveloped, and even for those whose voices, while in agreement with the Holy See, were pressured into silence.

Ultimately, there were aspects of the Final Document which the Holy See was unable to support. Certain key portions of the Document allow for — indeed encourage — access to "legal" abortion. The Holy See has always affirmed that human life begins at the moment of conception, a fact increasingly supported by science as it has discovered that the moment of conception enacts the creation of a new human being, genetically and biologically distinct from mother or father. Furthermore, the child developing inside the womb does so actively, on its own — given the necessary nutrition and protection. The new life does not develop passively as would, for example, a sculpture carved from a block of marble at the hands of a sculptor.

With regard to the other major issue of the Conference — development of persons and nations — the Holy See was once again in disagreement with those voices who attempted to solve problems of this sort solely by means of population control. While significant lip service was paid to other aspects of development, including education and basic health care, the complete absence of any funding targeted for these initiatives revealed the true import given them by this international conference. Why was the Holy See one of the few who linked development with the need for international sharing of resources and technology? Why were the discussions on international sharing and cooperation so few and, at that, so quiet? And what really were the agendas of those who wished to wrap the Conference in a bow of "sexual and reproductive health," pushing for abortion as a means of family planning?

As this work indicates, the Holy See and the Catholic Church promoted human life — all human life — as being worthy of primordial concern, with respect for each individual's innate dignity to be nurtured and safeguarded in the family, and to ultimately achieve his or her full potential. This was contrary to the view of many present at the Cairo Conference who promoted a concept of human life as an inconvenience or a calamity. And the Holy See will continue to don the armor of Truth in affirming and protecting the dignity, development and human rights of all men, women and children, never to deny the rights *(or even human existence)* of one over the other.

May we come to a greater understanding of the Holy Father's words offered prior to the Conference, when he stated that: "All development worthy of the name must be integral, that is, it must be directed to the true good of every person and of the whole person. True development cannot consist in the simple accumulation of wealth and in the greater availability of goods and services, but must be pursued with due consideration for the social, cultural and spiritual dimensions of the human being." (*Address of Pope John Paul II to Dr. Nafis Sadik, Secretary General of the 1994 International Conference on Population and Development and Executive Director of the United Nations Population Fund*, 18 March 1994, n. 4).

**MESSAGE OF
HIS HOLINESS POPE JOHN PAUL II
TO MRS. NAFIS SADIK
SECRETARY GENERAL OF THE
1994 INTERNATIONAL CONFERENCE ON
POPULATION AND DEVELOPMENT AND
EXECUTIVE DIRECTOR OF THE UNITED NATIONS POPULATION FUND
VATICAN, 18 MARCH 1994**

1.   I greet you, Madam Secretary General, at a time when you are closely involved in preparing the 1994 International Conference on Population and Development, to be held in Cairo in September. Your visit provides an occasion for me to share with you some thoughts on a topic which, we all agree, is of vital importance for the *well-being and progress of the human family*. The theme of the Cairo Conference takes on a heightened significance in the light of the fact that the gap between the rich and the poor of the world continues to widen, a situation which poses an ever increasing threat to the peace for which mankind longs.

The global population situation is very complex; there are variations not simply from continent to continent but even from one region to another. United Nations studies tell us that a rapid decrease in the global rate of population growth is expected to begin during the 1990s and carry on into the new century. At the same time, growth rates remain high in some of the least developed nations of the world, while population growth has declined appreciably in the industrialized developed nations.

Basic ethical principles

2.   The Holy See has carefully followed these matters, with a special concern to make accurate and objective assessments of population issues and to urge global solidarity in regard to development strategies, especially as they affect the developing nations of the world. In this we have derived

benefit from participation in the meetings of the United Nations Population Commission and from the studies of the United Nations Population Division. The Holy See has also participated in all the regional preparatory meetings of the Cairo Conference, gaining a better understanding of regional differences and contributing to the discussion on each occasion.

In accordance with its specific competence and mission, the Holy See is concerned that proper attention should be given to *the ethical principles* determining actions taken in response to the demographic, sociological and public policy analyses of the data on population trends. Therefore, the Holy See seeks to focus attention on certain *basic truths*: that each and every person — regardless of age, sex, religion or national background — has a dignity and worth that is unconditional and inalienable; that human life itself from conception to natural death is sacred; that human rights are innate and transcend any constitutional order; and that the fundamental unity of the human race demands that everyone be committed to building a community which is free from injustice and which strives to promote and protect the common good. These truths about the human person are the measure of any response to the findings which emerge from the consideration of demographic data. It is in the light of authentic human values — recognized by peoples of diverse cultures, religious and national backgrounds across the globe — that all policy choices must be evaluated. No goal or policy will bring positive results for people if it does not respect the unique dignity and objective needs of those same people.

Human development and the family

3. There is widespread agreement that a population policy is only one part of an overall development strategy. Accordingly, it is important that any discussion of population policies should keep in mind the actual and projected development of nations and regions. At the same time, it is impossible to leave out of account the very nature of what is meant by the term "development," All development worthy of the name must be integral, that is, it must be directed to the true good of every person and of the whole person. True development cannot consist in the simple accumulation of wealth and in the greater availability of goods and services, but must be pursued with due consideration for the social, cultural and spiritual dimensions of the human being. Development programmes must be built on justice and equality, enabling people to live in dignity, harmony and peace. They must respect the cultural heritage of peoples and Nations, and those social qualities and virtues that reflect the God-given dignity of each and every person and the divine plan which calls all persons to unity. Importantly, men and women must be active agents of their own

development, for to treat them as mere objects in some scheme or plan would be to stifle that capacity for freedom and responsibility which is fundamental to the good of the human person.

4.   Development has been and remains the proper context for the international community's consideration of population issues. Within such discussions there naturally arise questions relating to the transmission and nurturing of human life. But to formulate population issues in terms of individual "sexual and reproductive rights," or even in terms of "women's rights" is to change the focus which should be the proper concern of governments and international agencies. I say this without in any way wishing to reduce the importance of securing justice and equity for women.

Moreover, questions involving the transmission of life and its subsequent nurturing cannot be adequately dealt with except in relation to *the good of the family*: that communion of persons established by the marriage of husband and wife, which is — as the *Universal Declaration of Human Rights* affirms — "the natural and fundamental group unit of society" (art. 16.3). The family is an institution founded upon the very nature of the human person, and it is the proper setting for the conception, birth and upbringing of children. At this moment in history, when so many powerful forces are arrayed against the family, it is more important than ever that the Conference on Population and Development should respond to the challenge implicit in the United Nations' designation of 1994 as the "International Year of the Family" by doing everything within its power to ensure that the family receives from "society and the State" that protection to which the same *Universal Declaration* says it is "entitled" (*ibid*). Anything less would be a betrayal of the noblest ideals of the United Nations.

Responsible parenthood

5.   Today, the duty to safeguard the family demands that particular attention be given to securing for husband and wife the liberty to decide responsibly, free from all social or legal coercion, the number of children they will have and the spacing of their births. It should not be the intent of governments or other agencies to decide for couples but, rather, to create the social conditions which will enable them to make appropriate decisions in the light of their responsibilities to God, to themselves, to the society of which they are a part, and to the objective moral order. What the Church calls *"responsible parenthood"* is not a question of unlimited procreation or lack of awareness of what is involved in rearing children, but rather the empowerment of couples to use their inviolable liberty wisely and responsibly, taking into account social and demographic realities as well as

their own situation and legitimate desires, in the light of objective moral criteria. All propaganda and misinformation directed at persuading couples that they must limit their family to one or two children should be steadfastly avoided, and couples that generously choose to have large families are to be supported.

In defence of the human person, the Church stands opposed to the imposition of limits on family size, and to the promotion of methods of limiting births which separate the unitive and procreative dimensions of marital intercourse, which are contrary to the moral law inscribed on the human heart, or which constitute an assault on the sacredness of life. Thus, sterilization, which is more and more promoted as a method of family planning, because of its finality and its potential for the violation of human rights, especially of women, is clearly unacceptable; it poses a most grave threat to human dignity and liberty when promoted as part of a population policy. Abortion, which destroys existing human life, is a heinous evil, and it is never an acceptable method of family planning, as was recognized by consensus at the Mexico City United Nations International Conference on Population (1984).

6. To summarize, I wish to emphasize once again what I have written in the Encyclical *Centesimus annus:* "It is necessary to go back to seeing the family as the sanctuary of life. The family is indeed sacred: it is the place in which life - the gift of God - can be properly welcomed and protected against the many attacks to which it is exposed, and can develop in accordance with what constitutes authentic human growth. In the face of the so-called culture of death, the family is the heart of the culture of life. Human ingenuity seems to be directed more towards limiting, suppressing or destroying the sources of life — including recourse to abortion, which unfortunately is so widespread in the world — than towards defending and opening up the possibility of life" (n. 39).

Status of women and children

7. As well as reaffirming the fundamental role of the family in society, I wish to draw special attention to *the status of children and women*, who all too often find themselves the most vulnerable members of our communities. Children must not be treated as a burden or inconvenience, but should be cherished as bearers of hope and signs of promise for the future. The care which is essential for their growth and nurture comes primarily from their parents, but society must help by sustaining the family in its needs and in its efforts to maintain the caring environment in which children can develop. Society ought to promote "social policies which have the family as their

principal object, policies which assist the family by providing adequate resources and efficient means of support, both for bringing up children and for looking after the elderly, so as to avoid distancing the latter from the family unit and in order to strengthen relations between generations" (*Centesimus annus,* n. 49). A society cannot say that it is treating children justly or protecting their interests if its laws do not safeguard their rights and respect the responsibility of parents for their well-being.

8. It is a sad reflection on the human condition that still today, at the end of the twentieth century, it is necessary to affirm that *every woman* is equal in dignity to man, and a full member of the human family, within which she has a distinctive place and vocation that is complementary to but in no way less valuable than man's. In much of the world, much still has to be done to meet the educational and health needs of girls and young women so that they may achieve their full potential in society.

In the family which a woman establishes with her husband she enjoys the unique role and privilege of motherhood. In a special way it belongs to her to nurture the new life of the child from the moment of conception. The mother in particular enwraps the newborn child in love and security, and creates the environment for its growth and development. Society should not allow woman's maternal role to be demeaned, or count it as of little value in comparison with other possibilities. Greater consideration should be given to *the social role of mothers*, and support should be given to programmes which aim at decreasing maternal mortality, providing prenatal and perinatal care, meeting the nutritional needs of pregnant women and nursing mothers, and helping mothers themselves to provide preventive health care for their infants. In this regard attention should be given to the positive benefits of breast-feeding for nourishment and disease prevention in infants, as well as for maternal bonding and birth-spacing.

Valid implications of population growth

9. The study of population and development inevitably poses the question of *the environmental implications of population growth. The ecological issue too is fundamentally a moral one.* While population growth is often blamed for environmental problems, we know that the matter is more complex. Patterns of consumption and waste, especially in developed nations, depletion of natural resources, the absence of restrictions or safeguards in some industrial or production processes, all endanger the natural environment.

The Cairo Conference will also want to give due attention to morbidity and mortality, and to the need to eliminate life-threatening diseases of every sort. While advances have been made that have resulted in an increased life span, policies must also provide for the elderly and for the contribution that they make to society in their retirement years. Society should develop policies to meet their needs for social security, health care and active participation in the life of their community.

Migration is likewise a major concern in examining demographic data, and the international community needs to ensure that the rights of migrants are recognized and protected. In this regard I draw special attention to the situation of migrant families. The State's task is to ensure that immigrant families do not lack what it ordinarily guarantees its own citizens, as well as to protect them from any attempt at marginalization, intolerance or racism, and to promote an attitude of convinced and active solidarity in their regard (cf. *Message for World Migration Day*, 1993-94, n.1).

Moral significance of Conference issues

10. As the preparations for the *Cairo Conference* proceed, I wish to assure you, Madam Secretary General, that the Holy See is fully aware of the complexity of the issues involved. This very complexity requires that we carefully weigh the consequences for the present and future generations of the strategies and recommendations to be proposed. In this context, the draft final document of the Cairo Conference, which is already being circulated, is a cause of grave concern to me. Many of the principles which I have just mentioned find no place in its pages, or are totally marginalized. Indeed, certain basic ethical principles are contradicted by its proposals. Political or ideological considerations cannot be, by themselves, the basis on which essential decisions for the future of our society are founded. What is at stake here is the very future of humanity. *Fundamental questions* like the transmission of life, the family, and the material and moral development of society, *need very serious consideration.*

For example, the international consensus of the 1984 Mexico City International Conference on Population that "in no case should abortion be promoted as method of family planning" is completely ignored in the draft document. Indeed, there is a tendency to promote an internationally recognized right to access to abortion on demand, without any restriction, *with no regard to the rights of the unborn*, in a manner which goes beyond what even now is unfortunately accepted by the laws of some nations. The vision of sexuality which inspires the document is individualistic. Marriage is ignored, as if it were something of the past. An institution as natural, universal and fundamental as the family cannot be manipulated without causing serious damage to the fabric and stability of society.

The seriousness of the challenges that Governments and, above all, parents must face in the education of the younger generation means that we cannot abdicate our responsibility of leading young people to a deeper understanding of their own dignity and potentiality as persons. What future do we propose to adolescents if we leave them, in their immaturity, to follow their instincts without taking into consideration the interpersonal and moral implications of their sexual behavior? Do we not have an obligation to open their eyes to the damage and suffering to which morally irresponsible sexual behavior can lead them? Is it not our task to challenge them with a demanding ethic which fully respects their dignity and which leads them to that self-control which is needed in order to face the many demands of life?

I am sure, Madam Secretary General, that, in the remaining period of preparation for the Cairo Conference, you and your collaborators, as well as the nations which will take part in the Conference itself, will devote adequate attention to these deeper questions.

None of the issues to be discussed is simply an economic or demographic concern, but, at root, each is a matter of profound moral significance, with far-reaching implications. Accordingly, the Holy See's contribution will consist in providing an ethical perspective on the issues to be considered, always with the conviction that mankind's efforts to respect and conform to God's providential plan is the only way to succeed in building a world of genuine equality, unity and peace.

May Almighty God enlighten all those taking part in the Conference.

**LETTER OF
HIS HOLINESS POPE JOHN PAUL II
TO THE WORLD'S HEADS OF STATE
VATICAN, 19 MARCH 1994**

Mr. President,

The international community recently began its celebration of the International Year of the Family, a timely initiative promoted by the United Nations Organization.

The International Conference on Population and Development, also organized by the UN and to be held in Cairo in September 1994, likewise represents one of the important events of this year. International leaders will thus have an opportunity to reconsider the reflections and commitments of the previous Conferences on these themes held in Bucharest (1974) and Mexico City (1984). But public opinion is especially looking to the Cairo meeting for guidelines for the future, conscious as it is of the important matters everyone clearly recognizes to be at stake, including the well-being and development of peoples, the growth of world population, the rise of the median age in some industrialized countries, the fight against disease and the forced displacement of whole peoples.

The Holy See, in conformity with its mission and using the means at its disposal, willingly associates itself with all these efforts to serve the human family throughout the world. On 26 December last, the Catholic Church also inaugurated a "Year of the Family," for the purpose of encouraging all the faithful to engage in a deeper spiritual and moral reflection on this human reality, fundamental to the lives of both individuals and societies.

I myself decided to address all families personally by writing them a Letter. It re-states the fact that every human being is "called to live in truth and in love" (n. 16), and that the family unit continues to be the "school of life" where the tensions between independence and communion, unity and diversity are lived out on a unique and primary level. It is in the family, I believe, that we find a human resource which produces the best creative energies of the social fabric. This is something which every State ought carefully to safeguard. Without infringing on the autonomy of a reality which they can neither produce nor replace, civil authorities have a duty, in effect, to strive to promote the harmonious growth of the family, not only from the point of view of its social vitality but also from that of its moral and spiritual health.

This is why the draft of the final document of the forthcoming Cairo Conference was of particular interest to me. I found it a disturbing surprise.

The innovations which it contains, on the level both of concepts and wording, make this text a very different one from the documents of the Conferences of Bucharest and Mexico City. There is reason to fear that it could cause a moral decline resulting in a serious setback for humanity, one in which man himself would be the first victim.

One notes, for example, that the theme of development, on the agenda of the Cairo meeting, including the very complex issue of the relationship between population and development, which ought to be at the centre of the discussion, is almost completely overlooked, so few are the pages devoted to it. The only response to the population issue and to the urgent need for an integral development of the person and of societies seems to be reduced to the promotion of a lifestyle the consequences of which, were it accepted as a model and plan of action for the future, could prove particularly negative. The leaders of the nations owe it to themselves to reflect deeply and in conscience on this aspect of the matter.

Furthermore, the idea of sexuality underlying this text is totally individualistic, to such an extent that marriage now appears as something outmoded. An institution as natural, fundamental and universal as the family cannot be manipulated by anyone.

Who could give such a mandate to individuals or institutions? The family is part of the heritage of humanity! Moreover, the *Universal Declaration of Human Rights* clearly states that the family is "the natural and fundamental group unit of society" (Art. 16,3). The International Year of the Family should therefore be a special occasion for society and the State to grant the family the protection which the *Universal Declaration* recognizes it should have. Anything less would be a betrayal of the noblest ideals of the United Nations. Even more serious are the numerous proposals for a general international recognition of a completely unrestricted right to abortion: this goes well beyond what is already unfortunately permitted by the legislation of certain nations.

Indeed, reading this document — which, granted, is only a draft — leaves the troubling impression of something being imposed: namely a lifestyle typical of certain fringes within developed societies, societies which are materially rich and secularized. Are countries more sensitive to the values of nature, morality and religion going to accept such a vision of man and society without protest?

As we look towards the year 2000, how can we fail to think of the young? What is being held up to them? A society of "things" and not of "persons." The right to do as they will from their earliest years, without any constraint, provided it is "safe." The unreserved gift of self, mastery of one's instincts, the sense of responsibility — these are notions considered as belonging to another age. One would have liked, for example, to find in these pages some attention to the conscience and to respect for cultural and ethical values which inspire other ways of looking at life. We may well fear that tomorrow those same young people, once they have reached adulthood, will demand an explanation from today's leaders, for having deprived them of reasons for living because they failed to teach them the duties incumbent upon beings endowed with intelligence and free will.

In writing to you, I have not only wished to share my deep concern about the draft of a document. Above all I have wished to draw your attention to the serious challenges which need to be faced by those taking part in the Cairo Conference. Questions as important as the transmission of life, the family, the material and moral development of societies: all these undoubtedly call for deeper reflection.

That is why I am appealing to you, who are concerned for the good of your own people and of all humanity. It is very important not to weaken man, his sense of the sacredness of life, his capacity for love and self-sacrifice. Here we are speaking of sensitive issues, issues upon which our societies stand or fall.

I pray that God will grant you discernment and courage, and enable you to join the very many people of good will, both in your own country and throughout the world, in blazing new paths, where all can walk hand in hand and together build a renewed world which will truly be a family, the family of peoples.

ADDRESSES OF
HIS HOLINESS POPE JOHN PAUL II
AT THE GENERAL AUDIENCE AND BEFORE THE ANGELUS

GENERAL AUDIENCE, ST. PETER'S SQUARE
6 APRIL 1994

At the end of the General Audience the Holy Father said:

Before passing to the Final Blessing, and before singing the *Regina Coeli* we should stress once again the importance of the Cairo Meeting during this Year of the Family. The family is the first and basic community of love and life. This year is dedicated to the family, by the Church, but initially by the United Nations in every civil community.

We are concerned lest this Year of the Family become a Year *against* the Family. And it could easily become the Year *against* the Family if these plans, to which a response has already been given, were really to become the plans of the World Conference in Cairo, which is scheduled for September.

We protest! I have written to all the Presidents in the world, above all to the Heads of State but also to the Presidents of the Episcopal Conferences, to invite them to reflect and truly to protect and defend the family. I repeat this during this great audience in Easter week because Easter tells us of the victory of life over death.

We cannot walk into the future while planning the systematic death of the unborn! We can only walk with a civilization of love that welcomes life.

ANGELUS, ST. PETER'S SQUARE
17 APRIL 1994

1. I have already had occasion, also in writing to the Heads of State of

the entire world, to express my sad surprise regarding some orientations which have emerged during the preparation for the International Conference on Population and Development, convened by the United Nations at Cairo for the coming month of September.

No one will fail to see the importance of this meeting, which faces some of the greatest challenges which today confront humanity. The themes which are on the agenda are not, in fact, questions about the simple "technical" organization of social life, to be left exclusively to economists, sociologists and politicians; they concern a vital sphere in which all of us are directly involved. What is at stake is the manner in which we understand human life in the essential sectors of sexuality and the family. In the face of such complex questions no one can opt out, as if these questions did not concern them.

This is the reason why today I wish to give further echo to this deep-felt anxiety of mine, appealing to all consciences, to the free souls who do not let themselves be caught in the network of the logic of blocks or of economic or political interests. I turn to those who know how to react to pervasive models of an illusion of freedom and of a false progress, which, examined in the depth, constitute forms of slavery and of regression, because they weaken man, the sacred character of life and the ability to achieve a true sense of love. Anything which violates the moral norm is never a victory, but a defeat for mankind and makes it a victim of itself.

2. In this International Year of the Family we would have expected a rediscovery and a relaunching of the principle affirmed in the *Universal Declaration of Human Rights*, according to which the family is "the fundamental group unit of society" (art. 16,3). Because of this character, the family is not an institution which one can change whenever one pleases: the family belongs to the most sacred heritage of humanity, from its very origins. The family precedes the State, which is obliged to recognize it and to safeguard it on the basis of socio-ethical motives which can be easily understood and can never be overlooked.

Anything which threatens the family, threatens man. This is all the more true when there is talk of a so-called "right to abortion." It is more urgent than ever to react to models of behaviour which are the fruit of a permissive and hedonistic culture, for which disinterested self-giving, control of one's instincts, a sense of responsibility are presented as concepts linked with a long-past era. I ask myself: to what type of society will such an ethical permissiveness lead? Are there not already enough worrying symptoms which make us anxious about the future of humanity?

3. I entrust these questions to the maternal heart of Mary. It is not my intention to give way to pessimism or alarmism: but I consider it my absolute duty to strongly raise the voice of the Church with regard to such an important matter. May Our Blessed Mother speak to hearts, make these words of mine reach beyond ideological and political barriers, so that on these fundamental arguments one will seek and will find a renewed consensus among all men and women of truly good will.

ANGELUS, ST. PETER'S SQUARE
12 JUNE 1994

Dear Brothers and Sisters,

1. Today I wish to return to the Encyclical *Veritatis splendor* to propose once again some basic principles of moral life. The Encyclical's point of departure is Christ's dialogue with the young man (cf. Mt. 19:19:16), who asked him: "Teacher, what must I do to gain eternal life?" Jesus answered him: "...If you wish to enter into life, keep the commandments" (Mt. 19:17). And when the young man asked "Which ones?," Jesus replied by quoting the Ten Commandments. This dialogue shows that the desire for eternal life is inherent in human beings, a desire whose realization is conditioned by observance of the commandments, that is, the fulfillment of moral norms, the principles of conduct given by God and revealed in Sacred Scripture.

2. Inviting the young man to observe the Decalogue, Jesus only repeats the same commandments which God, in his majesty as supreme Legislator, had given the Israelites through Moses from the summit of Mount Sinai. Through the Commandments God had made a covenant with Israel: Moses, together with his people, was found to observe them, and God, for his part, had guaranteed the Israelites entry into the promised land. Observance of the Commandments is the condition for attaining eternal life, symbolized by entering the promised land.

3. The same law, revealed by God through Moses and confirmed by Christ in the Gospel (cf. Mt. 5:17-19), was written in human nature by the Creator. This is what we read in St. Paul's Letter to the Romans: "For when the Gentiles who do not have the law by nature observe the prescriptions of the law, they are a law for themselves, even though they do not have the law" (Rom 2:14). Thus the moral principles shown by God to the Chosen People through Moses are the same that he inscribed in the nature of the human being. Therefore, by following what from the beginning is part of his nature, every individual knows that he must honour his father and mother and respect life: he is aware that he should not commit adultery, nor steal, nor give false

witness; in a word, he knows that he should not do to others what he would not want done to himself.

4.   In his Letter to the Romans, St. Paul adds: "They show that what the law requires is written on their hearts" (Rom 2:15). Conscience is presented as a witness, both by accusing man when he violates the law written in his heart, and by justifying him when he is faithful. Therefore, in accordance with the Apostle's teaching, there is a law intimately linked to man's nature as an intelligent and free being, and this law is echoed in his conscience: for man, to live at peace with his conscience means living at peace with the law of his own nature, and, vice versa, living in accord with this law means living in accord with his conscience; obviously, with a true and upright conscience, that is, with a conscience that correctly interprets the contents of the law written in human nature by the Creator.

5.   Recollection of this teaching contained in Sacred Scripture and in particular in the Letter to the Romans, has always been important in the history of the Church and of humanity. During the current year it is particularly urgent, especially regarding our basic duties concerning the family and life, which are so closely linked. First of all, in the International Year of the Family that basic human right, the right to life, must be strengthened. This right cannot be denied, for example, by legalizing the suppression of human life, especially of the unborn.

6.   With the recitation of the Angelus we turn our thoughts and hearts to Mary, Mother of the Word who became flesh (cf. Jn 1:14). Coming into the world, the Son of God wants us to have life and have it more abundantly (cf. Jn 10:10). Let us pray to Him, through the intercession of the Mother of Life, so that the divine law written in the heart of every man may be respected; so that in particular the right to life of every human being conceived may be respected. Only by observing God's law can we attain eternal life!

ANGELUS, ST. PETER'S SQUARE
19 JUNE 1994

Dear Brothers and Sisters,

1.   Continuing the reflection I began last Sunday on the natural law written by God in the heart of every human being, today I would like to talk about the topic of the family, on which the Church and society are focusing special attention this year. The family is the primary cell of society and is solidly grounded in the natural law that links all people and cultures. It is

urgently necessary to be aware of this aspect, to which I am planning to return on the coming Sundays.

Indeed, the Church's insistence on the ethics of marriage and the family is frequently misunderstood, as though the Christian community wished to impose on all society a faith perspective valid only for believers. It was apparent, for example, in several reaction to the disapproval I openly expressed when the European Parliament proposed to legitimize a new type of family based on the union of homosexuals.

In fact, marriage, as a stable union of a man and a woman who are committed to the reciprocal gift of self and open to creating life, is not only a Christian value, but an original value of creation. The loss of this truth is not a problem for believers alone, but a danger for all humanity.

2. Today, unfortunately, a creeping relativism spurs people to doubt the very existence of objective truth. There are echoes of the well-known question which Pilate asked Jesus: "What is truth?" (Jn 18:38). This scepticism leads to a false concept of freedom that recognizes no ethical limits and seeks to reformulate the most obvious natural data according to its own will.

Of course, man always discovers the truth in a limited way and can be called a pilgrim of truth. But this is quite different from relativism and scepticism. Experience actually shows that, however darkened or weakened our intellect is by a variety of influences, it can understand the truth of things, at least when it is a question of those basic values that make the existence of individuals and society viable. These are impressed upon each person's conscience and are a common heritage of humanity. Does not conscience appeal to this when it condemns crimes against humanity, even if they are endorsed by some legislator? In fact, precisely because it has been engraved on the heart by God, the natural law is prior to all man-made laws and is the measure of their validity.

3. May the Blessed Virgin guide all the families of the world to a deep awareness of God's plan. May the Year of the Family become for them a time of reflection and renewal. May children, who have the right to the warmth of families worthy of the name — and they need it more than ever! — benefit from this in particular.

ANGELUS, ST. PETER'S SQUARE
26 JUNE 1996

Dear Brothers and Sisters,

1. Today I would like to continue our reflection of marriage and the family and the natural law. The family is based on the love between a man and woman, a love understood as the profound, reciprocal gift of self also expressed in the sexual, conjugal union.

The Church is sometimes accused of making sex a "taboo." The truth is quite different. In the course of history, in contrast to Manichaean tendencies, Christian thought developed a positive, harmonious view of the human being, recognizing the significant, priceless role that masculinity and femininity play in human life.

Moreover, the biblical message is unequivocal: "God created man in his own image ... male and female he created them" (Gn 1:27). In this assertion is engraved the dignity of every man and woman, in their equality of nature but also in their sexual diversity. It is a fact that deeply concerns the constitution of the human being. "In fact it is from sex that the human person receives the characteristics which, on the biological, psychological and spiritual levels, make that person a man or woman" (*Persona humana*, n.1).

I stressed this point recently in the *Letter to Families*. Here is what I said: "Man is created 'from the very beginning' as male and female: the life of all humanity — whether of small communities or of society as a whole — is marked by this primordial duality. From it there derive the 'masculinity' and the 'femininity' of individuals, just as from it every community draws its own unique richness in the mutual fulfilment of persons" (n.6).

2. Sexuality, then, belongs to the Creator's original plan and the Church cannot fail to hold it in high esteem. At the same time, however, she must ask everyone to respect it in its inmost nature.

As a dimension inscribed in the totality of the person, sexuality has a specific "language" of its own at the service of love and cannot be lived at the purely instinctual level. It must be controlled by man as a free, intelligent being.

This does not mean, however, that it can be manipulated arbitrarily. It actually has its own unique psychological and biological structure, aimed at both communion between man and woman and at the birth of new persons. Respecting this structure and this unbreakable connection is not "biologism" or "moralism" but concern for the truth of what it means to be human, to be a person. In virtue of this truth, which can also be grasped by the light of reason, so-called "free love," homosexuality and contraception are morally unacceptable. It is really a question of behaviour that distorts the essential meaning of human sexuality, preventing it from being put at the service of the person, of communion and of life.

3. May the Blessed Virgin, the model of femininity, tenderness and self-control, help everyone, the men and women of our time, not to trivialize sex, not to trivialize it in the name of a false modernity. Let young people, women and families look to her. May Mary, Mother most chaste, enlighten the representatives of nations so that at the forthcoming meeting in Cairo they will make decisions inspired by the authentic human values underlying the civilization of love for which we hope.

ANGELUS, ST. PETER'S SQUARE
3 JULY 1994

Dear Brothers and Sisters,

1. Returning to our discussion of conjugal love, today I would like to reflect on an essential property of marriage: its unity. The bond arising from valid marital consent is by its nature one and exclusive, and requires of both spouses the obligation of a lasting, mutual fidelity.

In a vivid image, Sacred Scripture teaches that husband and wife are called to "one flesh" (Gn 2:24). It is actually a covenant of love that involves the couple's whole spiritual and physical life. Through the union of their bodies, they express the depth and finality of their mutual gift.

Precisely in the light of this characteristic totality of the marital covenant one understands why sexual union must take place exclusively in marriage, which on the personal and social levels seals the choice of a complete communion of life.

Only in this context can husband and wife fully live "that primordial wonder which led Adam on the morning of creation to exclaim to Eve: 'This at last is bone of my bones and flesh of my flesh' (Gn 2:23). This same wonder is echoed in the words of the Song of Solomon: 'You have ravished my heart, my sister, my bride, you have ravished my heart with a glance of your eyes' (Song of Songs 4:9)" (*Letter to Families*, n. 19).

2. This is true: from a historical standpoint, the principle of matrimonial

unity has met with doubts due to a variety of socio-cultural influences. With regard to the duty of fidelity, then, the allurements of human weakness are unfortunately before our eyes, especially in those circles where there is little moral sense and sexual activity is reduced to a mere erotic experience or to the exploitation of others for one's own pleasure.

However, deviations cannot in fact lessen the objective, universal moral law, which is firmly rooted in human nature itself. Is not the promise to be the only man and the only woman for each other part of authentic conjugal love? This is precisely why we suffer so much when we feel abandoned or betrayed by the man or woman we love and from whom we have the right to expect a total response of love. This witness of love and unity is also the most natural expectation of children, who are the fruit of one man and one woman's love. And they require this love with every fibre of their being.

May the Blessed Virgin teach everyone the meaning of love. May Mary look with motherly devotion particularly upon the many difficulties encountered by married couples in a society such as ours in which there are few ethical standards but countless temptations. May the Mother of Fairest Love help young people preparing for marriage to lay solid foundations for their mutual commitment in order to live it faithfully throughout their earthly lives.

ANGELUS, ST. PETER'S SQUARE
10 JULY 1994

1. Continuing our Sunday reflections on the family in the year dedicated to this institution, today I would like to draw your attention to the scourge of divorce, which is unfortunately so widespread. Although in many cases it is legal, this does not prevent it from being one of the great failures of human civilization.

The church knows she is "swimming against the tide" when she proclaims the principle of the indissolubility of the marriage bond. All the service she owes to humanity obliges her constantly to insist on this truth, appealing to the voice of conscience, which even under the heaviest of influences is never completely extinguished in man's heart.

I know well that this aspect of marital ethics is among the most demanding, and that sometimes truly difficult, if not really tragic, marriage situations arise. The Church tries to be aware of these situations and to appear as the merciful Jesus. Even in the Old Testament the value of indissolubility had become blurred, so that divorce was tolerated. Jesus explained the concession of the Mosaic Law by the "hardness of the human heart," and did not hesitate to propose again God's original plan in all its force, as was stated in the Book of Genesis: "Therefore a man leaves his father and his mother and cleaves to his wife, and they become one flesh" (Gn 2:24), adding: "So they are no longer two, but one. What therefore God has joined together, let no man put asunder" (Mt 19:6).

2. Some might object that such a saying is understandable and applicable only within a horizon of faith. This is not so! It is true that for Christ's disciples indissolubility is further reinforced by the "sacramental" nature of marriage, a sign of the spousal union between Christ and his Church. But this "great mystery" (Eph 5:32) does not exclude, but rather implies, the ethical demand of indissolubility even at the level of the natural law. It is unfortunately the "hardness of heart" denounced by Jesus that continues to make the universal perception of this truth difficult, or to lead to cases in which it appears virtually impossible to live. However, when one reasons calmly and keeps the ideal in mind, it is not difficult to agree that the permanence of the marriage bond springs from the very essence of love and the family. We love one another truly and absolutely only when we love forever, in joy and in sorrow, in good times and in bad. Do not children themselves have the utmost need of the indissoluble union of their own parents, and are they not themselves frequently the first victims of the tragedy of divorce?

3. May the Holy Family of Nazareth, where Jesus, Mary and Joseph lived an exemplary experience of supernatural and human love, be the model for every family. May Mary most holy come to the aid of couples in crisis, helping them to rediscover the freshness of their first love. May this Year of the Family not pass in vain and may it enable everyone to rediscover the marvelous beauty of God's plan.

ANGELUS, CASTEL GANDOLFO
17 JULY 1994

Dear Brothers and Sisters,

1. Today I would like to draw your attention to another basic aspect of conjugal love: its intrinsic openness to life. The *Catechism of the Catholic Church* stresses this when it points out that the spouses' love "naturally tends to be fruitful. A child does not come from outside as something added on to the mutual love of the spouses, but springs from the very heart of the mutual giving, as its fruit and fulfillment" (CCC, n. 2366).

Grasping the mysterious greatness of this event is of fundamental importance. As I wrote in the *Letter to Families*, "God himself is present in human fatherhood and motherhood... Indeed, God alone is the source of that 'image and likeness' which is proper to the human being, as it was received at Creation. Begetting is the continuation of Creation" (n.9).

Certainly this theme finds particular resonance with believers. However, its value can also be recognized by pure reason which, in the miracle of nascent human life, is forced to acknowledge something that goes far beyond itself. This cannot fail to have implications on the ethical level too: what concerns the begetting of human life cannot be treated as if it were a mere biological event subject to any sort of manipulation.

2.   The Church's teaching about "responsible parenthood" is based on this essential anthropological and ethical foundation. Unfortunately, Catholic thought is often misunderstood on this point, as if the Church supported an ideology of fertility at all costs, urging married couples to procreate indiscriminately and without thought for the future. But one need only study the pronouncements of the Magisterium to know that this is not so.

Truly, in begetting life the spouses fulfill one of the highest dimensions of their calling: they are God's co-workers. Precisely for this reason they must have an extremely responsible attitude. In deciding whether or not to have a child, they must not be motivated by selfishness or carelessness, but by a prudent, conscious generosity that weighs the possibilities and circumstances, and especially gives priority to the welfare of the unborn child. Therefore, when there is a reason not to procreate, this choice is permissible and may even be necessary. However, there remains the duty of carrying it out with criteria and methods that respect the total truth of the marital act in its unitive and procreative dimension, as wisely regulated by nature itself in its biological rhythms. One can comply with them and use them to advantage, but they cannot be "violated" by artificial interference.

3.   Let us ask Blessed Mary for the gift of wisdom of heart, so necessary for clear vision in this sensitive matter, which is subject to the perversions of a hedonistic and permissive culture. May she enlighten married couples to live their service to life with a great sense of responsibility and to make their families true "sanctuaries of life."

**ANGELUS, CASTEL GANDOLFO
24 JULY 1994**

Dear Brothers and Sisters,

1.   One of the central problems of the forthcoming Conference organized by the United Nations in Cairo on "population and development" is the so-called "demographic explosion." This complex phenomenon is the subject of assessments that do not always converge. According to some statistical findings and predictions, humanity as a whole is growing at a rate that in the future could create difficulties for human coexistence itself. In many nations, however, a worrisome crisis in the birth rate has been observed.

The Church is familiar with the problem and does not underestimate its significance. Precisely for this reason she has, even recently, promoted and encouraged in-depth studies, taking into consideration the statistical data and evaluating the ethical and pastoral implications.

She recognizes the responsibilities States have in this sensitive area. The *Catechism* explicitly states that public authorities can "intervene to orient the demography of the population" (CCC, n. 2327). These interventions obviously presuppose a sense of responsibility on the part of families. As I have already recalled, husband and wife must make their decision to procreate according to a reasonable plan based on a generous and, at the same time, realistic assessment of the welfare of the child to be born and of society itself, in the light of objective moral criteria. These points were also stated in the Holy See's Message to the United Nations, to those responsible for preparing the final document of Cairo (cf. *Message to Mrs. Nafis Sadik*, L'Osservatore Romano English edition, 23 March 1994, pp. 1-2).

2.   In this matter, therefore, family ethics confronts the ethics of public policy. The ethical dimension also puts precise limits on the intervention of States and of the international community. For example, it is never legitimate to intervene with "authoritarian, coercive measures" (CCC, n. 2372) aimed at usurping the couple's primary and inalienable responsibility. Encouraging the use of immoral means, especially abortion, to regulate births, is also unacceptable. Here is one of the points of radical difference between the Church and some orientations now coming to the fore. Truly, how can we not be disturbed by the fact that vast sums of money have been allocated for distributing ethically impermissible contraceptives, while development of the great potential of "natural family planning" has been rejected? The latter, in addition to being less costly, certainly "helps couples maintain their human dignity while exercising responsible love." (cf. Appeal of the Cardinals in defence of the family, *L'Osservatore Romano*, English edition, 22 June 1994, p. 7).

Obviously, for a correct solution to demographic policy more intense efforts must be made to increase natural and economic resources and to distribute them more fairly, as well as to promote a proper international cooperation in the development of disadvantaged countries.

3. Let us call upon the Blessed Virgin to open the eyes of all who are responsible for the future of humanity. Certainly the problems are serious and weighty. But God's help will not be wanting, if we remain steadfast in his law. By her motherly prayers, may Mary most holy obtain for us a deep conversion of heart.

ANGELUS, CASTEL GANDOLFO
31 JULY 1994

Dear Brothers and Sisters who have come here to Castel Gandolfo, who have gathered in St. Peter's Square and who are listening to me on radio and television.

1. Returning to the theme of responsible parenthood, today I would like to underscore a specific requirement of the love with which spouses are called to beget life. They must want the child with an unconditional and sacrificial love, and avoid exploiting it for their own interests or personal gratification.

Certainly the newborn child is also a gift for the parents. Is it not true that a baby's smile can revive a somewhat tired, faded marital love? Nevertheless, this gift must be sought and accepted with deep respect and with awareness of the new creature's transcendent dignity.

The Council teaches that "man is the only creature on earth whom God willed for its own sake" (*Gaudium et spes*, n. 24). All creation, in a certain sense, is pointed towards man, whose "genealogy" — as I wrote in the *Letter to Families* (n. 9) — goes well beyond the parents and directly involves the creative intervention of God. Man alone is both a corporeal and spiritual being, called to an eternal, supernatural destiny. Parents therefore must imitate God's unconditional love, desiring the child "for its own sake" with full respect for its autonomy and originality.

2. Unfortunately, in the sensitive area of begetting life there are also worrying symptoms of a culture that is anything but inspired by true love. This seems obvious whenever newborn life is excluded or even suppressed; but paradoxically, it is also the case when life is "demanded" at any cost and morally disordered means are used to this end. In fact, technologies of human generation — such as artificial insemination, hiring a surrogate mother, and so forth — are spreading at a growing rate and pose grave ethical problems. Among other serious implications one need only recall that in these kinds of procedures the human being is defrauded of his right to be

born from an act of true love and in accordance with normal biological processes, and is thus marked from the beginning by psychological, legal and social problems that will accompany him throughout life.

As a matter of fact, the legitimate desire for a child cannot be interpreted as a sort of right to a child, to be fulfilled at any cost. This would mean treating the child as if it were a thing! As for science, it has the duty to support the natural generative processes, not the task of artificially substituting them. All the more so, since the desire for children can also be fulfilled through the legal institution of adoption, which deserves to be better organized and promoted, and through other forms of service and social commitment, such as expressions of hospitality towards the many children who in various ways have been deprived of a family.

3. May Mary Most Holy help all couples to appreciate the greatness of their mission. By looking to the Holy Family of Nazareth, may fathers and mothers make every effort to want and accept their children with great respect for their own personality. May unconditional love for every human being be the inspirational force for building a civilization worthy of the name.

ANGELUS, CASTEL GANDOLFO
7 AUGUST 1994

Dear Brothers and Sisters,

1. At the 1984 International Population Conference held in Mexico City, it was rightly stated that "in no way should abortion be promoted as a method of family planning." I hope, we hope, that this directive will be forcefully reaffirmed at the forthcoming Conference in Cairo. Should the opposite policy be asserted instead, in order further to legitimize the legal practice of abortion, humanity would suffer another great breakdown of right and justice.

The following moral principle applies not only for individuals but also for States and the international community: "Human life must be respected and protected absolutely from the moment of conception. From the first moment of his existence, a human being must be recognized as having the rights of a person — among which is the inviolable right of every innocent being to life" (CCC. n. 2270).

The Council did not hesitate to describe abortion as an "abominable crime" (*Gaudium et spes*, n. 51). The basis for this severe judgement is not only the word of Revelation, but also that of human reason. Today science itself offers its own confirmation of the embryo's human nature, assuring us that from the moment of conception it is an original and biologically autonomous being, endowed with an inner pattern of development that will unfold without loss of continuity until full maturity. Precisely for this reason God's commandment, "You shall not kill," applies to the embryo no less than to individuals already born.

2. The State has the task of guaranteeing and fostering respect for the life of each human being in every possible way. Freedom of conscience and choice cannot be invoked against this duty, because respect for life is the basis of all other rights, including those of freedom. As the *Catechism of the Catholic Church* states: "The inalienable right to life of every innocent human individual is a constitutive element of a civil society and its legislation" (CCC, n. 2273), since "the moment a positive law deprives a category of human beings of the protection which civil legislation ought to accord them, the State is denying the equality of all before the law. When the State does not place its power at the service of the rights of each citizen, and in particular of the more vulnerable, the very foundations of a State based on law are undermined" (Congregation for the Doctrine of the Faith, Instruction *Donum vitae*, ch. III).

3. Let us beseech the Virgin Mother of God to enlighten the conscience of leaders and to help humanity safeguard the respect owed to the dignity and value of every human life from the moment of its conception. May Mary, who had the privilege of carrying the Lord of Life in her womb, enable parents to respect the life they are called to beget, society to support mothers at risk with effective measures, government to pass laws always and only at the service of life.

4. As we now turn to the Blessed Virgin in our Angelus prayer, today too we wish to recall the noble figure of my predecessor, Pope Paul VI, the anniversary of whose death occurred yesterday. In his luminous magisterium he always courageously emphasized the dignity of every human being and the inviolable value of his life.

ANGELUS, CASTEL GANDOLFO
14 AUGUST 1994

Dear Brothers and Sisters,

1. Continuing our discussion of the family, today I would like to make special mention of woman, who has a particular and irreplaceable role in the family.

There are those who reproach the Church for insisting too much on woman's mission in the family and for overlooking the question of her active presence in the various areas of social life. Actually this is not the case. The Church is well aware of how much society needs the feminine genius in all aspects of civil society and insists that every form of discrimination of women be eliminated from the workplace, culture and politics, while still respecting the proper nature of femininity: an inappropriate leveling of roles would not only impoverish social life, but would ultimately deprive woman herself of what is primarily or exclusively hers.

These many forms of violence and exploitation, which rather openly commercialize women and trample on their dignity, must be vigorously rejected. Hence it is appropriate for the preparatory document of the forthcoming International Conference in Cairo to devote its attention to improving women's status in the world.

2. It is against this horizon of esteem and appreciation for femininity in all its expressions that the discussion of woman's mission as mother, a decisive mission for the fate of humanity, must be viewed. As I wrote in the Apostolic Letter *Mulieris dignitatem*, it could be said that through motherhood God has entrusted the human being to woman in a special way (cf. n. 30).

This is why woman has the primary responsibility for defending life from the moment of conception. Who better than a mother understands the miracle of life developing in her womb?

Unfortunately, woman often meets objective difficulties that make her task as mother more burdensome, even to the point of heroism. Often, however, this unbearable load is caused by indifference and inadequate assistance, due to legislation that pays scant attention to the value of the family, and to a widespread and distorted culture which unduly excuses man from his family responsibilities and, in the worst cases, inclines him to look upon woman as an object of pleasure or a mere reproductive device. Against this oppressive culture, every legitimate effort must be made to promote the authentic emancipation of women. However, in this task, the dignity of woman and the defence of life go together, and one hopes that the Cairo Conference will also be courageously viewed in this perspective.

3. Mary, Mother of the Son of God made man, is the consummate image of femininity. In her, God's plan for woman was fulfilled in an exemplary manner. Let all women, particularly the mothers of the world, look to her so that they fully realize and live the greatness of their mission.

**ANGELUS, CASTEL GANDOLFO
28 AUGUST 1994**

Dear Brothers and Sisters,

1. With the Cairo Conference on "Population and Development" imminent, and in the context of the International Year of the Family which we are now celebrating, I want to again turn to the very important topic of the institution of the family.

In particular, I would like to express my concern about the tendency in the preparatory document of the above-mentioned Conference to understand sexuality in a too individualistic key, without giving sufficient value to the social implications that are at the basis of the institution of marriage and family.

The need for such an institution is found within human nature itself. "Man," Aristotle said, "is, by his very nature, more inclined to live in pairs than to affiliate politically, because the family is something which precedes and which is more necessary than the State" (*Nicomachean Ethics*, VIII, 12). The *Universal Declaration of Human Rights* interprets this fact when it presents the family as "the natural and fundamental element of society" (art. 16).

It would be serious if the Cairo Conference, because of its concern to confront the problem of rapid population growth, instead of orienting itself toward the promotion of a culture of responsible procreation, were to content itself with accepting or directly favoring a sexuality apart from ethical references, and above all from the specific responsibility that men and women assume, reciprocally and before the community, when they give their conjugal consent.

2. It is true: today you sometimes hear judgements and proposals on this issue that are very surprising. But the psycho-biological structure of human sexuality is an objective fact that, in spite of the fragility of human behavior and the variety of opinions, does not cease to point toward the profound and stable union between man and woman in marriage, rendering them responsible for the life that springs from such a union. Before being a question of faith, it is an anthropological fact that demands simple rational reflection.

In reality, what is at stake is the future of the family and of society itself. In the more developed nations, where the demographic problem is one of a lack rather than excess, there are already several alarming signs of a morality of life and interpersonal relationships greatly in crisis. If you think, for example, of drugs, violence, the lack of ideals and values, the lack of meaning and respect for life, the indifference toward the elderly, the insecurity of youth ... In face of such disquieting situations, does not the need arise to make an appeal for the indispensable recovery of the family's role and responsibility?

3. May the Virgin Mary, to whom we faithfully address our prayer, open the eyes of humanity in this crucial passage of its history. May leaders obtain the courage necessary for wise and prudent choices, conforming to the design of God. May men and women of our time rediscover the meaning of marriage and the family and live it with joy, fidelity and responsibility.

Only in this way is it possible to construct a better, more serene and solid future for the whole of humanity.

National Report of the Holy See
in Preparation for the
International Conference on Population and Development
23 March 1993

Introduction

1.   Due to the particular nature of the Holy See, this *Report of the Holy See* has a different character to those of the other States participating in the European Population Conference.

2.   The Holy See follows with interest the current trends concerning population and development questions both within the European region of the United Nations as well as on a worldwide basis. This report will draw attention to some of the principal trends in demographic development and population policies in the region which have specific human and ethical consequences, illustrating the perception and the policy of the Holy See on the more pertinent questions.

I.   Population growth and age structure

3.   The ageing of the population is one of the particular marks of the current demographic situation of certain parts of the region and is likely to spread to other areas in the near future.

4.   Improvements in health care services have led to an increase in life expectancy. At the same time there has been over recent years a marked drop in fertility rates or a stabilization of these rates in many cases below replacement level. This has resulted in an imbalance in the population structure, with an increasingly large group of ageing persons and smaller group of children and youth. The imbalance in the population structure can be alleviated only in a limited way through immigration.

5.   This phenomenon of an ageing population combined with a drop in fertility has resulted in a reduced *work-force* in a number of countries which has not been completely compensated for by the introduction of modern technology. The change in the proportions between those who are economically active and those who are dependent has created strains on pension and health-care services, at a period when the overall economic climate is already producing cut-backs. It would seem that these trends are likely to become more acute and that to a greater extent the responsibility for the care of the aged and chronically ill will be assigned to the family and the

community.

6.	Governments should provide more resources to enable both the family and local communities to undertake this task, where necessary, by reassigning resources from institutional to community-based programmes. Experience in other areas, however, shows that the community must be prepared to assume this task through programmes of sensitization, community education and, where necessary, training programmes for those who work with the elderly. In many parts of the region, Church-based organizations have played an important role, alongside other voluntary and community organizations, in taking the lead in providing innovative services of support, companionship and solidarity for the elderly, as well as developing programmes which help to insert the elderly actively into society.

7.	While welcoming those factors which have contributed to the increase in life expectancy, European and North-American society must also face some underlying questions linked with the current situation. What are the long-term social, cultural economic and ethical consequences for a society which does not replace itself? How can one assure the rejuvenation of a society which seems to have lost its desire to transmit its identity and values through a flourishing new generation? To what extent are the ageing of European society and a certain resistance toward encouraging childbearing mutually interrelated? To what extent do they together contribute to the evolution of a pessimistic vision of life?

II. International migration

8.	The phenomenon of widespread international migration, with considerable variation from one area to another, is also one of the characteristics of the European and North-American region today. It is a phenomenon which meets with an ambivalent response. International migration is a key question to be examined in the context of the movement towards unification in Europe and the search for stability in a new political climate, as well as in the context of the development of an enlarged North-American market.

9.	The social impact of large numbers of incoming asylum seekers, refugees, migrant workers and their families, has in places caused violent reactions which, in turn, weaken the democratic consensus needed for any sustainable policy dealing with such large population movements. The cultural differences between the migrants and the local population also arouse concerns about national identity or priority access to employment and services. There is indeed a sense in which the *economic will* to have additional manpower to compensate for the ageing of the general population clashes with an *emerging political will* which emphasizes the negative aspects of immigration and which advocates greater controls and even expulsions.

10. The Holy See hopes that the existing international instruments which give protection and assistance to asylum seekers will not be weakened. However, it is today more difficult to distinguish voluntary and involuntary migration since the element of free choice is hardly the principal reason for people deciding to move abroad. The *push factor* is usually the dominant reason for emigration today. Armed conflicts, political oppression, poverty, the degradation of the environment, demographic imbalances, the lack of safety nets for basic needs in moments of crisis and the lack of peoples' participation in decision-making, all lead to emigration as a way of escaping conditions of life which have become seemingly unbearable.

11. The responsibility of the international community to extend protection and assistance becomes more challenging. It requires an adjustment of juridical instruments and international structures. Thus, while preserving the refugee regime based on the *Geneva Refugee Convention* of 1951 and its additional *Protocol* of 1967, support should also be given to those legislative measures for the acceptance of newcomers — who for well-founded reasons cannot be repatriated — which most developed countries have generally enacted in recent years. Despite such signs of increased awareness of the problems of involuntary migrants, some States tend more and more to determine arbitrarily the criteria for fulfillment of their international obligation towards asylum seekers, with policies which aim at reducing the number of entries and discouraging new requests for asylum.

12. It should be recognized that, if well planned, immigration can be a positive element in the construction and renewal of the Region (Western Europe, newly Independent States, North-America) and in its relations with the rest of the world. Immigrants make an important contribution to the economy of the *host country*. Contact between persons of different talents and cultures has historically been a source of civilization's advancement.

13. A reasonable acceptance of immigrants can also be a contribution to the development of the *countries of origin*, because of the alleviation of the competition for jobs, the transfer of skills and technology on their eventual return and the actual remittances sent back by migrants.

14. On a *regional level*, individual States cannot overlook the fact that the presence, within any part of the region, of a large number of persons who are excluded from social, economic and political participation constitutes an overall threat to democracy and peaceful coexistence. Since Europe and

North America will remain areas of attraction for new immigrations, the consideration of their inclusion requires greater coordination of the various multi-lateral fora dealing with immigration policies, information gathering, and the study of the root causes which give rise to migration. It should also be recalled that migrations can help regional integration, security and development, for example, by linking the offer and demand for manpower.

15. The assumption is, however, that most people would not move if they could enjoy decent living conditions at home. Unwanted migration is prevented by development. New forms of cooperation should be encouraged which aim at sustaining local economies, at local job creation and at trade liberalization. Joint programmes should be developed in order to share know-how in management and business skills as well as to share appropriate new technologies.

16. Integration is an important aspect of immigration policy. But the recommended integration requires measures aimed at safeguarding the fundamental human rights of all the migrants on the territory and ensuring the respect of their cultural identity.

17. A serious commitment to integration requires, among other factors: access to *citizenship* and its benefits for those who have resided for a long time in the host country, and especially for the second generation of migrants who have grown up there; the right to family reunification; education in schools which respects cultural and religious diversity.

18. A *caveat* should be expressed concerning *temporary migrations*, since experience has shown that they tend to evolve into permanent migrations with much weaker social protection. While programmes of temporary transfer of manpower for purposes of training and for well-defined forms of economic assistance can be beneficial, large scale temporary migrations risk becoming a source of cheap labour with damage to family life.

19. Emigration has considerable consequences in the area of foreign relations and international contacts should be intensified in this area, so that a better directed international policy can be developed. Questions of an underground labour market and the exploitation of clandestine immigrants should receive appropriate attention in the international domain.

II. Policy in the area of fertility and the family

20. The Holy See has always stressed in its reflection on population questions the central role and value of the family. As the basic unit of

society, the family should enjoy the support of a wide-ranging social policy in order that it can offer the particular stability which it brings to *society*, through its role of education, socialization and caring. In addition to being a juridical, social and economic unit, the family is a community of love and solidarity, which is uniquely suited to teach and transmit cultural, social, ethical, spiritual and religious values, essential for the well-being of its own members and of society. The family is, in fact, the place where different generations meet and help one another harmonize the rights of individuals with the other demands of social life.

21. Society as a whole thus has an interest in developing a policy which *benefits and supports* the family. The Holy See thus endorses the affirmation of the *World Declaration on Nutrition* (1992) which affirms "we fully recognize the importance of the family unit in providing adequate food, nutrition and a proper caring environment for meeting the physical, mental, emotional and social needs of children and other vulnerable groups, including the elderly ... We therefore undertake to strengthen and promote the family unit as the basic unit of society." In developing countries the family unit is also perhaps the most important unit for the effective delivery of health care and social services.

22. Recent studies indicate that most people enter marriage and found a family in the expectation that their experience will be stable and rewarding. Research also indicates stability and ordered care as essential for the healthy development of children.

23. Family social policy should aim at establishing a social environment and a climate favourable to stability. For this reason the Holy See stresses that public authorities have a responsibility to uphold the institutional and juridical character of marriage and that the situation of non-married couples should not be placed on the same level as marriage duly contracted.

24. Concerning *fertility* the Holy See advocates responsible parenthood, which emphasizes the responsible planning of family size. Decisions concerning the spacing of births and the number of children to be born belong to the spouses and not to any other authority. The spouses are called to make free and responsible decisions which take into full consideration their duties towards themselves, their children already born, the family and society, in accordance with objective moral norms as well as their own cultural and religious traditions.

25. The concrete decisions of couples are influenced by many external factors. The Holy See welcomes social and economic measures which compensate, at least partly, for cost of child-bearing and child-rearing,

including measures which recognize the contribution to society of women who choose to work in the home and which allow special social protection for relatively large families (those with more children or those who care for elderly family members).

26. The lack of such social protection, as well as the lack of adequate housing at reasonable rates, prevents some couples who might wish to do so from having a larger family. Material incentives alone cannot, however, reverse an overall negative attitude towards having children which has penetrated European and North American society. In recent years one can, however, observe some change in trends, such as a greater recognition of family stability or a revaluation of *maternity* as an important dimension of women's identity.

27. The Holy See supports the use of the natural methods for the regulation of fertility, not only for ethical reasons, but because these methods respect the health of women and men by avoiding the possibility of dangerous side-effects. Both unity and equality among the spouses are strengthened through the use of these methods, which by their very nature enlist the full involvement and commitment of the man to understand and respect his spouse. In the allocation of public funds these methods should receive appropriate support for their role in achieving or spacing pregnancies.

28. The Holy See is opposed to all forms of voluntary abortion. It must be noted that in both Europe and North American *abortion legislation* is generally permissive. It is also true, however, that both legislation and public consensus throughout the region recognize, with the last International Population Conference, that abortion should not be promoted as a means of family planning.

IV. Mortality and health

29. In Europe and North America, the overall high level of health care standards has produced noticeable results in improving health and prolonging a healthy life. But one encounters today what Pope John Paul II has called a "paradox of abundance," a new range of health problems linked with the affluent and consumerist life-style of the developed nations. This life-style makes excessive demands on natural resources both within the region and outside it. The life-style of developed nations is indeed one of the major causes of environmental degradation in the poorer nations.

30. Unbalanced eating habits, lack of exercise, substance abuse and irresponsible sexual behaviour have led to the emergence of a range of health

problems which are typical of the developed regions, bringing with them extremely heavy financial burdens for society. Sexually transmitted diseases represent a serious problem which can only be ultimately solved through a greater sense of responsibility and personal restraint as regards sexual behaviour. Other diseases such as tuberculosis, once thought to have been eliminated, are on the increase in various parts of the region. Traffic accidents and accidents in the workplace with resultant traumata also negatively affect the overall health expenditures in the region.

31. In many of the countries of Central and Eastern Europe the overall *environmental degradation* still has very serious effects on the health of the population. In the region in general, more effort must be made in order to identify sources of atmospheric and soil pollution which create serious health hazards.

32. Thus the Holy See advocates continuing improvements in both pre- and post-natal *health care for mothers and children*, with a view to reducing infant and maternal mortality and improving maternal and child health standards.

33. In the light of the ageing of the population of the region, greater attention should be given to the provision of home-based care and self-care for the aged, which will permit them to remain active participants in society in respect of their dignity and rights, including the right to life itself.

V. International cooperation

34. The title of the 1994 Cairo International Conference will be *Conference on Population and Development*. The experience of recent years has shown that population and development are interrelated. Heavily funded population and family planning programmes over the past decades have often failed to achieve their desired aim because they ignored the development of the people and the nation for which such programmes were designed. On the other hand, where social development takes place, especially through the education of women and improved maternal and child care, population growth has been reduced. A decline in population growth rates takes place when people are confident that their existing children can survive.

35. In many cases, population control programmes are not sufficiently sensitive to the cultural and religious traditions of people and are thus perceived as foreign and unjustly imposed.

36. The Holy See strongly insists that in international population

programmes couples should be free to make their own responsible choices about family size and the spacing of births, be exempt from coercion and undue pressure from governments or other organizations and also that their cultural and religious rights be fully respected. The Holy See is concerned about the increasing use of *sterilization* as a means of population control, especially in developing countries. Sterilization is the family planning means most open to abuse on human rights grounds, especially among the poor or the illiterate. Sterilization, because of its finality (or irreversibility) is also objectionable because it contradicts cultural attitudes regarding childbearing and leaves no opportunity for future changes in childbearing plans. The extremely high proportions of women in some developing countries who have been sterilized is a cause of very grave anxiety.

37. The Holy See calls for transparency regarding the terms in which multilateral and bilateral international agreements concerning economic aid are elaborated, in order to avoid the imposition of targets for demographic growth or the conditioning of aid on acceptance of specific family planning programmes. In all programmes of international developmental cooperation more attention must be paid to the traditions and specific requirements of the people of developing nations.

38. In recent years, within the international community there is mention of a presumed *right to family planning for all individuals and couples*. At times out of concern at the increase in promiscuity among adolescents, governments and private organizations have advocated an ever wider diffusion of family planning services among youth. Cut off from all forms of moral education, and without respect for the rights of parents, such campaigns have only contributed to the spread of sexual promiscuity among the young, without taking into consideration the resultant damage to their physical, psychological and moral health.

Address by
His Eminence Angelo Cardinal Sodano
Secretary of State,
on the Position of the Holy See Regarding the
International Conference on Population and Development
at the Special Assembly for Africa of the Synod of Bishops
Vatican, 21 April 1994

Last Sunday, 17 April, many Synod Fathers heard the Holy Father's appeal in defense of the ethical values of life and the family. It was a message directed to "all people of truly good will," which has had a wide echo in world public opinion. The Holy Father made an appeal

> ". . . to all consciences, to free minds, that they not allow themselves to be ensnared by the logic of taking-sides or economic and political interests. I address (he said) all those who are able to resist the spreading models of fatuous freedom and false progress, which, seen in depth, turn out instead to be forms of slavery and regression because they undermine humanity, the sacred character of life and the capacity for true love. Whatever violates the moral law is never a victory, but a serious setback for man and makes him a victim of himself.
>
> In this International Year of the Family, we expected that the principle asserted by the *Universal Declaration of Human Rights* that the family is 'the natural and fundamental group unit of society' (art. 6, n. 3), would be rediscovered and reasserted. Because of its character, the family is not an institution which can be modified at will: the family belongs to humanity's most fundamental and sacred heritage! It even has priority over the State, which is obliged to recognize it and has the duty to protect it on the basis of clearly understandable ethical and social actions which can never be neglected.
>
> A threat to the family is, in fact, a threat to mankind. This is all the more true in the case of a presumed 'right to abortion.' Today it is more urgent than ever to react against models of behaviour which are the fruit of a hedonistic, permissive culture, for which the unreserved gift of self, mastery of one's instincts, the sense of responsibility seem to be notions belonging to another age. I ask: to what kind of

society will this ethical permissiveness lead? Are there not already worrying symptoms that make us fear for humanity's future?"

1. In the face of this sad situation, some Synodal Fathers expressed the wish to have more precise information about the origin and purpose of the next International Conference on Population and Development, to be convoked by the U.N. in Cairo next September.

In particular I felt that it was a matter of urgency to furnish information on the subject, after I heard the intervention made here in the hall in the course of the Ninth General Congregation, last Friday, 15 April, by Archbishop Nicodemus Kirima of Nyeri, Kenya, who drew attention to the necessity of defending the African family against attacks coming from outside.

In the face of this reality, I believe it opportune to explain briefly to the Synod Fathers what the Holy See has done and is doing so that the next International Conference on Population and Development may really contribute to the good of humanity and not end by undermining those basic values which are the sure foundation of the individual and communal life of humanity.

2. The International Conference on Population and Development, scheduled to meet in Cairo, 5-13 September 1994, comes after those held at ten year intervals in Bucharest (1974) and Mexico City (1984).

The Holy See showed a great interest in this theme because, as Pope Paul VI affirmed at the Angelus of Sunday 18 August 1974, on the eve of the Bucharest meeting: "The life of humanity is at stake." As everyone knows, the Holy See, although present in the United Nations with "Observer" status, takes part in these International Conferences as a Member with full rights, in as much as they are open to Member States of the U.N. and States Members of the specialized agencies of the United Nations system, some to which the Holy See belongs as a Member.

Before the Bucharest Conference, 28 March 1974, Pope Paul VI received Mr. Antonio Carrillo Flores, Secretary General of the World Conference on Population, and Mr. Rafael Salas, Executive Director of the United Nations Fund for Population Activities (UNFPA). At that time he entrusted to them a message which explained the principles which guide the Holy See's position on demographic questions.

3. In *Bucharest* (19-30 August 1974) the Holy See's Delegation, led by

then Bishop Edouard Gagnon, contributed to the work of the Conference by presenting a moral perspective and an orientation regarding fundamental values, and by offering amendments both with regard to principles (respect for life; the right of couples to determine the size of their families; the promotion of women, including their vocation as wives and mothers) and in relation to the family (against the plan to extend on a massive scale to all the world's inhabitants the means to avoid births).

At the end of the work, a "Plan of Action" was adopted by consensus, without a vote. The Holy See could not be part of the final consensus. While it declared itself satisfied with the reorientation and with certain changes in the "Plan of Action," it was unable to give its assent to the document, because it contained too many ambiguous, imprecise or unacceptable points. Among these were, for example:

— procreation outside of the family ("couples and individuals");
— the lack of an ethic which respects the principles governing human life;
— an open door to abortion and sterilization;
— a lack of protection for a couple's rights, by leaving the interpretation of those rights to each government.

Many recommendations tended to open the way to national policies which the Holy See could not approve.

4. Ten years later, another International Conference of the United Nations on Population took place in Mexico City (6-14 August 1984).

That same year, on 7 June, His Holiness Pope John Paul II received in Audience Mr. Rafael Salas, Secretary General of the Conference and Executive Director of the United Nations Fund for Population Activities (UNFPA). Once again, the message which the Holy Father consigned to him contained the principles underlying the position which would be set out during the Conference by the Delegation of the Holy See.

The Holy See had earlier raised this matter with the Episcopal Conferences in two circular letters which provided basic information about the major themes to be discussed and presented the position of the Holy See in relation to them.

The Mexico City Conference remained in the framework of the Bucharest Plan of Action, the principles and objectives of which continued in force.

The Delegation of the Holy See, headed by Monsignor Jan Schotte, then Vice-President of the Pontifical Commission for Justice and Peace, made a significant contribution regarding substance, language and amendments.

At the end of the Conference, the Delegation of the Holy See considered that the final Recommendations represented an improvement of the Plan of Action and that they contained several sound proposals. Particularly significant was Recommendation 18 (e): "in no case should abortion be promoted as a method of family planning." That Recommendation also urged Governments "to take necessary measures to help women to avoid abortion... and, where possible, to provide humane treatment and counseling to women who have had recourse to abortions."

Even so, the Holy See decided not to adhere to the final consensus, for several reasons:

— the prerogatives belonging to married couples with regard to sexual intimacy and parenthood were being extended to individuals ("couples and individuals"), including adolescents;
— morally unacceptable methods of family planning were being adopted
— some measures found therein had implications for the right of national sovereignty.

5. While the Conferences of Bucharest (1974) and Mexico City (1984) were devoted to the theme of population alone, this year, for the Cairo Conference, for the first time the subject of development was added: "International Conference on Population and Development."

The Holy See took part with its own Delegation in the regional meetings held on the five continents during 1992 and 1993: in Bali (Indonesia) for Asia and the Pacific, in Dakar (Senegal) for Africa, in Geneva (Switzerland) for Europe and North America, in Amman (Jordan) for Western Asia and in Mexico City for Latin America and the Caribbean.

In May 1993, the second session of the Preparatory Committee of the Conference was held in New York, while the third session, presently (4-22 April) being held in the same city, is drawing up the final document to be approved by the Cairo Conference.

The Holy See has observed that from Bucharest 1974 to the present there has been a shift of emphasis: at first a government-centred vision prevailed, one which was not opposed to coercive measures being adopted by national administrations (how many abuses have been denounced by the Bishops of various regions of the world!). Now another approach has come to the fore, one which puts women's rights at the center of the debate, including a right to abortion, considered as if it were a human right, with no consideration for the life of the child which has been conceived. Every woman, and every man, would be entitled to make any "choice" whatever in the realm of procreation.

6. In view of the forthcoming Cairo Conference, the Conference Secretariat recently published the draft of a final document, which immediately caught the attention of the Holy See because of the serious moral implications it contained.

It was also apparent that the aspect of development, so fundamental for the countries which you, my Brother Bishops from Africa, represent, was given such little attention as to merit only 6 pages out of a total of 83 in the draft.

"The Holy See absolutely cannot agree with the numerous references to abortion, the vague definitions about 'various types of families,' the encouragement given to adolescents to adopt a sexually free lifestyle, with the consequent diffusion of methods of contraception. Unfortunately, the document proposes a model of education deprived of ethical values, and it is therefore contrary to the Christian model." These were the words I used in a letter written to the Presidents of the world's Episcopal Conferences last 19 March, the Solemnity of St Joseph:

> The door which some would now like to open in order to permit access to abortion is the so-called "unsafe abortion." In order to avoid the death of the mother — so the thinking goes — it is necessary to legalize abortion. And this, if approved, will be proposed as the plan of action for all the countries of the world. With good reason, you, the Bishops of Africa, are deeply concerned about this.

> Without elaborating on themes which have already been discussed with all the Episcopal Conferences, I would simply like to add that — in the words of the Holy Father — "the idea of sexuality underlying this text is totally individualistic," and that the family is considerably compromised by its neglect of, among other things, the rights of parents with regard to the raising of their children.

All this, one should note, has taken place during 1994, which the United Nations Organization itself has declared the "International Year of the Family." The Catholic Church has willingly joined this celebration by setting aside a "Year of the Family," from the Feast of the Holy Family in 1993 to the Feast of the Holy Family in 1994.

7. The Holy Father, in receiving Mrs. Nafis Sadik, Secretary General of the Cairo Conference and Executive Director of the United Nations Fund for Population (UNFPA), last 18 March, explained the principles underlying the papal Magisterium on the subject of population, and did not fail to address the question of the proposed document.

As mentioned earlier, I myself sent a letter, on the Solemnity of St. Joseph, to all the Presidents of Episcopal Conferences, following upon another letter, sent in December 1993, which provided information on the major themes to be discussed at the Cairo Conference. I enclosed a copy of the draft document and a Note containing observations made by various experts from throughout the world who had been consulted on the matter.

8. The Holy Father then wished, through the Diplomatic Corps accredited to the Holy See, that the respective Governments should be informed of the position of the Holy See on the themes of the family, development and population. In a meeting which I called, presentations on these issues were made by Alfonso Cardinal López Trujillo, President of the Pontifical Council for the Family, by Roger Cardinal Etchegaray, President of the Pontifical Councils for Justice and Peace and "Cor Unum," and by Archbishop Jean-Louis Tauran, Secretary for Relations with States.

9. The Holy Father decided in the end to write a personal letter to every Head of State to let them know of his surprise and of his concerns with regard to the future of the family institution, which "belongs to the patrimony of humanity" and which precedes the State.

This was an exceptional initiative, wished by the Pope, because what is at stake is of exceptional importance for the destiny of humanity. If I may read some significant passages from the Letter:

> "... the draft of the final document of the forthcoming Cairo Conference was of particular interest to me. I found it a disturbing surprise.
>
> The innovations which it contains, on the level both of concepts and wording, make this text a very different one from the documents of the Conferences of Bucharest and

Mexico City. There is reason to fear that it could cause a moral decline resulting in a serious setback for humanity, one in which man himself would be the first victim.

One notes, for example, that the theme of development, on the agenda of the Cairo meeting, including the very complex issue of the relationship between population and development, which ought to be at the centre of the discussion, is almost completely overlooked, so few are the pages devoted to it. The only response to the population issue and to the urgent need for an integral development of the person and of societies seems to be reduced to the promotion of a lifestyle, the consequences of which, were it accepted as a model and plan of action for the future, could prove particularly negative. The leaders of the nations owe it to themselves to reflect deeply and in conscience on this aspect of the matter.

Furthermore, the idea of sexuality underlying this text is totally individualistic, to such an extent that marriage now appears as something outmoded. An institution as natural, fundamental and universal as the family cannot be manipulated by anyone.

Who could give such a mandate to individuals or institutions? The family is part of the heritage of humanity! Moreover, the *Universal Declaration of Human Rights* clearly states that the family is 'the natural and fundamental group unit of society' (Art. 16,3). The International Year of the Family should therefore be a special occasion for society and the State to grant the family the protection which the *Universal Declaration* recognizes it should have. Anything less would be a betrayal of the noblest ideals of the United Nations. Even more serious are the numerous proposals for a general international recognition of a completely unrestricted right to abortion: this goes well beyond what is already unfortunately permitted by the legislation of certain nations.

Indeed, reading this document — which, granted, is only a draft — leaves the troubling impression of something being imposed: namely a lifestyle typical of certain fringes within developed societies, societies which are materially rich and secularized. Are countries more sensitive to the values of nature, morality and religion going to accept such a vision of man and society without protest?"

10. In New York at this time the third session of the Preparatory Committee of the Cairo Conference is being held. The Holy See is present along with the 183 member countries of the United Nations (among these, the 53 African States). The Delegation of the Holy See is led by Monsignor Diarmuid Martin, Secretary of the Pontifical Council for Justice and Peace, and is composed of several experts from various continents, assisted by Archbishop Renato R. Martino, Permanent Observer of the Holy See to the United Nations.

I can assure the African Bishops that the Holy See's Delegation is working very hard, in the midst of misunderstandings and, not unrarely, open hostility, because of the amoral mentality prevailing in certain circles, particularly among the more industrialized societies.

In truth of course, there are also various Delegations which in the Preparatory Committee have demonstrated a great sensitivity in defending and promoting those values which are at the foundation of every civilization. I do not wish to cite the names of the countries which have most distinguished themselves in this work, in order to avoid giving offence to anyone.

It is certain however that we are in the presence of "challenges which face humanity today," as the Holy Father said on 7 April. It is necessary to go on enlightening the consciences of Catholics and of all people of good will regarding both the moral values involved, as well as the irreparable damage which could come for society on a world-wide level from a "civilization" built on the permissive foundations proposed by many States in the course of the meeting in New York.

11. Venerable Brothers in the Episcopate,

We are faced with a serious pastoral problem: the formation of the consciences of our faithful with regard to themes like the promotion of a model of the family which would be in accord with God's plan, the promotion and defence of the sacred character of human life, the education of young people in a way that is worthy of humanity, in which the disinterested gift of oneself, the control of one's instincts and a feeling of responsibility will prevail over models which are the fruit of a hedonistic and permissive culture.

In this context, the first task of Pastors is that of the moral formation of the faithful, inviting them to adhere to the Magisterium of the Church and not leaving them to be guided by personal relativistic positions.

A second task should also be considered: the positions of governments in general should reflect the thinking in their countries about this matter. In the elaboration of a national position, the Catholic Church should make its own viewpoint known. Otherwise there is a risk that small groups with a determined ideological leaning, and sometimes directed by foreign organizations, will impose their own point of view as the national position. In this regard, it would be well for Catholic groups (such as Catholic Action and other movements) to establish themselves as non-governmental organizations (NGOs): one only needs to consider how many health-care workers or educators or agents in family matters the Church has serving the peoples of Africa!

Coming from countries which are closer to nature, you are very conscious of family values and life values. As Bishops of Africa, you also have the responsibility to guide the young Churches entrusted to your care along the paths which correspond to God's project for the human person, for the family and for humanity. It is a great enterprise, as great as every apostolic enterprise. Of course, there are many who do not wish to hear either the voice of natural law or the voice of revealed law. But there is comfort in the words of Jesus who also said to us: "They have heard my voice, they will hear yours as well." Our duty is to continue to work, to plant the seed of truth, natural and revealed, in the depth of people's consciences. There will always be comfort in the parable of the Sower: much of the seed was lost because it fell on arid ground. But there was also seed which fell on fertile ground and produced abundant fruits of goodness. *Quod faxit Deus!*

STATEMENT BY
HIS EMINENCE ALFONSO CARDINAL LÓPEZ TRUJILLO
PRESIDENT OF THE PONTIFICAL COUNCIL FOR THE FAMILY
TO THE DIPLOMATIC CORPS ACCREDITED TO THE HOLY SEE,
VATICAN, 25 MARCH 1994

*Underlying Values of the Charter of the Rights of the Family
of the Holy See*

The Apostolic Exhortation *Familiaris consortio* recalls that "...marriage and the family constitute one of the most precious of human values" (n. 1). Indeed, the family is "the first and vital cell of society," the "principle and foundation of human society" (*Apostolicam actuositatem*, n. 11) and the "most effective means for humanizing and personalizing society" (F.C., 43). Moreover, the Holy Father observes that the family "makes an original contribution in depth to building up the world, by making possible a life that is properly speaking human, in particular by guarding and transmitting virtues and values" (F.C., 43).

Because of the great esteem which the Church has for the family, the Holy Father John Paul II greeted and gladly welcomed the celebration of the International Year of the Family. On 6 June of last year, he announced the celebration of the Year of the Family, in the Church.

The *Charter of the Rights of the Family* by the Holy See is an instrument of dialogue and encouragement for a coherent policy in favor of the Family through adequate legislation in the different nations. It was requested and recommended during the Synod of Bishops on the Family which took place in 1980. After consultation with the Episcopal Conferences, the *Charter* was published on 22 October 1983. As the Preamble states, the Holy See urges "all States, International Organizations, and all interested Institutions and persons to promote respect for these rights, and to secure their effective recognition and observance" (Preamble, M).

1. The family: an essential value

The Charter is based on the confidence and hope in convincing public authorities that "...the family is an indispensable and essential value of the civil community" (F.C., 45). It also responds to the phenomenon — which is not negligible — of lack of recognition and violations to which the rights of the family are subjected, and which make their observation urgent for the very destiny of humanity whose future passes through this Institution. This is what the Holy Father, tireless defender of the Family, denounced in the

Apostolic Exhortation *Familiaris consortio*: "institutions and laws unjustly ignore the inviolable rights of the family and of the human person; and society, far from putting itself at the service of the family, attacks it violently in its values and fundamental requirements" (n. 46). We are facing the painful paradox in which the family, instead of being helped in its mission, is many times the "victim of society" and the object of unjust aggression (cf. *ibid*, n. 46).

In recalling some of the underlying values of this *Charter*, which in this International Year are most timely and important — in fact, "The rights of the family are closely linked to the rights of the person" (*Letter to Families*, n. 17) — it is good to stress that the family, a natural institution, based on marriage, is a precious value. It would be incomprehensible if this celebration were not to promote and help the family. This quality of the family has often been ignored or obscured with the corresponding symptoms of moral erosion in societies which the Pope has no doubt about describing as "sick", as he does in his recent *Letter to Families*. Our civilization, with its many positive aspects "...is a society which is sick and is creating profound distortions in man" (n. 20). Once again it is the heart-rending contrast between the family, which should be the "center and the heart of the civilization of love" (*ibid.*, n. 13), and the possibility of "a destructive anti-civilization" in societies which have symptoms of a "profound crisis of truth" in the confusion of an accentuated "crisis of concepts" (*ibid.*, n. 13).

In the face of this crisis of truth and values, it must be recalled that the community of life and love, which is the family, constitutes a value. This was solemnly proclaimed by the Second Vatican Council. The institution of marriage has its stability through divine ordainment, through a sacred bond which does not depend on human will, for "the common good of the partners, of the children and society" (*Gaudium et spes*, 48). It would be a painful wound inflicted on the family and on marriage, as an obstacle and limitation to the harmonious development and improvement of the human person, or as a threat to his or her freedom. Is this not perhaps the image which some communications media manipulate and transmit? The very basis of the *Charter of the Rights of the Family* is a loyal and coherent appreciation for this good, this central value which is part of a sound conscience of humanity and emerges spontaneously from the human heart and behavior when people are not artificially asphyxiated by cultural and even political projects. These are disconcerting new elements which offer alternative models for life and social progress that, in the end, are not substantial ones.

The confusion becomes structural, we might say, when it is introduced like a virus into the veins and arteries of the social body in the form of laws with the contours of what can be called a "social sin" (Apostolic

Exhortation, *Reconciliatio et poenitentia*, n. 16), or an attempt against "human ecology" (*Centesimus annus*, n. 39), which creates "profound distortions in man" (*Letter to Families*, n. 20). Laws which threaten the family and the sacred gift of life in an attack against the "sanctuary of life" create the most serious distortions in the social fabric and, to an even greater extent, when certain "ideologies have weakened societies."[1]

Therefore, when human rights are abused on the sacred terrain of the rights of the family, confusion leads to a systematic oblivion with regard to all moral reference. The victims are the spouses, the children (first of all) and society which becomes empty and torn.

With prophetic vigor, the Holy Father has indicated this ethical frame of reference for society and the State in the Encyclical *Veritatis splendor*: "These (moral) norms in fact represent the unshakable foundation and solid guarantee of a just and peaceful human coexistence ..." (n. 96). "The fundamental moral rules of social life thus entail specific demands to which both public authorities and citizens are required to pay heed. Even though intentions may sometimes be good, and circumstances frequently difficult, civil authorities and particular individuals never have authority to violate the fundamental and inalienable rights of the human person. In the end, only a morality which acknowledges certain norms as valid always and for everyone, with no exception, can guarantee the ethical foundation of social coexistence, both on the national and international levels" (n. 97).

The *Charter* represents a request for the justice owed to the family and life in the framework of basic human rights. Focus is made directly on natural marriage. Because of its focus as a natural institution, reference is not made to it as a sacrament.

2. The family, based on marriage, as a stable institution

Allow me to recall some reflections to you: "Friendship (today we would say love) between husband and wife is recognized as natural; man, in fact, is by nature more inclined to live in pairs than affiliate politically, because the family is something which precedes and which is more necessary than the State." "Parents love their children because they consider them a part of themselves, and children love their parents because they are derived from them." Lastly, children are considered a bond: "It is for this reason that

---

[1] St. Augustine said: "Remota igitur iustitia, quid sunt regna (i.e., political powers), nisi magna latrocinia?" *(De Civitate Dei 4,4)*.

spouses without any children separate more readily; children, in fact, are a common good for both, and what is common maintains unity."

One might be inclined to think that these are recent anthropological and pastoral considerations that grew up in the garden of the Church. What must be recognized as natural is seen in all its strength. As you know, these texts come from the *Nicomachean Ethics* (VIII, 12) written by Aristotle between the years 366-345 B.C.

We might ask ourselves how the idea has spread so widely that the family cannot be defined by making reference to the numerous transformations it has undergone, the variety of models in different epochs and religious cultures. One constant feature must be accepted, a permanent structure, a natural institution which is based on the stable relationship between a man and a woman and between parents and children, a reality which is a universal fact that has always existed. Its beginning cannot be identified historically nor is it possible to predict its end. Sociologists accept Levi-Strauss' definition as valid and sufficient: "The family is a more or less lasting union, which is socially approved, between a man and a woman and their children."[2]

The tendency is well-known which surfaced in the recent Resolution of the European Parliament and takes advantage of what is ethereal, imprecise and undefined in order to introduce homosexual and lesbian unions with the rights of a family. This is one result of avoiding a definition of the family. Therefore, just about everything could fall under this heading! In opposition to the constant universal feature of the family, alternatives which claim to substitute its function through other community forms and deny its formative mission of persons have shown themselves to be without substance.

---

[2] The synthetic comment given by the sociologist Mario Campanini regarding duration and social approval is effective: "In all cultures there are two fundamental forms of relationships between the sexes: pre- or extra-marital relations which are classified as occasional; those directed toward stability and which give rise to a union projected over time. Marriage marks as a norm the institutional passage from an existing or projected sexual relationship, which has an occasional character, to one which has the character of lastingness in time. In this second group of relationships the family is placed." With regard to social approval, there is this comment: "In all cultures (...) there are forms of prohibited cohabitation (...) or at least less tolerated ones. On the other hand, there are other forms which are allowed, approved and even encouraged or imposed" (GIORGIO CAMPANINI, *Realtà e Problemi della Famiglia contemporanea*, Ed. Paoline, Turin, 1989, pp. 12 and 13). These are constant features in the concept of the family. In order to go deeper into this question, it is useful to consult the word "family" as developed by P. DONATI in *Nuovo Dizionario di Sociologia*, Ed. Paoline.

The profoundness of the natural institution is denied which has its roots in God's design of creation, "ab initio," and which is not the product of the latest social consensus. For the "philosopher," the family was already "prior to, and more necessary than the State" with everything this implies regarding a certain "sovereignty" of that community. On this subject the Holy Father offers extremely rich considerations in his *Letter to Families* (cf. n. 17).

The tendency exists, and still exerts great influence, as we can see in some writings about the Year of the Family, based on the supposition that the family is the result of a social agreement or consensus that is changeable and mutable, with transformations that are at the mercy of the will of legislators. Of course, this position is more pronounced and radical when God is denied and therefore the truth about man is threatened in its essential roots.

The *Charter of the Rights of the Family* offers the following as a definition:

> "The family is based on marriage, that intimate union of life in complementarity between a man and a woman which is constituted in the freely contracted and publicly expressed indissoluble bond of matrimony, and is open to the transmission of life" (Preamble, B).

3. The risk of "privatization" of the family

The declarations in favor of the social importance of the family and the treatment to which it is subjected are not always in harmony. On the one hand, the family can be seen as something "private," thus losing its social importance, as a place for affection and emotions that is placed under the spouses' exclusive responsibility. The State would only have the mission of acting as a notary at its beginning and end. In that case, the positive aid which could be offered to the family as such would fall into secondary place, such as adequate forms of protection, guarantees and mediation within the criteria of the principle of subsidiarity.

Furthermore, a certain mentality tends toward complacent adaptation when social erosion, disorder or crises take place, and solutions, in a pro-divorce sense, are facilitated. This turns into a mentality and even a pressure which does not serve stability, but dissolution.

Today, experts in sciences related to the family point out the enormous social costs of all sorts, not least of which are the economic costs, which the trauma of broken families involve and which, in some societies, includes the idea of the inevitability of crises. The usual victims are the children. Many studies show that these children have serious learning problems in school, and that there is a tendency towards violence in children and young people from broken homes.

The human costs are very high and obvious and have lessened ingenuousness and enthusiasm for the peace and tranquility which divorce is supposed to assure.

The State cannot limit itself to following the footprints and oscillations of marriage, like a sort of electrocardiogram that records the deterioration of families.

Some nations are beginning to look with concern at the dangers related to the threats against, and the manipulation of human life in its origin and see the urgency of a defense worthy of the name of human life from the moment of conception until natural death. This is also one of the areas of special emphasis in the *Charter* which concern us.

The phenomenon of "privatization" and a concept of systematic or effective lack of concern for the family, despite its very serious social effects, joins with another tendency which harms the fundamental right of the family: putting the family, based on marriage, on the same plane with free, consensual unions and "de facto" forms of cohabitation which are increasingly tolerated, accepted and recognized.

It is one thing, through adequate instruments and social policies in many situations, for instance, to protect women, but it is another to level marriage with what does not attain its dignity before society (cf. Art. 1, C).

We find ourselves before the grave new political and cultural problem of systematic omissions by the State and, all the more so, by a legal apparatus which threatens the unity and stability of the family and is against life. The family is the "sanctuary of life" and it must be respected in an authentic "human ecology." All of this is affected, for instance, by population, educational, housing and fiscal policies which deserve special attention.

4. Rights of the family and family rights

Here there is a distinction which must be kept in mind in formulating the corresponding policies. The rights of the family recognize and take on the members who live and realize themselves within the family as one integrated subject. The family as such is recognized as a value and a need.

Basically, Article 5 refers to this: "The family has the right to exist and to progress as a family." Also in paragraph A: "Public authorities must respect and foster the dignity, lawful independence, privacy, integrity and stability of every family." The rights of the family require that real family policies be drawn up. This is considered in article 9: "Families have the right to be able to rely on an adequate family policy on the part of public authorities in the juridical, economic, social and fiscal domains, without any discrimination whatsoever."

On the other hand, family rights focus on the members of the family separately without any direct reference to the family as a community or a special unit.

Perhaps it would be good to mention another possible distinction: the distinction between policies of the family and for the family. In the first type, there is an effort to point out that families will be associated in some way with the formulation of policies, and their experience and ability to follow and verify their outcome or difficulties are recognized. Here the family is somewhat a protagonist in the political area as article 8(A) considers: "The family has the right to exercise its social and political function in the construction of society. Families have the right to form associations with other families and institutions, in order to fulfill the family's role suitably and effectively, as well as to protect the rights, foster the good and represent the interests of the family."

Social policies are absolutely necessary. This is considered in a special way in article 9(B), in which social security measures are advocated according to need. However, it is important to point out that social policies are more or less connected with the rights of the family to the extent, as one author points out, that they tend to consider the needs of persons taken individually rather than as part of the family group taken as a unit.

There is also a tendency to favor structures rather than home assistance as, for example, with regard to the elderly.

Conclusion

I have mentioned some of the presuppositions or underlying values of the *Charter of the Rights of the Family*.

It would be good to mention some other values and principles such as the central role of children in the family, as God's most precious gift to marriage (cf. *Gaudium et spes*, n. 50).

This aspect has been deepened through more mature and committed awareness as in the U.N. *Convention on the Rights of the Child*, or the *Hague Convention on International Adoption* which invokes "the higher interest of the child" (cf. Art. 4,d.e.f). The fundamental basis is the right which helps children be conceived in a stable home out of an act of authentically human love, and therefore really have a father and a mother and be brought up in a responsible community of life and love.

I have limited myself to some considerations which, in my opinion, enable greater understanding of the *Charter* which can greatly stimulate dialogue and the search for family policies in this Year of the Family.

STATEMENT BY
HIS EMINENCE ROGER CARDINAL ETCHEGARAY
PRESIDENT OF THE PONTIFICAL COUNCIL FOR JUSTICE AND PEACE
AT A MEETING FOR AMBASSADORS ACCREDITED TO THE HOLY SEE
VATICAN, 25 MARCH 1994

*The Integral Development of Peoples in the Major Appointments
of International Life*

For a development without models...

Nothing is more common in contemporary language than the word "development." But, at the same time, nothing is more fluid, indeed more ambiguous. It bears the mark of its origins, that is the era of the 60s, when many Third-World countries, by acceding to independence, broke into contemporary history and tried to find their place among the countries that had developed before them, at times even at their expense. Immediately, and by contrast, the word "under-development" came into use, followed by the expression "developing," as if all one had to do was to struggle to attain a predetermined model or to run along a path where some are ahead and others behind. The classification that labels some countries as "least developed" (LDC), others as "newly industrialized" (NIC), or with "economies in transition" (CEEC), would lead us to believe that development is guided solely by the western model, while it is actually every bit as much a problem for the developed countries. There is a serious temptation to propose or to accept a model of development as if it were a suit "off the rack" or a newly built factory turned over "with keys in hand."

To illustrate this danger, I shall take the example of poverty, one of the three themes of the Summit of Copenhagen (1995). Obviously, nothing is more urgent than the struggle against poverty, that gaping wound in the side of humanity. But, what country does poverty claim as its home, and what poverty are we talking about? Is not poverty of being more crippling than poverty of not having? Are not the "new poverties" that the developed countries now exude, a warning signal of the precariousness of societies that live in abundance? Do not the so-called rich countries have to discover the values proper to so-called poor countries? Still more, should they not recognize the value of and adopt a certain form of poverty that will help them to focus more on the gratuitousness of relations than on what they can get out of these relations? All of these questions, which are like to many drills boring deep into the idea of development, must neither brake the struggle against social inequalities nor block the questioning of the structures of a society that feeds on these inequalities.

...unless it is the model of the whole person

From the time of the first Development Decade, declared by the United Nations in 1960, immense efforts have been made, among which that which has allowed India, then on the edge of famine, to meet the challenge of self-sufficiency through the Green Revolution, in a country that now numbers almost 900 million inhabitants. Yet, today, the results of development are indeed meager, despite so much generous, intelligent and coordinated action. Disappointed or deceived by the models of development that they created for themselves or that were imposed on them, both persons and peoples have reached the point where they have begun to doubt the very possibility of development and to wonder if that star towards which they were heading was nothing more than a dead star. The gaps are wider than ever; the inequalities are more crying than ever; and even Sub-Saharan Africa seems to be disappearing into the sands of forgetfulness.

Yet, drawing on the lessons of this painful history, development is beginning to take on new qualifiers that broaden and deepen the concept. The GNP (Gross National Product) is no longer the standard measure of progress; other indices now seem necessary, among which the Index of Human Development (IHD) launched by the UNDP (United Nations Development Programme) in 1990, not without causing a storm in certain countries that were afraid that the measure of development aid would be gauged by those freedoms and human rights that they assess in terms of variable geometry. But this positive evolution in the reports and programmes of international institutions remains insufficient. It is not enough to give a human face to economy; rather economy must be placed in the heart of the person. Development is first and foremost the ongoing movement of history by which the human person seeks to attain the fullness of his or her being as a person.

And we can affirm that, in this upward movement, Christians play a decisive role. Their action, enlightened by the social thought of the Church, is, without a doubt, the most audacious as well as the most coherent. From the time of the Second Vatican Council, reasserting a theme dear to Pope John XXIII (cf. *Mater et magistra*), *Gaudium et spes* states, in an astounding way, that "Economic development must remain under man's direction; it is not to be left to the judgment of a few individuals or groups possessing too much economic power, nor of the political community alone, nor of a few strong nations. It is only right that, in matters of general interest, as many people as possible and, in international relations, all nations, should participate actively in decision making" (n. 65, §1). Three years later, in 1967, Pope Paul VI expressed the same thought in the Encyclical *Populorum progressio*, using the by now famous formula: "towards man's complete development and the development of all mankind" (No. 5) ... "promote the good of every man and of the whole man" (n. 14). Finally, for the twentieth anniversary of *Populorum progressio*, Pope John Paul II published his own encyclical, *Sollicitudo rei socialis*. In a climate of incertitude, indeed of skepticism, he wanted to launch a new development as a lever still capable of energizing the world. Like a bolero, this encyclical insistently hammers out, in every key, that true development is "measured and oriented according to the reality and vocation of man seen in his totality, namely according to his interior dimension" (n. 29). And as if he wanted to shake up those who were too bound to an economic conception, the Pope invented a startling word: "over-development," an ironic expression by which he denounces the deceptive content which characterizes a "so-called civilization of consumption" (n. 28).

Some appointments on the calendar of development

In today's setting, development — true development — appears to be an arduous combat, even a war of attrition. Under-development is a far more difficult task than had ever been experienced; but John Paul II has made it an urgent moral imperative, and no one can evade this imperative. We should, therefore, be very happy that the United Nations has explicitly linked development to its major concerns, be it the environment (Rio 1992), population (Cairo 1994), to be prolonged by Beijing on women in 1995. The Copenhagen Summit of 1995 should give development itself a "social" consistency that will enable it to face new challenges. In this chronology, it is regrettable that Copenhagen will not take place before Cairo.

All of these appointments have been or will be, we hope, so many fires lit, converging in such a way that they highlight and throw new light on the unique figure of the human person and his role on the planet. But experience has shown, alas, that nothing can be taken for granted, and that the most elementary convictions can be tossed about, according to the whims of ideologies or simply by carelessness. In this sense, the implementation of Agenda 21, adopted by consensus at Rio, is an acid test to see whether it is not merely a catalogue of pious desires as are so many such documents within the United Nations. And the test is all the more significant in that it deals with a development which is called "sustainable," that is one, according to the definition of the Brundtland Commission: "that meets the needs of the present without compromising the ability of future generations to meet their own needs."

Development put to the test of Cairo

These days, eyes are on the draft final document of the Cairo Conference that will be examined starting Easter Monday in New York. The Pope has just referred to it in his *Message to Mrs. Nafis Sadik*, Secretary General of this Conference (Cf. *L'Osservatore Romano*, 19 March 1994). What could be glimpsed in Bucharest in 1974, what had already sprung into view in Mexico City in 1984, that is the link between population and development, has become the heart of this coming Conference. In his *Message*, the Pope recognized that "a population policy is only one part of an overall development strategy." Population-development should actually be considered one word with two terms, where the accent can be placed neither on one nor on the other without running the risk of one absorbing the other. Will people know how to talk this way in Cairo, when we see that the draft final document skirts the reflection on development? Will people realize that, if the Church (and she is not alone) is so sensitive to everything that touches life, the family, it is simply because of her concern for true development? In 1979, from the tribune of the United Nations, John Paul II had already declared that it came down to respecting "a constant rule of the history of humanity;" namely "the pre-eminence of the values of the spirit defines the proper sense of earthly material goods and the way to use them." For this reason, it is up to spouses, in the first place, to make joint and responsible decisions, that are both informed and free, concerning procreation (cf. *Populorum progressio*, n. 37; *Familiaris consortio*, n. 33-35). In this regard, the U.N. was close to the Roman Magisterium at the time of the first International Conference on Human Rights in 1968 in Teheran, where both stressed the primary rights of married couples, rather than of the State. This closeness of position has unfortunately been weakened through the affirmation in subsequent U.N. documents of rights regarding procreation with no regard to marriage and the family.

But the concrete question remains: how can this freedom and this responsibility best be carried out in face of accelerated population growth? A Church that fights so strongly for the integral development of persons and peoples is not afraid to address the highly complex question of the regulation of human fertility. She recognizes that the problem is not only one of individual or conjugal ethics, but also of social ethics, because a whole series of mutually interactive factors comes into play, that are not only economic but political and cultural as well.

But the Church is also well aware that her own reflection on this subject is still inchoative and requires a great deal of circumspection in face of doomsday scenarios or simply when she observes that, on the spot, reality is not always and everywhere what it was thought to be in theory. The nature of the link between demographic growth and economic growth remains the object of controversies that some try to solve by recourse to such slogans as "less poverty thanks to fewer people" or the contrary "fewer people thanks to less poverty." The second maxim seems to be just as infelicitous as the first if development is merely considered a reliable and irreproachable contraceptive method. Love, procreative love, transcends, but does not ignore, every aspect of our earthly condition.

In the extraordinary human adventure, it is fortunate that the international community has chosen development as the thread that links its major appointments in order to give them spirit and life. But, for that very reason, this threat must be a golden one, that is to say it must be the best possible conductor of authentic and integral development, the only one that fulfills the expectations of persons and of peoples. Every country invited to these international appointments must see to it that development not simply be considered a sign to be hung out but rather a splendid fire kept ablaze by each of them.

STATEMENT BY
HIS EXCELLENCY ARCHBISHOP JEAN-LOUIS TAURAN
SECRETARY FOR RELATIONS WITH STATES,
AT A MEETING FOR AMBASSADORS ACCREDITED TO THE HOLY SEE
VATICAN, 25 MARCH 1994

The countries which you so worthily represent had the occasion over the past year and a half to follow closely the regional Conferences on Population and Development which took place in each continent, as well as other meetings, organized by the various regional offices of the United Nations, which were held in preparation for the International Year of the Family.

The Delegates of your countries have noted the presence of Delegations of the Holy See at regional meetings in such diverse cities as Beijing (People's Republic of China), Cartagena (Colombia), Valletta (Malta), Denpasar, Bali (Indonesia), Dakar (Senegal), Geneva (Switzerland), Amman (Jordan) and Mexico City. They will also have met with Delegates of the Holy See at the Second Session of the Preparatory Committee of the Conference on Population and Development, held at New York in May 1993, as will also be the case at the 3rd Preparatory Committee in New York in a few days time.

You might ask: Why this great interest on the part of the Holy See? It is not just an interest of the moment. It is a characteristic of the concern of the Church, and particularly of the Holy Father John Paul II, for the human person. The theme of population touches the most important issues of life and thus touches the dignity of the human person in a special way. The Church "cherishes a feeling of deep solidarity with the human race and its history" (*Gaudium et spes*, n. 1) and follows with attention the development of all peoples, especially those who are most in need (cf. Paul VI, *Populorum progressio*, n. 1). The human being and the family, from which he or she cannot be dissociated, "constitute the way of the Church" (John Paul II, *Letter to Families*, n. 2).

In this short talk, let me simply give examples of some themes which are the object of the concern of the Holy See, and illustrate the basic thrust of the message which the Holy See wishes to present. I had originally intended to speak in a more general way, but since a number of the concerns and worries of the Holy See have been particularly accentuated in this period of immediate preparation for the Cairo Conference on Population and Development, I will make reference especially to the recently published Draft Final Document of that Conference, which will be discussed at the Final

Preparatory Committee Meeting which, as you know, will take place from the 4 — 22 April in New York.

1. Relationship between population and development

Conferences on Population have taken place at ten year intervals: Bucharest in 1974 and Mexico City in 1984. For the 1994 Conference in Cairo, the theme has been broadened to read "Population and Development," but the reality has not always reflected this title, either during the Preparatory Meetings or in the Draft Final Document, which dedicates only 6 pages out of 83 to the topic of development.

Cardinal Etchegaray has already explained in greater detail something of the wealth of the Church's teaching on development and of its application in population questions.

"True development cannot consist in the simple accumulation of wealth and in the greater availability of goods and services" but must be pursued with "due consideration for the social, cultural and spiritual dimensions of the human person" (cf. John Paul II, *Sollicitudo rei socialis*, n. 9).

Population policy is only one part of development policy. Development policy, in fact, involves a whole range of health, nutritional, agricultural, educational, demographic, economic and political dimensions, as well, of course, as the deeper moral, spiritual and religious dimensions. True development is not respected when one factor, population growth, is singled out as the sole obstacle to development. Health problems, agricultural problems, educational problems, etc., will only be resolved when they are faced for what they are: health problems, agricultural problems, educational problems, etc. They will not be resolved if they are simply attributed "en bloc" to "the population problem;" such an attitude will only prolong their eventual solution.

There are some who would say that the major key to resolving the economic problems of developing countries is reducing population growth rates. However, one should look at the evidence presented, for example, at the Latin American regional preparatory meeting, which noted, on the one hand, that "one of the most outstanding demographic changes in Latin America and the Caribbean in the past 25 years is the pronounced decline in fertility, from 6 to 3.5 children per woman, which reduced the annual average population growth rate to 2% by the second half of the 1980s" and, on the other hand, that "the region took a giant step backward" in the 1980s "in terms of real per capita output — which dropped, by the end of 1989, to its lowest levels in 13 years — and experienced heavy macroeconomic imbalances and the deterioration of the social context as well."

It is the conviction of the Holy See that only through an international effort in favour of the integral development of the person and of society can we adequately respond to the problem of population and development in a manner which respects the dignity of the person. Otherwise, one runs the risk of supporting an ideological policy in which those who live in the less developed countries of our planet are considered the object rather than the active and creative subjects of policies: or, in another way, one risks also that policies will be decided in terms of the priorities of the wealthy countries rather than the needs of the people who aspire to development while maintaining their own cultural traditions and values, so necessary to guarantee the stability of societies.

2. The family

Another central element of the Holy See's policy on population and development is the family. The *Universal Declaration on Human Rights* describes the family as "***the*** natural and fundamental group unit of society" (art. 16,3), and adds that "it is entitled to protection by society and the State." The contribution that the family makes to the stability of society is irreplaceable, especially because of its mission of education, socialization and caring.

Cardinal López Trujillo has shown how the *Charter of the Rights of the Family* of the Holy See sets out a coherent agenda for the defence and the protection of the family in today's world. In this International Year of the Family, the international community must do everything in its power to see that the family does receive that protection to which it is entitled. As the Holy Father said in his Message to the Secretary General of the Cairo Conference, "anything less would be a betrayal of the noblest ideals of the United Nations."

One cause of concern to the Holy See is the fact that in the Draft Final Document for the Cairo Conference there is a tendency to qualify the term family with phrases like "in all its forms" and to refer to it not as ***the*** but as "***a*** basic unit of society," thus distorting the special recognition which the family deserves.

Another concern is that an institution as natural, fundamental and universal as marriage is practically absent from the text of that Document and is ignored in the formulation of its concrete recommendations.

There are certain values and institutions which are determining for the good of humanity, and have been witnessed to throughout history as they are witnessed to today in all cultures.

The international community must be very cautious in the face of the temptation to put aside such fundamental values and institutions on the basis of short-lived social experiences which, in fact, are limited to certain geographical and cultural regions, and which have given no evidence that they will stand the test of time as to whether they really contribute to the stability and good of society.

The Holy See stresses that public authorities have a responsibility to uphold the institutional and juridical character of marriage and that the situation of non-married couples or same sex unions should not be placed on the same level as marriage duly contracted between a man and a woman.

As Bishop Sgreccia, Secretary of the Pontifical Council for the Family, noted at the Valletta preparatory meeting for the International Year of the Family, there is a paradox in today's world: while mankind has rediscovered, as it were, nature in the forms which are external to the human person (the environment), there is the risk of destroying the nature which is within us (the family) — (cf. *L'Osservatore Romano*, 19 May 1993, p. 2).

3. Human life

The human person is at the centre of population concerns. Population policies touch on the deepest aspects of what it is to be a human person. In this context, the Holy See stresses, particularly, respect for human life and for its transmission.

The Draft Final Document persistently uses innovative language concerning "reproductive rights," "reproductive health," "reproductive services." Nowhere in the text is there a full definition of the content, the extent or the limits of these terms. There is, in fact, no internationally accepted definition of reproductive rights. The term appears neither in the text of the Teheran or of the Vienna International Human Rights Conferences nor is it to be found explicitly in the principal human rights instruments of the United Nations.

What is happening here? Is this an attempt to introduce into the language of International Organizations a new expression? At first sight, reproductive health could refer to safeguarding the health of men and women in their cooperation in the transmission of life. On the other hand, in the current situation of lack of clarity, "reproductive rights" could be a convenient way of introducing abortion as a fundamental human right without any limitations or conditions whatsoever.

Such an interpretation is reinforced by the fact that at the recent meeting of the Commission on the Status of Women a resolution was introduced by one Delegation asking Governments to protect "women's reproductive rights, including access to safe, voluntary and legal abortion." During negotiations, this language was fortunately removed because a number of nations were not ready to approve an internationally recognized right to abortion.

I ask you to reflect on the juridical consequences of inventing rights on the basis of political or ideological interests, or of affirming rights whose content is not clearly defined and which may be deliberately left vague so that they can be exploited ideologically. This would be an extremely dangerous path for the international community, as past experiences show.

Returning to the question of abortion policy, the 1984 Mexico City International Conference on Population approved by consensus a recommendation (n. 18e) which stated that "in no case should abortion be promoted as a method of family planning." The same Recommendation also urged governments "to take appropriate steps to help women avoid abortion... and whenever possible, provide for the humane treatment and counseling of women who have had recourse to abortion."

Similarly, the Latin American Consensus of the 1993 Mexico City regional Conference on Population and Development affirmed that while abortion is a major public health issue in the countries of the region, none of them accepts abortion as a method of regulating fertility (cf. Latin American Consensus of the 1993 Mexico City Regional Population and Development Conference, n. II.3.6).

Nowhere does the Draft Final Document take up these statements which stress that abortion is not an appropriate means of family planning. No attention is given to the fact that many countries do not wish the promotion of abortion to be part of their development policy.

There is no international consensus on a generalized right to abortion. The Constitutions of several countries affirm clearly the equal rights of the unborn. Almost no country in its national legislation permits an absolute right to abortion, a right which could be deduced from some affirmations of the

Draft Final Document, at times explicitly, at times in vaguer terms.

The Document is concerned about the health problems caused by what is called "unsafe abortion," but the term is not defined. At times, the terms "unsafe" and "illegal" abortion are used as identical. On other occasions, "unwanted births" and "unsafe abortion" are placed together. No reference is made to any worldwide study of unsafe abortion and there is no data as to its worldwide incidence. A recent United Nations study document (WHO/MSM/92.5) notes in fact that "the legality or illegality of (abortion) services, however, may not be the defining factor of their safety." Simply legalizing abortion is not the answer.

It is hard to find the evidence on which the Draft Final Document bases its affirmations. It states, for example, without any indication or reference, that "in some countries as many as half of maternal deaths may result from unsafe abortions, many others result from the absence of the most basic antenatal, maternity and post-natal care" (n. 1.13). Vague and unsubstantiated statements of this kind are clearly unscientific and can easily mislead the reader to arrive at ideologically predisposed conclusions. This vague and generic language is phrased in such a way that the person who tries to refute it is left open to the accusation of not caring for the life of mothers.

4. Use of statistics

Speaking of vague language, it should be noted that there is an extremely loose and selective use of statistics throughout the Document, both concerning population growth as well as regarding sexual behaviour and unmet family planning needs. The role of the more technical United Nations Population Division seems to have been diminished in the preparations for the Conference. The entire scientific apparatus of the statistical references in the Draft Final Document is inadequate by professional standards and needs to be completely reexamined. Once again, I stress that it is important to eliminate the use, for ideological purposes, of scientific data, as well as the use of inaccurate presentation or vague language.

On a matter which is so delicate and has in the past been open to much ideological abuse — think, for example, of the doomsday "prophecies" on population explosion, which have not materialized — the very objectivity of the reflection of the Cairo Conference will depend on the correct and balanced use of the best scientific information available.

5. Adolescents

Another very serious concern of the Holy See is that of the vision of sexuality contained in the Draft Final Document and which is proposed especially for adolescents. The view of sexuality that it stresses is individualistic in the extreme.

In the face of the problems caused by sexual promiscuity among certain sectors of young people, the Document tends to present, as the only solution, "information and services which can help protect them from unwanted pregnancies and sexually transmitted diseases." There is little or no recognition of the interpersonal dimensions of sexuality. There is no reference to the consequences or to the moral implications of their sexual activity. Is this not the way to promote a promiscuity which would create more problems than it solves? It would appear that the international community has lost the courage needed to offer to the younger generations a more challenging view of their sexuality and of the responsibilities which sexual behaviour brings with it.

What kind of future do we really offer young people if entire societies abdicate their responsibility to indicate some basic common moral positions which foster that self-control which is an essential aspect of maturity in every aspect of life?

There is in certain areas a worrying promiscuity among young people and it is difficult to convince them of the validity of moral norms. This "social pathology" cannot be ignored, but "illness" should not become the criterion to guide the "healthy."

The Draft Document in fact tends to affirm the right of all individuals to establish their own sexual life style. The only norm that remains is the right to be sexually active, but without accepting the consequences or the responsibilities involved. Many of you are parents and you know well that preparing children for a healthy and happy future requires a broader vision of life than this.

6. "Goals" and sterilization

The Holy See has always expressed its concern about coercion in family planning programmes, and, linked with this question, the establishment by Governments, or International Organizations or Agencies, of quantitative goals, targets or quotas. Population is not simply about numbers; it is about people, about individual human persons with their own dignity, it is about persons who suffer in the tragedies caused by certain policies which, on the basis of numbers, have attempted to impose solutions which do not respect fundamental human rights.

The Draft Final Document favours quantitative goals with regard to the provision of universal access to family planning and reproductive health services as part of development policy. It is more negative however in dealing with targets or quotas for the recruitment of clients in family planning programmes and stresses that such targets should not be imposed on family planning providers. The Document also asks Governments to introduce systems of monitoring and controlling abuses by family planning providers. Over the years the Holy See has drawn attention to the existence of many abuses in this area, beginning, of course, with programmes which were not exempt from explicit coercion. However, there are more subtle forms of coercion, especially when incentives are offered to the poor or the illiterate, who may not be fully aware of the consequences of their decisions. This applies particularly to the use of sterilization in developing countries. Sterilization is the family planning means most open to abuse on human rights grounds. Because of its finality or irreversibility, in addition to moral objections, it contradicts cultural attitudes regarding childbearing and leaves no opportunity for future changes in childbearing plans. The extremely high proportions of women in some developing countries who have been sterilized has been a cause of very grave concern to the Holy See for years and is now finally the object of parliamentary inquiry in some countries.

There is a second area of concern which does not deal directly with coercion but with the knowledge or full information of participants in family planning programmes. It is a question of the control of methods and products which are used in developing countries, which at times do not respect standards which are normal in the country of production. This is particularly risky in areas in which overall health care standards for women are inadequate and the use or the experimentation with inferior quality family planning products can thus be a cause of greater health risk.

7. Cultural, ethical, spiritual and religious values

In all its interventions during the period of preparation for the Cairo Conference, the Holy See has stressed the need in population programmes to respect the cultural, ethical, spiritual and religious values of peoples. The Holy See is convinced that population questions, the family, the transmission of life are deeply embedded in the traditions and cultures of peoples. The worldwide experience of the Church also offers her an opportunity to appreciate how much these cultural factors are linked to the conservation of the fundamental values of humanity. The question of values is absent from the Draft Final Document, except for the specific reference to the indigenous people. The Document tends to impose its own world view which is that of a particular sector of the Western or industrialized world.

Indeed it proposes vast and pervasive programmes of education towards this world view entering into all sectors of society from health care to recreation, from the mass media to schools from their earliest stage.

In the regional preparatory Conferences of Bali, Dakar, Amman and Mexico City there was sensitivity to the importance of cultural and ethical factors, and their documents make some reference to respect for convictions, principles, beliefs and cultural diversity. However, one must note that delegations of the wealthier nations consistently objected to any form of what they called "moralizing language" even though the programmes that they support would constitute or endorse major changes in the moral climate of all our societies.

The Holy See is well aware that on occasion its interventions in the area of family life and population are not understood or are even misinterpreted. Why? Perhaps it is because in a world characterized by purely utilitarian values, "it is difficult to recognize and respect the hierarchy of the true values of human existence" (John Paul II, *Centesimus annus*, n. 29,b).

It is encouraging however that even in this climate there are more and more people who are dissatisfied and who realize that the solution to today's problems requires that we look in greater depth at the questions involved. Many of them look to the person of the Holy Father as a source of moral and spiritual values, without which there is a risk of building a "civilization" which has within it the seed of its own decadence. "The Church can never abandon her religious and transcendent mission on behalf of man" (John Paul II, *Centesimus annus*, n. 55).

8. Conclusion

Your Excellencies,

As you can see, the international community is called at the Cairo Conference to reflect on subjects which are of extreme importance for the coming years.

Because of the serious moral implications involved, the Holy See cannot give explicit or implicit support, for example, to abortion, the changed concept of family that emerges, the encouragement among adolescents of a liberal sexual lifestyle with no reference to ethical values, which in the long term can only bring damage to individuals and to society.

For this reason, I would ask you to transmit to your Governments as soon as possible — the time available is very limited — a Note which has been prepared with the collaboration of experts from various countries and which will be made available to you at the end of the meeting. This Note explains some of the problematic language and tendencies that the Holy See finds in the text.

In transmitting this Note, I would ask you to invite your Governments to reflect on the consequences, both for your own country and for society on the world level, of what is involved in many of the recommendations contained in the Draft Final Document.

I hope that in the period before the Conference, and especially at the Preparatory Committee meeting of 4-22 April 1994, the international community will draw attention to the deeper questions that I have outlined.

You will also find a copy of the Message which the Holy Father, last Friday, handed to the Secretary General of the Conference, Mrs. Nafis Sadik, whom he received in audience, and which presents very clearly the concerns and values which inspire the Holy See's position.

On my part, I can assure you that your countries' Delegations to the Preparatory Committee of 4-22 April in New York will find the members of the Holy See's Delegation always ready to collaborate in a constructive way.

STATEMENT BY THE COLLEGE OF CARDINALS MEETING IN EXTRAORDINARY CONSISTORY, PROPOSED BY HIS EMINENCE JOHN CARDINAL O'CONNOR ARCHBISHOP OF NEW YORK
VATICAN, 14 JUNE 1994

We the Cardinals of the Catholic Church, gathered in Extraordinary Consistory from throughout the world, express our strong solidarity with Pope John Paul II in his pastoral concern for the family, his clear teaching on the true nature of the family, his firm defence of the dignity and the rights of the family and his insistence that the family be free of coercion, particularly in regard to questions of procreation.

With the Holy Father, we see the family as both the way of the Church and the way of society. Any effort to oppose the individual to the family must ultimately have disastrous consequences, as is tragically evident today in so many nations.

We call on the nations of the world to seize the opportunity that will be afforded by the United Nations International Conference on Population and Development, to be held in Cairo in September 1994. This Conference could be of enormous benefit to all peoples of the world if it focuses on the family, the family, that is, in the traditional and natural sense of that term. Rather than approaching the Conference with an attitude of despair and of exaggerated fear concerning population trends, we urge especially the wealthy and powerful nations to offer hope by way of promising and providing resources for development, which is an essential element in meeting the needs of increasing population.

We are not unaware of population trends from various experts who offer a variety of opinions. Regardless of the dimensions of the problem, however, it cannot be legitimately resolved by the introduction or imposition of artificial, unnatural or immoral means. It should be clear, for example, that the destruction of human life through abortion will never serve as a gateway to a rational and civilized life for the society that practices it. We regret that many who promulgate widespread usage of artificial contraception, and are willing to expend large sums of money to support this approach to population control, often refuse even to investigate the great potential of natural family planning, which can be inexpensively taught and helps couples maintain their human dignity while exercising responsible love. Education and development are far more effective responses to population trends than are coercion and artificial forms of population control.

The failed social policies of many developed countries should not be foisted on the world's poor. Neither the Cairo Conference nor any other forum should lend itself to cultural imperialism or to ideologies that isolate the human person in a self-enclosed universe, wherein abortion on demand, sexual promiscuity and distorted notions of the family are proclaimed as human rights or proposed as ideals for the young. Rights separated from responsibilities inevitably destroy one another, just as the human will that defies the divine will leads the human person to self-destruction.

In this Year of the Family, we pray that all the nations of the world will recognize that the family is the way for society, and for this we ask the blessing of Almighty God.

Intervention of
His Excellency Bishop James T. McHugh, STD
Bishop of Camden, New Jersey,
Member of the Holy See Delegation
to the 26th Session of the
United Nations Population Commission,
Session I of the Preparatory Committee for the International
Conference on Population and Development
New York, 28 February 1991

Madame Chairperson,

I would like to comment on some of the topics mentioned by Mr. Horlacher in his report:

> Relation of population and development
> Relation of population and environment
> Implications of changing age structure

The Holy See maintains that demographic policies or population policies should be placed in the overall context of socio-economic policies that include an emphasis on the overall well-being of society, and of families and children.

Demographic policies should be based on respect for human dignity and human rights and a commitment to protect and sustain human life from conception to natural death. There should also be a commitment to socio-economic development which includes international assistance to developing nations. Thus, international development efforts should be expanded, as evidenced in many other United Nations meetings and Conventions.

It is important that population policies maintain safeguards for families to make decisions regarding family size without outside coercion or pressure. There is always a danger that population policies may limit or compromise the freedom of the spouses to have their desired number of children.

In regard to environment, there is a delicate relationship between the environment and population trends. There is often a tendency to see all population growth as a threat to the environment. At the same time, there is considerable evidence to remind us that consumption patterns — especially in developed nations with lower population growth rates — are a major threat to the environment. Protection of the environment is a serious moral responsibility. The Holy See Delegation maintains that:

> "Today the ecological crisis has assumed such proportions as to be the responsibility of everyone ... its various aspects demonstrate the need for concerted efforts aimed at establishing the duties and obligations that belong to individuals, peoples, States and the international community. This not only goes hand in hand with efforts to build true peace, but also confirms and reinforces those efforts in a concrete way" (Pope John Paul II, *World Day of Peace Message*, 1990).

Finally, perhaps there should be more emphasis on ageing. I realize this has been mentioned before in our consideration of the changing age structure. In any case, the first paragraph of the *Concise Report* that we considered at our opening session shows a projected increase in the proportion of persons age 65 and over and a corresponding decline in the proportion of persons age 15 and under. This dramatizes the complexities of population trends and signals future difficulties in regard to socio-economic conditions, particularly in regard to maintaining a work force. In terms of priority, continued consideration should be given to the implications of changing age structure.

Thank you, Madame Chairperson.

INTERVENTION OF
HIS EXCELLENCY BISHOP ELIO SGRECCIA
SECRETARY OF THE PONTIFICAL COUNCIL FOR THE FAMILY
AT THE MEETING OF THE EUROPEAN POPULATION CONFERENCE
IN PREPARATION FOR THE
INTERNATIONAL CONFERENCE ON POPULATION AND DEVELOPMENT
GENEVA, 26 MARCH 1994

From 23-26 March 1993 the European Population Conference, organized jointly by the European Economic Commission, the Council of Europe and the United Nations Fund for Population Activities, was held in Geneva, Switzerland. The regional meeting (which includes all of Europe, the United States, Canada and Israel) was held in preparation for the United Nations International Conference on Population and Development planned for September 1994, Cairo, Egypt. The following is a translation of the French language address given by the head of the Holy See's Delegation on the final day.

Mr. President,

1. During this European Population Conference, the principal qualitative and structural elements of the population situation in the region have been amply identified. Nevertheless, in regard to policies and strategies for the future, it would be appropriate, in our opinion, to put greater stress on the ethical, cultural and spiritual factors that can play a decisive role in solving the problems and disadvantages indicated and that can contribute to the more harmonious development of the positive elements already present in our societies.

2. These ethical and cultural factors can help better define and obtain an appropriate, acceptable quality of life for those populations involved in the "new demographic revolution," and also foster closer and more positive relations of solidarity between States.

To this end it is appropriate to highlight four factors: a) the responsibility factor; b) the family principle; c) a new solidarity; and d) the new horizons of scientific research.

a) The *principle of responsibility* (H. Jonas), without diminishing the value of individual freedom on which the Western democracies are based, can give to the meaning of life and human action a more marked orientation toward the global good of the person and society.

It is important to rediscover this principle and to give it its proper place in healthcare management, particularly in healthcare education and respect for the body, so that the concept of "responsible" parenthood can become the sole way to approach, with respect for human rights, the question of birth regulation. This principle will likewise be useful for better defending the lives of individuals before and after birth, as well as that of the environment.

In recent years thinkers, philosophers and scientists of all tendencies have invoked this principle of responsibility towards the environment and future generations, in the context of what has been called "the ethic of the future," and "protecting the survival of humanity and ethnic diversity."

In this perspective of responsibility and an ethic of the future for the region, we ask that the spread of education in responsible parenthood with the methods that respect life, health and biological ecology be encouraged. There are reliable methods compatible with a sense of responsibility and respect for life, through the natural regulation of fertility and the justifiable spacing of births. The struggle against the social scourge of abortion can and should take place by means of a clear, resolute education in responsible procreation.

b) Another decisive factor is the *stability and harmony of the family*: it is called the "family principle."

Psychology and the social sciences have sufficiently shown the damage, deviancy and violence resulting from the affective deficiency that children and adolescents can suffer.

It is not enough to promote social policies for individual family members, such as children, the disabled, the elderly. Policies that address the family as a whole are necessary in order to reinforce its ability to remain united and to raise and support children.

In this regard, one can envisage many intervention strategies: assistance for women, especially during pregnancy, re-evaluation of domestic work, parental leave for the sake of the children's education, economic measures to support procreation and large families or those family members who are in difficulty. What the State spends in this way on the family can be recouped from the prevention of many social ills.

c) The third principle is a *new solidarity* that, in our region, has been damaged by individualism and utilitarianism.

This solidarity should be shown, as Pope John Paul II recalled in the

Encyclical *Centesimus annus*, in relation to underdeveloped areas, including those found outside our region. It is from these regions, in fact, that the destabilizing elements and restless immigrations that are so deeply affecting us come.

The problems connected with the fear of overpopulation and hunger would be better solved if all people were allowed access to harmonious and accelerated economic development.

Global disarmament has not been directed, as was desirable and possible, towards helping developing countries. On the other hand, easy access to weapons and the clandestine trafficking in nuclear material tend to encourage the solution of political problems by violence, producing tension and wars, which are the cause of new migrations.

This new solidarity must be extended to the emigrants in our region, by encouraging a culture of diversity capable of establishing a multicultural and multiracial society, which offers migrants and refugees the opportunity to participate in the structures and decisions of the host society. In this regard it is fitting not to ignore the universally recognized right to repatriation in one's own homeland. On this point the Holy See has been able to make a significant contribution to the conclusions of this Conference.

d) Fourth, it is important to open up *new horizons for scientific research*.

Science, which has sometimes been subjected and diverted to building tools of death and for negatively affecting populations, could, on the contrary, help create new conditions favouring the quality of life.

Scientific research can help perfect the methods for determining fertility, for preventing and treating the causes of infertility, and for preventing nutritional disorders.

In order to preserve the environment, the progress achieved for transforming energy and in the area of biotechnology have made it possible to perfect methods that reduce pollution and even produce biological agents capable of purifying some of the causes of pollution.

Experimental research in the field of biotechnology can also contribute to the improvement of farm produce and zootechny in developing countries so as to meet the increase in population.

In this regard we would like to recall the statement of John Paul II:

"These new conditions must be met not only with scientific reasoning, but more importantly with recourse to all available intellectual and spiritual energies. People need to rediscover the moral significance of respecting limits; they must grow and mature in the sense of responsibility with regard to every aspect of life" (Pope John Paul II, *Address to the Pontifical Academy of Sciences*, 22 November 1991; cf. *L'Osservatore Romano,* English edition, 2 December 1991).

Thank you.

STATEMENT BY
MONSIGNOR DIARMUID MARTIN
UNDER-SECRETARY, PONTIFICAL COUNCIL FOR JUSTICE AND PEACE AND HEAD OF DELEGATION OF THE HOLY SEE TO THE LATIN AMERICAN AND CARIBBEAN REGIONAL CONFERENCE ON POPULATION AND DEVELOPMENT MINISTERIAL PLENARY MEETING
MEXICO CITY, 3 MAY 1993

Mr. Chairman,

I wish to thank the President, the Government and the people of Mexico for the remarkable hospitality and the quiet efficiency which we have experienced in these days.

I also thank UNFPA and the U.N. Economic Commission for Latin America and the Caribbean for the invitation extended to the Holy See to be present at this Conference as an Observer.

The Holy See has been represented at all the Regional Preparatory Conferences for the 1994 Cairo Conference. This has helped the representatives of the Holy See to appreciate more deeply what there is in common, and where differences exist, in the concrete situations, the anxieties, the aspirations and the hopes of the men and women who live in our world today.

It is clear that the aspirations of these people will be realized and their problems resolved only through common efforts, through a renewed movement of solidarity, through a realization of the common responsibility of all to serve our earth and all its people, especially the poorest.

Mr. Chairman,

I would like to make some specific comments on the content of our work and especially on the Latin American Consensus document.

1. *The relationship between population and development*

The Latin American and Caribbean Conference recognizes the complexity of this relationship. It is a relationship which was examined at the 1974 Population Conference in Bucharest and again in 1984 at Mexico City. But it is an ever present question both in theory and above all in real practice.

Population programmes alone do not resolve the problems of economic growth. The elimination of poverty, especially through education, is on the other hand a pre-condition for the application of population policies which wish to respect the dignity of people.

When we speak about population we speak about people. Development is *for* people. Development is *through* people. In every country of the world, as has been repeated by many Delegations here, people constitute the most important resource of any nation.

But development is above all *of* people. It is human development. It involves every aspect of people's lives. It involves nutrition, health, work, education and what we call "quality of life." But it also involves culture, traditions, values and religious convictions: the deepest dimensions of human existence.

Each of us knows the debt we owe to the traditions and values we have inherited from our families, our cultures and our nations. Cultural traditions and religious values are real dimensions of human life and the life of society. They belong to what it is to be human.

Mr. Chairman,

In speaking of the relationship between development and population, the Holy See shares what has been said by many Delegations about the problem of external debt in this continent.

The question of foreign debt was a subject of a special document of the Office of the Holy See to which I am attached, published already six years ago, which called on the solidarity of all the protagonists in this question to find an urgent solution.

The debt problem hinders progress in many areas and because of the use of important resources for debt re-payment, at times strangles progress in human development.

One has to ask the question if the time has not come to take a radical new look at this problem and to bring about an end to this particular chapter of the history of North-South relations.

2. The questions of traditions and values is important when we speak of *the future generations*.

There has been discussion at this Conference about adolescents and indeed the Consensus Document speaks about adolescents on various occasions.

My Delegation is concerned that the solutions proposed be integral, especially regarding the significance of sexuality for adolescents both now and for their future.

Too often, solutions are presented which look only at the avoidance of pregnancy or the transmission of sexually transmitted diseases. But sexuality is a much wider concept. Adolescents must be guided towards seeing sexuality within the context of mature and lasting human relationships and of respect between men and women.

Many of the appeals which the Conference has made for greater sharing by men in family responsibilities will remain a dead-letter if one does not begin to teach young people the concept of responsibility.

We will teach our young people only a mechanical notion of sexuality if we do not educate them to values, responsibility and morality.

To carry out this education adequately we must strengthen the family, so that it can exercise its unique role in the transmission of values.

3. Speaking of shared responsibility, my Delegation has noted the references in the documents of the Conference to *periodic abstinence*.

The modern methods of natural family planning, chosen by many in this region, are especially interesting in that they require the commitment of both men and women and thus foster the unity of couples and the integration of the family unit. They require men to change their attitudes and behaviour towards their spouses.

These methods — according to the generally accepted terminology — are not contraceptive methods. They are not methods which control fertility by surgical or chemical means, but require a change in behaviour. They do not have the side effects of chemical or hormonal methods.

It is to be hoped that the terminology of this and future meetings will respect the nature of the natural methods through the use of appropriate terminology which does not label them contraceptives.

4. *The education of women* is another aspect of this Conference — as

indeed of the other regional Conferences — which my Delegation wishes to support, not just as an aspect of population policy. Women's contribution is a wealth and a resource which society has a right to draw upon.

But this also calls for an adequate response from society, through appropriate social and fiscal policies which will permit women, if they freely choose to do so, to take their part in the work force, and which will also give due recognition and support to those women who choose to dedicate themselves to their family and to contribute in this way to the welfare of society.

5. I wish also to join my support to those Delegations which have spoken about the questions of *refugees*, who constitute a large section of the population of some countries of this region.

If we talk about the hopes and aspirations of people, then our hearts must turn to the many refugees who wait and hope to return to the land to which they belong and from which they draw their culture and traditions and in which they have their family roots.

Mr. Chairman,

My Delegation recognizes many positive elements in the documents of this Conference, especially regarding the relationship between development and population. Hopefully these aspects will inspire the future reflection of the preparatory process for the Cairo Conference and also our own reflection and action for the good of the people we serve.

STATEMENT BY
HIS EXCELLENCY ARCHBISHOP RENATO R. MARTINO
APOSTOLIC NUNCIO, PERMANENT OBSERVER OF THE HOLY SEE
TO THE UNITED NATIONS
AND HEAD OF THE DELEGATION OF THE HOLY SEE
TO THE SECOND SESSION OF THE PREPARATORY COMMITTEE
FOR THE INTERNATIONAL CONFERENCE ON POPULATION AND
DEVELOPMENT
NEW YORK, 17 MAY 1993

Mr. Chairman,

The Holy See welcomes the concept adopted as the theme of the forthcoming International Conference by the title that links population to development. This marks a significant evolution, and reflects the correct view of many countries, especially the developing countries, that all great issues — such as environment at the Rio Conference of last year and population at the forthcoming Cairo Conference — cannot be separated from, and even less opposed to, the integral development of any society and of all the human beings that constitute it.

The relationship between population and development was examined in detail at Bucharest (1974) and at Mexico City (1984) and next year at Cairo that examination must be taken a step further. A Conference on population and development must above all place in evidence that sustainable development is about people, about the hopes, anxieties and aspirations of women and men of today and tomorrow, of the various generations of the one human family.

Looked at this way, development must take on a new face. It must not only be centered on economics and production, but above all it must be centered on the manner in which we make use of the resources of the earth, so that our brothers and sisters in every part of the world can live longer and more satisfying lives, today and in the future.

This means working towards new definitions of sustainable development, which looks at improving the quality of life of people, at standards of equity in international relationships and in the sharing of wealth and technology, at social and human development, which respects what is deepest in human traditions and in the cultural and religious convictions of people.

The existence of poverty, and indeed of large pockets of extreme poverty, both in the developing and in the industrialized worlds, is the clearest indication — or should one not say indictment — of the fact that we have not yet achieved sustainable development.

Sustainable development requires that people, especially peoples of the developing countries, become the real protagonists of development, with greater equality of opportunity and greater participation in the economic, social and political lives of their countries. Only when development is integral will it be truly human. Only when poverty is eradicated will people be truly in a position to exercise real choices and fully assume their responsibilities in a manner which responds to the dignity and the rights of each person.

The reduction in population growth rates on its own has not automatically been accompanied by economic growth or by a reduction in poverty. The resources of our earth were originally created for the benefit of all humanity. Development must thus aim at restoring this original common destiny. Today this requires above all an examination of lifestyles and of forms of exploitation of the resources of the earth for the exclusive benefit of a few. It requires ways of guaranteeing an equitable sharing of technology. It involves an equitable access of all, especially the poorest, to markets, without encountering protectionist measures. The question of the external debt of the poorest countries must be looked at in a new manner, so that it does not create a circle of indebtedness from which it is not possible to break out.

Programmes of structural adjustment must also take into account that in the long term the greatest resource of any country is its people. Poverty will be passed on from one generation to the next if such programmes do not give greater priority to investment in education, for boys and girls, primary health care especially for mothers and young children. Attention must also be given to programmes which help people to cope with changes in production and in the labour market, especially in the face of growing urban poverty.

In speaking of a renewed concept of sustainable development which is people-centered, the Holy See wishes to stress that more emphasis should be given to the place of the family in development. The *Universal Declaration of Human Rights* of 1948, and many other United Nations instruments, have stated that "the family is the natural and fundamental group unit of society and is entitled to protection by society and the State." Especially in developing countries, the family is a vital element for the effective and integrated delivery of health and social services. Concerted action in favour of the family should promote increased solidarity with its vital role. Parents must be supported in their fundamental right and duty to transmit along with life the cultural, ethical, social, spiritual and religious values essential to the well-being of the members of the community of love and solidarity which is the family, and of society as a whole. The observance of the 1994 International Year of the Family should offer great opportunity for the strengthening of the family.

My Delegation has taken due note of the interventions made during this Meeting. One of the major calls we have heard, Mr. Chairman, is the one to focus on people when dealing with the issues of Population — and particularly on their rights to full, sustainable development. The centrality of the human being in all development concerns figures most prominently as the First Principle of the Rio Declaration and surfaces again in the interventions made in this Committee. This is an appropriate echo of the Declarations made at the five Regional Population Conferences held respectively in Bali, Dakar, Geneva, Amman, and Mexico City, in which the Holy See had the privilege of participating as an Observer.

It has been gratifying to note both in the interventions, as well as in the advance documentation of the Preparatory Committee, the outline of a large mosaic of issues which any serious examination of population must consider. When speaking of population, one cannot only address demographic concerns since they are not synonymous terms. Attention must be drawn to the full range of population issues such as: *inter alia,* the family and its continuing need for societal support; the issues of the ageing including the continuing and changing needs of the elderly; the mentally and physically disabled; sustainable development with particular emphasis on education and information; refugees and migrants, both within and beyond national boundaries; the full integration of women and the girl child in development; maternal and child health and child survival strategies; and the responsible planning of family size and spacing of births. Thus, without losing sight of demographic concerns, due regard must be given to the full range of population issues just mentioned.

Vast displacements of population have plagued our century and continue to be the cause of unmeasurable sufferings. The causes of these vast movements of millions of refugees and migrants within and outside national boundaries cannot be ignored any longer and need to be courageously addressed.

The blessings of modern medicine and of improved nutritional and environmental conditions have increased life expectancy, while at the same time have presented new challenges for the care of the elderly whose right to life and dignity must be upheld. As for the mentally and physically disabled, the care of the weakest members of society has been and will always be the real measure of the degree of civilization reached by any society. The Holy See views with increasing alarm sporadic calls, particularly from the more materialistically concerned societies, for dependent, "non-producing" members of the human family to be considered as expendable. Such calls are increasingly cloaked in language related to individual rights and are made more particularly insidious for this very reason. There is a lurking danger in the Western model of increasingly consumeristic societies of persons being "defined" and their "value" correlated to their current economic contribution to the community. To measure the value of a human life by standards of economic costs versus productivity is barbaric.

Human life itself is the foundation of all legal rights and the moment that human beings are entrusted with the decision as to what is human or what is not, all order and the expendability of all other rights hangs in the balance. For this reason, the Holy See will unceasingly insist on the basic right to life for all human beings whether they be vigorous and economically independent, or weaker and dependent due to old age, infirmity, or disabling afflictions, or simply due to their dependence on a mother's life-giving nourishment from the moment of conception. God's graces extend to each and every member of the human family, and human laws should at least respect the basic right to life of all of our sisters and brothers.

Calls for any ratification of voluntary abortion under the guise of other perceived rights begs the question of the most fundamental and inalienable right of any human being to life. The opening of the right to life to interpretation is done only at the greatest of peril. Mr. Chairman, there are too many instances, of recent and even immediate memory, of individuals or societies taking it upon themselves to interpret who is or is not human, or who is or is not worthy of life. The statement of the 1984 International Conference, Recommendation 18 (e), should be retained and emphasized. The consensus agreed that as one step in reducing mortality and morbidity, governments should take appropriate steps to help women avoid abortion and to provide treatment and counseling for women who have had recourse to abortion. The consensus also clearly stated that "in no case should abortion be promoted as a method of family planning."

The various documents before us draw our attention to the synergism which exists between the various population and development concerns. It is thus imperative to seek to fully comprehend the various interlinkages between development and population activities. For instance, recent studies have pointed out that many parents in developing countries look to their progeny as a means of financial support for their old age — a replacement, if you will, for lacking social security. Eliminating one of the major future economic constraints for young couples, especially in developing countries, by addressing the full range of needs of the elderly, will have the added effect of providing them their due freedom and far greater selflessness in the responsible planning of their family size. Moreover, the security provided by appropriate Maternal Child Health Care will do much to alleviate the fear amongst parents of not having a sufficient number of children to survive infancy. Thus there is a growing recognition that there is no quick fix or panacea for demographic problems, and particularly irrelevant are those programmes and activities which do not take into account the full scope of developmental aspects in their approach to population issues.

Similarly, while population growth continues to remain a concern in certain areas of the world, many of the more developed areas must take a hard and careful look at their own long-term social security planning when faced with increasing numbers of aged being supported by fewer younger working adults. Further, appropriate heed must be given to the perplexing problem in certain countries of their population growth rates having fallen to such an extent that they face non-replacement levels if current trends continue unabated.

As regards human procreation, I would like to repeat here a paragraph from my Statement at the Conference on Environment and Development in Rio de Janeiro on 4 June 1992:

> "The position of the Holy See regarding procreation is frequently misinterpreted. The Catholic Church does not propose procreation at any cost. It keeps on insisting that the transmission of, and the caring for human life must be exercised with an utmost sense of responsibility. It restates its constant position that human life is sacred; that the aim of public policy is to enhance the welfare of families; that full respect be assured to the parents' God-given right to determine in full responsibility the size of their own family. What the Church opposes is the imposition of demographic policies and of methods for limiting births which are contrary to the liberty, dignity and conscience of the human being. At the same time, the Holy See does not consider people as mere numbers, nor only on economic terms. It emphatically states its concern that the poor be not singled out as if, by their very existence, they were the cause, rather than the victims, of the lack of development."

The concept of responsibility and of the couple's right to be free from all coercions in determining the spacing of births and the size of the family was already stated by the International Conference on Human Rights at Teheran (1968), and I quote: "Parents have a basic human right to determine freely and responsibly the number and the spacing of their children."

In the statements of Delegations as well as in the preparatory documents there have been further calls to this freedom from all forms of coercion, such as economic pressure directed to persons or to sovereign states under the guise of developmental assistance.

The Church has constantly upheld this principle of freedom from coercion, stressing that the decision regarding the frequency of births and the size of the family be a free, informed and mutual decision by the couple, based on their conscientious assessment of their responsibilities to God, themselves, their children and family and the society of which they are part, respecting the objective moral order and the licit methods of spacing or limiting pregnancies.

In concluding, Mr. Chairman, I express the sincere hope of the Holy See that the International Conference on Population and Development will be a positive event in our history. May the sovereign countries that participate in it wisely and courageously rededicate themselves to the service of all the people of the world, planning the way for their genuine development.

Thank you, Mr. Chairman.

Statement by
Monsignor Frank J. Dewane
Member of Delegation of the Holy See
to the Second Session of the Preparatory Committee
for the International Conference on Population and Development
New York, 18 May 1993

On Cluster 4 :
Population distribution: Internal and International Migration

Mr. Chairman,

My Delegation's comments will focus on international migration. However clear references will be made to areas which also impact internal migration. The Delegation of the Holy See approaches this topic of Cluster Four, as it does all issues relating to Population and Sustainable Development, from the perspective of the "Centrality of the Human-Being."

While the phenomenon of widespread international migration demonstrates considerable variation from one area of the world to another, this phenomenon often meets with an ambivalent response. Yet the international community has a responsibility to extend protection and assistance, including but certainly not limited to adjustment of juridical instruments and international structures. Despite signs of increased awareness of the problems of involuntary migrants, some states tend more and more to determine arbitrarily the criteria for fulfillment of their international obligation toward asylum seekers with policies which aim at only reducing the number of entries and discouraging new requests for asylum.

It should be recognized that immigration can be and is a positive element in many countries and in the relations of the country with the rest of the world. Immigrants make an important contribution to the economy of the host country. Contact between persons of different talents and cultures has historically been a source of civilization's advancement.

Since the theme of the 1994 International Conference is "Population and Development," it must be acknowledged that a reasonable acceptance of immigrants can be a contribution to the "development" of countries of origin because of the alleviation of the competition for jobs, the transfer of skills and technology on their eventual return and the actual remittance sent back by migrants.

The accepted assumption is that most people would not move if they could enjoy decent living conditions at home. Unwanted migration is preventable by development. New forms of cooperation should be encouraged which aim at sustaining local economies, at local job creation and at trade liberalization. Joint programs should be developed in order to share know-how in management and business skills as well as to share appropriate new technologies.

Integration is an important aspect of immigration policy. But the recommended integration requires measures aimed at safeguarding the fundamental human rights of all the migrants in the territory and ensuring the respect of their cultural identity. While the theme of integration as been mentioned often at this PrepCom, the suggestion of strategies has been noticeably absent. A serious commitment to integration requires, among other factors: access to citizenship and its benefits for those who have resided for along time in the host country, and especially for the second generation of migrants who have grown up there; the right to family reunification; education in schools which respects cultural and religious diversity.

At this point my Delegation would like to express a caveat concerning temporary migrations, since experience has shown that they tend to evolve into permanent migrations with much weaker social protection. While programs of temporary transfer of manpower for purposes of training and for well-defined forms of economic assistance can be beneficial, large-scale temporary migrations risk becoming a source of cheap labor with damage to family life.

In conclusion, Mr. Chairman, the questions which surround underground labor markets and the exploitation of clandestine immigrants should receive appropriate attention in the international domain. It is the hope of the Delegation of the Holy See that this topic will find its way into this forum for discussion and consideration.

Thank you, Mr. Chairman.

STATEMENT BY
MR. JOHN M. KLINK
MEMBER OF DELEGATION OF THE HOLY SEE
TO THE SECOND SESSION OF THE PREPARATORY COMMITTEE
FOR THE INTERNATIONAL CONFERENCE ON POPULATION AND
DEVELOPMENT; NEW YORK, 19 MAY 1993

*On Cluster 5 : Resource Allocation, Resource Mobilization,
The Role of Governments and Other Sectors*

Mr. Chairman,

My Delegation attaches particular importance to this cluster as it represents the real teeth of concrete actions in favor of population and development. It bears noting, however, that it is our understanding that there will most probably be recommendations for action at the end of each chapter or section of the final document which may again be resynthesized in a final section. As some items would thus be repeated, their importance will be enlarged accordingly. Thus, my Delegation's comments regarding this cluster would similarly apply to such repetitions or syntheses of this text.

In the interest of time I will not address myself to the positive aspects of the document, but will limit my comments to those areas where my Delegation feels there is a particular lack or need for revision.

In this context, allow me to say that the distinguished Delegate from Sweden has pointed accurately to the overall limitation of the document, in that it focuses almost exclusively on reproductive health concerns rather than broad concerns.

Mr. Chairman,

My Delegation sees the question of freedom from coercion to be one which should be assured on several planes. The most important is that of assuring the freedom of couples to make their own informed decisions regarding the responsible planning of family size and spacing of births without coercion. The other important plane is that which regards the sovereignty of nations not to be pressured to adopt population policies. Our Delegation thus views with concern the wording throughout the document, but particularly of Paragraph 18, regarding a possible implied linkage of developmental assistance with increased involvement in family planning activities.

In relation to the issue of the freedom of potential recipients, we feel it important that there be clear language regarding respect for cultural, religious and social traditions. If population activities are to be truly synergistic with development activities, the importance of the respect for such traditions which is key to success in development, must also be given its due importance as the key to any population activities. Thus, the language of these documents should carefully reflect this concern.

Mr. Chairman,

I would like to also point to other specific language which we feel should be revised or enlarged. Specifically, in Paragraph 5, we are unclear as to why the wording limits development to only, and I quote, "a wide spectrum" of population, rather than noting the right to development of all peoples. It is the Holy See's firm belief, Mr. Chairman, that all persons have the right to development, in its many facets — physical, educational and spiritual. For this reason, we maintain it to be imperative that the right to development never be obscured in any section of the documents, but particularly when discussing resource allocation.

In light of my previous comments we feel that this paragraph should contain specific reference to the sovereignty of countries and freedom from linkages between developmental assistance and conformation to population policies.

I would also like to make reference to Paragraph 7, and here my Delegation would again suggest that specific language regarding respect for rights and freedom from coercion in keeping with the respect for cultural, religious and social traditions be included.

Regarding the references in the document to IEC activities for youth and adolescent groups, we would first question the distinction to be made between youth and adolescents and what criteria would be used in this definition.

Most importantly, however, the proposed provision of reproductive health and counseling services to these groups needs to again carefully take into consideration the rights of parents as the ones primarily responsible for the education and upbringing of their children. Parents have the right to fulfill their duties and responsibilities in this regard without coercion and this should be mentioned in this context.

Again, in Paragraph 9, we question why youth and adolescents are grouped together in the same paragraph with the elderly. The elderly obviously deserve the due attention of a separate paragraph at the least.

Finally, Mr. Chairman, we would like to question the continued use of the *Amsterdam Declaration* as a reference almost on a level as an international Convention or other consensus document. This is not the case with the *Amsterdam Declaration*, given that the participants were limited in number and the majority of nations were not present during its debates or conclusions. In this we take note of similar comments made by the U.S. Delegation regarding their objection to inclusion of other non-consensus documents.

Thank you, Mr. Chairman.

Statement by
Monsignor Joseph A. DeAndrea
Member of the Delegation of the Holy See
before the Second Committee of the 48th Session of the
General Assembly, on Item 96:
International Conference on Population and Development
New York, 5 November 1993

Mr. Chairman,

The Annotated Outline of the Final Document of the International Conference on Population and Development (A/48/430/Add.1) deserves a more detailed analysis than the time constraints of this meeting allow. With that in mind, my Delegation will attempt to briefly summarize its comments.

Concerning Part One: My Delegation insists, along with other Delegations, that the recognition of the human person, in his/her dignity and rights, be clearly stated as the premise that guides all the subsequent Statements and proposals regarding population and development. Should this be neglected, the whole exercise would lack a firm and permanent foundation and become disconnectedly technocratic.

Turning to Part Two: My Delegation affirms the need to emphasize the strong linkage of the problems of sustainable development, of economic growth and of sharing world's resources with the issue of population. This demands a much stronger call to solidarity than is expressed in the document: clear and increased action in favour of debt relief, of technology transfers, of true educational and occupational opportunities, of radical changes in the scandalous patterns of consumption and waste are what is really necessary, more than simply underlining population stabilization, serious as this issue may be in some areas. Developing countries could perceive this latter one sided emphasis as an attempt by more affluent countries to camouflage their reluctance in facing their obligations toward a realistic help for sustainable development.

My Delegation shares profoundly the concerns expressed about the complex problems of migrations, of indigenous peoples, of the ageing population and of disabled persons. Time does not allow for a more detailed examination of these problems, but my Delegation repeats its long-standing view that all efforts at addressing these problems must take into full consideration the fundamental dignity and inalienable rights of each person in these groups. Due to their difficult situations, they have a special claim not only to protection and assistance, but to a truly human acceptance and to the real appreciation of the values they represent and contribute, beyond the narrow limits of economic productivity.

The Holy See takes note of the references in the document to "unsafe abortion," to extending reproductive rights with the possibility of including abortion as a family planning method. There is also the proposal that the laws of some countries regulating abortion or declaring abortion illegal in certain cases should be reviewed and possibly changed.

This Delegation calls attention to and supports Recommendation 18(e) of the Recommendations for the Further Implementation of the World Population Plan of Action adopted by strong consensus after extended discussion at the 1984 International Conference on Population. Recommendation 18(e) addresses two important issues, first "in no case should abortion be promoted as a method of family planning." Many nations, citing demographic policies and medical data, strongly affirmed and continue to affirm that abortion should not be promoted as a family planning method nor encouraged as a means of spacing or limiting births. In the discussion it was clear that legalizing abortion does not make it safe and that even if legal, it is not an appropriate means of family planning. Secondly, the Recommendation also urged governments "to take appropriate steps to help women avoid abortion ... and whenever possible, provide for the humane treatment and counseling of women who have had recourse to abortion."

Admittedly this is a difficult area because of the wide divergence of laws in various countries. The 1984 International Conference recognized the complexity. Documents in preparation for the 1994 Conference should not attempt to override the 1984 consensus nor should they try to impugn the laws of most nations that recognize that abortion is an inappropriate method of family planning.

My Delegation concurs in stating that changes in the attitudes and behaviour of both men and women are necessary conditions for achieving full gender equality and insists that the reproductive process is the responsibility of both spouses, the man and the woman. For this reason, it is surprising that, while at various points the current draft document calls for use and availability of contraceptive methods, no mention is made of natural family planning which has as its central point the full and responsible participation of both man and woman in the planning of family size.

My Delegation is also especially concerned with the proposed section on The Family, Its Roles, Composition and Structure. In some cases the language of the text is a departure from established United Nations language. For instance, the *Universal Declaration of Human Rights* states that "The family is the natural and fundamental group unit of society and is entitled to protection by society and the State." The text under preparation weakens the force of that language in stating that "The family, in its many forms, is a basic unit of society and it is the social institution within which child-bearing and child-rearing occur."

The text further speaks of social policies "supporting the plurality of family forms." Member nations have well established laws and policies to support the family, the spouses and the children, and these laws and policies should not be called into question or weakened to accommodate new social trends or experiments.

Thank you, Mr. Chairman.

STATEMENT BY
MONSIGNOR DIARMUID MARTIN
UNDER-SECRETARY OF THE
PONTIFICAL COUNCIL FOR JUSTICE AND PEACE
AND HEAD OF THE DELEGATION OF THE HOLY SEE TO
THE THIRD SESSION OF THE PREPARATORY COMMITTEE FOR THE
INTERNATIONAL CONFERENCE ON POPULATION AND DEVELOPMENT
NEW YORK, 5 APRIL 1994

The Holy See has followed with interest the entire phase of the preparation for the Cairo Conference up to this moment. It was pleased to take part especially in the Regional Preparatory Conferences, as well as in the earlier sessions of this Preparatory Committee and the meetings of the Population Commission.

The presence of the Holy See in these activities is a sign of the importance that it attaches to the themes which will be discussed here over the coming days, and later on this year in Cairo. An overall view of the positions of the Holy See can be found in the Message which the Holy Father, Pope John Paul II consigned to the Secretary General of the Conference, Mrs. Nafis Sadik, on the occasion of her recent visit to the Vatican. The text of this Message is available to all Delegations.

The theme of the Cairo Conference — Population and Development — as Pope John Paul noted in that Message, is "of vital importance for the well-being and progress of the human family." "None of the issues to be discussed," he continued, "is simply an economic or demographic concern, but, at root, each is a matter of profound moral significance, with far-reaching implications."

It is important, in the first place, during these weeks of intense work and discussion, never to lose contact with the deepest aspects of the subjects under consideration and their significance for the human person and for society. Subjects which so intimately concern the well-being and the welfare of humanity, the transmission and the protection of human life, such fundamental institutions as marriage and the family, and responsible stewardship of the earth's resources and its environment must be approached with caution, indeed with reverence and respect. We live in a world which is marked all too often with predominantly utilitarian values. But decisions about the human person cannot be measured only or even primarily in utilitarian terms. When we proclaim, as the principles outlined in the Draft Final Document rightly do, drawing from the Rio Declaration, that "human beings are at the centre of concerns for sustainable development," we already clarify the vision of development we wish to foster.

Human-centred development, person-centred development, is one which is holistic, centred on an integral understanding of the destiny and the potentialities of the person, while at the same time taking into account interpersonal and societal relationships.

The ethical and moral dimensions of the responsibilities of persons and their behaviour, of their rights and duties, belong clearly within such integral reflection. Ethics is a real dimension of human existence, which cannot be measured in economic or utilitarian terms, but without which the human person and human society can never progress towards full development.

One of the principal concerns of the Delegation of the Holy See regarding the Draft Final Document is its lack of a clear ethical vision. It is not simply a question of a different ethical evaluation of one or other particular situation or circumstance. The document is marked in fact by an extremely individualistic understanding of the person and of human sexuality. It accepts, almost as an unrestricted right, that each individual including adolescents from an early age, may be "sexually active." While the Draft Final Document recognizes the negative consequences that some recent changes in social patterns have brought, the only response it offers is to indicate the possible means to avoid pregnancy or sexually transmitted diseases. No indications are offered as to how society intends to discourage behaviour which the text itself describes as "high-risk" regarding the health of persons. No indications are given of ways in which young people can be led to understand that mature sexual behaviour requires an appreciation of the deeper interpersonal dimensions, and of the self-restraint that is necessary to show respect and love for the other.

In reflection on the rights and duties involved in the decisions of couples concerning the number of their children and the spacing of births, the expressions of the Teheran Human Rights Conference are often quoted. In the twenty-five years or so since that Conference, the reflection on one aspect of the Teheran formulations has however been neglected: "parents," the text reads, "have a basic human right to decide freely and *responsibly* on the number and spacing of their children... ." If anything there has been, in these years, a fear of making more explicit what this notion of responsibility means.

Ethical demands and responsibility cannot be determined by a superficial analysis of the behaviour patterns of the day, especially when some of these patterns are commonly judged to be immature or even irresponsible. Society cannot abdicate its responsibility of indicating the fundamentals of what responsible behaviour is, and of effectively challenging, especially young people, to reach personal and human maturity, which inevitably involves more respectful behaviour towards others.

A reading of the Draft Final Document can leave one with the impression that it is marked by that reticence towards a coherent moral vision which is characteristic of certain industrialized countries. It does not seem to take into consideration, or fully grasp, the extent to which cultural, ethical, spiritual and religious values are deeply rooted in the traditions of other peoples, especially developing countries.

The lack of a coherent ethical vision underpinning a document which deals with fundamental questions concerning the future of humanity is extremely worrying. In such an ethical vacuum, the document attempts to establish principles, at times of an ideological, at times of an operational nature. A society, an international community, which is based on principles which do not have a clear vision or philosophical underpinning is doomed to disintegration.

In an analogous way, it would be extremely dangerous for the international community to proclaim new "fundamental human rights" which, rather than being based on what is essential to the dignity of the human person and the common good of humanity, are based on individual preference or on a particular ideology. The international community has justifiably been very sparing in creating "new rights" or in amplifying the application of the well-recognized human rights. To dilute the content of human rights is to weaken gravely their impact and the ability of the international community to demand their absolute respect.

The Delegation of the Holy See would therefore like to see more clearly defined the precise content, extent and *limits* of the proposed concept of "reproductive rights." My Delegation appreciates the value and necessity of reproductive health as part of a person's overall well-being, both men and women. This includes a commitment to the fostering of all those physical, psychological, economic, social and cultural factors which would ensure that conception, pregnancy, birth and child nurturing are guaranteed, in optimal conditions, for women. Such concerns would embrace, naturally, also those educational measures, including moral education which will lead young people to mature sexual behaviour and to respectful family relations. It involves efforts to eliminate sexual violence, to remove other abuses and mutilations, especially of women. It involves the appropriate treatment and prevention of infertility. The Holy See will support such a notion of "reproductive health": one that is open to the creation of an environment where women and men can make free and responsible decisions that will enable them to procreate, without endangering their own health or that of the children they bear.

However, the Holy See cannot support any concept of "reproductive rights" which would include abortion as an appropriate means of family planning or the notion of an internationally recognized fundamental right to abortion.

The Holy See also finds unacceptable the Document's continual implication that family planning and contraception are synonymous terms. This is underlined by the total absence of any reference in the Draft Final Document to natural family planning. The Holy See supports the use of the natural methods for the regulation of fertility, not only for ethical reasons, but because these inexpensive methods respect the health of women and men by avoiding the possibility of dangerous side-effects and enlist the full involvement and commitment of the man.

In the course of the discussions, the Delegation of the Holy See is most willing to work together with other Delegations in these meetings in presenting and elaborating formulations of appropriate language, to develop or to clarify existing sections of the Draft Final Document.

The same will apply, Mr. Chairman, to other aspects of the document under consideration and which I will not develop at this moment. Most of these areas have been indicated in the Message which Pope John Paul has addressed to the Secretary General, such as the relationship of population policy to development policy in general, the centrality of the family and its right to support from society and the State, the dignity of women and the need for men to assume greater responsibility for family life.

The aim of the interventions of my Delegation will be above all to deepen the awareness which our final document will show for the fundamental ethical truths which are involved in our reflection. We stand before serious questions about the future of humanity which challenge us to provide convincing answers. But we must also approach such questions, as I have said, with a certain reverence and respect, aware of the modesty and limitations of the contribution that even such an important Conference can bring.

REPORT OF
MONSIGNOR DIARMUID MARTIN,
SECRETARY OF THE PONTIFICAL COUNCIL FOR JUSTICE AND PEACE,
AT THE SPECIAL ASSEMBLY FOR AFRICA OF THE SYNOD OF BISHOPS
— 22ND GENERAL CONGREGATION —
ON THE WORK OF THE THIRD SESSION OF THE PREPARATORY
COMMITTEE FOR THE
INTERNATIONAL CONFERENCE ON POPULATION AND DEVELOPMENT
NEW YORK, 28 APRIL 1994

I. What happened in New York

The final session of the Preparatory Committee for the Cairo International Conference on Population and Development concluded in New York late on Friday last.

The New York meeting had before it an 82 page document, with 16 different chapters, covering a very broad series of topics on population policy in general. Only 7 pages were dedicated to the theme of development.

On much of what was presented there was general agreement, or at least enough agreement to arrive at formulations around which general consensus could be arrived. There was, however, no agreement on a number of essential areas, some of which are of very special concern to the Church, and indeed to persons of all religions and none.

Before moving on to deal in some detail with those areas, it might be helpful to draw attention to some aspects of the draft programme of the Conference which have not received as much attention as they deserve.

The first is money. The United Nations draft document calls for dramatic increases in the amount of international development funding which should be earmarked for population activities. It asked that population-directed funds should be increased from 1.4% of all development funds to at least 4%, that is an increase from US$ 5 billion to at least US$ 13 billion by the year 2000. Much of this money would come from increased donations, especially from the United States of America and Japan. But a great deal would have to come from cutting back spending on other areas of development, in the areas of education, health care, industrial development and disaster relief.

In addition to such an unprecedented increase in the funds which might become available, the results of the Preparatory Committee constitute a real change in the basic philosophy which will inspire such a massive intervention.

Ten years ago, at the Mexico City Population Conference, the doomsday prophecies of uncontrolled population growth and the threat that it proposes to the earth's resources and its security were dominant themes. The answers were indicated in government-centred programmes of population education, and in reaching certain targets and goals for the provision of family planning services. The Holy See was almost alone in stressing the fact that the decisions to be made concerning the number and spacing of births belong to married couples, responsibly exercising their vocation, and not in the first place to governments.

Now ten years later, the priorities of population policies have changed. At New York there was hardly any mention of the doomsday visions and even some criticism of the former government-centred policies, considered as coercive and demeaning to women, just as the Holy See had been saying for some time.

That does not, unfortunately, mean that the preparation for the Cairo Conference has come around to positions closer to those of the Holy See: far from it. The New York meeting made it abundantly clear that the Cairo Conference will be a Conference about lifestyles, rather than about numbers or about development as more traditionally understood.

It will be a Conference on lifestyles starting out from a very specific vision. At the conclusion of the New York meeting, for example, the Secretary General of the Conference said that the work was a victory for *individuals* and for the right of individuals to make choices. It would be wrong to think that the word "individual" in this case was just a synonym for the person or for man or the human being. What is at stake is a philosophical vision, linked especially to views of some Northern European countries and the United States, based on an exaggerated individualism, which colours every aspect of the text and leaves the way open to a broadly libertarian interpretation of its proposals.

In the discussions on the theme of the family, for instance, many Delegations wished not to refer to the family as *the* fundamental unit of society, as the *Universal Declaration of Human Rights* does. One Delegate said that his society is now marked by an atomization and an individualism, the result of which was that his society could no longer identify itself with the *Universal Declaration*. The question is, what right has any International Conference to export such visions and impose them on societies where the family and the community are greatly respected and, in fact, constitute the guarantee of stability and cohesion for society?

One of the new concepts proposed for approval by the Cairo Conference is that called *reproductive health*, with the consequent *reproductive rights*. These terms are so new that there is no satisfactory translation for them. They could, of course, be considered in a positive way, if they were orientated to helping women to exercise their vocation to maternity in optimal health conditions, providing education, primary health care, emergency services and post-natal care for mother and child. But they are interpreted, in fact, in an ideological way. As used, they refer to prerogatives of individuals without any reference to marriage.

Abortion is included as one of the essential parts of the definition of reproductive health. The term reproductive rights is interpreted by many in terms of a radical "pro-choice" position, in which the woman would be assigned the exclusive right to make the decision to terminate her pregnancy.

The consequences of such new concepts are of especial interest to the Church in Africa, where the Church is in fact a major — in some cases the only — supplier of the healthcare services, especially at grass roots level and among the poor. The Delegation of the Holy See made it very clear that it would block any suggestion which would make more difficult or compromise this work of the Church by the inclusion in any national healthcare agendas of measures which the Church-based services cannot endorse.

On the specific theme of *abortion*, the Conference was divided into three groupings:

— One, found in the Secretariat text, stressed the serious problem of the danger to women's health caused by the complications of abortions, but then asked governments to re-examine legislation on abortion and to move towards the affirmation of an exclusive right of women to make decisions about their pregnancies. In practice, abortion on demand.

— A less radical solution stressed simply that in the circumstances where abortion is legal, it should be medically safe.

— The Holy See and others stressed that all efforts should be made to assist women to avoid abortion, but that the legalization of abortion does not resolve the problems.

In any case, all the references concerning abortion in the documents have remained "in brackets." This is a procedural method to show that the preparatory meeting could come to no agreement and the question will be rediscussed at Cairo. Some reports affirm that this constituted "a defeat of the Holy See." Such reports do not take into account that it was the clear intention of some Delegations to have abortion-related texts approved already in New York, alongside the other approved texts. And this did not occur!

On a number of occasions, those who propose that abortion be included as a generalized component of population policy, stressed that abortion is already legalized in some way in most States, and that therefore the International Community should recognize this as a reality. Such affirmations are based on a superficial interpretation of statistics and take no account of the fact that even in countries where abortion is legalized, there is no national consensus of the citizens on the question, and very often the majority of citizens do not want to see abortion as a family planning means and much less so as part of development aid programmes.

A more attentive examination to the statistical evidence available would indicate that a high incidence of maternal death can be correlated, not to the availability or not of legalized abortion, but to the complex of factors included in the Human Development Index, which concern the overall level of health, educational and development factors in a country. The problem of women's health will be best resolved through investment in improving health services for women, not by the further promotion of abortion.

Statistics presented to the Committee showed that it is also naive to suggest that the number of abortions will be reduced simply by making a wide range of family planning services available. The statistics for the United States for example indicate that it has a very high rate of what is called "contraceptive prevalence" and at the same time one of the highest abortion rates in the world.

Finally, the individualistic philosophy of the Conference is noticeable in the attempts to extend the availability of all reproductive health care and family planning services to *adolescents and to children*, and to assure absolute confidentiality for young people, on the basis that "sexual-activity" is not simply a fact but almost a personal or individual right for all young people.

The Holy See fought hard to reaffirm and guarantee the rights and responsibilities of parents, as recognized already in international documents. Whereas it was not possible to arrive at finalized terminology of this question, the pressure from African and Islamic countries is so strong that a favourable solution will hopefully be found.

II. What can be done?

Only a few months remain before the Cairo Conference begins, the first of the major population conferences to be held in Africa. What can be done in these months ahead?

One of the dominating impressions that I had during the New York meeting was that only one side of the picture was emerging, only one lifestyle was being presented. Being against such lifestyles was equated with being against progress. But such a form of progress is not shared by so many people in every part of the world and of all beliefs.

What is happening in the preparations for the Cairo meeting is something which concerns the future of humanity. It concerns institutions such as marriage and the family which have been recognized as central to society since its very origins. What is involved is the sacred character of human life and the enormous responsibility and dignity assigned to parents as stewards of its transmission. It involves the future stability of our societies and of the very values which so many families throughout the world are struggling to transmit and defend.

I was greatly struck by the fact that at the New York meeting dealing with family and women's issues, with the questions of the transmission of life, the responsibilities of adolescents, there was much talk of gender equity and equality, of reproductive rights, and of individual choices, but two words were completely absent. One was *marriage*, an institution which seems sadly to have been put aside as irrelevant or emarginated. The other was *love*: love is the most central concept, to be rediscovered, to be protected and fostered, if the family is to carry out its mission, as a true community of life and love. A closed, exaggerated individualism, on the other hand, can only extinguish love.

To overcome this one-sidedness, it is important that the viewpoint of the vast majority of the population of Africa, as well as of other continents, be made more evident. The Church has a special interest, as I have said, in seeing that its enormous contribution in the healthcare and educational sectors not be compromised. But it has a deeper concern: a concern for the defence of humanity, for the authentic values of the various cultures and for the entire Christian heritage.

Concretely, the Church should work on four fronts:

— In the first place, its agencies should be more familiar with what is being elaborated nationally as regards population and health *policies*, also through actively intervening with the appropriate authorities of their countries to guarantee that such procedures are not left exclusively to interested groups. Sometimes the highest authorities are unaware of what is being done in their name or in the name of their nation.

— In the second place, there should be greater *dialogue* with the leaders of other Christian communities as well as with the leaders of other great religions, who certainly share our concerns especially with regard to the future lifestyles of the younger generations.

— The Church has a leadership role and a responsibility to *enlighten society*, to draw attention through all the means at our disposal to what is at stake in these issues, so that politicians and other leaders are not tempted to overlook the deeper questions concerning the future of humanity which are at stake in the period of preparation for the Cairo Conference.

— Finally, the Church must use these coming months to develop a more intense effort of *prayer and witness*, especially of married couples and families themselves. Perhaps the international community surrenders too easily to compromise positions because it has lost heart and confidence. The Church, with the strengths that are its own, must be in the forefront in renewing confidence in the family and in showing that, with the help of the Almighty, families in all parts of the world are willing and able to face the challenges that are posed to them.

REMARKS OF
HIS EXCELLENCY BISHOP ELIO SGRECCIA,
SECRETARY OF THE PONTIFICAL COUNCIL FOR THE FAMILY,
ON A REPORT OF THE PONTIFICAL ACADEMY OF SCIENCES
VATICAN, 19 JUNE 1994

The study of populations, their quantitative dynamics and the rates of growth or decline according to age bracket, of their relationship with the earth's resources, of the phenomena of birth, mortality, migration, etc., form the domain of a young discipline: demography.

In recent decades, due especially to world conferences on the topic of population considered in relation to the earth's resources, this discipline has acquired vast public, political and moral interest.

In view of the forthcoming Cairo Conference to be held in September, already preceded by a series of regional conferences and more recently, by the final session of the Preparatory Committee that worked on drawing up a draft of the Final Document to be submitted to the national representatives of States, different opinions on the problem and international policies confronted each other.

The Holy See, which will attend the Conference as an official member, has always taken part in these meetings and submitted its proposal within the framework of respect for scientific results and of pronounced moral concern. The topic is loaded with human issues, because it involves the procreative responsibility of parents, respect for life, for the family and for marriage, the family's autonomy with regard to State authority and the eventual ideological and economic positions of the political power and of the economically stronger nations over those developing.

In this light, the Holy See has mobilized its institutions, each in the sector of its own competence, to help clarify this problem which appears complex in itself. The press has referred to the Holy Father's *Statements before the Angelus*, his personal *Letter* to all Heads of State and in his *Message* to the Secretary General of the Conference, the Director General of the United Nations Population Fund, Dr. Nafis Sadik.

The Pontifical Council for the Family has recently published a document as an *Instrumentum laboris* entitled: *"Ethical and Pastoral Dimensions of Population Trends,"* in which among other things, the teaching of former Pontiffs on this subject is summarized and dealt with from the ethical and pastoral point of view that prevails in the Church.

Academy of Sciences not a department of the Holy See

Among these, there would have to be a contribution from the Pontifical Academy of Sciences. Already in 1991, this Academy dedicated one of its study weeks to the theme "Population and Resources," with the participation of the members and other experts. Publication of the *Acts* of this study week is still awaited, but in the last few days a *Report* edited by some members and consultors of the Academy itself was published. This document is not a summary of the work presented, but an illustration of the salient data and problems, accompanied by some considerations by the editors.

It was especially this latest publication, consisting of a few pages of text meant for the general public, that sparked off polemics, since the press interpreted certain expressions as indicating a position contrary to the Holy Father's appeals and his firm stands. It was written that the Holy See had changed its thinking, recommending indiscriminate birth control. It was wrongly claimed that there were tensions and polemics among its own institutions.

It should be immediately pointed out that the Pontifical Academy of Sciences is not a department of the Holy See and thus does not share in the Church's pastoral responsibilities. It is a prestigious institution sponsored by the Holy See and founded by Pius XI, but it is autonomous; it even has some non-Catholic members and its institutional aim is "to seek the truth in the area of the various sciences" (*Report*, Preface), providing the Pope and the dicasteries of the Holy See with certain and up-to-date knowledge.

The above-mentioned statement by the Pontifical Academy was intended, especially in the reports which will appear in the *Acts*, as a contribution to the issue based on scientific data.

In fact, demography is based on statistically verified data and is examined according to this discipline's specific method; with this data it then works out what seems to be the most consistent interpretation.

As can be seen from the preface to the *Report*, it was not intended by the compilers to interfere in the development of the Church's ethical and pastoral position, but to offer "a contribution free from technicalities (...) for those who have pastoral roles at various levels of responsibility."

Providing and interpreting statistical data with regard to the population is a demographic task and comes within the scope of the Pontifical Academy of Sciences. Nevertheless, while the data is generally undebatable, the interpretations can vary widely. This is clearly stated in the Academy of Sciences' *Report* itself: it is regrettable that the daily press, in referring to the document, did not grasp this clarification.

On pages 13 and 14 of the *Report*, after an explanation of current world demographic trends, two foreseeable hypotheses are discussed: one of high growth, almost 11 billion for the year 2025, an another of average growth, 8.5 billion for 2025.

It should be noted that the difference between the hypotheses for high growth and that for average growth is 2.5 billion in about 30 years. This means that even among experts, no certain or absolute predictions are made.

Number of children cannot be imposed

Further examples of hypotheses that subsequently differ when the facts are verified can be cited from other documents. Thus, for example, the document of the Pontifical Council for the Family points out that "considered by observers as reliable, the census of November 1991 in Nigeria, the most populated country in Africa, registered 88.5 million inhabitants. The previous official estimate indicated 122.5 million inhabitants, that is, an overestimation of 34 million people!" (*Ethical and Pastoral Dimensions of Population Trends*, n. 13, footnote n. 8).

The reference to the average of 2.3 children, as indicated in the Academy of Sciences' *Report*, pages 13 and 15, should be read and judged in this perspective. It states: "...it is therefore unthinkable — without present knowledge — that we could indefinitely sustain a fertility rate that would appreciably diverge from the average of two children per couple; in other words, from what is necessary to guarantee generational replacement, taking into account responsibility for future generations."

This percentage of 2.3 children is a scientifically valid fact, as an average general statistic to replace the deaths of the two parents plus some deaths in youth.

But obviously this is not the case if applied to individual families, because the overall average should include unmarried people who also die and must be replaced by births, to say nothing of ethical considerations. This is why nobody can impose a fixed number of children on a family.

Furthermore, this percentage would not be valid were it applied to a single nation or a single continent such as Africa, for example, where the high infant mortality rate, infectious diseases and now AIDS account for an increasingly high number of deaths.

It is known that the average birth rate for Europe, and for Italy in particular, is well under 2.3, and should therefore lead to opposite conclusions if we do not wish to suffer "irreparable consequences."

These irreparable consequences to which the text refers thus have a general significance and can have it in opposite directions. Furthermore, if there is one thing on which all demographers agree it is that, as regards the growth and decline of populations, no safe forecasts can be made for the future other than in the short term. Again on the subject of predictions for the future, two further factors should be considered. The first is that when a population enters a process of better healthcare conditions that bring down infant mortality and many other causes of death, there is a temporary growth rate caused precisely by this factor and not exclusively by the increase in births; once a better healthcare standard is reached, the growth rate tends to fall off.

In general, when a population enters a phase of high economic development, the birthrate tends to drop by itself, without planned interventions; indeed, it sometimes risks falling below the replacement level, as has happened particularly in European countries and is also happening in some countries on the other continents.

Then there is the legitimate hope that economic and nutritional factors may also improve: the same document of the Pontifical Academy of Sciences also refers to these factors, on pp. 35-38 and 43-44.

Hence we cannot understand how this data, especially the mention of the replacement percentage between births and deaths, can have been interpreted by the press to imply a change of attitude by the Holy See with regard to birth rate problems. This information does not say as much; it is general technical information from which no indication of a moral norm for individual couples can be inferred.

Responsible parenthood must respect divine law

Nevertheless, the Church's concern at the moment has nothing to do with explanatory hypotheses, nor with discussing the need to encourage a sense of procreative responsibility. Procreation is an act of true conjugal responsibility and on this point, long before the *Report* issued by the Academy of Sciences, precise reminders were made to the extent that the

Catholic Church's position is also internationally known as one based on the principle of responsible procreation: "Free to choose the number of children they desire, the couple must be equally free to use natural methods for the responsible regulation of their fertility, for serious reasons and in conformity with the teaching of the Church" (*Ethical and Pastoral Dimensions of Population Trends*, n. 76).

As regards this teaching, one need only recall what John Paul II said to the participants in the study week promoted by the Pontifical Academy of Sciences, on "the relationship between world population and natural resources" in November 1991: after having mentioned that "the Church, as 'an expert in humanity,' upholds the principle of responsible parenthood," the Pope explained that "population growth has to be faced" not only be economic means which have a profound effect on social institutions but also "by the exercise of a responsible parenthood which respects the divine law" (*L'Osservatore Romano*, English edition, n. 48, 2 December 1991, p. 6).

The specifically ethical point today is to be aware of who must exercise this responsibility and of what the duty of the State or the role of healthcare policies should be. On this point, the Church claims the autonomy of parents' ethically informed conscience. The State, as Paul VI already declared, can give information about "suitable measures," without imposing them, "provided that these be in conformity with the moral law and that they respect the rightful freedom of married couples. Where the inalienable right to marriage and procreation is lacking, human dignity has ceased to exist" (Encyclical *Populorum progressio*, n. 37).

Even less can certain prevailing economic forces and international organizations exercise directly or indirectly, openly or dishonestly, financial influence or pressures on individual families to limit the number of children.

Problems today concern this boundary line, and the duties of clarity and of civil and Christian consistency are essential.

The ethical problem is even more acute when one thinks of the means suggested for birth control, means that are incompatible not only with Catholic morality but with respect for the dignity of the human person, human rights, healthcare and the dignity of woman.

To state that the Church may have changed her doctrinal position on the basis of mere assertions in the Academy of Sciences' *Report* is the result of a superficial reading or perhaps represents an effort by some commentators to weaken the Holy See's position on the international scene by means of presumptuous and misleading information.

BRIEFING BY
DR. JOAQUÍN NAVARRO-VALLS
DIRECTOR OF THE HOLY SEE PRESS OFFICE
ON THE DRAFT PROGRAM OF THE
INTERNATIONAL CONFERENCE ON POPULATION AND DEVELOPMENT
VATICAN, 8 AUGUST 1994

The Holy Father paid special attention to the demographic, sociological and social analyses of the data on demographic tendencies. He has made his own substantial contribution — and will continue to do so — taking adequate initiatives. The Holy See has participated in all the regional preparatory meetings of the Cairo Conference. The Holy See is interested in a *consensus* on the well-being and progress of the human family. It is not interested in — and considers unacceptable — a sectorial or ideological consideration dominated by demographic strategy that does not take into consideration the basic questions concerning the family or the moral and material development of society, such as the dignity of women or the rights of parents as well as children. Moreover, we cannot allow the rights of the unborn to be ignored completely, as if these rights did not even exist. We are interested in a *consensus* on the true well-being of men and women and not in a *consensus* on words or even less on slogans. The Holy Father is well aware that this question concerns the future of humanity.

— In devising measures and practically oriented initiatives to favor human development, the Holy See "seeks to focus attention on certain *basic truths*: that each and every person — regardless of age, sex, religion, or national background — has a dignity and worth that is unconditional and inalienable; that human life itself from conception to natural death is sacred; that human rights are innate and transcend any constitutional order; and that the fundamental unity of the human race demands that everyone be committed to building a community which is free from injustice and which strives to promote and protect the common good" (John Paul II, *Message to the Secretary General of the International Conference on Population and Development*, 18 March 1994, n. 2).

— The Draft Final Document of the Cairo Conference on Population and Development was determined in the Preparatory Meeting of New York which ended on 22 April. It reviewed the previous 83 page document, and the major part of the chapters were revised. There was general agreement on a considerable part of it; 10% of the texts remain in brackets due to a lack of agreement. Certain basic concepts remain in brackets all throughout the document: a clear sign of the lack of consensus demonstrated in the Preparatory Meeting of New York.

— Two chapters concretely present aspects that offend the dignity of the person and these focus mainly on the lack of *consensus*: Ch. 7, "Reproductive Rights, Reproductive Health and Family Planning," and Ch. 8, "Health, Morbidity and Mortality."

Chapter 7. Here you find the kernel of the idea the Cairo Conference is trying to propose. In New York, the great difficulty this chapter presented was already evident. At the root of this difficulty are two concepts: reproductive health and reproductive rights. We find these concepts more than one-hundred times in the entire document. Both come from the working documents of the WHO (World Health Organization) that was, however, not approved formally or definitively by this assembly. These concepts contain positive elements ("the right to have access to adequate health services to eliminate the risks involved during pregnancy and delivery..."). However, among the methods to promote "reproductive health" was cited the term "fertility regulation," which (according to the texts available at the New York meeting) includes abortion. *Thus abortion is considered an essential component of "reproductive health."*

Par. 7.4 proposes access to "reproductive health" services to all individuals of all ages (thus, also for adolescents). And among the services offered it wants to make abortion available.

Obviously, it is not possible to maintain positions that accept abortion as an essential measure of health policies, whether at the national or international level, and even less so, as a part of international development policies.

Some of the references to young people in this chapter have raised a strong doubt among various Delegations to the New York Conference. It was asserted, for example, that services of "reproductive health" for adolescents must "safeguard their right to privacy and confidentiality." These efforts to ensure unlimited rights of adolescents and children to be sexually active and to be assisted by centers administrated by the State without any reference to their parents are characteristic of a good part of the entire Draft Final Document. Naturally, this language has remained in brackets.

One can say that the two key concepts of this chapter — "reproductive health" and "sexual health" — are tremendously ambiguous. Given the lack of clarification, the concept of "sexual health" could be applied, for example, to a whole series of sexual activities that are not reproductive in nature, particularly homosexual relations. Because what is at stake is the affirmation of the rights governments must uphold, this ambiguity is unacceptable for ethical reasons, as well as for the pure need for scientific reliability.

— On abortion: the draft of the document deals with the question of abortion in different ways under three major headings:

1. Abortion as a women's health problem

It is often said that the Cairo Conference speaks of abortion only to express concern for the many women who die as a result of poorly performed abortions, whether legal or illegal. Par. 8.25 deals with the issue, stressing that all efforts should be made to discourage abortion.

But the text then asks governments to review their laws on abortion and to provide medical care to women who decide to terminate their pregnancies.

The European Union proposed an alternative text stressing that "in the circumstances where it is legal ... it should be safe;" (an interesting assertion clearly admitting that the legalization of abortion does not make it safe.

The risks to maternal health will be best resolved by increased investment in the overall standard of health care, not by increased abortion.

2. The right to abortion

But the Draft Final Document goes much further than expressing concern for women's health problems of a right to abortion.

The definition of reproductive health is found in Par. 7.1 and includes the phrase "rights ... to safe, effective, affordable and acceptable means of fertility regulation of their choice." World Health Organization definitions note that the term "fertility regulation" includes both the concepts of family planning and abortion. So, wherever the term *reproductive health* appears in the text it automatically endorses a "right to safe, effective, affordable and acceptable abortion."

The term *affordable* would mean that governments would have to subsidize abortions. In the current text, the "right" is presented in a totally unqualified way, and would thus accept abortion for any reason or at any time in the pregnancy. The only criterion presented for permitting abortion is the *choice* of the woman. Naturally, this sounds very close to *abortion on demand*.

Par. 7.4 urges governments to provide reproductive health services by the year 2015, "to all individuals *of all ages*" and explicitly lists *pregnancy termination* among the services to be provided. This text, speaking of "all ages," would extend the "right to abortion" also to adolescents.

In fact Par. 7.43 urges countries "to remove legal, regulatory and social barriers to sexual and reproductive health information and care for *adolescents* ... and such services for adolescents must safeguard their right to privacy and confidentiality. *This would eliminate the rights of parents and family to be informed about teenage abortions.*

3. Abortion and family planning

Par. 7.22 which stresses that "abortion should in no case be promoted as a means of family planning" — taking up the consensus language of the 1984 Mexico City Population Conference and the texts of the legislation of many countries — remains bracketed due to the consistent opposition of some Western nations.

Many governments — among these, for example, the U.S. administration — have said that they do not want to accept abortion as a method of "family planning." Thus, they have insisted that the foregoing formulations remain in brackets.

In recent interviews Mrs. Sadik has made the statement on abortion: "We are not proposing its legalization." Taking into consideration all that has been said up until now, our reading of the Document leads us to believe otherwise.

Briefing by
Dr. Joaquín Navarro-Valls
Director of the Holy See Press Office
in view of the International Conference in Cairo
on Population and Development
Vatican, 31 August 1994

The Holy See Delegation to the International Conference on Population and Development is going to Cairo with the idea of making a contribution to obtaining a document of consensus. Never, on the part of the Holy See, was the idea ever considered not to participate in the work of the International Conference on Population and Development. It is, in fact, opportune to recall that the presence of the Holy See has been assiduous and constant in all the regional preparatory meetings. The Holy See thus feels strongly involved in the formulation of the principles and the working out of solutions in this international meeting.

The Holy See is well aware of the complexity of problems connected with the material and moral development of mankind. But, at the same time, it knows it is acting in a field which does not regard joint, ideological, geopolitical or sectorial interests. The themes which will be discussed in Cairo touch on, in a particular way, the respect for and dignity of each human person.

This awareness of the Holy See also comes from the concrete situations in which the Church operates — through, for example, her 21,757 worldwide health institutions, 1,800 of which are found in Africa alone. It is in these receiving points, in the service of women, maternity, childhood, and whoever is found to be suffering, that the Church feels and proclaims day by day the inviolable right to dignity given to each member of the human family.

It is also on these bases that the Holy See feels it can and must state — in Cairo as in every other circumstance — that the multiple solutions which can be applied to solving the complex *human* problems, cannot go against, nor violate, nor much less humiliate, the rights and dignity of the *human person*.

Together with the complexity of the problems, the Holy See is not unaware of the positive aspects contained in the draft document of the Cairo Conference. But at the same time the Holy See cannot be silent on the serious lacks, the imprecisions and the ambiguities of language, the unproven statements and the very *social philosophy* which is in the draft document which will soon be discussed at the Cairo Conference.

Ambiguity of language

What cannot be passed over in silence is the ambiguous language which runs through a great part of the draft document and is found especially in the points which constitute the fundamental nucleus of the ideas which the Conference is proposing to promote. Once again, today, on the vigil of the opening of the work, reference must be made to several concrete examples.

The first regards the concepts of "reproductive health" and of "sexual health," two terms which appear more than one-hundred times in the draft document, and are quoted exclusively from working documents of the World Health Organization, without having ever been approved by WHO itself or by other international assemblies. It can again be observed how too often, in the draft document, one makes reference to "rights" never sanctioned nor recognized by the international community.

Emblematic of this is the case of Para. 7.1 on "reproductive health" which, while containing some elements that can be appreciated, also contains reference to "the right to have access to methods of fertility regulation which are safe, efficacious, accessible and acceptable." It is, in effect, abortion on demand, since in the definition of the World Health Organization — according to texts presented in the third preparatory conference of New York — the term "fertility regulation" includes abortion. Abortion is thus considered as an essential component of "reproductive health." In the repeated ambiguity of this language is excluded every limitation to abortion which is proposed as a possibility in whatever moment of the pregnancy and for whatever reason.

One must recall in this regard that there is no form whatsoever of international consensus on a generic "right to abortion." Such a "right" could, precisely, be deduced from several of the statements contained — sometimes in an implicit way, other times explicitly — of the draft document.

Mr. Al Gore, vice-president of the U.S.A., and member of the American Delegation, recently stated that "the United States have never sought, nor do they seek nor will they seek to establish an international right to abortion." The draft document, which has the U.S. administration as its principal sponsor, contradicts, in reality, Mr. Gore's statement.

The imprecision, the approximation of terms, is not just a matter of lexicon terminology. Treating as it does of rights to be inserted into the norms and laws of single countries, it seems necessary to study more deeply and completely to give a precise and definite meaning to concepts which concern human behavior which have deep cultural and ethical implications.

Among the language ambiguities must be singled out the statement — in Para. 7 — on "reproductive rights" as a prerogative of "couples and *individuals.*" What meaning can such a concept have? It would be justified to think that such a biological absurdity can legitimize the will of man to "subdue" the woman to satisfy his "reproductive right."

Also in this chapter one finds the extremely loose and selective use of statistics, both in the order of population growth as well as moral conduct and to the not-reached objectives of "family planning" programs. The technical role of the UN's Division for Population would thus seem changed around. The entire scientific apparatus of the means of statistical surveys, judging from references in the draft document, appears totally inadequate and shows that it needs a complete revision.

The family

If ambiguity of language runs all through the draft document, it is more explicitly so — in the negative — regarding the consideration of the family.

This, I must emphasize, is one of the great concerns of the Holy Father. In fact, in the document there exists the tendency to identify, and then to assimilate the term with expressions that humiliate not only its nature but also its *social and biological function.* Next to the family, one finds the reference to phrases such as "in its every form." It is not a casual fact that consequently an institution so natural, fundamental and universal as marriage, is practically absent in the document text. Family, procreation and marriage are treated in the draft with an equal diffidence, as if it were dealing with three independent variables.

Adolescents

In referring to adolescents and youth, the draft document shows the most glaring limitations, above all, on sexuality. The vision indicated is that of an exaggerated individualism, which does not leave any room for a dimension of interpersonal relationships. The sole preoccupation of the document seems to be to affirm the right of everyone to live the sexuality according to their own lifestyle.

It is on this level that the draft proposes consequently the affirmation of practically unlimited sexual rights not only to adolescents, but also to children. Besides all public institutions or assistance centers, there is not any reference in this section to the role of parents. There is, instead, the desire to cancel out all responsibility on the part of mothers and fathers, asking governments explicitly to "remove every social barrier to sexual health and to information and medical assistance to adolescents." The medical assistance that the draft asks of governments includes abortions. And it affirms that these "health services" "must" safeguard the right of adolescents to privacy, to confidentiality and to respect" (Para. 7.43). This formulation would take away the rights of parents and the family to be informed not only of the access to contraception but also to abortion by adolescents.

***

It deals with concepts absolutely unreconcilable not only with the Christian ethic, but also with the most elementary rights of the person as they are expressed in the culture and the social formulations of millions of people throughout the world.

They are obscure points that prevent the whole document from offering a view equal to a humanity called to face the road toward the future.

Also, in the title of the Conference there is a reference to the future, where it speaks — for the first time — of Development besides Population. Yet one fact betrays the depth of such a projection: in the 113 pages of the draft on development there are only seven actually dedicated to it.

We should remember that population policies are only a part of development policy. In fact, they include the whole gamut of areas: nutrition, medicine, agriculture, education, demographics, economics, and politics, together with more profound aspects, moral and spiritual dimensions. True development will not be respected if only demographic data is considered as the obstacle to development.

We must also remember that the more developed countries have balanced the relationship between population and resource through the use of all these elements, without recourse to any brutal formulas that in this draft are being paradoxically proposed for countries less developed.

These are some of the concepts that risk transforming the Cairo Conference into a session called to sanction a *lifestyle* current in minority circles of certain opulent societies and which propose - or impose - as a universal model and as — *social philosophies* to all humanity of today.

More unacceptable still is the pretense of presenting this operation of *social engineering* under the category of *human rights*.

In reality what strongly emerges from the whole draft is exactly this fact: the will to impose these points of view, as the dominant ideas of all political societies. And this without being respectful to the emerging, less developed cultures of our society.

This is basically the theme of the Cairo Conference.

Statement by
His Excellency Archbishop Renato R. Martino
Apostolic Nuncio, Permanent Observer of the Holy See to the United Nations and Head of the Delegation of the Holy See to the International Conference on Population and Development
Cairo, 7 September 1994

Mr. President,

The Delegation of the Holy See wishes in the first place to express its particular appreciation to the President, the Government and the People of Egypt for the welcome that we have all received in this city of Cairo and for the excellent arrangements that have been made for the Conference.

Our meeting in these days represents the culmination of a period of intense reflection and activity on the part of the international community on a number of important challenges which all of us must face in the coming years. Pope John Paul II has stressed rightly that these challenges touch on crucial issues. They concern the future of humanity.

The period of preparation, which has lasted a number of years, has shown that population policy, if it is to respond to these challenges, cannot simply be about numbers. It must deal with the conditions in which all the people of the world are called to live. It is about the solidarity that must be fostered among peoples so that humanity can become more and more a true family.

The Holy See has taken an active and constructive part in the preparatory period, fully respecting the procedures of the Conference, entering into dialogue with the various participants at all levels, while remaining true to its own particular position and status in the international community.

1. This Conference deals not only with global statistics or the complex question of population growth rates, which have in recent years been noticeably decreasing. The very title "International Conference on Population and Development" shows that our task involves the search for a better management and a more equitable distribution of the goods of this earth, which in God's design were destined to be shared as the common heritage of all. *Population policy* must always be seen as part of a more comprehensive *development policy*. Both are, in fact, about the same reality, namely, the centrality of the human person and the responsibility of all to

guarantee that every individual person can live in a manner which respects his or her dignity. The great biblical tradition describes the human person as being created as nothing less than "in the image of God." The purpose of this Conference should be to ensure that every person on this earth can live in conditions which truly reflect that dignity. While many development issues are treated in the various chapters of the Draft Final Document, the Holy See finds that the Chapter dealing explicitly with the relationship between population and development is disproportionately small with respect to the document as a whole.

Population growth or decline affects the lives of people who strive to live in dignity and security, but who are thwarted by fragile political and socio-economic structures. Development strategies require equity in the distribution of resources and technology within the international community and access to international markets. The servicing of the external debt of the poorest nations strangles their social development. Measures are needed to make available, on priority terms, the technology required for improvements in agriculture, clean water supply, food security and distribution, and healthcare, especially to overcome those infectious diseases which greatly contribute to maternal and child mortality.

2   This Conference addresses in a special way the position of *women* within population and development policies. Already ten years ago, at the Mexico City Population Conference, the Holy See Delegation stressed that population policies must address as a priority the advancement of women's level of education and health care, especially primary healthcare. In both developed and developing countries, the Catholic Church has been and is deeply involved in providing a wide range of education and health care services, with special attention to women and children, especially the poor.

Throughout the world, also in countries with only a minority Catholic population, tens of thousands of hospitals, clinics, dispensaries, as well as other facilities for mother and child health and the care of the elderly, are run by the Catholic Church or funded by Catholic donors. Such healthcare facilities, along with Church structures for formal and informal education, contribute to the advancement of women in such a way as to foster their active participation in the development process and to remove the often excessive burdens which women in developing countries must bear. Much remains to be done in this area and the Holy See, as well as members of the Church in various parts of the world, remain ready to cooperate in achieving this goal.

3.   Population policies have a particular place in development policies, as they involve at the same time *global* questions and the *most intimate* area

of the lives of men and women: the responsible use of their sexuality and their mutual responsibility concerning human reproduction.

Responsible decisions concerning the number of children and the spacing of births belong to parents, who must be free from all coercion and pressure from public authorities, which should however ensure that citizens have accurate information on the various demographic factors involved. The Holy See, following on its longstanding and consistent position, welcomes the affirmations of this Conference which stress that coercion be excluded from all aspects of population policy. It is to be hoped that these affirmations will be scrupulously put into practice by all the nations participating here and that nations and the international community will be vigilant in eliminating abuses associated with family planning programmes.

In the past, population policies were structured in such a way that they often tended towards coercion and pressure, especially through the setting of targets for providers. Women were the primary victims. Subtle forms of coercion and pressure have also resulted from a misrepresentation of demographic data which induces fear and anxiety about the future.

This Conference must mark the beginning of a new and deeper reflection on population policy. Respect for life and for the dignity of the human person must be the ultimate guiding norm for such a policy. This policy should foster the family based on marriage and must sustain parents, fathers and mothers, in their mutual and responsible decisions with regard to the procreation and education of children. The Draft Final Document, in fact, draws attention to the need to foster family stability, for the positive effects that such stability brings to society.

The Holy See does not support a notion of procreation at all costs. Its respect for the sacred significance of the transmission of human life makes it stress, even more than others, the *responsibility* which must characterize the decisions of parents as to whether, at a given moment, they should have or not have a child. This responsibility concerns not only their own personal fulfillment, but their responsibilities to God, to the new life that they will mutually bring into the world, to their existing children and their family, as well as to society, in a correct hierarchy of moral values.

Lack of responsibility in the area of human sexuality cannot but be a cause of concern to everybody. It is women and children who are most often the principal victims of such irresponsible behaviour. Much remains to be done to educate and form men to more responsible behaviour and to their own sharing in responsibilities concerning the procreation and the education of children. Lack of responsibility in sexual behaviour is also due to the fostering today of attitudes of sexual permissiveness, which focus above all on personal pleasure and gratification.

One of the great concerns of the Holy See about the Draft Final Document is that, while in identifying behaviour which the text itself considers "high-risk" or undesirable, all too often it limits itself primarily to suggestions as to how the "risks" can be reduced or contained, shying away from proposing a change in such behaviour at its roots. No one can deny that society must be aware of the health consequences of irresponsible or immature behaviour, but one has to ask: what will be the long-term consequences of the abdication by society of its responsibility to challenge and to attempt to change such undesirable behavioural patterns? Even more so, what happens when society tacitly accepts such irresponsible behaviour as normal?

The Church's position on responsible parenthood is well known, although at times it is misunderstood. Some here might consider it too demanding for today's man and woman. But no way of fostering the deepest respect for human life and the processes of its transmission is going to be an easy one. Responsibility brings burdens. Responsibility demands discipline and self-restraint.

4.   Human life is so important that its transmission has been entrusted not simply to a series of mechanical biological processes. New life, from its very beginnings, has the right to be generously welcomed into the loving and stable communion of the family, the natural and fundamental group unit of society. The family belongs to the heritage of humanity, precisely because it is the place where the stable relationship of a man and a woman is transformed into a caring institution for the responsible transmission and nurturing of new life.

The problems which families have to face are well known. It is commonplace, likewise, to attribute many of the problems concerning social disintegration to a breakdown in family structures. Few, however, have the courage to develop creative programmes to strengthen the family and to concretely assist parents in the exercise of their rights and in carrying out their duties and responsibilities. Society must give primary recognition to the extraordinary contribution which parents render to society's own good, and translate that recognition into effective support on the level of cultural, fiscal and social policy. The Holy See strongly rejects any attempts to weaken the family or to propose a radical redefining of its structure, such as assigning the status of family to other lifestyle forms.

5.   The transmission of life begins with the intimate relationship of

parents and is entrusted to parental love. The responsible transmission of life and the loving care of parents belong together. The Holy See cannot endorse methods of family planning which fundamentally separate those two essential dimensions of human sexuality, and will express its position on such methods through an appropriate reservation. The Holy See is also concerned — and must express this concern — about some specific family planning methods, which while not explicitly treated in the Conference texts, are obviously included under the general term "family planning services." This concern touches especially programmes of sterilization, a family planning method which is generally irreversible, and thus excludes a change in decisions about child bearing, and is the family planning method most open to abuse on human rights grounds, especially when promoted among the poor or the illiterate.

The natural methods of family planning receive only passing mention in the Draft Plan of Action, despite the fact that a substantial number of families wish to use these methods, not only for moral reasons, but also because they are scientifically effective, inexpensive, without the side effects often associated with hormonal and technical methods, and because they foster, in a unique manner, the cooperation and mutual respect of both partners, especially through requiring a more responsible attitude on the part of men.

6. The Holy See is particularly concerned about the manner in which the question of abortion has been treated in the preparation of this Conference.

International consensus language urges governments to "take appropriate steps to help women to avoid abortion, which in no case should be promoted as a method of family planning, and whenever possible, to provide for the humane treatment and counseling of women who have had recourse to abortion." The Holy See is hopeful that the Conference will reaffirm this principle.

While there are many texts in the document which would clearly infer a desire of nations to reduce the number of abortions and to remove the conditions which lead women to have recourse to abortions, there have been efforts by some to foster the concept of "a right to abortion" and to establish abortion as an essential component of population policy. Texts under negotiations ask that countries reexamine their legislation on abortion and countries are urged, in similar texts, to provide in the coming years, services of "pregnancy termination" for persons "of all ages." Should current bracketed texts be approved, they would endorse "pregnancy termination." without setting any limits, any criteria or any restrictions on such practices, as integral parts of reproductive health services. Through the possible approval of other bracketed language, addressed to the entire international community, such unrestricted access to abortion might be elevated to the level of a right.

None of these new tendencies emerged during the regional preparatory Conferences. The concept of a "right to abortion" would be entirely innovative in the international community and would be contrary to the constitutional and legislative positions of many States, as well as being alien to the sensitivities of vast numbers of persons, believers and unbelievers alike.

7. The Holy See supports efforts which may emerge from this Conference to provide for the reduction of maternal and infant mortality and to ensure improvements in the conditions of women's health and child survival. These are important in themselves. The dignity of individual people is at stake. The existence of high levels of maternal and infant mortality in any part of the world is a wound in the image of a modern world which prides itself on its high level of material, scientific and technical progress.

At the same time, there is need to strengthen counseling services to support women faced with difficulties regarding their pregnancies and to provide humane treatment following the negative consequences of induced abortions.

On many occasions in the preparatory work of this Conference, the Holy See has stressed that it will support, and contribute to the putting into practice of, a concept of "reproductive health" which is understood as a holistic vision of health concerns in the area of reproduction, that is, a vision which embraces men and women in the entirety of the personality, mind and body, and which is oriented towards a mature and responsible exercise of their sexuality.

While such a concept must look to the good of each and every individual, it cannot overlook that fact that human sexuality is of its very nature *interpersonal*. Reproductive health must take into account the formation of people in those areas which will lead them to be responsible and respectful in their behaviour. The current text is largely individualistic in its reflection and as such tends to be lacking in its appreciation of the very nature of human sexuality.

8. In today's world, in which many problems exist concerning irresponsible behaviour in the area of sexuality, and in which women in particular are exploited, the education of adolescents towards mature and

responsible sexual behaviour is essential. The principal responsibility in this area belongs to parents, whose rights are recognized in numerous international instruments. All efforts must be made to guarantee parents the full exercise of these rights and to assist them to carry out their responsibilities and duties. The task of rearing children belongs in the first place to parents, not to the State. The Holy See hopes that texts under negotiation will clearly endorse the rights, duties and responsibilities of parents in this area, will draw attention to the negative aspects of premature sexual activity for young people and will endeavour to foster mature behaviour on the part of adolescents.

Mr. President,

At the beginning of my intervention, I noted that the Holy See had followed the preparatory period for this Cairo Conference with great attention and in respectful dialogue with all the participants. I can assure you, that when the good of the people of this world is at stake, the Holy See and the institutions of the Catholic Church throughout the world will continue, in collaboration with the nations of the international community, to make their specific contribution, and indeed to intensify their traditional concrete service of basic education and care, in complete respect for human life and for the development of peoples in solidarity.

Statement by
His Excellency Archbishop Renato R. Martino
Apostolic Nuncio, Permanent Observer of the Holy See
to the United Nations
and Head of the Delegation of the Holy See
at the Concluding Session of the
International Conference on Population and Development
Cairo, 13 September 1994

Mr. President,

My Delegation thanks you for your guidance of our work and for the welcome we have received.

Our Conference, attended by persons of various traditions and cultures, with widely differing viewpoints, has carried out its work in a peaceful and respectful atmosphere. The Holy See welcomes the progress that has been made in these days, but also finds that some of its expectations have not been met. I am sure that most Delegations share similar sentiments.

The Holy See knows well that some of its positions are not accepted by others present here. But there are many, believers and non-believers alike, in every country of the world, who share the views we have expressed. The Holy See appreciates the manner in which the Delegations have listened to and taken into consideration views which they may not always have agreed with. But the Conference would be poorer if these views had not been heard. An International Conference which does not welcome voices that are different would be much less a consensus conference.

As you well know, the Holy See could not find its way to join the consensus of the Conferences of Bucharest and Mexico City, because of some fundamental reservations. Yet, now in Cairo for the first time, development has been linked to population as a major issue of reflection. The current Programme of Action, however, opens out some new paths concerning the future of population policy. The document is notable for its affirmations against all forms of coercion in population policies. Clearly elaborated Principles, based on the most important documents of the international community, clarify and enlighten the later chapters. The document recognizes the protection and support required by the basic unit of society, the family founded on marriage. Women's advancement and the improvement of women's status, through education and better healthcare services, are stressed. Migration, the all too often forgotten sector of population policy, has been examined. The Conference has given clear indications of the concern that exists in the entire international community about threats to women's health. There is appeal to greater respect for religious and cultural beliefs of persons and communities.

But there are other aspects of the Final Document which the Holy See cannot support. Together with so many people around the world, the Holy See affirms that human life begins at the moment of conception. That life must be defended and protected. The Holy See can therefore never condone abortion or policies which favour abortion. The Final Document, as opposed to the earlier documents of the Bucharest and Mexico City Conferences, recognizes abortion as a dimension of population policy and, indeed of primary health care, even though it does stress that abortion should not be promoted as means of family planning and urges nations to find alternatives to abortion. The Preamble implies that the Document does not contain the affirmation of a new internationally recognized right to abortion.

My Delegation has now been able to examine and evaluate the Document in its entirety. Mr President, on this occasion the Holy See wishes, in some way, to join the consensus, even if in an incomplete, or partial manner.

First, my Delegation joins the consensus on the *Principles*, as a sign of our solidarity with the basic inspiration which has guided, and will continue to guide our work. Similarly, it joins the consensus on Chapter V on the *Family*, the basic unit of society.

The Holy See joins the consensus on chapter III on *Population, Sustained Economic Growth and Sustainable Development*, although it would have preferred to see a more detailed treatment of this subject. It joins the consensus on Chapter IV, *Gender Equality, Equity and Empowerment of Women* and Chapters IX and X on *Migration Issues*.

The Holy See, because of its specific nature, does not find it appropriate to join the consensus on the operative chapters of the Document (Chapters 12-16).

Since the approval of Chapters 7 and 8 in the Committee of the Whole, it has been possible to evaluate the significance of these Chapters within the entire Document, and also within healthcare policy in general. The intense negotiations of these days have resulted in the presentation of a text which all recognize as improved, but about which the Holy See still has grave concerns. At the moment of their adoption by consensus at the Main Committee my Delegation already noted its concerns about the question of abortion. The Chapters also contain references which could be seen as accepting extra-marital sexual activity, especially among adolescents. They would seem to assert that abortion services belong within primary health care as a method of choice.

Despite the many positive aspects of Chapters 7 and 8, the text that has been presented to us has many broader implications, which has led the Holy See to decide not to join the consensus on these Chapters. This does not exclude the fact that the Holy See supports a concept of reproductive health, as a holistic concept for the promotion of the health of men and women, and will continue to work, along with others, towards the evolution of a more precise definition of this and other terms.

The intention, therefore, of my Delegation is to associate itself with this consensus in a partial manner compatible with its own position, without hindering the consensus among other nations, but also without prejudicing its own position with regard to some sections.

Nothing that the Holy See has done in this consensus process should be understood or interpreted as an endorsement of concepts it cannot support for moral reasons. Especially nothing is to be understood to imply that the Holy See endorses abortion or has in any way changed its moral position concerning abortion or on contraceptives or sterilization nor on the use of condoms in HIV/AIDS prevention programmes.

* * *

I would ask, Mr. President, that the text of this Statement and the annexed Note formally indicating our reservations be included in the Report of the Conference.

RESERVATIONS OF THE HOLY SEE TO THE PROGRAMME OF ACTION ADOPTED AT THE INTERNATIONAL CONFERENCE ON POPULATION AND DEVELOPMENT CAIRO, 13 SEPTEMBER 1994

The Holy See, in conformity with its nature and its particular mission, by joining in the consensus to parts of the Final Document of the International Conference on Population and Development, Cairo, 5-13 September 1994, wishes to express its understanding of the Programme of Action of the Conference.

1. Regarding the terms "sexual health" and "sexual rights," and "reproductive health" and "reproductive rights," the Holy See considers these terms as applying to a holistic concept of health, which embrace, each in their own way, the person in the entirety of his or her personality, mind and body, and which foster the achievement of personal maturity in sexuality and in the mutual love and decision-making that characterize the conjugal relationship in accordance with moral norms. The Holy See does not consider abortion or access to abortion as a dimension of these terms.

2. With reference to the terms "contraception," "family planning," "sexual and reproductive health," "sexual and reproductive rights," and "women's ability to control their own fertility," "widest range of family planning services" and any other terms regarding family planning services and regulation of fertility concepts in the document, the Holy See's joining the consensus should in no way be interpreted as constituting a change in its well-known position concerning those family planning methods which the Catholic Church considers morally unacceptable or on family planning services which do not respect the liberty of the spouses, human dignity and the human rights of those concerned.

3. With reference to all international agreements, the Holy See reserves its position in this regard, in particular on any existing agreements mentioned in this Plan of Action, consistent with its acceptance or non-acceptance of them.

4. With reference to the term "couples and individuals," the Holy See reserves its position with the understanding that this term is to mean married couples and the individual man and woman who constitute the couple. The Document, especially in its use of this term, remains marked by an individualistic understanding of sexuality which does not give due attention to the mutual love and decision-making that characterizes the conjugal relationship.

5.   With reference to Chapter V, the Holy See interprets this chapter in the light of Principle 9, that is, in terms of the duty to strengthen the family, the basic unit of society, and in terms of marriage as an equal partnership between husband and wife.

6.   The Holy See places general reservations on Chapters VII, VIII, XI, XII, XIII, XIV, XV and XVI. This reservation is to be interpreted in terms of the Statement made by the Delegation in the plenary meeting of the Conference on 13 September 1994. We request that this general reservation be noted in each of the above-mentioned chapters.

Statement of
His Excellency Archbishop Renato R. Martino
Apostolic Nuncio, Permanent Observer of the Holy See to the United Nations,
before the Plenary Session of the U.N. General Assembly on Item 158: Report on the International Conference on Population and Development
New York, 18 November 1994

Mr. President,

The Delegation of the Holy See has taken note of the *Report on the International Conference on Population and Development*. I am pleased to have this opportunity to address the United Nations General Assembly on this Item, and to comment on the Programme of Action.

It is well-known that Catholic Organizations are involved in a wide array of development activities as well as humanitarian assistance programmes throughout the world. These undertakings focus on education and basic health care, always considering their primary component, the human being and his/her integral development. Therefore, the Holy See is keenly interested in the issues which were addressed by the Conference.

Consistent with its own moral convictions and teachings, the Holy See ultimately associated itself through a partial consensus on selected chapters, and supported specific sections in the Document.

The Holy See notes that the International Conference on Population and Development has affirmed the application of universally recognized human rights standards to all aspects of population programmes. While fundamental human rights represent a common good for all humanity on its path towards peace, it is necessary in this context to note clearly that when one speaks of rights one is actually concomitantly defining duties. It is the international community which is given not only the priority, but also the duty to promote and protect all human rights "in a just and balanced manner." However, as the Programme of Action so clearly states, "the International Conference on Population and Development does not create any new international human rights."

The majority of the principles, as set forth in the Document, make a substantial contribution to the understanding of the entire Programme of Action. The Chapter on Principles expresses, with greater specificity and clarity than any other chapter, the basic inspiration which guided the work of the Conference and must continue to guide its implementation. My Delegation is pleased to find in the chapeau of Chapter 2, and thus as a concept implied throughout the Document, that the implementation of the recommendations contained in the Programme of Action be done in each State "with full respect for the various religious and ethical values and cultural backgrounds of its people, and in conformity with universally recognized international human rights." These points, as well as non-coercion, are central in the implementation of population-related policies.

The first four principles all address aspects of the human being; and this is done prior to referring to the role of the State. My Delegation is pleased to see that the concept of the importance of the human being and its prioritization in all issues related to sustainable development, already enshrined in the Rio Declaration, is carried forward in the Programme of Action.

The Holy See Delegation welcomes the Conference's linkage of population and development as an important focus of consideration, emphasizing the right to development in the Principles when it states: "The right to development is a universal and inalienable right and an integral part of fundamental human rights, and the human person is the central subject of development." The Conference notes the fact that population policies must be considered within the context of overall development. However, the Holy See had hoped for a more comprehensive treatment of the relationship between population and development, with appropriate attention given to specific development strategies in which the developed nations would manifest a stronger commitment and establish some priorities. This would have addressed issues such as the transfer of technology and the results of progress in medicine, alleviation of external debt, and development of new markets for developing nations.

The Holy See wishes to stress its support for that portion of the Document which provides for strengthening the family. Indeed, the family is the basic unit of society and, as such, is entitled to comprehensive protection and support by governments. The family belongs to the sacred heritage of humanity and to the future of the human race. But the family is based on marriage — a permanent, faithful, mutual relationship — between a man and a woman. It involves partnership and mutual respect and is committed to the bearing and rearing of children and the guidance of adolescents. However, the Programme of Action, in many instances, does not adequately take into consideration the concrete application of the rights and responsibilities of parents in the context of the family, and particularly their important continuing responsibilities as regards the guidance of adolescents. It is hoped that in the implementation of the Programme of

Action the responsibility of States to respect parental rights and duties will be closely adhered to.

The ICPD properly recognized that women must be full and equal participants in development. This means that women must also enjoy equal opportunity in education, primary health care, professional career choices and employment opportunities in order for them to meet their basic human needs and to exercise their human rights. It is hoped that a more objective treatment of women's true roles and responsibilities will be taken up in Beijing in 1995.

An important issue in the Programme of Action is that of reproductive healthcare. In expressing concern over the high rates of morbidity and mortality in many countries, the Programme of Action appropriately makes reduction of child and maternal mortality one of its primary objectives. My Delegation continues to be concerned about the health of each and every human being, including his/her reproductive health. The Holy See's great concern for the unacceptable incidence of maternal death in various parts of the world is evidenced in its commitment to maintain a vast network of healthcare facilities and programmes throughout the world run by Catholic Organizations. At the same time, however, the Holy See cannot, does not and will not accept abortion as a component of reproductive healthcare.

Throughout the ICPD process, the Holy See made clear its grave concern regarding the treatment of the issue of abortion in the Programme of Action. The Holy See spoke strongly in favor of the value of every human life, including the life of the unborn child. The deliberate destruction of the unborn is inconsistent with respect for human life and puts in jeopardy all other human rights which have the very right to life as their cornerstone. Any compromise of this most fundamental of all human rights is particularly dangerous as part of a social or demographic policy promoted by States whose duty it is to protect life.

Although the Cairo Programme of Action has reconfirmed that abortion is not to be promoted as a method of family planning, it dangerously hints at condoning the legalization and provision of abortion services within the context of population-related policies. My Delegation would like to see more concerted efforts emerge to give concrete actualization to those sections of the Programme of Action which urge "governments (to) take appropriate steps to help women avoid abortion." No new internationally recognized right to abortion can be implied by the Document since the Preamble, as noted earlier, states that the ICPD does not create any new international human rights.

The Holy See recognizes that sexuality is an important aspect of personal identity. It is not difficult to understand that sexuality finds its proper and deepest expression within a context of reciprocity. The Programme of Action, however, invokes a policy on sexuality that does not give due consideration to that dimension of reciprocity which is the expression of mutual love and decision-making within a stable, conjugal relationship, and instead presents an individualistic and permissive approach to sexual behavior, even for adolescents, which undermines an appropriate understanding of human dignity and the moral responsibility of each person. A permissive attitude toward sexual behavior undermines the family, parenthood and the well-being of the child, and results in a highly destabilizing effect on society as a whole.

While attention was often given to the rights of women and men, there was a notable absence of concern about the rights of children, except in the Principles. My Delegation firmly believes that every child, from the moment of conception, is a person in his or her own right, and thus deserves legal protection and support. At Cairo the Holy See reminded the international community that at the moment in which new human life is created, there are no longer two participants — man and woman — but a third, the child. That is why the expression "safe abortion" is ambiguous: abortion is never safe for one of the persons involved; the child, already conceived, dies. Sadly, since children are the weakest and most vulnerable members of our society, they are easily exploited, marginalized, and even eliminated. If we are truly concerned about our future, then we must invest in our children.

Concerning the movement of peoples, the Holy See supported the Chapters on international and internal migration, but would have preferred a consensus on a more firm commitment toward the reunification of families.

Mr. President,

The Holy See was pleased to take part in the ICPD, to express its position and to make efforts to forge a consensus with other nations. For this reason, some areas of disagreement remain, not only for the Holy See but for a substantial number of States whose large number of reservations to the Document are a matter of record. The Holy See, while offering partial consensus, enumerated its difficulties with various wordings in the ICPD Programme of Action in its final Statement at the Conference and in the Holy See's reservations to this Document.

The Holy See hopes that all parties charged with the responsibility for the implementation of the ICPD Programme of Action keep at the forefront of their endeavours the respect for the dignity of all persons. Backed by such inspiration, one can be confident in achieving a full solidarity for the integral development of all human beings.

Thank you, Mr. President.

Interview given to Vatican Radio by His Excellency Archbishop Renato R. Martino Apostolic Nuncio, Permanent Observer of the Holy See to the United Nations Head of the Delegation of the Holy See to the International Conference on Population and Development Cairo, 30 August 1994

Q. - How would you say current relations between the Holy See and the U.N. are faring following the latest tensions over the Cairo Conference?

A. - Our relations are — as they have always been — based on a tradition of mutual collaboration while respecting each other's role. I would like to take advantage of the opportunity given to me by Vatican Radio to clear up a misunderstanding which is widely diffused: it is believed that the document, the draft document, which will be presented in Cairo, is already an official document of the United Nations. It is not. Even though it was prepared by the Secretariat of the Conference at the United Nations Fund for Population Activities (UNFPA), the draft is only a basis for discussion. The international community will amend it and adopt it in Cairo and will present it at the United Nations General Assembly. The document will become official only after the Assembly's adoption. All the criticism and the accusations are not directed at the United Nations per se. I believe these remarks are necessary because they contribute to a sound, democratic argumentation which can be found in any parliament when attempting to formulate and elaborate a final document that must be agreed upon by all.

Q. - All eyes are on the upcoming Cairo event. What has contributed to such worldwide interest?

A. - I think the interest is due to the ongoing, animated debate regarding the Plan of Action. Even the person who is least concerned with international matters is now interested in the Conference. I think the Holy Father has contributed to the worldwide interest with his numerous interventions particularly because he realizes what is at stake: the future of all humanity. The Pope has also written to the Heads of State. In doing so, he has encouraged everyone to reflect — and not only those directly involved.

Q. - The subjects to be discussed at the Conference are many but the impression has often been that discussions will focus on abortion and contraception ...

A. - The Cairo event has become the Conference on abortion and contraception. It should not be the case. Problems regarding population are many, and each one deserves consideration. Development is the other issue which will be discussed — after all, the title of the Conference is "Population and Development." Only 7 of the document's 113 pages are dedicated to development.

Q. - Is the abortion issue the core of the problem or is it a mere simplification?

A. - The Document principally affirms reproductive rights and reproductive health. These terms are the backbone of the document, since they appear over one hundred times. The definition of "reproductive health" includes the "the right of men and women to be informed and to have access to safe, effective, affordable and acceptable methods of fertility regulation of their choice." The World Health Organization's (WHO) definition of "fertility regulation" includes the concept of family planning and the concept of abortion. Therefore, it is clear that each time health is quoted, abortion is implied.

Q. - If this plan were accepted, what would be the consequences?

A. - If it were to be accepted, then, as the Pope has said, humanity will be faced with a serious threat. Until now the right to life was considered evident and sacred. If this principle were to be thrown away, the consequences would be disastrous. Although experts do not even agree on the problem of overpopulation and of the carrying capacity of the planet earth, there are those who have embarked on a new and aberrant "moral mission" to limit population growth. These new "missionaries" go to extremes: they either deny scientific evidence that the human embryo is indeed human, or they give the State the power over life and death. The ghosts of the past regimes — which were thought to be dead and buried — are now haunting the Cairo Conference.

Q. - Is it true that we're facing the explosion of a "population time bomb?"

A. - I'm not an expert, but a month ago I had a U.N. notice (which only now the press has picked up on) which cited a 1.57 per cent increase in population growth from 1990 to today, while for the same period the U.N. had forecast a growth of 1.73 percent. The United Nations Population Division believes that it marks the resumption of the trend of declining population growth rates even in large areas of the developing world. It greatly lowers the predicted number of inhabitants forecast for the years 2015 and 2050. I've been told that, even in an extremely hypothetical situation where the world's population would be concentrated in one percent of the earth's surface, a family of five could live comfortably on one third of an acre. The population density would be 14.6 people per acre, which is still less than the density of the Boston area which is around 19.5 people per acre. Hypothetically, the world's population could live comfortably in one of the largest States of the United States, like Texas, Alaska or Nevada. In addition, the U.N. Food and Agriculture Organization has a report which will be presented at the Cairo Conference, entitled "Agriculture towards the Year 2010," which says it will be possible to feed in a stable way the billions of people forecast to live on our planet. The FAO says that for now world population is not a problem of numbers, but more a problem of the uneven distribution of food and other goods. At this point, I wish to reaffirm that the Church's position, which the Holy Father recently highlighted in the Angelus, is not simply procreation at any cost but a responsible fatherhood and motherhood brought about through means which are rooted in the nature of procreation itself.

Q. - The Delegations, including the Holy See, have put some debatable parts of the Cairo draft document in parentheses. Are there chances for the greater consensus on these issues which will also satisfy the Holy See?

A. - The Delegations are going to Cairo to eliminate these parentheses and to make the document which will be adopted one which reflects consensus. The Holy See will do everything possible to contribute to this process.

INTERVIEW GIVEN TO VATICAN RADIO BY HIS EXCELLENCY ARCHBISHOP RENATO R. MARTINO APOSTOLIC NUNCIO, PERMANENT OBSERVER OF THE HOLY SEE TO THE UNITED NATIONS AND HEAD OF THE DELEGATION OF THE HOLY SEE TO THE INTERNATIONAL CONFERENCE ON POPULATION AND DEVELOPMENT CAIRO, 2 SEPTEMBER 1994

Human Development, not Population Control

Q. - Contrary to what most people have heard, the Cairo Conference is not only about population problems as in Bucharest in 1974 or Mexico City ten years later. It's also about development and especially its relationship with population.

A. - Authentic human development cannot be appropriately addressed when one factor, population growth, is singled out as its primary obstacle. Rather, authentic development involves a whole range of complex issues, including education, health, nutrition, agriculture, economics, politics, and demographics. While these issues are by their very nature inter-related, it is disingenuous not to deal with them on their terms. Problems in these areas will only be resolved by true solidarity which seeks to improve the conditions of persons in less developed nations rather than using economic pressures to limit their number. Human development is more than material well-being. "True development," according to John Paul II, "does not consist in the simple accumulation of wealth and in the greater availability of goods and services, but must be pursued with due consideration for the social, cultural and spiritual dimensions of the human person" (*Sollicitudo rei socialis*, 9).

Q. - The Cairo draft document seems to draw a cause and effect relationship between population growth and underdevelopment.

A. - The Cairo document fails to note that in several parts of the world, population growth has not hindered economic development, but has stimulated it. Historically, there are few examples of countries that have combined an extended period of population decline with economic growth. While responsible stewardship should lead to the wise use of natural resources, scientific data indicate that the scarcity of exhaustible resources is at most a minor restraint on economic growth. In the Holy See's view, the human organization of societies and the just distribution of goods are primary factors in enabling nations to meet the full range of their developmental needs. These factors should be given due importance in any international document on Population and Development.

Q. - How does education, especially of women, play an important role in this delicate relationship between population growth and development?

A. - The Holy See first raised the importance of education to development, especially for women, at the 1984 Mexico City Conference. According to the Cairo document, 75% of illiterate persons in the world are women. The Holy See fully agrees that the increase in education of women and girls will contribute to their greater dignity and advancement, to a postponement of the age of marriage, and to a correspondingly natural reduction in the size of families. Moreover, as mothers become better educated, the survival rate of their children will increase (para. 11.3). All countries should consolidate the progress made in the 1990s towards providing universal access to primary education (cf. para. 11.6).

Q. - Is there the risk of a new sort of cultural colonialism with the efforts to promote development?

A. - Any and all development programs must be built on justice and equality, rather than on a cultural hegemony of one region over others. Programs must respect the free autonomy and cultural heritage of nations. "Men and women must be active agents of their own development, for to treat them as mere objects in some scheme or plan would be to stifle that capacity for freedom and responsibility which is fundamental to the good of the human person" (John Paul II, *Address to Dr. Nafis Sadik*, March 1994). It is the conviction of the Holy See that any development program must respect the dignity of the person in all moral and ethical dimensions. What should be avoided at all costs is the imposition of an ideological policy in which those who live in less developed countries are considered more objects rather than active creators of their own future.

INTERVIEW GIVEN TO VATICAN RADIO BY HIS EXCELLENCY ARCHBISHOP RENATO R. MARTINO APOSTOLIC NUNCIO, PERMANENT OBSERVER OF THE HOLY SEE TO THE UNITED NATIONS AND HEAD OF THE DELEGATION OF THE HOLY SEE TO THE INTERNATIONAL CONFERENCE ON POPULATION AND DEVELOPMENT CAIRO, 3 SEPTEMBER 1994

Women's dignity is not promoted by contraception and abortion

Q. - The United Nations Conference on Population and Development in Cairo seems to offer a unique opportunity to reaffirm the dignity of women and their role in the family and world today. What is the Holy See's position on this issue?

A. - The Holy See strongly supports the Cairo document's call for increased attention to the status of women — and children — who all too often find themselves the most vulnerable members of our communities. According to the Cairo document, more than two-thirds of the 960 million illiterate adults in the world are women. Of the 130 million children in the world who are not enrolled in primary schools, 70 percent are girls. And we must not forget the plight of refugee and displaced women, who must often bear a disproportionate share of the burdens of war and oppression. At the Cairo Conference, the Holy See's efforts will be guided by profound respect for women's personal dignity and recognition of the need to provide women with the equality which is the basis of the right of all to share in the process of full development. As it now stands, the language in the Cairo document calls for increased access to abortion, and also attempts to establish abortion as a reproductive "right." Such measures would seriously threaten the dignity of women and fail to address their real needs.

Q. - The Holy See has always tried to make sure that parents can freely and responsibly choose the number of children they want to have or adopt. How will the Holy See make this an objective in Cairo?

A. - At the Cairo meeting, the Holy See will be working closely with other Delegations to ensure greater support for programs that aim at: decreasing maternal mortality; providing prenatal and perinatal care; meeting the nutritional needs of pregnant women and nursing mothers; and helping mothers to provide preventive healthcare for their infants. Concrete steps must be elaborated to promote the dignity of women, and to eliminate all forms of exploitation, abuse and violence aimed at women. This is the first indispensable step to allow the couple to decide in total freedom and responsibility the number of children and their spacing.

Q. - Often the Church and the Holy See are accused of not doing enough to promote the needs of women today. What do you think about that?

A. - The Holy See's advocacy for women's development is manifested in its vast world-wide network of institutions such as schools, mother-child health, and nutrition programs, hospitals, and international development agencies. While this long history of the promotion of the integral development of women has benefitted vast numbers, much remains to be accomplished. As Pope John Paul II pointed out in his pre-conference message, "it is a sad commentary on the human condition that still today, at the end of the twentieth century, it is necessary to affirm that every woman is equal in dignity to man, and a full member of the human family ... ." In this regard, the Pope stressed that "much still has to be done to meet the educational and health needs of girls and young women so that they may achieve their full potential in society."

INTERVIEW GIVEN TO VATICAN RADIO BY HIS EXCELLENCY ARCHBISHOP RENATO R. MARTINO APOSTOLIC NUNCIO, PERMANENT OBSERVER OF THE HOLY SEE TO THE UNITED NATIONS AND HEAD OF THE DELEGATION OF THE HOLY SEE TO THE INTERNATIONAL CONFERENCE ON POPULATION AND DEVELOPMENT CAIRO, 4 SEPTEMBER 1994

Holy See supports chapter in Cairo Draft Document on Migrants and Refugees

Q.- *The Holy See will give its full support to the principal points of the Cairo Draft Plan of Action on refugees and migrants, while calling attention to the inadequacy of the financial commitments which have been undertaken in this regard. Your Excellency, what are the principal points of the Draft to which the Holy See has made a notable contribution?*

A.- Among the objectives are the following:
- to address the root causes of documented and undocumented migration and reduce pressures leading to refugee movements;
- to encourage more cooperation and dialogue between countries of origin and countries of destination in order to maximize the benefits of migration while also reducing the number of refugees and undocumented migrants;
- to facilitate the reintegration process of returning migrants and refugees.

Q.- *The vast displacements of people, both within and outside of national boundaries, continue to be one of the major causes of concern for the human family. Archbishop Martino, can you give us any figures relating to this tragedy?*

A.- The number of migrants and refugees is staggering. It is estimated that there are more than 120 million in the world, half of whom are in developing nations. Each year countries in the developed world receive about 1.4 million persons, roughly two-thirds coming from developing countries. In 1993 there were 19 million refugees. In 1994 this figure was over 20 million which, as the Holy Father said, was a "tragic wound in the side of humanity."

All nations should seek to satisfy the needs of the common good. The common good requires the creation of an environment centered upon respect for humanity and embodying the rights of each person, group, or associative entity.

The international community must be especially concerned with recognizing and protecting the rights of all displaced persons. "The first point of reference should not be the interests of the State or national security, but the human person, so that the need to live in a community, a basic requirement of all persons, will be safeguarded."

Q.- The denial of the human rights of refugees and migrants is, unfortunately, a frequent occurrence. From the standpoint of International Law, what can be done to address this situation?

A.- The Holy See encourages all States that have not done so to accede to all international conventions on migrants, refugees and asylum-seekers. All other States must be encouraged to comply with those regulations more rigorously, especially the Convention of 1990 regarding the "Protection of the Rights of Migrant Workers and Their Families."

Furthermore, all States should ensure that migrants, refugees, and asylum-seekers are provided with those basic goods and services that are guaranteed to its own citizens. The State should promote a culture of solidarity, protecting migrants and refugees from any attempt at marginalization or racism. This includes safeguarding against all forms of discrimination, especially in areas of wages and working conditions. The State should also facilitate those conditions that would enable migrants and refugees to have their families with them.

Q.- How is the Holy See concretely engaged in working for refugees?

A.- Over the centuries the Holy See has been at the forefront of efforts aimed at providing basic human services to all displaced persons. Currently, these humanitarian efforts are carried out by a multitude of Catholic agencies throughout the world.

Solidarity between nations is absolutely necessary to help alleviate the unjust structures that can bring about vast displacement of peoples. Human solidarity, as witnessed by any community that welcomes refugees and by the commitment of national and international organizations who care for them, is a source of hope for the real possibility of living together in fraternity and peace.

**INTERVIEW GIVEN TO VATICAN RADIO BY
HIS EXCELLENCY ARCHBISHOP RENATO R. MARTINO
APOSTOLIC NUNCIO, PERMANENT OBSERVER OF THE HOLY SEE
TO THE UNITED NATIONS
AND HEAD OF THE DELEGATION OF THE HOLY SEE TO THE
INTERNATIONAL CONFERENCE ON POPULATION AND DEVELOPMENT
CAIRO, 16 SEPTEMBER 1994**

Q.- The media gave a lot of coverage to the Cairo Conference. How would you evaluate the way public opinion was informed on this important event?

A.- The media's wide coverage of the Cairo Conference was justified by the fact that the future of humanity depends in great measure on the topics that were discussed. The debate focused on the complexity of the document which produced understandable difficulties — often oversimplified by the mass media by presenting two opposing sides on each issue: like abortion *yes*, abortion *no*; or contraception *yes*, contraception *no*; or traditional families *yes* or traditional families *no*, and so forth. And even further mystifying and far from reality was the portrayal of a Conference split between the Vatican, Islamic Countries and Developing Countries on the one side, united against all of the others.

Of course at the Conference — given the convictions and the ideas put forward and the moral respect for the Pope — the Holy See was able to play an important, widely recognized, and in a certain sense persuasive role. And as declared throughout the Conference preparatory phase to the meeting itself, the Holy See always worked to arrive at consensus, and never division within the Conference, nor through so-called "holy alliances" and "secret pacts." The adopted solution of "partial consensus" with reservations on certain unacceptable points in the document — allowed the Holy See to define its position on population and development problems in the best way, showing solidarity with the international community in the search for appropriate solutions. And this was the case with the other countries who shared the positions held by the Holy See.

Q.- You've often spoken about the unacceptable points in the Final Document, but could you outline some of the main improvements in the text which the Holy See was able to obtain?

A.- I would like to emphasize that the Holy See, *along with other countries*, was able to obtain improvements in the text. I state briefly: This document does not create any new international human rights, particularly relating to abortion. Human beings are at the centre of concerns for sustainable development. States should reduce and eliminate unsustainable patterns of production and consumption. Everyone has the right to education and in the case of the child this responsibility lies in the first place with parents. Everyone has the right to seek and to enjoy in other countries asylum from persecution, while countries should provide proper treatment and adequate social welfare services for documented migrants and for their families.

Among the general principles we obtained the inclusion of the "full respect for the various religious and ethical values and cultural backgrounds of all people." In addressing international migration it is noted that rights of "persons belonging to ethnic, religious or linguistic minorities ... be respected." As regards the family, Principle 9 identifies the family as "the basic unit of society and as such should be strengthened" and "is entitled to receive comprehensive protection and support. Marriage must be entered into with the free consent of the intending spouses, and husband and wife should be equal partners." In addressing education, reference is made to "taking into account the rights and responsibilities of parents and the needs of adolescents." We succeeded to reintroduce the Mexico language that "abortion should not be promoted as a means of family planning."

Q.- Could the Holy See's "partial consensus" on the Cairo Document with its concepts like "sexual and reproductive rights," "sexual and reproductive health," be interpreted as the beginning of a change in Catholic morals on issues like premarital relationships, contraception, homosexuality and abortion?

A.- Absolutely not. That's why the consensus was only partial. While I appreciate the overall concepts you've highlighted such as "sexual and reproductive rights" and "sexual and reproductive health," the Holy See made it unequivocally certain that this does not imply any change in Catholic morals whatsoever. The Church will continue to make sure that such concepts are clearly understood and respected in its healthcare institutions. These ideas comprise a global vision of health which encompasses the entire person, body and soul, and aims to secure sexual maturity, reciprocal love and a personal control in marital relationships with respect to moral norms. Therefore, the Church's stand on abortion, contraception, homosexuality, premarital relationships, remains — and I repeat — remains absolutely unchanged, and that includes the prohibition of the use of condoms in AIDS prevention programs. We did not expect in any way to convince everyone of our positions. At the same time the Holy See cannot but express its disappointment that an International Conference could support national laws which allow abortion or even include abortion as part of primary healthcare.

Press Release
Issued by the Delegation of the Holy See during the International Conference on Population and Development
Cairo, 5 September 1994

Resource allocations

The Programme of Action of the International Conference on Population and Development sets out three goals (Par. 1.18) that it describes as "mutually supporting and of critical importance to the achievement of other important population and development objectives." In their order of appearance, these are 1) education, especially for girls; 2) child and maternal mortality reduction; and 3) universal access to family planning and reproductive health services. The Holy See supports all three goals, with some reservations about the forms the third should take. "We are especially alarmed that the Programme's allocation of resources will channel tens of billions of dollars to the last item (Par. 13.17) and nothing at all to education or the reduction of mortality," a spokesman of the Holy See said today.

The Catholic Church, through its almost one-hundred thousand health and medical facilities, runs the most extensive network of health services for people around the world, especially in poor and remote areas. "We can speak with no little experience about global health needs," the spokesman said. The Cairo Programme plans to devote $10-20 billion over the near future to family planning and reproductive health, 65 per cent of which, it says, will be needed to set up a delivery system. "We find this an unwise and ineffective use of resources," the spokesman said.

Just last year, for example, UNICEF argued that modest investments in emergency obstetrical care could quickly reduce maternal mortality by one-half. If the Cairo Conference regards this question as critically important and one of the mutually reinforcing steps it wishes to take, it should show it by devoting some funds to this issue. At present, the Programme merely encourages nations to recognize the need, "the costs of which should be met by overall health sector budgets" (13.16.b).

On education, specifically of girls, the Programme's recommendations are, if anything, weaker: "The education sector will also require substantial and additional investments in order to provide universal basic education and to eliminate disparities in educational access owing to gender, geographical location, social or economic status, etc" (Par. 13.17). This is true — added the Holy See spokesman — but "`substantial and additional investments' by whom if not by the program itself?"

The Cairo Programme talks a great deal about ways of empowering people to take responsibility for their own development but "unfortunately, as it stands, it only pays lip service to issues like reduction of maternal mortality and increases in education; all the money, we fear, is headed elsewhere," added the spokesman.

Press Release
Issued by Delegation of the Holy See to the International Conference on Population and Development
Cairo, 6 September 1994

Statement by Dr. Joaquín Navarro-Valls, Director of the Holy See Press Office and Spokesman for the Delegation of the Holy See

The Holy See's participation in the International Conference on Population and Development springs from its characteristic and constant concern for mankind. It takes a profound interest in and acts on all issues that affect the dignity of the human person, and participates in numerous areas of social policy, focusing on the development of persons and of society. Specific areas include respect for human rights, social justice, healthcare, education, and migrants.

The Holy See has participated in all of the regional preparatory meetings of the Cairo Conference and has worked to achieve a consensus on the well-being and progress of the human family, on the true well-being of all men and women.

Population policy is not about numbers but about people. The Holy See publicly acknowledges that there are serious problems connected with population growth. However, the global population situation is too complex to allow for unqualified generalizations. There are variations, not simply from continent to continent, but from one region to another. United Nations studies indicate that growth rates remain high in some of the least developed nations of the world, while population growth has declined appreciably worldwide, reaching this year the lowest levels since World War II. In the industrialized developed nations, the decline is such that it creates in many cases its own set of problems.

In addressing population issues, it is important to remember that a population policy is only one aspect of an overall development strategy. Accordingly, any discussion of population policies should take into account the actual and projected development of nations and regions. Unfortunately, the Draft Final Document devotes only 7 out of 113 pages directly to development issues.

Among its many positive points, the Draft Final Document appropriately focuses on issues of education and health care — services which the Church has traditionally provided, especially for women and children. The Catholic Church has an extensive network of health services in the world with almost 100,000 facilities, large and small.

However, there are some approaches in the Document which the Holy See finds objectionable. One that has already gained significant attention is that of the provision of abortion services. While the Holy See recognizes that a woman may be faced with serious difficulties in connection to a pregnancy, the Delegation would argue that she should be provided with better, higher and free medical assistance, with compassionate counseling, and, if she does not want to keep the child, access to adoption services. Such difficulties do not warrant the violation to the right to life.

Another objection of the Holy See is the provision (para. 7.43) of information and services to adolescents with no mention of the rights and duties of parents. Both the *Universal Declaration of Human Rights* and the *Convention on the Rights of the Child* provide for the parents' primary involvement in the upbringing of their children and these rights are not adequately taken into account by the Draft Final Document in its current form.

Both of these issues have serious implications for the well-being of the family, an institution of fundamental importance for the proper development of persons and of society.

On the matter of contraceptives, the Holy See Delegation made a Statement at the last Preparatory Committee of the Conference indicating that it would not delay the negotiations with continued debate on this issue. It thus offered to remove the brackets around the term "family planning" as soon as appropriate language is inserted in the text to the effect that abortion not be promoted as a means of family planning. The Delegation has taken a reservation on the use of the term "family planning," indicating that the Holy See will interpret it in accordance with the teaching of the Catholic ethic. However, as several States at that time were unwilling to exclude abortion from the definition of family planning, no consensus was reached and the brackets remain on this term throughout the text at this point in negotiations.

The position of the Holy See has an ethical foundation. It is put forth as being in the best interest of the person and of society, and is therefore oriented towards good public policy. For example, the institution of the family has always been given significant importance in religious traditions, but failure to safeguard the family results in serious damage to the fabric and stability of society as a whole.

This is reflected in the fact that the same position is held by those of other religious or ethical convictions and of no particular religious conviction.

The Holy See favors qualitative, person-centered goals, not quantitative ones. It looks for the integral development of the person and society. It believes that true development is not respected when one factor, population growth, is singled out as the sole obstacle to development.

Thus, while the Draft Document contains many positive elements, the Holy See cannot give explicit or implicit support to those parts of the document regarding abortion, the weakening of several family-related terminologies, the effective encouragement among adolescents of a liberal sexual lifestyle free of parental rights with no reference to ethical values — all of which in the long term can only bring damage to individuals and society.

Press Release
Issued by the Delegation of the Holy See during the International Conference on Population and Development
Cairo, 8 September 1994

Responsible Parenthood

No one can oppose responsible parenthood: The Holy See supports efforts in the International Conference on Population and Development Draft Plan of Action to make people better informed and more effective in exercising their rights to determine family size and the spacing of children by ethically acceptable methods. But the idea of responsible parenthood is mixed in with so many other goals in the draft document that it is necessary to distinguish more clearly what both parenthood and responsibility mean.

Ideally, parents should be a man and a woman joined in marriage who have wed to support one another and their children by their union. The support of single parent families in the document is proper as a response to difficult situations in which people may find themselves, often through no fault of their own. But, however, we should not obscure the importance of the intact married couple as the accepted and desired way people around the world exercise responsible parenthood.

Similarly, good information service and programs to encourage sexual self-control among adolescents contribute to forming adults to mature and healthy notions of sexuality. Some of the measures foreseen by the programme deliberately aim at providing adolescents from a very early age with confidential access to a wide range of consulting services with access also to controversial reproductive controls like contraceptives and even abortions without prior parental knowledge or involvement. Encouraging responsible parenthood should include what the U.N. *Universal Declaration of Human Rights* describes as the prior right of parents "to choose the kind of education that shall be given to their children." The Cairo document often gives the impression that parents exercising their responsibilities towards their children *after* they are born are the enemies, rather than the allies, of "responsible parenthood."

Responsible parenthood can only mean, in the final analysis, the free, informed, and mutual decision of a married couple about the most intimate matters in their married lives. Reciprocity requires education to raise the status of women in societies as is the need to involve them in family responsibilities: information may be needed to enable people to make good decisions (though this seems less the case in the developing world than the document argues).

MESSAGE OF
MOTHER TERESA OF CALCUTTA
TO THE UNITED NATIONS INTERNATIONAL CONFERENCE ON
POPULATION AND DEVELOPMENT
CAIRO, 7 SEPTEMBER 1994

Whatever you did unto one of the least, you did unto me

On the last day, Jesus will say to those on His right hand, "Come, enter the Kingdom. For I was hungry and you gave me food, I was thirsty and you gave me drink, I was sick and you visited me." Then Jesus will turn to those on His left hand and say, "Depart from me because I was hungry and you did not feed me, I was thirsty and you did not give me to drink, I was sick and you did not visit me." These will ask Him, "When did we see You hungry, or thirsty or sick and did not come to Your help?" And Jesus will answer them, "Whatever you neglected to do unto one of the least of these, you neglected to do unto Me!"

As we have gathered here to pray together, I think it will be beautiful if we begin with a prayer that expresses very well what Jesus wants us to do for the least. St. Francis of Assisi understood very well these words of Jesus and His life is very well expressed by a prayer. And this prayer, which we say every day after Holy Communion, always surprises me very much, because it is very fitting for each one of us. And I always wonder whether, 800 years ago when St. Francis lived, they had the same difficulties that we have today. I think that some of you already have this prayer of peace — so we will pray it together.

Let us thank God for the opportunity He has given us today to have come here to pray together. We have come here especially to pray for peace, joy and love. We are reminded that Jesus came to bring the good news to the poor. He had told us what is that good news when He said: "My peace I leave with you, My peace I give unto you." He came not to give the peace of the world, which is only that we don't bother each other. He came to give the peace of heart which comes from loving — from doing good to others.

And God loved the world so much that He gave His Son — it was a giving. God gave His Son to the Virgin Mary, and what did she do with Him? As soon as Jesus came into Mary's life, immediately she went in haste to give that good news. And as she came into the house of her cousin, Elizabeth, Scripture tells us that the unborn child — the child in the womb of Elizabeth — leapt with joy. While still in the womb of Mary, Jesus brought peace to John the Baptist who leapt for joy in the womb of Elizabeth.

And as if that were not enough, as if it were not enough that God the Son should become one of us and bring peace and joy while still in the womb of Mary, Jesus also died on the Cross to show that greater love. He died for you and for me, and for that leper and for that man dying of hunger and that naked person lying in the street, not only of Calcutta, but of Africa, and everywhere. Our Sisters serve these poor people in 105 countries throughout the world. Jesus insisted that we love one another as He loves each one of us. Jesus gave His life to love us and He tells us that we also have to give whatever it takes to do good to one another. And in the Gospel Jesus says very clearly: "Love as I have loved you."

Jesus died on the Cross because that is what it took for Him to do good to us — to save us from our selfishness in sin. He gave up everything to do the Father's will — to show us that we, too, must be willing to give up everything to do God's will — to love one another as He loves each of us. If we are not willing to give whatever it takes to do good to one another, sin is still in us. That is why we, too, must give to each other until it hurts.

It is not enough for us to say: "I love God," but I also have to love my neighbor. St. John says that you are a liar if you say you love God and you don't love your neighbor. How can you love God whom you do not see, if you do not love your neighbor whom you see, whom you touch, with whom you live? And so it is very important for us to realize that love, to be true, has to hurt. I must be willing to give whatever it takes not to harm other people and, in fact, to do good to them. This requires that I be willing to give until it hurts. Otherwise, there is no true love in me and I bring injustice, not peace, to those around me.

It hurt Jesus to love us. We have been created in His image for greater things, to love and to be loved. We must "put on Christ" as Scripture tells us. And so, we have been created to love as He loves us. Jesus makes Himself the hungry one, the naked one, the homeless one, the unwanted one, and He says, "You did it to Me." On the last day He will say to those on His right, "whatever you did to the least of these, you did to Me, and He will also say to those on His left, whatever you neglected to do for the least of these, you neglected to do it for Me."

When He was dying on the Cross, Jesus said, "I thirst." Jesus is thirsting for our love, and this is the thirst of everyone, poor and rich alike. We all thirst for the love of others, that they go out of their way to avoid harming us and to do good to us. This is the meaning of true love, to give until it hurts.

I can never forget the experience I had in visiting a home where they kept all these old parents of sons and daughters who had just put them into an institution and forgotten them — maybe. I saw that in that home these old people had everything — good food, comfortable place, television, everything, but everyone was looking toward the door. And I did not see a single one with a smile on the face. I turned to Sister and I asked: "Why do these people who have every comfort here, why are they all looking toward the door? Why are they not smiling?"

I am so used to seeing the smiles on our people, even the dying ones, smile. And Sister said: "This is the way it is nearly every day. They are expecting, they are hoping that a son or daughter will come to visit them. They are hurt because they are forgotten." And see, this neglect to love brings spiritual poverty. Maybe in our own family we have somebody who is feeling lonely, who is feeling sick, who is feeling worried. Are we there? Are we willing to give until it hurts in order to be with our families, or do we put our own interests first? These are the questions we must ask ourselves, especially as we begin this year of the family. We must remember that love begins at home and we must also remember that "the future of humanity passes through the family."

I was surprised in the West to see so many young boys and girls given to drugs. And I tried to find out why. Why is it like that, when those in the West have so many more things than those in the East? And the answer was: "Because there is no one in the family to receive them." Our children depend on us for everything — their health, their nutrition, their security, their coming to know and love God. For all of this, they look to us with trust, hope and expectation. But often, father and mother are so busy they have no time for their children, or perhaps they are not even married or have given up on their marriage. So the children go to the streets and get involved in drugs or other things. We are talking of love of the child, which is where love and peace must begin. These are the things that break Peace.

But I feel that the greatest destroyer of peace today is abortion because it is a war against the child, a direct killing of the innocent child, murder by the mother herself. And if we accept that a mother can kill even her own child, how can we tell other people not to kill one another? How do we persuade a woman not to have an abortion? As always, we must persuade her with love and we remind ourselves that love means to be willing to give until it hurts. Jesus gave even His life to love us. So, the mother who is thinking of abortion should be helped to love, that is, to give until it hurts her plans, or her free time, to respect the life of her child. The father of that child, whoever he is, must also give until it hurts.

By abortion, the mother does not learn to love, but kills even her own child to solve her problems. And, by abortion, the father is told that he does not have to take any responsibility at all for the child he has brought into the world. That father is likely to put other women into the same trouble. So abortion just leads to more abortion. Any country that accepts abortion is not teaching its people to love, but to use any violence to get what they want. This is why the greatest destroyer of love and peace is abortion.

Many people are very, very concerned with the children of India, with the children of Africa, where quite a few die of hunger, and so on. Many people are also concerned about all the violence in this great country of the United States. These concerns are very good. But often these same people are not concerned with the millions who are being killed by the deliberate decision of their own mothers. And this is what is the greatest destroyer of peace today — abortion which brings people to such blindness.

And for this I appeal in India and I appeal everywhere: "Let us bring the child back." The child is God's gift to the family. Each child is created in the special image and likeness of God for greater things — to love and to be loved. In this Year of the Family we must bring the child back to the center of our care and concern. This is the only way that our world can survive because our children are the only hope for the future. As older people are called to God, only their children can take their places.

But what does God say to us? He says: "Even if a mother could forget her child, I will not forget you. I have carved you in the palm of my hand." We are carved in the palm of His hand; that unborn child has been carved in the hand of God from conception and is called by God to love and to be loved, not only now in this life, but forever. God can never forget us.

I will tell you something beautiful. We are fighting abortion by adoption — by care of the mother and adoption for her baby. We have saved thousands of lives. We have sent word to the clinics, to the hospitals and police stations: "Please don't destroy the child; we will take the child." So we always have someone tell the mothers in trouble: "Come, we will take care of you, we will get a home for your child." And we have a tremendous demand from couples who cannot have a child — but I never give a child to a couple who has done something not to have a child. Jesus said, "Anyone who receives a child in my name, receives me." By adopting a child, these couples receive Jesus but, by aborting a child, a couple refuses to receive Jesus.

Please don't kill the child. I want the child. Please give me the child. I am willing to accept any child who would be aborted and to give that child to a married couple who will love the child and be loved by the child.

From our children's home in Calcutta alone, we have saved over 3,000 children from abortion. These children have brought such love and joy to their adopting parents and have grown up so full of love and joy.

I know that couples have to plan their family and for that there is natural family planning. The way to plan the family is natural family planning, not contraception. In destroying the power of giving life, through contraception, a husband or wife is doing something to self. This turns the attention to self and so it destroys the gift of love in him or her. In loving, the husband and wife must turn their attention to each other as happens in natural family planning, and not to self, as happens in contraception. Once that living love is destroyed by contraception, abortion follows very easily.

I also know that there are great problems in the world — that many spouses do not love each other enough to practice natural family planning. We cannot solve all the problems in the world, but let us never bring in the worst problem of all, and that is to destroy love. And this is what happens when we tell people to practice contraception and abortion.

The poor are very great people. They can teach us so many beautiful things. Once, one of them came to thank us for teaching her natural family planning and said: "You people who have practiced chastity, you are the best people to teach us natural family planning because it is nothing more than self-control out of love for each other." And what this poor person said is very true. These poor people maybe have nothing to eat, maybe they have not a home to live in, but they can still be great people when they are spiritually rich.

When I pick up a person from the street, hungry, I give him a plate of rice, a piece of bread. But a person who is shut out, who feels unwanted, unloved, terrified, the person who has been thrown out of society — that spiritual poverty is much harder to overcome. And abortion, which often follows from contraception, brings a people to be spiritually poor, and that is the worst poverty and the most difficult to overcome.

Those who are materially poor can be very wonderful people. One evening we went out and we picked up four people from the street. And one of them was in a most terrible condition. I told the Sisters: "You take care of the other three; I will take care of the one who looks worse." So I did for her all that my love can do. I put her in bed, and there was such a beautiful smile on her face. She took hold of my hand as she said: "Thank you" — and she died.

I could not help but examine my conscience before her. And I asked:

"What would I say if I were in her place?" And my answer was very simple. I would have tried to draw a little attention to myself. I would have said: "I am hungry, I am dying, I am cold, I am in pain," or something. But she gave me much more — she gave me her grateful love. And she died with a smile on her face.

Then there was the man we picked up from the drain, half eaten by worms and, after we had brought him to the home, he only said, "I have lived like an animal in the street, but I am going to die as an angel, loved and cared for." Then, after we had removed all the worms from his body, all he said, with a big smile, was: "Sister, I am going home to God" — and he died. It was so wonderful to see the greatness of that man who could speak like that without blaming anybody, without comparing anything. Like an angel — this is the greatness of people who are spiritually rich even when they are materially poor.

We are not social workers. We may be doing social work in the eyes of some people, but we must be contemplatives in the heart of the world. For we must bring that presence of God into your family, for the family that prays together, stays together. There is so much hatred, so much misery, and we with our prayer, with our sacrifice, are beginning at home. Love begins at home, and it is not how much we do, but how much love we put into what we do.

If we are contemplatives in the heart of the world with all its problems, these problems can never discourage us. We must always remember what God tells us in Scripture: "Even if a mother could forget the child in her womb — something impossible, but even if she could forget — I will never forget you."

And so here I am talking with you. I want you to find the poor here, right in your own home first. And begin love there. Bring that good news to your own people first. And find out about your next-door neighbors. Do you know who they are?

I had the most extraordinary experience of love of neighbor with a Hindu family. A gentleman came to our house and said: "Mother Teresa, there is a family who has not eaten for so long. Do something." So I took some rice and went there immediately. And I saw the children — their eyes shining with hunger. I don't know if you have ever seen hunger. But I have seen it very often. And the mother of the family took the rice I gave her and went out. When she came back, I asked her: "Where did you go? What did you do?" And she gave me a very simple answer: "They are hungry also." What struck me was that she knew — and who are they? A Muslim family

— and she knew. I didn't bring any more rice that evening because I wanted them, Hindus and Muslims, to enjoy the joy of sharing.

But there were those children, radiating joy, sharing the joy and peace with their mother because she had the love to give until it hurts. And you see this is where love begins — at home in the family.

So, as the example of this family shows, God will never forget us and there is something you and I can always do. We can keep the joy of loving Jesus in our hearts, and share that joy with all we come in contact with. Let us make that one point — that no child will be unwanted, unloved, uncared for, or killed and thrown away. And give until it hurts — with a smile.

Because I talk so much of giving with a smile, once a professor from the United States asked me: "Are you married?" And I said: "Yes, and I find it sometimes very difficult to smile at my spouse, Jesus, because He can be very demanding — sometimes." This is really something true. And there is where love comes in — when it is demanding, and yet we can give it with joy.

One of the most demanding things for me is traveling everywhere — and with publicity. I have said to Jesus that if I don't go to heaven for anything else, I will be going to heaven for all the traveling with all the publicity, because it has purified me and sacrificed me and made me really ready to go to heaven.

If we remember that God loves us, and that we can love others as He loves us, then America can become a sign of peace for the world. From here, a sign of care for the weakest of the weak — the unborn child — must go out to the world. If you become a burning light of justice and peace in the world, then really you will be true to what the founders of this country stood for. God bless you!

Intervention by
Mr. John M. Klink
Member of the Holy See Delegation
to the UNICEF Executive Board on Document E/ICEF/1995/12:
"UNICEF Follow-up to the
International Conference on Population and Development"
New York, 23 March 1995

Mr. President,

My Delegation is taking the floor today on the item of UNICEF Follow-up to the International Conference on Population and Development (Document E/ICEF/1995/12).

As is known, Mr. President, the Holy See Delegation was active in its participation in the Cairo Conference — particularly since it was our Delegation's strong conviction that the matters being pursued in Cairo were of universal significance, dealing as they did with issues fundamental to the very fabric of our societies as we know them. What was clear from the document which emerged from Cairo was that it made great headway in considering and advancing matters of common concern, such as the sustainable development of all peoples — and that such development must be based primarily on the advancement of education — especially for women and girls.

What was also clear from Cairo, Mr. President, is that there remained issues of fundamental difference as was made clear from the extraordinarily large number of reservations and declarations made by participating States regarding their interpretation of the document and its outcomes.

Mr. President, the history of international conferences is replete with acknowledgments of differing viewpoints and attempts at accommodation and compromise — with some more successful and some less. The privilege of this Executive Board of UNICEF, however, Mr. President, is to participate in the history of one of the unique endeavors of humankind — a ship whose course is guided by the brightly visible star amidst otherwise dark and troubled nights — this star which all can see as clear as can be is the commonality of humankind's efforts on behalf of children.

I think I need not point out, Mr. President, that UNICEF alone amongst the specialized agencies of the United Nations, not only inspires a sense of common purpose, it also depends on it for its very vitality. The generosity of the world community is the lifeblood not only of UNICEF's extraordinary ability to engender trust amongst its beneficiaries, but the lifeblood of its fiscal health as well. No one I think, Mr. Chairman, should take either of these two aspects of UNICEF's success for granted.

It is thus that my Delegation comes to this Board to express its concern that the document before us would evidently seek to swap its long-standing priorities for children's health and education and duplicate the work of other agencies whose mandated job it is to handle the family planning and overall reproductive health of adults. Our Delegation's simple question is: is this the intent of the majority of UNICEF's private sector donor community?

My Delegation does not wish to enter into the specific discussions in this fora as to the pluses or minuses of family planning or the various approaches to reproductive health as these are questions which in my Delegation's opinion go beyond not only the mandate, but the competence of UNICEF. My Delegation's point is simply that other agencies such as UNFPA and WHO receive funding from governments specifically to do just this sort of activity. Thus, why should UNICEF enter into a duplicative and therefore wasteful endeavor with funds for which it must be held accountable by individual donors throughout the world.

These donors have until now remained confident that their money donated to UNICEF is being used for the simple and basic needs of children such as Oral Rehydration Therapy, Immunization, Basic Nutrition and Basic Education. My simple question, Mr. President, is: does UNICEF have sufficient funds at its disposal to accomplish these basics that it can now afford the luxury of doing the mandated work of WHO and UNFPA as well?

Mr. President, if I may make a brief reply to the suggestions that abortion be included in UNICEF programming efforts made by two Delegations, one can only imagine what donor reaction would be should the United Nations Children's Fund, which is charged with the care of the world's children, become charged in any way with promoting the death of the most vulnerable of all children — the unborn! For the Holy See Delegation and for many millions of donors, it would represent the end of UNICEF as we know it.

Mr. President, the swapping of UNICEF's priorities is obvious even from the summary on the first page of the document E/ICEF/1995/12. While the ICPD Programme of Action deals with a host of issues not the least of which from UNICEF's proud history would be the family (which is the subject of a full chapter in the ICPD document) the vital importance of education (another full chapter of the ICPD), and the child, (yet another full chapter of the Cairo document), UNICEF would seem in this document to have gotten the politically correct or incorrect fever to place these in a backseat position. Further, while ICPD dedicates two full chapters to migrants and their concerns, the document before us does not dedicate even a paragraph to this vital concern.

What *is* given the highest priority is the "reproductive health of women and youth." As an afterthought it notes that "UNICEF also will expand its efforts to provide universal access to basic education, improve gender equity and enhance the status of girls and women in society." Then it provides the further explanation which ironically points to the very duplication of efforts upon which it is about to become engaged: "these efforts will be carried out in close collaboration with the United Nations Population Fund and other organizations actively engaged in these issues."

Similarly, the very essence of the Cairo document regarding the need to empower women also takes a back seat. As an example, the document before us notes in paragraph 6 that "the Conference advanced consensus on the need to promote gender equality and equity *in order to achieve reproductive health for all people as well as to achieve sustainable population growth"* (italics ours). Mr. President, I ask whether this is the best or even a reasonable summary of the ICPD's reasons for promoting gender equality and equity. In this regard, my Delegation's stance at the ICPD, which was in agreement with the entirety of the Delegations present, was that gender equality and equity are a good in themselves and should never be seen as a mere vehicle to promote reproductive health or sustainable population growth.

Mr. President, my Delegation is gratified with the corrigendum noted by Mr. Gautam, the Acting Deputy Director of Programming, that the wording in paragraph 7, "promoting a small family norm," has been deleted. We are gratified since it has been my Delegation's firm understanding that regardless of the backs and forths of the negotiations of the last several years in the important international conferences such as Rio and Cairo, that what was being promoted was the ability for women and men to decide responsibly and freely as to the number and spacing of their children, not that those women and men who freely choose to have a larger family should be marked or targeted as "abnormal." The coercion which all States have recently committed themselves to staunchly avoid should not become the *modus operandi* of the United Nations Children's Fund as is called for in the document before us. Individual donors, Mr. President, I am convinced, would not want any United Nations organization, let alone the United Nations Children's Fund, to define the "norm" for any family in any country.

While the document before us does not fail to mention many of the other facets of UNICEF's work it is as if it remained fixated on one, and only one aspect of the wealth of the ICPD Programme of Action. Mr. President, what we would appear to have here is a serious "cart before the horse" problem. For the document of an agency whose very essence is the well-being of children not to address its family-related activities, the importance of its important role in favor of migrants and refugees, and to put the proverbial "cart" of reproductive health before the "horse" of the education of children and women — and even gender equity itself — is to put at risk the very faith and vision which has guided the agency as a success story apart from all others.

Mr. President, it should be noted that the draft resolution in the document calls for the endorsement of this Executive Board of its contents. In doing so it asks for its members to endorse language which not only goes beyond consensus language reached over multiple months of consultations, but even inadvertently challenges in a very real sense gender equity and gender equality itself.

For all of the above reasons, Mr. President, my Delegation would suggest that a full endorsement of this document as suggested in the draft resolution cannot and should not be given by this Board. Further, my Delegation would support the suggestion made that UNICEF should not become engaged in or reopen the discussions of Cairo. It is inconceivable that the interests of the children of the world will be served by the forced entry by UNICEF, their international protector, into the rancorous debate of the International Conference on Population and Development of Cairo upon which no absolute consensus ever emerged.

Finally, Mr. President, my Delegation has noted various references to the need for some organization to fill in for UNFPA in those countries in which it is not present. As it is my Delegation's understanding that it is not UNICEF itself, but the national governments themselves which carry out development activities in each country with the help of UNICEF and other U.N. agencies, then it remains questionable for it to be proposed that UNICEF take over activities outside of its original mandate such as those of UNFPA, when assistance can be given directly to the governments in question, should they desire it.

Thank you, Mr. President.

Intervention of
Mr. John M. Klink
Member of the Holy See Delegation
to the Third Regular Session of the UNICEF Executive Board
on Agenda Item 6: E/ICEF/1995/12/Rev.1:
"UNICEF Follow-up to the
International Conference on Population and Development"
New York, 20 September 1995

Mr. Chairman,

My Delegation has read with interest the paper before us on UNICEF Follow-up to the International Conference on Population and Development and would like to thank the Secretariat for its preparation of this report and express its appreciation to Dr. Richard Jolly for his clarifying comments made this morning, by way of introduction, wherein he verbally indicated that it is *not* UNICEF policy to become involved in abortion or in contraceptive distribution.

As noted in the document, the ICPD reaffirmed what has been one of the most important tracking points in UNICEF's "bible" — that is, that family planning and women's reproductive health are and must be directly tied to development. Education, especially of girls and women, is key to development. The greater the education of young women and the more they can count on the survivability and health of their children, the more likely that they will make responsible decisions regarding the planning of family size.

The emphasis, however, is on the total education of girls and women: the responsible planning of family size cannot be seen as an end in itself, and not as a magical shortcut to development.

My Delegation thus would see UNICEF's follow-up to the ICPD as simply a more energetic follow-up on its traditional strategy of synergistic, overall development focused on the whole human being and especially on women's education and development.

As my Delegation had occasion to mention in my previous intervention this morning on the UNICEF Health Strategy, it is imperative that UNICEF not get sidetracked into highly controversial actions — especially regarding adolescent sexuality. My Delegation has noted calls by certain Delegations for UNICEF to become highly involved in sexual education for girls and boys — Mr. Chairman, here we go far beyond even the still undefined and already highly problematic area of adolescents! Should this occur, the risk in our opinion is inevitable to a wide range of donor support.

Further, Mr. Chairman, in my Delegation's view "complementarity" of U.N. Agencies should not become a code word for a hand-off of responsibilities which should be those of other agencies. We support the need to avoid the danger of duplication by the various U.N. agencies, but even greater is the danger of UNICEF becoming the "water-carrier" for other agencies whose mandate is precisely for population activities as opposed to UNICEF's specific mandate for children.

While some Delegates have mentioned what they term a new "consensus" in favor of sexual rights and reproductive health following the Beijing Conference, it should be recalled that sexual rights paragraphs, even in Beijing, were deleted following two weeks of seemingly unending debate; and further, that despite these deletions, the final document contains some 43 formal Reservations regarding these controversial issues from concerned States who participated in that Conference.

Finally, Mr. Chairman, I would like to follow-up on a point made by the distinguished Delegate of Italy and state that the inclusion of encouragement to UNICEF in Paragraph 2(c) of the Draft Decision in this document — to provide not only family planning information, but also family planning services — is unacceptable to our Delegation. This wording would seem to imply opening the door to UNICEF not only for general family planning information, but also for contraceptive distribution, sterilization, etc., thus going far beyond what Dr. Jolly has just indicated in his helpful commentary this morning is on-going UNICEF policy. My Delegation considers this an important point and requests that the wording of the draft decision match what the reality is — particularly to reassure those donors who have a right to such reassurance.

Thank you, Mr. Chairman.

Chapter Seven

THE WORLD SUMMIT FOR SOCIAL DEVELOPMENT

Copenhagen, Denmark

6 - 12 March 1995

Chapter Contents

The World Summit for Social Development
Copenhagen, Denmark;
6 - 12 March 1995

Addresses of His Holiness Pope John Paul II before the Angelus 365
    St. Peter's Square, 26 February 1995 365
    St. Peter's Square, 5 March 1995 366
    St. Peter's Square, 12 March 1995 367

Statement by His Eminence Angelo Cardinal Sodano,
    Secretary of State of His Holiness, at the
    World Summit for Social Development
    Copenhagen, 12 March 1995 369

Statement of Interpretation and Reservations of the Holy See
    to the Declaration and Programme of Action of the
    World Summit for Social Development
    Copenhagen, 12 March 1995 374

Statement by His Eminence Roger Cardinal Etchegaray,
    President of the Pontifical Council for Justice and Peace,
    to the Annual Session of the United Nations Economic and
    Social Council (ECOSOC), on the topic of the
    World Summit for Social Development
    Geneva, 30 June 1993 375

Statement by Monsignor Diarmuid Martin,
    Under-Secretary of the Pontifical Council for Justice and Peace,
    Head of the Holy See Delegation to the First Session of the
    Preparatory Committee for the World Summit for Social
    Development; New York, 3 February 1994 378

Statement by Monsignor Diarmuid Martin,
    Under-Secretary of the Pontifical Council for Justice and Peace,
    Head of the Holy See Delegation to the First Session of the
    Preparatory Committee for the World Summit for Social
    Development; New York, 7 February 1994 383

Comments by Monsignor Diarmuid Martin,
    Secretary of the Pontifical Council for Justice and Peace,
    Head of the Holy See Delegation to the Preparatory Committee
    for the World Summit for Social Development
    New York, 22 August 1994 386

362 Chapter Seven

Comments by Monsignor Diarmuid Martin,
    Secretary of the Pontifical Council for Justice and Peace,
    Head of the Holy See Delegation to the Preparatory Committee
    for the World Summit for Social Development, on the Section:
    "Reduction and Elimination of Widespread Poverty"
    New York, 23 August 1994 388

Comments by Monsignor Frank J. Dewane,
    Member of the Holy See Delegation to the Preparatory Committee
    for the World Summit for Social Development, on the Section:
    "Social Integration"; New York, 24 August 1994 390

Comments by Monsignor Frank J. Dewane,
    Member of the Holy See Delegation to the Preparatory Committee
    for the World Summit for Social Development, on the Section:
    "The Declaration"; New York, 25 August 1994 391

Statement by Dr. Joaquín Navarro-Valls,
    Director of the Press Office of the Holy See, on the
    World Summit for Social Development
    Vatican, 28 February 1995 393

Statement by Monsignor Diarmuid Martin,
    Secretary of the Pontifical Council for Justice and Peace,
    Head of the Holy See Delegation to the Preparatory Committee
    for the World Summit for Social Development
    Copenhagen, 7 March 1995 397

Interview of Dr. Joaquín Navarro-Valls,
    Director of the Press Office of the Holy See, after the
    Inauguration of the World Summit for Social Development
    Copenhagen, 8 March 1995 401

Holy See Press Conference by Dr. Joaquín Navarro-Valls,
    Msgr. Diarmuid Martin and Mrs. Patricia Donahoe,
    during the World Summit for Social Development
    Copenhagen, 9 March 1995 402

Intervention of Monsignor Diarmuid Martin,
    Secretary of the Pontifical Council for Justice and Peace,
    at the 34th Session of the Commission for Social Development, on
    Item 5: "Priority Subject: World Summit for Social Development"
    New York, 18 April 1995 405

Intervention of His Excellency Archbishop Renato R. Martino,
    Apostolic Nuncio, Permanent Observer of the Holy See
    to the U.N., before the Plenary Session of the U.N. General

Assembly, on Item 161: "World Summit for Social Development" New York, 8 December 1995 408

(The Appendix contains no related documents for this chapter.)

ADDRESSES OF
HIS HOLINESS POPE JOHN PAUL II
BEFORE THE ANGELUS

ANGELUS, ST. PETER'S SQUARE
26 FEBRUARY 1995

After reciting the Angelus and imparting his Blessing, the Holy Father spoke of the UN World Summit for Social Development, to be held in Copenhagen, Denmark, beginning on 6 March. He expressed his wish for the meeting's success and prayed that it be a further step towards world solidarity. The Pope spoke in Italian.

We spoke of the role of women as teachers of peace. If we really want to build peace, we must not forget that today, even more than in the past, it is closely linked with development: I remember the words of my venerable predecessor Pope Paul VI: "The new face of peace is development."

The World Summit for Social Development, organized by the United Nations, will open in Copenhagen, Denmark, on 6 March next.

Heads of State or Government from across the world will meet in the desire to fight poverty together by creating new jobs and promoting social integration: a commitment that will help overcome so many forms of marginalization.

With all my heart I wish success to this important meeting.

The human person and his dignity must always be at the centre of every development endeavour, especially wherever societies and nations are planning their future.

It is an effort that involves the whole international community and every individual, because each of us is called to work together in making the world more human and fraternal.

May the prayers we offer during these days obtain the necessary light and strength for government leaders so that the Copenhagen Summit will mark a step forward towards the world solidarity we hope for and desire.

ANGELUS, ST. PETER'S SQUARE
5 MARCH 1995

Dear Brothers and Sisters,

1.   Tomorrow in Copenhagen the World Summit for Social Development to which I referred last Sunday will begin. I would like first of all to express my deep appreciation to the United Nations Organization, which has organized this important Conference and supervised its preparation. I respectfully greet the Heads of State and Government and the Delegations which will be taking part in the work. I sincerely hope that this meeting will mark the beginning of a new phase in humanity's journey, in which the well-being of individuals and peoples will be the focus of the attention and efforts of world leaders.

This Summit gathers the highest authorities of almost all countries in their search for common directives to combat poverty, to create work for all and to foster social integration. These are objectives which certainly require that economic incentives and legislative measures be set up, but which are first and foremost rightly seen as questions of dignity, human rights, peace and security for everyone. It is truly a good sign that these tasks will be faced not only in a political and economic, but also in an ethical and spiritual perspective, putting the human person at the heart of social development and not economic laws. Indeed, economies must effectively meet human needs.

2.   Every human being has equal dignity; a particularly great dignity for believers, who recognize God's image in him. Nevertheless, great inequalities exist among men. There are striking differences between certain developing countries, which are frequently afflicted with famine, the lack of education and sickness, and the developed countries, where the phenomena of heightened consumerism even go so far as to cause environmental imbalances. Then we must not forget the sometimes excessive gap between rich and poor within a single nation.

In this context, it should not be forgotten that unemployment is not only an economic fact but a personal tragedy for many. In this way the unemployed find themselves excluded from full participation in social life. To create new job opportunities is a profoundly human task, since through work the individual fulfills himself as a person and plays the lead role in his own development in a cooperative relationship with others.

3. Social integration, the endeavour to overcome the many forms of marginalization, is a highly valuable objective. It is important that societies be open places, where everyone may feel welcome with equal freedom, rights and duties. I would like to draw attention to two aspects, indispensable if such a great goal is to be achieved.

The first is religious freedom, which is actually the basis and synthesis of many freedoms, as the Conference recognizes. The second is the role of the family, an important factor in social integration. When the family is unable to fulfill its tasks, the whole community suffers the negative consequences. It is advantageous to all that families feel their stability is assisted and reinforced at both the economic and legislative levels.

Social development is a great work for the common good, to which we are all called to contribute.

I entrust the work of this World Summit for Social Development to the intercession of Mary Most Holy, so that this broad international meeting may offer real reasons to hope for a more welcoming and fraternal world.

ANGELUS, ST. PETER'S SQUARE
12 MARCH 1995

After reciting the Angelus and imparting his Blessing, the Holy Father spoke of the U.N. World Summit for Social Development, held in Copenhagen, Denmark. The Holy Father's remarks concerning the Conference follow.

The World Summit for Social Development, ending in Copenhagen today, has brought to the attention of world public opinion the inequalities that exist between rich and poor nations and the impending tragedies in the lives of a large part of humanity. These unfortunately are the result of a world which, in forgetting God, often ends by debasing man's dignity. I hope that the Copenhagen meeting may be a sign of hope for the poor on every continent and the premise for building a world of freedom and solidarity.

We entrust these wishes and our Lenten commitment to Mary, so that she may help every Christian to be transformed into a concrete sign of God's vivifying love, in order to proclaim to all, especially those who are suffering and all who are lonely and abandoned, the joy of the Easter Resurrection.

STATEMENT BY
HIS EMINENCE ANGELO CARDINAL SODANO
SECRETARY OF STATE
AT THE WORLD SUMMIT FOR SOCIAL DEVELOPMENT
COPENHAGEN, 12 MARCH 1995

Mr. President,
Distinguished Heads of State and Heads of Government,
Mr. Secretary-General of the United Nations,
Ladies and Gentlemen,

Humanity is now taking leave of a century marked by two World Wars, the Cold War and numerous other regional and local conflicts which have destroyed immense human and material resources. It urgently needs a stable peace, and in order to achieve this peace humanity requires that the world's goods, which according to God's plan are destined for all, should be justly and peaceably shared. We cannot disappoint peoples' expectations!

Our world is drawing near to a new millennium, with enormous technology at its disposal. There is now an opportunity, truly extraordinary in the history of humanity, to undertake action aimed at overcoming the poverty which still marks the world in so many ways.

This World Summit represents a significant step in a movement which ought to result in the commitment of States, civil society and many citizens to give practical shape to the basic principle in the documents of this meeting: *human beings are at the centre of development.*

1. From the time that the World Summit was first announced, Pope John Paul II has given it his decisive support. He has now entrusted me with the responsibility of expressing his heartfelt gratitude to the Secretary-General of the United Nations and to all who have worked with him in promoting this historic meeting of Heads of State or Government.

In a special way I greet Ambassador Juan Somavía who spearheaded the Summit and has guided its preparation. The Holy See also wishes to thank the Authorities of Denmark for the cordial welcome they have extended for this meeting.

2. It is known to all that the mission of the Catholic Church is specifically religious. Even so, she does not neglect but resolutely faces the concrete situations in which men and women live in our world, above all situations which harm their transcendent dignity. A witness to this concern

are the more than 270,000 Church educational and welfare institutions, spread across all the continents. Side by side with these institutions are many groups and movements, all of which are committed to human advancement and to fostering the freedom of individuals and peoples. This network of institutions is looking to the World Summit as a significant event, capable of giving a fresh impulse to social development.

3.   A society which is not rooted in solid ethical values is a society without direction. It lacks the necessary foundation upon which the sought-after social development can be built and sustained.

For this reason the Holy See is pleased to recognize that, right from the outset of the formulation of the Principles of the Declaration of this Summit, the commitment to promote a vision of social development which is "political, economic, *ethical and spiritual* ... with full respect for religious and ethical values and the cultural patrimony of persons" has been emphasized (Declaration, Principles and Objectives, n. 22). This statement echoes in a timely way what the late Pope Paul VI had affirmed in 1967 in one of his most significant magisterial pronouncements, the Encyclical *Populorum progressio*: "The development we speak of cannot be restricted to economic growth alone. To be authentic, it must be well rounded; it must foster the development of each human being and of the whole human being" (n.14).

4.   In this context, I take the liberty of recalling what the Summit's documents affirm many times concerning respect for the *religious values* of peoples and individuals. The common values of the great religions are intimately linked to the most profound aspirations of humanity: the spiritual and transcendent dimension of the human person, the ability to make a gift of self, solidarity among peoples and the harmony which should exist among individuals and between them and the created world.

Respect for religious values does not consist only in mere tolerance. Rather its aim should be to enable believers to contribute to society's development with the religious inspiration which is their most valuable possession. History and recent events testify to the commitment offered by believers in bringing relief and compassion to those living in poverty and social and cultural marginalization as well as enabling them to become themselves protagonists of their own development.

5.   Indeed, if we wish to work with generous hearts for the social development of our societies, what is needed today is the involvement of everyone. The decisions made by Governments will offer an essential framework for social development. But if these steps are not accompanied

by the active participation of civil society, they will have very little effect.

In this respect it will be necessary to recover the sense of community, interdependence and solidarity which link individuals, generations, families and peoples. And, as Pope John Paul II states, solidarity "is not a feeling of vague compassion or shallow distress at the misfortunes of so many people, both near and far. On the contrary, it is a firm and persevering determination to commit oneself to the common good; that is to say, to the good of all and of each individual because we are all really responsible for everyone else" (Encyclical Letter *Sollicitudo rei socialis*, n. 38, published on the 20th anniversary of *Populorum progressio).*

The presence at our Summit of such a great number of non-governmental organizations shows how many people are convinced of the duty of solidarity. The Holy See is a witness to how very generous has been the response to appeals for solidarity in situations of tragic suffering existing in today's world. The authorities should be encouraged by these signs and recognize in them a true desire to seek a decisive political orientation in this regard. They should not let themselves be disheartened by the pressures of groups which reject solidarity or are guided by purely self-centred interests. Exaggerated nationalism, especially, is one of today's principal obstacles to development.

6. For this reason, the institutions to be safeguarded above all are the ones which promote effective solidarity between individuals, generations and peoples.

Undoubtedly, the first of these institutions to be safeguarded is the *family,* the basic unit of society. The family, founded on marriage, is an institution which has belonged to the heritage of humanity from its very beginning. It is to be defended and fostered. It is essential to restore confidence in the family and to create a cultural climate which offers it the necessary stability to carry out its function of raising children and preparing them for life in society.

It is urgently necessary that States should offer families proper recognition for the social value of their efforts, also through necessary financial support. If society counts so much on the educational mission of parents, it should foster their rights and responsibilities, particularly in the sphere of the transmission of values and the very difficult task of guiding children towards upright and responsible behaviour.

7. Furthermore, the principle, reaffirmed several times in the Summit's documents, that "the person is at the centre of sustainable development"

should also be applied to laws in the sphere of economics. Pope John Paul II has affirmed that, even prior to the system of the exchange of goods and the free market, there exists something due the person given their very nature, by reason of his lofty dignity (cf. *Centesimus annus,* n. 34, published to mark the centenary of *Rerum novarum*).

We should avoid building economic systems on the creation of false needs or on the petty exploitation of the frailty of the weak.

8. In order to guarantee that economic development will spread throughout the world, international integration is needed, according to a plan of cooperation. It is therefore essential that all nations, especially the poorer nations, should effectively be able to participate actively in international trade. For this reason the Holy See appreciates the concept of "participation," which can thus become a key to interpreting the documents of this Summit.

I wish to recall that the principle of freedom, certainly essential to economic development, goes beyond the movement of capital and resources. It also embraces human mobility which is a phenomenon of our times. People are not merely instruments of the economy. Migrant workers and their families have fundamental rights, and their work, which contributes to the economic good of the countries which receive them and to the welfare of their citizens, should always enjoy just social protection.

9. The role of women has been prominent at this World Summit. Development can only be achieved when women, in equal partnership with men, are enabled to participate fully in the social and economic order, especially through their access to education. However, many obstacles must be overcome. Therefore, protecting women and children against exploitation, trafficking and harmful and cruel practices and seeking societal and economic recognition of women's unremunerated work are some of the initiatives proposed and strongly supported by the Holy See at this Summit and throughout its preparatory stages.

10. On this occasion one cannot remain silent about the scourge of war, which in various parts of the world continues to debase the dignity of many people. Far from promoting human integration, it causes very deep and damaging wounds, wounds which will need many generations before they are healed. Recourse to arms does not bring about relations of peace and harmony between peoples. All too often today, people are cruelly and deliberately abused and their most basic needs used as pawns in armed conflict. It has been written that, in the course of the last year alone, more than five million people died due to armed conflicts. Without peace, the development of peoples will never come about, just as without development

there will never be peace. These two factors are inseparable in the present international situation.

11.   Mr. President, to acknowledge that the human person is at the centre of development is also an act of confidence in the human person and in the human ability to overcome, with God's help, the forces of evil and to find the material and spiritual resources in order to respond to the challenge offered by the themes of this Summit. From the moment when the World Summit for Social Development was first announced, the Holy See has encouraged this initiative. It is linked, now more than ever, to all States and to all men and women of goodwill in the task of charting a new era of cooperation for the integral development of humanity.

Statement of Interpretation and Reservations of the Holy See to the Declaration and Programme of Action of the World Summit for Social Development
Copenhagen, 12 March 1995

The Holy See, in conformity with its nature and particular mission, in joining the consensus at the World Summit for Social Development, held in Copenhagen from 6 to 12 March 1995, wishes to express its understanding of some concepts used in the documents of the Summit.

1. The Holy See reaffirms the reservation it expressed at the conclusion of the International Conference on Population and Development, held in Cairo from 5 to 13 September 1994, which is included in the report of that Conference, concerning the interpretation given to the term "reproductive health." In particular, the Holy See reiterates that it does not consider abortion or access to abortion as a dimension of reproductive health or reproductive health services.

2. The Holy See's joining the consensus on the term "family planning" should in no way be interpreted as constituting a change in its well-known position concerning those family planning methods that the Catholic Church considers morally unacceptable or concerning family planning services that do not respect the liberty of spouses, human dignity and the human rights of those concerned.

3. The Holy See, in line with the *Universal Declaration of Human Rights*, stresses that the family is the basic unit of society and is based on marriage as an equal partnership between husband and wife.

4. With reference to all international agreements and instruments mentioned in the documents of the Summit, the Holy See reserves its position in a manner consistent with its acceptance or non-acceptance of them or of any expression found in them.

5. Nothing that the Holy See has done in this consensus process should be understood or interpreted as an endorsement of concepts that it cannot support for moral reasons. Especially, nothing is to be understood to imply that the Holy See endorses abortion or has in any way changed its moral position concerning abortion or on contraceptives, sterilization or the use of condoms in HIV/AIDS prevention programmes.

The Holy See asks that these reservations be included in the report of the Summit.

STATEMENT BY
HIS EMINENCE ROGER CARDINAL ETCHEGARAY
PRESIDENT OF THE PONTIFICAL COUNCIL FOR JUSTICE AND PEACE
TO THE ANNUAL SESSION OF THE
UNITED NATIONS ECONOMIC AND SOCIAL COUNCIL (ECOSOC)
ON THE TOPIC OF THE WORLD SUMMIT FOR SOCIAL DEVELOPMENT
GENEVA, 30 JUNE 1993

(the original was delivered in French)

Mr. President,

The Holy See is particularly interested in the preparation for the World Summit for Social Development organized by the United Nations Economic and Social Council (ECOSOC). The development of individuals and peoples is one of the Church's main concerns in her religious mission as the social Encyclicals show, especially those of Paul VI (*Populorum progressio*, 1967) and of John Paul II (*Sollicitudo rei socialis*, 1987).

I think that this Summit is all the more timely since numerous countries, disappointed or betrayed by development models which they have created for themselves or which were imposed on them, have come to have doubts about development itself and to believe that the star they had been reaching for is nothing but a meteorite. In the face of this atmosphere of uncertainty or even scepticism, despite so many intelligent and generous strategies promoted by "decades of development," the preparation for the Summit would like to revitalize development as a potential mechanism to energize humanity and restore confidence to man. But everything depends on the ideal of the human person we affix to the banner of development. There is no development without the integral development of the individual. There is no development without the common development of the human race.

The Secretary General's report appears to me to be a good approach if new deadlocks and new disappointments are to be avoided. Along these lines the Holy See wishes to offer some reflections based on its universal experience.

The problem of development is not confined to developing countries, but it is also a problem of developed countries. It is not a question of a footrace where some sprint ahead and others fall behind, and where it would suffice to accelerate the rhythm in order for some to catch up with the others by a sudden burst of imitation. The classification that qualifies certain countries as "less advanced" (LAC) or others as "newly industrialized" countries (NIC) would suggest that development is exclusively guided by Western experience. There is a great temptation to offer a model like a ready-to-wear garment or a factory ready for immediate production. I hope that the Summit presents a wide-open platform where all, on a human scale, may seek together a new and original development, to bring about a wholesome solidarity leading to interdependence.

To illustrate this wish, I take the example of poverty, which is to be one of the three priority topics of the Summit. Certainly, there is nothing more urgent than fighting against the "massive and tenacious" poverty (report by the Secretary General), this gaping wound in the side of humanity; but in which countries is it present and what sort of poverty is it? Is not the poverty of *being* more damaging than the poverty of *having*? Should not the so-called rich countries discover the intrinsic values of the so-called poor countries, and let themselves be questioned by them, in order to promote them? Is not the "new poverty" generated by developed countries indicative of the precarious nature of the affluent societies? Further, should not one dare to assume a certain poverty as a value expressed in a lifestyle, to the extent that it helps one to count on the gratuitousness of relationships rather than on profit? Nevertheless, all these searching questions which put development to the test will not be able to check the struggle against social inequalities nor call into question the structures of a society which thrives on these same inequalities.

The Holy See is glad to see that the human and social dimension is receiving increased and ever closer attention in the reports and programmes of the international financial institutions and specialized agencies of the United Nations. Along these lines, Rio in 1992, Vienna in 1993, Cairo in 1994, Copenhagen in 1995, have been or will be so many kindled and converging fires, which will cause the original figure of the human person and his or her central place in the heart of creation to emerge and be enhanced. Development therefore becomes the privileged place where man learns how to hope: a development whose source rises in the land of each people, whose dynamism is drawn from formation, responsibility, and the participation of each, a development whose guarantee is democracy, a development whose driving force and crowning achievement are human rights.

The World Summit's noble ambition is to gather and to reinforce the common values that enable the human vessel to progress towards a development that, in the photographic sense of the word, gradually reveals man to himself. Mr. Director, your lucidity and tenacity reassure us that the tiller is in good hands. But we cannot leave it all to you: this "high-level segment" is telling you so. For its part, the Holy See would like to assure you that in its educational task, it will make its own contribution beyond the bounds of this establishment, to translate into the vernacular a U.N. language which must reach the most popular sectors on every continent. In particular, the Church is seeking to raise development to the very level of a moral obligation, relying on a vision of the human family understood according to the plan of creation, in its unity and basic equality.

Underdevelopment is even worse an evil than one imagines. Development is a more difficult task than one realizes. It has assumed the aspect of a fierce combat and even a war of attrition. The disenchanted world needs to be told again that everything is possible for those who believe in the human person and I dare to add, to those who believe in God ... it is one and the same thing.

The ECOSOC has opened a great construction site where all have their place, which they will maintain all the better once they see concretely that by working for themselves they are working for their brothers and sisters.

Statement by Monsignor Diarmuid Martin
Under-Secretary of the
Pontifical Council for Justice and Peace
Head of the Holy See Delegation to the
First Session of the Preparatory Committee for the
World Summit for Social Development
New York, 3 February 1994

Mr. Chairman,

Among the various initiatives planned for the 50th anniversary of the United Nations, the World Summit for Social Development must have a special place. One of the aims of the Summit must be to establish a closer link between the United Nations and the people of the world. It must become a People's Summit — not just in the sense of a slogan — but as a sign of a renewed point of interest and contact between the United Nations and all its component structures and agencies with the fundamental needs and aspirations of the people of the world.

The peoples of the world aspire to peace and to security, both important pillars of the United Nations agenda. But in concrete they experience peace in the level in which they live out their social progress. Where their social and employment situations are insecure or precarious, where they are excluded from participating in the decisions that concern them, where they live in poverty — especially extreme poverty — they live in insecurity, and the very peace they yearn for is insecure.

Pope Paul VI already in 1969 proclaimed that development is the new name for peace. The barometer by which the peoples of the world measure peace is human and social development.

The fact that so many NGOs have shown clear interest in the preparation of the Summit, either through coming to New York to assist in this PrepCom, or through their active participation in the activities on a national level, is a sign that many people and grass root organizations have understood the basic insight which underlines the Summit.

Mr. Chairman,

It is not easy to move from a basic insight to structuring the concrete content and working method of a World Summit. But that is our task. It is easy to be skeptical about the feasibility of the project. You yourself, however, have reminded us that in recent years, in international political life, many things which seemed impossible, were possible.

What is at stake in the Summit is, among other things, the establishing of a new form of confidence in the part of the citizens — the people of the world — in the institutions of the international community. If we succeed we can not only bring a contribution to the reform of the United Nations, but above all bring to the Organization an injection of confidence from the people of the nations and of the world community. We work for a People's Summit, in which the national and international institutions pledge themselves to be more people-centered, but also in which the institutions can receive that support of people, without which they inevitably fail.

How then can we move from insight to reality? There are two fundamental levels which must be developed together. On the one hand, we must focalize more clearly on the vision which inspires our work, and secondly we must show through concrete proposals that this vision works.

The Summit for Social Development is something new and original in the activity of the United Nations and the dialogue among States, which have the fundamental responsibility for social policy. But to maintain that originality we will have to clarify the common vision that inspires our work.

What is it that is original in our concept? What precisely do we mean by Social Development? Already 50 years ago, the *Charter of the United Nations* spoke of promoting social progress and better standards of life in larger freedom, of tolerance and living together in peace and with one another as good neighbours, of higher standards of living, full employment and social advancement.

If we, 50 years later, wish to be more successful than those who went before us, then we must renew our own vision, the vision which inspires the United Nations itself. Above all we must renew our confidence, commitment and investment in the human person and in people, our most precious resource.

We must look again at the *centrality of the human person*, as was stressed in Principle 1 of the Rio Declaration, and work to ensure that the dignity of the human person is respected. We do that by, above all, working to see that the potential of the human person is realized and fostered. This involves scrupulous respect for human rights, for the right to life, and for the right to be a protagonist in the development of the resources of the world, and in the political, economic and social life of our nations.

The more our focus is aimed at the centrality of people and their potential, the more we can examine which are the areas in which investment in social expenditures should be directed. Obviously, primary concern should be dedicated to survival, to basic healthcare and the elimination of those diseases which threaten the survival especially of children, to nutrition, to education and especially the improvement of the basic education of women, a most important force in development potential, to improving the basic technical and technological abilities and formation of the young, so that they can become active participants of the economic development of their nation. The exclusion of vast sectors of our peoples from being able to contribute to building society through their own work is one of the greatest collective violations of people's rights and of exclusion from the mainstream of social progress in today's world. It is also a waste of valuable human resources.

But our vision must accompany this thrust on the centrality of the human person with reflection on the nature of the human family and on solidarity among peoples, who have a right to a share in the goods of the earth, which are in their origin destined for all, and must be responsibly administered by all.

The fundamental basis of all solidarity is the recognition that we all belong to the one human family and that we have a right to participate in development and to a share in the fruits of development. The Summit for Social Development — if it is to be a success — must not only work toward solidarity, but it must be marked by solidarity and inspired by solidarity. A Summit which recognizes the mutuality of needs and means which characterize the various regions of the world will reflect that basic sense of solidarity also in its working methods.

Solidarity means not only recognizing the needs of others, much less just sympathy. Solidarity means recognition of interdependence and must result in shared participation. Sustainable economic growth requires the participation of people and the ability to harness their potential. The same applies to democracy. The end of totalitarian systems — whether of a military or ideological kind — has not automatically resulted in implanting full democracy in various parts of the world. The reforms needed to underpin lasting democracy will only succeed if they are set within economic and social policies which foster social participation and take careful note of all their social consequences, especially for the poorest.

The social consequences of growth and economic reform cannot be overlooked. When growth does not result in social equity or social justice it carries within itself a self-destroying element.

Our final document must apply this principle in many specific areas. One would have to draw attention, for example, to the level of corruption which can enter into the public service and which requires constant monitoring. Great disservice is done through lack of overall responsibility in the use of resources which causes disenchantment on the part of citizens. Attention should be drawn to the disproportion between spending on armaments and on social spending. The free-market system is the system best suited to the development of a sound economy. But there are also some basic needs which the market does not satisfy and where public authorities have the responsibility to bring correctives and eliminate abuses (Cf. Pope John Paul II, Encyclical Letter *Centesimus annus* n. 34). Lack of equity, discrimination in access to social services, lack of efficiency in the working of these services, all lead to a weakening of the bond between people and State. The Summit, while maintaining the principle that responsibility for social policy remains with the nations, should clearly enunciate some basic internationally respected principles in these and other areas.

In speaking of the delivery of social services, it would be impossible in this International Year of the Family not to mention the potential of the *family* as a factor for social integration and progress. The Summit must work to enable the family to carry out its functions as the basic social — and socializing — group unit of society. The work of the family in the transmission of values and traditions is also a contribution to social integration.

The same should also be applied to voluntary organizations and to the other components of civil society, which constitutes the wealth of any true democracy and an essential part of the fabric of society.

The concept of the solidarity of the human family also draws our attention to the need, in order to foster social development, to see that all the members of the human community can grow in a climate that fosters both diversity and harmony, as should be the case with any family. Social disintegration is among the biggest challenges to development and peace. Examples of social disintegration can be found on the local and community level, through the weakening of family and community links, through the growth of criminality and the spread of drugs. On an international level we find that very often in analyzing many conflicts, which are all too easily described as nationalistic, ethnic or religious, the real roots can in fact be traced to the inability of one or both of the parties to achieve a desired level of social development.

Mr. Chairman,

The field that is opened out to us in our preparation for the World Summit is vast. Social development is a theme which goes way beyond what has been traditionally considered, either as social policy or as development policy. The danger of becoming dispersed in our reflection is great. But we must recall that the insight underlying the Summit is valid. Putting that insight into practice is possible. Indeed it is necessary. No other model of development will in fact succeed.

STATEMENT BY
MONSIGNOR DIARMUID MARTIN
UNDER-SECRETARY OF THE
PONTIFICAL COUNCIL FOR JUSTICE AND PEACE
AND HEAD OF THE DELEGATION OF THE HOLY SEE
TO THE FIRST SESSION OF THE PREPARATORY COMMITTEE FOR THE
WORLD SUMMIT FOR SOCIAL DEVELOPMENT
NEW YORK, 7 FEBRUARY 1994

Mr. Chairman,

The problem of poverty is one of the great ethical problems of our sophisticated and developed world. Ethics can help us clarify and focus on the challenges and the significance of poverty. Solutions, however, require economic and political decisions.

1. **Definition of poverty**

In the definition of poverty economic and technical indicators are important. But fundamentally poverty must be defined by its opposite. We must reaffirm that all individuals and social groups have a right to live in conditions which enable them to provide for personal and family needs and to share in the life and progress of the local community. Poverty is the absence of essential necessities to which every man, woman and child has a right.

The actual conditions in which a great number of people are living are an insult to their innate dignity and are a threat to the authentic and harmonious progress of the world community.

The person who is poor enjoys the same rights and dignity as every other person. This should be reflected in all the initiatives that the community, the State or the international community take in their behalf. Poverty offends their dignity. Our response should not humiliate people even more. We should always bear this in mind in reflecting on the quality of the services which are provided to the poor.

2. **The question of transition**

Many countries today find themselves in situations of economic transition. These are the countries explicitly so-called, especially in Central and Eastern Europe. Others are going through a similar process of moving to a different form of economic system. Certain African countries are undergoing rapid political, economic and social change, very often in a very difficult climate.

We need in those situations an ethics and a politics for transition. The fight against poverty requires economic reforms and stability. But what are we going to say of a situation in which one of the first effects of a process which is to lead to democracy and a market economy is that the poor get poorer? That the weak find their situation even more precarious? The experience of many nations present here is that the existing safety nets which are part of adjustment and transition programs are not sufficient.

Perhaps the present structures of the U.N. system which deal with economic adjustment and monetary reform are not adequate or appropriate and there may be a need for a new pillar or focal point of that system which has the mandate to identify and to respond to the social dimensions of such economic adjustment.

But we should never forget that the greatest wish of the poor is to get out of their poverty. They do not wish to remain forever in a safety net, but to get up and stand on their own two feet.

An ethics of transition should especially identify those types of intervention, even in the transition period, which enable and empower people to become part of that new social system which is to be the end point of transition.

The transition involves not only the economic system, but also the people and the ability of people to participate and benefit from that system. This involves access to resources, to credit, to training and re-training, to cooperation, to organizations and to the market.

3.   **The international debt question**

The problem of repayments on external debt is a serious problem with social consequences. In many developing countries debt repayment strangles the possibility of investment in social development.

When history looks back at the current international debt crisis, it will be remembered as a particular and short chapter of economic history. We must remember that this chapter had a beginning at a specific moment, in a special economic situation.

The debt crisis involves the responsibility of many and — let us say it — also the lack of responsibility on the part of many. It is important to remember that there was irresponsible lending, irresponsible spending, irresponsible monitoring of what was happening.

What is now important for the good of all is that this chapter of economic history not drag on indefinitely but also end at a particular moment, if we are to have social progress in developing countries. At the very least, the favorable terms which have been proposed should be more effectively applied.

But the resolution of the effects of the debt question requires at the same time a renewed sense of responsibility, equity and transparency in the economic management of developing countries. A number of interventions last week spoke of the question of corruption. Corruption in the economic sphere has a twofold negative effect. It reduces confidence in real needed investment. And the poor rightly become more disenchanted when they see resources they so badly need being wasted.

Thank you, Mr. Chairman.

Comments by Monsignor Diarmuid Martin
Secretary of the Pontifical Council for Justice and Peace
and Head of the Holy See Delegation
to the Preparatory Committee for the
World Summit for Social Development
on the Section "An Enabling Environment"
New York, 22 August 1994

I would like to make some comments on the concept of human security, which is emerging as a central theme of our reflection.

Human security offers a hopeful concept which points to a new manner in which national and global security can be conceived. Everyone will be happy to see the world move from a concept of security based on military means to one where human concerns are placed at the center.

But it may not be quite so easy to pass from one vision of security to the other, if we do define human security and not look in greater depth at the differences between the two ways of understanding security. It is not enough that we change the adjective *military* to *human*: what must change, above all, is the way we understand and apply the word security. If we do not bring about a change in mentality among nations, then, to adapt the words of the Secretary General this morning, we will be fighting tomorrow's battles with other weapons, but which are still yesterday's.

What was the basic context of yesterday's security debate? Confrontation, inequality in the relationships between States, the legacy of colonialism, trade imbalances and economic exploitation. The security interests of States and blocks were argued and fought out often in distant parts of the world, which had other problems which were not faced. Security concepts shaped the relationship between States and between governments and their people. Super-power strategies of security stressed containment and management.

The move from old security concepts, both international and national, will require a much greater change of mentality than we might appreciate and may not take place overnight. Without a radical change of mentality in which security becomes people's security, then human security could turn out to be simply a new system of social management in the name of security; interventions in the name of human security could turn out to be interventions to contain social unrest or avoid social threat; social investments could be conditioned on political conformity, in the name of national or regional security or indeed in terms of the national security interests of other countries; warfare could be replaced only by international welfare, rather than a system in which people are enabled to take their development interests and priorities into their own hands, in such a way as they can build their own security.

One has only to look at the manner in which some debates, in various parts of the world, concerning immigration are conducted in the name of security, to see that security can be used to back up fear rather than to promote solidarity.

Human security, or more precisely people's security, can only be a totally different kind of security which must radically change the relationship between States to one of solidarity, and the manner in which governments should exercise the mandate they receive from people to a relationship of participation, to human advancement and respect for human rights.

Briefly on the question of debt relief, especially in Africa, and of structural adjustment programs, I would strongly support what our text, and what the Secretary General and various other speakers have said today. Social concerns must receive greater attention, indeed priority attention, in all structural adjustment programs. Perhaps it might be useful in our later reflection of possible new orientations in the United Nations system and its working to propose also a structural adjustment in that very system, which would guarantee a stronger institutional voice for social and humanitarian concerns within or alongside the Bretton Woods Institutions, so that social considerations are more adequately, systematically and organically taken into account in all global trade negotiations and programs for monetary and economic reforms.

COMMENTS BY MONSIGNOR DIARMUID MARTIN SECRETARY OF THE PONTIFICAL COUNCIL FOR JUSTICE AND PEACE AND HEAD OF THE HOLY SEE DELEGATION TO THE PREPARATORY COMMITTEE FOR THE WORLD SUMMIT FOR SOCIAL DEVELOPMENT ON THE SECTION "REDUCTION AND ELIMINATION OF WIDESPREAD POVERTY"; NEW YORK, 23 AUGUST 1994

The Draft Plan of Action stresses that the struggle against poverty constitutes a moral obligation for the international community. This moral obligation has been repeated on so many occasions in similar documents. Yet poverty, and what is called extreme poverty, continues to persist in all parts of the world today.

The World Summit on Social Development, if it is to be worthy of its name, must at the very least set out clear goals for the elimination of extreme poverty within a determined period. These goals should address especially the questions of basic nutrition, shelter, education and health services. Such goals must be realistic, not in the traditional sense that they have a reasonable chance of success. No, they must be realistic goals in the sense that they involve a determined commitment on the part of the international community to their realization on time.

One of the most difficult tasks of the Summit, but perhaps the task on which its success hinges, is that of forging a viable link between the social and economic parts of its agenda. The Plan of Action must, therefore, pay greater attention to the interrelationship between the core themes. The elimination of poverty depends to a great degree on the evolution of creative and viable economic models.

My Delegation wishes in particular to endorse what is said in para. 34 concerning the fact that "efforts to reduce and eliminate poverty are a major contribution to growth." Social development, in fact, has an instrumental value in accelerating economic growth. Expenditures on improving human capabilities have the potential to yield a return to society as high as return on physical investment. This is clear, for example, from an analysis of the rate of return on expenditure in education. On the other hand, countries that neglect human development not only delay the expansion of human capabilities, they also undermine the country's long-term potential rate of economic growth.

Development, in the past, has been too much associated with expanding the supply of commodities. A new concept of social development must focus on the welfare of individuals in a society and must be seen in terms of the expansion of their capabilities for functioning and of their freedom to achieve combinations of functioning. The Plan of Action must, in this context, be clear on its concept of growth. It must look at the relationship between economic growth, on the one hand, and equity and freedom, on the other. There is no need to have a trade-off between economic growth and equity, given the right balance of policies. Indeed without some form of equity, a concern for human needs and respect for human rights, in the broad sense, political stability is not possible and without political stability investment and growth cannot be sustained.

A notion of grassroots and participatory development is one example of an economically viable program of poverty eradication. It is premised on the fact that people have creativity, knowledge and wisdom, and can be trusted. Grassroots development can help to keep the local economic surplus in the hands of the poor and set in motion a new accumulation process, but also establish an all-round development in their lives, which is sustainable, that is ecologically sound and rational in its use of natural resources and which better responds to concrete needs. Participation can also reduce the cost of public services by shifting responsibility from central and local government (where costs are high) to the grassroots level (where costs are low).

A participatory development process, with people as its subject, should start simply and build gradually on the people's own awareness of their economic, political and ecological reality. The consequent improvement of their resource position and technological capability, through collective effort, would impart also greater community consciousness, which would in turn create the social substructures for further progress in the areas of education and better healthcare services. It could also have the effect of encouraging regional development, discouraging the process of urbanization and the move by the poor to large cities, which are in fact very often least able to cope with their problems.

A people's summit, a true notion of people's security, must make it very clear that investment in people is the best way to overcome poverty, and also makes economic sense.

COMMENTS BY MONSIGNOR FRANK J. DEWANE MEMBER OF THE HOLY SEE DELEGATION TO THE PREPARATORY COMMITTEE FOR THE WORLD SUMMIT FOR SOCIAL DEVELOPMENT ON THE SECTION "SOCIAL INTEGRATION"
NEW YORK, 24 AUGUST 1994

Mr. Chairman,

My Delegation will be brief in commenting on Chapter IV of the Draft Program of Action.

In discussing social integration, or a culture of participation, education for all is most important, and must be given priority consideration. Emphasis should be placed on the quality of education and the reduction of wide divergence, especially for women and the poor. This must include an education to values and to the spiritual dimensions of the person.

As was heard several times this morning, social participation is an area which calls for a more dynamic treatment of the family — as a means of social support and in the delivery of social services. Measures must be developed to assist families living in conditions of poverty or on the borderline of poverty who are, in many cases, penalized by tax systems. It is as the basic unit of society that the family passes on the moral and ethical values which foster and are part of the concept of social integration.

The disruptive and destructive factor of violence is a major barrier to social integration in many societies. This violence is manifest in various forms and to varying degrees, in some States marginalizing segments of the society — both perpetrators and victims.

In conclusion, the role and responsibility of the media as an instrument to foster social integration is deserving of added consideration. The media can be central to the formation of values which a society manifests toward all its members and toward the diverse groups which constitute the society.

Thank you, Mr. Chairman.

COMMENTS BY
MONSIGNOR FRANK J. DEWANE
MEMBER OF THE HOLY SEE DELEGATION TO THE
PREPARATORY COMMITTEE FOR THE
WORLD SUMMIT FOR SOCIAL DEVELOPMENT
ON THE SECTION "THE DECLARATION"
NEW YORK, 25 AUGUST 1994

The Delegation of the Holy See is of the opinion that the Declaration should present a vision and do this in a concise manner. However, this vision must come from a stated context and that context is where the world is today. Therefore, the entire Declaration may not necessarily all appear in positive terms. This vision must secure the commitment, hopefully not limited to the political realm, of governments, a commitment needed to translate the Social Summit into action for all.

The vision presented must also incorporate the centrality of the human person with reflection on the nature of *people security* and on *solidarity* among the peoples of the world. The fundamental basis of all solidarity is the recognition that we belong to the one human family.

For some it may be too abstract to speak of one human family in the broad sense. However, at the entrance of the Conference Room this morning there was a poster which read, "Build the smallest democracy at the heart of society." This poster is part of the celebration of the International Year of the Family. The family, the basic unit of society, offers the most natural of units to serve for the delivery of social services and as a means of social support. Yesterday we heard the central role of the family noted several times and it was referred to as the "pillar for social cohesion" and as "the building brick of society." This pillar, this building brick, should certainly be central to the Declaration.

In the text before us, my Delegation notes with particular interest the section of the Declaration on "the moral fibre of contemporary societies." It welcomes the opportunity to openly address and promote social values in a moral context. Still another section calls for "an intellectual, aesthetic and spiritual renewal." These are themes which often do not find resonance in these halls and are components deserving of discussion and consideration in the context of the World Summit for Social Development and in particular in this Declaration.

This brings my Delegation to echo what was mentioned earlier today by the distinguished Representative of Slovenia, that what may be made here is not simply a political commitment but a political/ethical commitment — a moral commitment.

Mr. Chairman, in conclusion the Delegation of the Holy See supports those calling for special consideration in this text to the social development needs of the African continent.

Statement by
Dr. Joaquín Navarro-Valls
Director of the Press Office of the Holy See
on the World Summit for Social Development
Vatican, 28 February 1995

On 11 and 12 March a World Summit for Social Development will be held in Copenhagen, organized by the United Nations — in conformity with Resolution n. 47/92 of the General Assembly — at the level of Heads of State or Government. The Summit will be preceded by a meeting of Delegations specifically designated by the respective Governments, from 6 to 10 March.

Parallel to the World Summit, a Conference of non-governmental organizations (NGOs) will be organized.

All the member States of the United Nations and Permanent Observers, as well as the representatives of specialized agencies, have been invited to take part in this Summit.

The importance of the World Summit in Copenhagen is obvious: it is the first time in history that the international community, under the aegis of the United Nations Organization, will meet in the framework of a Conference to deal with the topic of social development. In this case there is no question of it being a North-South Convention or a meeting to evaluate the extent of the needs in certain sectors in each country. The Copenhagen Summit, in which 130 Heads of State or Government will take part, will draft strategic policies and concrete operational measures, in some cases with very clear time limits, aiming to promote social development on a world scale.

Participants in the World Summit — representatives of the Governments of both developed and developing countries — will sign the solemn commitment to adopt the resolutions of the Copenhagen Summit for dealing with the problems of unemployment, poverty and the lack of social development at both national and international levels.

The World Summit will examine and approve two documents: a Declaration and a Plan of Action.

The Programme of Action, 77 pages long, which includes strategies, procedures and measures to implement the principles and commitments contained in the Declaration, consists of five chapters. The first chapter proposes creating an environment suitable for social development. The second lists a series of operative decisions to eradicate poverty. The third envisions practical measures to create employment and to reduce unemployment. The fourth addresses the topic of social integration. The fifth spells out criteria for the application and evaluation of the measures adopted.

The last paragraph of the Declaration will adopt the resolution to convoke a session of the General Assembly in the year 2000 to review and evaluate the global application of the resolutions adopted at the Copenhagen Summit, and to examine the possible need for new initiatives.

The Holy See has staunchly upheld this initiative since it was formulated in 1992. Moreover, the Holy See has taken part in the three preparatory sessions for the Summit and made an effective contribution to drafting the two documents that will be approved in Copenhagen. It trusts and expects that the governments represented at the World Summit will assume the commitments subscribed to at the meeting, with measures in conformity with their respective social systems.

At the International Conference on Population and Development in Cairo, the Holy See Delegation repeatedly expressed the need to face developmental problems in a way that is both global and daring, rather than by focusing separately on the complex issues connected with poverty, which can be simplistic and sometimes heavily ideologized. The World Summit in Copenhagen welcomes this recommendation.

Some data make it possible to put the Copenhagen Summit in the right perspective. More than one billion people are currently living in a state of absolute poverty and they are mostly concentrated in the developing countries. A large number of people in these countries, most of whom are women, do not enjoy regular access to an income and resources, nor to basic social services. Unemployment is a scourge that affects all countries to a greater or lesser degree. Out of two billion people of working age, only 800 million have stable employment. About 770 million people die each year from causes directly linked to poverty. To a disproportionate degree, women bear the burden of poverty, which at times amounts to marginalization, suffer exclusion from decision-making processes, have greater difficulty in finding a place in educational institutions or even lack recognition of their basic human rights. More women than men live in utter poverty with predictable and tragic consequences for themselves and their children.

Although poverty concerns mainly the developing countries, in every country, even the affluent ones, there are "pockets of poverty" with unemployment, lack of social services, no access to education, undernourishment, etc. The North-South dimension is not an exclusively international yardstick; in fact, in all countries, even the developed, there is a domestic "North-South" phenomenon of affluence and poverty.

The Catholic Church has established and directs 170,433 educational institutions scattered throughout the world, institutions which cover the whole educational cycle from nursery school to university. In 1993, the number of students in these educational institutions amounted to 45,322,828. Many of these institutions are in Third World countries.

In the area of education and healthcare assistance, the Catholic Church directs 100,231 institutions all over the world, of which a considerable number are found in developing countries. These institutions range from hospitals or dispensaries to leprosaria, rest homes for the elderly, orphanages, family counseling centres or specialized centres for assistance to the seriously handicapped.

In addition, the Catholic Church has promoted a worldwide network of 985 national Catholic organizations dedicated to the promotion and distribution of financial resources for social and spiritual development. This network, in turn, is complemented by more than 20 well-known international aid organizations.

These figures make it possible to state that the Catholic Church today is one of the world's leading institutions in the field of education and social assistance and in the fight to eliminate the causes of poverty.

The Holy See Delegation, which brings with it the incomparable, age-old experience of the Catholic Church in the various fields of social development in the five continents, is going to Copenhagen determined to make an in-depth contribution — its contribution has already been decisive during the preparatory process for the Summit — in the legitimate hope that this first World Summit for Social Development may lead to a greater awareness of responsibilities and to a serious commitment at the international level. We believe that the World Summit offers an important opportunity to each country to make a serious commitment.

Some points of the documents that will be approved in Copenhagen could be improved or enriched. Nevertheless, overall they represent a collection of valid ideas and suggestions for implementation beyond the national level.

In them we find deep harmony with the Church's social teaching. On various points of the Agenda and the Plan of Action one can recognize echoes of the Church's social teaching, and in particular, of the recent social Encyclicals such as *Centesimus annus*. The Declaration to be approved in Copenhagen stresses that "our society must more effectively respond to the material and spiritual needs of individuals and their families" (Declaration, 2). The human being is considered the subject of development. The Document describes "the family as the basic unit of society and recognizes that it plays a key role in social development and as such, should be supported, with attention to the rights, abilities and responsibilities of its members" (Principles and Goals, h). Social development and social justice are achieving peace and security, both within and among peoples (Declaration, 5).

The Holy See Delegation, to which encouraging attention has been paid during the preparatory phase, is going to Copenhagen with the desire to help decisively overcome, in some circles, a certain scepticism as to the results of this Summit.

On the one hand, official funding for development has decreased by about 8 per cent in the past two years. Very few countries have accepted, for the moment, the proposal to direct 0.7 per cent of their gross national product to furthering development. On the other, this loss has been partially compensated for by private funding and interventions.

If, on the one hand, it seems legitimate to speak of a crisis of solidarity, on the other there are signs which justify a certain optimism. The presence in Copenhagen of thousands of representatives of the 2,400 NGOs will doubtless represent a moral support for the Delegates of the governments taking part in the Summit.

Among other things, the Holy See Delegation will give particular attention to the subject of immigrants' rights (Declaration, Commitment, 4), to absolute respect of human dignity, to equality and fairness between women and men, to the promotion and protection of women's human rights and their participation in social, political, economic and cultural leadership (Commitment, 5).

Furthermore, our Delegation intends to help reach a consensus on the topics of reducing military expenditure and the arms trade, particularly those weapons which have indiscriminate effects on civilian populations (Programme of Action, para. 71); and on reducing to the point of canceling the foreign debt of the less developed countries (Commitment, 8, n).

STATEMENT BY
MONSIGNOR DIARMUID MARTIN,
SECRETARY OF THE
PONTIFICAL COUNCIL FOR JUSTICE AND PEACE
AND HEAD OF THE HOLY SEE DELEGATION TO THE
WORLD SUMMIT FOR SOCIAL DEVELOPMENT
COPENHAGEN, 7 MARCH 1995

Mr. Chairman,
Distinguished Delegates,

1. If our work in these days is a success, then this World Summit and this city of Copenhagen will be remembered by history as a significant moment in humanity's struggle to overcome the scourge of poverty. If our work in these days fails, then this Summit will quickly be forgotten as just another well-intentioned but fruitless event. The decision rests with us. The responsibility is ours.

In offering you, Mr. Chairman, the congratulations of my Delegation on your election as Chairman of our proceedings, through you I wish to express the appreciation of the Holy See for all those who have worked in the preparation of the Summit. I express a special word of appreciation for Ambassador Juan Somavía who not only guided, but also inspired, our work over the past years. The Danish Government and the people of Denmark have shown us such warm hospitality.

I chose my opening words, Mr. Chairman, quite deliberately, because in many rather skeptical media comments on this Summit, setting the task of working towards the eradication of poverty has been written off as something unrealistic. Certainly our programmes should be realistic. If anything, we should face such a task with a certain humility, knowing from past experience how our plans have not always come to fruition. But mere scepticism, and lack of concrete action, in the face of the extent of extreme poverty in today's world, would simply be unworthy of humankind.

2. Most of us before coming here will have been asked: "What difference will the Copenhagen Summit make?" The answer to that question will hopefully be found in a key word we use throughout our Declaration. That word is *commitment*. The leaders of the world's nations come together at this Summit not just to study, to analyze, to reflect on or to discuss poverty, productive employment and social integration. They come, individually and collectively, to commit themselves, and to commit themselves publicly. They will make a promise to those one billion people

in today's world who live in abject poverty, to do something concrete and definitive about their situation. The actions we propose must naturally be adapted to the special needs and situation of individual countries. But they cannot be realized without the support of all, without the support of the community of nations. We all know how past actions or failure to act have contributed to the lack of social development and to current inequities. With our commitment, we now promise to initiate what Pope John Paul II called, in speaking on the past two Sundays about our Summit, "a new phase on the path of humanity."

It is on the degree and on the strength of our commitment that the hope of the Summit hinges.

3. Our reflection today is principally on the theme of poverty. It is the core issue which, perhaps more than any other, has attracted the attention of public opinion.

The documents of the Summit have rightly seen the connection between poverty and economic factors. We must look at the type of economic environment we wish to create. Eliminating poverty means, among other things, permitting all people, especially women and persons with disabilities, to be active participants in the economy and in society. The effectiveness of our economic systems to meet the needs of people must be constantly evaluated. A system which leaves substantial sectors of a nation or a community on the margins, unable actively to contribute their talents to society and to the economy, has failed those persons. And further, such a system, apart from all considerations of a moral nature, does not make good economic sense.

In section (e) of our Commitment 1 on *an enabling economic environment* for social development, we will endorse certain essential aspects of an economic system geared to fight the root causes of poverty. We recognize the value and importance of dynamic, open and free markets, but we also see the need for intervention, to the extent necessary, to provide an ethically-based juridical framework within which the market can work, and we stress the role of governments in harmonizing economic and social development, especially through basic social protection. Finally, we see the need to do more to enable people living in poverty to bring their own contribution. All of these factors must be fostered in an economic system which is at the service of a person-centred sustainable development.

Persons living in poverty have the same dignity as every other person. Persons living in poverty have potential which they have a right to see recognized. Very often, those who are living in poverty may know best how to improve their economic situation. But they are not heard or they do not have access to credit or training. This is especially true of women in many areas.

There are people living in poverty and people living in affluence in all countries and there is a North and a South in every country, in every city, in every community. Poverty and unsustainable lifestyle exist side-by-side. All too often it is a question of existing side-by-side, without any contact. An invisible line divides many of our societies and communities and people rarely even know the conditions on the other side. At times the quality of the services offered by the same authorities varies enormously, with those offered to the poorest being inferior to others.

4. Just as persons living in poverty must be given the opportunity to become protagonists of the economy and society, the poorest countries must be enabled to take their place as true partners in international economic activities and in international life. Our documents mention the specific needs of the countries of Africa, the countries of South Asia with substantial concentrations of people living in poverty, the countries with economies in transition, the Small Island Developing States. Each of these groups has very specific problems which require the support of the community of nations.

Our texts rightly look at two special aspects of economic life linked to poverty and especially to the situation of the poor countries. The first is that of external debt. We have not yet reached complete agreement on the manner in which to finally address this question. We all know, however, the history of the current international debt situation. It is a history with a specific beginning, in particular economic circumstances. We have to recognize that this history has been marked, among other aspects, by irresponsible spending, but also by irresponsible lending. Just as this situation had a particular beginning, we must set our minds towards bringing it rapidly to a definitive conclusion. The best available terms must be applied — and applied rapidly — so that normal patterns of credit, lending and investment, especially in the social sphere, can be restored. The resolution of the international debt problem is an economic question, but is also a question of political will. Surely that will can be found.

The debt problem is linked also with that of adjustment, which is in its turn linked to transition. By their nature both these terms point to something, to some important aim, towards which we are working. Transition and adjustment must also be looked on in a people-centred manner. We wish to move towards democratic, socially-oriented market economies, so that the needs of people can be better addressed, so that people can make the fullest use of their potential. People are prepared to accept hardship when they know that they are on the road to something better. But when the initial sustained impact with the desired reality brings with it a situation in which the poorest are the first to suffer even more, we cannot be surprised when the very goal towards which we are moving becomes discredited in their eyes. Adjustment or transition means also that those who were marginalized in the older system must be provided with the training needed to make them the protagonists of the new.

5. I wish, Mr. Chairman, finally to look at the relationship between the family and poverty. The institution of the family must receive comprehensive protection and support. The rights, capabilities and responsibilities of the individual members can indeed be fostered through the experience of this first human community, this first school of social values. Parents must be helped and sustained in their irreplaceable contribution to society. Their task today can be an extraordinarily difficult one. But without the contribution of parents, society would be the poorer. Parents want the best for the children and their rights should be protected. Special attention should be given to those families who care for disabled or elderly members, and for single-parent families, especially those headed by women, who are often exposed to extremely precarious situations.

Mr. Chairman,

The Holy See strongly endorses the basic ideas which have inspired this World Summit. At a time when, in many sectors, we are confronted with a drop in financial resources for social and developmental programmes, it is encouraging to note that the caring institution of the Catholic Church, as also those of other religious and voluntary organizations, receive continued generous community support. In the face of signs of receding solidarity, of fatigue, this network of institutions is firmly committed to an agenda of solidarity.

These organizations, witnesses of an active participatory society, commit themselves, Mr. Chairman, to realize the aims of our Summit, and its implementation, for the good of all people.

INTERVIEW OF
DR. JOAQUÍN NAVARRO-VALLS,
DIRECTOR OF THE PRESS OFFICE OF THE HOLY SEE,
AFTER THE INAUGURATION OF THE
WORLD SUMMIT FOR SOCIAL DEVELOPMENT
COPENHAGEN, 8 MARCH 1995

Vatican Information Service (VIS), 8 March 1995 — Speaking to journalists after the inauguration of the World Summit for Social Development in Copenhagen, Dr. Joaquín Navarro-Valls, Director of the Press Office of the Holy See, noted that "the question is, will the Summit be able to translate the enormous hopes expressed, not only by public opinion but also by the Delegations present, into operative realities?"

"Why I say this," he continued, "is because there seems to be a certain dose of skepticism in some Western countries." He added that "there is no discussion on the content of the draft of the Declaration, which in general is good enough, but on having the courage to actualize the points mentioned in the Final Document ... because these principles involve changes in political positions." He explained it is precisely this skeptical position that the Delegation from the Holy See is trying to overcome.

On the central theme of social development, he added "one cannot resolve the problems through free market forces alone; it is necessary to introduce social correctives based on serious ethical reflection." Moreover, he explained: "All countries, including the rich ones, have serious social problems. They, too, must follow the directives of world strategy on development."

Navarro-Valls said that "statesmen and economists should recognize the role of certain jobs in society, such as domestic work, and realize the adjustments they require." At this moment he also recalled that "very few developed countries follow the recommendation to allocate 0.7% of their Gross National Product (GNP) as an official fund for development."

On a question about "reproductive health," Navarro-Valls answered that "what is missing is a clarification on this concept ... It is like not really knowing what is in the box."

HOLY SEE PRESS CONFERENCE BY
DR. JOAQUÍN NAVARRO-VALLS,
MSGR. DIARMUID MARTIN AND MRS. PATRICIA DONAHOE
DURING THE WORLD SUMMIT FOR SOCIAL DEVELOPMENT
COPENHAGEN, 9 MARCH 1995

Vatican Information Service (VIS), 10 March 1995 — Msgr. Diarmuid Martin, head of the Holy See Delegation to the World Summit for Social Development in Copenhagen, Patricia Donahoe and Joaquín Navarro-Valls, both members of the Delegation, held a Press Conference at the Summit's Bella Center yesterday afternoon in which they outlined the concerns of the Holy See at this Summit and what it hoped to see accomplished.

Navarro-Valls, Holy See Press Office Director, chaired the Conference and took questions from the journalists.

Msgr. Martin, in an opening statement, referred to the three issues being addressed in Copenhagen at the Summit — poverty, unemployment and social integration — and said that it was "a crime to the conscience of humanity" that more than one billion people in the world are living in poverty.

On both unemployment and under-employment, he said, "it is the Holy See's concern that people who find themselves in these situations are not able to contribute to society the talents that they have and thus are not able to realize their human dignity. It is a very strong principle of the social teaching of Pope John Paul II that work belongs to the very dignity of the human person."

He pointed out in this regard that the Holy See "had initiated a proposal at this Summit by looking at the idea of new approaches to work and of giving societal recognition to unpaid work and also of proposing language which would insert such work into the national statistics of Gross National Product (GNP). We put this concept into the text and want to keep it open and in front of the international community."

Turning to the issue of social integration, he said the Holy See "places great emphasis on education, in particular the fight against illiteracy. There are 950 million illiterate people in the world, two-thirds of whom are women. People cannot take their real part in society if they are unable to read and write. We supported all references to persons with disabilities and we also introduced a phrase we consider important dealing with the arms trade and arms expenditures, not only asking that overall expenditures be reduced and money be given to social expenditure but that certain types of arms which are particularly injurious and have indiscriminate effects — an example would be land mines — be mentioned in the text."

Msgr. Martin said that, although these concepts were absent from the preparatory sessions, when the Holy See introduced them, people took note. "It often happens that when something becomes an issue of public opinion, leaders will then act on it."

He said that the Holy See has placed strong emphasis on the family which "at certain moments in the draft, seemed to be missing. The concept of the family is essential to any concept of social development."

Asked if the Holy See would make reservations to parts of the Final Document, Msgr. Martin responded that meetings were still continuing on a number of points in the Summit document and said he would have to see the final text before definitively answering this question.

"If the Summit is a success, to whom does the merit go?" asked one journalist. Msgr. Martin replied: "In the first place it goes to the organizers who had the courage to call such a Summit, to put on the agenda of the United Nations the problems of ordinary people. Secondly, much will depend on public opinion which will drive these issues to the center of attention."

Patricia Donahoe, answering a question on the reunification of families of migrants, said that there was not much opposition to reunification but there was concern for the rights of the child, especially in cases of families where the child might be abused, who in this case should be protected.

Both Msgr. Martin and Patricia Donahoe responded to questions regarding the definition of the family used in the document. Mrs. Donahoe stated that the definition was essentially that coming from the Cairo document and Msgr. Martin added: "The definition was taken from Cairo with one exceptional change or addition. It speaks of also respecting the rights of individual family members. The basic principle of this definition is that it asserts, reaffirms, and endorses the concept of the family as the basic unit of society which is entitled to comprehensive support."

Msgr. Martin stated that "one of the most important things the Holy See has tried to do here is be supportive, to draw attention to the fact that, even though we don't agree with every detail of the program, the theme that was chosen is central to anybody who is concerned about the dignity of humankind. We will continue as we always have done in the types of services to peoples of all faiths, or none, who are in need." He illustrated to the journalists graphs depicting the Roman Catholic Church's 270,664 educational, welfare and health institutions throughout the world.

INTERVENTION OF
MONSIGNOR DIARMUID MARTIN
SECRETARY OF THE
PONTIFICAL COUNCIL FOR JUSTICE AND PEACE
AT THE 34TH SESSION OF THE
COMMISSION FOR SOCIAL DEVELOPMENT
NEW YORK 18 APRIL 1995

Item 5: Priority subject: World Summit for Social Development

The World Summit for Social Development was the most significant and innovative moment in recent years in international reflection on social development. It is obvious that the Summit should receive the consideration of this Commission. It is also inevitable that the innovative nature of the Summit will have significant effects on the work of the Commission for the future.

The question of follow-up is of greater importance in the case of the World Summit on Social Development than in the case of all the other recent and upcoming International Conferences, because:

— it was the first Summit of its kind;

— it was truly innovative in its work: it set out, for the first time, in an integrated way, the notion and the policy implications of "people-centred sustainable development";

— it does not, like the other Conferences, have a clear single principal follow-up body within the U.N. system.

If the question of follow-up is not urgently addressed, there is the danger that the Summit's work and originality will be lost, precisely to that sectoral approach which the Summit wished to avoid.

The work of follow-up is urgent, but it cannot be done by simple superficial changes of formulae. It requires systematic examination within the U.N. system, within the U.N. Secretariat and within the integrated and comprehensive examination of the results of the series of International Conferences which have touched on social issues.

This meeting, at this moment so soon after the conclusion of the Copenhagen Summit, cannot do more than set the scene for that long-term follow-up. But it must be seen to do precisely that: to set the scene for the examination by ECOSOC for a truly effective programme of application of the Summit's programme.

This could perhaps most easily be achieved by a brief Resolution or paper, which recalls and puts into focus the originality of the approach of the Summit: an originality which must not be lost, but an originality which — precisely because it looked at social development in an integrated context — is hard, as yet, to fit into existing structures and reflection.

Such a Resolution might draw on the language of the Copenhagen documents themselves, around which there is already consensus, to indicate a series of areas where the Summit stressed an integrated vision of social development and to which this Commission, at the minimum, feels it must draw the attention of ECOSOC.

The Resolution could draw on, among others, such themes as:

— (Para. 6, Declaration): Economic development, social development and environmental protection are interdependent and mutually reinforcing components of sustainable development;

— (Art. 21, c, Declaration): Social development is a national responsibility, but cannot be successfully achieved without the collective commitment and efforts of the international community;

— (Commitment 1): Social development requires the creation — and the consistent evaluation — of an appropriate economic, political, social, cultural and legal environment;

— (Para. 2, Declaration) The core issues of Copenhagen are interlinked and affect every country. People-centred social development must find ways and institutions to ensure that this linkage is not lost;

— (Para. 94, 95, Programme of Action): The follow-up of the Summit involves the entire UN system, with each organism responding according to its own mandate, but with an adequate reviewing and monitoring process to oversee integration.

There are two other points which, according to my Delegation, must find some echo in any Resolution if it is to be true to the spirit of the Copenhagen Summit. These are:

- the role of civil society: Participation was a key concept of the Summit. The long term success of the Summit will depend not only on governments and international organizations, but on the ability to set in motion and keep alive a popular movement, a sense of concern among people for the importance of a concept of development centred on the human person.

In the long run, political will is created and sustained by popular thinking. The Summit follow-up must change not only government policies and international organizations. It must reach the way in which people think and commit themselves on social questions. Ways must be found to permit the contributions of people to reach policy makers on an international level.

- the centrality of the fight against absolute poverty. This is the aspect which caught greatest public attention. The Heads of State were seen to say: the existence of widespread absolute poverty in today's world is a scandal which cannot be accepted. The urgency of this primary commitment must not be lost.

Mr. Chairman,

The Resolution could finally note the need, within the overall evaluation and follow-up process to Copenhagen, to examine the specific role of the Commission for Social Development and its working methods, in order to make it a more effective instrument at the service of ECOSOC in the application of the Copenhagen Summit.

Intervention of
His Excellency Archbishop Renato R. Martino
Apostolic Nuncio, Permanent Observer of the Holy See
to the United Nations
at the 86th Plenary Meeting of the Fiftieth Session
of the General Assembly
on Item 161: "World Summit for Social Development"
New York, 8 December 1995

1. Within the framework of the various recent International Conferences, the World Summit for Social Development holds a special place. At Copenhagen, for the first time, the community of nations attempted to examine in an integrated manner those factors which influence, in a positive and in a negative way, human and social development. Heads of State and Government committed themselves to build a "culture of cooperation and partnership" to respond to the needs of all, especially those most affected by human distress.

The Summit marked an important moment in our understanding of the word *development*. The term development, since the Copenhagen Summit, can never again be separated from its essential human and social dimensions. The centrality of the human person in the development process, a principle recognized already in the Rio Declaration, has been more firmly anchored as essential to any true notion of development.

When the Copenhagen Summit speaks of "people-centered sustainable development" it clearly wishes this centrality of the human person to be the key to the interpretation of that phrase. We can truly speak of development only when the needs and the security of all persons and communities are respected and guaranteed. We can speak of true development only when the rights of all are respected and when all persons and communities have access to what they need to exercise their rights effectively.

The manner in which governments approach the follow-up to the Summit will be a sign of the seriousness with which they wish to respond to the commitments, solemnly made at Copenhagen, by their Heads of State or Government.

2. The Summit emphasized the primary responsibility of national governments for social development, while at the same time recognizing that social development "cannot be successfully achieved without the collective commitment and efforts of the international community" [Copenhagen Declaration, n. 26, (c)]. Precisely on the level of the international

community, the Summit on Social Development, unlike the other recent international Conferences, does not have one clear focal point within the United Nations system to coordinate its follow-up. The Summit touched on areas which are the competence of various bodies and specialized agencies. It is important, however, that the follow-up process does not lose anything of the integrated approach to the questions that characterized the Summit's own originality. The Commission for Social Development might assume, within the United Nations system, a particular role in the follow-up and development of this integrated approach. It is to be hoped that the Commission for Social Development can be strengthened and rendered more effective, in order to become a focal point for the witness of the United Nations system to social development as a priority of its activity.

3. The Summit also recognized the special contribution which non-governmental organizations and "civil society" are called to play in social development. All actors in the area of social development are called to foster a renewed sense of solidarity in today's world, both within individual countries and on the international level.

The human person can only reach full development in a spirit of community and solidarity with others. No individual, no community, no economic unit can live in isolation from others. The recognition of the interdependence of all nations only strengthens the aspiration for greater solidarity. A process of globalization, without the safeguard of a determined ethic of solidarity, can only result in rendering existing imbalances more acute. Development and peace depend on the ability of persons and peoples to establish bonds of solidarity. Pope John Paul II, in his speech to the General Assembly on 5 October last, expressed this desire for greater solidarity, asking that the international community become a "family of nations." "The idea of family," the Pope noted, "immediately evokes something more than simple functional relations or a mere convergence of interests. The family is by nature a community based on mutual trust, mutual support and sincere respect. In an authentic family the strong do not dominate; instead, the weaker members, because of their weakness, are all the more welcomed and served" (n. 14).

The same spirit of solidarity must be a mark of relationships within each nation. In speaking about the theme of poverty, in the context of the Social Summit, Pope John Paul posed a question concerning the alternatives with which each society is faced today: "Do we want a civilization of love which involves all humanity, or a civilization of individual withdrawal, where love is absent and which leads inexorably to a world 'which does not know where it is going'"? (*Address to the Pontifical Council "Cor Unum"*, 27 October 1995, n. 2). Even since the commitments made at Copenhagen, however, we can see further signs emerging, in various parts of the world, of a kind of individual and collective withdrawal from a true spirit of solidarity. Such a withdrawal into individual and collective isolationism is not worthy of a world which possesses unprecedented possibilities of resolving the most urgent problems of social development. We must see that the noble commitments of the World Summit are not allowed to evaporate, even in the face of the current financial difficulties which almost all nations are facing.

4.   The spirit of solidarity must be a mark of economic systems. The Copenhagen Summit stressed clearly the importance of "dynamic, open, free markets." It also recalled, however, the need for appropriate intervention "to prevent or counteract market failure, promote stability and long term investment, ensure fair competition and ethical conduct, and harmonize economic and social development." In the same context it stressed the need for programmes "that would entitle and enable people living in poverty and the disadvantaged, especially women, to participate fully and productively in the economy and society" [Commitment 1, (e)].

       Whereas the Summit's final documents do not set out to present a comprehensive and complete vision of the role of the economy at the service of the human community, there are many references which call for innovative approaches in this area. It is to be hoped that in the future, some of these areas will be the subject of greater investigation and research. Providing access for all to opportunities for economic security and development is a major challenge for the future. An economic system which leaves large sectors of the population on its margins, without access to its benefits and opportunities, especially employment, is not a just one, and indeed makes bad economic sense. An economic system must foster the widest participation and contribution of all. "Poverty cannot be definitively eradicated," Pope John Paul adds, "unless the poor themselves take their own destiny in hand and are involved in the conception and implementation of programmes directly concerning them. Only in this way will they rediscover their dignity" (*Address to "Cor Unum,"* n. 5).

5.   The Delegation of the Holy See wishes to draw special attention to the commitments and promises made at Copenhagen concerning the question of external debt, especially that of the poorest countries. There is need for greater cooperation between nations and international organizations to monitor, and alleviate, the effects of debt burdens, especially on the ability of countries to dedicate the necessary funds to social needs. The Commitment to "develop techniques of debt conversion applied to social development programmes" [Commitment 7 (c)] as well as that concerning "the immediate implementation" of certain favourable measures for the

poorest countries, must not remain a dead letter.

6.   At Copenhagen, the Heads of State recognized the fact that "our societies must respond more effectively to the material and *spiritual needs* of individuals, their families and the communities in which they live throughout our diverse countries and regions" (Copenhagen Declaration, n. 3). Again, it is stressed that the vision of social development endorsed by the Summit and its participants was a "political, economic, ethical and spiritual vision" (Copenhagen Declaration, n. 25). Indeed, one of the preparatory seminars for the Summit was precisely on the subject of the "Ethical and Spiritual Dimensions of Social Progress." There can be no vision of social progress or social development which does not finally come to examine in depth the need for a renewal of the "human spirit" and which does marvel at the innate goodness and inherent dignity of humankind, while at the same time stopping in the face of the evil that human beings are capable of inflicting on their brothers and sisters.

Governments are aware of the limits of their mandate and sphere of competence in this area. But experience shows how much it is necessary to face our challenges today in the field of social development with a spirit of compassion, responsibility and courage. We know that many of the great social wounds which mark our era, especially as the result of war and conflicts, can only be healed in the context of forgiveness and reconciliation, and full respect for the rights of individuals and communities.

These are ethical and spiritual values which we all recognize as essential for social development. Our programme for the future requires us to look more closely at them and at the type of society we wish to create and transmit to the coming generations. Governments must facilitate all those who wish to make their contribution to such a process of reflection and action. They must ensure that a climate for dialogue and the building of community can be constructed at all levels of society. The richness of the diversity of cultural traditions must be welcomed and embraced. The inspiration which so many persons derive from their religious belief must be allowed to flourish for the good of society. The cultures and religious sentiments of all, and in particular of indigenous people, must be fully respected by governments and international organizations. The family must be supported so that it can more effectively provide its irreplaceable role in a changing world. These are all aspects which belong to the heritage of humankind. Their protection is demanded as a fundamental right. A legitimate respect for pluralism in our societies, should not result in a weakening of our commitment to those common values, without which society will only lose its sense of cohesion and direction.

The Holy See desires to offer its full cooperation in the process of the follow-up to the World Summit for Social Development. The Pontifical Council for Justice and Peace has been assigned special responsibility within the Holy See to follow this task and it will intensify its efforts to contribute through study, reflection and the coordination of various Catholic institutions, around all the principal themes of the Summit in a spirit of cooperation.

Chapter Eight

THE FOURTH WORLD CONFERENCE ON WOMEN

Beijing, China

4 - 15 September 1995

Chapter Contents

The Fourth World Conference on Women
Beijing, China;
4 - 15 September 1995

Message of His Holiness Pope John Paul II
    to Mrs. Gertrude Mongella, Secretary General of the
    Fourth World Conference on Women
    Vatican, 26 May 1995 419

Message of His Holiness Pope John Paul II
    to the Delegation of the Holy See to the Fourth World Conference
    on Women; Vatican, 29 August 1995 425

Addresses of His Holiness Pope John Paul II at the General Audience
    and before the Angelus 429
    Angelus, St. Peter's Square, 1 January 1995 429
    Angelus, St. Peter's Square, 5 February 1995 430
    Angelus, St. Peter's Square, 12 February 1995 431
    Angelus, St. Peter's Square, 19 February 1995 433
    Angelus, St. Peter's Square, 26 February 1995 434
    Angelus, St. Peter's Square, 18 June 1995 435
    Angelus, St. Peter's Square, 25 June 1995 436
    Angelus, St. Peter's Square, 9 July 1995 437
    Angelus, Les Combes - Valle d'Aosta, 16 July 1995 439
    Angelus, Castel Gandolfo, 23 July 1995 440
    Angelus, Castel Gandolfo, 30 July 1995 441
    Angelus, Castel Gandolfo, 6 August 1995 442
    Angelus, Castel Gandolfo, 13 August 1995 443
    Angelus, Castel Gandolfo, 15 August 1995 444
    Angelus, Castel Gandolfo, 20 August 1995 446
    Angelus, St. Peter's Square, 27 August 1995 447
    Angelus, St. Peter's Square, 3 September 1995 448
    General Audience, 6 December 1995 449

National Report of the Holy See in Preparation for the
    Fourth World Conference on Women
    30 May 1994 453

Statement by Ms. Sheri Rickert,
    Member of the Holy See Delegation, at the 38th Session
    of the Commission on the Status of Women, on Preparations
    for the Fourth World Conference on Women
    New York, 9 March 1994 467

Statement by Monsignor Frank J. Dewane,
        Member of the Holy See Delegation, at the Second Asian and
        Pacific Ministerial Conference on Women in Development
        Jakarta, Indonesia, 9 June 1994 471

Statement by Monsignor Candido Rubiolo,
        Member of the Delegation to the Sixth Regional Conference
        on the Integration of Women in the Economic and Social
        Development of Latin America and the Caribbean
        Mar del Plato, Argentina; 25-29 September 1994 475

Statement by Bishop Paul Josef Cordes,
        Secretary, Pontifical Council for the Laity, at the High-Level
        Regional Preparatory Meeting for the Fourth World Conference
        on Women; Vienna, 18 October 1994 479

Statement by Ms. Sheri Rickert,
        Member of the Holy See Delegation, at the Fifth African
        Regional Conference on Women (Preparatory Meeting
        to the Fourth World Conference on Women)
        Dakar, Senegal, 19 November 1994 483

Statement by His Excellency Archbishop Renato R. Martino,
        Apostolic Nuncio, Permanent Observer of the Holy See
        to the U.N., before the Third Committee of the General Assembly,
        on Item 97: "Advancement of Women"
        New York, 5 December 1994 487

Statement by Ms. Sheri Rickert,
        Member of the Holy See Delegation at the 39th Session of the
        Commission on the Status of Women, on Preparations for the
        Fourth World Conference on Women
        New York, 15 March 1995 491

Statement by His Excellency Archbishop Renato R. Martino,
        Apostolic Nuncio, Permanent Observer of the Holy See
        to the U.N., at the 39th Session of the Commission on the
        Status of Women, on Preparations for the Fourth World
        Conference on Women
        New York, 16 March 1995 493

Statement by His Excellency Archbishop Jean-Louis Tauran,
        Secretary for Relations with States, on the Holy See's Position
        on the Draft Platform for Action for the Fourth World
        Conference on Women; Vatican, 26 May 1995 497

Briefing by Dr. Joaquín Navarro-Valls,

Director of the Holy See Press Office, on the topic of the
Fourth World Conference on Women
Vatican, 20 June 1995 505

Second Briefing by Dr. Joaquín Navarro-Valls,
    Director of the Holy See Press Office, on the topic of the
    Fourth World Conference on Women
    Vatican City, 25 August 1995 514

Statement by Professor Mary Ann Glendon,
    Head of the Delegation of the Holy See to the
    Fourth World Conference on Women
    Beijing, China, 5 September 1995 523

Statement by Professor Mary Ann Glendon,
    Head of the Delegation of the Holy See, at the Concluding
    Session of the Fourth World Conference on Women 531

        and Reservations and Statements of Interpretation of the
        Holy See 533

        and Statement of Interpretation of the Term "Gender" 536
    Beijing, China, 15 September 1995

Press Release issued by the Delegation of the Holy See during the
    Fourth World Conference on Women
    Beijing, 9 September 1995 537

Press Release issued by the Delegation of the Holy See during the
    Fourth World Conference on Women
    Beijing, 15 September 1995
    "Holy See Challenge: Real Commitment, not Paper Promises" .. 539

Statement by His Excellency Archbishop Renato R. Martino,
    Apostolic Nuncio, Permanent Observer of the Holy See
    to the U.N., before the Third Committee of the General Assembly,
    on Item 107: "Advancement of Women: Report of the
    Fourth World Conference on Women"
    New York, 16 November 1995 541

Intervention of Mr. John Klink,
    Member of the Holy See Delegation to the UNICEF
    Executive Board, on Document E/ICEF/1996/3:
    "UNICEF Follow-up to the Fourth World Conference on Women"
    New York, 25 January 1996 545

418 *Chapter Eight*

See Appendix for the following related documents:

Message of His Holiness Pope John Paul II
    for the celebration of the World Day of Peace,
    "Women: Teachers of Peace"
    Vatican, 1 January 1995 821

Letter of His Holiness Pope John Paul II to Women
    Vatican, 29 June 1995 829

Message of His Holiness Pope John Paul II for
    World Migration Day
    Vatican, 10 August 1995 839

Message of Pope John Paul II for the 30th World
    Communications Day — "The Media: Modern Forum
    for Promoting the Role of Women in Society"
    24 January 1996 845

Statements regarding "Catholic for a Free Choice" 849
    - United States Catholic Conference Press Release
        Washington, D.C., 16 March 1995 849
        (two attachments):

        a) Statement by His Eminence William Cardinal Keeler
           NCCB/USCC President, Washington, D.C.
           16 March 1995 850
        b) Statement by the Administrative Committee of the
           National Conference of Catholic Bishops,
           Washington, D.C., 4 November 1993 851

    - Holy See Mission Press Release
        "Holy See Delegation Questions Accreditation of
        'Catholics for a Free Choice'"
        New York, 17 March 1995 853

    - Holy See Mission Press Release
        "Holy See Delegation Challenges NGO Accreditation
        of 'Catholics for a Free Choice' to United Nations
        Women's Conference"
        New York, 21 March 1995 854

MESSAGE OF
HIS HOLINESS POPE JOHN PAUL II
TO MRS. GERTRUDE MONGELLA
SECRETARY GENERAL OF THE
UNITED NATIONS' FOURTH WORLD CONFERENCE ON WOMEN
VATICAN, 26 MAY 1995

1. It is with genuine pleasure that I welcome you to the Vatican, at a time when you and your collaborators are engaged in preparing the *United Nations Fourth World Conference on Women*, to be held in Beijing in September. There, the attention of the world community will be focused on important, urgent questions regarding the dignity, the role and the rights of women. Your visit enables me to express deep appreciation for your efforts to make the Conference, on the theme of "Action for Equality, Development and Peace," the occasion for a serene and objective reflection on these vital goals, and the role of women in achieving them.

The Conference has raised high expectations in large sectors of public opinion. Conscious of what is at stake for the well-being of millions of women around the world, the Holy See, as you are aware, has taken an active part in the preparatory and regional meetings leading up to the Conference. In this process, the Holy See has discussed both local and global issues of particular concern to women not only with other Delegations and organizations, but especially with women themselves. The Holy See's Delegation, which has itself consisted mostly of women, has heard with keen interest and appreciation the hopes and fears, the concerns and demands of women all over the world.

Solutions must be based on the inherent dignity of women

2. Solutions to the issues and problems raised at the Conference, if they are to be honest and permanent, cannot but be based on *the recognition of the*

inherent, inalienable dignity of women, and the importance of women's presence and participation in all aspects of social life. The Conference's success will depend on whether or not it will offer *a true vision of women's dignity and aspirations*, a vision capable of inspiring and sustaining objective and realistic responses to the suffering, struggle and frustration that continue to be a part of all too many women's lives.

In fact, the recognition of the dignity of every human being is the foundation and support of the concept of *universal human rights*. For believers, that dignity and the rights that stem from it are solidly grounded in the truth of the human being's creation in the image and likeness of God. The *United Nations Charter* refers to this dignity in the same instance as it acknowledges the equal rights of men and women (cf. Preamble, para. 2), a concept prominent in almost every international human rights instrument. If the potential and aspirations of many of the world's women are not realized, this is due in great part to the fact that their human rights, as acknowledged by these instruments, are not upheld. In this sense, the Conference can sound a needed warning, and call governments and organizations to work effectively to ensure the legal guarantee of women's dignity and rights.

3.   As most women themselves point out, *equality of dignity* does not mean "sameness with men." This would only impoverish women and all of society, by deforming or losing the unique richness and the inherent value of femininity. In the Church's outlook, women and men have been called by the Creator to live in profound communion with one another, with reciprocal knowledge and giving of self, acting together for the common good with the complementary characteristics of that which is feminine and masculine.

A unique role in humanizing society

At the same time we must not forget that at the personal level one's dignity is experienced not as a result of the affirmation of rights on the juridical and international planes, but as the natural consequence of the concrete material, emotional and spiritual care received *in the heart of one's family*. No response to women's issues can ignore women's role in the family or take lightly the fact that every new life is *totally entrusted* to the protection and care of the woman carrying it in her womb (cf. Encyclical Letter *Evangelium vitae*, 58). In order to respect this natural order of things, it is necessary to counter the misconception that the role of motherhood is oppressive to women, and that a commitment to her family, particularly to her children, prevents a woman from reaching personal fulfillment, and women as a whole from having an influence in society. It is a disservice not only to children, but also to women and society itself, when a women is made to feel guilty for wanting to remain in the home and nurture and care for her children. A mother's presence in the family, so critical to the stability and growth of that basic unity of society, should instead be recognized, applauded and supported in every possible way. By the same token society needs to *call husbands and fathers to their family responsibilities*, and ought to strive for a situation in which they will not be forced by economic circumstances to move away from the home in search of work.

4.   Moreover, in today's world, when so many children are facing crises that threaten not only their long-term development, but also their very life, it is imperative that the security afforded by responsible parents — mother and father — within the context of the family be re-established and reaffirmed. Children need the positive environment of a stable family life that will ensure their development to human maturity — girls on an equal basis with boys. The Church historically has demonstrated in action, as well as in word, the importance of educating the girl-child and providing her with health care, particularly where she may not otherwise have had these benefits. In keeping with the Church's mission and in support of the goals of the Women's Conference, Catholic institutions and organizations around the world will be encouraged to continue their care and special attention to the girl-child.

5.   In this year's *World Day of Peace Message*, on the theme of "Women: Teachers of Peace," I wrote that the world urgently needs "to heed the yearning for peace which they [women] express in words and deeds and, at times of greatest tragedy, by the silent eloquence of their grief" (*1995 World Day of Peace Message*, No. 4). It should in fact be clear that "when women are able fully to share their gifts with the whole community, the very way in which society understands and organizes itself is improved" (No. 9). This is a recognition of *the unique role which women have in humanizing society* and directing it towards the positive goals of solidarity and peace. It is far from the Holy See's intentions to try to limit the influence and activity of women in society. On the contrary, without detracting from their role in relation to the family, the Church recognizes that women's contribution to the welfare and progress of society is incalculable, and the Church looks to women to do even more to save society from the deadly virus of degradation and violence which is today witnessing a dramatic increase.

There should be no doubt that on the basis of their equal dignity with men "women have a full right to become actively involved in all areas of public life, and this right must be affirmed and guaranteed, also, where necessary, through appropriate legislation" (*1995 World Day of Peace Message*, No. 9). In truth, in some societies, women have made great strides in this direction, being involved in a more decisive way, not without overcoming many obstacles, in cultural, social, economic and political life (cf. *ibid.*, No 4). This is a positive and hopeful development which the Beijing Conference can help to consolidate, in particular by calling on all countries to overcome situations which prevent women from being acknowledged, respected and appreciated in their dignity and competence. Profound changes are needed in the attitudes and organization of society in order to facilitate the participation of women in public life, while at the same time providing for the special obligations of women and of men with regard to their families. In some cases changes have also to be made to render it possible for women to have access to property and to the management of their assets. Nor should the special difficulties and problems faced by single women living alone or those who head families be neglected.

Women bear hardest burden of abortion

6. In fact, development and progress imply access to resources and opportunities, *equitable access* not only between the least developed, developing and richer countries, and between social and economic classes, but also *between women and men* (Cf. Second Vatican Ecumenical Council, Constitution on the Church in the Modern World, *Gaudium et spes*, 9). Greater efforts are needed to eliminate discrimination against women in areas that include education, health care and employment. Where certain groups or classes are systematically excluded from these goods, and where communities or countries lack basic social infrastructures and economic opportunities, women and children are the first to experience marginalization. And yet, where poverty abounds, or in the face of the devastation of conflict and war, or the tragedy of migration, forced or otherwise, it is very often women who maintain the vestiges of human dignity, defend the family, and preserve cultural and religious values. History is written almost exclusively as the narrative of men's achievements, when in fact its better part is most often moulded by women's determined and persevering action for good. Elsewhere I have written about man's debt to woman in the realm of life and the defense of life (cf. Apostolic Letter *Mulieris dignitatem*, 18). How much still needs to be said and written about man's enormous debt to woman in every other realm of social and cultural progress! The Church and human society have been, and continue to be, measurelessly enriched by the unique presence and gifts of women, especially those who have consecrated themselves to the Lord and in him have given themselves in service to others.

7. The Beijing Conference will undoubtedly draw attention to the *terrible exploitation of women and girls* which exists in every part of the world. Public opinion is only beginning to take stock of the inhuman conditions in which women and children are often forced to work, especially in less developed areas of the globe, with little or no recompense, no labour

rights, no security. And what about the sexual exploitation of women and children? The trivialization of sexuality, especially in the media, and the acceptance in some societies of a sexuality without moral restraint and without accountability, are deleterious above all to women, increasing the challenges that they face in sustaining their personal dignity and their service to life. In a society which follows this path, the temptation to use abortion as a so-called "solution" to the unwanted results of sexual promiscuity and irresponsibility is very strong. And here again it is the woman who bears the heaviest burden: often left alone, or pressured into terminating the life of her child before it is born, she must then bear the burden of her conscience which forever reminds her that she has taken the life of her child (cf. *Mulieris dignitatem*, 14).

A radical solidarity with women requires that the underlying causes which make a child unwanted be addressed. There will never be justice, including equality, development and peace, for women or for men, unless there is an unfailing determination to *respect, protect, love and serve life* — every human life, at every stage and in every situation (cf. *Evangelium vitae*, 5 and 87). It is well known that this is a primary concern of the Holy See, and it will be reflected in the positions taken by the Holy See Delegation at the Beijing Conference.

8. The challenge facing most societies is that of upholding, indeed strengthening, woman's role in the family while at the same time making it possible for her to use all her talents and exercise all her rights in building up society. However, women's greater presence in the work force, in public life, and generally in the decision making processes guiding society, on an equal basis with men, will continue to be problematic as long as the costs continue to burden the private sector. In this area the State has a duty of subsidiarity, to be exercised through suitable legislative and social security initiatives. In the perspective of uncontrolled free-market policies there is little hope that women will be able to overcome the obstacles on their path.

Many challenges face the Beijing Conference. We must hope that the Conference will set a course that avoids the reefs of exaggerated individualism, with its accompanying moral relativism, or — on the opposite side — the reefs of social and cultural conditioning which does not permit women to become aware of their own dignity, with drastic consequences for the proper balance of society and with continuing pain and despair on the part of so many women.

9. Madame Secretary General, it is my hope and prayer that the participants in the Conference will appreciate the importance of what is to be decided there, and its implications for millions of women throughout the

world. A great sensitivity is required in order to avoid the risk of prescribing action which will be far removed from the real-life needs and aspirations of women, which the Conference is supposed to serve and promote. With Almighty God's help may you and all involved work with enlightened mind and upright heart so that the goals of equality, development and peace may be more fully realized.

From the Vatican, 26 May 1995

MESSAGE OF
HIS HOLINESS POPE JOHN PAUL II
TO THE DELEGATION OF THE HOLY SEE TO
THE FOURTH WORLD CONFERENCE ON WOMEN
VATICAN, 29 AUGUST 1995

Dear Mrs. Glendon
and Members of the Delegation of the Holy See
to the Fourth World Conference on Women,

As you prepare to leave for Beijing, I am happy to meet you, the Head of the Delegation of the Holy See to the Fourth World Conference on Women, and the other Members of the Delegation. Through you, I extend my best wishes and prayers to the Secretary General of the Conference, to the participant nations and organizations, as well as to the authorities of the host country, the People's Republic of China.

My wishes are for the success of this Conference in its aim to guarantee all the women of the world "equality, development and peace," through full respect for their equal dignity and for their inalienable human rights, so that they can make their full contribution to the good of society.

Over the past months, on various occasions, I have drawn attention to the positions of the Holy See and to the teaching of the Catholic Church on the dignity, rights and responsibilities of women in today's society: in the family, in the workplace, in public life. I have drawn inspiration from the life and witness of great women within the Church throughout the centuries who have been pioneers within society, as mothers, as workers, as leaders in the social and political fields, in the caring professions and as thinkers and spiritual leaders.

The Secretary General of the United Nations has asked the

participating nations at the Beijing Conference to announce concrete commitments for the improvement of the condition of women. Having looked at the various needs of women in today's world, the Holy See wishes to make a specific option regarding such a commitment: *an option in favour of girls and young women.* Therefore, I call all Catholic caring and educational institutions to adopt *a concerted and priority strategy directed to girls and young women, especially to the poorest*, over the coming years.

It is disheartening to note that in today's world, the simple fact of being a female, rather than a male, can reduce the likelihood of being born or of surviving childhood; it can mean receiving less adequate nutrition and health care, and it can increase the chance of remaining illiterate and having only limited access, or none at all, even to primary education.

Investment in the care and education of girls, as an equal right, is a fundamental key to the advancement of women. It is for this reason that today:

— I appeal to all the educational services linked to the Catholic Church to guarantee equal access for girls, to educate boys to a sense of women's dignity and worth, to provide additional possibilities for girls who have suffered disadvantage, and to identify and remedy the reasons which cause girls to drop out of education at an early stage;

— I appeal to those institutions which are involved in health care, especially primary health care, to make improved basic health care and education for girls a hallmark of their service;

— I appeal to the Church's charitable and development organizations to give priority in the allocation of resources and personnel to the special needs of girls;

— I appeal to Congregations of Religious Sisters, in fidelity to the special charism and mission given to them by their Founders, to identify and reach out to those girls and young women who are most on the fringes of society, who have suffered most, physically and morally, who have the least opportunity. Their work of healing, caring and educating, and of reaching to the poorest is needed in every part of the world today;

— I appeal to Catholic Universities and centres of higher education to ensure that, in the preparation of future leaders in society, they acquire a special sensitivity to the concerns of young women;

— I appeal to women and women's organizations within the Church and active in society to establish patterns of solidarity so that their leadership and guidance can be put at the service of girls and young women.

As followers of Jesus Christ, who identifies himself with the least among children, we cannot be insensitive to the needs of disadvantaged girls, especially those who are victims of violence and a lack of respect for their dignity.

In the spirit of those great Christian women who have enlightened the life of the Church throughout the centuries and who have often called the Church back to her essential mission and service, I make an appeal to the women of the Church today to assume new forms of leadership in service and I appeal to all the institutions of the Church to welcome this contribution of women.

I appeal to all men in the Church to undergo, where necessary, a change of heart and to implement, as a demand of their faith, a positive vision of women. I ask them to become more and more aware of the disadvantages to which women, and especially girls, have been exposed and to see where the attitude of men, their lack of sensitivity or lack of responsibility may be at the root.

Once again, through you, I wish to express my good wishes to all those who have responsibility for the Beijing Conference and to assure them of my support, as well as that of the Holy See and the institutions of the Catholic Church, for a renewed commitment of all to the good of the world's women.

From the Vatican, 29 August 1995

**ADDRESSES OF
HIS HOLINESS POPE JOHN PAUL II
AT THE GENERAL AUDIENCE
AND BEFORE THE ANGELUS/REGINA COELI**

**ANGELUS, ST. PETER'S SQUARE
1 JANUARY 1995**

Beloved Brothers and Sisters, Happy New Year!

1.   On the first day of 1995 I wish everyone a happy New Year. May it be a truly serene and joyful year for all!

"The Lord look upon you kindly and give you peace!" (Num 6:26). Beloved brothers and sisters, with these words from Sacred Scripture, I wish to express to you my most cordial greetings for the year which has just begun, asking God for the gift of peace for families, for nations and for the whole of humanity.

May the Lord grant us *his* peace! This is our constant entreaty, which should be supported by concrete gestures and initiatives. How many opportunities do we have to reflect upon the urgent need to build peace! 1995, for example, reminds us of the end of the sorrowful events of the Second World War. Fifty years have also past since the appalling tragedy of Hiroshima and Nagasaki which has profoundly marked the conscience of the people of our time.

Recalling these events and observing the regions of the world where fighting unfortunately continues, how can we not hope that the new year may finally bring the longed for Peace to every corner of the earth? This is our ardent wish, the wish that we want to enhance by constant prayer to the Child laid in the crib. May "the Prince of Peace," (Is 9:5) who came into the world to offer men reconciliation and true peace, give us peace; and make us all builders of peace.

2. Continuing the reflection I began in my *Message* last year, the "Year of the Family," for today's occasion I have had a Message sent to all the Heads of State on the topic: *"Women: Teachers of Peace."* In it, I emphasized the significant contribution which women can make to achieving a peace which affects every aspect of human existence. I addressed them, inviting them to "become teachers of peace with their whole being and in all their actions. May they be witnesses, messengers and teachers of peace in relations between individuals and between generations, in the family, in the cultural, social and political life of nations, and particularly in situations of conflict and war" (n. 2).

3. May Mary guide them in this demanding mission. At the beginning of the new year which marks the first stage in the preparations for the Great Jubilee of the Year 2000, we turn our gaze to her. The Church today invokes her as "Mother of God," Mother of the "Prince of Peace."

O Mary, inspire the leaders of nations with resolutions of dialogue and reconciliation, guide the efforts made by people of goodwill; above all, sustain women in their natural vocation as teachers of peace in the family, in society and in every social context.

ANGELUS, ST. PETER'S SQUARE
5 FEBRUARY 1995

Dear Brothers and Sisters,

1. In this year's Message for the *World Day of Peace,* I reflected on the role that women are called to play as "teachers of peace." In this respect, I pointed out how history is filled with "marvelous examples of women" who, sustained by faith and love, "have been able successfully to deal with difficult situations of exploitation, discrimination, violence and war" (n. 5).

Today and on the coming Sundays I would like to recall the concrete witness of several female figures who distinguished themselves in the Church's history precisely by their work in promoting peace.

2. I would like to draw your attention today to St. Birgitta of Sweden, who lived from 1303 to 1373. She played an important role in the Europe of her time. It is not difficult to grasp the timeliness of her message in some regions of the continent. Although the process of unification has begun, there are still today disconcerting and absurd outbursts of fratricidal hatred, and the

threatening clash of weapons can be heard.

In St. Birgitta's time too, the force of passionate feelings endangered the peace and serenity of peoples. Bitter clashes of interest often provoked bloody conflicts, and even within the Church moments of painful tension occurred.

Birgitta's witness shines brightly against this background. From the northern edges of Europe she felt called to a mission of peace, which led her to Rome and made her Christ's messenger to the ecclesial and civil authorities of the time.

3. In this work she expressed all her femininity, tempered by a profound experience of God. Gentle and firm at the same time, Birgitta was able first of all to impart to her children — and she had eight — a love of harmony and peace. One need only recall that her daughter, Catherine, is also honoured as a saint! But her recognized gifts as a teacher also brought her prestigious responsibilities in the princely circles where she grew up.

Nevertheless, the qualitative leap in her enterprising femininity occurred when her founding of the Order of the Most Holy Saviour enabled her to embrace the "contemplative" life to the full. It was not a flight from the world: on the contrary, the depth of her mystical experience permitted her to become the privileged echo of God's voice for the Church and for society. The Pope himself, residing at that time in Avignon, received Birgitta's insistent and effective plea to return to his "natural" See of Rome. Today the Church continues to praise God for the gift of this exceptional woman.

4. Our thoughts now turn to Mary, the model for Birgitta and for all the saints. May Mary, who combined in herself both the beauty and the power of femininity according to God's plan, be close to every woman with her effective help.

May she instill, particularly in the women of our time, an ever deeper and more active awareness of their mission of peace and help them become messengers of religious and moral values, the only possible way to build a true and lasting peace.

ANGELUS, ST. PETER'S SQUARE
12 FEBRUARY 1995

Dear Brothers and Sisters,

1.　Continuing my reflection on women's mission of peace, today I would like to present St. Catherine of Siena's witness.

There is something incredible about the life of this woman who died at the age of only 33 years, after playing a primary role in the Church of her time. The secret of her exceptional personality was the inner fire that devoured her: a passion for Christ and for the Church.

To Catherine, consumed by such fire, the situation of Christianity in that difficult period of the second half of the 14th century seemed unbearable. She considered it a disaster that the Pope should remain far from Rome, his natural See. It seemed scandalous to her that Christian princes were unable to live peaceably together.

So she became a messenger of peace. Her passionate words spread in all directions. They were motherly words, characterized by intrepid firmness and persuasively sweet. Around her something happened which seemed humanly impossible. The hardness of hearts melted away and everyone began once more to experience the joy of families or of entire communities where peace had been restored. Catherine of Siena's experience is an exemplary case of what I wrote about in my *Message* at the beginning of the year: "When women are fully able to share their gifts with the whole community, the very way in which society understands and organizes itself is improved, and comes to reflect in a better way the substantial unity of the human family" (n. 9).

2.　"Women: Teachers of Peace." The cry with which Catherine turned to Pope Gregory XI to encourage him to be a herald of peace among Christians is well known: "Peace, peace, peace, my sweet father, and no more war!" (*Letter* 218). She wrote similar words to sovereigns and princes and did not hesitate to undertake difficult journeys to instill in opponents sentiments of reconciliation.

Of course, we must recognize that she was also a daughter of her time, when, justly eager to defend the holy places, she adopted the then prevailing mentality that this task could be accomplished even by recourse to fighting. Today we ought to be grateful to the Spirit of God, who has enabled us to understand ever more clearly that the appropriate way to deal with problems that can arise in relations between peoples, religions and cultures, one which is also most in harmony with the Gospel, is that of patient, firm and respectful dialogue.

Nevertheless Catherine's zeal remains an example of brave, strong love, an encouragement to devote our efforts to all possible strategies of constructive dialogue in order to build an increasingly stable and far-reaching peace.

3. Let us call upon Mary Most Holy, Queen of Peace, so that the Church may become an ever more effective sacrament of unity for the whole human race: unity, to be built up first and foremost in relations between Christ's followers; unity to be fostered in every corner of the world torn by tension and war. May she inspire enterprising and courageous women like Catherine of Siena, who, in the Church and in society, will make themselves weavers of unity and peace.

ANGELUS, ST. PETER'S SQUARE
19 FEBRUARY 1995

Dear Brothers and Sisters,

1. In my *Message for the World Day of Peace* I urged women to be "witnesses, messengers and teachers of peace in relations between individuals and between generations, in the family, in the cultural, social and political life of nations" (n. 2; *L'Osservatore Romano* English edition, 14 Dec. 1994, p. 1). Many female figures have carried out and continue to carry out this task in an exemplary way. Among them I would like to point out St. Frances Xavier Cabrini, patroness of immigrants, an area of the apostolate which is still very timely today.

We can only marvel at all Mother Cabrini achieved. Born in Lombardy in the middle of the last century, she devoted herself to immigrants who, in the United States and other American countries, encountered various difficulties in finding their place in society. She organized schools, nurseries, colleges, hospitals and orphanages for them, all with little means, trusting solely in divine Providence. Love for the Sacred Heart of Christ inspired and sustained her. "The Sacred Heart," she confided one day, "is in such a hurry to do things that I cannot manage to keep up with him." And it was Christ whom she recognized and served in the faces of the immigrants to whom she sought to be an affectionate and untiring "mother."

2. Her work, a real miracle of charity, was a remarkable contribution to the cause of peace, a true pedagogy of peace. With her keen insight, Mother Cabrini realized that it was not enough to offer immigrants material support. It was necessary to help them to be fully integrated into the new society, without losing the authentic values of their own culture. Although she did not renounce her love for Italy, she herself took American citizenship and became deeply involved with the people among whom God had called her

to carry out her mission.

It is easy to understand the timeliness of such witness. Because of the growing migrations which bring millions of people from one nation to another, from one continent to another, especially from the developing countries to prosperous societies, today and perhaps even more in the future there is a need for mutual understanding, acceptance and integration. Clearly, then, in order to build this future we need men and women of peace. In particular, we need motherly hearts like that of Mother Cabrini, with the rich potential of a feminine soul refined by Gospel charity.

3. We entrust to Our Lady the process of integration among peoples, in the multicultural and multiracial society of our time. May Mary teach acceptance and solidarity to us all. May all who come from distant countries feel understanding from their host communities; may they always be respected and loved as brothers and sisters. May the Mother of the Lord give women a deep awareness of their irreplaceable role in building a society rich in human warmth and generous brotherhood.

ANGELUS, ST. PETER'S SQUARE
26 FEBRUARY 1995

Dear Brothers and Sisters,

1. Among the women who served the cause of peace, today I would like to recall a "martyr" of our century whom I myself had the joy of raising to the honours of the altar in 1987: the Carmelite, Edith Stein.

Like so many other victims of Nazi cruelty, she was killed in the concentration camp of Auschwitz. Of Jewish descent and raised in the traditions of her ancestors, for her choosing the Gospel, a decision reached after painful searching, did not mean the rejection of her cultural and religious roots. Christ, known in the footsteps of St. Teresa of Avila, helped her instead to interpret the history of her people in the most profound way. With her gaze fixed on the Redeemer, she learned the wisdom of the Cross, which made her capable of a new solidarity with the sufferings of her brothers and sisters.

To be united with the sorrow of the God made man, by offering her life for her people, became her great longing. She faced deportation and the prospect of "martyrdom" with the inner awareness that she was going to "die for her people." Her sacrifice is a cry of peace, a service to peace.

2.　　Edith Stein is also exemplary for the contribution she made to the advancement of women. I wrote in my *Message for the World Day of Peace* that the building of this basic value "can hardly overlook the need to acknowledge and promote the dignity of women as persons" (n. 4). Here Edith Stein played a significant role, dedicating herself for many years before her monastic seclusion to activities for the recognition of women's rights: those belonging to every human being and those specific to their femininity. When speaking of woman, she liked to stress her calling as "wife and mother," but she also extolled the role to which she is called in every aspect of cultural and social life. She herself was a witness to this socially active femininity, winning esteem as a scholar, lecturer and teacher. She was also highly regarded as a woman intellectual, who with wise discernment could utilize the contributions of contemporary philosophy to seek the "full truth about things" in the continual effort to combine the demands of reason and those of faith.

3.　　To the Blessed Virgin we particularly wish to entrust today harmony and peace among the believers of different religions: God is love, and by his nature he unites and does not divide those who believe in him. Jews and Christians in particular cannot forget their unique brotherhood, which is rooted in the providential design of God who accompanies their history.

Mary, Daughter of Sion and Mother of the Church, pray for us!

ANGELUS, ST. PETER'S SQUARE
18 JUNE 1995

Dear Brothers and Sisters,

1.　　In the course of the Fourth World Conference on Women organized by the United Nations in Beijing for next September, the international community will be called to reflect on a series of problems concerning the status of women in our time. I would like to express immediately my deep appreciation of this initiative. The theme chosen is in fact extraordinarily important, not only for women, but for the very future of the world, which depends so much on the awareness women have of themselves and on the proper recognition which should be guaranteed to them. Therefore the Church looks hopefully to all that is being done in this regard and considers it a true "sign of the times," as my venerable predecessor John XXIII pointed out in his Encyclical *Pacem in terris* (n. 22). A "sign of the times" that highlights an aspect of the full truth about the human being which cannot be ignored.

Unfortunately, awareness of the identity and value of women has been obscured in the past — and still is today, in many cases — by various forms of conditioning. Indeed, they have been and are often culpably disregarded and offended by unjust and even violent practices and behaviour. All this, on the threshold of the third millennium, is really intolerable! As the Church joins in denouncing all injustices that weigh on women's condition, she intends to proclaim God's plan in a positive way, so that a culture may develop that respects and welcomes "femininity."

2. As I have had more than one occasion to stress, and particularly in the Apostolic Letter *Mulieris dignitatem*, the affirmation of woman's dignity must be the basis of this new culture, since she, like man and with man, is a person, that is, a creature made in the image and likeness of God (cf. n. 6); a creature endowed with a subjectivity from which stems her responsible autonomy in leading her own life. This subjectivity, far from isolating people and setting them in opposition is, on the contrary, a source of constructive relationships and finds its fulfilment in love. Women, no less than men, are fulfilled "in a sincere giving of self" (*Gaudium et spes*, n. 24). This subjectivity is the basis of a specific way of being for woman, a way of "being feminine," which is enriching and indeed indispensable for harmonious human coexistence, both within the family and in society.

3. May the Blessed Virgin help men and women in our time clearly understand God's plan for femininity. Called to the highest vocation of divine motherhood, Our Lady is the exemplary woman who developed her authentic subjectivity to the full. May Mary obtain for women throughout the world an enlightened and active awareness of their dignity, gifts and mission.

ANGELUS, ST. PETER'S SQUARE
25 JUNE 1995

Dear Brothers and Sisters,

1. Respect for the full equality of man and woman in every walk of life is one of civilization's great achievements. Women themselves, with their deeply-felt and generous daily witness, have contributed to this, as have the organized movements which, especially in our century, have put this subject before world attention.

Unfortunately even today there are situations in which women live, *de facto* if not legally, in a condition of inferiority. It is urgently necessary to cultivate everywhere a culture of equality, which will be lasting and constructive to the extent that it reflects God's plan.

Equality between man and woman is in fact asserted from the first page of the Bible in the stupendous narrative of creation. The Book of Genesis says: "God created man in his own image, in the image of God he created him;" (Gn 1:27). In these brief lines we see the profound reason for man's grandeur: he bears the image of God imprinted on him! This is true to the same degree for male and female, both marked with the Creator's imprint.

2.   This original biblical message is fully expressed in Jesus' words and deeds. In his time women were weighed down by an inherited mentality in which they were deeply discriminated. The Lord's attitude was a "consistent protest against whatever offends the dignity of women" (*Mulieris dignitatem*, n. 15). Indeed he established a relationship with women which was distinguished by great freedom and friendship. Even if he did not assign the Apostles' role to them, he nevertheless made them the first witnesses of his Resurrection and utilized them in proclaiming and spreading God's kingdom. In his teaching, women truly find "their own subjectivity and dignity" (*ibid.*, n. 14).

In the footprints of her divine Founder, the Church becomes the convinced bearer of this message. If down the centuries some of her children have at times not lived it with the same consistency, this is a reason for deep regret. The Gospel message about women however has lost none of its timeliness. This is why I wanted to present it once again with all its richness in the Apostolic Letter *Mulieris dignitatem*, which I published on the occasion of the Marian year.

3.   One can already perceive the immense dignity of women by the sole fact that God's eternal Son chose, in the fullness of time, to be born of a woman, the Virgin of Nazareth, the mirror and measure of femininity. May Mary herself help men and women to perceive and to live the mystery dwelling within them, by mutually recognizing one another without discrimination as living "images" of God!

ANGELUS, ST. PETER'S SQUARE
9 JULY 1995

Dear Brothers and Sisters,

1.   Tomorrow my *Letter to Women* will be published. In it I have wished to address all the women in the world, directly and almost confidentially, to express to them the Church's esteem and gratitude, and at the same time to propose once again the main lines of the Gospel message

concerning them.

Today, continuing the topic I began a few Sundays ago, I wish particularly to reflect on the complementarity and reciprocity which mark the relationship between the persons of the two sexes.

In the biblical account of creation, we read that after creating man God took pity on his loneliness and decided to give him a helper fit for him (Gn 2:18). But no creature was able to fill this void. Only when the woman taken from his own body was presented to him, could the man express his deep and joyful amazement, recognizing her as "flesh of [his] flesh and bone of [his] bones" (Gn 2:23).

In the vivid symbolism of this narrative, the difference between the sexes is interpreted in a deeply unitive key: it is, in fact, a question of the one human being who exists in two distinct and complementary forms: the "male" and the "female." Precisely because the woman is different from the man, nevertheless putting herself at the same level, she can really be his "helper." On the other hand, the help is anything but unilateral: the woman is a "helper" for the man, just as the man is a "helper" for the woman!

2. This complementarity and reciprocity emerges in every context of coexistence. "In the 'unity of the two,'" I wrote in my Apostolic Letter *Mulieris dignitatem*, "man and woman are called from the beginning not only to exist 'side by side' or 'together,' but they are also called to exist mutually 'one for the other'" (n. 7).

The most intense expression of this reciprocity is found in the spousal encounter in which the man and the woman live a relationship which is strongly marked by biological complementarity, but which, at the same time goes far beyond biology. Sexuality in fact reaches the deep structures of the human being, and the nuptial encounter, far from being reduced to the satisfaction of a blind instinct, becomes a language through which the deep union of the two persons, male and female, is expressed. They give themselves to one another and in this intimacy, precisely to express the total and definitive communion of their persons, they make themselves at the same time the responsible co-workers of God in the gift of life.

3. We ask the Blessed Virgin to help us to be aware of the beauty of God's plan. In the special mission entrusted to her, Mary brought all her feminine richness, first to the family of Nazareth and later to the first community of believers. May the men and women of our time learn from her the joy of being fully themselves, establishing mutual relations of respectful and genuine love.

ANGELUS, LES COMBES - VALLE D'AOSTA
16 JULY 1995

Dear Brothers and Sisters,

1.   Today, too, in this splendid place in the mountains, I would like to continue the talks I have been developing over the past few weeks. The fact can never be sufficiently stressed that woman must be appreciated in every area of her life. However, it must be recognized that, among the gifts and tasks proper to her, her vocation to motherhood stands out particularly clearly.

With this gift woman assumes almost a "foundational" role with regard to society. It is a role she shares with her husband but it is indisputable that nature has assigned to her the greater part. I wrote about this in *Mulieris dignitatem*: "Parenthood — even though it belongs to both — is realized much more fully in the woman, especially in the prenatal period. It is the woman who 'pays' directly for this shared generation, which literally absorbs the energies of her body and soul. It is therefore necessary that the man be fully aware that in their shared parenthood he owes a special debt to the woman" (n. 18).

Woman's singular relationship with human life derives from her vocation to motherhood. Opening herself to motherhood, she feels the life in her womb unfolding and growing. This indescribable experience is a privilege of mothers, but all women have in some way an intuition of it, predisposed as they are to this miraculous gift.

2.   The maternal mission is also the basis of a particular responsibility. The mother is appointed guardian of life. It is her task to accept it with care, encouraging the human being's first dialogue with the world, which is carried out precisely in the symbiosis with the mother's body. It is here that the history of every human being begins. Each one of us, retracing this history, cannot fail to reach that moment when he began to exist within his mother's body, with an exclusive and unmistakable plan of life. We were "in" our mother, but without being confused with her: in need of her body and her love, but fully autonomous in our personal identity.

The woman is called to offer the best of herself to the baby growing within her. It is precisely by making herself "gift," that she comes to know herself better and is fulfilled in her femininity. One could say that the fragility of her creature demands the best of her emotional and spiritual resources. It is a real exchange of gifts! The success of this exchange is of inestimable value for the child's serene growth.

3. Mary, whom we invoke today under the title of Our Lady of Mount Carmel, experienced this to the full, having received the task of generating, in time, the eternal Son of God. In her the vocation to motherhood reached the summit of its dignity and potential. May the Blessed Virgin help women to be ever more aware of their mission and encourage the whole of society to express every possible form of gratitude and active closeness to mothers!

ANGELUS, CASTEL GANDOLFO
23 JULY 1995

Dear Brothers and Sisters,

1. It is a "sign of the times" that woman's role is increasingly recognized, not only in the family circle, but also in the wider context of all social activities. Without the contribution of women, society is less alive, culture impoverished, and peace less stable. Situations where women are prevented from developing their full potential and from offering the wealth of their gifts should therefore be considered profoundly unjust, not only to women themselves but to society as a whole. Of course, the employment of women outside the family, especially during the period when they are fulfilling the most delicate tasks of motherhood, must be done with respect for this fundamental duty. However, apart from this requirement, it is necessary to strive convincingly to ensure that the widest possible space is open to women in all areas of culture, economics, politics and ecclesial life itself, so that all human society is increasingly enriched by the gifts proper to masculinity and femininity.

2. In fact, woman has a genius all her own, which is vitally essential to both society and the Church. It is certainly not a question of comparing woman to man, since it is obvious that they have fundamental dimensions and values in common. However, in man and in woman these acquire different strengths, interests and emphases and it is this very diversity which becomes a source of enrichment.

In *Mulieris dignitatem* I highlighted one aspect of feminine genius, that I would like to stress today: woman is endowed with a particular capacity for accepting the human being in his concrete form (cf. n. 18). Even this singular feature which prepares her for motherhood, not only physically but also emotionally and spiritually, is inherent in the plan of God who entrusted the human being to woman in an altogether special way (cf. ibid., n. 30). The woman of course, as much as the man, must take care that her sensitivity does not succumb to the temptation to possessive selfishness, and must put it at the service of authentic love. On these conditions she gives of her best, everywhere adding a touch of generosity, tenderness, and joy of life.

3. Let us look at the Blessed Virgin's example. In the narrative of the wedding at Cana, John's Gospel offers us a vivid detail of her personality when it tells us how, in the busy atmosphere of a wedding feast, she alone realized that the wine was about to run out. And to avoid the spouses' joy becoming embarrassment and awkwardness, she did not hesitate to ask Jesus for his first miracle. This is the "genius" of the woman! May Mary's thoughtful sensitivity, totally feminine and maternal, be the ideal mirror of all true femininity and motherhood!

ANGELUS, CASTEL GANDOLFO
30 JULY 1995

Dear Brothers and Sisters,

1. In the *Message* which last 26 May I addressed to Mrs. Gertrude Mongella, Secretary General of the forthcoming Beijing Conference, I made the observation that because of a new appreciation of woman's role in society, it would be appropriate to rewrite history in a less one-sided way. Unfortunately, a certain way of writing history has paid greater attention to extraordinary and sensational events than to the daily rhythm of life, and the resulting history is almost only concerned with the achievements of men. This tendency should be reversed. "How much still needs to be said and written about man's enormous debt to woman in every other realm of social and cultural progress!" (*ibid.*, n. 6). With the intention of helping to fill this gap, I would like to speak on behalf of the Church and to pay homage to the manifold, immense, although frequently silent, contribution of women in every area of human life.

2. Today in particular, I would like to call to mind woman as teacher. It is an extremely positive fact that in countries where the school system is more developed, the presence of women teachers is constantly increasing. We can, of course, hope that this greater involvement of women in education will lead to a qualitative leap in the educational process itself. It is a well-founded hope, if one considers the deep meaning of education, which cannot be reduced to the dry imparting of concepts, but must aim at the full growth of man in all his dimensions. In this respect, how can we fail to understand the importance of the "feminine genius"? It is also indispensable for the initial education in the family. Its "educational" effect on the child begins when he is still in his mother's womb.

But woman's role in the rest of the formational process is just as important. She has a unique capacity to see the person as an individual, to understand his aspirations and needs with special insight, and she is able to face up to problems with deep involvement. The universal values themselves, which any sound education must always present, are offered by feminine sensitivity in a tone complementary to that of man. Thus the whole educational process will certainly be enriched when men and women work together in training projects and institutions.

3. May the Holy Virgin guide this rediscovery of the feminine mission in the field of education. Mary had a unique relationship with her divine Son: on the one hand she was a docile disciple, meditating on his words in the depths of her heart; on the other, as his mother and teacher, she helped his human nature to grow "in wisdom and in stature, and in favour with God and man" (Lk 2:52). May the women and men who work in the field of education and are committed to building man's future, look to her!

ANGELUS, CASTEL GANDOLFO
6 AUGUST 1995

Dear Brothers and Sisters,

1. Today I would like to introduce our reflection on woman's role, a reflection accompanying us during the weeks of preparation for the Beijing meeting, with a mention of the Servant of God, Paul VI, who died here in Castel Gandolfo exactly 17 years ago.

Speaking of Maria Montessori in 1970, on the occasion of the centenary of her birth, he remarked that the secret of her success, in a certain sense the very origin of her scientific merits, should be sought in her soul or in that spiritual sensitivity and feminine outlook which enabled her to make the "vital discovery" of the child and led her to conceive of an original form of education on this basis (cf. *Insegnamenti di Paolo VI*, VIII [1970], 88).

The name of Montessori is clearly representative of all women who have made important contributions to cultural progress. Unfortunately, in looking objectively at historical reality, we are compelled to notice with regret that, even at this level, women have suffered the effects of systematic marginalization. For too long their opportunities for expression outside the family have been denied or restricted, and the women who, despite being thus penalized, succeeded in asserting themselves have had to be very enterprising.

2. It is time, therefore, to close the gap between the cultural

opportunities for men and women. I deeply hope that the forthcoming Beijing Conference will provide a decisive impetus in this direction. This will benefit not only women but culture itself, since the vast and variegated world of thought and art has a greater need of their "genius" than ever. Let this not seem a gratuitous assertion! Cultural activity calls into question the human person as a whole, in the twofold complementary sensitivity of man and woman.

This is always important, but especially when the ultimate questions about life are at stake. Who is man? What is his destiny? What is the meaning of life? These decisive questions do not find a satisfactory answer in the laboratories of positive science, but they profoundly challenge man and require, so to speak, a "global thinking" that can harmonize with the sphere of mystery. To this end, how could the contribution of the feminine mind be undervalued? Women's increasingly qualified entrance, not only as beneficiaries but also as protagonists, into the world of culture in all its branches from philosophy to theology, from the social to the natural sciences, from the figurative arts to music, is a very hopeful sign for humanity.

3. Let us turn our gaze trustingly to the Blessed Virgin. Like the other women of her time, she bore the burden of an age when little room was allowed them. Yet the Son of God did not hesitate, in some ways, to learn from her! May Mary obtain for all the women in the world a full awareness of their potential and their role at the service of a culture which is ever more truly human and in conformity with God's plan.

ANGELUS, CASTEL GANDOLFO
13 AUGUST 1995

Dear Brothers and Sisters,

1. A long history, for the most part unrecorded, testifies to the privileged role women have always played in situations of suffering, sickness, marginalization and old age, when the human being proves especially frail and in need of a friendly hand.

In some cases, one could say that woman's vocation to motherhood makes her more sensitive to understanding needs and sympathetic in giving a caring response. When a conscious altruistic attitude and, above all, the strength of faith and Gospel charity are added to these natural endowments, true miracles of dedication occur. The Church's history is filled with them. For example, I like to recall the work carried out three centuries ago by St. Louise de Marillac, in the footsteps of St. Vincent de Paul. Charity knew no bounds in this tireless woman's heart. The sick, the deprived, the elderly, abandoned children, those condemned to hard labour, she served them all with a mother's love and used her rare practical talent for organization. In 1960, John XXIII fittingly proclaimed her the heavenly patron of all those who do Christian social work (cf. AAS LII [1960] 556-568).

2. But in Christian communities and in civil society, how many women have become angels of consolation to countless suffering people? I would like to renew the Church's gratitude to them! Thanks to the women who devote themselves to children, to the suffering, to the elderly: in the family, in hospital wards, in mission dispensaries, in a whole range of public and private institutions, in volunteer work. In all these spheres the presence of women who are able to combine singular gifts of generosity, practicality, intuition and tenderness with the necessary professionalism, is irreplaceable. It is comforting to note how many women today are dedicated to the medical profession, one of those which together with competence demands a large dose of humanity. Those who have had this experience know well that no sick person is cured by medicine alone: warmth, understanding, listening, fraternal encouragement make all the difference to him. Everyone dedicated to medical and paramedical service is called to this. But who can deny that women often have a special talent for the more delicate and human aspects of this exacting vocation? What can be said about so many nurses? In my experience, I have much to say in gratitude to these sisters, these nurses, especially in the hospitals where I have stayed. I am thinking in particular of Sr. Ausilia.

3. In our world, where despite scientific and economic progress so much poverty and marginalization continue to exist, extra courage is really necessary. May women continue to remain in the first ranks in this task.

May Mary Most Holy bless the vast numbers of women who provide social and healthcare assistance and work in the various fields where human solidarity is needed, and obtain for us all that we may experience the joy of serving with love.

Angelus, Castel Gandolfo
15 August 1995

Dear Brothers and Sisters,

1. Today the Church celebrates the Assumption of Mary Most Holy into heaven. The Lord has done "great things" (Lk 1:49), preserving from the corruption of death the woman who brought the world the Giver of Life. The

Second Vatican Council called upon her as "a sign of certain hope and comfort" (*Lumen gentium*, n. 68);

Thus, Mary is resplendent as the "beginning and the pattern of the Church" (preface for the Assumption), already fulfilled in her person by virtue of Christ's paschal mystery, that saving destiny to which God calls every human creature from eternity. On their earthly pilgrimage, believers look to Mary, the "woman clothed with the sun" (Rv 12:1), as a bright star showing us the goal to strive for on our daily journey.

Her Assumption into heaven is not only the culmination of her particular vocation as the Mother and disciple of the Lord Jesus, but also an eloquent sign of God's fidelity to the universal plan of salvation aimed at the redemption of every man and of all men.

2. Femininity finds its full expression in Mary, Virgin and Mother, since the personal qualities that distinguish woman from man were able to be expressed in her in their full splendour. In looking at her, every woman can discern the authentic affirmation of her own dignity and value.

How could we not entrust to Mary, on today's liturgical solemnity, the women of the whole world, so that, conscious of their own vocation, they may generously make their indispensable contribution to every area of human advancement, especially to the defence of life? Through her intercession, may the forthcoming Conference in Beijing shed full light on the genuine values which every woman has to offer. Thanks to the constructive participation of all the Delegations, a significant contribution will be made to the cause of woman and to her mission in the contemporary world.

3. The Solemnity of Mary's Assumption into heaven reminds us that Mary has returned to the Father's house in body and soul, to the heavenly Jerusalem, the city of peace towards which we are all journeying. This is the reason why the Church, which addresses the Mother of the Lord by the title of Queen of Heaven, also loves to invoke her with the fitting name of Queen of Peace. May she, Queen of the Heavenly Jerusalem, abode of peace, constantly intercede with the Son for her children, pilgrims in history, so that the longed-for good of peace and harmony may spread to every corner of the earth.

May the Blessed Virgin protect all humanity; in particular, may she protect the victims of injustice, hatred and violence. May she obtain peace for the world and especially for the lands tormented by war. May Mary truly be a sign of certain hope and comfort for all.

Mary assumed into heaven, pray for us!

ANGELUS, CASTEL GANDOLFO
20 AUGUST 1995

Dear Brothers and Sisters,

1. Doubtless one of the great social changes of our time is the increasing role played by women, also in an executive capacity, in labour and the economy. This process is gradually changing the face of society, and it is legitimate to hope that it will gradually succeed in changing that of the economy itself, giving it a new human inspiration and removing it from the recurring temptation of dull efficiency marked only by the laws of profit. How can we fail to see that, in order to deal satisfactorily with the many problems emerging today, special recourse to the feminine genius is essential? Among other things, I am thinking of the problems of education, leisure time, the quality of life, migration, social services, the elderly, drugs, health care, ecology. "In all these areas a greater presence of women in society will prove most valuable," and "it will force systems to be redesigned in a way which favours the processes of humanization which mark the 'civilization of love'" (*Letter to Women*, n. 4).

2. Nevertheless, it is clear that increasing the role of women in the frequently harsh and demanding structures of economic activity must take into account their temperament and particular needs. Above all it is necessary to respect the right and duty of woman as mother to carry out her specific tasks in the family, without being forced by need to take on an additional job. What would society truly gain — even at the economic level — if a shortsighted labour policy were to prejudice the family's endurance and functions?

The safeguarding of this basic good, however, cannot be an alibi with regard to the principle of equal opportunity for men and women also in work outside the family. Flexible and balanced solutions should be found which can harmonize the different needs. In fact — as I wrote in my recent *Letter to Women* — "Much remains to be done to prevent discrimination against those who have chosen to be wives and mothers. As far as personal rights are concerned, there is an urgent need to achieve real equality in every area: equal pay for equal work, protection for working mothers, fairness in career advancements, equality of spouses with regard to family rights and the recognition of everything that is part of the rights and duties of citizens in a democratic State" (n. 4).

3. Dear brothers and sisters, let us entrust this great challenge of our era to the Blessed Virgin's intercession! Her home in Nazareth was a place of work. Mary, like any good housewife, was busy with domestic tasks while Joseph, with Jesus beside him, worked as a carpenter. May working women look to the hard working and holy family of Nazareth, and may society be able to find suitable ways to increase their role to the full.

ANGELUS, ST. PETER'S SQUARE
27 AUGUST 1995

Dear Brother and Sisters,

1. As the Beijing Conference is now close at hand, today I would like to stress the importance of a greater involvement of women in public life.

A long tradition has seen mostly men involved in politics. Today more and more women are asserting themselves even at the highest levels of representation, national and international.

This process should be encouraged. Politics, in fact, geared as it is to promoting the common good, can only benefit from the complementary gifts of men and women. Of course, it would be naive to expect "miracles" from this alone. It is especially true that for women no less than for men, the quality of politics is measured by the authenticity of the values which inspire them, as well as by the competence, commitment and moral consistency of those who dedicate themselves to this important service.

In every case women are showing that they can make as skilled a contribution as men, a contribution which indeed is proving particularly significant, especially with regard to the aspects of politics that concern the basic areas of human life.

2. How great, for example, is the role they can play on behalf of peace, precisely by being involved in politics, where the fate of humanity is largely decided.

Dear brothers and sisters, peace is the most pressing need of our time. A collective effort is more than ever necessary to restrain the frenzy of arms. However, peace is not limited to the silence of cannons. It becomes concrete with justice and freedom. It needs a spiritual atmosphere rich in basic elements such as the sense of God, a taste for the beautiful, love for the truth, the option for solidarity, the capacity for tenderness and the courage of forgiveness. How can we not recognize the valuable contribution which woman can make to promoting this atmosphere of peace!

3. Let us call upon the Blessed Virgin, Queen of Peace, so that she may turn her gaze to those countries of the world where unbridled hatred has caused destruction and death for too long. In this regard, my thoughts cannot but turn to the thousands of mothers, wives and daughters, who in the countries of the former Yugoslav Republic — whether they are Croats, Serbs or Muslims — are still forced to abandon their homes and their loved ones, and are often the object of inhuman treatment and exposed to a very uncertain future. I am particularly troubled by the grave news from Banja Luka. I am close to the zealous and generous Bishop Franjo Komarica, who is almost helplessly witnessing the forced expulsion of his priests, religious and faithful. It is their desire and their right to be able to continue living in their own homes, remaining there as a sign of the reconciliation for which they long and of the coexistence of peoples of different nationalities and religions, which is still possible.

May those responsible for all this suffering open their eyes! May the women on opposing sides, especially the mothers, give one another their hand symbolically in a chain of peace, as if to compel the governments, those fighting and the people to regain their trust in the validity of negotiations and the prospects of peaceful coexistence.

ANGELUS, ST. PETER'S SQUARE
3 SEPTEMBER 1995

Dear Brothers and Sisters,

1. Last Tuesday, as I met the Holy See's Delegation to the Fourth World Conference on Women, which starts in Beijing tomorrow, I confirmed the Church's commitment on behalf of women and I asked the communities and institutions of the Church to make concrete gestures particularly in service to girls and adolescents, especially the poorest.

Today I appeal to the whole Church community to be willing to foster feminine participation in every way in its internal life.

This is certainly not a new commitment, since it is inspired by the example of Christ himself. Although he chose men as his Apostles — a choice which remains normative for their successors — nevertheless, he also involved women in the cause of his Kingdom; indeed, he wanted them to be the first witnesses and heralds of his Resurrection. In fact, there are many women who have distinguished themselves in the Church's history by their holiness and hardworking ingenuity. The Church is increasingly aware of the need for enhancing their role. Within the great variety of different and complementary gifts that enrich ecclesial life, many important possibilities are open to them. The 1987 Synod on the Laity expressed precisely this need and asked that "without discrimination women should be participants in the life of the Church and also in consultation and the process of coming to decision" (Propositio 47; cf. *Christifideles laici*, n. 51).

2. This is the way to be courageously taken. To a large extent, it is a question of making full use of the ample room for a lay and feminine presence recognized by the Church's law. I am thinking, for example, of theological teaching, the forms of liturgical ministry permitted, including service at the altar, pastoral and administrative councils, Diocesan Synods and Particular Councils, various ecclesial institutions, curias, and ecclesiastical tribunals, many pastoral activities, including the new forms of participation in the care of parishes when there is a shortage of clergy, except for those tasks that belong properly to the priest. Who can imagine the great advantages to pastoral care and the new beauty that the Church's face will assume, when the feminine genius is fully involved in the various areas of her life?

3. May the Blessed Virgin, model of the Church and ideal of femininity, accompany and sustain the efforts of all the people of goodwill who are involved in the Beijing Conference. May the Mother of the Lord help all humanity to progress in their respect for and promotion of women's true dignity! May she obtain for the Christian community to be ever more faithful to God's plan, following the example of the great women who have embellished its history!

GENERAL AUDIENCE, VATICAN
6 DECEMBER 1995

1. As I have already explained in the preceding catecheses, the role entrusted to Mary by the divine plan of salvation sheds light on the vocation of woman in the life of the Church and society by defining its difference in relation to man. The model represented by Mary clearly shows what is specific to the feminine personality.

In recent times some trends in the feminist movement, in order to advance women's emancipation, have sought to make her like man in every way. However, the divine intention manifested in creation, though desiring woman to be man's equal in dignity and worth, at the same time clearly affirms her diversity and specific features. Woman's identity cannot consist in being a copy of man, since she is endowed with her own qualities and prerogatives, which give her a particular uniqueness that is always to be fostered and encouraged.

These prerogatives and particular features of the feminine personality attained their full development in Mary. The fullness of divine grace actually fostered in her all the natural abilities typical of woman.

"Let it be done to me according to your word"

Mary's role in the work of salvation is totally dependent on Christ's. It is a unique function, required by the fulfillment of the mystery of the Incarnation: Mary's motherhood was necessary to give the world its Saviour, the true Son of God, but also perfectly man.

The importance of woman's co-operation in the coming of Christ is emphasized by the initiative of God, who, through the angel, communicates his plan of salvation to the Virgin of Nazareth so that she can consciously and freely cooperate by giving her own generous consent.

Here the loftiest model of woman's collaboration in the Redemption of man — every man — is fulfilled; this model represents the transcendent reference point for every affirmation of woman's role and function in history.

2. In carrying out this sublime form of cooperation, Mary also shows the style in which woman must concretely express her mission.

With regard to the angel's message, the Virgin makes no proud demands nor does she seek to satisfy personal ambitions. Luke presents her to us as wanting only to offer her humble service with total and trusting acceptance of the divine plan of salvation. This is the meaning of her response: "Behold, I am the handmaid of the Lord; let it be done to me according to your word" (Lk 1:38).

It is not a question of a purely passive acceptance, since her consent is given only after she has expressed the difficulty that arose from her intent to remain a virgin, inspired by her will to belong more completely to the Lord.

Having received the angel's response, Mary immediately expresses her readiness, maintaining an attitude of humble service.

It is the humble, valuable service that so many women, following Mary's example, have offered and continue to offer in the Church for the growth of Christ's Kingdom.

3. The figure of Mary reminds women today of the value of motherhood. In the contemporary world the appropriate and balanced importance is not always given to this value. In some cases, the need for women to work in order to provide for the needs of their family and an erroneous concept of freedom, which sees child care as hindrance to woman's autonomy and opportunities, have obscured the significance of motherhood for the development of the feminine personality. On the contrary, in other cases the biological aspect of childbirth becomes so important as to overshadow the other significant opportunities woman has for expressing her innate vocation to being a mother.

In Mary we have been given to understand the true meaning of motherhood, which attains its loftiest dimension in the divine plan of salvation. For her, being a mother not only endows her feminine personality, directed towards the gift of life, with its full development, but also represents an answer of faith to woman's own vocation, which assumes its truest value only in the light of God's covenant (cf. *Mulieris dignitatem*, n. 19).

4. In looking attentively at Mary, we also discover in her the model of virginity lived for the Kingdom.

The Virgin *par excellence*, in her heart she grew in her desire to live in this state in order to achieve an ever deeper intimacy with God.

For women called to virginal chastity, Mary reveals the lofty meaning of so special a vocation and thus draws attention to the spiritual fruitfulness which it produces in the divine plan: a higher order of motherhood, a motherhood according to the Spirit (cf. *Mulieris dignitatem*, n. 21).

Women sow the seeds of the civilization of love

Mary's maternal heart, open to all human misfortune, also reminds women that the development of the feminine personality calls for a commitment to charity. More sensitive to the values of the heart, woman shows a high capacity for personal self-giving.

To all in our age who offer selfish models for affirming the feminine personality, the luminous and holy figure of the Lord's Mother shows how only by self-giving and self-forgetfulness towards others is it possible to attain authentic fulfillment of the divine plan for one's own life.

Mary's presence therefore encourages sentiments of mercy and solidarity in women for situations of human distress and arouses a desire to alleviate the pain of those who suffer: the poor, the sick and all in need of help.

In virtue of her special bond with Mary, woman has often in the course of history represented God's closeness to the expectations of goodness and tenderness of a humanity wounded by hatred and sin, by sowing in the world seeds of a civilization that can respond to violence with love.

NATIONAL REPORT OF THE HOLY SEE
IN PREPARATION FOR
THE FOURTH WORLD CONFERENCE ON WOMEN
30 MAY 1994

PRESENTATION

1. The Holy See is a subject of international law acting in accordance with its religious, moral and spiritual purposes. It is the central and supreme organ of government of the Catholic Church, which is spread throughout the world and has almost one thousand million members divided into 2,759 ecclesiastical circumscriptions.[1] The specific mission of the Catholic Church consists, in the first place, in preaching the Gospel, that is, in proclaiming the Christian faith to all mankind; it likewise entails a pastoral responsibility towards all who profess that faith.

Given the nature of the Holy See, this *Report* is different in character from those presented by the other groups taking part in the preparation for the Fourth World Conference on Women.

The Holy See wishes in this way to make its own specific contribution to this Conference, which will constitute an important step in the promotion of the dignity of women and their place in society.

2. The *Report* is in conformity with the indications of the Conference Secretariat. In its introduction, it presents an evaluation of the overall changes in the situation of women which have taken place in the last decade. It then sets forth the Holy See's analysis with regard to critical areas of concern which are examined with reference to three main themes:

    a.   *Equality*: The Holy See considers women and men as being of equal dignity in all areas of life, but without this always implying an equality of roles and functions.

    b.   *Development and Peace*: The Holy See calls for a proper appreciation of the capacities of women who are qualified to take full part in building society and creating a climate of peace, especially in the areas of education and of political and economic life.

    c.   *Violence*: The Holy See regards any kind of violence to

---

[1] Statistics drawn from the *Annuario Pontificio*, 1994 edition.

which women are subjected, inasmuch as it represents a denial of their essential rights and a violation of their dignity, as having an effect on the whole of society.

Next, the Holy See offers an evaluation of the juridical safeguards which presently exist in various crucial areas.

Finally, it presupposes strategic actions and goals for the future.

INTRODUCTION

Global changes

3.   Following the adoption of the *"Forward-Looking Strategies for the Advancement of Women"* by the Nairobi Conference (1985), a number of important changes have taken place on the international level and in different parts of the world; these have had an effect on the condition of women and its development.

4.   In particular, the Holy See notes the following tendencies, together with their limitations and their ambiguities:

1) In the framework of the recognition and application of "human rights" within the international community, there is general evidence of a greater awareness of the dignity of women as human persons, and of women's basic rights.

2) Growing democratization has expanded the possibilities for the full-time participation of women in the various sectors of education, economic life, culture and politics.

3) The collapse of myths and utopias associated with the dominance of ideologies in the Sixties and Seventies, has brought with it a tendency to move beyond a radical "feminism"; complete uniformity or an undifferentiated leveling of the two sexes is no longer seen as a goal; instead, there is a growing sensitivity to the "right to be different," in other words, the "right to be a woman."

4) This tendency to acknowledge unity in diversity is a source of enrichment for human development, and frees women from a blind race towards self-realization seen in terms of patterns and styles drawn from a predominantly masculine society. It is more attentive to the reciprocity, complementarity and cooperation between women and men in the family and

in the various areas important for the building of a more human world.

5) A "liberation" of women, based on viewing family life and motherhood as a hazard and a handicap, is being seen more and more clearly as a fallacy. Such a "liberation," which often leaves women alone and unsatisfied, helps to show that any genuine human promotion — whether of woman or of man — is supported by being part of a family, based on marriage between a woman and a man, an authentic community of love and life, and an irreplaceable setting for the human growth of every individual.

6) The elimination of forms of discrimination against women requires not only adequate legislation but also new attitudes and patterns of behaviour on the social, cultural and spiritual levels.

7) In order to get beyond certain approaches to the advancement of women which are excessively tied to conditions in highly industrialized societies, the international community needs to pay closer attention to the situation of the great majority of women living in the various developing countries. These women are often the victims of poverty, the consequences of which can be seen in the precariousness of living conditions, the absence of health services and schools, and by the break-up of the family because of emigration and seasonal work. The absence of their husbands requires these women to take responsibility for the material and moral support of their families. Neo-liberal models, when applied in an excessive degree, tend to eliminate all the mechanisms of social policy which benefit excluded or marginalized sectors, particularly women and their families living in situations of extreme poverty.

8) In contemporary societies we see the appearance of new ways in which women are alienated and exploited as objects. These have developed as a result of a hedonistic and individualistic culture, and have frequently been aggravated by the images spread by the media.

9) The profound transformations which the revolution in technology is presently bringing about in the sphere of production and labour — as well as forms of restructuring involving job transfers, permanent recycling, the reduction of working hours, the development of part-time employment, more personalized and flexible jobs — can help in the search for a new balance between paid employment, family commitments, leisure time and volunteer work.

10) While today the dissolution of political and military blocs seems to provide a better guarantee of international security, local conflicts are nonetheless on the increase: these conflicts affect populations, with dramatic

repercussions on their environment and on their living conditions in the family and in society. The sectors of the population not directly involved in combat — including women — experience these consequences just as severely.

Juridical evaluation

5. The development of the world situation favours a greater juridical protection of women by the international community. The method followed for proposing specific norms which will have an impact on the internal legislation of each State deserves close examination. It responds to the need to define criteria common to all countries permitting a uniform protection of fundamental rights, as well as eliminating every form of discrimination between various subjects, discrimination which produces inequality before the law between men and women.

6. In fact, the danger of discrimination is found not only in direct action exercised by the State apparatus in all its guises, but also — and often this is the greatest danger — in omissions on the part of State institutions. This is seen in the limited recourse of even absence of recourse to legislative, executive, administrative, or judicial means in order to guarantee real parity in the enjoyment of fundamental rights and liberties.

7. Consequently, reflection at the international level and the normative measures flowing from it aim at: a) avoiding or eliminating discrimination between men and women (according to the formula: non-discrimination/without distinction/without restriction); b) favouring conditions of equality between men and women; c) combating obstacles which prevent the attainment of equality between men and women.

8. This action of the international community and its institutions concentrates on the factors of a social, cultural, economic and political nature which appear to be the causes of discrimination and obstacles to equality. But the very development of international juridical instruments shows that, in spite of efforts to eliminate the causes, discrimination and inequality have not, in fact, disappeared. It is necessary to take into consideration other factors, hitherto judged to be secondary with regard to discrimination. In the light of the experience gained in the decade following the Nairobi Conference, legal systems, both national and international, need to appreciate the fact that true equality between women and men at the level of fundamental rights will only be attained if the specificity of women is safeguarded and that it will not be possible to reach true equality if *diversity* is ignored.

CRITICAL AREAS OF CONCERN

I. EQUALITY

9. The Holy See would like the point of reference for a reflection on equality to be that of respect for the dignity of the human person.

10. The traditional and constant teaching of the Catholic Church affirms the equal dignity of women and men. Both are creatures of God, fashioned in his image and likeness. Men and women are human beings to the same degree.

11. In developing the concept of an equal dignity, the teaching of the Catholic Church would like to underline that men and women must be respected and considered as equal in their existence as persons.

12. At present, the struggle against all discrimination is bearing fruit in many areas of women's lives, and juridical protection is theoretically assured to them.

13. However, the life of women remains more uncertain and more vulnerable than that of men. Too often women alone carry most of the responsibilities for the family, the education of the children, and the material side of daily life. This causes feelings of dissatisfaction and fatigue which is shown partly by the fact that they cannot develop their full potential or participate actively in public life.

14. Moreover, as material profit is an essential criterion in our societies, a person tends to be considered only in terms of what he or she can produce, to the neglect of the personal growth of the individual, the ignoring of individual characteristics and the elimination of less "profitable" traits. This model of society is particularly hurtful to women and to their self-esteem, since a large part of the tasks they carry out are not "profit-earning": for example, everything concerning education and service.

15. This is why it is necessary to pursue reflection and action on questions concerning the equal dignity of men and women, which presupposes a proper application of various juridical directives and a great respect for human dignity.

16. Lack of awareness of and commitment to women's rights makes itself felt in many areas: ignorance of concrete conditions in the life of women, lack of respect for women's maternal and family role by comparison with

other public occupations and careers, the absence of firm control of violence against women, ineffective assistance for women who are poor, immigrant, illiterate, etc.

17. In order that these recognised rights may be applied, on the one hand society must make room for women's self-expression, and on the other hand help men and women to know these rights.

18. Social relations between men and women need to be studied, so that the active participation of women in social, political and cultural life may be promoted with a view to a shared involvement in the sum total of community responsibilities.

19. In this context, programmes for equal rights between women and men must also take into account the specific role of women in motherhood. Motherhood, the fruit of the married union between a man and a woman, should be given more protection. Any limit imposed on maternity prevents women from fulfilling themselves as persons.

20. The setting up of plans to encourage the promotion of women is closely connected to the correct interpretation of rights and to their application in the concrete circumstances of the life of individuals and of society. This is why women must be able to share in the making of decisions which concern them.

21. The promotion of women must take into account facts which often escape the quantitative domain and which introduce a qualitative dimension linked to the fact that women have a particular relationship with everything that concerns the gift of life.

22. It is right to emphasise the importance and weight of women's work in the family home: it must be recognised and valued to the full. So great is the "task" of a woman who gives birth to a child and then nourishes it, takes care of it and contributes to its education, especially during its early years, that she has no cause to fear comparison with any professional work. This must be clearly recognised, on the same level as any other right related to work. Motherhood, with all the hard work which it brings, should be financially compensated. The mother's work in the home must be recognised and respected by reason of its value for the family and for society.

23. Family policies must ensure conditions favourable to the balance between professional life and family life for each of the spouses.

24. Remuneration for work must be sufficient to start and to support a

family, either by means of an appropriate wage, a "family wage," or by other social measures such as family benefits or payment to the parent who works in the home; it must be large enough for the mother of the family not to be obliged to work outside the home to the detriment of family life, especially the education of the children.

II. DEVELOPMENT AND PEACE

25. Women themselves become powerful agents for development to the extent that they are aware of their abilities and rights. They also contribute actively towards ensuring that the family plays a role in development. It is therefore in the interest of the whole of society to allow the expression of what one might call the "genius" proper to women.

26. Three areas which are particularly apt for woman's participation in the construction of society may be noted: education, politics and the economy.

Education

27. It is within the framework of an overall understanding of development, that is to say one aiming not only at economic growth but also the growth of the human person considered in his or her unity, that consideration has been given in the last few decades to the urgent need for basic education, including literacy training, and for a basic formation for all. To a great extent women have benefitted from these programmes, even though the statistics on literacy are still alarming.

28. Women's sharing in this basic education enables them to express with greater awareness and more actively the traditional culture of which they are the guardians and which they try to keep alive in a changing world, despite migrations and also despite the destruction connected with armed conflict. Women thus make it possible for a nation's culture, which is a factor of unity and peace, to remain alive.

29. Women not only have a responsibility for passing on cultural and traditional values but they also play a part in the ethical aspect of education.

Politics

30. All citizens have a right and duty to participate in public life for the

sake of the common good. There are many ways of participating both for men and for women. But political life in the strict sense, in its structures and functioning, remains an essentially masculine world.

31. To be truly credible in its service of the common good, politics must not be cut off from the problems of daily life or from individual initiatives. Women, who in the home exercise a major role in welcoming others and in ensuring the growth of the family community, actively contribute to establishing the link between political life and private life, if they have the opportunity to express themselves publicly. It is therefore necessary to offer the maximum scope and help to intermediate groups and institutions, to family, social, cultural and religious associations within which men and women work together.

32. Women also owe it to themselves to be present in political life taken in a strict sense, by devoting themselves to public affairs in a spirit of service. To the extent that they come to be present more and more in this sphere, women can work from the inside, without fear of being considered as exceptions to the norm.

33. While the desire to establish parity in political structures can be considered as progress, in no case should women's participation be used as a means of propaganda or as a subject of political campaigning.

Economy

34. Women carry a greater burden than men of the various effects of economic crises and the consequences of still unsolved economic tensions: unemployment, immigration, lack of health care, housing, etc. To it they more directly bear the cares of daily family life.

35. In general, women's contribution to the economy is acknowledged as at least equal to men's. Nevertheless, in various sectors, this contribution is not yet valued at its true worth nor properly remunerated. We have already spoken of work in the family; the work which women do in the rural world and in the unplanned economy also needs to be recognised.

36. In the economic world, account must be taken not only of women's ability to produce goods but also of their aptitude for developing services. The service sector, though it is in full expansion, remains poorly paid and it is here that a majority of women are employed (for example, 85% of the world's nursing personnel is made up of women).

37. The aim of these various considerations is to develop mechanisms which would enable women to have a minimum of economic resources, since it is they who create goods essential for human life. Certainly this is a general problem which raises the question of the high earnings attached to certain activities, or even to dealings in finances, and the low earnings or none at all attached to many other activities, which means that women remain poor in spite of their work.

38. The presence and activity of women are essential at the levels where decisions about economic and social life are made. Together with men, they are the subjects and objects of the whole of socio-economic life.

III. VIOLENCE

39. Violence towards women occurs on the physical, sexual, psychological and moral levels. But in reality all violence which touches women in one way or another affects them in the integrity of their being. The person, body and spirit, cannot be divided, and the body itself is a whole which must be respected in its unity. For this reason it is impossible to act effectively against violence without considering the unity of the person.

40. In addition, violence done to a person cannot be considered as an isolated act. It must be taken in relation to the human community of which both the perpetrator and the victim are members.

41. It is the absence in society of respect for the dignity of the person which explains the violence committed against women in contradiction of their most basic rights. Likewise, it is the manipulation of women's image in the media and in the advertising industry which has profoundly harmful effects on behaviour towards women.

42. It would be difficult to imagine anything more radically and directly opposed to the affirmation of the equality of men and women than the pornography trade. It is always surprising to see how equality is solemnly proclaimed, while pornography is permitted or at least tolerated by public opinion and exploited by the media. Closely linked to pornography, to the extent that it is difficult to distinguish them, are the forms of advertising which use women as objects to promote certain products.

43. The lack of an overall policy on prostitution gives rise to contradictions in the way it is viewed juridically: prostitution is at one and the same time accepted, forbidden, penalized or taxed. Prostitution is, in effect, considered to be an individual matter, a free act. In reality this is very rarely

the case.

44. The sexual exploitation of young girls through prostitution has reached international proportions and is causing much grave physical, emotional and moral harm, degrading the human person for the sake of profit, and most often leaving the person incapable of returning to a normal life.

45. It is still more difficult to denounce and stop rape, a particularly violent expression of lack of respect for the dignity of women. Women who have been attacked physically and morally very often find themselves unable to lodge a complaint in a way which justice is prepared to accept.

46. Mention must also be made of violence towards women used as a repressive measure in wartime. It is a matter of urgency to bring into play every mechanism of support for civilian populations in cases of armed conflict. The international community must condemn rape, internment, the displacement of peoples and the breaking up of families.

47. There is a further type of violence which families experience through the imposition from outside of various programmes which particularly concern the obligatory control of the number of births, forced sterilization and the encouragement of abortion.

EVALUATION OF JURIDICAL SUPPORTS

48. When the situation is analyzed at the world level, it can easily be seen that international legislation tends to favour a convergence between States through the emergence of uniform criteria for the protection of women. This trend has manifested itself along two interrelated paths, the consequences of which differ, however, in internal legislation.

49. The first path is that of producing declarations, recommendations, and even international conventions on various aspects of the situation of women. It is a question of measures adopted by the Institutions of the United Nations system and by Regional Organizations. Some of these measures affect women directly, while others refer to the fundamental rights of the human person. This output constitutes in itself a normative point of reference insofar as it is translated into regulations in the internal legislation of States or at the very least into criteria inspiring this legislation.

50. To this path has come to be added little by little at the international level a policy concerning women, the result of the work of Intergovernmental

Organizations and of International Conferences on the main topics linked to women, their rights and their equal sharing in social life, in order to promote authentic *development* and to guarantee conditions for *peace*. Indeed, the Conferences in Mexico (1985), Copenhagen (1980) and Nairobi (1985) considered the questions of equality, development and peace. The next Conference in Beijing in 1995 will also follow the same path.

51. As for the content of the norms foreseen for the juridical protection of women, it is easy to see that having tackled the question of civil and political rights, it is now the turn of education, women's work, and the problems resulting from it: maternity, working conditions, equality and family responsibilities. Lately, the elimination of every kind of discrimination against women has been the focus of international legislation. Such a perspective imposes on the international community the obligation not only to study at greater depth the topics linked to the rights of women, but above all to determine more exactly the content of these rights, ensuring that the juridical protection of women both at the international level and within each State is in no way weakened.

52. The next World Conference on Women will take place in a very heterogeneous geo-political context. By way of example, one can point to the discrimination which is becoming more marked due to the increasing gap between North and South; likewise, the certainty that international action cannot concern solely the demand for women's rights, since it is first of all necessary to discover the common elements among different cultures which determine a similar diversity in the condition of women. In this light, it is essential to overcome the tendency to separate the demand for rights and their juridical formulation from any reference to the ethical order, because this would involve a total relativizing of the statements of principle demanding that women should be protagonists of a future of equality, development and peace.

STRATEGIC ACTIONS AND OBJECTIVES FOR THE FUTURE

53. Fortunately, the discussion about the status of women is no longer seen only as a limited area of research regarding society's future, but is an essential element of a process the success of which will shape humanity's destiny. Consequently, the presence of women is rightly considered as indispensable in every sphere of life and in the very places where decisions are made.

54. On the other hand, women themselves, by actively participating in every sector of development, make possible a true reciprocity between men

and women. It can be seen that more and more women are claiming their place, not like men, but with men. Both women and men, in mutual respect, together bear responsibility for the future of humanity.

55. However, it really seems that there will always remain something proper to women which is imponderable and essential at the same time. In his Apostolic Letter *Mulieris dignitatem*, on the dignity of women, published on 15 August 1988, Pope John Paul II says that "God entrusts the human being to her in a special way" and the "woman is strong because of her awareness of this entrusting" (No. 30). The Catholic Church looks to Mary, the woman through whom the new and everlasting Covenant of God with humanity has its beginning; the "Virgin full of courage" invites men and women who imitate her "to establish on earth the civilization of truth and love" (Post-Synodal Apostolic Exhortation *Christifideles laici,* 64). Following this powerful inspiration, innumerable feminine figures in the Church have exercised considerable sway on the events of history and humanity.

56. The different forms of community life, beginning with the family, furnish a good place of apprenticeship for putting into practice the specific mission of women and the relative roles of men and women at the service of society. Within the Catholic Church, parish communities, movements and associations, as well as Religious Congregations, guarantee a large measure of this formation.

57. The Holy See wishes to pursue endeavours in favour of women for equality, development and peace at three levels: reflection, formation and action. Its primary objectives are the following:

- to strengthen awareness of the dignity of the person and the person's inalienable rights;
- to enable women to put their abilities to use in order to participate in their own development and in that of society;
- to ensure a fair balance of workforces in society, by recognizing the importance of family work;
- to promote the access of women to positions of responsibility in every sphere of life, including politics;
- to continue the struggle against all forms of poverty, and in particular against unemployment and the marginalization which follows from it;
- to do everything possible to eliminate illiteracy;
- to guarantee at every age a family-life education which includes education in responsible parenthood.

58. The Holy See, to the extent that it is in its competence, wishes to serve the aspirations of women for equality, development and peace. It is interested in all initiatives which can foster the attainment of these aims. For its own part, it contributes to the development of an awareness of the responsibility of men and women to serve the common good, so that everyone may feel responsible for everyone else. It encourages all undertakings which serve the solidarity of men and women, the care of the most deprived and peace-making efforts which can be undertaken with the help of women and families. At the international level, it supports International Catholic Movements and Organizations which participate with their members in achieving the goals of the United Nations.

STATEMENT BY
MS. SHERI RICKERT
MEMBER OF THE HOLY SEE DELEGATION
AT THE 38TH SESSION OF THE COMMISSION ON THE STATUS OF WOMEN
ON PREPARATIONS FOR THE FOURTH WORLD CONFERENCE ON WOMEN
NEW YORK, 9 MARCH 1994

Madame Chairperson,

The Fourth World Conference on Women provides an important opportunity for all to move closer to attaining the goals of equality, development and peace — objectives that are becoming more crucial, but arguably more difficult to attain, in today's world. The Delegation of the Holy See looks forward to making its contribution to this effort.

In recent years, the Holy See has argued repeatedly in support of women's interests. It has spoken out against the injustices of a discrimination based on gender, since women as well as men are created in the image and likeness of God. For the same reason, women are not to be placed at a disadvantage due to their gender, but should receive a responsible and fuller share in the whole of societal life, with reverence for their rights and duties in accordance with women's unique and essential richness.

The following are those issues concerning women that my Delegation considers of key importance for the Conference. I will present the Holy See's perspective on these issues and related actions to address the critical areas.

It should be evident that every person and all of society is harmed when a woman's inherent dignity is not recognized, and she is given less than the equal treatment she is due. Legal, juridical and judiciary measures are necessary to address particular violations of the human rights of women, and may help to remedy some injustices. Fundamentally, however, the authentic advancement of women requires a change in attitude on the part of those who are unaware of or who ignore a woman's human dignity and rights.

Attitudes are shaped largely through education starting at an early age. Since this education generally begins and continues in the family, the family constitutes the fundamental educating community. The values of mutual respect for every person's dignity, more than being "taught," must be witnessed to in the family setting. A child needs to be wanted, loved and respected regardless of the gender of the child, to see other children treated the same way, and to see his or her mother and father treat one another with equal dignity. A child who is raised in this type of environment is more likely to continue living these values later in life. By the same token, other institutional efforts to change a negative or oppressive attitude toward others will have limited success if this fundamental education in the family is not provided.

Mother Teresa recently gave an Address in which she spoke about the major crises facing our time. She traced the root of these problems to the family, and proposed that "maybe in our own family, we have somebody who is feeling lonely, who is feeling sick, who is feeling worried. Are we there? Are we willing to give until it hurts in order to be with our families, or do we put our own interests first?" These are the questions we must ask ourselves, especially as we begin this Year of the Family. We must remember that love begins at home and we must remember that "the future of humanity passes through the family."

One important reason to promote the concept of equal dignity in the family is to reduce the incidence of domestic violence — a widespread but largely hidden threat to girls and women in every part of the world. Violence against the woman in the home not only poses a serious threat to her own physical and emotional well-being, but if she has children who witness the abuse, it can result in a cycle of violence that will be repeated through subsequent generations. Domestic violence counselors say that violence is learned behavior; therefore, it is not uncommon to find that a perpetrator of abuse was raised in a family where violence occurred. A child who grows up repeatedly exposed to violent conduct may come to believe that violence is acceptable behavior.

Unfortunately, too many families today lack the environment that can support and strengthen relationships based on mutual dignity. There exist both biases inherited from previous generations and external pressures that contribute to familial discord. But to ignore or abandon the family's role in striving to establish woman's equal dignity would be to undertake efforts that will be far more difficult, perhaps even futile, elsewhere. For this reason, the Platform for Action should explicitly recognize the importance of the family in establishing the bases for equality, development and peace for women. It should call on international agencies, governments, nongovernmental organizations, the media and other sectors of society to promote and support a positive family environment, and to refrain from any action that would interfere with the creation and sustenance of such an environment.

In this regard, the role of public communication needs to be emphasized. Given modern technology, the media in particular can make an important contribution to the promotion of the dignity of women, both by promoting positive images of women and through educational programs. But it can also harm women's status and well-being in numerous direct and indirect ways: by employing negative portrayals of women; by propagating degrading values and models of behavior; by broadcasting pornography and graphic depictions of brutal violence by and against women; by promoting violence as a way to dissipate tension and to solve problems; by inculcating moral relativism in relationships; by carrying exploitative advertising that appeals to base instincts; and by glorifying false visions of life that obstruct the realization of mutual respect between women and men. In the Platform for Action, the Fourth World Conference on Women should call upon the media to fulfill its public responsibilities by developing and observing a code of ethics that includes a commitment to promoting women's dignity.

Madame Chairperson,

Violence in the context of conflict situations also has a serious impact on women, and such violence seems to be growing both in scope and in gravity. There are currently over 30 conflicts in the world, and some sources predict that by the year 2000 this number will increase to 45. Practically every new conflict brings with it a new wave of refugees and displaced persons, most of whom are women and children. Therefore, the more than 14 million women and children who are refugees today are likely to be joined by significantly more in the five years following the Beijing Conference; the Platform for Action needs to devote more attention to their plight.

While equality, development and peace are goals for all in the upcoming Conference, these words have special significance for refugee women. The term "equality" must have a different emphasis when one is alone in the struggle to survive; "development" must seem more daunting when one is in a foreign country, or when it involves building a life from the ashes of utter destruction; "peace" must seem more difficult when one must reconstruct one's own life, as well as family and community relationships, in spite of lingering distrust, hatred and the remnants of death.

For these reasons, refugee women should be given priority in the international agenda. When it proves impossible for women and children to remain safely in their homes, the international community should not only remove obstacles from, but should also facilitate, their escape from conflict areas. They must be given refuge in a secure environment, with security measures commensurate with their increased vulnerability.

Many refugee women today do not receive sufficient humanitarian assistance, and a renewed awareness and commitment to provide this assistance is crucial. In addition, it would be to everyone's advantage to provide these refugees with counseling, education and training resources. Such human resource development minimizes the pain and the harmful effects of exile, enables the refugees to contribute to the well-being of the host community, and prepares them to rebuild their own communities when they are able — safely and in dignity — to return home. While the financial commitment necessary for such an endeavor may seem great, the benefits — and the necessity — far outweigh the cost, and is essential if the goals of the Conference are to be realized for the many victims of war.

One cannot focus on the plight of refugee and displaced women, without also calling to mind the many women who permanently live in a state of extreme poverty. To be resolved, this problem will require the political will to satisfy the rights of all the marginalized poor specifically, their right to have equal access to the resources necessary to live a dignified existence. The situation of women in poverty will not improve if everyone in their particular social class or geographic area is excluded from the education, basic resources, social benefits, science, technology or trade opportunities available to others. If this Conference leads to the achievement of fundamental equality — the equality which is the basis of the right of all to share in the process of full development — then it will have contributed significantly to realizing its goals, not only for women, but for all people.

Thank You, Madame Chairperson.

STATEMENT BY
MONSIGNOR FRANK J. DEWANE
MEMBER OF THE HOLY SEE DELEGATION
AT THE SECOND ASIAN AND PACIFIC
MINISTERIAL CONFERENCE ON WOMEN IN DEVELOPMENT
JAKARTA, INDONESIA, 9 JUNE 1994

Madame Chairperson,

The Holy See Delegation is pleased to participate in the Second Asian and Pacific Ministerial Conference on Women in Development. My Delegation would like to take this opportunity to thank all those who have sponsored and helped to organize this meeting.

There are several concerns that my Delegation would like to express regarding the review and appraisal of the implementation of the Nairobi Forward-Looking Strategies for the Advancement of Women. Many of these concerns have already been elaborated upon by the Holy See Delegation at prior meetings of the Commission on the Status of Women. One regards the central role of the family in shaping attitudes about and teaching respect in gender relationships. In addition, due recognition must be given to the many women who assume important responsibilities as spouses and mothers; in considering social policy, governments should show a deep appreciation for the undeniable social value of women's work in the family, and work to address the difficulties these women face in fulfilling their responsibilities.

In this regard, one cannot ignore the growing incidence of domestic violence in practically every culture, economic class, and region of the world. Contrary to those who propose that this trend indicates the failure of the family, this increase in violence is actually one of the many alarms being sounded for the need to strengthen and promote the well-being of the family.

The media also has a crucial role to play in the development of perceptions about and the treatment of women and girls. The role of the media is expanding, both in terms of its influence on individual societies and its bridging effects between every country and culture. While this influence can be positive, it can also have serious negative consequences. Therefore, my Delegation continues to advocate a call on the media to develop and observe a code of ethics that includes a commitment to promoting women's dignity.

The growing and deepening problem of poverty, and the consequent greater impact it is making on women and their children, is evident in every region including that of Asia and the Pacific. Not infrequently, poverty is concealed as a fundamental cause under the more obvious violations against the rights of women. And yet a closer examination reveals the major role that poverty, particularly in the context of under-development, plays in regards to major issues, including the trafficking of women and girls, prostitution, mistreatment and abuse of migrant women workers, and domestic violence.

For example, women and girls in the lower economic strata of every country, particularly from rural areas, reportedly are the ones most vulnerable to sexual exploitation. Many women feel forced to seek employment abroad in order to support both themselves and their families, due to the poor economies in which they live and the lack of training and employment opportunities. The stress placed on families as a result of economic depravation can be a major contributing factor in cases of domestic violence.

Legal measures and the enforcement of laws designed to protect women in such situations obviously are necessary and should be strengthened, as well as social services aimed at providing safe shelter, counseling and rehabilitation. But these are only temporary and partial solutions. If these problems, as well as the scourge of poverty itself, are to be meaningfully resolved, then concrete action must be taken to address the economic conditions that give rise to women's vulnerability and abuse.

Even when it does not give rise to opportunities for violating the rights of women, poverty can still prevent women from attaining their basic needs. This is particularly true for rural women, who cannot dream of attaining an education or safeguarding their long-term physical well-being as long as their time and energy are directed towards day-to-day survival. Also for them, the creation of a sustainable economic base is a fundamental necessity.

One idea that is being raised in the international forum is that of focusing a greater percentage of international aid and domestic budgets on fostering the productive activity of the low income and poor populations. Some countries and non-governmental organizations are sponsoring income-generating skill training programs in poor areas, and there are some efforts to increase the access of poor and low-income entrepreneurs to credit and financial resources. But a far greater commitment in this area is needed.

Such programs, while necessarily including administrative oversight and regulations, must respect the human dignity of their beneficiaries. In addition, the financing for such endeavors should not be diverted from other social programs for the poor and disadvantaged, particularly in the areas of education, primary health care, and disease control. And in connection with what was stated earlier, authorities and organizations should provide for the professional promotion of women and at the same time safeguard those who have undertaken roles as mothers and educators. Women must be able to contribute their own abilities to the common good and the social and economic context; yet this "requires that labour should be structured in such a way that women do not have to pay for their advancement by abandoning what is specific to them and at the expense of the family, in which women as mothers have an irreplaceable role" (Pope John Paul II, *Laborem exercens*, n. 19).

An important advance for the human rights of women has been the growing consensus in the international community on the need to eliminate prenatal sex selection through the abortion of female fetuses. It is being recognized that this practice is one component of the broader social injustice of "son preference," and yet it results in the greatest injustice of all — the denial of the right to life. Mother Teresa has made what is now a generally well-known quote: "Any country that accepts abortion is not teaching its people to love, but to use any violence to get what they want. This is why the greatest destroyer of love and peace is abortion." And this is why my Delegation advocates not only eliminating abortion of the unborn girl child, but promoting the value of all human life from the moment of conception.

This promotion also extends to the value of the life of a mother who is faced with an unexpected pregnancy. An argument is often made, such as that in the document before this Committee concerning "Women in Social Development" (E/ESCAP/RUD/SOCWD/2), para. 35, that legal abortions are safe, and that if abortion were legalized everywhere, it would reduce the incidence of maternal mortality resulting therefrom.

Information from various United Nations agencies indicates that there are serious concerns regarding maternal health in some countries where abortion is available "on demand," but where the healthcare facilities in general are poor. Even when an abortion is conducted "under proper medical care," it is known to carry risks for the woman's well-being and life.

The answer to unplanned pregnancies is not found in the legalization or the increased availability of abortion, which results in the death of the unborn child and has adverse consequences for the mother and society in general. The answer must begin with the recognition of the economic and social factors which cause women to have recourse to abortion and recognition of the value of all human life, female as well as male, unborn as well as adult.

The term "reproductive rights" is included in the documentation "Women in Social Development." This term is at present being discussed in a parallel process — it is not consensus language and its components are unclear. The term "reproductive rights" is neither used nor defined in universal human rights instruments, not in the context of the Teheran Human Rights Conference nor of the World Conference on Human Rights held in Vienna less than one year ago. In reflection on the rights and duties involved in the decision concerning the number of children and spacing of births, that stated at the time of the Teheran Human Rights Conference is often quoted: "Parents," the text reads, "have a basic right to decide freely and responsibly on the number and spacing of their children... ." If anything, there has been in the years since the Conference a fear of making more explicit what the notion of responsibly means.

In conclusion, the proposals being raised by my Delegation are not simple and would require a sincere effort by all concerned to resolve the problems presented. But the problems that women, their families and their societies face are not simple, and must be dealt with by confronting the fundamental causes, together with respect for the inherent dignity of the human person, if they are to be overcome. It is only through such efforts that the goals of equality, development and peace can truly be attained.

Thank you, Madame Chairperson.

STATEMENT BY
MONSIGNOR CANDIDO RUBIOLO
HEAD OF THE HOLY SEE DELEGATION AT THE
SIXTH REGIONAL CONFERENCE ON THE INTEGRATION OF WOMEN
IN THE ECONOMIC AND SOCIAL DEVELOPMENT
OF LATIN AMERICA AND THE CARIBBEAN
MAR DEL PLATO, ARGENTINA, 25-29 SEPTEMBER 1994

Madame President:

The Delegation of the Holy See wishes, first of all, to express its gratitude to the Government of Argentina for the hospitality it has extended to us, as well as for the dedication of all who have, in one way or another, helped to organize the Sixth Regional Conference on the Integration of Women in the Economic and Social Development of Latin America and the Caribbean, which will serve at the same time to prepare for the Fourth World Conference on Women (Beijing, 1995).

1.   The Holy See attends, with Observer status, all Regional Preparatory Meetings of this World Conference. This helps our Delegation to study in depth the problems encountered in the various regions of the world and to assess the different ways in which these problems are perceived in the various geographic areas.

2.   The Regional "Programme of Action for Women in Latin America and the Caribbean, 1995-2001," which is a contribution to the Fourth World Conference on Women, is structured around six basic topics: Gender Equality; Social Integration; the Participation of Women in the Responsibilities and Benefits of Development; the Reduction and Relief of Poverty Among Women; the Participation of Women in Decision-Making and the Empowerment of Women; Human Rights, Peace and Violence and the Sharing of Family Responsibilities.

Since each of these points is of great interest to the Holy See, my Delegation wishes to suggest a few ideas, with a view to contributing to their study.

3.   The Holy See firmly supports all efforts at enabling women to enjoy their rights in society effectively and peacefully. It feels that, when studying equal rights, the reference criterion is respect for the dignity of the human being. The traditional and constant teaching of the Catholic Church has been to assert the equal dignity of men and women, both creatures of God, human beings that are equal in every respect and complement each other.

4. The complementarity of men and women, their equality in their diversity, the right "to be a woman" and thus to be present in all areas of the social economic and political life enriches human development and sets woman free from having to affect her self-realization according to the ways and lifestyles of a society that, by its organization, is mainly masculine, and thus to build a more humane world.

5. Women today have better legal protection within the International Community. Nevertheless, my Delegation notes, as is repeatedly expressed in the documents submitted at this forum, that there is still a great difference between the precepts of the law stated at the international level and the practical application of such principles. This can be seen in the limited, or even sometimes in the lack of available remedies of a legislative, executive, administrative or judicial nature, to guarantee true equal rights and fundamental freedoms at the level of the State's institutions.

6. Practical application of the above at the international level is intimately linked with an appropriate interpretation of rights and their application in concrete situations. That is why women must be able to share in decision-making, by taking an active part in the political life which, by its structures and its operation, is still an essentially masculine world.

7. This integration of women in the decision-making processes is intimately linked with the question of women's work. Women's right to be integrated in the labour world, on an equal footing with men, cannot be achieved so long as differences and — inevitably — costs weigh down on those who provide the work. Society will have to implement appropriate legislative and social security measures.

Furthermore, the Delegation of the Holy See believes that the rights of women who decide to join the labour force must not allow the rights of women who decide to work at home, in order to devote more time to their families, to be forgotten.

Family policies must ensure favourable conditions and a proper balance between the professional and family lives of both spouses. Work must be sufficiently remunerated to allow for the establishment and support of a family, either through adequate salaries to support it, or through social measures such as family allocations or remuneration for one of the spouses' work at home.

8. Violence against women, whether physical, sexual, psychological or moral, is a phenomenon which cannot be ignored. In fact, any violence involving women affects their whole being. Of particular concern is the

increase in family violence, in practically all cultures, all classes of society and all regions.

Further examples of violence are abuse in the workplace, pornography, prostitution, rape, compulsory control of the number of births, enforced sterilization and incentives for abortion.

Any type of violence infringes the most elementary rights of women and can be ascribed to a lack of respect for a person's dignity. Such is also the case with regard to the manipulation of women's image in the mass media and the advertising industry; such manipulation adversely affects behaviour towards women.

It is to be hoped that policies will be instituted requiring the mass media to establish and to follow ethical rules of conduct promoting the dignity of women.

9. Closely related to the issue of violence is the question of poverty, which is also intimately linked with the problem of migrations and its heavy impact on the lives of women, who often bear the brunt of the consequences of the lack of means of subsistence. Many are the cases of split families, where the wives, abandoned by their husbands, are left to bear alone the responsibility of looking after the children and the elderly members of the nuclear family.

The Holy See supports all efforts at helping women in such situations, through social services, housing, counseling offices, reinsertion into the labour force. Many of these solutions are, nevertheless, temporary. To find definitive solutions to these problems, measures must be taken, with the participation of these same women, aimed at producing an integral improvement of society. It is, of course, a worldwide problem, that also shows the need for a review of the high rewards given certain activities against the small or nonexistent remuneration of many others, a fact that accounts for women remaining poor despite their work.

10. The draft "Regional Program of Action for Women in Latin America and the Caribbean 1996-2001," also presents, among its strategic objectives, consideration of women's health in an integrated, even-handed way and according to the various stages of their lives. In the various international forums, the Delegation of the Holy See supports the need for the promotion of health services for women. Even in countries where Catholics are in the minority, there are thousands of Catholic hospitals, clinics, dispensaries as well as other kinds of institutional structures.

This promotion also extends to cases where women have to face unwanted pregnancies. It is often argued that, if abortion were legal, women's mortality rate from such causes would be reduced. However, information from various United Nations agencies indicates that the mothers' health gives rise to grave concerns in some countries where abortion is free, but where health conditions are poor. Even when abortion is performed with due medical attention, it carries risks for the woman. On the other hand, the Holy See cannot fail to show its opposition to the voluntary elimination of a defenseless human being, whatever the circumstances. The answer must be found in the solution to the social and economic problems which cause women to resort to abortion, much to their inner suffering, in the majority of cases.

With regard to the expressions "reproductive health" and "reproductive rights," the Holy See considers them as concepts that refer to the person in an integral manner, to the entire bodily and spiritual personality, oriented towards maturity in the sexual field and in the mutual love which characterizes marital relations, in accordance with the moral norm.

11. Women's full participation in the social, cultural, economic and political life requires an effort on the part of society in the area of training at all levels. On one hand, women have a right of access to training that enables them to participate in public life and find fulfillment in the family circle.

Men, too, need training, in learning to look upon women with full respect for their rights.

The Delegation of the Holy See trusts that the full realization of women's rights will not be a feminine question only, but a matter that concerns all of society.

Statement of
His Excellency Bishop Paul Josef Cordes
Secretary, Pontifical Council for the Laity
at the High-Level Regional Preparatory Meeting for the Fourth World Conference on Women
Vienna, 18 October 1994

Madame President,

1. I wish to begin by expressing my Delegation's gratitude to the Austrian Government for the hospitality which it is extending to this important Meeting in preparation for the Fourth World Conference on Women, to be held in Beijing in 1995. Likewise, we express appreciation to all who have worked to prepare this Meeting.

The Holy See has taken an active part, in its Observer status, in all of the Regional Preparatory Meetings and is very conscious of the diversity which exists in different geographical regions in relation to the conditions in which women live and work, and in the way their dignity and rights are perceived and respected.

2. A clear and uncompromising recognition by the international community that the human rights of women are an inalienable, integral and indivisible part of universal human rights is needed as the basis for progress in the context of the United Nations Conference on Women. Much must still be done to ensure that this fundamental principle is acknowledged, safeguarded and applied, juridically and practically. Only then will it be possible for the international community to tackle effectively the task of eradicating all forms of discrimination on grounds of gender and promoting the full and equal participation of women in political, civil, economic, social and cultural life at all levels. The Holy See wishes to see widespread and enlightened attention being given to the principles involved, so that these efforts on behalf of women and their equal treatment in society will indeed be favourable to them, and not become simply another form of an ideological and cultural clash of ideas or interests.

3. Europe is living a moment of transition and change. While enormous difficulties and challenges lie ahead, there is still much room for a positive outlook on the way this continent will develop over the next decades. It would add insult to injury if the extremely necessary and valuable contribution of women to this better future is not recognized and properly esteemed. The Catholic Church has a two thousand year presence in Europe, and in every epoch has experienced the vital influence of women in

humanizing society. My Delegation therefore wishes to express the hope that the many positive elements of the Draft Regional Platform for Action will indeed help the forthcoming World Conference on Women to give an effective impulse not only to the cause of promoting the dignity and rights of women but also to ensuring their real sharing in the processes of development.

4. I take this opportunity to underline some aspects of the Holy See's understanding of the equal dignity and rights between women and men. We see this equality as arising from the very origin of the human person in the order of creation; that is, as preceding any theory, consensus or declaration on their significance. We see this equality in the context of a true complementarity between the two sexes, and not as a complete uniformity or an undifferentiated leveling of real differences. In fact, we are conscious of women's and men's "right to be different." Consequently, and almost paradoxically, we see the need to affirm a woman's "right to be a woman." And we see in this right the true foundation of women's dignity and their most radical and important contribution to authentic development in all its forms.

We are convinced that this acknowledgment of unity in diversity is a source of enrichment for human development, and frees women from a blind race towards self-realization seen in terms of patterns and styles drawn from a predominantly masculine society. This way of approaching the question of equality in no way hinders women's greater role; rather it enables women to affirm their own specific qualities and merits. This way of looking at the question of women's rights is more attentive to reciprocity, complementarity and cooperation between women and men, both in the family and in every other activity aimed at building a more human world, and therefore involves a true "liberation" of women from the dominion of models of social structure and behaviour too often shaped by past male "privilege."

5. The International Year of the Family has provided the context for a widespread and fruitful reflection on this basic unit of society. A "liberation" of women, consisting in seeing family life and motherhood as a humiliating burden, a handicap or hazard, is a clearly false liberation, for it neither respects women nor leads to genuine human development, since every human being has an innate need to belong to a community of love and life as the irreplaceable setting for his or her human growth. That community is the family, built on marriage between a man and a woman, a community which no other institution can adequately replace. In promoting equal rights between women and men, account must therefore be taken of the specific role of women in motherhood. Motherhood must be protected if women's rights are to be a reality. To impose coercive limits on maternity is to prevent

many women from fulfilling themselves as persons.

       The family exercises a fundamental role in transmitting the patrimony of values — social, religious and cultural — which constitutes a people's identity and which therefore plays such an important part in every individual's self-awareness and self-realization. Today, the handing on of that patrimony is made difficult by the breakdown of families caused by migration for economic reasons, the increase in the number of refugees due to conflicts, and the internal weakening of family life due to new pressures in consumer and media-saturated societies. We all see that it is women and children who bear the greatest burden in such situations. The Holy See encourages legislative measures aimed at defending, facilitating and fostering family life, as the best source of society's stability and well-being, and as a necessary condition for protecting women's rights.

6.   In regard to labour and the economy, the Holy See stands for a real equality of opportunity for women, with the application of legislation suited to overcoming unjust discrimination and capable also of changing long-standing attitudes which do not value women's contribution as its true worth, especially in relation to work in the home, in the rural world and the unplanned economy. Together with men, women are the subjects and objects of the whole of socio-economic life. They have a corresponding right to be present where decisions about economic and social life are made.

7.   Furthermore, and with no less emphasis, my Delegation wishes to express the very grave concern of the Holy See in relation to increasing violence against women. In Europe very recently we have been witnesses of terrible crimes committed against women and young girls in the name of an abhorrent ideology of ethnic purity and superiority. Violence against women, adults and children, even within the home, seems to be increasing at an alarming rate. Pornography, which is radically and directly opposed to the affirmation of the equality of men and women, is permitted or at least widely tolerated. Moreover, certain forms of advertising use women in a way that is far from respectful of their dignity. The Holy See considers that Governments and the international community ought to feel a serious responsibility to take effective measures against this endemic violence which goes against women precisely as women.

8.   Finally, in the Gospel of Matthew we read: "It is written, 'Man shall not live by bread alone, but by every word that proceeds from the mouth of God'" (4:4). This saying reminds us that there are values which are not just material, but spiritual and transcendent, without which people cannot fully understand or achieve the meaning of their lives. Women in particular, being more closely connected with the mystery of giving and nurturing life, are

generally more sensitive to those values, including religious values, which play such an important part in motivating individuals and groups to commit themselves with enlightened generosity to serving the common good, and thus sustain solidarity and the struggle against all forms of poverty. The Holy See is anxious to see more attention being given to the real application of freedom of conscience and of religion to all women.

9. The Holy See hopes that the Fourth World Conference on Women will effectively contribute to the authentic progress of women's rights. The Catholic Church on its part will continue to work everywhere for the advancement of women, especially through the education of consciences, both of men and of women, regarding the inalienable God-given dignity of every human being.

Thank you, Madame President.

STATEMENT BY
MS. SHERI RICKERT
MEMBER OF THE HOLY SEE DELEGATION
AT THE FIFTH AFRICAN REGIONAL CONFERENCE ON WOMEN,
(PREPARATORY MEETING TO THE
FOURTH WORLD CONFERENCE ON WOMEN)
DAKAR, SENEGAL, 19 NOVEMBER 1994

The Holy See Delegation is pleased to be here in Dakar to participate in the Fifth African Regional Conference on Women, part of the preparations for the World Conference on Women. My Delegation would like to take this opportunity to thank the people of Senegal for their warm welcome, and the Secretariat and all those involved in the Conference preparations for their efforts.

While the agenda for this meeting includes many serious issues concerning women that merit extensive consideration, time obviously does not allow for adequate treatment of all of them. Therefore, this Statement will focus only on those issues that present perhaps the greatest challenge but also the greatest potential for advancing Africa's women, and thereby the African people.

Respect for and development of all human life, including that of women, requires peace (cf. *Catechism of the Catholic Church*, No. 2304). Women cannot achieve equality or economic or social advancement if their own lives and the existence of the society in which they live is constantly threatened. Therefore, one of the most critical issues for the women of this region is that concerning the pervasive wars, political conflicts and civil strife. It is also an issue for which a political solution is available, even if the political will is not yet evident for achieving it — that of halting the excessive transfer and accumulation of conventional arms.

While the State has the right, even the obligation, to defend its people, morally it should not possess military means beyond that necessary to assure its legitimate defense. The failure to abide by this principle has two adverse consequences: the risk of the violent use of force increases with excessive accumulations, and the public expenditures for such arms, particularly when they result in an increase in external debt, squander resources desperately needed in social service sectors.

The implications of this situation for women is obvious. Weapons do not discriminate on the basis of gender or age — women and their children are killed and maimed as readily as the combatants themselves. There are areas in Africa where the number of handicapped women is rapidly increasing, women injured by land mines in fields where they were foraging for food in order to feed their families. A disproportionately large number of the refugees and displaced persons are women, who in turn face greater danger as a result of their lack of protection and increased vulnerability. At a time when Africa's women are confronted with high rates of female illiteracy, disease and premature mortality, some countries are spending more on their military sector than on the health and educational sectors combined. This regional conference presents a unique opportunity to address the weapons industry, governments and the international community, and to raise awareness of the effects of the trade and excessive accumulation of arms on the status of women.

The situation of rural women is also worthy of significant attention. They, in particular, suffer from numerous forms of discrimination and from the inadequacy or absence of development efforts. In many communities women undertake heavy farm labor in difficult environmental conditions, with no time to attend educational programs — assuming they are available. The Catholic Church, through its educational programs for women, has experienced the positive impact that education can have not only on the well-being of women, but also on the family, community and country. The participants to this Meeting would do well to seek the means to overcome discriminatory attitudes regarding the education of the girl child, to ease the workload of rural women so that they have time to learn, and to increase access to educational services.

While the international community has oftentimes recognized the importance of women's education, little has been done to finance and implement action programs to make educational access a reality. This regional conference would greatly benefit the cause for improving women's status by emphasizing the need to make education a priority at the Fourth World Conference on Women.

Women, and particularly rural women, would also benefit from a greater commitment in confronting the major basic health problems in the region, particularly infectious and parasitic diseases. Such a commitment, together with the construction and maintenance of safe water and sanitation facilities, would not only address humanitarian concerns but would also further development efforts by providing women with the time and physical strength they need to undertake productive activity.

In order that productive activity be worthwhile, poor women in turn need a sustainable economic base in their community in which to work. One approach to creating such a base is to increase the access of poor and low-income entrepreneurs to credit and financial resources. Catholic Church agencies that provide village banking services in Africa are experiencing promising results with this approach, as are others who are attempting to assist the poor — mostly women — in this way. Given this experience, a greater percentage of international aid and domestic budgets should be used to foster the productive activity of the low-income and poor populations.

A development strategy must take into account not only the interests and well-being of women, but also of their families. While children play an important part in most women's lives, a wife and mother is often provided with little support in caring for the family from either society or her husband. Pope John Paul II has referred to the fact that "Unfortunately, (a) woman often meets objective difficulties that make her task as mother more burdensome, even to the point of heroism. Often, however, this unbearable load is caused by indifference and inadequate assistance, due to legislation that pays scant attention to the value of the family, and to a widespread and distorted culture which unduly excuses man from his family responsibilities and, in the worst cases, inclines him to look upon woman as an object of pleasure or a mere reproductive device." Against this oppressive culture, the Pope has asked that every legitimate effort be made to promote the authentic emancipation of women.

This necessarily includes measures to combat the growing incidence of violence against women at every level of society. A woman has the right to feel secure and to seek self-fulfillment both within her family and outside the home. Educational and legislative actions should focus on sustaining the family as a peaceful and mutually-supportive institution and on addressing those instances in society where the inherent dignity of women is violated.

The media has a central role to play in the perceptions a society has about women. This role is expanding, due to the media's influence and in its bridging effects between countries and cultures. It should be encouraged to further its positive role, but also reminded of its obligation to balance the right to freedom of expression with respect for fundamental human rights and women's dignity. My Delegation would advocate a recommendation that the media develop and observe a code of ethics that includes a commitment to promoting human rights and dignity, including that of women.

In identifying those who can contribute to the authentic advancement of women, one must not forget that women themselves have an indispensable role to play, through the education they provide within the family, their opposition to situations of violence, and their efforts through the workplace and the political process. The Holy See Delegation has found it strange that some are calling for women's greater participation in the armed forces, at the same time that armed conflicts are being condemned for their negative impact on women. This seems to convey divergent messages — women want to be proponents of peace, but they also want equality with men in an activity which is often a source of violence.

As was mentioned before, the issues are serious and they are many. It is the hope of my Delegation that courage will be found to focus upon and tackle those issues which may be most difficult, but that have the greatest importance for women. Such an endeavor will mean success not only for the interests of the African people, but by contributing to the Fourth World Conference on Women, also for the interests of the world.

STATEMENT BY
HIS EXCELLENCY ARCHBISHOP RENATO R. MARTINO
APOSTOLIC NUNCIO, PERMANENT OBSERVER OF THE HOLY SEE
TO THE UNITED NATIONS
BEFORE THE THIRD COMMITTEE OF THE 49TH SESSION
OF THE GENERAL ASSEMBLY
ON ITEM 97: ADVANCEMENT OF WOMEN
NEW YORK, 5 DECEMBER 1994

Mr. Chairman,

While the item concerning the Advancement of Women is routinely discussed by this Committee, it has particular importance this year in view of the Fourth World Conference on Women that will take place next September. Therefore, my Delegation is pleased to take this opportunity to comment on some of the Holy See's priorities and concerns regarding this issue.

Even though the Conference has the general theme of Equality, Development and Peace, many are urging that the issue of peace be given particular attention, given that a state of peace is required before measures to achieve development and equality can be successful. This is particularly evident today, when conflicts are increasing in their frequency and severity at all levels of society and throughout the world. Not only is peace a prerequisite to equality and development, but years of work to attain economic and social progress can be lost within a matter of weeks if peace itself is not maintained. Therefore, the upcoming Women's Conference should focus both on establishing means to achieve peace in order to further the advancement of women, and on the advancement of women in order to achieve peace.

Peace in any and all aspects of society requires recognition of the equal dignity of every human person, including that of women in relation to men. Pope John Paul II has described this relationship as "equality in diversity," noting that "perfection for woman is not being like man, becoming masculine to the point of losing her specific feminine qualities, but her perfection — which is also a secret of affirmation and of relative autonomy — is to be a woman, equal to man but different."

This difference is apparent primarily in the family, where the woman undertakes the unique role of wife and mother. In today's world, in practically every culture and society, more women are undertaking professional and other economic activity, and contributing with their own abilities to their communities' well-being. At the same time, they are seeking ways to balance these endeavors with their irreplaceable role within the family. The Pope has spoken on behalf of women in this emerging trend, stating that "it is necessary to avoid the risk that the family and humanity suffer a loss which impoverishes them, since women can never be replaced in begetting and rearing children. The authorities should therefore provide for the professional promotion of women and at the same time safeguard her vocation as a mother and educator with appropriate legislation."

Such legislation may include, for instance, provisions that accord the work of women within the family its social value, and that include this work within national labor accounting systems. Governments may also encourage flexible work schedules for parents, and incentives for the reintegration of older women into the work force.

The safeguarding of women in the family also requires measures to address domestic violence, a serious problem for women that seems to be growing in almost every society. More effective mechanisms need to be developed and implemented to deal with these crises, and to protect the institution of the family as a place of security and self-fulfillment for every one of its members. The need for public education in this regard is evident, as well as established means for legal redress when a woman's human rights are violated. Education concerning these means should be provided not only to women, but also to men, in the hope that awareness of the equal dignity of women, and the sanctions imposed for violating that dignity, would help to prevent abuses from occurring.

Another important concern for women and their families is the provision of essential social services including education and health care. This is particularly the case for rural women, who are among the poorest of the poor and yet are a vital component for the continued existence and the well-being of their communities. Concrete means should be established to help them attain their rights to education, to physical and mental health and to development. Such means would involve not only providing educational and healthcare facilities, but just as importantly, creative means for development. Humanitarian agencies of the Catholic Church have seen how the provision of basic assistance, such as the local establishment of self-sustaining economic initiatives, comprehensive credit assistance programs, and projects as small as the digging of a water well, have transformed the lives of rural women, their families and their communities.

On a global scale, the role of the media, in all its forms — audio, visual and print — and its influence on the advancement of women, needs to be examined. Those responsible for the media should be encouraged in its promotion of positive images of women and of respectful gender relationships, as well as the provision of educational programs to further personal and societal well-being. However, there is a growing recognition of the need for the media industry to be accountable for its programming, not only to the financial interests that support it, but also to the various societies to which its programs are transmitted. This is particularly the case where those exposed to the media may be in a different country or region from that of the financial sponsor, and have widely varying cultural, moral and ethical standards. Currently, many communities have little economic or political influence over the kind of programming that is broadcast, and no ability to address concerns such as the importation of pornography, graphic depictions of brutal violence, or exploitative advertising.

The need for accountability is not to deny in any way the right "to seek, receive and impart information and ideas through any media and regardless of frontiers"; it is to recognize that the media has a responsibility to seek the necessary balance between freedom of expression and respect for fundamental human rights and human dignity, including the rights and dignity of women. A possible means of achieving this balance would be to call upon those who own and operate the media, public or private, to develop and observe an international code of ethics that includes a commitment to promoting and protecting women's dignity and rights.

The treatment of women's issues requires an integral approach, taking into consideration not only a woman's material, psychological and social well-being, but her spiritual and religious aspirations as well. Women have the fundamental right, as do all people, to freedom of thought, conscience and religion. For these reasons, it is disturbing to my Delegation that efforts have been made recently in various international fora to avoid or delete any positive reference to religion or spirituality in relation to women. Such action is not necessary in order to denounce the violence being perpetuated against women by those who claim to act in the name of religion; in fact, the Holy See joins in this denunciation. At the same time, religious and spiritual beliefs are an important aspect of most women's lives — and must be acknowledged and respected as such.

Conflict and related violence are affecting an increasing number of women and their children, and the Holy See has often expressed its hope that they will receive increased attention and compassion. The women in refugee and displaced populations should also receive priority consideration as they often carry the burden of ensuring the welfare of their families. Another concern of my Delegation is the suffering endured, particularly by women and children, as a result of internationally-imposed sanctions. Whoever is to blame for the creation of conflict or the failure to resolve it, it is certainly not this innocent sector of the population. And yet, they are precisely the ones to suffer the greatest harm — and for the longest period of time — as a result of economic sanctions.

Protective measures should be undertaken by all concerned parties to shield the most vulnerable from the effects of any conflict situation. Such measures should not be mere verbal considerations, but means that effectively provide women with access to sufficient amounts of food, clean water, sanitary living conditions and medical care and supplies. Of course, these means are only part of a solution — what women truly want, and what they truly need, is peace. Recent international developments have illustrated the importance of continued and sincere dialogue between opposing parties in order to achieve this end.

Mr. Chairman,

It is the sincere hope of the Holy See Delegation that these and other critical issues will be addressed in a meaningful way during the preparations for and at the Fourth World Conference on Women, as this Conference provides the opportunity for everyone, women and men, to achieve peace and greater opportunities for equality and development.

Thank you, Mr. Chairman.

STATEMENT BY
MS. SHERI RICKERT
MEMBER OF THE HOLY SEE DELEGATION AT THE
39TH SESSION OF THE COMMISSION ON THE STATUS OF WOMEN
ON PREPARATIONS FOR THE FOURTH WORLD CONFERENCE ON WOMEN
NEW YORK, 15 MARCH 1995

Madame Chairperson,

My Delegation would like to express its appreciation to the Secretariat for the work which has been carried out in preparing the documentation in E/CN.6/1995/L.4 with add 1, add 2 and add 3. These documents concern the "List of Non-Governmental Organizations Recommended for Accreditation" to the Fourth World Conference on Women presently before this session of the Commission on the Status of Women.

The Delegation of the Holy See wishes to draw attention to the listing in: E/CN.6/1995/L.4/Add 1 number 59 (Catholics for a Free Choice - United States of America); E/CN.6/1995/L.4/Add 2 number 62 (Católicas por el Derecho a Decidir [Oficina Central de la Red Latinoamericana] - Uruguay) and number 63 (Católicas por el Derecho a Decidir A.C. - Mexico); E/CN.6/1995/L.4/Add 3 number 69 (Católicas Pelo Direito De Decidir - Brazil).

The name of the non-governmental organization in question is "Catholics for a Free Choice." It is the position of my Delegation that the organizational listings in question are misleading by the use of their title. Thus my Delegation cannot approve of their accreditation.

The organization in question uses the word "Catholic" in its title and yet publicly maintains positions contrary to those held by the Catholic Church, particularly on the issue of the right to abortion. Any group claiming to speak for Catholics, while at the same time assuming and promoting positions totally contrary to the Catholic Church's moral teaching, cannot be recognized as Catholic.

In the case of the entry number 59 in E/CN.6/1995/L.4/Add 1, the organization in question has listed its affiliation as being in the United States of America. However, the highest civil and canonical Catholic body of that country, the United States Catholic Conference and the National Conference of Catholic Bishops respectively, has issued a public statement noting that "Catholics for a Free Choice" is not an authentic Catholic organization, and has no affiliation, formal or otherwise, with the Catholic Church and merits no recognition as a Catholic organization.

Madame Chairperson, my Delegation again states that it does not and cannot approve the inclusion of these non-governmental organizations for accreditation.

Thank you, Madame Chairman.

STATEMENT OF
HIS EXCELLENCY ARCHBISHOP RENATO R. MARTINO
APOSTOLIC NUNCIO, PERMANENT OBSERVER OF THE HOLY SEE
TO THE UNITED NATIONS
AT THE 39TH SESSION OF THE
COMMISSION ON THE STATUS OF WOMEN
ON PREPARATIONS FOR THE FOURTH WORLD CONFERENCE ON WOMEN
NEW YORK, 16 MARCH 1995

Madame Chairperson,

It is with great pleasure that the Holy See Delegation takes this opportunity to address the Commission on the Status of Women in view of the Commission's preparations for the Fourth World Conference on Women. Given the importance of the task that lies ahead, it is indeed fortunate that we will have your leadership and guidance. The Delegation of the Holy See expresses appreciation to the Conference Secretariat, and to all who have worked so diligently to prepare for this meeting.

The occasion of the Fourth World Conference on Women should be a cause for international celebration, reflection, and motivation: celebration in recognition of all women, their contribution to the world and the progress that has been achieved; reflection, on those areas in which women's hopes and expectations have yet to be realized, and also areas in which their situation unfortunately has worsened; motivation, to address these areas with concrete, realistic solutions for the benefit of women themselves, their families, our societies and our world.

On 1 January 1995, Pope John Paul II dedicated his annual *Message for the World Day of Peace* to the theme "Women: Teachers of Peace," emphasizing women's participation in the various aspects of social life. "When women are able fully to share their gifts with the whole community, the very way in which society understands and organizes itself is improved, and comes to reflect in a better way the substantial unity of the human family... The growing presence of women in social, economic and political life at the local, national and international levels is thus a very positive development. Women have a full right to become actively involved in all areas of public life, and this right must be affirmed and guaranteed... ."

The quality of public life in general depends on every person's experience, education and well-being in private life, particularly in the family. For this reason, a woman's role in the family, particularly of those women who undertake the care and formation of their children, must be recognized and deeply appreciated. Many of us realize the influence that our mothers have had in our own lives, and know that a mother's attention and love has no substitute for personal growth and development. Unfortunately, there are also many in our societies who, for a variety of reasons, have not known the nurturing love of a mother. Not only these individuals, but our societies as a whole, have suffered as a result.

In the same way, society is disadvantaged to the extent that women are precluded from contributing their perspectives, experiences and talents to other aspects of social life, and women themselves justly criticize their arbitrary exclusion. Yet in order to participate meaningfully, every person, including women, requires a minimal amount of societal support. This minimum includes an education, a secure place to call home with safe water and sanitation facilities, access to health care and the utilization of development resources. It is a sad discrepancy that while significant international attention is being given to increasing women's participation in leadership and decision-making, the most basic of needs of so many women are still unattended. The illiteracy rate among women continues to be unacceptably high, the number of women living in poverty is increasing, and many women must still fear death from childbirth and medically preventable and treatable diseases, because they are not provided with even simple medical assistance.

The Draft Platform for Action justifiably places significant attention on addressing these areas. My Delegation hopes that those actions on behalf of the disadvantaged and the poor will not simply be printed words, but that the necessary political and financial means to implement them will be provided.

A woman has a right to expect the necessary support and protection not only from public authorities, but also within her home. Parents have a duty and a responsibility to provide and care for their daughters as well as their sons. The world community should be concerned at the growing scandals involving the girl-child from the earliest stages of life, including neglect, physical and sexual abuse, child labor, son preference, prostitution and pornography. In this regard, the Holy See Delegation encourages and would support the addition of a Critical Area of Concern on the girl child, as has been proposed by other Delegations.

While the critical role of mothers in the formation and care of their children is generally recognized, the role of men in accepting their responsibilities as husbands and fathers largely has been neglected, or relegated solely to the provision of financial support. Statistics alone reveal the danger of ignoring men's responsibility in the family. An increasing number of female-headed households are struggling with poverty, and in some societies, a rise in juvenile delinquency, drug addiction, and violence is related to an increased number of children growing up without a father.

Adolescents, boys as well as girls, should be made aware of and appreciate their physical dignity and the importance of respect for themselves and others. To this end, adolescents should be taught the importance of abstinence before marriage, not only to safeguard their own and others' physical, emotional and spiritual well-being, but also as a responsibility towards the creation of new life. Once a man becomes a father, he has an obligation to learn together with the mother how best to meet the various needs of their child, and to share responsibility for meeting those needs.

Governments also should be sensitive to the hardship created for women when their husbands are missing due to a lack of local employment opportunities, or as a result of war or human rights violations. Women suffer greatly as a result of disintegration of the family, and greater priority must be given by society to strengthening family life, and to maintaining the unity of and stability within the family, for the benefit of every one of its members.

One means by which governments should contribute to women's security, including unity in the family, is to significantly reduce the international arms trade and military expenditures. The intra- and international violence that is occurring in our world, together with the forced movements of refugees and displaced persons, is not only due to the violence and hatred of individuals. The proliferation of death, mutilation and destruction would not be possible if the weapons being used, particularly those which are especially injurious and have indiscriminate effects, were not produced and sold in some parts of the world, and then purchased at the expense of peaceful development and social needs in others. Women who have lost family members, suffered exile and severe hardship, and experienced dismemberment, torture and death have a right to demand the halt of the excessive weapons trade — and they have a right to be heard.

The international community is becoming increasingly aware that women are experiencing violence not only in war and conflict situations, but within the home as well. The legal systems of some countries have recognized domestic violence as a violation of women's human rights, and make it punishable as such. While this should be the case in every country, attempts must also be made to address the root causes of domestic violence. In many cases this will involve not only education on the rights and dignity of women, but also drug and alcohol treatment, counseling, and measures to confront stress caused by unemployment and poverty.

Education, in the broadest sense, is a critical element in the way women are perceived and treated by others. This education occurs today to a great extent through the mass media, and includes the negative values that are being transmitted internationally, including the promotion of violence and sexual irresponsibility, the assault of pornography on the dignity of women and pornography-related violence, and the exploitation of women in advertising. The passive acceptance of these portrayals of women on television screens, in music, and in magazines is leading to their presumed acceptability in day-to-day life. The media should not only present positive portrayals of women and increase women's participation, but those responsible for the media's content should be held accountable for the negative influence that it has on the lives of women.

Madame Chairperson,

While more attention appropriately is being given to many of the human rights of women, more should also be given to respect for women's right to freedom of thought, conscience and religion. A diminishing respect for this right can be perceived in several ways, including the reluctance by some in secular societies to recognize that religion can and does play an important positive role in women's lives. Women's freedom of conscience is important, and should be addressed by the international community.

The Holy See Delegation hopes that agreement can be reached on means to address these issues and others during the coming weeks, and assures you, Madame Chairperson, of our complete cooperation towards this end.

Thank you, Madame Chairperson.

Statement by
His Excellency Archbishop Jean-Louis Tauran
Secretary for Relations with States of the Holy See:
The Position of the Holy See on the Draft Platform for Action for the Fourth World Conference on Women
Vatican, 26 May 1995

1. The Beijing Meeting will be the Fourth World Conference on Women organized by the United Nations, following those held in Mexico City (1975), Copenhagen (1980) and Nairobi (1985). The theme will be: "Equality, Development and Peace." The Secretary General of the Conference is Mrs Gertrude Mongella, from Tanzania.

As you know, the September Meeting has been prepared by a series of regional meetings:

— Asia-Pacific (Jakarta, June 1994);
— Latin America-Caribbean (Mar del Plata, September 1994);
— Europe (Vienna, October 1994);
— Western Asia (Amman, November 1994);
— Africa (Dakar, November 1994).

Finally, the 39th Session of the Commission on the Status of Women was held in New York from 15 March to 7 April last, to continue drawing up the "Platform for Action" to be adopted by the Conference in Beijing.

The Holy See has taken part in all these meetings with a Delegation of women from different countries and from different social backgrounds and professional experiences.

Dr. DiNicola has just mentioned the Catholic Church's concern for the dignity of women and for women's contribution to the life of society.

The international community and the juridical instruments drawn up by multilateral diplomacy have given increased legal protection to women. But there is a significant difference between what is juridically affirmed at the international level and its concrete application. The Holy See is especially concerned that the Beijing Meeting should clearly highlight and adopt new measures capable of putting into effect what has been affirmed at the universal level on the dignity, rights and role of women in society.

2. The draft document studied in New York presents the following subjects: poverty, education, health, violence against women, the effects of persecution and armed conflicts, women's part in economic structures, in structures of power and decision-making, the lack of suitable mechanisms for the promotion of women, human rights, the influence of the mass media, women and the natural environment, and the specific theme of female children and adolescents.

The document of about 120 pages constitutes a noteworthy effort to free women from constraints which certain experiences of the past or cultural conditioning have imposed on them.

Having said this, the Holy See is perplexed by the tendency throughout the document to impose a certain specific Western model of "the promotion of women," a model which ignores the values of women who for the most part live in other regions of the world. I would like briefly to recall certain important concepts which give rise to a certain preoccupation:

a) The family, which is often presented in a negative way: even as an environment where discrimination is learned. One is amazed to see that on various occasions the word "mother," when presented in a positive context, has been put in brackets. Without idealizing relationships within the family, one cannot reasonably propose as the only model, today and for the future, a Western type of household, which is often characterized by an absence of children and not infrequently by deviations which cause psychological imbalances and weakness in its most vulnerable members.

b) On the question of *abortion* there has been no positive development. We find the same expressions as at Cairo. The Holy See's Delegation will therefore have to repeat in Beijing what Pope John Paul II has written in his Encyclical *Evangelium vitae*, namely that the decision to have an abortion is tragic and painful for the mother and that no reason, however serious, can ever justify the deliberate killing of an innocent human being (cf. No. 58).

c) Attention is also given to the theme of *education*, which the Holy See considers of great importance. It has not been possible to ensure that the text will favour parents' choice in obtaining a good education for their children. Also refused has been the proposal to guarantee the rights of women and of girls to freedom of conscience and religion in educational institutions. For the Holy See it is important that account be taken of what the *Universal Declaration of Human Rights* states: that parents have the right to choose the kind of education their children are to receive.

d) Another question on which the Holy See has expressed itself many times is that of *poverty*. The document devotes an important part to this issue, which finds the Holy See substantially in agreement. Nevertheless, one wonders with concern why there is opposition to the introduction of the principle, many times reaffirmed by International Documents, that "the human being is at the centre of sustainable development." This principle was adopted, for example, by the Rio de Janeiro Declaration on the Environment and Development, and also accepted by the Cairo Conference on Population and Development. At the recent Summit on Social Development at Copenhagen the principle was again reaffirmed when reference was made to the need for a "people centered" development.

e) The Document also devotes an important section to the *effects of persecution and armed conflicts on women*. On various occasions the Holy See has made clear its position in this regard. It has constantly denounced the use of immense resources for buying weapons rather than for meeting essential social needs; it has also spoken out about the effects of armed conflicts on women. Wars cause death and the separation of family members and reduce whole peoples to desperate conditions, with consequences which are especially burdensome to women, forced to flee their own land with their children and the oldest members of the family.

The Holy See notes with satisfaction that this chapter presents as the Document's strategic objective the promotion of women's contribution to the culture of peace. You will recall that the Pope devoted his *Message for the World Day of Peace* this year precisely to "Women: Teachers of Peace."

f) The Document devotes *little attention* to the many problems faced by *women emigrants*, although it does refer to them in other contexts, on various occasions.

In emigration, the major burden of care for the family frequently falls upon women. This situation often imposes upon them the heaviest tasks: women are in effect forced to do two jobs, and this is even more demanding if they have to look after their children.

For this reason the Holy Father stated a short time ago that the increased number of women involved in migration in recent times calls for a change of perspective in the framing of migration policies.

g) The problem of women in relation to work is appropriately considered at various points. Women have a right to be part of the work force and to enjoy equal conditions with men. It is not the task of the Holy See to offer practical solutions to problems of social and labour policy, but there is certainly a need for a profound change which will enable women to become fully a part of economic, social, cultural and political life. This involves respect for the necessary conditions for this to occur, in such a way that a responsible choice to have children and to bring them up does not force women to abandon for good their involvement in public life. The Holy See thus supports whatever efforts are necessary to promote family policies which will ensure conditions favourable to a balance between professional life and family life on the part of both spouses.

On the other hand there are millions of women who have chosen to work in the family. The importance and difficulty of household work should be even more fully recognized and esteemed in view of its value for the family and the community. Motherhood, with the commitment and the responsibilities which it involves, should not fear comparison with any type of professional commitment and should receive recognition in economic terms.

The Holy See has always emphasized the importance of the family as defined by the *Universal Declaration of Human Rights* as "the natural and fundamental group unit of society" (Art. 16.3), which has a right to protection by society and the State.

While the Holy See recognizes the specific and important role of mothers in raising their children, an equally unique and important role in the family and in the education of children belongs, as mentioned earlier, to the father, not only because he is normally the breadwinner but also because of his many responsibilities for the promotion of the family in its various aspects.

h) Another subject on which the Holy See expresses agreement is that of *violence against women*, violence which may be physical, sexual, psychological or moral. Every act of violence against women affects in one way or another their whole being. Very appropriately the Document takes into consideration the exploitation of young girls forced into prostitution, a problem which has reached international dimensions. This degradation causes great physical, emotional and moral harm, cheapens individuals and very often leaves them incapable of returning to normal living.

The Document also finds the Holy See in agreement in its condemnation of violence against women as a means of repression in times of war.

But another type of violence against women also exists: the violence of the varying programmes imposed on them such as mandatory birth control, forced sterilization, the forced use of contraceptives or pressure to have abortions. This kind of violence has not found its way into the Document. The Holy See has always expressed its grave concern at the number of women who are the victims of sterilization campaigns conducted especially in developing countries. This practice constitutes a grave violation of the rights of women who are even more vulnerable when they have minimal economic resources and little formal education.

i. With regard to *health care* the Holy See accepts the principle that women have a right to the highest level of physical and mental health. Ability to enjoy this right is essential to their well-being and to the possibility of their taking part in public life and living their private life with dignity.

It is therefore surprising that in the Document, dedicated to defending all women's right to health, tropical diseases are mentioned only twice, whereas there are at least forty references to health problems related to sexuality (AIDS, reproductive health, sexually transmitted diseases, fertility control, abortion, etc.). But from data published by the World Health Organization we learn that, according to recent statistics, which probably underestimate the real situation, the number of cases of tropical diseases is estimated at between 650 and 850 million per year. On the other hand, according to the same Organization the estimated number of AIDS cases for 1994 was four million.

j) It is a serious matter that the draft Document ignores the idea of *religion*. The Holy See has obviously been especially concerned to ensure that the Document will contain a clear reference to respect for *ethical and religious values*, as also a reference to the *cultures of peoples*.

This affirmation, accepted in previous international meetings, for example the Conference on Population and Development at Cairo and the Summit on Social Development at Copenhagen, has not yet been accepted. Without this reference there is a risk that the Document will exert pressure on the weakest peoples to adopt ways of life and thinking which reflect other cultures and traditions and are foreign to their own cultural context, and thus cause them to lose precious values of their own civilization and way of life.

In the text under consideration, religion (and it is very sad to have to say so) is considered only in negative contexts. Nevertheless we must recognize and respect the fact that religion plays a central role in the life of millions of women and men. If the United Nations wishes to represent all peoples it cannot overlook the fundamental spiritual dimension of a large part of humanity.

3. I would now like to mention *certain more technical problems*, which in fact touch upon basic questions:

> — the universal nature of human rights,
> — certain problems of language,
> — the accusation leveled at the Holy See of wishing to re-open the Cairo debate.

a) The universal nature of human rights

One noted at New York a resistance on the part of some countries to stating that all human rights — and therefore also those of women — are universal. Their universality was expressed at the recent International Conference on Human Rights in Vienna: "The universal nature of these rights and freedoms is beyond question" (*Vienna Declaration*, Section I, para. 1).

It would be extremely dangerous for women and children if the task of promoting human rights were now left to the competence of individual States, according to national or local criteria.

b) Problems of language

The definition of the word "*gender*." A difficulty arose in the last days of the meeting of the Preparatory Committee in New York: some Delegations requested a clarification of the definition of this term, which is used frequently in the Document.

The Holy See has defended the right of every Delegation to ask for and receive explanations of the term, and it supports the endeavours of the Contact Group which at the moment is working on a simple and quick solution.

The expressions "*sexual orientation*" and "*lifestyle*"

Already at Cairo the Holy See expressed its concern at the inclusion in an international text of terms which prove ambiguous. There do not exist definitions of "sexual orientation" or "lifestyle," and still less an international document which recognizes a right to them. To us it seems very risky that a Government should commit itself to specific actions in relation to expressions of which the precise meaning is unclear. In this regard, it could for example happen in the future that pedophilia might be considered a "sexual orientation."

I now move on to the last point:

c) The accusation leveled at the Holy See of wishing to re-open the Cairo debate

This accusation is unjust. In point of fact, we consider it dangerous to re-open discussion on statements and texts on which it proved possible to find a balanced understanding after long months of difficult negotiations.

Thus it is not acceptable even to quote, outside their context, the paragraphs of the Cairo Document. The whole Cairo Document is to be interpreted in the light of the Preamble and the Principles of Chapter Two.

In particular, Chapter Seven, concerning "reproductive rights and reproductive health," specifies that this Chapter must be "especially guided by the principles contained in Chapter Two."

The Preamble of Chapter Two states: "The implementation of the recommendations contained in the Programme of Action is the sovereign right of each country, consistent with national laws and development priorities, with full respect for the various religious and ethical values and cultural backgrounds of its people, and in conformity with universally recognized international human rights."

If this reference and others were to be omitted, the meaning of the above-mentioned paragraphs of the Cairo Document would undergo a radical change.

As in Cairo last year, various paragraphs dealing with educating and informing adolescents in matters pertaining to sexuality seek to eliminate the responsibility of parents.

It has so far proved difficult to secure the introduction in all cases of the concept finally agreed upon at the end of the Cairo Conference and re-used by the recent Social Summit in Copenhagen, namely that access of adolescents to education, programmes and services, etc. in matters pertaining to sexuality must be "consistent with the *Convention on the Rights of the Child* and recognizing the rights, duties and responsibilities of parents and other persons legally responsible for children."

The Holy See's Delegation has asked for the introduction of the same criterion whenever specific actions involving minors are proposed, but so far the statement remains in brackets.

It is the intention of the Holy See to contribute as much as possible to the success of the Beijing Conference, by listening to everyone and presenting its own point of view. The Holy See is aware that, even though its own positions are not accepted by all, there are many people, both believers and non-believers, who share its vision and wish their voice to be heard.

In questions touching so intimately upon the nature of the human person and personal responsibilities in the matter of life and social coexistence, it is important to call things by their proper names without giving in to pretense and easy compromises or falling into outright self-deception.

The Holy See's Delegation has the advantage of the experience of Christian communities, and those belonging to the Catholic Church in particular, which have always benefitted from the contribution and witness of holy and distinguished women in the society of their time. Apart from the exceptional figure of the Virgin Mary, we can mention Birgitta of Sweden, Catherine of Siena, Frances Xavier Cabrini and Edith Stein, to name but a few.

It is the conviction of the Holy See that the complementarity of woman and man, their equality in diversity, the "right to be a woman" and to be "co-protagonist" in all sectors of social and political life enriches human development.

Our Delegation will therefore go to Beijing aware of its responsibility, sustained by the universal vision of the Catholic Church and determined to cooperate with everyone in order to affirm "a new life-style, consisting in making practical choices — at the personal, family, social and international level — on the basis of a correct scale of values: the primacy of being over having, of the person over things." These are words of Pope John Paul II in his latest Encyclical Letter *Evangelium vitae* (No. 98).

BRIEFING BY
DR. JOAQUÍN NAVARRO-VALLS
DIRECTOR OF THE PRESS OFFICE OF THE HOLY SEE
ON THE TOPIC OF THE
UNITED NATIONS FOURTH WORLD CONFERENCE ON WOMEN
VATICAN, 20 JUNE 1995

The Fourth World Conference on Women, organized by the United Nations, will take place in Beijing from September 4 to 15, 1995. It was preceded by the Conferences of Mexico City (1975), Copenhagen (1980) and Nairobi (1985).

Habitually these world conferences are preceded by regional meetings and meetings of the Preparatory Commission (Prep-Comm); this last one was held in New York (USA). The regional meetings in preparation for the Peking Conference took place in Jakarta, June 1994 (for Asia and the Caribbean); Vienna, October 1994 (for Europe); Amman, November 1994 (for Western Asia) and Dakar, November 1994 (for Africa).

The Holy See, which has Permanent Observer status at the U.N. and that will send a Delegation to Beijing, participated in all the regional meetings as well as the preparatory sessions of March-April. In the Delegation were present women of various nations, different walks of life and professional experience.

Following the established custom in these world conferences, the Delegates will meet in Beijing to work on the Draft Platform for Action with the intention of arriving at a consensus on the Final Document. Also a Final Declaration is expected to be made at the Beijing Conference.

The Draft Platform for Action is written in English, containing 112 pages, with 362 paragraphs (often with sub-paragraphs). It is divided in the following manner:

Chapter I	(par.	1-5)	Mission Statement
Chapter II	(par.	6-42)	Global Framework
Chapter III	(par.	43-46)	Critical Areas of Concern
Chapter IV	(par.	47-285)	Strategic Objectives and Actions
Chapter V:	(par.	286-345)	Institutional Arrangements
Chapter VI:	(par.	346-362)	Financial Arrangements

Chapter IV treats the themes of poverty, education, health, violence against women, effects of persecution and armed conflicts, participation in economic structures, power and decision-making processes, the lack of an adequate mechanism for the promotion of women, human rights, women and the media, women and the environment, the rights and issues of children and adolescents.

* * *

This Fourth World Conference will deal with topics such as dignity, the rights and the roles of women in every aspect of social life, equality and human development. The point of departure for every consideration made by the Holy See is the human dignity of women, which is the foundation for the concept of universal human rights recognized by the *United Nations Charter* (Preamble, par. 2).

The document that will be discussed in Beijing — *Proposals for Consideration in the Preparation of a Draft Declaration and the Draft Platform for Action* — favors the operative aspects of the varied topics. The Holy See shares this definition: the dignity of women in too many social and geographical contexts is far from being fully recognized.

We think the moment has come to create universal agreement in order to bridge the gap between what is being affirmed juridically at the international level and the concrete applications; between proposals and legal regulations; between the rhetoric and real hopes of many women. Aspirations that extend from the safety of the work environment in and out of the home to the educational arena, from the overcoming of every form of violence to the complete integration of educational structures, from an adequate health assistance to a real freedom of choice within marriage.

The Holy See recognizes the considerable efforts made to identify topics and circumstances that hinder the historical path toward women's freedom. The Platform for Action rightly calls the attention of governments to many concrete topics, among which are poverty and illiteracy — mainly female problems — as well as those of prostitution, pornography, the treatment of women, etc.

At the same time, the Holy See sees in this Document pressure of an ideological character that seems to want to impose on women all over the world a particular social philosophy belonging to some sectors of Western countries.

If, on the one hand, the Document wishes to liberate women from certain cultural conditioning, on the other hand, it seems to want to impose a Western model of female advancement which does not take into account the values of women in the majority of the countries around the world.

The dignity of women and universal human rights

One has the right to think that the unanimous goal in Beijing will be to attain a common operative effort to defend the dignity of women and the promotion of their universal human rights. Incidentally, it becomes paradoxical and incomprehensible that the word "dignity" — referring to women — appears systematically within brackets throughout the Document. In the same way the term "universal" is placed in brackets when referring to the human rights of women (cf. par. 2, 4, 11, 14, 43, etc. of the Platform of Action).

One reason, among many, why the Holy See has insisted that the Platform for Action include some reference to the universality of human rights is that women in many countries do not enjoy the human rights recognized by the International Declarations. We think that it is not possible to promote and defend that which has not been defined. If every country limits itself to promoting generic rights of women not defined on an international level, then this Conference will not represent any progress in the area of human rights for the majority of the world's women.

Lack of continuity with respect to previous international documents

In many places the Document does not maintain a continuity with preceding ones and often with United Nations Declarations. For example, paragraph 12, which the Holy See Delegation proposed be included, appears in brackets, even though its contents come from the World Conference on Human Rights (Vienna 1993). We maintain that when one speaks of Human Rights there should be a general consensus on their content and, if possible, reference to international documents.

In the whole text and especially in the section dedicated to health and the education of adolescents the annotation "taking into account the rights and duties and responsibilities of parents..." (cf. 107 (i), 107 (l), 107 (m), etc.), that appeared in the preceding international documents, is placed in brackets. This lack of continuity is all the more disconcerting because the annotation of paragraph 107(i) was approved by the Heads of State/Government or by their representatives some weeks before the Summit on Social Development in Copenhagen (6-12 March 1995).

A similar reservation should be expressed on paragraph 107 (j) which, as it is formulated, cancels out the statement, "In no case will abortion be promoted as a method of family planning," an affirmation agreed upon at the International Conferences in Mexico City (1984) and Cairo (1994).

Ideological imbalance

The recurrence of certain concepts illustrates in some way the implied social philosophy of the Draft Document. One can find, for example, that the term "gender" appears around 300 times; "mother/motherhood" appear fewer than 10 times, while the terms "sex/sexual/sexuality" appear about one hundred times. From this point of view the document appears to be extraordinarily unbalanced.

This ideological unbalance is more evident, for example, in the section that proposes the defense of women's right to health. While the Document talks 40 times about health problems related to sexual life (AIDS, reproductive health, sexually transmitted diseases, fertility control, etc.), only in two cases are tropical diseases mentioned. While the World Health Organization estimates, for example, 4 million cases of HIV infection in 1994, the same World Health Organization estimates the cases of tropical diseases during the same period as hovering between 650 and 850 million.

Sometimes one gets the impression there is a preconceived attitude. It is not understandable why "natural family planning" was put in brackets when speaking of techniques for the regulation of births (par. 110 h); and even why the request to inform women of the risks to their health caused by "hormonal contraception, abortion and promiscuity" was put between brackets (par. 110 e).

Linguistic ambiguity

Already on the occasion of the Cairo Conference the Holy See, together with many other Delegations, had expressed a real concern about the insertion of ambiguous terms into an international text. Much of the difficulty to reach a "consensus" at Cairo came from this semantic ambiguity. The ambiguities of international language are often a way to avoid a concrete resolve to carry out what is expressed.

Some terms in the document are often vaguely defined: "sexual orientation" and "lifestyle" lack a precise definition, and moreover, no juridical recognition in an international document exists for either one. This semantic and conceptual ambiguity could lead one to consider, for example, pedophilia as simply a mode of "sexual orientation," thus easily acceptable as a "right" (cf. 232 h). The term "sexual orientation," proposed by some Western countries, was not accepted by developing countries.

Some aspects of particular interest: violence against women

The Holy See agrees with the emphasis that the Platform for Action places on physical, sexual, psychological and moral violence against women (par. 113 ff.). For the Holy See this topic is a priority. Very fortunately the document takes into consideration the exploitation of young girls steered into prostitution, a phenomenon that has reached international dimensions. The Holy See also agrees on condemning — as it has done repeatedly — the violence against women as a means of repression in times of war, as well as the genital mutilation of women, the topic proposed by the Holy See Delegation at the Copenhagen Summit and agreed upon through much negotiating effort.

The Holy See would like, however, a more decisive and radical condemnation of every kind of violence, as well as psychological, against women, including forced sterilization, forced use of birth control or induced abortion. The Holy See has always expressed its real concern about the number of women who have been made objects of systematic sterilization plans which take place especially in developing countries. Such practices constitute a grave violation of the rights of women, and still more indefensible when they are funded from scarce economic and educational resources.

The Holy See Delegation proposed that these practices be included in paragraph 115 among the violations of the rights of women. Some Delegations have wanted to put this proposal in brackets.

At the same time the proposal of the insertion of the phrase "female feticide" (par. 115, 125 i, etc.) was made among the acts of violence whether against the mother or against the unborn daughter. Also this insertion was placed in brackets. Some Delegations have suggested the substitution with the eugenic euphemism "prenatal sex selection," obviously not acceptable to the Delegation of the Holy See.

In paragraph 40, the Holy See Delegation would like to have added to the list of attacks against young girls — limitations of the access to food, to education and to health care — also the denial of the very access to life ("and even life itself").

Family

Surprisingly the theme of family and motherhood receives scarce attention and little space in a document of nearly 120 pages on women. Already in Chapter II the concept of the family as "the fundamental unit of society..." (cf. par. 30), is placed within brackets, in contrast with the *Universal Declaration of Human Rights*, art. 16,3. In fact, all of paragraph 30 will go to Beijing in brackets.

On the topic of the advancement of women, the Holy See certainly shares the emphasis on the importance of their full participation in all the activities of social life. Nevertheless, it is contrary to all evidence to think that this emphasis should cancel out the unique role of women in the family: a role that does not exhaust all the personal resources of femininity but one rather which is specific to women. Obviously this point of view is shared by the immense majority of women all over the world and by the societies to which they belong.

Juridical regulations on the family should also guarantee women the fundamental right to be mothers. Indeed laws should create conditions — environmental, legal, economic, etc. — favorable to the practice of motherhood. Perhaps the moment has come to affirm that the struggle for equal dignity between men and women implies also the recognition of woman's being as different and the need to be treated in a different way.

Among these differences, for example, it is the right of a woman who also works outside the home not to be a victim of discrimination, undue pressures and particular difficulties because of her maternity. She also has the right to be defended against the daily micro-violence, and in certain cases from domestic violence also.

It is the conviction of the Holy See, as has been recognized already in Copenhagen, that the work of women, at present not remunerated, should be recognized adequately; work which nevertheless has a definite social value. None of this is mentioned in the Beijing document.

Emigration

The Holy See attributes great importance to the rights of emigrant women, the number of whom, for various reasons, is continually increasing. It maintains that new migration situations — particularly in regard to women — must be taken into consideration by the corresponding policies of the States, especially by those who are economically more privileged. This topic has already gathered ample consensus at the Conference in Cairo.

The Document addresses this theme in various places. It is nevertheless the opinion of the Holy See that the attention paid in this regard is insufficient, as are also insufficient the proposals suggested, which seem to represent a step backward with respect to Cairo.

Rights and responsibilities of parents

In all cultures parents are particularly interested in the education of their children and the exercise of their duty especially with respect to minors. The Holy See, making these concerns its own, maintains that in Beijing no formula should be accepted that goes against the *Universal Declaration of Human Rights*, which establishes the right of parents to choose the type of education they desire for their own children. Along these same lines of incomprehensible negation of certain universal rights, the proposal to guarantee the rights of women and girls freedom of conscience and of religion in educational institutions has been refused in the document that is going to Beijing.

Even more serious is the attempt to deprive parents of their responsibility in relation to programs and public services offered in the area of sexuality, including abortion.

In the Cairo Conference and at the Copenhagen Summit the recommendation to governments was approved, according to which educational programs and the rendering of these services to children and adolescents was to be put into action "consistent with the *Convention on the Rights of the Child* and recognizing the rights, duties and responsibilities of parents and other persons legally responsible for children." At the Copenhagen Summit these formulations were agreed upon by all the Heads of State or Governments, or by their representatives. In the preparatory document of Beijing this recommendation was put between brackets. The Holy See Delegation asked for the adoption of the same criterion every time specific actions regarding minors is proposed, but at the present time it still remains between brackets (cf. par. 108 g, 109 b, 281 c, etc.).

From "Vatican Information Service," 21 June 1995 (VIS) - After outlining the Holy See's position for the September 4-15 United Nations-sponsored World Conference on Women in Beijing, Holy See Press Office Director Joaquín Navarro-Valls made additional remarks and answered questions asked by journalists.

He noted that, in its contacts with other countries and institutions in recent months, the Holy See has discovered that "the consensus is growing daily" on its position for the Conference on Women. "We want Beijing to be a big success," he stated.

The first question concerned the issue of "gender," a term whose meaning was questioned by several Member States at the Beijing PrepCom (Preparatory Committee) held in New York from 15 March to 7 April (1995). This term, the director explained, has traditionally been used in U.N. documents to mean "sex," that is, "masculine" and "feminine," man or woman. In fact, when the English word "gender" is translated into French or Spanish, it becomes the equivalent of "sex," "man" or "woman." A special committee was set up by the U.N. to study this term, following the request of some who wished to expand its definition to include, for example, transsexuals and homosexuals. Navarro-Valls reported on the results of that study and said that the meaning of the word "gender" remains unchanged from traditional U.N. use.

Asked about the composition of the Holy See Delegation to Beijing, he responded that there would be twenty members, that the Holy Father was evaluating the possibilities, and that women would form, as they have in the past for International Conferences, a great part of the Delegation. Names will be announced at a later date.

To a question on what these International Conferences mean on a practical level, Joaquín Navarro-Valls replied: "These Conferences offer a Final Document on a specific theme which is proposed to the international community but which is not binding on the single nations. They are not laws. The U.N. is not a legislative organ. Every country has its parliament. The fact that these documents — from Cairo, Copenhagen, and from Nairobi ten years ago — are not binding does not mean they do not have a value. They are a collective reflection which has a supranational level. These documents can have an influence, can be important, for example, when the nations of the world come to agree on one, two or ten points of action set forth in that specific document and then act on a national level."

"Why does the Holy See participate in these Conferences?" he added, in answer to the same question. "It participates because the beautiful part of these Conferences is that they are, in some way, an appeal to consciences." He quoted a member from another Delegation at the Cairo Conference who said he felt the fundamental contribution of the Holy See was its proposing to the international community an ethical dimension to the problems that everyone would be discussing. Navarro-Valls said "this is useful, this serves a purpose."

"What are the indispensable principles for the Holy See in view of the Beijing Document and Conference?" asked a reporter. The press office director responded: "The Holy See will insist on two things: the human dignity of the woman and the universal human rights of the woman."

The Holy See will not reach a "holy alliance" with Islam to form a united front in the face of the topics that will be discussed at the Beijing Conference, said Navarro-Valls, who rejected the allegation made regarding the Holy See Delegation at the Cairo Conference. "Some Muslim representatives have wanted to present their concerns about some of the themes of the Peking Document through international organizations. We have agreed to speak with them. However, although there are some areas of general interest for both them and us, there are some substantial differences between Christianity and Islam on themes such as women, family, etc., that do no permit us to arrive at any type of operative agreement."

One journalist asked about the practice of aborting female fetuses, as occurs for example in China. Joaquín Navarro-Valls went back to the issue of human rights: "The important thing is to recognize that human rights are universal, and that consequently, it is not up to each country to decide what they are, because otherwise, we enter the realm of arbitrariness."

Briefing by
Dr. Joaquín Navarro-Valls
Director of the Press Office of the Holy See
on the topic of the Fourth World Conference on Women
Vatican, 25 August 1995

With the Fourth World Conference on Women imminent, the Holy See finds it opportune to make known the position of its Beijing Delegation. In defining its position the Holy See has been attentive to and has taken into account the desires, concerns and just demands of millions of women on the five continents. It has listened also to the voice of millions of non-Catholic women, from all cultural and religious traditions, who participate in educational programs and those of human and spiritual promotion in place in more than 300,000 Catholic institutions world-wide. At least half of the beneficiaries of these institutions are non-Catholics and a significant number of them come from developing countries.

The Holy See has supported the Fourth World Conference on Women from the time of its convocation and its Delegations have participated in all phases of the preparatory process: Regional Conferences, Preparatory Committees, etc., making its contribution.

The Holy See wants the Conference in Beijing to be an occasion for reflection, and above all, to take operative decisions that promote the dignity, the rights and the holistic development of women. To reach these objectives it is necessary that the Conference boldly assume a perspective decidedly in favor of women.

The Delegation of the Holy See wants to commit its efforts toward the liberation of women from the heavy load of certain cultural and socially negative conditioning, which, in many places, have also kept women from being conscious of their own dignity. The Holy See hopes that new constraints will be avoided in Beijing, those that impose on women a social minority philosophy which misunderstands the daily concrete needs and deepest hopes of the majority of women within developed countries, as well as, and especially, in developing countries.

During the Conference's preparatory process a tension between two very distant positions emerged.

The first seems to reduce the human person — woman in this case — to social functions that must be overcome; it is paradoxical that the struggle for equality with man ends up in denying women the most intimate truth of their existence. Three main characteristics of this feminism are: a negative attitude toward the family, a critical support for abortion and an angry anthropology in which feminine problems are linked solely to sexuality and contraception.

The second considers women and men equal co-partners — and not enemies — in the immense task of bettering humanity. It affirms the equal dignity of woman, her right to responsible motherhood, and denounces the totalitarian ideology that, in the name of governments and totalitarian anthropologies, tries to pit the State against the family, women against men and children, or rich against poor.

Inevitably this confrontation of positions influences also the North-South tension, which is very visible in this preparatory phase.

The draft of the Platform of Action is a basis of discussion for the Conference on Women. It is alarming that more than 50% of the text has not obtained a consensus and goes to Beijing in brackets. If this Document is to mirror women's hopes at this time in history, its contents must be all the more open to real facts which up until now have not sufficiently been taken into account. The Holy See hopes that its contribution and that of the other Delegations present at Beijing will help eliminate from the current Platform certain exaggerated tendencies present in a few pages, which are not respectful of the cultural pluralism among women in today's world.

Some thematic fundamentals of the Platform for Action are part of an agreed language, recognized in preceding documents of the U.N., mainly in the *Universal Declaration of Human Rights* (1948), in the *Declaration of the Rights of the Child* (1959), in the *Declaration of Vienna on Human Rights* (1993), in the International Conference on Population and Development (1994) and the World Summit on Social Development (1995). It is disturbing that at the Beijing Conference some formulations contained in these Documents today appear in brackets.

The Holy See will insist that the content of these documents already approved by the international community be respected. The Operative Platform that will be approved at Beijing must not ignore continuity with preceding international documents.

Other basic points of the Holy See's position at Beijing:

1. The dignity of women

Men and women enjoy the same identical dignity. The dignity of women is prerequisite to any recognition on the part of the State. Without a clear understanding of the meaning of human dignity discrimination will never be avoided. Women are — and have been historically — the first to suffer. In reality discriminatory practices against women, in all their forms, are no other than the expression of a lack of recognition of the equal dignity of women. With compulsory contraception, sterilization, genital mutilation, discrimination in work, etc. one can see the lack of respect regarding women's dignity, especially when they are poor and not sufficiently educated.

1.1 Women and men are the illustration of a biological, individual, personal and spiritual complementarity. Femininity is a unique and specific characteristic of woman, as masculinity is of man. This difference — by reason of equal dignity — must find in practice juridical recognition in various legal systems. A woman cannot accept the parameters imposed by and through men within her familial as well as professional life. Women have the right to choose between: having a profession, being simultaneously a mother and carrying on a profession, and being a mother and dedicating all her activity to the home.

1.2 In the Document the word "dignity" (of women) is found unexplainably in brackets (par. 43, 225, etc.). The Holy See has always given importance to the dignity of women — of men and women — because from this reality it follows that all human beings deserve the same respect. Furthermore, the first Principle of the *Rio Declaration* (1992) affirms that "human beings are the center of concern for a sustainable development."

2. Equal dignity for all women

The dignity of a poor woman is identical to that of a rich woman. Women represent the majority of the world's poor, the less educated and those who count for less in political terms. Only the particular attention of the Conference to the inalienable dignity of each woman can avoid discrimination founded on "pragmatic" reasoning.

3. Human rights of women

Human rights by their nature are universal. The rights of women are an integral part of human rights, which are valid for all human beings in all time and all places. The universality of human rights has been recognized by many international legal documents, in particular, by the *Universal Declaration of Human Rights* (1948) and by the *Declaration of Vienna on Human Rights* (1993).

Human rights are not "concessions" of the State, for the simple fact that they are based in the very structure of the human being, and they are antecedent to every social and political organization. Women and men share the same human nature. All legal documents on human rights recognize that human nature is unique.

4. Women and family

Statistics show on the average that nine women out of ten get married and five out of six have children. This fact cannot be ignored by the Beijing Document.

The family is the fundamental unit of society. For this reason there needs to be special protection of it by society. This fact has been recognized and emphasized in international documents on human rights up to the present time.

Nevertheless in their discussion of the subject a few States did not include the family among the above cited objectives of social policy. This attitude seems to ignore the accords on the topic recognized by the final documents of the International Conference on Population and Development in Cairo (1994) and in the World Summit on Social Development of Copenhagen (1995). One would hope that on such an important topic as the family the accords agreed upon less than a year ago and the commitments made in the conferences and international summits will find their full application in the Beijing Document.

4.1 There is no substitute for the family. The roles of a father and mother are different but of equal importance: both are complementary. A woman has a right to protection by society in her role as mother. Society must recognize the social value of woman's work in the family.

5. A woman's work within the family today is the object of serious discrimination especially in Western countries where, one might add, it is becoming almost impossible for a woman to dedicate herself solely to the home. If society organizes itself uniquely on the criteria of productivity, motherhood will certainly be the victim. The "social value" of work in the home has been publicly proclaimed, but it still has not been translated into an adequate legal recognition, at least with regard to economic remuneration. This paradox is found in the Platform of Action: every time a study and consequent decision to give economic recognition for domestic work was suggested, the text was put in brackets (see. par. 158, 209 f, g, etc.).

6. In the Platform of Action there is an alarming tendency to speak of the family solely in negative terms. Instead of underscoring the duties of the State regarding the family and of discussing more adequate family policies, there is an almost conscious non-advertence to the crucial, social importance of the family. In contrast to the Document approved at Cairo (1994), which has one entire chapter on the family, and that of Copenhagen (1995), which has a section on the family, it is alarming that the preparatory Document for Beijing does not include any chapter on the family. This is one aspect which broadly demonstrates the ideological weight that the Platform of Action carries. The absence in the Document of practically any consideration of the role and work of women in the family arouses suspicion. The paragraph is still in brackets.

7. The feminization of poverty

It is necessary that the Conference propose measures to avoid the phenomenon of the "feminization of poverty." The fundamental causes are found above all in the instability of the family, in the lack of protection of motherhood and the abandonment of the home by fathers. It is also a result of an irresponsible non-advertence on the part of the rich countries to their duties toward women in the developing countries, including those that find themselves forced to emigrate. It cannot be resolved, as some think, by mechanically applying enforced plans of population control.

8. Physical and psychic violence

Physical violence against women includes not only rape, war, genital mutilation, forced prostitution and arranged marriages, but also forced contraception, sterilization and abortion. Besides this, when violence exists in a family, most often the victims are women. It is widely documented that in many countries, in the campaign for demographic control, often there is no respect for the "informed consent," nor is a woman fully informed about the effects of medicines or medical techniques. Equally many cases of forced sterilization as part of oppressive programs of population control have been recorded. These practices — which are just mentioned or completely absent in the Platform of Action — certainly violate all the fundamental human rights of women and are totally unacceptable.

9. Women and peace

The role of women as educators of peace in society, in family, political, national and international life can never be emphasized enough. Their contribution to family life, teaching children respect, love, understanding, and caring for one another, is greater and more important than any scholastic program. The family is the first school — and in many underdeveloped countries, the only one.

Practical experience as much as academic social psychology teaches that the mother has a fundamental ability in maintaining the peace and in resolving conflict, and that she plays the principal role as mediator within the family. She can keep members of the family united through her continued effort of mediation. And even this obvious fact appears in brackets in par. 141.

10. Women and education

Access to education, on all levels, is a focal point in the liberation and promotion of women. Education is the prerequisite for access to employment, to personal autonomy, and to complete participation in economic, social and political life. In a respectable social and cultural context, women do not need to have children simply to guarantee their own future. Education is the road that averts poverty. The Holy See cannot help but cite in this area its own experience, down through the centuries and still active today in more than 300,000 social welfare institutions world-wide, many of these specializing in the education of women of all cultures and religions.

11. Women and health

The ideological imbalance present in the Platform for Action is more evident in the chapter devoted to health. The Document gives preference to sexually transmitted diseases or those which refer to reproduction.

These represent only a part of women's health problems. Other diseases, such as tropical ones — which each year become more contagious and cause more deaths than sexually transmitted diseases — are not given serious consideration.

The greatest limitation in the measures proposed is that women's health is considered in a reproductive context only. When "seen through the lens of fertility control, the notion of health is distorted beyond all recognition" (*The Lancet*, 22-VII-95, p. 195). The general picture that emerges in this chapter is not only a non-comprehensive one, but not even representative of the interests and concrete needs of women, especially of women in developing countries.

While in one of its first paragraphs the Document refers to the increase predicted in sexually transmitted diseases, in the chapters on health, promiscuity is not discouraged in any way, but even presumed. To discourage promiscuity could be an ethical topic, but certainly it is also a medical topic and an important element in the orientation of social policy.

12.   The unbalanced emphasis in this chapter on so-called "reproductive rights," "safe sex" and "safe abortion" runs the risk of altering the aim and the sense of this Conference. While the official theme of the Conference is "action for equality, development and peace," it has already been presented as a Conference "on the rights of women and their reproductive health." This reduction again penalizes the interests of the majority of women.

13.   Abortion and human rights

The Holy See continues to insist that there exists no human right to abortion because this contradicts the human right to life. The human right to life is a fundamental human right: all others stem from it. Human life deserves respect in any circumstance. A life in a poor country or in a developing country must be as much respected as any human life in the wealthy West.

Abortion is not a problem uniquely concerning women; it involves also men and society. Surprisingly, this aspect is absent in the Platform of Action. In this way, a woman is condemned to isolation just in that moment of her life when she needs solidarity the most. The irresponsibility of men, and often of society, is at the root of many abortions.

14.   Rights, duties and responsibility of a mother and father

In all cultures, independent of political systems, parents consider it their personal responsibility to educate their children and to exercise their duties toward minors. The *Declaration of Human Rights* recognizes this principle establishing the right of parents to choose the type of education for their progeny. This principle has been placed in brackets in the Platform of Action.

More serious yet is the pretense of depriving parents of their responsibility regarding the choice of programs and public services in the area of sexuality, including abortion, (par. 107). At Cairo and at Copenhagen the recommendations to governments were approved, according to which services to minors and adolescents have to be offered and carried out "in accordance with the *Convention on the Rights of the Child* and in recognition of the rights, duties and responsibility of the parents and of other persons responsible for minors." Some Western States seem to have changed their opinion on this point, now finding it difficult to affirm in the Beijing Document the very commitment made only six months ago at Copenhagen. On this point one would hope one can count on the good will and good sense of the Delegations going to Beijing.

15. Spiritual dimensions of a woman's life

The serious problems of our world require that society answer not only the material needs of women, but also the spiritual dimensions of their lives. Every form of extremism can have a negative impact on women, but it is undisputable that religion plays a central and positive role in the life of millions of women throughout the world, and is a part of the expectations that they have for the future. The Draft Document presses for plurality and tolerance in many sections, but the sole reference in the whole Document to the spiritual and religious dimension of a woman's life is found in brackets.

* * *

The Holy See goes to Beijing with the desire and the purpose of making its own contribution so that the Fourth World Conference on Women can reach a universal "consensus" on the urgent topics of interest to women today. It has been said that the Conference would be "a very effective way to get the world together." This objective can be reached if the Conference succeeds in making everyone conscious of women's rights; if it offers the means to protect motherhood, the family, and the needs of women in professional life; if it succeeds in eradicating violence and the feminization of poverty; and if it finds effective ways to protect women emigrants and the population migrating between the South and the North of the world.

Certainly the world will not get together if in the Conference there is an attempt to impose, particularly on developing countries, a Western product, a socially reductive philosophy, which does not even represent the hopes and needs of the majority of Western women.

Statement of
Professor Mary Ann Glendon
Head of the Delegation of the Holy See
to the Fourth World Conference on Women
Beijing, 5 September 1995

Madame Chairperson,

The Delegation of the Holy See wishes first of all to express its special thanks and appreciation to the Government of the People's Republic of China, to whom it gladly renews the cordial and respectful good wishes of Pope John Paul II. The warm reception we have received from the authorities and from the people here in Beijing and the efficient manner in which the arrangements for the Conference have been managed have further helped to make this World Conference such a memorable experience.

1. We are celebrating the Fourth World Conference on Women. Our Conference follows on a series of other International Conferences which will surely mark the international social climate, as we move to the end of this millennium and to the beginning of the new one. From Rio de Janeiro to Vienna, from Cairo to Copenhagen and now here in Beijing, the community of nations and each single State have been focusing their attention on the significance and the practical consequences of what was affirmed in the first principle of the *Rio Declaration*, namely, that "Human beings are at the centre of the concern for sustainable development."

Today, more than ever, our task is to move from aspiration to action. We must see that what has been affirmed at the universal level becomes a reality in the everyday lives of women in all parts of the world. The historical oppression of women has deprived the human race of untold resources. Recognition of the equality in dignity and fundamental rights of women and men, and guaranteeing access by all women to the full exercise of those rights will have far-reaching consequences and will liberate enormous reserves of intelligence and energy sorely needed in a world that is groaning for peace and justice.

During the preparations for this Conference, the Holy See has listened carefully to the hopes, fears and daily concerns of women in various parts of the world and from different walks of life, as well as to their criticisms. Pope John Paul II has directly addressed the concerns of the Conference in numerous talks and encounters, especially in his recent personal *Letter to Women*. He has acknowledged the deficiencies of past positions, including those of the Catholic Church, and has welcomed this initiative of the United Nations as an important contribution to a global improvement in the situation of women in today's world.

Holy See's views represent aspirations of many

The Delegation of the Holy See, headed by a woman and composed mainly of women with varied backgrounds and experiences, applauds the purpose of the draft Platform of Action to free women at last from the unfair burdens of cultural conditioning that have so often prevented them even from becoming conscious of their own dignity.

The views of the Holy See represent the aspirations of many people, believers of all faiths and non-believers alike, who share the same fundamental vision and wish it to be known. It is only when different viewpoints are sensitively listened to and appreciated that one can arrive at a true discernment of situations and a consensus on how to remedy them.

2. I will draw attention, therefore, to some of the many points where my Delegation concurs with the Platform of Action, while at the same time I will also indicate some areas which my Delegation feels ought to have been developed in a different manner.

At times in the preparatory process, the Holy See has had strenuously to emphasize that marriage, motherhood and the family, or the adherence to religious values, should not be presented only in a negative manner. To affirm the dignity and rights of all women requires respect for the roles of women whose quest for personal fulfillment and the construction of a stable society is inseparably linked to their commitments to God, family, neighbor and especially to their children.

The position of women is linked with the fate of the entire human family. There can be no real progress for women, or men, at the expense of children or of their underprivileged brothers and sisters. Genuine advances for women cannot overlook the inequalities that exist among women themselves. Enduring progress for women must be rooted in solidarity between young and old, between male and female, as well as between those who enjoy a comfortable standard of living with ample access to basic needs and those who are suffering deprivation.

At the same time, it should be clear that promoting women's exercise of all their talents and rights without undermining their roles within the family will require calling not only husbands and fathers to their family responsibilities, but governments to their social duties.

Because so many women face exceptional difficulties as they seek to balance greater participation in economic and social life with family responsibilities, this Conference rightly places a high priority on the right of women to effectively enjoy equal opportunities with men in the workplace as well as in the decision-making structures of society, especially as they affect women themselves.

Justice for women in the workplace requires in the first place the removal of all forms of the exploitation of women and young girls as cheap labour, all too often at the service of the lifestyle of the affluent. It requires equal compensation and equal opportunities for advancement, while addressing also the added responsibilities they may bear as working mothers, and according special attention to the problems of women who are the sole providers for their family.

Furthermore, effective action on behalf of working mothers requires recognition of the priority of human over economic values. If efficiency and productivity are considered the primary goals of society, then the values of motherhood will be penalized. The fear of reinforcing certain stereotypes concerning the roles of women should not prevent this Conference from clearly addressing the special challenges and the real-life needs and values of those millions of women who dedicate themselves to motherhood and family responsibilities, either on a full-time basis or who reconcile them with other activities of a social and economic nature. Our societies offer far too little tangible recognition or concrete assistance to those women who are struggling to do a decent job of raising children in economically trying circumstances. For our Conference not to face these issues would be to render true equality for the majority of the world's women even more elusive.

The Holy See, at this Conference, as it did also on the occasion of the World Summit on Social Development, stresses the importance of finding new ways of recognizing the economic and social value of women's unremunerated work, in the family, in the production and conservation of food and in a wide range of socially productive work within the community. Women must be guaranteed measures of economic and social security which reflect their equal dignity, their equal rights to ownership of property and access to credit and resources. The effective contribution of women's work to economic security and social well-being is often greater than that of men.

Everyone has the right to education

3. I wish to return, now, to the fact that so many women today do not have access to those basic rights which belong to them as human beings, to

the extent, in fact, as I have said, that they are often even unaware of their own dignity. I return to this theme to indicate some areas of special concern and commitment of the Holy See for the coming years.

It is well-known that the Catholic Church, in its manifold structures, has been a pioneer and leader in providing education to girls in both developed and developing countries, and often in areas and cultures where few groups were willing to provide equal educational opportunities to both girls and boys.

Every human person has the right to be helped to make the fullest use of the talents and abilities they possess and thus, as the *Universal Declaration of Human Rights* asserts, "everyone has the right to education." Universal access to basic education is, indeed, an established goal of all nations. Yet in today's world, of the scandalously high number of persons who are illiterate, over two-thirds are women. Of the millions of children who are not enrolled in basic education, about seventy percent are girls. What is to be said of the situation in which the simple fact of being a girl reduces the likelihood of even being born, of survival or of then receiving adequate education, nutrition and health care?

On August 29 last, His Holiness Pope John Paul II committed all of the over 300,000 social, caring and educational institutions of the Catholic Church to a concerted and priority strategy directed to girls and young women, and especially to the poorest, to ensure for them equality of status, welfare and opportunity, especially with regard to literacy and education, health and nutrition and to ensure that they can, in all circumstances, continue and complete their education. The Holy See has made a special appeal to the Church's educational institutions and religious congregations, on their own or as part of wider national strategies, to make this commitment in favour of the girl child a reality. This is, in fact, a commitment already assumed at the Copenhagen Summit for Social Development and the Holy See, as on that occasion, places itself side by side with all the governments of the world to work in collaboration with them on such programmes of education. More and more it is recognized that investment in the education of girls is the fundamental key to the later full advancement of women.

The question of education is closely linked with the question of poverty and the fact that the majority of those who today live in abject poverty are women and children. Efforts must be strengthened to eliminate all those cultural and legal obstacles which impair the economic security of women. The reasons specific to each region or economic system which render women more likely to bear the heavier burden of poverty must be addressed. No part of the world is without its scandal of poverty which strikes women most. Every society has its specific pockets of poverty, of groups of persons especially exposed to poverty, at times within sight of others whose patterns of consumption and lifestyle are all too often insensitive and unsustainable. The "feminization of poverty" must be of concern to all women. Its social, political and economic roots must be addressed. Women themselves must be in the forefront in the fight against the inequalities among women in today's world, through the concrete caring and direct solidarity with the poorest among women.

May I draw attention here to the extraordinary work that has been done, and is being done today, by a category of women whose service is so often taken for granted: that of religious sisters. In their communities they have developed innovative forms of female spirituality. From their communities, they have developed forms of solidarity, caring and leadership for and among women. They are examples of how religious principles are for so many women today a source of inspiration in fostering a new identity for women and a source of perseverance in the service and advancement of women.

Holy See condemns coercion in population policies

4. The Holy See also recognizes the need to address the urgent specific healthcare needs of women. It supports the special emphasis of the Conference Documents on expanding and improving women's health care, especially since so many women in today's world do not even have access to a basic healthcare centre. In such a situation, the Holy See has expressed its concern regarding a tendency to focus privileged attention and resources on the consideration of health problems related to sexuality, whereas a comprehensive approach to the health of all women would have to place greater emphasis on such questions as poor nutrition, unsafe water and those diseases that afflict millions of women each year, taking a vast toll on mothers and children.

The Holy See concurs with the Platform of Action in dealing with questions of sexuality and reproduction, where it affirms that changes in the attitudes of both men and women are necessary conditions for achieving equality and that responsibility in sexual matters belongs to both men and women. Women are, moreover, most often the victims of irresponsible sexual behaviour, in terms of personal suffering, of disease, poverty and the deterioration of family life. The Conference Documents, in the view of my Delegation, are not bold enough in acknowledging the threat to women's health arising from widespread attitudes of sexual permissiveness. The Document likewise refrains from challenging societies which have abdicated their responsibility to attempt to change, at their very roots, irresponsible attitudes and behaviour.

The international community has consistently stressed that the decision of parents concerning the number of their children and the spacing of births must be made freely and responsibly. In this context, the Catholic Church's teaching on procreation is often misunderstood. To say that it supports procreation at all costs is indeed a travesty of its teaching on responsible parenthood. Its teaching on the means of family planning is often regarded as too demanding on persons. But no way of ensuring deep respect for human life and its transmission can dispense with self-discipline and self-restraint, particularly in cultures which foster self-indulgence and immediate gratification. Responsible procreation also requires especially the equal participation and sharing of responsibility by husbands, something which will only be achieved through a process of changing of attitudes and behaviour.

The Holy See joins with all participants in the Conference in the condemnation of coercion in population policies. It is to be hoped that the recommendations of this Conference to this effect will be adhered to by all nations. It is also to be hoped that, in order to arrive at informed consent, couples will be provided with clear information about all possible health risks associated with family planning methods, especially where these are at an experimental stage or in cases where their use in certain nations has been restricted.

There is clear consensus within the international community that abortion should not be promoted as a means of family planning and that all efforts must be made to eliminate those factors which lead women to seek abortions. Pope John Paul II has emphasized, in speaking of the responsibility for a women's tragic and painful decision to have an abortion, "before being something to blame on the woman," there are occasions when "guilt needs to be attributed to men and to the complicity of the general social environment." All who are genuinely committed to the advancement of women can and must offer a woman or a girl who is pregnant, frightened and alone a better alternative than the destruction of her own unborn child. Once again, concerned women must take the lead in the fight against societal practices which facilitate the irresponsibility of men while stigmatizing women, and against a vast industry that extracts its profits from the very bodies of women, while at the same time purporting to be their liberators.

All violence against women must be stopped

The Conference has, however, rendered a great service by casting a spotlight on violence towards women and girls, violence which may be physical, sexual, psychological or moral. Much more needs to be done in all our societies to identify the range and the causes of violence against women. The extent of sexual violence in the industrialized nations, as it becomes more evident, comes often as a shock to their populations. The fact of the use, in this twentieth century, of sexual violence as an instrument of armed conflict has stunned the conscience of humanity.

All such forms of violence against women should be condemned and social policies to eliminate the causes of such violence should be given priority consideration. More must be done to eliminate the practice of female genital mutilation and other deplorable practices such as child prostitution, trafficking in children and their organs and child marriages. Society must also reach out to all those who have been the victims of such violence, ensuring that justice be applied to the perpetrators of such violence, as well as offering the victims holistic healing and rehabilitation into society.

The question of violence experienced by women is also linked to those factors which underlie the widespread hedonistic and commercial culture which encourages the systematic exploitation of sexuality and especially reduces women to the role of sex objects. Should the Conference not condemn such attitudes, it could well be accused of condoning the very root causes of much violence against women and girls.

Finally, I feel that greater attention could have been drawn to the needs of specific categories of women, especially within changing social and economic environments. I will simply mention here elderly women, who are among those who experience special problems in all our societies.

Madame Chairperson,

The title of our Conference is "equality, development and peace." We must move from a vision of human persons looked on as mere instruments or objects to one in which every person can fully realize her or his dignity and full potential. Our century has been a century of unprecedented scientific progress, but one also which has seen horrific conflicts and wars. In the midst of a culture of death, it has been very often women who have safeguarded and promoted a civilization of love, preserving the vestiges of human dignity throughout the darkest days and years. Ignored, underestimated and taken for granted, the beneficent influence of women has radiated throughout history, enriching the lives of successive generations.

It is to the future that we must now look. The freer women are to share their gifts with society, and to assume leadership in society, the better are the prospects for the entire human community to progress in wisdom, justice and dignified living.

The Delegation of the Holy See hopes that this Conference and the name of the great city of Beijing will be remembered by history as an important moment in which, by advancing women's freedom and dignity, we will have contributed to building a civilization of love, where every woman, man and child can live in peace, liberty and mutual esteem, with full respect for their rights and responsibilities; a civilization where life and love can flourish; a civilization where the culture of death shall have no dominion.

May Almighty God accompany us and sustain us in our task.

STATEMENT BY
PROFESSOR MARY ANN GLENDON
HEAD OF THE HOLY SEE DELEGATION,
AT THE CONCLUDING SESSION OF THE
FOURTH WORLD CONFERENCE ON WOMEN
BEIJING, 15 SEPTEMBER 1995

Madame President,

"When one looks at the great process of women's liberation," one sees that the journey has been a difficult one, with its "share of mistakes," but headed toward a better future for women. Those are the words of Pope John Paul II. And he goes on to say: "This journey must go on!" The Holy See Delegation joins its voice to his: This great journey must go on!

Women's voyage has been marked by false starts and disappointments, as well as by luminous achievements. There have been times, as in the industrial revolution, when old forms of oppression were exchanged for new, as well as times when intelligence and good will have triumphed.

The Documents before us reflect that complex and uneven history of women's search. They are full of promise, but often short on concrete commitment, and in certain respects one could ask if the long-term consequences will really serve the good of women.

The Delegation of the Holy See has worked hard, in a constructive way and in a spirit of good will, to make the Documents more responsive to women. Certainly, the living heart of these Documents lies in their sections on the needs of women in poverty, on strategies for development, on literacy and education, on ending violence against women, on a culture of peace, and on access to employment, land, capital, and technology. My Delegation is pleased to note a close correspondence between these points and Catholic social teaching.

My Delegation would be remiss in its duty to women, however, if it did not also indicate several critical areas where it strongly disagrees with the text.

My Delegation regrets to note in the text an exaggerated individualism, in which key, relevant, provisions of the *Universal Declaration of Human Rights* are slighted — for example, the obligation to provide "special care and assistance" to motherhood. This selectivity thus marks another step in the colonization of the broad and rich discourse of universal rights by an impoverished, libertarian rights dialect. Surely this international gathering could have done more for women and girls than to leave them alone with their rights!

Surely we must do more for the girl child in poor nations than give lip service to providing access to education, health and social services while carefully avoiding any concrete commitment of new and additional resources to that end.

Surely we can do better than to address the health needs of girls and women by paying disproportionate attention to sexual and reproductive health. Moreover, ambiguous language concerning unqualified control over sexuality and fertility could be interpreted as including societal endorsement of abortion and homosexuality.

A document that respects women's dignity should address the health of the whole woman. A document that respects women's intelligence should devote at least as much attention to literacy as to fertility.

Finally, Madame President,

Because my Delegation is hopeful that out of these Documents, which are in some ways at odds with themselves, the good for women will ultimately prevail, it wishes to associate itself with the consensus only on those above-mentioned aspects of the Documents that the Holy See considers to be positive and at the service of the real well-being of women.

Unfortunately, the Holy See's participation in the consensus can be only a partial one because of numerous points in the Documents which are incompatible with what the Holy See and other countries deem favorable to the true advancement of women. These points are indicated in the Reservations which my Delegation has annexed to this Statement.

My Delegation is confident that women themselves will overcome the limitations of and bring out what is best in these Documents. As John Paul II has so well put it, "The path that lies ahead will be long and difficult, nevertheless we must have courage to set out on that path and the courage to go on to the end."

I would ask that the text of this Statement, the Reservations formally indicated below, as well as the Statement of Interpretation of the term "gender" be included in the report of the Conference.

RESERVATIONS

The Holy See, in conformity with its nature and particular mission, in partially joining the consensus on the Documents of the Fourth World Conference on Women, wishes to express its position regarding those Documents, and make Reservations on some of the concepts used in them.

1.   The Holy See wishes to reaffirm the dignity and worth of women and the equal rights of men and women and regrets the failure of the Platform for Action to explicitly reassert this concept.

2.   The Holy See, in line with the *Universal Declaration of Human Rights*, stresses that the family is the basic unit of society and is based on marriage as an equal partnership between husband and wife, to which the transmission of life is entrusted. It regrets that in the Platform for Action references were not made to such a fundamental societal unit without banal qualifying language (cf. *Strategic Objective* L. 9).

3.   The Holy See can only interpret such terms as "women's right to control their sexuality," "women's right to control ... their fertility," or "couples and individuals," as referring to the responsible use of sexuality within marriage. At the same time, the Holy See firmly condemns all forms of violence against and exploitation of women and girls.

4.   The Holy See reaffirms the Reservations it expressed at the conclusion of the International Conference on Population and Development, held in Cairo from 5 to 13 September 1994, which are included in the Report of that Conference, concerning the interpretation given to the terms "reproductive health," "sexual health" and "reproductive rights." In particular, the Holy See reiterates that it does not consider abortion or abortion services to be a dimension of reproductive health or reproductive health services. The Holy See does not endorse any form of legislation which gives legal recognition to abortion.

5.   With regard to the terms "family planning" or "widest range of family planning services" and other terms concerning family-planning services or regulation of fertility, the Holy See's actions during this Conference should in no way be interpreted as changing its well-known position concerning those family planning methods that the Catholic Church considers morally unacceptable or concerning family planning services that do not respect the liberty of spouses, the human dignity or the human rights of those concerned. The Holy See in no way endorses contraception or the use of condoms, either as a family planning measure or in HIV/AIDS

prevention programmes.

6. The Holy See maintains that nothing in the Platform for Action or in other documents referenced therein is to be interpreted as requiring any health professional or health facility to perform, cooperate with, refer or arrange for services to which they have objections on the basis of religious belief or moral or ethical conviction.

7. The Holy See interprets all references to the term "forced pregnancy" as a specific instrument of armed conflict, in the context in which that term appears in the Vienna Declaration and Programme of Action, Part II, par. 38.

8. The Holy See interprets the term "gender" as described in the Statement annexed to these Reservations.

9. The Holy See does not associate itself with the consensus on the entire Chapter IV Section C, concerning health; it wishes to place a general reservation on the entire section and it would ask that this general reservation be noted in the chapter. This section devotes a totally unbalanced attention to sexual and reproductive health in comparison to women's other health needs, including means to address maternal mortality and morbidity. Furthermore, the Holy See cannot accept ambiguous terminology concerning unqualified control over sexuality and fertility insofar as it could be interpreted as a societal endorsement of abortion or homosexuality. The reservation on this chapter does not, however, indicate any reduction in the Holy See's commitment towards the promotion of the health of women and the girl child.

10. The Holy See does not join the consensus and expresses a reservation on par. 232(f), with its reference to a text (par. 97) on a right of women to "control over their sexuality." This ambiguous term could be understood as endorsing sexual relationships outside heterosexual marriage. It asks that this reservation be noted on the paragraph. On the other hand, however, the Holy See wishes to associate itself with the condemnation of violence against women asserted in par. 97, as well as with the importance of mutuality and shared responsibility, respect and free consent in conjugal relations as stated in that paragraph.

The Holy See, with regard to the entire section on human rights, with the exception of quotations from or restatements of already existing human rights instruments, expresses its concern about an excessive individualism in its treatment of human rights. The Holy See further recalls that the mandate of the Fourth World Conference on Women did not include the affirmation of new human rights.

11. With regard to the phrase "Women's Rights are Human Rights," the Holy See interprets this phrase to mean that women should have the full enjoyment of all Human Rights and Fundamental Freedoms.

12. With regard to all references to international agreements, the Holy See reserves its position in this regard, in particular on any existing international agreements mentioned in the Documents, consistent with its manner of acceptance or non-acceptance of them.

The Holy See requests that these Reservations, together with the annexed Statement of Interpretation on the term "gender," be included in the Report of the Conference.

Beijing, 15 September 1995.

STATEMENT OF INTERPRETATION OF THE TERM "GENDER" BY THE HOLY SEE DELEGATION

In accepting that the word "gender" in this Document is to be understood according to ordinary usage in the United Nations context, the Holy See associates itself with the common meaning of that word, in languages where it exists.

The term "gender" is understood by the Holy See as grounded in biological sexual identity, male or female. Furthermore, the Platform for Action itself (cf. N. 193, c) clearly uses the term "both genders."

The Holy See thus excludes dubious interpretations based on world views which assert that sexual identity can be adapted indefinitely to suit new and different purposes.

It also dissociates itself from the biological determinist notion that all the roles and relations of the two sexes are fixed in a single, static pattern.

Pope John Paul II insists on the distinctiveness and complementarity of women and men. At the same time, he has applauded the assumption of new roles by women, stressed the degree to which cultural conditioning has been an obstacle to women's progress, and exhorted men to assist in "the great process of women's liberation" (*Letter to Women*, 6).

In his recent *Letter to Women*, the Pope explained the Church's nuanced view in the following way: "One can also appreciate that the presence of a certain diversity of roles is in no way prejudicial to women, provided that this diversity is not the result of an arbitrary imposition, but is rather an expression of what is specific to being male and female" (11).

Beijing, 15 September 1995

Press Release issued by the Delegation of the Holy See during the Fourth World Conference on Women
Beijing, 9 September 1995

After five days of negotiations at the Fourth World Conference on Women, the Holy See Delegation has expressed its concern that a minority coalition is vigorously blocking efforts to bring the Beijing Draft Declaration and Programme of Action into conformity with the *United Nations Universal Declaration of Human Rights*, and other basic human rights documents. The European Union figures prominently in this group that is impeding consensus.

Pointing out that the Conference participants have no authority to undermine the pillars of the human rights tradition, spokesperson Dr. Joaquín Navarro-Valls cited five respects in which the positions of such Delegations are at odds with foundational human rights documents and principles. He criticized the Delegations' selective use of human rights language.

1. Where the *Universal Declaration* provides that "recognition of the inherent dignity" and equal rights of all human beings is the "very foundation of freedom, justice and peace," a determined coalition of Beijing negotiators is making vigorous efforts to remove all references to human dignity from the Beijing Draft.

2. The *Universal Declaration* recognizes marriage as a fundamental right and provides that "the family is the natural and fundamental group unit of society and is entitled to protection by society and the State." At Beijing, the Draft Document casts marriage and the family negatively as impediments to women's self-realization (e.g. as associated with violence). Several negotiators, moreover, are pressing to change "family" to the politically correct and ambiguous word "families" — which lends itself to the interpretation that any group of unrelated people may call itself a family.

3. The *Universal Declaration* provides that "Everyone has the right to freedom of thought, conscience and religion ... (including) freedom, either alone or in community with others and in public or in private, to manifest his religion or belief in teaching, practice, worship and observance." At Beijing, an active coalition has aggressively sought to remove all references to religion, morals, ethics and spirituality, except where religion is portrayed negatively (e.g., as associated with intolerance or extremism).

4. The *Universal Declaration* provides that "Motherhood and childhood

are entitled to special care and protection." Beijing negotiators have quashed references to motherhood except where it appears in a negative light.

5. The *Universal Declaration* and the *Convention on the Rights of the Child* make special provision for parents' rights and responsibilities concerning the education and upbringing of their children. Beijing negotiators are attempting to eliminate all recognition of parental rights and responsibilities from key sections of the draft — even rejecting direct quotations from the *Convention on the Rights of the Child*.

The Holy See Delegation, in calling attention to these surprising positions, expressed puzzlement about the stances of these negotiators — in view of the fact that most of their own national constitutions mirror the above-cited provisions of the international human rights documents. Surely the provisions of the *Universal Declaration of Human Rights* should not be so casually brushed aside.

Press Release
Issued by the Holy See Delegation
during the Fourth World Conference on Women
15 September 1995

"Holy See Challenge:
Real Commitment, Not Paper Promises"

Equality, poverty, education, resources, violence, the environment, and peace are the principles of the Beijing Platform for Action. These same themes are central pillars of the social teaching of the Church, the Holy See stressed in announcing today that it would associate itself *in part, and with reservations*, with the Conference consensus.

In her Final Statement to the Beijing Conference, Delegation leader Mary Ann Glendon quoted Pope John Paul II's *World Day of Peace Message* in which he said of women's liberation: "This journey must go on!"

The Holy See was sharply critical of the Conference Documents, however, for "paper promises" unbacked by financial commitments and for "preoccupation with sexual issues" at the expense of important interests of women, especially women to whom the Catholic Church has a special mission — poor women, indigenous women, migrants and refugees.

The sections on poverty, education, peace, and resources for development, said Delegate Katherine Hawa Hoomkwap, a former commissioner of health from Nigeria, are the "very heart of the Program of Action," yet are likely to remain empty promises without real change of heart and behavior on the part of affluent nations and classes.

The Holy See noted with great regret that the sections on human rights reflect an increasing colonization of the great universal human rights tradition by an impoverished, libertarian rights dialect. The Documents actually put women at risk by using rights language selectively, and by blurring the distinctions between the basic rights of all human beings everywhere and rights that merely exist under one or another nation's law.

In refusing to join the section of the Program of Action relating to women's health, the Holy See criticized the Document for its obsession with reproductive matters at the expense of the holistic approach to the health problems of women. "One must ask," said Dr. Navarro-Valls, "whose interests are being promoted here? Women's? Or those who want to get rid of poverty by getting rid of poor people?" The Holy See pointed out that its view of the health sections is shared even by non-Catholic experts, such as the British medical journal *Lancet* (7/22/95), describing the sections as expressing a "new colonialism" designed to control rather than to liberate women. Similarly, Harvard population economist Amartya Sen has charged that by giving priority to "family planning arrangements in the third world countries over other commitments such as education and health care," international policy-makers and conferences "produce negative effects on people's well-being and reduce their freedoms." (*New York Review of Books*, 9/22/94). "The last thing women in the Third World need now are new forms of colonialism," said Spokesman Joaquín Navarro-Valls.

Dr. Navarro-Valls described the Conference Documents as "perplexing": with one face looking toward women's freedom and dignity, and another regarding women almost paternalistically. He compared the Documents to a garden planted by many gardeners where nutritious grains are surrounded by opportunistic weeds that threaten to engulf the whole.

In associating itself with such a mixed document, he said, the Holy See has been guided by the characteristic approach of John Paul II to other flawed human enterprises — seeking to lift up and develop what is true and helpful while naming and vigorously denouncing what is false and harmful to human flourishing.

Beijing, 15 September 1995

STATEMENT BY
HIS EXCELLENCY ARCHBISHOP RENATO R. MARTINO
APOSTOLIC NUNCIO, PERMANENT OBSERVER OF THE HOLY SEE
TO THE UNITED NATIONS
BEFORE THE THIRD COMMITTEE OF THE GENERAL ASSEMBLY
ON ITEM 107: "ADVANCEMENT OF WOMEN:
REPORT OF THE FOURTH WORLD CONFERENCE ON WOMEN"
NEW YORK, 16 NOVEMBER 1995

Mr. Chairman,

It is not merely coincidental that the Fourth World Conference on Women took place during the United Nations' celebration of its Fiftieth Anniversary and of the world's achievements over the past five decades. This Conference provided, in the words of Pope John Paul II, "an auspicious occasion for heightening awareness of the many contributions made by women to the life of whole societies and nations. This contribution is primarily spiritual and cultural in nature, but socio-political and economic as well. The various sectors of society, nations and States, and the progress of all humanity, are certainly deeply indebted to the contribution of women!" (Pope John Paul II, *Letter to Women*, n.8.)

But obviously, the Beijing Conference was not only a celebration of what women are accomplishing on behalf of themselves and of all society; it also produced a Document that identifies critical areas of concern, that is intended to address them and thereby ensure greater progress in the advancement of women in the future.

The Holy See Delegation to the Conference, composed mostly of women from every region of the world and from a variety of backgrounds, was pleased with the outcome of major portions of the Beijing Declaration and Platform for Action. The attention provided to the girl-child serves to address the often-ignored fact that the status and well-being of women depends upon the status they are accorded from the earliest stages of life. Education has been affirmed as an essential tool for achieving the goals of the Conference, and the success of the numerous other provisions in the Platform will depend on whether the actions to provide all girl-children and women with at least a basic education are taken seriously.

The Beijing Report is noteworthy in numerous other respects. It recognizes the need to strengthen the role of women in order to further development efforts, and also to strengthen domestic and international development measures in order to improve the situation of poorer women.

It recognizes the disproportionate burden that poverty imposes on women, and suggests means to overcome this economic blight that is spreading and deepening throughout the world. The sections on poverty, education, and resources for development are the "very heart" of the Platform, but a sincere change of heart and behavior on the part of affluent nations and social classes will be necessary to realize these objectives.

Governments and other relevant sectors of society should be encouraged to back up these proposed actions with the necessary financial resources, so as to compensate for the unfortunate absence of such a commitment in the Document itself. Even before the Conference began, Pope John Paul II responded to the call for concrete commitments by issuing a special appeal to all Catholic education, health and other relevant institutions to mobilize their personnel and resources in order to meet the needs of girls and women, particularly the most disadvantaged.

The Holy See also strongly endorses measures to prevent violence against women, to alleviate the suffering of those who have been the victims of violence and to take effective action against the perpetrators. While significant public attention has appropriately been given to the tragedy of domestic violence, the world community must not forget, nor lessen its commitment to overcoming, the suffering endured by millions, particularly women and children, in civil and international conflicts. This includes refugee women and children, who are having to cope not only with their own personal fatigue in seemingly hopeless situations, but also with the fatigue of host countries and potential donors whose compassion and assistance are essential to their continued survival.

Unfortunately, Mr. Chairman, the Holy See was not able to join the consensus on the entire Beijing Report, due to its strong disagreement and disappointment with certain aspects of the Document. While the human dignity inherent in women as well as in men was reaffirmed in the Declaration, the Holy See Delegation was surprised and dismayed at the strong opposition encountered in attempts to state this truth in the Platform for Action. To expressly fail to recognize the importance of human dignity is to threaten the very basis upon which human rights are founded, as well as the conceptual basis for actions against unjust discrimination and sexual, economic and other forms of human exploitation — all of which are important issues for women addressed in the Platform.

The Holy See had also hoped to see a broad range of health concerns addressed in the Platform and concrete means to address the serious problems women face in this area, particularly the poorest women and those living in the poorest regions. Yet the actions in the health section and other related paragraphs provide an imbalanced and largely superficial treatment of the major health needs of most of the world's women. Relatively scant attention is given to essential aspects for health such as access to safe drinking water, proper sanitation facilities and adequate housing. Even though provisions related to "reproductive health," "reproductive rights" and "unsafe abortion" are extensively presented, attempts to enumerate measures needed to lower maternal morbidity and mortality rates related to childbirth were rejected. In fact, the apparent obsession of some Delegations with women's sexuality and with limiting reproduction is reflected by the emphasis given to these issues, while concrete means to address women's overall health needs that would require a financial commitment have been avoided or studiously qualified.

An additional concern applies to ambiguous terminology that could imply endorsement of certain sexual and reproductive practices that would have been unacceptable to a very large number of Delegations if stated explicitly. The ideological bias in reproductive health care was also evident when many Delegations resisted the proposal to inform women of the health risks related to hormonal contraception, promiscuity and abortion. Yet this bias did not achieve consensus, as evidenced by the extensive number of reservations made on certain paragraphs in the health section and other related paragraphs in the Beijing Report. The Statement by the Holy See Delegation has also been included, and provides further detail of the Holy See's reservations and concerns.

On the other hand, the Holy See applauds the recognition given to the importance of the role of women in the family, and to the social significance of maternity, motherhood and the role often played by women in the care of family members. In this regard, it is important that the Platform reaffirmed the family as being the basic unit of society, and as such entitled to comprehensive protection and support. However, it is disconcerting that a number of Delegations, representing countries that unequivocally affirmed this principle in the *Universal Declaration of Human Rights*, now insist on repeatedly qualifying "the family" as existing in various forms. One would have to question whether such qualification does not potentially undermine the very commitment of the State and society to provide the family with protection and support, and thereby the well-being of women and children within the family.

While reaffirming the unique role of women in the family, the Holy See also attributes importance to the Beijing Report's emphasis on the need for women to be present in social, economic and political life at the local, national and international levels. As Pope John Paul has stated, when women are allowed such participation, "the very way in which society understands and organizes itself is improved, and comes to reflect in a better way the substantial unity of the human family." Thus he added that "Women have a full right to become actively involved in all areas of public life, and this right must be affirmed and guaranteed, also, where necessary, through appropriate legislation" (Pope John Paul II, *1995 World Day of Peace Message*, n. 9). Effective follow-up measures are needed to ensure the right of women to enjoy equal opportunities and conditions with men in the workplace, as well as in other structures of society.

The reaffirmation of the universal nature of all human rights and fundamental freedoms was a significant achievement in the Platform. This reaffirmation is essential if everyone in the world community is to accept that human rights are as inherent in women as they are in men, and they are to be respected regardless of where one lives or to which social or economic class one belongs.

It is particularly significant that the Declaration and the Platform for Action recognize the importance of conscience and religion in the lives of women and men, and affirms these aspects both as human rights and as contributing to the advancement of women. It is therefore to be expected that these rights, together with other social, civil, cultural and political rights, will be acknowledged in the practical implementation of the Beijing Report.

Mr. Chairman,

The Holy See has associated itself with those aspects of the Beijing Report that it considers to be positive and in the best interest of women. As the Head of the Holy See Delegation, Professor Mary Ann Glendon noted in her concluding Statement at the Conference that there is reason to be confident that women themselves will overcome the limitations of and bring out what is best in these Documents.

INTERVENTION OF
MR. JOHN M. KLINK
MEMBER OF THE HOLY SEE DELEGATION
TO THE UNICEF EXECUTIVE BOARD ON DOCUMENT E/ICEF/1996/3:
"UNICEF FOLLOW-UP TO THE FOURTH WORLD CONFERENCE ON WOMEN"
NEW YORK, 25 JANUARY 1996

Mr. President,

As is well known, the Holy See was an active participant in the negotiations of the Plan of Action of the Fourth World Conference on Women. Pope John Paul II has continued to place strong emphasis on women's development and on the equal footing which the girl-child should enjoy in programmes associated with the developmental basics of education, health and nutrition and protection from all forms of abuse. This is a priority which the Holy See has been encouraged to see reflected in the history of UNICEF activities in favor of children and mothers and which it had hoped to see emerging as a UNICEF priority in its follow-up to the Beijing Women's Conference.

Mr. President, while my Delegation finds some sections of the Document to reflect forward-looking strategies in terms of the rights to education for the girl-child and in terms of the rights of the girl-child to be free from abuse, it is deeply disturbed to see UNICEF's strong voice fall mute and its protective gaze drift decidedly away from the girl-child in terms of her rights to basic health care.

Thus, appropriately, under the Section I: "A. Girl's education," UNICEF proclaims its clear goal of "eliminating gender discrimination in basic education" and immediately outlines the means to judge the future success of its endeavors: "it will seek to ensure gender equality in the achievement of the goals of universal access to basic education and completion by at least 80 per cent of primary school-age children by the year 2000."

My Delegation would strongly applaud the Document's identification of obstacles to this goal and especially that of "weak parental partnerships/educational demand" which as the Document states, "calls for parents and other key actors to be active participants in building a consensus for girls' education." Clearly, full involvement and motivation of parents as regards the importance of ensuring that their female children — as well as their male ones — are provided equal access to education is key to the achievement of the basic education of the girl-child.

Again, my Delegation would commend UNICEF's efforts to seek universal recognition of the rights of the girl-child (as well as all children) as outlined in various human-rights instruments and in particular in the *Convention on the Rights of the Child*. While fully concurring with UNICEF's role as a general advocate for women's human rights and a specific advocate for those special rights of women which particularly impact on children, my Delegation would question whether UNICEF's role as the special advocate for the *Convention on the Rights of the Child* should become in any way compromised or marginalized by what would appear to be a growing equality of its commitment to advocacy for the *Convention on the Elimination of All Forms of Discrimination Against Women*. Clearly, UNICEF is *the* United Nations' advocate for children's rights and this priority must never be displaced or diluted with other issues which do not specifically bear on the fulfillment of this advocacy for *children.*

Mr. President, as regards the Document's treatment of health for the girl-child to which I made earlier reference, my Delegation expresses its concern that non-adolescent girls have been inadvertently, but further, marginalized. The risk in the strategy of prioritizing adolescent girls' health to the *exclusion* of pre-adolescent girls is not only that girls remain at the "back of the line" in terms of basic health campaigns such as immunization, Mother/Child Health, ORT, elimination of Guinea Worm Disease and a dozen other former UNICEF priorities, in comparison to boys, but that now they face the added potential marginalization of a "back-of-the-line politics" behind both boys *and* female adolescents. While the health section of the Document opens with the statement that "the health of women and girls is becoming an increasingly important programming area for UNICEF," *no* further mention is made of pre-adolescent girls nor is *any* health program envisioned therein for their benefit.

Mr. President, I would invite all of the Delegations here present to refer to the Beijing Platform for Action's Section on the Elimination of Discrimination against the Girl Child in Nutrition and Health (Para 281). As will be noted, this section in the Platform for Action begins its treatment of the subject by concentrating on "girls" rather than on "adolescent girls." While "adolescent girls" are also subsequently addressed, "girls" in general are the first priority of this special section of the Beijing Platform for Action. Thus, my Delegation finds it puzzling at best that the Document produced by the United Nations Children's Fund on UNICEF's proposed follow-up to the Beijing Conference should *ignore* the girl-child's health needs when on the contrary, *the Beijing Platform for Action itself goes to great lengths to highlight the health needs of the girl-child*.

The second effect of this singular emphasis on adolescents' health,

Mr. President, is to swerve the vaunted UNICEF health vehicle from its stated path of *basic* health for children to a further narrowing of UNICEF's health concerns for adolescents to reproductive health alone. One would be led to conclude from the health section of this Document that once arrived at adolescence, the only health service needed by adolescent girls is in terms of reproductive health. The final paragraph of this section in fact synthesizes the entire "Health Strategy for UNICEF" (approved only at the last Board Session with the proviso that it be implemented bearing in mind the critical comments of the Board). By mentioning "child health" only after a litany pertaining only to reproductive health, *The Report on the "Health Strategy for UNICEF"* (E/ICEF/l995/11/Rev.1) recommends the promotion of an integrated approach to reproductive health services for women, including reproductive health education, family planning, prenatal and post-natal services, delivery care, prevention and management of sexually transmitted diseases/AIDS and *child care*." To my Delegation this would amount to a serious misreading of the UNICEF Health Policy document resulting in a trivialization of children's health. To our Delegation, the question looms large as to whether UNICEF's donor base on which it depends for at least half of its support would continue as generously as in the past knowing that UNICEF's follow-up to the Beijing Women's Conference, and particularly to UNICEF's follow-up to that Conference's chapter on the girl-child, will put child health care at the "back of the line" of its priorities.

Again, in the Child's rights section of the Document, para. 16 calls for "the implementation of intersectoral programmes that address the evolving capacities of children, in particular girls, in the areas of nutrition, education, reproductive health... ." Once again, no reference is made to girls' health outside of "reproductive health." Similarly, in the UNICEF emergency programme section of the document, the UNICEF basics of ensuring girls' basic nutrition, health and education have disappeared to be replaced by "reproductive health care." Clearly, girls, particularly in emergencies, have health needs apart from reproductive health.

Finally, Mr. President, my Delegation cannot help but observe that the other policy papers previously approved by the UNICEF Board — even that on family planning — find no cross reference in this text. Especially missing is any reference to UNICEF's traditional mandate, or to its comparative advantage in terms of *information, education and communication* rather than *service* provision.

Mr. President, my Delegation is appreciative of, and has taken careful note of, the helpful comments made by Mr. Gautam during this Board Session that UNICEF's stated policies remain in effect that UNICEF does not distribute contraceptives, does not advocate any particular type of contraceptive use over another and never engages in abortion or abortion related activities, but feels that such assurances should be not only spoken at Board meetings, but should be written in the Board documents relating to reproductive health — precisely to alleviate the concerns expressed by a large number of Board members during this Session.

Mr. President, my Delegation would appeal to the Secretariat to ensure that preconsultations precede the publication of important draft documents such as the one before us. Again, it would appeal to the Secretariat to ensure that drafts of the Board minutes are shared not only with Member States, but also with Observer States to provide the latter an opportunity to review these and submit possible corrections/revisions prior to their final publication. This is of growing importance as increasing Board Decisions make reference to these minutes. It would appeal to the Board to ensure that the document regarding UNICEF's follow-up to the Beijing Women's Conference be revised to reflect UNICEF s priority of "children first!" Surely, UNICEF should be the last to put the girl-child at the "back of the line," even by an unintentional backpedaling from its priorities regarding the health of the girl-child.

Thank you, Mr. President.

Chapter Nine

THE SECOND UNITED NATIONS CONFERENCE ON HUMAN SETTLEMENTS

Istanbul, Turkey

3 - 14 June 1996

Chapter Contents

The Second United Nations Conference on Human Settlements (Habitat II)
Istanbul, Turkey;
3 - 14 June 1996

Address of His Holiness Pope John Paul II
    to Participants at a Meeting sponsored by the
    European Bureau for the Environment
    (Non-Governmental Organizations of Europe and the
    Mediterranean Basin); 7 June 1996 553

Addresses of His Holiness Pope John Paul II in conjunction with the
    Angelus and Regina Coeli Prayers 555
    Regina Coeli, St. Peter's Square, 26 May 1996 555
    Angelus, St. Peter's Square, 2 June 1996 555
    Angelus, St. Peter's Square, 9 June 1996 556
    Angelus, St. Peter's Square, 16 June 1996 557

Address of His Excellency Archbishop Paul Josef Cordes,
    President of the Pontifical Council "Cor Unum," at the
    International Colloquia organized by the
    International Catholic Centre for UNESCO
    Venice, Italy, 28 March 1996 559

Intervention of His Excellency Archbishop Renato R. Martino,
    Apostolic Nuncio, Permanent Observer of the Holy See
    to the U.N. and Head of the Holy See Delegation to the
    U.N. Conference on Human Settlements (Habitat II)
    Istanbul, 4 June 1996 567

Intervention of Monsignor Diarmuid Martin,
    Secretary of the Pontifical Council for Justice and Peace,
    at the High Level Segment of the U.N. Conference
    on Human Settlements (Habitat II)
    Istanbul, 13 June 1996 572

Statement by His Excellency Archbishop Renato R. Martino,
    Apostolic Nuncio, Permanent Observer of the Holy See
    to the U.N. and Head of the Holy See Delegation to the
    U.N. Conference on Human Settlements (Habitat II)
    Istanbul, 14 June 1996 575

    and Reservations and Statements of Interpretation 575

Chapter Nine

Statement by Mother Teresa of Calcutta,
    Missionaries of Charity,
        to the U.N. Conference on Human Settlements (Habitat II)
        28 May 1996 577

Address to His Holiness Pope John Paul II
    by His Excellency Archbishop Renato R. Martino,
    Apostolic Nuncio, Permanent Observer of the Holy See
    to the U.N., on the occasion of the Papal Audience to the
    Members of the Holy See Delegation to the U.N. Conference
    on Human Settlements (Habitat II)
    Vatican, 17 June 1996 579

Address of His Holiness Pope John Paul II
    to the Members of the Holy See Delegation to the
    U.N. Conference on Human Settlements (Habitat II)
    Vatican, 17 June 1996 581

Statement by His Excellency Archbishop Renato R. Martino,
    Apostolic Nuncio, Permanent Observer of the Holy See
    to the U.N., before the Second Committee of the General Assembly,
    on Item 96: "Sustainable Development and International
    Economic Cooperation: (e) Human Settlements and
    (f) Eradication of Poverty"; New York, 30 October 1996 582

(The Appendix contains no related documents for this chapter.)

Address of
His Holiness Pope John Paul II
to Participants at a Meeting sponsored by the European Bureau for the Environment (Non-Governmental Organizations of Europe and the Mediterranean Basin)
7 June 1996

(translated from the original French)

Dear Friends,

1. On the occasion of the meeting of Delegates of the Non-Governmental Organizations of Europe and the Mediterranean Basin on the topic of fiscal reform and the environment, which is taking place in Rome, I am pleased to welcome you. I cordially greet Mr. Armando Montanari, President of the European Bureau for the Environment, whom I thank for his kind words, and Mr. Raymond Van Ermen, Secretary General.

At the time when we are celebrating World Day of the Environment in the perspective of Habitat II, the United Nations Conference which is currently being held in Istanbul, your reflection addresses a review of the issues concerning lasting human development and interreligious dialogue in the area surrounding the Mediterranean.

2. As I said at the time of the Rio de Janeiro Conference on Environment and Development four years ago, modern man is led to ask a fundamental question which can be described as both ethical and ecological. How can accelerated development be prevented from turning against man? How can one prevent disasters that destroy the environment and threaten all forms of life, and how can the negative consequences that have already occurred be remedied?

The Catholic Church continues to be attentive to the maintenance and protection of the environment as well as to problems concerning development, in accordance with her own anthropological viewpoint, shared by people of goodwill and by noble religious traditions. The environment and development both involve the human person, the centre of creation. Economic and political decisions regarding the environment must therefore be made to serve individuals and peoples.

Man's vocation is to "cultivate" and subdue the earth which God has entrusted to him. Among creatures, he is the only being who is responsible for the consequences of his action, not only for himself but also for future generations for whom we must prepare a habitable world. No one can claim the goods of the earth for himself. As Ambrose of Milan said, "the fruitfulness of all the earth must be fruitfulness for all" (*De Nabuthe*, 7, 33).

3. In the social domain this truth must be expressed by the firm will to live and act in solidarity with our brothers and sisters, with a view to the common good. It is impossible for a single person or group to determine their own needs with regard to the environment, while ignoring the rest of humanity. Indeed, it is more than obvious today that the way we treat nature has consequences for our earth as a whole. Education in international solidarity and respect for the environment is urgently needed today.

Human beings, individually and collectively, are more than ever responsible for the future of the globe, for the glory of God and the good of creation. One cannot fail to appreciate the awareness of the local, national and international civil authorities and their concern for dialogue and cooperation in building a truly habitable rural and urban environment, without failing to preserve the necessary space for families, places of worship and human formation. I hope that the participants in the Habitat II Conference will find suitable responses to guarantee man's basic material needs without forgetting, however, the cultural and spiritual dimensions. Creativity and a sense of solidarity and responsibility should be fostered in order to create "living spaces" where people, children and families can achieve their best, because for his well-being and growth, the human being is deeply affected by his habitat.

4. In this spirit, I encourage you to pursue the service you are carrying out with our contemporaries, in order to create an ever more human world, as I hope your meetings will be crowned with success. I willingly grant my Apostolic Blessing to you all, to your colleagues and to those who are dear to you.

ADDRESSES OF
HIS HOLINESS POPE JOHN PAUL II
BEFORE THE ANGELUS AND AFTER THE REGINA COELI,

REGINA COELI, ST. PETER'S SQUARE
26 MAY 1996

On Sunday, 26 May 1996, the Solemnity of Pentecost, the Holy Father, after praying the Regina Coeli, said:

In the light of Pentecost, I would like to turn my thoughts to the United Nations Conference, Habitat II, which will be held in Istanbul on 3-14 June next. How could one fail to grasp the importance of this event? Man's life is deeply influenced by his "habitat." Creativity, solidarity and a sense of responsibility are required to design authentic "living environments." To undertake such a demanding task, the help of the Spirit of God is truly necessary!

I hope that humanity will be inspired by the great civilizations of the past, which were able to find suitable answers for satisfying material needs without forgetting man's inner yearnings.

May the Blessed Virgin, to whom the gaze of the Christian people is turned with particular devotion during this month of May, help us to organize "habitats" that are open to spiritual values, to respect for nature and to the demands of solidarity.

My blessing to all.

ANGELUS, ST. PETER'S SQUARE
2 JUNE 1996

On Sunday, 2 June, at the end of the Mass to celebrate the canonization of three new saints, the Holy Father spoke of the forthcoming Habitat II Conference in Istanbul, Turkey, saying:

Tomorrow the Second United Nations Conference on Human Settlements will open in Istanbul. It will be a valuable opportunity to reflect on the difficult problems of a world being rapidly urbanized. This is an issue which must be faced with a culture inspired by an integral conception of man and society. Particular attention must be paid to the needs of the family, the basic cell of society. The family must always remain the natural place where the person begins life and receives his first, fundamental acceptance: in the family different generations grow in loving and respecting one another, and in communicating the most authentic values of life.

In the "home," spouses exercise their rights and, by attending to their own responsibilities, bring their marital plan to maturity. May the Habitat II Conference sensitize States to supporting this commitment.

Through their intercession, may the Mother of Christ and the three saints raised today to the honours of the altar help all who are working for the success of this Conference, so that it may mark a milestone in the authentic progress of the whole human family.

ANGELUS, ST. PETER'S SQUARE
9 JUNE 1996

Dear Brothers and Sisters,

1. This last week was marked by the liturgical celebration of the Solemnity of Corpus Christi, which is celebrated today in Italy and in other nations. In the sacrament of the Body and Blood of Christ, the Church recognizes the source and culmination of her life. The Eucharist makes the one sacrifice of Golgotha mysteriously present. Christ himself becomes the nourishment of his people.

It is a mystery of life, according to Jesus' promise: "He who eats my flesh and drinks my blood has eternal life" (Jn 6:54). It is a reality of communion as the Apostle Paul recalls: "Because there is one bread we who are many are one body" (1 Cor 10:17). It is a source of love for the Church's life, which inspires and nourishes the plan for a society of openness and solidarity, with particular concern for the very poor.

2. This thought brings me back again to the Habitat Conference taking place in Istanbul, to make myself the voice of those who have no voice, and to invite the peoples' representatives involved in reflecting on human settlements to focus their attention on the poor, children, women, the elderly and the marginalized.

The task of eradicating poverty and that of the civil organizing of life together in both the rural and urban areas of the globe must go hand in hand. We must not be resigned to the scene of the great city outskirts where crowds of poor people throng, seeking some makeshift shelter and searching for barest essentials among the crumbs of a consumerism unfortunately often wasteful and indifferent. The right to housing, the right to an honest job, are integral to a single plan of social life, which must provide dignified living conditions for everyone, without discrimination. Every city should feel committed to becoming a city for everyone.

How can we forget that entire peoples pour into the richest cities from regions of poverty and lands of suffering: emigrants, displaced persons and refugees who hope to escape want and fear? If modern metropolises are often places of freedom, they can nonetheless manifest indifference, loneliness and new forms of poverty. This is a challenge to be taken up with promptness, broad-mindedness and a united sense of responsibility.

3. Let us entrust these urgent world needs to the motherly care of the Blessed Virgin, who gave birth to Jesus, the Son of God, and laid him in a manger because — as the Gospel tells us — there was no room for her and her husband Joseph in the inn in Bethlehem (cf. Lk 2:7). Indeed, who better than Mary can understand the hardship and humiliation of those who lack food and lodgings? May Mary instill in us the necessary sentiments and intentions so that our "habitats" may more and more take on the face of solidarity.

ANGELUS, ST. PETER'S SQUARE
16 JUNE 1996

Dear Brothers and Sisters,

1. The Second United Nations Conference on Human Settlements, to which I have directed my thoughts several times in recent Sundays, closed last Friday in Istanbul with a unanimous affirmation of the right to housing for every person with his family. This outcome is to be greeted with satisfaction. It raises the hope that this natural human aspiration, already protected by previous declarations and international commitments, will be more and more a focus of concern for all States.

It is not right for anyone — still less for public authorities responsible for the common good — to disregard the tragic situation of so many individuals and entire families forced to live on the street or to be content with inhospitable, makeshift shelters. It is also sad that so many young people, because of the difficulty in finding housing, often due to the lack or uncertainty of work, must postpone their marriage for a long time or even forgo the starting of their own family. Therefore, may this renewed expression of the international ethical and juridical conscience enjoy success; as it confirms the right to housing for all, it also stresses the close connection of this right with the right to start a family and to have an adequately paid job.

2. On the threshold of the new millennium, these viewpoints must be considered the firm basis of a great strategy for reducing as much as possible the gap between rich and poor countries and for eliminating the inequalities in the higher-income nations themselves. The Istanbul Conference has forcefully brought to humanity's attention the need for an ever better harmonizing of development and economic progress with solidarity and concern for the less fortunate. I make a heartfelt appeal to the authorities of all countries to take this task firmly in hand and make it a priority in their political decisions.

Ensuring a suitable "habitat" for everyone is demanded by the respect owed to every human being and, therefore, is a measure of civilization and the condition for a peaceful, fraternal society. By virtue of his human dignity, every person must be guaranteed a lodging which offers not only physical shelter but a suitable place for satisfying his social, cultural and spiritual needs.

3. May the Blessed Virgin help all to overcome selfish temptations and to open their heart to the needs of their brothers and sisters. If States have precise duties in providing housing, much also depends on the sensitivity of private individuals. Moreover, how can political guidelines inspired by justice and solidarity be promoted, if these values are not woven into the fabric of society as a whole? I hope that everyone — particularly those who appeal to the Gospel of Christ — will develop a greater sensitivity to the concrete, urgent issue of the right to housing.

ADDRESS OF
HIS EXCELLENCY ARCHBISHOP PAUL JOSEF CORDES
PRESIDENT OF THE PONTIFICAL COUNCIL "COR UNUM"
AT THE INTERNATIONAL COLLOQUIUM ORGANIZED BY THE
INTERNATIONAL CATHOLIC CENTRE FOR UNESCO
VENICE, ITALY, 28 MARCH 1996

Your Excellency,
Ladies and Gentlemen,

The Holy See would like to take this opportunity to confirm the continued importance and priority which the Catholic Church attributes to the topic and issue to be dealt with at the second International Conference on Human Settlements (Habitat II). The Church and its members have long taken an active role, and continue to do so today, in providing for the homeless and those in need of adequate shelter. Thus, in sharing "the joys and hopes, the grief and anxieties of people of our time" (Second Vatican Council, *Gaudium et spes*, I), the Church proclaims the Gospel and offers her contribution in the midst of the problems affecting the existence and destiny of individuals and peoples.

Today, most alarming are the large numbers of human beings, and families, who have no homes. This phenomenon of the lack of adequate shelter is not only found in less developed countries. We see this in Rome every day; I have seen it in Germany, my native country, and on a recent visit to the United States it was clearly evident when I visited the Samaritan House in Denver. An absolute priority must be given to ensuring everyone has the minimum conditions for a decent life. The Church's response strives to foster a habitat which fully meets human requirements as well as material and spiritual needs.

Turning to the message of Christ in the Gospel, there is ample reference for our reflection. As happened in Bethlehem, which "had no place in the inn" (Lk. 2: 7) for the poor one who was the Son of God. Today we see that there is no room for many throughout the world, all the more regrettable in so far as they frequently coexist at a short distance from the luxury and waste of sumptuous residences. The charity to which we are called is often identified by Christ and serves as a reminder for each one of us to heed the call of the great number of homeless or those without adequate shelter. Christ identifies with the homeless at the Last Judgement in saying "I was a stranger, and you sheltered me" (Mt. 25: 35). In the Gospel we see those who strive to follow Christ, and Jesus tells them, "Foxes have holes, and birds of the air have nests, but the Son of man has nowhere to lay his head" (Lk. 9: 58). Thus we can see in the faces of the homeless, the face of Christ.

In addition to Scripture, the concern of the Church for housing, and its insistence in calling for adequate shelter and housing for all, flows from among other considerations, the following three points:

— adequate shelter/housing is important if a person is to find fulfilment, both as an individual and as a member of a family and society;

— the witness that the Church seeks to give in collaborating in the search for a solution to the problems of the poor, including adequate housing, is a sign of the presence of the kingdom of God;

— the mission of the Church consists in helping to make society more human.

In this contextual framework, the act of providing adequate shelter and housing for another person is a concrete expression, not of simple social assistance, but an expression of the Gospel message and of the works of mercy, in that they are also works of Christian faith.

An analysis of various housing programmes conducted through the Church, and encouraged and promoted by the Holy See, would be an extensive undertaking. However, if we examine how it is that the local Churches, parishes in a diocese, address the problems of adequate shelter, three basic ways are identifiable.

1. Material help is given to provide shelter to homeless families. This facilitates the construction of houses for families, emergency shelters, and group centres, especially for the young and elderly. In many cases, these programmes are coupled with the development of infrastructures for the stocking and distribution of food, dispensaries, treatment of drinking water, transportation services, schools, cultural and recreative community centres.

2. Education and community development is given a particular importance in housing programmes so as to promote and develop each person, family and community. In this way efforts go far beyond material aid. Efforts are taken to develop local techniques, to produce building materials locally and to involve the family in the work to be done. This action of the local Churches also aims at the development and social integration of the homeless and those without adequate shelter.

The local Churches in the developing world have been able to count on the support and solidarity of ecclesial communities in developed countries. Many housing programmes exist that are the product of the generosity of members of these Christian communities. Such programmes are also financed or coordinated by organizations linked together in Caritas Internationalis or other similar organizations and institutions.

3. Local Churches actively dialogue with authorities in view of legislation and housing policies that are favourable to the poor. This communication with competent authorities attempts to urge them to take appropriate action. The Church repeatedly requests and supports political and economic initiatives aimed at providing housing for the homeless and low-cost housing schemes with favourable mortgage conditions. It encourages the creation of funds for long term, low interest rate loans as well as plans for land programmes, so that families can build their own home. Local Churches also collaborate in initiatives undertaken by public and private institutions in supporting such initiatives as housing programmes by trade unions, cooperatives, solidarity associations and private initiatives. Civil engineering concerns, architectural schools and universities are also encouraged to engage in community development projects.

Habitat II and the Holy See Delegation

The Holy See does not intend, nor has it undertaken efforts, to enter into technical considerations of Habitat II or to turn to political solutions, even though it is not unaware of the difficulties, problems and real possibilities at such levels. The Holy See has ventured to contribute, in conformity with its moral and spiritual position, to the preparations for Habitat II through its attendance at the three meetings of the Preparatory Committee and other consultations. However, I am pleased to say that in my presenting some positions of the Holy See today, you will hear many of the themes reflected in the "15 Propositions" prepared by the "NGO Standing Committee at UNESCO" for Habitat II.

The human being is at the centre of our concerns

The Holy See Delegation has continually asserted that all efforts and undertakings related to development must place the human being at the centre of our concerns. This was a concept that the Holy See Delegation to the United Nations Conference on Environment and Development held in Rio in 1992, proposed as the first principle there and it was adopted. It is the human being which is now identified in the draft text of the Habitat Agenda, as being at the centre of concerns for sustainable development, including adequate shelter for all and sustainable human settlements.

This concept of the centrality of the human being means that the need for adequate shelter for all must be addressed in a serious and forthright manner. Housing and shelter are part of the essential minimum in life, corresponding to a biological need, together with food and health, not to mention the major spiritual effects. Therefore it is right to be concerned about the quality of life for each and every human being and whether that is enhanced or diminished by their housing. The subsequent action presupposes political and material choices, but more fundamentally, it raises and attempts to bring to the forefront moral and spiritual dimensions.

In keeping with this centrality of the human being, the Holy See Delegation, along with others, has supported language in the lead paragraph of the "Goals and Principles" endorsing an ethical and spiritual vision of human settlements based on principles of human dignity. This particular reference to human dignity has been rejected by some States and remains in brackets as does the reference to the ethical and spiritual vision of human settlements. The Holy See Delegation continues to support this broader contextual framework in the lead paragraph rather than using strictly social and economic factors.

The family

Throughout the negotiating process the Holy See Delegation has placed an emphasis on the recognition of the importance of the family, the basic unit of society, in addressing problems related to shelter. The Delegation continues to call for the consideration and insertion of additional language regarding the family in the Document.

While the principle on "the family," which appears in the section titled "Goals and Principles," includes a reference noting that "the rights, capabilities and responsibilities of family members must be respected," there is a portion in the "Preamble" regarding the responsibilities, duties and rights of parents in addressing the shelter needs of their children and this language remains in brackets. The Delegation of the Holy See supports the lifting of the brackets from around this parental language since it supports the position that parents do have responsibilities, duties and rights in this realm and this should be clearly recognized. This parental duty encompasses the education of their children in the running and upkeep of their home and should prepare the children to collaborate tomorrow in the improving and perfecting of human settlements. This is not, should not be, and cannot be, the sole domain of the State.

Space is a fundamental requirement of a truly human habitat, especially for the family. Cramped housing is a major obstacle to individual development and still more to the development of family life. The quality of life of the couple and of the family unit grouped around this couple, is such an essential value, rooted in the nature of the human race, that it cannot be sacrificed under the pretext of technological and social necessity or an over-emphasis on individualism.

The right to housing

The Delegation of the Holy See has continually supported the right to housing in the discussions during the Preparatory process and continues to do so. However, it has been the legal or juridical aspects of this question of the "right to housing" which has become controversial, especially for a few large Delegations. The Holy See Delegation, while commenting on the juridical components of this question, has attempted to broaden the discussion to encompass the ethical and moral dimensions which merit, in fact deserve, equal treatment to that of the juridical components of the right.

The Holy See, in publishing its *Charter on the Rights of the Family* explicitly states that "the family has the right to decent housing, fitting for family life and commensurate to the number of its members, in a physical environment that provides the basic services for the life of the family and the community" (Art. 11).

Marginalized and vulnerable groups

In recognizing that human beings are at the centre of our concerns, it is to be understood that this includes all human beings. However, for numerous reasons, which will not be gone into at this point, certain groups need to be given added consideration in the Habitat Agenda. The Church is very conscious that the lack of decent housing threatens the dignity and rights of the poor.

The Holy See Delegation proposed and continually advocated the inclusion of a principle on the eradication of poverty which is now found in the Document. This has been an effort to call attention to the poor of the world and to advocate a call for wide-spread cooperation and solidarity in favour of those in need of adequate shelter. It is encouraging to note, not only that the number of programmes continue to increase in this area, but also that an education in the spirit of solidarity and responsibility of aiding the poor is spreading.

Additional considerations are needed in the Document, especially in the commitments, so as not to exclude those unable to enter into the financial and economic mechanisms advocated in the text, precisely because of being poor. The ethical and moral dimension of this issue also needs to be given consideration within the text.

The Holy See Delegation has advocated additional consideration within the text of vulnerable groups such as refugees, displaced persons, disabled persons, migrants, street children to mention but a few. However, there has been an attempt by some to label all children and all women, for example, as vulnerable. This simply is not reality and caution should be employed in this labeling of broad categories as vulnerable. Some children and some women are in need of assistance due to situations not limited to age or gender. Those who are in need should be provided for from the available resources.

Community facilities including places of worship

Facilities providing collective services are necessary in communities, some for material needs and others that meet cultural and spiritual requirements.

Due to its unique nature, the Holy See Delegation proposed that a place should be reserved beside the houses of men and women and their families for the house of God. Thus, particular importance should be given to the inclusion of planning for places of worship in the overall planning and development of human settlements. Cooperation between religious officials and the town planning authorities is desirable. By its interior and exterior beauty, this place of worship should be a symbol of faith and hope in the supernatural destiny of each one of us. As an architectural piece it should blend harmoniously with the city's other monuments.

Historically, urban development has resulted in the creation of districts, and even new towns, where the problem of building places of worship was acute. Sometimes even the need for such buildings was and is today questioned, on the grounds that priority should be given to housing construction or because it is considered that the practice of religion and the expression of faith do not necessitate that closed spaces should be exclusively given over to religious services. However, the Holy See Delegation wishes to note that neither personal nor social dimensions of life can find fulfilment in purely earthly activities. Every human being has spiritual needs. The values which these aspects of shelter and places of worship foster and promote, both in human settlements and among their occupants, are crucial and central to sustainable human settlements.

Rural-urban balance

Throughout this Intervention the remarks made and observations given have not been limited or defined by only citizens. The Holy See has advocated the treatment of human settlements as encompassing both urban and rural questions and issues, both urban and rural development, as the draft of the Habitat Agenda now indicates. Unless there is a rural-urban synergism in the approach to human settlements, there will be no solution in either the rural setting or the urban area. The basis for this view lies in the visible and invisible interconnections and linkages between rural and urban areas. These should not be seen as mutually exclusive and competing areas.

Conclusion

Human settlements and the provision of adequate shelter for all in sustainable human settlements provides a privileged field of human collaboration. The needs are immense. Adequate shelter should be a priority aim of national policy and of international cooperation and solidarity. These efforts are not only to meet the problem of the suffering, but also the hope of greater justice and the promotion of human dignity.

The Second International Conference on Human Settlements provides us all with the opportunity to make a contribution. We look forward to hearing the voices of those here present as the issues unfold over the next two days. We do this as Christians carrying with us the treasure of God's revelation.

Human settlements may not initially seem to be an obvious focus of our reflections as members of the Church. However, we can discover in the Bible interesting indications for our theme.

In the perspective of Revelation the *city* is the foundation of Cain. After having killed his brother it is written: "Cain ... built a city, and called the name of the city after the name of his son, Enoch" (Gen. 4: 17). This indicates that the Bible sees the city as such in a sinful light. This link between the human guilt and the human settlement, therefore necessitates that the act of salvation touch not only every human being, but even the settlement. This salvation is fulfilled step by step when God speaks to His people and sends His Son, whose death and resurrection make everything new — even the city. And so marvelously, the institution of guilt and sin — the city — becomes by God's grace the most meaningful image of salvation and perfect beauty. As we read in the Book of Revelation for the last days, "And I saw the holy city, New Jerusalem, coming down out of heaven from God... Behold the dwelling of God is with men. He will dwell with them and they shall be his people and God himself will be with them..." (Rev. 21: 2ff).

INTERVENTION OF
HIS EXCELLENCY ARCHBISHOP RENATO R. MARTINO
APOSTOLIC NUNCIO, PERMANENT OBSERVER OF THE HOLY SEE
TO THE UNITED NATIONS AND HEAD OF THE
DELEGATION OF THE HOLY SEE TO THE
SECOND UNITED NATIONS CONFERENCE ON
HUMAN SETTLEMENTS (HABITAT II)
ISTANBUL, 4 JUNE 1996

Mr. President,

I would like to take this opportunity to express the thanks of the Holy See Delegation to the Government and people of Turkey and to the population of the city of Istanbul. In a special way I wish to convey to them the cordial best wishes of His Holiness Pope John Paul II. We are gratified by the very warm welcome which we have received since our arrival in this historic city. In addition, it is most heartening to note that this Conference is off to a good and auspicious start, a reflection of the careful planning and the untiring efforts which have been put forth by our hosts.

1. Mr. President, this Conference represents a milestone in the recent work of the International Community. Previous gatherings have reflected upon such questions as the Environment, Poverty, Social Development and the role of Women. Now, in this last International Conference of this century and this millennium, we are here to consider the question of "Human Settlements." We might say that, at the end of all of our recent discussions, we are returning home.

Indeed, human settlements are our homes. These are the places where children are born and raised by parents to be the productive and contributing citizens of the next generation. Here is where all of the values of life and the elements which form culture are transmitted from adults to the young. This is where the elderly, in their declining days, are cared for by loving individuals who wish to repay with gratitude what they received from them in the past. The home is where the sick receive devoted attention which cannot be provided by even the finest of hospitals. Home is the place to which so many refugees, migrants and displaced persons long to return, to finally know that their exile is over.

New possibilities from solidarity and the human spirit

It is obvious that when we are dealing with questions of home and human settlements, we are dealing with a very practical matter. Sadly, inadequate shelter is a part of life for many people spread throughout the world, in all countries and cultures. Homelessness and a lack of adequate shelter are not theoretical questions. Their elimination is not merely a matter of economics and planning. Rather, the efforts which we expend to eliminate these offenses against the very dignity and worth of each human person are the measure of our commitment to and solidarity with our less fortunate brothers and sisters.

For this reason, the Holy See has noted with satisfaction that the focus of this International Conference is on two very important goals: Adequate Shelter for All and Sustainable Human Settlements Development in an Urbanizing World. Indeed the task of facilitating the provision of adequate shelter for all is, one might say, the bottom line. Our first and most important task is to strive toward providing access to shelter for all people, whether they live in major urban centers or undeveloped rural areas. The statement of this goal properly expresses the context of our deliberations.

At the same time, a particular focus on shelter needs within cities is not out of place. The contemporary phenomenon of mega-cities presents numerous challenges. Undeniably, large numbers of people dwelling side by side can place stress on the infrastructure and the delivery of essential services within a city, as well as on the local environment. Nevertheless, we must not be pessimists. For every challenge or difficulty resulting from people residing in cities, there are also vast new possibilities arising out of solidarity and the human spirit. While we must not avert our gaze from problems, we must keep in mind that, historically, it is cities which have been the centers of learning, culture and religious expression in many societies. We have every reason to be confident that solutions can be found and provisions made so that even the large cities of today can contribute to the good of all.

2. Mr. President, the Holy See does indeed believe that adequate shelter and housing are a right of each and every person. This has been stated on numerous occasions, including the *Address of His Holiness Pope John Paul II to the General Assembly of the United Nations* on 2 October 1979 when he said, "Permit me to enumerate some of the most important human rights that are universally recognized: the right to life, liberty and security of person; the right to food, clothing, housing, sufficient health care, rest and leisure; the right to freedom of expression, education and culture; the right to freedom of thought, conscience and religion, and the right to choose a state of life, to found a family and to enjoy all conditions necessary for family life... ."

The Holy See believes that the right to housing is already recognized in international instruments such as the *Universal Declaration of Human Rights* (N. 25), as well as in the *International Covenant on Economic, Social and Cultural Rights* (Article 11, 1). But we should not restrict ourselves merely to a discussion and an exegesis of such juridical texts, as important as they may be. In truth, the right of each person to adequate shelter flows from a spiritual, moral and ethical vision which is based in a recognition of human dignity. For this reason, the Holy See is particularly pleased that the very first Principle of the *Rio Declaration on Environment and Development* which states: "Human beings are at the centre of concerns for sustainable development," has been enshrined in the Document proposed for our consideration, and applied to the themes of "adequate shelter for all and sustainable human settlements." Because this Conference is and must be committed to what is good for people, this point must be clearly stated .

Parents have primary responsibility for housing

3. The Holy See also strongly supports the assertion that the family is the "basic unit of society and as such should be strengthened." This principle has been affirmed at previous International Conferences and Summits, and it merits repeating at this gathering. This is an eminently fitting consideration for a Conference on Human Settlements because experience shows that it is families, and not isolated individuals, who inhabit the vast majority of homes.

Indeed, in every society, it is the family which is the primary vehicle for social stability and cohesion. Such stability is an essential condition for harmonious and well-functioning human settlements. Further, it is precisely the family which is the greatest provider of care, assistance and support in moments of need. Therefore, policies which encourage the formation of strong families and stable marriages are the best way to eliminate one of the underlying causes of homelessness.

Naturally, the most basic relationship within the family is that between parents and children. For this reason, it should also be clearly recognized that it is parents who have the primary duty and responsibility to provide for the housing needs of their children. The role of the State and of society is to assist and enable parents to fulfill this task.

4. My Delegation would like to commend the efforts which have been made so far to highlight the needs of those who are vulnerable, and especially of people who are living in poverty. Indeed, this is an aspect of our deliberations which we believe requires still more emphasis in the Document before us. Particular attention must be paid to the sad plight of refugees, displaced persons and migrants. Even while we discuss the shelter needs of

people in rural and urban areas, we must not lose sight of the shelter needs of so many who are often forced to live in the squalor and inadequacy of camps in various parts of the world. Such people have a particular claim on our attention since they have some of the greatest need, and yet they are often met with indifference or even rejection. And how frequently, in such situations, it is women and children who bear the brunt of the suffering, often separated from their husbands and fathers. However, we must recognize that we cannot eliminate this kind of shelter problem without the courage and resolve to find solutions to the conflicts which leave so many of these people in situations of vulnerability. Indeed where there is no peace, Sustainable Human Settlements Development simply will not be possible.

There are others whose vulnerability must also be considered. These would include street children, disabled persons and women living in poverty, to name just a few of these groups. Their specific shelter needs should be highlighted as well, especially because their voices too often go unheeded.

5. By means of Resolution 48/183 of 21 December 1993, the General Assembly proclaimed 1996 to be the "International Year for the Eradication of Poverty." The world leaders participating in the World Summit for Social Development restated this decision in the 2nd Commitment of the *Copenhagen Declaration*. We must keep this in mind in the course of our discussions. There is an undeniable link between poverty and shelter needs. Indeed it would not be enough if the International Community were to facilitate the access to shelter but not link this to the elimination of poverty. This is another facet of the respect which we owe the worth and dignity of every human person. We should strive to give to each one the necessary means to raise him or herself out of poverty. Furthermore, there will always be some who because of their poverty or other circumstances will be unable to benefit from even the most well intentioned and well designed market mechanisms. Their needs must also be met.

Due attention must be paid to religious buildings

6. Mr. President, all human settlements, be they urban or rural, large or small, are not simply places to live and to take refuge from the elements. Settlements are also a means of expression of the human soul. Our host city of Istanbul is a vivid example of how cities all over the world serve also as a statement of the culture of their inhabitants. Often, too, settlements are filled with and sometimes centered on monuments which are part of their history. In this way cities become an expression of the great continuity of the human race with those who have gone before, while they reflect also an implicit desire to be one with those who will come after. We therefore must

not allow human settlements to become simply a matter of functionality. It is imperative that consideration be given to the preservation of cultural and historical heritage.

In this same vein, we must not overlook the spiritual nature of the inhabitants of settlements. Throughout the world, in all ages of history as well as in the present, religious belief has played an enormous role in the lives of countless individuals, families and communities. Indeed, how many are the cities which, at their very beginning, were in fact founded and centered upon a cathedral, a church, a mosque, a synagogue, a temple, a shrine or some other religious building. For people of various religions, free access to a place of worship and the vivid expression of their faith as manifested by the presence of a religious building, is an essential part of their life and of their community. This fact was recognized in the final Document of Habitat I which stated, "Places of worship, especially in areas of expanding human settlements, should be provided and recognized in order to satisfy the spiritual and religious needs of different groups in accordance with freedom of religious expression" (Guidelines for Action, N. 17). For this reason, due attention must be given in our deliberations and in the final Document to the need for religious buildings in our human settlements.

Mr. President, in closing, I would like to restate the appreciation of the Holy See for the efforts being made by this Conference to respond to the pressing global problem of the poor in need of adequate shelter, and I would repeat the words of Pope John Paul II during his visit to the Centre of the United Nations for Habitat in Nairobi when he said that the Church

> "... gladly join[s] hands with all people of good will in the worthy efforts being made to provide adequate housing for the millions of people in today's world living in absolute destitution. ... I assure you of the Church's great interest in and support for your commendable endeavours to provide housing for the homeless and to safeguard the human dimension of all settlements of people."

It is the hope of my Delegation that the discussions, deliberations and the decisions of this Conference will truly achieve these lofty goals.

Thank you, Mr. President.

INTERVENTION OF
MONSIGNOR DIARMUID MARTIN
SECRETARY OF THE PONTIFICAL COUNCIL FOR JUSTICE AND PEACE
AT THE HIGH LEVEL SEGMENT OF THE
UNITED NATIONS CONFERENCE ON HUMAN SETTLEMENTS
(HABITAT II)
ISTANBUL, 13 JUNE 1996

Mr. President,
Mr. Secretary General of the United Nations,
Your Excellencies,
Ladies and Gentlemen,

My Delegation wishes to express its congratulations to you, Mr. President, and to the authorities and people of the Republic of Turkey on the successful outcome of this Conference, which your country has hosted with graciousness and efficiency.

My congratulations go also to the General Secretary of the Conference, to the Secretariat and to all who have collaborated in facilitating the work of the Conference.

My Delegation has stressed on various occasions that it is fitting that the final Conference of the current series of International Conferences of the United Nations should be dedicated to the theme of Adequate Shelter for All and Sustainable Human Settlements Development. The very first principle of the *Rio Declaration*, at the first Conference of this series, states that the "Human beings are at the centre of concerns for sustainable development." At the end of the series, after all the complexities and controversies of our negotiations, after all the agreements and at times disagreements, we have come back once again concretely to those same human beings, in the place where they live and work, suffer and flourish: the home.

The Holy See has continuously stressed the equal importance of the two themes of this Conference: Adequate Shelter for all and Sustainable Human Settlements. Seen from the point of view of the individuals, family and the communities of our world, these two themes cannot be separated. Every child, woman and man needs both the intimacy of the home and the possibility of human enrichment and growth which the community in which they live offers them. Adequate shelter is not simply a roof over one's head. It is a much broader, richer notion which permits all persons to live in dignity and to realize themselves fully, in individual achievement, in their family life at home, at school, at work, in recreation and the enjoyment of creation, in worship, and in working and living together in safety and harmony.

One of the principal achievements for which this Conference will be remembered is the outcome of its negotiations on the right to adequate housing, for all persons and their families. The *Universal Declaration of Human Rights* recognized this right clearly within the fundamental vocabulary of human rights language. At Istanbul we have taken this right from the textbooks and have given it a new concrete embodiment. Governments have committed themselves to the promotion and protection of this right and to its application. And they have recognized this as a specific obligation. This action of our Conference will give new hope and confidence to many people concerning what the United Nations Organization can do in its mandate to serve the good of humankind.

Now it is up to the Governments of the participating States, to their partners, especially local authorities, and also to all the elements of civil society to make sure that our actions become reality. We must never allow the term "progressive realization," which we use, to hold us back from the obligation to achieve the "full realization" of this right.

The Holy See wishes to play its part, consistent with its own nature and mission, to give concrete realization to this right, and to lead to a broad-based commitment of society in this regard. Pope John Paul II, in the light of this Conference, has already announced that his annual *Message* at the beginning of the forthcoming Lent 1997, a period in which Christians fast and dedicate themselves to renewed commitment to those living in poverty, will be dedicated to the theme of homelessness. The aim is to mobilize the Church and especially all Church aid organizations to examine and commit themselves to seeking solutions to this ubiquitous crisis of our contemporary world.

To mark the occasion of this Conference and its aims, the Holy See wishes to recognize two significant housing initiatives, each of which embodies the aims and objectives of the Habitat Agenda:

The first is the "Fundacion de Viviendas del Hogar de Cristo," whose aim is to help in the design and construction of houses for families living in poverty. A contribution will be made to the programme of the Foundation, a Catholic voluntary organization, which has already built 7 million square meters of housing in Chile, Ecuador and Colombia. In this way, the Holy See wishes to show its recognition of all those community organizations which have taken a lead in providing concrete and durable solutions to the problems of the homeless.

The second award will be given to the head of the Catholic Diocese of Byumba in Rwanda, Bishop Servilien Nzakamwita, to achieve a programme of building or rehabilitating houses for refugees who have returned home. In this way the Holy See wishes to draw attention to the special needs of all those, who for various reasons, have been uprooted from their homes and who, upon returning, need assistance in reestablishing themselves and their families in security and harmony.

These awards, each of the modest amount of US$50,000, are but small symbols of recognition for concrete service for the homeless already begun, and are signposts for the type of community-based services which can ensure adequate shelter and more human and sustainable human settlements today.

The Holy See will accompany these gestures with a renewal of its commitment throughout the wide range of educational services with which it is associated to promote a greater awareness of the needs of the homeless and of the challenge of constructing settlements which truly reflect the dignity of the men and women who live in them.

Our Conference has recognized that the dramatic number of homeless persons in all parts of today's world and the critical situation regarding the living conditions of people in cities require urgent intervention at various levels. This effort involves special responsibilities for the international community. All of us are well aware of the financial restraints which governments are experiencing in today's global economy. The dilemma that thus arises can only be broken by the creation of a new climate of solidarity and a recognition that the fruits of creation are destined for the good of the whole human family. The fundamental global community is the human family itself. The process of economic globalization in general, and the continued growth of cities in particular, which is underway, will only serve the human family if accompanied by a global process of concern and solidarity. A new "political will" must be constructed, especially in the wealthier countries, which will recognize solidarity as more than just self interest, but as moral imperative for all.

This was also the message of Pope John Paul II, speaking about this Conference, when he stressed that today "every city should feel committed to becoming a city for everyone so that "our 'habitats' may more and more take on the face of solidarity."

STATEMENT BY
HIS EXCELLENCY ARCHBISHOP RENATO R. MARTINO
APOSTOLIC NUNCIO, PERMANENT OBSERVER OF THE HOLY SEE
TO THE UNITED NATIONS AND
HEAD OF THE HOLY SEE DELEGATION TO THE UNITED NATIONS
CONFERENCE ON HUMAN SETTLEMENTS (HABITAT II)
ISTANBUL, 14 JUNE 1996

Mr. President,

Our Conference, attended by persons of various traditions and cultures, with viewpoints that differ widely, has carried out its work in a peaceful and respectful atmosphere. The Holy See appreciates the way in which Delegates have listened to these viewpoints and considered these varying views. The Holy See welcomes the progress that has been made in these days, and expresses its desire that the Plan of Action of this Conference be faithfully undertaken.

Finding answers and solutions to issues surrounding the goals of adequate shelter for all and sustainable human settlements development is essential as the world family moves into the new millennium. Those goals are also essential for peace and security in the world around us, for all people.

The Holy See wishes to express its thanks to the government and people of Turkey and Istanbul. The success of this Conference is a reflection of the vitality of the Turkish people. The Holy See looks forward to the continued good will and cooperation that it has enjoyed with the people of this land for so many years.

As my Delegation has announced in the meeting of the main committee, I submit to this plenary meeting, the Reservations and Statements of Interpretation of the Holy See and ask that these be included in the Report of the Conference.

Reservations and Statements of Interpretation

The Holy See, in conformity with its nature and particular mission, joins the consensus on the Documents of the Second United Nations Conference on Human Settlements (Habitat II) and wishes to express the following Reservations and Statements of Interpretation regarding certain concepts used in them.

1. The Holy See reiterates the Reservations it expressed at the conclusion of the International Conference on Population and Development, held in Cairo from 5 to 13 September 1994, and which are included in the Report of that Conference, concerning the interpretation to be given to the terms "reproductive health," "sexual health" and "reproductive rights." In particular, the Holy See reiterates that it does not consider abortion or abortion services to be a dimension of reproductive health or reproductive health services. The Holy See for moral reasons does not endorse any legislation which gives legal recognition to abortion. With regard to the term "family planning" or other terms concerning family planning services, the Holy See's actions during this Conference should in no way be interpreted as changing its well-known position concerning those family planning methods that the Catholic Church considers morally unacceptable or concerning family planning services that do not respect the liberty of spouses, the human dignity or the human rights of those concerned.

2. The Holy See, in line with the *Universal Declaration of Human Rights*, stresses that the family is the basic unit of society and is based on marriage as an equal partnership between husband and wife, to which the transmission of human life is entrusted. It considers references to "various forms of the Family," in para. 18 of the Habitat Agenda, as references to different cultural expressions of the family as described above.

3. The Holy See understands the use of the term "gender" in this document in the light of its Statement made at the conclusion of the Fourth World Conference on Women held at Beijing, 4-15 September 1995, and included in the Report of that Conference.

4. With regard to all references to international agreements, in particular any existing international agreements mentioned in the documents, the Holy See reserves its position in a manner consistent with its acceptance or non-acceptance of these agreements and with any reservations it may have expressed.

5. The Holy See requests that these Reservations and Statements of Interpretation be inserted integrally into the Report of the Conference on Human Settlements (Habitat II).

STATEMENT BY
MOTHER TERESA OF CALCUTTA
MISSIONARIES OF CHARITY
TO THE UNITED NATIONS CONFERENCE ON HUMAN SETTLEMENTS
(HABITAT II)
28 MAY 1996

Dear Friends,

I am praying much for God's blessing on all who are taking part in the second "Habitat Conference." I hope this Conference will help everyone to bring peace, love and compassion to the world today. Compassion and love have to grow from within, from our union with God. And from that union, love for the family, love for our neighbors, love for the poor is a natural fruit.

Jesus came to bring us peace of heart which comes from loving, doing good to others. Abortion and partial-birth abortion are the killers of peace in this world, the greatest destroyers of peace, for if a mother can destroy her child, what is left but for us to kill each other. Love starts at home and lasts at home. By abortion and partial-birth abortion, the mother destroys the home and does not learn to love. And by abortion and partial-birth abortion, the father is told that he does not have to take responsibility for the child he has brought into the world. So, abortion just leads to more abortion. Any country that accepts abortion or partial-birth abortion is not teaching its people to love but to do violence to get what they want. The next step is assisted suicide for the elderly, seriously ill and the unwanted person.

The shut-in, the unwanted, the unborn, the partially-born, the unloved, the alcoholics, the dying destitutes, the abandoned and the lonely — all those who are a burden to the human society — they look to us for comfort. If we turn our back on them, we turn it on God. Therefore, I appeal to everyone of you — rich and poor, old and young, people of all nations, races and religions — to give your hands to serve God in His poor and your hearts to love Him in them. Since love begins at home, maybe Jesus is naked, hungry, sick or homeless in your own heart, in your family, in your neighbors, in the country you live in, in the world.

Where does love begin? In our own homes. When does it begin? When we pray together. The family that prays together, stays together. Prayer begets faith, faith begets love and love begets service on behalf of the poor. If faith is scarce it is because there is too much selfishness in the world. Faith, in order to be authentic, has to be generous and giving. Love and faith go hand in hand.

Let us remember what Jesus said: "Whatever you do to the least, you did it to Me." So let us pray.

God bless you.

Address to
His Holiness Pope John Paul II
by His Excellency Archbishop Renato R. Martino
on the occasion of the Papal Audience to the
Members of the Holy See Delegation
to the United Nations Conference on Human Settlements
(Habitat II)
Vatican, 17 June 1996

Holy Father,

We have returned from Istanbul, where we have had the honor to represent the Holy See at the Second United Nations Conference on Human Settlements.

I am happy to report to Your Holiness, without singling out any specific member of the Delegation, that each one has given completely of themselves, according to their talents and specific skills.

We are very tired but we are happy to have completed our task in fulfilling the instructions that Your Holiness sent to us. Our work, thanks be to God, was crowned with a comforting success.

In the final Document we have seen the solemn affirmation of the full and progressive right of all to a home; family values were affirmed, as were the rights and obligations of parents. More over, we could sense the determination of the international community to ensure adequate housing for all, including those most vulnerable, such as refugees, migrants and displaced persons.

Our Delegation made it a point to advocate the protection of human life in every stage.

These, in summary, were the more important aspects of our mission. As soon as possible, after some much needed moments of rest, we will present to our Superiors a detailed report of our participation in this important Conference. In the meantime, we implore Your Holiness to give us your blessing.

Address of His Holiness Pope John Paul II to the Members of the Holy See Delegation to the United Nations Conference on Human Settlements (Habitat II); Vatican, 17 June 1996

Dear Archbishop Martino,
Dear Friends,

    I am indeed happy to greet you, the members of the Holy See's Delegation to the United Nations' Second Conference on the Human Habitat which has just ended in Istanbul. In the course of these two weeks, you have taken part in discussions on what constitutes a home truly worthy of human beings, a home properly adapted to the needs of the family.

    Your principal concern at the Conference has been to put the inalienable dignity of the human person at the centre of everyone's attention, and to draw out the consequences for the international community of that dignity in relation to something as fundamental to people's well-being as the human habitat, the physical and social environment in which individuals and families work out their earthly destiny.

    I wish to thank you for your dedication and for your sensitivity to the real needs of people as regards housing and living conditions. Through your skill and commitment, you have made public opinion more clearly aware of the fact that the human habitat will not be truly human unless it also promotes the spiritual and moral development of the human person, and is open to the fraternal solidarity which springs from the social dimension of human life. Your contribution to the Conference was enlightened by the Christian ideal of the family, as experienced by Jesus in Nazareth, in the setting of a hard-working and peaceful life lived in the sight of God.

    As a token of my gratitude and of the appreciation which you have merited on the part of the Holy See, I cordially impart my Apostolic Blessing to you and to your dear ones.

Statement of
His Excellency Archbishop Renato R. Martino
Apostolic Nuncio, Permanent Observer of the Holy See to the United Nations
before the Second Committee of the 51ST Session of the General Assembly, on Item 96:
"Sustainable Development and International Economic Cooperation"
(e) "Human Settlements" and (f) "Eradication of Poverty"
New York, 30 October 1996

Mr. Chairman,

The theme before us today, "Human Settlements," is of great importance. For this reason, the Holy See was pleased that the final United Nations International Conference of this century and millennium, the meeting in Istanbul held this past June, dealt with this topic.

The theme of human settlements has very personal implications for every human being. Everyone knows that whatever form it takes, home is a part of one's life and one's identity. It is a place that human beings and the Family can call their own. It is there that many of the deepest experiences of life take place. It is there that experiences and wisdom are exchanged, and the values and traditions which make up our various cultures are passed down from one generation to another. The home is where all persons experience that inner freedom which comes from the one particular place where they always belong.

Because the Holy See is so convinced of the great importance of shelter for human life, it has continually emphasized, during its participation at the Istanbul Conference, that the dual themes of Habitat II, "Adequate Shelter for All" and "Sustainable Human Settlements Development" had to be given equal importance. It was pleased to see such a balance reflected in the final Document. The International Community thus committed itself not only to necessary long-term policies to improve the quality and provision of shelter, but it also recognized its moral obligation to see that each and every person has a fitting and worthy place to live.

My Delegation wishes to express once again its clear support for one of the principal achievements of the international community at the Habitat II Conference: that is, the reaffirmation of a right to adequate housing. Further, it was recognized that such a right, while subject to "progressive realization" must be "fully realized." By this decision, the United Nations and the International Community have shown a desire and a willingness to defeat one of the most immediate and widespread symptoms of poverty and inequality in the world.

At the same time, Habitat II rightly underscored the vital role of the family in the area of housing. It recognized, as previous Conferences had done, that "the family is the basic unit of society and as such should be strengthened." It also repeated what is contained in the *Universal Declaration of Human Rights*, which acknowledges that the right to housing applies to "oneself and one's family." My Delegation believes that proper respect, protection and assistance for families is a vital component of any program for development. In the area of shelter, common experience shows that the vast majority of dwellings are not inhabited by individuals living in isolation, but by families. This is the reality that must be taken into consideration and continually addressed as the Habitat Agenda moves to implementation. But in the wider context, it is the natural assistance given within the family which is the most basic support for those living in poverty. Again, it is common experience that people turn first to their families for assistance in time of need. It is other members of the family who have the best understanding of their problems and the solutions they require. Thus, my Delegation is convinced that in the area of development, respect for and promotion of the family is essential.

In the ongoing discussions about development, there are now frequent references to "an enabling approach." Chapter 7 of Agenda 21 outlines the concept of "an enabling approach to shelter development," and this idea is prominently taken up throughout the Habitat Agenda. Such an enabling approach is linked to the idea of markets which are said to "serve as the primary housing delivery mechanism" (N. 71) in many countries. Clearly, market forces have become a strong and even a determining factor in the provision of goods and the achievement of economic growth. It will become increasingly necessary for the International Community to study how to place these forces at the disposition of the poor and how to involve them and their needs in the context of the market, both within their own countries and on a global level.

It is here that we need real innovation and a new way of thinking. Specifically, ways must be found to integrate market forces, which at times are said to be based solely on the sometimes harsh economic realities of success and failure, with the social needs and commitments articulated by the international community, most recently in Istanbul. Clearly, as the Habitat Agenda states, governments retain the final obligation to assist the poor of their own countries. Such help can take many forms, including various means of direct assistance. But enough is not yet being done to help the poor to benefit from the economic growth which the market can bring. For example, more must be done to attract investment and therefore jobs into areas stricken by poverty. Globally, study must be made of how to increase the openness to and the availability of world markets for the sale of products coming from poor and underdeveloped areas. In the words of a document released last week by the Holy See entitled *"World Hunger, A Challenge for All: Development in Solidarity,"* importing countries have a responsibility "to remove barriers and to refrain from raising new ones to selectively keep out exports from countries where a major proportion of the population is suffering from hunger." In this context, the Holy See wishes to note that a deeper sense of "corporate responsibility" must be developed, so that even large transnational private actors acknowledge the duty to use their economic influence to contribute to economic and social development, especially in areas beset by poverty.

In the end, however, we must recognize that there will always be some people who, for a variety of reasons, are not able to benefit from free market mechanisms. We must see to the housing and social needs of these people as well.

Finally, Mr. Chairman, we should note that there is one factor which is a *sine qua non* when considering conditions which favor development: it is the need for peace. Perhaps more than any other single factor, war and violence bring about poverty and misery, and impede any hope of a better life. Sadly, in our day, warfare constantly targets cities, bringing about the destruction of buildings which offer shelter and serve as a place of employment. In rural areas, the widespread and often indiscriminate use of land mines renders land unusable for agricultural and other activities, and thus reduces the shelter of villages to places where the poor and hungry can simply try to stay covered from the elements. What is worse is that such weapons are frequently employed not for reasons of any military advantage or strategy, but simply as a means of terror. It is truly contradictory and scandalous for the world community to hold international meetings to discuss how to overcome poverty and misery, when at the same time various countries are producing and/or using the very weapons which contribute to such suffering.

The International Conference on Human Settlements which concluded its deliberations just four months ago was a very positive effort by the international community to address the shelter needs of the poor all over the world. But we know very well that it is possible to leave fine phrases and commitments as mere words written on paper. Housing is too important for that to be allowed to happen. The fulfillment of the commitments which were made in Istanbul will not only contribute to the lives of the poor, but they will also say much about those who are in a position to act. In the words of His Holiness Pope John Paul II, "Ensuring a suitable 'habitat' for everyone is demanded by the respect owed to every human being and, therefore, is a measure of civilization and the condition for a peaceful, fraternal society" (*Angelus Message*, 16 June 1996).

Chapter Ten

THE WORLD FOOD SUMMIT

Rome, Italy

13 - 17 November 1996

Chapter Contents

The World Food Summit
Rome, Italy;
13 - 17 November 1996

Address of His Holiness Pope John Paul II
   at the World Food Summit
   Rome, 13 November 1996 591

Intervention of His Eminence Angelo Cardinal Sodano
   Secretary of State of His Holiness,
   to the World Food Summit, FAO Headquarters
   Rome, Italy, 16 November 1996 595

      and Reservations and Statement of Interpretation of the Holy See
      to the Final Document adopted by the World Food Summit 598

Statement by His Excellency Archbishop Renato R. Martino,
   Apostolic Nuncio, Permanent Observer of the Holy See
   to the U.N., before the Second Committee of the General Assembly,
   on Item 97: "Sectoral Policy Questions, Food and
   Sustainable Agricultural Development"
   New York, 25 October 1996 599

See Appendix for the following related documents:

   Address of His Holiness Pope John Paul II
      at the Opening Session of the International Conference
      on Nutrition, sponsored by the Food and Agriculture
      Organization (FAO) and the World Health Organization
      (WHO); FAO Headquarters, Rome; 5 December 1992 855

   Address of His Holiness Pope John Paul II
      to Participants in the 28th Conference of the
      United Nations food and Agriculture Organization (FAO)
      Vatican, 23 October 1995 861

   Message of His Holiness Pope John Paul II
      to Mr. Jacques Diouf, Director-General of the Food
      and Agriculture Organization (FAO), for the
      Annual Observance of World Food Day
      12 October 1996 867

"World Hunger, A Challenge for All: Development in Solidarity",
  issued by the Pontifical Council "Cor Unum"
  Vatican, 4 October 1996 869

Statement by His Excellency Archbishop Renato R. Martino,
  Apostolic Nuncio, Permanent Observer of the Holy See
  to the U.N., before the Second Committee of the
  U.N. General Assembly, on Item 97:
  "Sectoral Policy Questions, Food and Sustainable
  Agricultural Development"
  New York, 25 October 1996 943

Statement by His Excellency Archbishop Renato R. Martino,
  Apostolic Nuncio, Permanent Observer of the Holy See
  to the U.N., at the UN/FAO Pledging Conference for the
  World Food Programme
  New York, 4 November 1996 946

ADDRESS OF
HIS HOLINESS POPE JOHN PAUL II
AT THE WORLD FOOD SUMMIT
ROME, 13 NOVEMBER 1996

(the original was delivered in French)

Mr. Director General,
Mr. Secretary General of the United Nations Organization,
Your Excellencies,
Ladies and Gentlemen,

1. I am particularly grateful to accept your kind invitation to speak to the Delegations of the 194 countries taking part in the World Food Summit. I thank you for your warm welcome. Sharing your concerns, I am anxious to acknowledge and encourage your efforts to come to the aid of those children, women, elderly people or families who are suffering from hunger or who are not properly nourished. To find an appropriate response to the tragic situations of many countries, you are responsible for studying the technical problems and proposing reasonable solutions.

2. In the analyses which have accompanied the work preparatory to your meeting, it is recalled that more than 800 million people still suffer from malnutrition and that it is often difficult to find quick solutions effectively to improve these tragic situations. Nevertheless, we must seek them together so that the starving and the opulent, the very poor and the very rich, those who lack the necessary means and others who lavishly waste them, no longer live side by side. Such contrasts between poverty and wealth are intolerable for humanity.

It is the task of nations, their leaders, their economic powers and all people of goodwill to seek every opportunity for a more equitable sharing of resources which are not lacking, and of consumer goods; by this sharing, all will express their sense of brotherhood. It requires "firm and persevering determination to commit oneself to the common good; that is to say to the good of all and of each individual, because we are all really responsible for all" (*Sollicitudo rei socialis*, n. 38). This outlook calls for a change of attitude and habits with regard to lifestyle and the relationship between resources and goods, as well as to increase awareness of others and their legitimate needs. It is to be hoped that your reflections will also introduce practical measures to combat food insecurity, which claims as victims too many of our brothers and sisters in humanity; for nothing will change at world level, if the leaders of nations do not put into practice the written Plan of Action you have drawn up to promote economic and food policies based not only on profit but also on sharing in solidarity.

3. As you have observed, demographic considerations alone cannot explain the poor distribution of food resources. We must abandon the sophism which consists in affirming that "if we are numerous, we are condemned to being poor." Man, by his intervention, can modify situations and respond to the increasing needs. Education guaranteed to everyone, equipment adapted to local realities, wise agricultural policies, equitable economic networks, can be so many factors which will produce positive effects in the long run. A numerous population can become a source of development for it involves the exchange of and demand for goods. This does not, of course, mean that demographic growth can be unlimited. In this area, each family has its own duties and responsibilities and State demographic policies must respect the dignity of human nature as well as the fundamental rights of individuals. To believe that any arbitrary stabilization of world population or even its reduction could directly solve the problem of hunger would nonetheless be an illusion: without young people's work, without the contribution of scientific research, without solidarity between peoples and generations, agricultural and nutritional resources would probably become less and less reliable and the poorest categories would remain below the poverty line and excluded from the economic circuit.

4. It should also be recognized that populations subjected to conditions of food insecurity are often restricted by political situations that prevent them from working and earning normally. Think, for example, of the countries ravaged by conflicts of all kinds or, sometimes, struggling beneath the stifling weight of an international debt, of refugees forced to leave their land and all too often deprived of help, of the peoples who are victims of embargos imposed without sufficient discernment. These situations require the practical application of peaceful means to settle controversies or differences which may arise, such as those proposed by the Plan of Action of the World Food Summit (cf. n. 14).

5. I am of course aware that among the most important long term

commitments are those concerning forms of investment in the agricultural and food sector. It seems essential here to make a comparison with the sums allocated for defense or the superfluous spending which is customary in the most developed countries. Urgent choices become necessary, both at national and international levels and at the level of the different communities and families, in order to identify significant ways of guaranteeing food security in the majority of countries. This is a peace factor which does not only consist in building up considerable food reserves, but especially in giving each individual and family the possibility of access to an adequate supply of food at all times.

6. Your intention is to make demanding commitments in these fields, especially as regards the economic and political dimension. You would like to find the most suitable measures to encourage local agricultural production and the protection of agricultural land, while safeguarding natural resources. The proposals contained in the Plan of Action aim, by political action and legal measures, at guaranteeing a just sharing of productive ownership, to promote the activities of agricultural and co-operative associations, and to protect market access for the benefit of rural populations. You have also drafted suggestions for international aid to the poorest countries and for a fair definition of the exchange rate and access to credit. All this will certainly be inadequate if efforts are not made to educate people to justice, solidarity and the love of all human beings who are their brothers and sisters. The elements contained in your different commitments could serve to boost good relations between peoples, by a constant exchange, a "real *culture of giving* which should make every country prepared to meet the needs of the less fortunate," as I said on the occasion of the 50th anniversary of the FAO, (cf. *Address*, 23 October 1995, n. 4; *L'Osservatore Romano* English edition, 1 November 1995, p. 7). Food security will be the fruit of decisions inspired by an ethic of solidarity, and not only the result of inter aid programmes.

7. In the Letter *Tertio millennio adveniente*, written in preparation for the Jubilee of the Year 2000, I proposed concrete initiatives of international solidarity. I felt it a duty to call for "reducing substantially, if not canceling outright, the international debt which seriously threatens the future of many nations" (n. 51). Last week, when I received the plenary assembly of the Pontifical Council for Justice and Peace, I reiterated the Church's esteem for some of the commitments made by the international community. I renew my encouragement here, for the measures taken to be followed up. For her part, the Church has decided to continue her efforts to enlighten those who have to make decisions with important consequences. In its recent document *World Hunger - A Challenge for All: Development In Solidarity*, the Pontifical Council "Cor Unum" expressed several proposals intended to foster a more equitable division of food resources which, thanks to God and human labour,

are not lacking today and will not be lacking in the future. Goodwill and generous policies must encourage human ingenuity, so that the vital needs of all can be met, also by virtue of the universal destination of the earth's resources.

8. Your Excellencies, Ladies and Gentlemen, you have understood; my encouragement is assured and the presence of an Observer Mission at the United Nations Food and Agriculture Organization should suffice to assure you of the interest with which the Holy See follows your work and your efforts to eliminate the spectre of hunger from the world. You know, besides, how many sons and daughters of the Catholic Church are present in numerous local organizations that are working to help the poorer countries improve their production and to discover on their own, "in full fidelity to their own proper genius, the means for their social and human progress" (Paul VI, *Populorum progressio*, n. 64).

I like to recall that the motto of the Organization which has welcomed us today is *"Fiat panis,"* and that it corresponds to the prayer dearest to all Christians, which Jesus himself taught them: "Give us this day our daily bread." Then let us work together without respite, so that everyone everywhere may have bread on his table to share. May God bless all those who produce it and are nourished by it!

INTERVENTION OF
HIS EMINENCE ANGELO CARDINAL SODANO
SECRETARY OF STATE OF HIS HOLINESS
TO THE WORLD FOOD SUMMIT
FAO HEADQUARTERS, ROME, 16 NOVEMBER 1996

AND

RESERVATIONS AND STATEMENT OF INTERPRETATION OF THE HOLY SEE TO THE FINAL DOCUMENT ADOPTED BY THE WORLD FOOD SUMMIT

Mr. President,
Mr. Director General,
Your Excellencies,
Ladies and Gentlemen:

My first duty is to thank you for the warm welcome which you gave to His Holiness Pope John Paul II in the opening ceremony of this World Summit!

He wished to renew to FAO the support of the Holy See and the whole Catholic Church for the noble initiatives which are being undertaken in order to guarantee food security for all the earth's inhabitants.

In fact, the existence of an Observer Mission of the Holy See to FAO, and the presence of a Special Delegation at this World Summit, demonstrates the enormous importance which the Holy See has always attributed to the activity of FAO, located here in the heart of old Rome in order to call all nations of the world to cooperate in such a vital area as that of Food and Agriculture.

We are all aware that what we are dealing with is a major problem of international cooperation. If millions of people are still marked by the damaging effects of hunger and malnutrition, the cause is not to be sought in lack of food.

Only last year, FAO acknowledged in its "Atlas of Food and Agriculture" that there is enough in the world to meet the energy needs of all, but unfortunately there is no uniformity in food production or distribution (cf. FAO, Dimension of Need and Resources, *Atlas of Food and Agriculture,* Rome 1995, p. 16). Our Organization had, in fact, already said this in the final Statement of the International Conference on Nutrition, held jointly with the World Health Organization (WHO) in 1992 (cf. *Final Report of the*

Conference, No. 1). What was said was that the earth's resources, taken globally, are capable of feeding all its inhabitants.

On the basis of these data, the Holy See maintains that the challenge of the present moment — to give food security to all the people on every continent — is not only an economic and technical challenge, but in the first place an ethical and spiritual one. It is a question of solidarity lived in the light of certain basic principles, which I would like to underline here briefly.

1) The *first principle* of our commitment to solidarity is respect for every human person. Whoever that person may be, he or she possesses inalienable rights. And for believers, every human person is created in the image and likeness of God himself. This is a teaching which can transform our whole vision of life, society and history.

2) The *second principle* is that of solidarity. If individual human beings possess their own inalienable dignity, when they need our help we are bound to give it to them. For us believers, this also constitutes a specific duty explicitly given to us by Christ. Throughout history, this principle has inspired the best moral and juridical traditions. Here in Italy, more than 800 years ago, the famous Decree of Gratian set down this rule: "Feed the man dying of hunger, because if you have not fed him you have killed him" (Distinction LXXXVI, c. 21).

3) A *third principle* inspiring our social activity is that of the universal destination of the goods of the earth. Consequently, whatever forms property may take, forms adapted to the legitimate institutions of the peoples, we hold that "attention must always be paid to the universal purpose for which created goods are meant. In using them, therefore, a man should regard his lawful possessions not merely as his own but also as common property in the sense that they should accrue to the benefit of not only himself but of others" (Second Vatican Council, *Gaudium et spes*, 69).

4) A *fourth principle* inspiring the Holy See's activity in the international sphere is the promotion of peace. Often people die of hunger because war is taking place where they live. The tragedy in Africa, in the region of the Great Lakes, clearly reminds us that the plague of poverty and hunger can be eliminated only if peace is restored between peoples.

Ladies and Gentlemen,

I have briefly spelled out the solidarity from which the Holy See seeks to draw inspiration in its desire to work with all Governments, with International Organizations and in particular with FAO, in order to eradicate from the world the scourge of hunger and to give everyone the possibility of having his daily bread.

It is for this reason that the Holy See joins the other Nations which have manifested their assent to the final Documents of the Summit. However, in view of its particular nature and mission, the Holy See would like to present certain Reservations and its own Interpretative Statement, and requests that they be included in the Final Report of this Summit.

Thank you.

(Reservations and Statement of Interpretation follow.)

Reservations and Statement of Interpretation of the Holy See to the Final Document Adopted by the World Food Summit

The Holy See joins the consensus on the final Documents of the World Food Summit (Rome, 13-17 November 1996) in conformity with its nature and mission and, with reference to paragraph 12 of the "World Food Summit Plan of Action," wishes to express its understanding of some concepts and terms used in the said Documents.

1. The Holy See reiterates its Reservations concerning the interpretation to be given to the term "reproductive health services" expressed in the Report of the International Conference on Population and Development (Cairo, 5-13 September 1994).

2. The Holy See reasserts that the stabilization of the world's population must not be achieved by national or international measures which deny the right of spouses to decide on procreation and the spacing of births.

3. With reference to the terms "family planning" and "family planning services," the consensus of the Holy See should in no way be interpreted as constituting a change in its well-known position concerning those family planning methods which the Catholic Church considers morally unacceptable, or concerning family planning services that do not respect the freedom of spouses, the human dignity or the human rights of those concerned.

4. The Holy See understands the use of the term "gender" in these Documents according to its Statement of Interpretation which was included in the Report of the Fourth World Conference on Women (Beijing, 4-15 September 1995).

5. With regard to all references to international agreements, declarations, resolutions and instruments mentioned in the Documents of the Summit, the Holy See reserves its position in a manner consistent with its formal acceptance or non-acceptance of them or of any expression found in them, in their related mechanisms or procedures of control and with any Reservations it may have expressed.

6. The Holy See requests that these Reservations and Statement of Interpretation be included integrally in the definitive Report of the World Food Summit.

STATEMENT BY
HIS EXCELLENCY ARCHBISHOP RENATO R. MARTINO
APOSTOLIC NUNCIO, PERMANENT OBSERVER OF THE HOLY SEE
TO THE UNITED NATIONS
BEFORE THE SECOND COMMITTEE OF THE
51ST SESSION OF THE GENERAL ASSEMBLY, ON ITEM 97:
"SECTORAL POLICY QUESTIONS, FOOD AND SUSTAINABLE
AGRICULTURAL DEVELOPMENT"
NEW YORK, 25 OCTOBER 1996

Mr. Chairman,

The topic of our consideration, "Food and Sustainable Agricultural Development," is obviously of primary importance. It is literally a matter of life and death. For this reason, during his *Address to the United Nations General Assembly* in 1979, His Holiness Pope John Paul II stated: "Permit me to enumerate some of the most important human rights that are universally recognized: the right to life, liberty and security of person; the right to food, clothing, housing, sufficient health care, rest and leisure; the right to freedom of expression, education and culture . . . " The fundamental importance of food as an essential component of the human right to an adequate standard of living has also been unequivocally asserted by the international community, most notably in the *Universal Declaration of Human Rights*, (N. 25), the *Universal Declaration on the Eradication of Hunger and Malnutrition* of 1974 (N.1), and the *World Declaration on Nutrition* of 1992. My Delegation strongly hopes that the right to food will be enshrined once more in the Document to be approved by the coming World Food Summit to be held in Rome in mid-November.

As the right to have enough to eat is fundamental and inalienable for every person and for their family, the international community and national governments have the obligation to see that everyone does indeed have sufficient food. For this reason, solutions which bring only temporary or occasional relief to the hunger suffered by our fellow human beings — especially by women and by girl children — are not satisfactory for the human family. Moreover, no one is exempt from the duty of providing such immediate aid, especially when food producing countries have at their disposal an abundance of goods.

In order to respond to this pressing need, there is much talk and reflection about how to achieve "food security" for all. Such a concept must be based in a desire for deeper solutions which flow from a profound solidarity among all people, rich and poor; citizens of countries which are developed and of those which are on their way to development. Food security must stress components such as: the production of a sufficient amount of food, a stable supply throughout the year, access to food for all, a proper and equitable distribution, and a commitment to producing the components of a balanced and healthy diet in keeping with the local nutritional practices.

Concrete efforts must be made to bring about true agrarian reform. In some countries, for example, 1% of the population controls 50% of the land. A more equitable distribution of land, with the consequent increase in participation in food production, especially by the poor, is an important component of any such solution. In this regard the right of women to have access to land must also be strongly reaffirmed.

Accompanying such a change must be a commitment to offer proper training and education, especially to small farmers, so that they can learn to maximize the results of their labors. Such training should stress sustainable agricultural practices which are suited to local realities and cultures.

On a global scale, sustainable agricultural development must be fostered by encouraging study and development of crops which produce a high yield. It is particularly important that, wherever possible, results of such development be made available to parts of the world where agricultural production is deficient. In addition, economic policies which result in an inadequate distribution of the already existing food which is sufficient to feed the world's population cannot be allowed to continue.

If the world is to have sustainable agriculture, the international community must acknowledge that peace is a prior and fundamental condition. Wars not only bring about poverty, they also breed famine by forcing massive displacements of peoples and render land either unsafe or unsuitable for growing food. Once again, the Holy See wishes to stress the urgent need for the cessation of the production, sale, stockpiling, export and use of land mines. How many people throughout the world are hungry precisely because they fear to use the land at their disposition, or because land mines have killed or maimed for life those who were being counted on to be the breadwinner of a family?

As we consider the conditions for food security and sustainable agriculture, we must admit that in our day there exist what Pope John Paul has called "structures of famine" (*Address to the Participants in the 28th Conference of the FAO*, 23 October 1995). These can be overcome only with an attitude of solidarity touching on every aspect of development: formation and use of capital, investments, surpluses, production, and distribution systems. Each phase has an underlying moral and ethical dimension. Indeed economic policies themselves cannot be separated from ethical considerations. As His Holiness has stated, "Individuals and whole peoples will be finally judged by history in relation to how they actually fulfill their obligation to contribute to the good of their fellow human beings. ... It is to be hoped that everyone — individuals, groups, private undertakings and public bodies — will take proper care of the most needy, beginning with the basic right to satisfy one's own hunger." (*Homily during the Mass at St. Peter's Basilica* to commemorate the fortieth anniversary of the FAO, 10 November 1985).

I would like to inform this Committee that just yesterday, the Holy See published a Document entitled, *"World Hunger - A Challenge for All: Development in Solidarity."* This serves as a more complete and articulated contribution of the Holy See to the discussion surrounding the scandal of hunger in a world which has the means to feed every person.

I would conclude by citing the *Message* of Pope John Paul to the Director General of the FAO on the occasion of World Food Day 1996. He stated, "Recent experience has also heightened humanity's awareness that technical solutions, however elaborate, are not effective if they lack the necessary reference to the central importance of the human person — the beginning and end of the inalienable rights of every individual, community and people. Among these rights there emerges the fundamental right to nutrition, but the actual putting into practice of this right cannot be seen merely as a goal to be striven for. This right, in fact, must inspire action aimed at promoting a life consistent with the demands of human dignity and free from those external constraints which, under any form, can limit freedom of choice and even compromise the survival of individuals, families and civil communities."

APPENDIX

APPENDIX

World Summit for Children; New York, USA
Letter of His Holiness Pope John Paul II to Children
in the Year of the Family, 13 December 1994 609

U.N. Conference on Environment and Development; Rio de Janeiro, Brazil
"Ecology and Population: Birth Rate Does Not Create
Greatest Drain on Resources," by
His Excellency Bishop James T. McHugh, STD,
Bishop of Camden, (from *L'Osservatore Romano*, English ed.,
n.35, 2 September 1992, p.2) 617

Intervention of His Excellency Archbishop Jean-Louis Tauran
Secretary for Relations with States, at the 19th Special Session
of the General Assembly of the United Nations; "Rio+5"
New York, 27 June 1997 621

International Conference on Population and Development; Cairo, Egypt
Letter of His Holiness Pope John Paul II to Families
"1994 – Year of the Family"
Vatican, 2 February 1994 623

Address of His Holiness Pope John Paul II
to a Gathering of Families from Around the World
Attending the World Meeting with Families
St. Peter's Square, 8 October 1994 687

Address *(excerpts)* of His Holiness Pope John Paul II to
Members of the Diplomatic Corps Accredited
to the Holy See; Vatican, 9 January 1995 693

"Charter of the Rights of the Family"
presented by the Holy See to all Persons,
Institutions and Authorities concerned with the
Mission of the Family in Today's World
Vatican, 22 October 1983 697

"Ethical and Pastoral Dimensions of Population Trends"
issued by the Pontifical Council for the Family
Vatican, 25 March 1994 711

Declaration of the Pontifical Academy for Life
issued by the Executive Board at their First Meeting
Vatican, 19 June 1994 755

Address of His Eminence Alfonso Cardinal López Trujillo,
  President of the Pontifical Council for the Family, at the
  Press Conference presenting the Proceedings of a
  Study Conference on Natural Family Planning Methods
  Vatican, 7 July 1994 757

Statement by His Eminence Alfonso Cardinal López Trujillo,
  President of the Pontifical Council for the Family,
  to the United Nations General Assembly, on the Occasion of
  the International Conference on Families
  New York, 19 October 1994 764

Report of His Eminence Alfonso Cardinal López Trujillo,
  President of the Pontifical Council for the Family, to the
  Twenty-Seventh General Congregation of the Synod
  of Bishops, on the Year of the Family and the
  Cairo Conference; Vatican, 28 October 1994 768

Selected Statements by Bishops' Conferences, Pro-Life Leaders
  and Organizations regarding the International Conference on
  Population and Development: 780

  - Letter of the Latin American Episcopal Council (CELAM)
      to Mrs. Nafis Sadik; 14 March 1994 780

  - Letter on behalf of the African Bishops,
      to Secretary-General Boutros Boutros-Ghali
      Rome, 23 April 1994 785

  - United States Cardinals and Conference President's
      Letter to President William Clinton
      29 May 1994 787

  - Statement by the United States Bishops at their
      June 1994 Meeting 790

  - European Bishops Declaration (President and Vice-
      Presidents of the Council of European
      Episcopal Conferences); 4 June 1994 793

  - Message of the Presidents of the Latin American Bishops'
      Conferences to the Leaders of the Region,
      Santo Domingo; 18 June 1994 795

  - European Bishops Issue Final Declaration
      4-5 July 1994 802

  - Canadian Bishops' Conference on Cairo Conference
      Letter to Prime Minister Jean Chrétien, 18 July 1994 .. 805

- German Bishops' Statement, 4 August 1994 806

- European Pro-Life Leaders Issue Declaration
    8-9 July 1994 807

- Knights of Columbus Statement, 13 September 1994 809

Speech by Mr. John M. Klink,
    Advisor, Permanent Observer Mission of the Holy See
    to the United Nations, to the organization
    "Women Affirming Life"; Washington, D.C.
    24 September 1994 811

Fourth World Conference on Women; Beijing, China

Message of His Holiness Pope John Paul II
    for the celebration of the World Day of Peace,
    "Women: Teachers of Peace"
    Vatican, 1 January 1995 821

Letter of His Holiness Pope John Paul II to Women
    Vatican, 29 June 1995 829

Message of His Holiness Pope John Paul II for
    World Migration Day
    Vatican, 10 August 1995 839

Message of Pope John Paul II for the 30th World
    Communications Day — "The Media: Modern Forum
    for Promoting the Role of Women in Society"
    24 January 1996 845

Statements regarding "Catholic for a Free Choice" 849
    - United States Catholic Conference Press Release
        Washington, D.C., 16 March 1995 849
        (two attachments):
        a) Statement by His Eminence William Cardinal Keeler
            NCCB/USCC President, Washington, D.C.
            16 March 1995 850
        b) Statement by the Administrative Committee of the
            National Conference of Catholic Bishops,
            Washington, D.C., 4 November 1993 851
    - Holy See Mission Press Release
        "Holy See Delegation Questions Accreditation of
        'Catholics for a Free Choice'"
        New York, 17 March 1995 853

- Holy See Mission Press Release
"Holy See Delegation Challenges NGO Accreditation
of 'Catholics for a Free Choice' to United Nations
Women's Conference"
New York, 21 March 1995 854

World Food Summit; Rome, Italy
Address of His Holiness Pope John Paul II
at the Opening Session of the International Conference
on Nutrition, sponsored by the Food and Agriculture
Organization (FAO) and the World Health Organization
(WHO); FAO Headquarters, Rome; 5 December 1992 855

Address of His Holiness Pope John Paul II
to Participants in the 28th Conference of the
United Nations Food and Agriculture Organization (FAO)
Vatican, 23 October 1995 861

Message of His Holiness Pope John Paul II
to Mr. Jacques Diouf, Director-General of the Food
and Agriculture Organization (FAO), for the
Annual Observance of World Food Day
12 October 1996 867

"World Hunger, A Challenge for All: Development in Solidarity,"
issued by the Pontifical Council "Cor Unum"
Vatican, 4 October 1996 869

Statement by His Excellency Archbishop Renato R. Martino,
Apostolic Nuncio, Permanent Observer of the Holy See
to the U.N., before the Second Committee of the
U.N. General Assembly, on Item 97:
"Sectoral Policy Questions, Food and Sustainable
Agricultural Development"
New York, 25 October 1996 943

Statement by His Excellency Archbishop Renato R. Martino,
Apostolic Nuncio, Permanent Observer of the Holy See
to the U.N., at the UN/FAO Pledging Conference for the
World Food Programme
New York, 4 November 1996 946

LETTER OF
HIS HOLINESS POPE JOHN PAUL II
TO CHILDREN
IN THE YEAR OF THE FAMILY

Dear Children,

Jesus is born

In a few days we shall celebrate Christmas, the holy day which is so full of meaning for all children in every family. This year it will be even more so, because this is the *Year of the Family*. Before the Year of the Family ends, I want to write to you, the children of the whole world, and to share with you in the joy of this happy time of year.

Christmas is the feast day of a Child, of a Newborn Baby. So it is your feast day too! You wait impatiently for it and get ready for it with joy, counting the days and even the hours to the Holy Night of Bethlehem.

I can almost see you: you are setting up the Crib at home, in the parish, in every corner of the world, recreating the surroundings and the atmosphere in which the Saviour was born. Yes, it is true! At Christmastime, the stable and the manger take centre place in the Church. And everyone hurries to go there, to make a spiritual pilgrimage, like the shepherds on the night of Jesus' birth. Later, it will be the Magi arriving from the distant East, following the star, to the place where the Redeemer of the universe lay.

You too, during the days of Christmas, visit the Cribs, stopping to look at the Child lying in the hay. You look at his Mother and you look at Saint Joseph, the Redeemer's guardian. As you look at the *Holy Family,* you think of your own family, the family in which you came into the world. You think of your mother, who gave you birth, and of your father. Both of them provide for the family and for your upbringing. For it is the parents' duty not only to have children but to bring them up from the moment of their birth.

Dear children, as I write to you I am thinking of when many years ago I was a child like you. I, too, used to experience the peaceful feelings of Christmas, and when the star of Bethlehem shone, I would hurry to the Crib together with the other boys and girls to relive what happened 2,000 years ago in Palestine. We children expressed our joy mostly in song. How beautiful and moving are the Christmas carols which in the tradition of every people are sung around the Crib! What deep thoughts they contain, and above all what joy and tenderness they express about the Divine Child who came into the world that Holy Night!

The days which follow the birth of Jesus are also feast days: so *eight days afterwards,* according to the Old Testament tradition, the Child was given a name: he was called *Jesus. After forty days,* we commemorate his presentation in the Temple, like every other first-born son of Israel. On that occasion, an extraordinary meeting took place: Mary, when she arrived in the Temple with the Child, was met by the old man Simeon, who took the Baby Jesus in his arms and spoke these prophetic words: "Lord, now let your servant depart in peace, according to your word; for my eyes have seen your salvation which you have prepared in the presence of all peoples, a light for revelation to the Gentiles, and for glory to your people Israel" (*Lk* 2:29-32). Then, speaking to his Mother Mary, he added: "Behold, this child is set for the fall and rising of many in Israel, and for a sign that is spoken against (and a sword will pierce through your own soul also), that thoughts out of many hearts may be revealed" (*Lk* 2:34-35). So already in the very first days of Jesus' life we heard the foretelling of the Passion, which will one day include his Mother Mary, too: on Good Friday she will stand silently by the Cross of her Son. Also, not much time will pass after his birth before the Baby Jesus finds himself facing a grave danger: the cruel king Herod will order all the children under the age of two years to be killed, and for this reason Jesus will be forced to flee with his parents into Egypt.

You certainly know all about these events connected with the birth of Jesus. They are told to you by your parents, and by priests, teachers and catechists, and each year you relive them spiritually at Christmas time together with the whole Church. So you know about these dramatic aspects of Jesus infancy.

Dear friends! In what happened to the Child of Bethlehem you can *recognize what happens to children throughout the world.* It is true that a child represents the joy not only of its parents but also the joy of the Church and the whole of society. But it is also true that in our days, unfortunately, many children in different parts of the world are suffering and being threatened: they are hungry and poor, they are dying from diseases and malnutrition, they are the victims of war, they are abandoned by their parents and condemned to remain without a home, without the warmth of a family of their own, they suffer many forms of violence and arrogance from grown-ups. How can we not care, when we see the suffering of so many children, especially when this suffering is in some way caused by grown-ups?

Jesus brings the truth

The Child whom we see in the manger at Christmas grew up as the years passed. When he was *twelve years old,* as you know, he went for the first time with Mary and Joseph from Nazareth to Jerusalem for the Feast of the Passover. There, in the crowds of pilgrims, he was separated from his parents and, with other boys and girls of his own age, he stopped to listen to the teachers in the Temple, for a sort of "catechism lesson." The holidays were good opportunities for handing on the faith to children who were about the same age as Jesus. But on this occasion it happened that this extraordinary boy who had come from Nazareth not only asked very intelligent questions but also started to give profound answers to those who were teaching him. The questions and even more the answers astonished the Temple teachers. It was the same amazement which later on would mark Jesus' public preaching. The episode in the Temple of Jerusalem was simply the beginning and a kind of foreshadowing of what would happen some years later.

Dear boys and girls who are the same age as the twelve-year-old Jesus, are you not reminded now of *the religion lessons* in the parish and at school, lessons which you are invited to take part in? So I would like to ask you some questions: What do you think of your religion lessons? Do you become involved like the twelve-year-old Jesus in the Temple? Do you regularly go to these lessons at school and in the parish? Do your parents help you to do so?

The twelve-year-old Jesus became so interested in the religion lesson in the Temple of Jerusalem that, in a sense, he even forgot about his own parents. Mary and Joseph, having started off on the journey back to Nazareth with other pilgrims, soon realized that Jesus was not with them. They searched hard for him. They went back and only on the third day did they find him in Jerusalem, in the Temple. "Son, why have you treated us so? Behold, your father and I have been looking for you anxiously" (*Lk* 2:48). How strange is Jesus' answer and how it makes us stop and think! "How is it that you sought me? Did you not know that I must be in my Father's house?" (*Lk* 2:49). It was an answer difficult to accept. The evangelist Luke simply adds that Mary "kept all these things in her heart" (2:51). In fact, it was an answer which would be understood only later, when Jesus, as a grown-up, began to preach and say that for his Heavenly Father he was ready to face any sufferings and even death on the cross.

From Jerusalem Jesus went back with Mary and Joseph to Nazareth where he was obedient to them (cf. *Lk* 2:51). Regarding this period, before his public preaching began, the Gospel notes only that he "increased in wisdom and in stature, and in favour with God and man" (*Lk* 2:52).

Dear children, in the Child whom you look at in the Crib you must try to see also the twelve-year-old boy in the Temple in Jerusalem, talking with the teachers. He is the same grown man who later, at thirty years old, will begin to preach the word of God, will choose the Twelve Apostles, will be followed by crowds thirsting for the truth. At every step he will confirm his extraordinary teaching with signs of divine power: he will give sight to the blind, heal the sick, even raise the dead. And among the dead whom he will bring back to life there will be the twelve-year-old daughter of Jairus, and the son of the widow of Naim, given back alive to his weeping mother.

It is really true: this Child, now just born, once he is grown up, as Teacher of divine Truth, *will show an extraordinary love for children.* He will say to the Apostles: "Let the children come to me, do not hinder them," and he will add: "for to such belongs the kingdom of God" (*Mk* 10:14). Another time, as the Apostles are arguing about who is the greatest, he will put a child in front of them and say: "Unless you turn and become like children, you will never enter the kingdom of heaven" (*Mt* 18:3). On that occasion, he also spoke harsh words of warning: "Whoever causes one of these little ones who believes in me to sin, it would be better for him to have a great millstone fastened round his neck and to be drowned in the depth of the sea" (*Mt* 18:6).

How *important children are in the eyes of Jesus!* We could even say that *the Gospel is full of the truth about children.* The whole of the Gospel could actually be read as the "Gospel of children."

What does it mean that "unless you turn and become like children, you will not enter the kingdom of heaven?" *Is not Jesus pointing to children as models* even for grown-ups? In children there is something that must never be missing in people who want to enter the kingdom of heaven. People who are destined to go to heaven are simple like children, and like children are full of trust, rich in goodness and pure. Only people of this sort can find in God a Father and, thanks to Jesus, can become in their own turn children of God.

Is not this the main message of Christmas? We read in Saint John: "And the Word became flesh and dwelt among us" (*Jn* 1:14); and again: "To all who received him, who believed in his name, he gave power to *become children of God*" (*Jn* 1:12). Children of God! You, dear children, are sons and daughters of your parents. God wants us all to become his adopted children by grace. Here we have the real reason for Christmas joy, the joy I am writing to you about at the end of this Year of the Family. *Be happy in this "Gospel of divine sonship."* In this joy I hope that the coming Christmas holidays will bear abundant fruit in this Year of the Family.

Jesus gives himself

Dear friends, there is no doubt that an unforgettable meeting with Jesus is *First Holy Communion,* a day to be remembered as one of life's most beautiful. The Eucharist, instituted by Christ at the Last Supper, on the night before his Passion, is a Sacrament of the New Covenant, rather, the greatest of the Sacraments. In this Sacrament, the Lord becomes food for the soul under the appearances of bread and wine. Children receive this Sacrament solemnly a first time in First Holy Communion — and are encouraged to receive it afterwards as often as possible in order to remain in close friendship with Jesus.

To be able to receive Holy Communion, as you know, it is necessary to have received *Baptism:* this is the first of the Sacraments and the one most necessary for salvation. Baptism is a great event! In the Church's first centuries, when Baptism was received mostly by grown-ups, the ceremony ended with receiving the Eucharist, and was as solemn as First Holy Communion is today. Later on, when Baptism began to be given mainly to newborn babies — and this is the case of many of you, dear children, so that in fact you do not remember the day of your Baptism — the more solemn celebration was transferred to the moment of First Holy Communion. Every boy and every girl belonging to a Catholic family knows all about this custom: First Holy Communion *is a great family celebration.* On that day, together with the one who is making his or her First Holy Communion, the parents, brothers, sisters, relatives, godparents, and sometimes also the instructors and teachers, generally receive the Eucharist.

The day of First Holy Communion is also *a great day of celebration in the parish.* I remember as though it were yesterday when, together with the other boys and girls of my own age, I received the Eucharist for the first time in the parish church of my town. This event is usually commemorated in a family photo, so that it will not be forgotten. Photos like these generally remain with a person all through his or her life. As time goes by, people take out these pictures and experience once more the emotions of those moments; they return to the purity and joy experienced in that meeting with Jesus, the One who out of love became the Redeemer of man.

For how many children in the history of the Church has the Eucharist been a source of spiritual strength, sometimes even heroic strength! How can we fail to *be reminded,* for example, *of holy boys and girls* who lived in the first centuries and are still known and venerated throughout the Church? Saint Agnes, who lived in Rome; Saint Agatha, who was martyred in Sicily; Saint Tarcisius, a boy who is rightly called the "martyr of the Eucharist" because he preferred to die rather than give up Jesus, whom he was carrying under the appearance of bread.

And so down the centuries, up to our own times, *there are many boys and girls among those declared by the Church to be saints or blessed.* Just as Jesus in the Gospel shows special trust in children, so his Mother Mary, in the course of history, has not failed to show *her motherly care for the little ones.* Think of Saint Bernadette of Lourdes, the children of La Salette and, in our own century Lucia, Francisco and Jacinta of Fatima.

Earlier I was speaking to you about the "Gospel of children": has this not found in our own time a particular expression in the spirituality of Saint Theresa of the Child Jesus? It is absolutely true: Jesus and his Mother often choose children and give them important tasks for the life of the Church and of humanity. I have named only a few who are known everywhere, but how many others there are who are less widely known! The Redeemer of humanity seems *to share with them his concern for others:* for parents, for other boys and girls. He eagerly awaits their prayers. *What enormous power the prayer of children has!* This becomes a *model for grown-ups themselves:* praying with simple and complete trust means praying as children pray.

And here I come to an important point in this Letter: at the end of this Year of the Family, dear young friends, it is to your prayers that I want to entrust the problems of your own families and of all the families in the world. And not only this: I also have other intentions to ask you to pray for. *The Pope counts very much on your prayers.* We must pray together and pray hard, that humanity, made up of billions of human beings, may become more and more the family of God and able to live in peace. At the beginning of this Letter I mentioned the unspeakable suffering which many children have experienced in this century, and which many of them are continuing to endure at this very moment. How many of them, even in these days, are becoming victims of the hatred which is raging in different parts of the world:

in the Balkans, for example, and in some African countries. It was while I was thinking about these facts, which fill our hearts with pain, that I decided to ask you, dear boys and girls, to take upon yourselves the duty of *praying for peace*. You know this well: *love and harmony build peace, hatred and violence destroy it*. You instinctively turn away from hatred and are attracted by love: for this reason the Pope is certain that you will not refuse his request, but that you will join in his prayer for peace in the world with the same enthusiasm with which you pray for peace and harmony in your own families.

Praise the name of the Lord!

At the end of this Letter, dear boys and girls, let me recall the words of a Psalm which have always moved me: *Laudate pueri Dominum!* Praise, O children of the Lord, praise the name of the Lord! Blessed be the name of the Lord from this time forth and for evermore! From the rising of the sun to its setting may the name of the Lord be praised! (cf. *Ps.* 112/113:1-3). As I meditate on the words of this Psalm, the faces of all the world's children pass before my eyes: from the East to the West, from the North to the South. It is to you, young friends, without distinction of language, race or nationality, that I say: *Praise the name of the Lord!*

And since people must praise God first of all with their own lives, do not forget what the twelve-year-old Jesus said to his Mother and to Joseph in the Temple in Jerusalem: "Did you not know that I must be in my Father's house?" (*Lk* 2:49). People praise God *by following the voice of their own calling*.

God calls every person, and his voice makes itself heard even in the hearts of children: he calls people to live in marriage or to be priests; he calls them to the consecrated life or perhaps to work on the missions... Who can say? Pray, dear boys and girls, that you will find out what your calling is, and that you will then follow it generously.

Praise the name of the Lord! The children of every continent, on the night of Bethlehem, look with faith upon the newborn Child and experience the great joy of Christmas. They sing in their own languages, praising the name of the Lord. The touching melodies of Christmas spread throughout the earth. They are tender and moving words which are heard in every human language; it is like a festive song rising from all the earth, which blends with the song of the Angels, the messengers of the glory of God, above the stable in Bethlehem: "Glory to God in the highest, and on earth peace among men with whom he is pleased!" (*Lk* 2:14). The highly favoured

Son of God becomes present among us as a newborn baby; gathered around him, the children of every nation on earth feel his eyes upon them, eyes full of the Heavenly Father's love, and they rejoice because God loves them. People cannot live without love. They are called to love God and their neighbour, but in order to love properly they must be certain that God loves them.

God loves you, dear children! This is what I want to tell you at the end of the Year of the Family and on the occasion of these Christmas feast days, which in a special way are your feast days.

I hope that they will be joyful and peaceful for you; I hope that during them you will have a more intense experience of the love of your parents, of your brothers and sisters, and of the other members of your family. This love must then spread to your whole community, even to the whole world, precisely through you, dear children. Love will then be able to reach those who are most in need of it, especially the suffering and the abandoned. What joy is greater than the joy brought by love? What joy is greater than the joy which you, O Jesus, bring at Christmas to people's hearts, and especially to the hearts of children?

Raise your tiny hand, Divine Child,
and bless these young friends of yours,
bless the children of all the earth.

From the Vatican, 13 December 1994.

"ECOLOGY AND POPULATION: BIRTH RATE DOES NOT CREATE GREATEST DRAIN ON RESOURCES" BY HIS EXCELLENCY BISHOP JAMES T. MCHUGH, STD BISHOP OF CAMDEN, NEW JERSEY, USA

(from L'Osservatore Romano, English edition, N.35, 2 September 1992, p.2)

The relation of population growth or decline to environmental concerns is complex and tenuous. Some claim that population growth constitutes a serious threat to the environment.

Concerns about the relationship of environmental problems to population emerged at the 1974 United Nations World Population Conference in Bucharest, Romania, and again in 1984 in Mexico City, Mexico.

There is widespread consensus that population issues and environmental concerns should always be considered in the overall context of socio-economic development. Both global and national development policies must take into account the implications of population growth and distribution, as well as the threats to the global environment from warfare, industrialization and urbanization. The U.N. Conference on Environment and Development has created renewed interest in the interaction between population, development and the environment, but there is little certainty as to how these factors interrelate or what can be done to avoid imbalances. In addressing this question it is important to begin with a review of the present population situation.

Analyses and forecasts of world population trends have changed continually during the past twenty years, and our knowledge of the causes of past trends and events has developed slowly. According to the most recent United Nations population reports the total population of the world was 5.3 billion persons at mid-year 1990. The rate of world population growth was 1.7 percent. It is projected that the rate will remain at 1.7 percent per year until 1995, after which it will resume its downward trend. The actual size of the world population is projected to be 6.3 billion persons in 2000 and 8.5 billion in 2025.

Since World War II, world population increased rapidly between 1950 - 1970. In the 1970s there was a sharp decline in the population growth rate, and from 1970 on a relatively constant growth rate. A new phase of the world's demographic history is expected to begin in 1995, issuing in a rapid decrease in the population growth rate. Note that population growth rates and trends differ considerably between the more developed and less developed regions and also among the major areas within these regions. Most developed nations face the problem of seriously declining growth rates and ageing populations. In most of Africa, Latin America and Asia, growth rates have begun to decline and the problem of rapid population growth exists now in only a small number of countries, mostly in sub-Saharan Africa and parts of Asia. The increase in world growth rates from 1950 to 1970 was due primarily to a decrease in mortality, not to an absence of birth control.

Increased life expectancy adds to population numbers

In regard to mortality, life expectancy at birth has increased steadily, but there are still wide divergences between the more developed and less developed nations. The latest projections see that divergence narrowing by 2020 - 2025. Mortality rates and trends vary according to regions and even within regions.

In summary, then, according to our most reliable estimates, at the global level rates of population growth have declined and population growth is neither rapid nor excessive. In the developed nations birth rates are generally at or below replacement level with low mortality and an ageing population. In developing nations birth rates are generally in decline and mortality rates are decreasing. In a small number of nations, mostly in sub-Saharan Africa and Western Asia, population growth is high and the development process has failed to take hold or is at a standstill. While population growth may be a contributing factor, it is difficult to show a definite causal link between population growth and environmental damage because of many other factors. For instance, in many poorer countries there is often lower overall consumption and the lower levels of development are traceable to the lack of economic and political infrastructures.

However, there are some patterns that merit attention. In most countries migration to cities has created great concentrations of population in these urban centres. Above and beyond the need for housing, education, health care and employment, the concentrations also put pressure on water supplies. The large industrial and technological complexes often contribute to atmospheric pollution by releasing gasses into the atmosphere that endanger the ozone layer. The concentration of gasses and the systematic destruction of forests can lead to greater problems, possibly affecting global climates.

It is also claimed that population growth will lead inevitably to soil erosion, desertification and deforestation. Such claims are part of the outmoded forecasting now rejected by population specialists as simplistic and often erroneous. Desertification is often the result of a complex mixture of factors — some due to human behaviour, some to climatic conditions. For instance, in Africa the livestock population increased from 295 million in 1950 to 521 million in 1983. Unquestionably this puts pressure on the land where the animals graze. But the growth of the animal population is partly attributable to cultural attitudes that see animals as sacred and not to be killed. Deforestation occurs because developing countries rely heavily on wood for fuel and because in some cases unregulated commercial logging has destroyed forests and woodlands. Population growth is not the major factor. As environmentalist Barry Commoner has noted: "in sum, the data both from an industrial country like the United States and from developing countries show that the largest influence on pollution levels is the pollution-generating tendency of the system of industrial and agricultural production, and the transportation and power systems. In all countries, the environmental impact of the technology factor is significantly greater than the influence of population size or of affluence." In fact, many of the dangers can be eliminated by more efficient pollution control technology and standards and by more careful conservation and protection of forest areas.

We have also learned that consumption patterns have a far more disastrous impact on the ecological balance than population growth alone. As a recent U.N. report states, "with barely 25 percent of the world's population, developed countries consume 75 percent of all energy used, 79 percent of all commercial fuels, 85 percent of all wood products, and 72 percent of all steel produced." Developed nations, with much smaller populations, also control the major portion of the world's wealth and financial investments and have become accustomed to a lifestyle of competition, consumption and waste that endangers resources and pollutes land and water areas.

The relationship of population growth to the environment also takes into consideration the impact on natural resources. Most resources are limited, even if plentiful or renewable. Unrestrained use endangers the supply and drives up the cost when there are shortages, which often creates inequities. But many of the resources once thought to be in dangerously short supply have been protected by conservation or recycling or by substitution of new materials, as for instance, the replacement of copper wire with fiber optics and the use of satellites to replace cables.

Will population limits solve environmental problems?

This brings us to the critical question. Is population limitation the only — or even the principal — way to safeguard the environment? The answer, in the minds of many scholars, is negative. Commoner argues that the assault on the environment cannot be contained or controlled, but must be prevented. Prevention involves redesigning the major industrial, agricultural, energy and transportation systems, realizing that such transformation may be costly in the short term. Commoner also argues that the costs will be greater on the developing countries and that the developed countries should help finance the transformation for those nations.

Whether or not that happens, the developing nations continually call on the developed world to share the new technologies that will ensure development and protect the global environment. That means favourable means of financing such ventures and some relief of external debt to free up needed capital. There is no simple or easy solution to these problems.

In conclusion, then, the argument has been made that unlimited population growth endangers a world of finite resources and destroys the fragile ecosystem, and thus, population growth must be restricted. But no one argues for absolutely unlimited population growth and moreover, as we have seen, present patterns of population growth alone are not the sole or primary cause of environmental problems. Nonetheless, with our present information base deficient and often uncertain, it is important to establish policies and strategies that protect the common good, that is, natural resources and the ecosystem both in the present and for succeeding generations. Such policies include restrictions on use and eventual replacement of the systems that pollute or endanger the global environment and a change in the patterns of human behaviour that destroy or waste precious resources. It becomes clear that the new solidarity called for by Pope John Paul II is absolutely necessary for the global management of the world's environmental problems. It is not simply a matter of counting heads and proclaiming that there are too many people. Rather it is a matter of adjusting our lifestyles and global strategies to protect, enhance and sustain human life as well as the global ecosystem.

INTERVENTION OF
HIS EXCELLENCY ARCHBISHOP JEAN-LOUIS TAURAN
SECRETARY FOR RELATIONS WITH STATES
AT THE 19TH SPECIAL SESSION OF THE GENERAL ASSEMBLY
OF THE UNITED NATIONS
"RIO + 5"
NEW YORK, 27 JUNE 1997

Mr. President,

Those who have spoken during these last days have proven the extent to which the concept of an environment worthy of human beings, as well as that of sustainable development, both of which were elaborated at the Rio Summit in 1992, have become part of our way of thinking.

The Holy See is pleased to note this since the Catholic Church has always believed that the cause of the environment is the cause of the human person who is at the same time both spiritual and material, the guardian and consumer of natural resources, and likewise of what is produced by our intelligence and technical abilities.

To speak of forests, water resources, pollution of the air, water or soil, as well as of human settlements, is to reflect upon living conditions and the survival of the whole of humankind. Agenda 21 said nothing less, when it specified that "Human beings are at the center of concerns for sustainable development. They are entitled to a healthy and productive life in harmony with nature."

That is why I am pleased to find these aspects present in the Final Document which has been submitted for our consideration. However, my Delegation cannot fail to repeat here the Reservations and Interpretations formulated by the Holy See at recent International United Nations Conferences and which are — let us not forget — an integral part of the Reports of those same Conferences. I am thinking in particular of the interpretation given to terms such as "reproductive health," "sexual health" and "family planning" which we find once more in the Document prepared at our meeting.

The results obtained at Rio — and even more so the commitments made there — make it our duty to protect nature in order to defend humanity. This must be done in a spirit of solidarity without underestimating the link existing between ecology, economics and equitable development.

A particular aspect of this problem, and one upon which I wish to insist, is the fate of the fifty million persons in the world who are displaced, in many cases as a result of an inadequate environment offering no assurance of human and economic security. Let us not forget them: they have a right to life, to adequate shelter and to a stable food supply.

The Holy See believes that one of the simplest and most efficacious methods through which the insights and resolutions of Rio are becoming a reality is education. From earliest childhood and the beginnings of schooling, parents and teachers, through the atmosphere they create and by their instruction and witness, can form young people to respect nature and to use its resources wisely. In this way they help them to develop attitudes of acceptance, sharing and giving.

In this very important task believers are in the front line. They wish to help their fellow men and women to go beyond mere respect for nature and a sharing of resources — which are, of course, absolutely necessary — in order to rediscover a sense of awe before the beauty of the natural elements, which can always inspire in us thoughts about the One who is always before us and whose very nature surpasses our own. The *Canticle of the Sun* of Francis of Assisi must surely be recalled here or, yet again, the paradoxical expression of a contemporary author who did not hesitate to speak of "the spiritual power of matter" (Teilhard de Chardin).

Mr. President, Ladies and Gentlemen, in granting me the privilege of being with you, Pope John Paul II wishes to express the confidence he has in each of the world leaders represented here so that, in his own words, we may study these questions "with sure ethical convictions, mastery of self, justice and brotherly love" (*Address to the Pontifical Academy of Sciences*, 22 October 1993). That we might all follow the path of participation, discussion and perseverance; this is my dearest wish.

Thank you, Mr. President.

LETTER OF
HIS HOLINESS POPE JOHN PAUL II
TO FAMILIES
1994 – YEAR OF THE FAMILY
VATICAN, 2 FEBRUARY 1994

Contents

1. Introduction
2. The family — way of the Church
3. The year of the family
4. Prayer
5. Love and concern for all families

I
The Civilization of Love

6. "Male and female he created them"
7. The marital covenant
8. The unity of the two
9. The genealogy of the person
10. The common good of marriage and the family
11. The sincere gift of self
12. Responsible fatherhood and motherhood
13. The two civilizations
14. Love is demanding
15. The fourth commandment: "Honour your father and your mother"
16. Education
17. Family and society

II
The Bridegroom is With You

18. At Cana in Galilee
19. The great mystery
20. Mother of fairest love
21. Birth and danger
22. "You welcomed me"
23. "Strengthened in the inner man"

Dear Families!

1. The celebration of the Year of the Family gives me a welcome opportunity to knock at the door of your home, eager to greet you with deep affection and to spend time with you. I do so by this *Letter*, taking as my point of departure the words of the Encyclical *Redemptor hominis,* published in the first days of my ministry as the Successor of Peter. There I wrote that *man is the way of the Church.*[1]

With these words I wanted first of all to evoke the many paths along which man walks, and at the same time to emphasize how deeply the Church desires to stand at his side as he follows the paths of his earthly life. The Church shares in the joys and hopes, the sorrows and anxieties[2] of people's daily pilgrimage, firmly convinced that it was Christ himself who set her on all these paths. Christ entrusted man to the Church; he entrusted man to her as the "way" of her mission and her ministry.

The family - way of the Church

2. Among these many paths, *the family is the first and the most important.* It is a path common to all, yet one which is particular, unique and unrepeatable, just as every individual is unrepeatable; it is a path from which man cannot withdraw. Indeed, a person normally comes into the world within a family, and can be said to owe to the family the very fact of his existing as an individual. When he has no family, the person coming into the world develops an anguished sense of pain and loss, one which will subsequently burden his whole life. The Church draws near with loving concern to all who experience situations such as these, for she knows well the fundamental role which the family is called upon to play. Furthermore, she knows that *a person goes forth from the family in order to realize in a new family unit his particular vocation in life.* Even if someone chooses to remain single the family continues to be, as it were, his existential horizon, that fundamental community in which the whole network of social relations is grounded, from the closest and most immediate to the most distant. Do we not often speak of the "human family" when referring to all the people living in the world?

---

[1] Cf. Encyclical Letter *Redemptor hominis* (4 March 1979), 14: *AAS* 71 (1979), 284-285.

[2] Cf. SECOND VATICAN ECUMENICAL COUNCIL, Pastoral Constitution on the Church in the Modern World *Gaudium et spes,* 1.

The family has its origin in that same love with which the Creator embraces the created world, was already expressed "in the beginning," in the *Book of Genesis* (1:1). In the Gospel Jesus offers a supreme confirmation: "God so loved the world that he gave his only Son" (Jn 3:16). The *only-begotten Son,* of one substance with the Father, "*God from God* and Light from Light," *entered into human history through the family:* "For by his incarnation the Son of God united himself in a certain way with every man. He laboured with human hands... and loved with a human heart. Born of Mary the Virgin, he truly became one of us and, except for sin, was like us in every respect."[3] If in fact Christ "fully discloses man to himself,"[4] he does so beginning with the family in which he chose to be born and to grow up. We know that the Redeemer spent most of his life in the obscurity of Nazareth, "obedient" (*Lk* 2:51) as the "Son of Man" to Mary his Mother, and to Joseph the carpenter. Is this filial "obedience" of Christ not already the first expression of that obedience to the Father "unto death" (*Phil* 2:8), whereby he redeemed the world?

The divine mystery of the Incarnation of the Word thus has an intimate connection with the human family. Not only with one family, that of Nazareth, but in some way with every family, analogously to what the Second Vatican Council says about the Son of God, who in the Incarnation "united himself in some sense with every man."[5] Following Christ who "came" into the world "to serve" (*Mt* 20:28), the Church considers serving the family to be one of her essential duties. In this sense both man and the family constitute "the way of the Church."

The year of the family

3. For these very reasons *the Church joyfully welcomes the decision* of the United Nations Organization *to declare 1994 the International Year of the Family*. This initiative makes it clear how fundamental the question of the family is for the member States of the United Nations. If the Church wishes to take part in this initiative, it is because she herself has been sent by Christ to "all nations" (*Mt* 28:19). Moreover, this is not the first time the Church has made her own an international initiative of the United Nations. We need but recall, for example, the International Year of Youth in 1985. In this way

---

[3] *Ibid.,* 22.

[4] *Ibid.*

[5] *Ibid.*

also the Church makes herself present in the world, fulfilling a desire which was dear to Pope John XXIII, and which inspired the Second Vatican Council's Constitution *Gaudium et spes*.

On the Feast of the Holy Family in 1993 the whole ecclesial community began the "Year of the Family" as one of the important steps along the path of preparation for the Great Jubilee of the Year 2000, which will mark the end of the second and the beginning of the third Millennium of the Birth of Jesus Christ. This Year ought to direct our thoughts and our hearts towards Nazareth, where it was officially inaugurated this past 26 December at a Solemn Eucharistic Liturgy presided over by the Papal Legate.

Throughout this Year it is important to discover anew the many *signs of the Church's love and concern for the family,* a love and concern expressed from the very beginning of Christianity, when the meaningful term *"domestic church"* was applied to the family. In our own times we have often returned to the phrase "domestic church," which the Council adopted[6] and the sense of which we hope will always remain alive in people's minds. This desire is not lessened by an awareness of the changed conditions of families in today's world. Precisely because of this, there is a continuing relevance to the title chosen by the Council in the Pastoral Constitution *Gaudium et spes* in order to indicate what the Church should be doing in the present situation: *"Promoting the dignity of marriage and the family."*[7] Another important reference point after the Council is the 1981 Apostolic Exhortation *Familiaris consortio*. This text takes into account a vast and complex experience with regard to the family, which among different peoples and countries always and everywhere continues to be the "way of the Church." In a certain sense it becomes all the more so precisely in those places where the family is suffering from internal crises or is exposed to adverse cultural, social and economic influences which threaten its inner unity and strength, and even stand in the way of its very formation.

Prayer

4. In this *Letter* I wish to speak not to families "in the abstract" but *to every particular family in every part of the world,* wherever it is located and whatever the diversity and complexity of its culture and history. The love

---

[6] Cf. Dogmatic Constitution on the Church, *Lumen gentium,* 11.

[7] Pastoral Constitution on the Church in the Modern World *Gaudium et spes,* Part II, Chap. 1.

with which God "loved the world" (*Jn* 3:16), the love with which Christ loved each and every one "to the end" (*Jn* 13:1), makes it possible to address this message to each family, as a living "cell" of the great and universal "family" of mankind. The Father, Creator of the Universe, and the Word Incarnate, the Redeemer of humanity, are the source of this universal openness to all people as brothers and sisters, and they impel us *to embrace them in the prayer* which begins with the tender words: *"Our Father."*

Prayer makes the Son of God present among us: "For where two or three are gathered in my name, I am there among them" (*Mt* 18:20). This *Letter to Families* wishes in the first place to be a prayer to Christ to remain in every human family; an invitation to him, in and through the small family of parents and children, to dwell in the great family of nations, so that together with him all of us can truly say: "Our Father!" Prayer must become the dominant element of the Year of the Family in the Church: prayer by the family, prayer for the family, and prayer with the family.

It is significant that precisely *in and through prayer man comes to discover in a very simple and yet profound way his own unique subjectivity:* in prayer the human "I" more easily perceives the depth of what it means to be a person. *This is also true of the family,* which is not only the basic "cell" of society, but also possesses a particular subjectivity of its own. This subjectivity finds its first and fundamental confirmation, and is strengthened, precisely when the members of the family meet in the common invocation: "Our Father." Prayer increases the strength and spiritual unity of the family, helping the family to partake of God's own "strength." In the solemn nuptial blessing during the Rite of Marriage, the celebrant calls upon the Lord in these words: "Pour out upon them [the newlyweds] the grace of the Holy Spirit so that by your love poured into their hearts they will remain faithful in the marriage covenant."[8] This "visitation" of the Holy Spirit gives rise to the inner strength of families, as well as the power capable of uniting them in love and truth.

Love and concern for all families

5. May the Year of the Family become a harmonious and universal prayer on the part of all "domestic churches" and of the whole People of God! May this prayer also reach families in difficulty or danger, lacking confidence or experiencing division, or in situations which *Familiaris*

---

[8] *Rituale Romanum, Ordo Celebrandi Matrimonium,* No. 74, editio typica altera, 1991, p. 26.

consortio describes as "irregular."⁹ *May all families be able to feel the loving and caring embrace of their brothers and sisters!*

During the Year of the Family, prayer should first of all be an encouraging witness on the part of those families who live out their human and Christian vocation in the communion of the home. How many of them there are in every nation, diocese and parish! With reason it can be said that these families make up "the norm," even admitting the existence of more than a few "irregular situations." And experience shows what an important role is played by a family living in accordance with the moral norm, so that the individual born and raised in it will be able to set out without hesitation on the road of the good, which *is always written in his heart*. Unfortunately various programmes backed by very powerful resources nowadays seem to aim at the breakdown of the family. At times it appears that concerted efforts are being made to present as "normal" and attractive, and even to glamourize, situations which are in fact "irregular." Indeed, they contradict "the truth and love" which should inspire and guide relationships between men and women, thus causing tensions and divisions in families, with grave consequences particularly for children. The moral conscience becomes darkened; what is true, good and beautiful is deformed; and freedom is replaced by what is actually enslavement. In view of all this, how relevant and thought-provoking are the words of the Apostle Paul about the freedom for which Christ has set us free, and the slavery which is caused by sin (cf. *Gal* 5:1)!

It is apparent then how timely and even necessary a Year of the Family is for the Church; how indispensable is *the witness of all families* who live their vocation day by day; how urgent it is *for families to pray* and for that prayer to increase and to spread throughout the world, expressing thanksgiving for love in truth, for "the outpouring of the grace of the Holy Spirit,"¹⁰ for the presence among parents and children of Christ the Redeemer and Bridegroom, who "loved us to the end" (cf. *Jn* 13:1). Let us be deeply convinced that this *love is the greatest of all* (cf. 1 *Cor* 13 :13), and let us believe that it is really capable of triumphing over everything that is not love.

During this year may the prayer of the Church, the prayer of families as "domestic churches," constantly rise up! May it make itself heard first by

---

⁹ Cf. Apostolic Exhortation *Familiaris consortio* (22 November 1981), 79-84: *AAS* 74 (1982), 180-186.

¹⁰ Cf. *Rituale Romanum, Ordo Celebrandi Matrimonium,* No. 74, ed. cit., p. 26.

God and then also by people everywhere, so that they will not succumb to doubt, and all who are wavering because of human weakness will not yield to the tempting glamour of merely apparent goods like those held out in every temptation.

At Cana in Galilee, where Jesus was invited to a marriage banquet, his Mother, also present, said to the servants: "Do whatever he tells you" (*Jn* 2:5). Now that we have begun our celebration of the Year of the Family, Mary says the same words to us. What Christ tells us, in this particular moment of history, constitutes a forceful call to a great prayer with families and for families. The Virgin Mother invites us to unite ourselves through this prayer to the sentiments of her Son, who loves each and every family. He expressed this love at the very beginning of his mission as Redeemer, with his sanctifying presence at Cana in Galilee, a presence which still continues.

Let us pray for families throughout the world. Let us pray, through Christ, with him and in him, to the Father "from whom every family in heaven and on earth is named" (*Eph* 3:15).

I

THE CIVILIZATION OF LOVE

"Male and female he created them"

6.	The universe, immense and diverse as it is, the world of all living beings, *is inscribed in God's fatherhood, which is its source* (cf. *Eph* 3:14-16). This can be said, of course, on the basis of an analogy, thanks to which we can discern, at the very beginning of the Book of Genesis, the reality of fatherhood and motherhood and consequently of the human family. The interpretative key enabling this discernment is provided by the principle of the "image" and "likeness" of God highlighted by the scriptural text (*Gen* 1:26). God creates by the power of his word: "Let there be...!" (e.g., *Gen* 1:3). Significantly, in the creation of man this word of God is followed by these other words: *"Let us make man* in our image, after our likeness" (*Gen* 1:26). Before creating man, the Creator withdraws as it were into himself, in order to seek the pattern and inspiration in the mystery of his Being, which is already here disclosed as the divine "We." From this mystery the human being comes forth by an act of creation: *"God created man in his own image,* in the image of God he created him; male and female he created them" (*Gen* 1:27).

God speaks to these newly-created beings and he blesses them: "Be fruitful and multiply, and fill the earth and subdue it" (*Gen* 1:28). The Book of Genesis employs the same expressions used earlier for the creation of other living beings: "multiply." But it is clear that these expressions are being used in an analogous sense. Is there not present here the analogy of begetting and of fatherhood and motherhood, which should be understood in the light of the overall context? No living being on earth except man was created "in the image and likeness of God." Human fatherhood and motherhood, while remaining *biologically similar* to that of other living beings in nature, contain in an essential and unique way a *"likeness" to God* which is the basis of the family as a community of human life, as a community of persons united in love (*communio personarum*).

In the light of the New Testament it is possible to discern how *the primordial model of the family is to be sought in God himself,* in the Trinitarian mystery of his life. The divine "We" is the eternal pattern of the human "we," especially of that "we" formed by the man and the woman created in the divine image and likeness. The words of the Book of Genesis contain that truth about man which is confirmed by the very experience of humanity. Man is created "from the very beginning" as male and female: the life of all humanity — whether of small communities or of society as a whole — is marked by this primordial duality. From it there derive the "masculinity" and the "femininity" of individuals, just as from it every community draws its own unique richness in the mutual fulfilment of persons. This is what seems to be meant by the words of the Book of Genesis: "Male and female he created them" (*Gen* 1:27). Here, too, we find the first statement of the equal dignity of man and woman: both, in equal measure, are persons. Their constitution, with the specific dignity which derives from it, defines "from the beginning" the qualities of the common good of humanity, in every dimension and circumstance of life. To this common good both man and woman make their specific contribution. Hence one can discover, at the very origins of human society, the qualities of communion and of complementarity.

The marital covenant

7.   The family has always been considered as the first and basic expression of man's *social nature*. Even today this way of looking at things remains unchanged. Nowadays, however, emphasis tends to be laid on how much the family, as the smallest and most basic human community, owes to the personal contribution of a man and a woman. The family is in fact a community of persons whose proper way of existing and living together is communion: *communio personarum*. Here, too, while always acknowledging the absolute transcendence of the Creator with regard to his creatures, we can see the family's ultimate relationship to the divine "We." *Only persons are capable of living "in communion."* The family originates in a marital communion described by the Second Vatican Council as a "covenant," *in which man and woman "give themselves to each other and accept each other."*[11]

The Book of Genesis helps us to see this truth when it states, in reference to the establishment of the family through marriage, that "a man leaves his father and his mother and cleaves to his wife, and they become one flesh" (*Gen* 2:24). In the Gospel, Christ, disputing with the Pharisees, quotes these same words and then adds: "So they are no longer two but one flesh. What therefore God has joined together, let not man put asunder" (*Mt* 19:6). In this way, he reveals anew the binding content of a fact which exists "from the beginning" (*Mt* 19:8) and which always preserves this content. If the Master confirms it "now," he does so in order to make clear and

---

[11] Pastoral Constitution on the Church in the Modern World *Gaudium et spes*, 48.

unmistakable to all, at the dawn of the New Covenant, the *indissoluble character* of marriage as the *basis of the common good of the family.*

When, in union with the Apostle, we bow our knees before the Father from whom all fatherhood and motherhood is named (cf. *Eph* 3:14-15), we come to realize that parenthood is the event whereby the family, already constituted by the conjugal covenant of marriage, is brought about "in the full and specific sense."[12] *Motherhood necessarily implies fatherhood,* and in turn, *fatherhood necessarily implies motherhood.* This is the result of the duality bestowed by the Creator upon human beings "from the beginning."

I have spoken of two closely related yet not identical concepts: the concept of "communion" and that of "community." "*Communion*" has to do with the personal relationship between the "I" and the "thou." "*Community*" on the other hand transcends this framework and moves towards a "society," a "we." The family, as a community of persons, is thus the first human "society." It arises whenever there comes into being the conjugal covenant of marriage, which opens the spouses to a lasting communion of love and of life, and it is brought to completion in a full and specific way with the procreation of children: the "communion" of the spouses gives rise to the "community" of the family. The "community" of the family is completely pervaded by the very essence of "communion." On the human level, can there be any other "*communion*" comparable to that *between a mother and a child* whom she has carried in her womb and then brought to birth?

In the family thus constituted there appears a new unity, in which the relationship "of communion" between the parents attains complete fulfillment. Experience teaches that this fulfillment represents both a task and a challenge. The task involves the spouses in living out their original covenant. *The children* born to them — and here is the challenge — *should consolidate that covenant,* enriching and deepening the conjugal communion of the father and mother. When this does not occur, we need to ask if the selfishness which lurks even in the love of man and woman as a result of the human inclination to evil is not stronger than this love. Married couples need to be well aware of this. From the outset they need to have their hearts and thoughts turned towards the God "from whom every family is named," *so that their fatherhood and motherhood will draw from that source the power to be continually renewed in love.*

Fatherhood and motherhood are themselves a particular proof of love;

---

[12] Apostolic Exhortation *Familiaris consortio* (22 November 1981), 69: *AAS* 74 (1982), 165.

they make it possible to discover love's extension and original depth. But this does not take place automatically. Rather, it is a task entrusted to both husband and wife. In the life of husband and wife together, fatherhood and motherhood represent such a sublime "novelty" and richness as can only be approached "on one's knees."

Experience teaches that human love, which naturally tends towards fatherhood and motherhood, is sometimes affected by a profound *crisis* and is thus seriously threatened. In such cases, help can be sought at marriage and family counseling centres, where it is possible, among other things, to obtain the assistance of specifically trained psychologists and psychotherapists. At the same time, however, we cannot forget the perennial validity of the words of the Apostle: "I bow my knees before the Father, from whom every family in heaven and on earth is named." Marriage, the Sacrament of Matrimony, is a covenant of persons in love. And *love can be deepened and preserved only by Love,* that Love which is "poured into our hearts through the Holy Spirit which has been given to us" (*Rom* 5:5). During the Year of the Family should our prayer not concentrate on the crucial and decisive moment of the passage from conjugal love to childbearing, and thus to fatherhood and motherhood? Is that not precisely the moment when there is an indispensable need for the "outpouring of the grace of the Holy Spirit" invoked in the liturgical celebration of the Sacrament of Matrimony?

The Apostle, bowing his knees before the Father, asks that the faithful "be *strengthened* with might *through his Spirit in the inner man*" (*Eph* 3:16). This "inner strength" is necessary in all family life, especially at its critical moments, when the love which was expressed in the liturgical rite of marital consent with the words, "I promise to be faithful to you always... all the days of my life," is put to a difficult test.

The unity of the two

8. Only "persons" are capable of saying those words; only they are able to live "in communion" on the basis of a mutual choice which is, or ought to be, fully conscious and free. The Book of Genesis, in speaking of a man who leaves father and mother in order to cleave to his wife (cf. *Gen* 2:24), highlights the *conscious and free choice* which gives rise to marriage, making the son of a family a husband, and the daughter of a family a wife. How can we adequately understand this mutual choice, unless we take into consideration the full truth about the person, who is a rational and free being? The Second Vatican Council, in speaking of the likeness of God, uses extremely significant terms. It refers not only to the divine image and

likeness which every human being as such already possesses, but also and primarily to "a certain similarity between the union of the divine persons and the union of God's children in truth and love."[13]

This rich and meaningful formulation first of all confirms what is central to the identity of every man and every woman. This identity consists in the *capacity to live in truth and love;* even more, it consists in the need of truth and love as an essential dimension of the life of the person. Man's need for truth and love opens him both to God and to creatures: it opens him to other people, to life "in communion," and in particular to marriage and to the family. In the words of the Council, the "communion" of persons is drawn in a certain sense from the mystery of the Trinitarian "We," and therefore "conjugal communion" also refers to this mystery. The family, which originates in the love of man and woman, ultimately derives from the mystery of God. This conforms to the innermost being of man and woman, to their innate and authentic dignity as persons.

In marriage man and woman are so firmly united as to become — to use the words of the Book of Genesis — "one flesh" (*Gen* 2:24). Male and female in their physical constitution, the two human subjects, even though physically different, *share equally in the capacity to live "in truth and love."* This capacity, characteristic of the human being as a person, has at the same time both a spiritual and a bodily dimension. It is also through the body that man and woman are predisposed to form a "communion of persons" in marriage. When they are united by the conjugal covenant in such a way as to become "*one flesh*" (*Gen* 2:24), their *union* ought to take place "*in truth and love,*" and thus express the maturity proper to persons created in the image and likeness of God.

The family which results from this union draws its inner solidity from the covenant between the spouses, which Christ raised to a Sacrament. The family draws its proper character as a community, its traits of "communion," from that fundamental communion of the spouses which is prolonged in their children. *"Will you accept children lovingly from God, and bring them up according to the law of Christ and his Church?,"* the celebrant asks during the Rite of Marriage.[14] The answer given by the spouses reflects the most profound truth of the love which unites them. Their unity, however, rather than closing them up in themselves, opens them towards a new life, towards

---

[13] Pastoral Constitution on the Church in the Modern World *Gaudium et spes,* 24.

[14] *Rituale Romanum Ordo Celebrandi Matrimonium,* No. 60. ed. cit., p. 17.

a new person. As parents, they will be capable of giving life to a being like themselves, not only bone of their bones and flesh of their flesh (cf. *Gen* 2:23), but an image and likeness of God — a person.

When the Church asks "Are you willing?", she is reminding the bride and groom that they stand *before the creative power of God.* They are called to become parents, to cooperate with the Creator in giving life. Cooperating with God to call new human beings into existence means contributing to the transmission of that divine image and likeness of which everyone "born of a woman" is a bearer.

The genealogy of the person

9.   Through the communion of persons which occurs in marriage, a man and a woman begin a family. Bound up with the family is the genealogy of every individual: *the genealogy of the person.* Human fatherhood and motherhood are rooted in biology, yet at the same time transcend it. The Apostle, with knees bowed "before the Father from whom all fatherhood [and motherhood] in heaven and on earth is named," in a certain sense asks us to look at the whole world of living creatures, from the spiritual beings in heaven to the corporeal beings on earth. Every act of begetting finds its primordial model in the fatherhood of God. Nonetheless, in the case of man, this "cosmic" dimension of likeness to God is not sufficient to explain adequately the relationship of fatherhood and motherhood. When a new person is born of the conjugal union of the two, he brings with him into the world a particular image and likeness of God himself: *the genealogy of the person is inscribed in the very biology of generation.*

In affirming that the spouses, as parents, cooperate with God the Creator in conceiving and giving birth to a new human being,[15] we are not speaking merely with reference to the laws of biology. Instead, we wish to emphasize that *God himself is present in human fatherhood and motherhood* quite differently than he is present in all other instances of begetting "on earth." Indeed, God alone is the source of that "image and likeness" which is proper to the human being, as it was received at Creation. Begetting is the continuation of creation.[16]

---

[15] Cf. Apostolic Exhortation *Familiaris consortio* (22 November 1981), 28: *AAS* 74 (1982), 114.

[16] Cf. POPE PIUS XII, Encyclical Letter *Humani generis* (12 August 1950): *AAS* 42 (1950), 574.

And so, both in the conception and in the birth of a new child, parents find themselves face to face with a "great mystery" (cf. *Eph* 5:32). Like his parents, the *new human being is also called* to live as a person; he is called *to a life "in truth and love."* This call is not only open to what exists in time, but in God it is also open to eternity. This is the dimension of the genealogy of the person which has been revealed definitively by Christ, who casts the light of his Gospel on human life and death and thus on the meaning of the human family.

As the Council affirms, man is "the only creature on earth whom God willed for its own sake."[17] Man's coming into being does not conform to the laws of biology alone, but also, and directly, to God's creative will, which is concerned with the genealogy of the sons and daughters of human families *God "willed" man from the very beginning and God "wills" him in every act of conception and every human birth.* God "wills" man as a being similar to himself, as a person. This man, every man, is created by God "*for his own sake.*" That is true of all persons, including those born with sicknesses or disabilities. Inscribed in the personal constitution of every human being is the will of God, who wills that man should be, in a certain sense, an end unto himself. God hands man over to himself, entrusting him both to his family and to society as their responsibility. Parents, in contemplating a new human being, are, or ought to be, fully aware of the fact that God "wills" this individual "for his own sake."

This concise expression is profoundly rich in meaning. From the very moment of conception, and then of birth, the new being is meant *to express fully his humanity,* to "find himself" as a person.[18] This is true for absolutely everyone, including the chronically ill and the disabled. "To be human" is his fundamental vocation: "to be human" in accordance with the gift received, in accordance with that "talent" which is humanity itself, and only then in accordance with other talents. In this sense God wills every man "for his own sake." *In God's plan,* however, the vocation of the human person extends beyond the boundaries of time. It encounters the will of the Father revealed in the Incarnate Word: *God's will is to lavish upon man a sharing in his own divine life.* As Christ says: "I came that they may have life and have it abundantly" (*Jn* 10:10).

Does affirming man's ultimate destiny not conflict with the statement

---

[17] Pastoral Constitution on the Church in the Modern World *Gaudium et spes,* 24.

[18] *Ibid.*

that God wills man "for his own sake?" If he has been created for divine life, can man truly exist "for his own sake?" This is a critical question, one of great significance both for the beginning of his earthly life and its end: it is important for the whole span of his life. It might appear that in destining man for divine life God definitively takes away man's existing "for his own sake."[19] What then is the relationship between the life of the person and his sharing in the life of the Trinity? Saint Augustine provides us with the answer in his celebrated phrase: "Our heart is restless until it rests in you."[20] This "restless heart" serves to point out that between the one finality and the other there is in fact no contradiction, but rather a relationship, a complementarity, a unity. By his very genealogy, the person created in the image and likeness of God, *exists "for his own sake"* and reaches fulfillment precisely by *sharing in God's life*. The content of this self-fulfillment is the fullness of life in God, proclaimed by Christ (cf. *Jn* 6:37-40), who redeemed us precisely so that we might come to share it (cf. *Mk* 10:45).

It is for themselves that married couples want children; in children they see the crowning of their own love for each other. They want children for the family, as a *priceless gift*.[21] This is quite understandable. Nonetheless, in conjugal love and in paternal and maternal love we should find inscribed the same truth about man which the Council expressed in a clear and concise way in its statement that God "willed man for his own sake." It is thus necessary that the will of the parents should be in harmony with the will of God. *They must want the new human creature in the same way as the Creator wants him:* "for himself." Our human will is always and inevitably subject to the law of time and change. The divine will, on the other hand, is eternal. As we read in the Book of the Prophet Jeremiah: "Before I formed you in the womb I knew you, and before you were born I consecrated you" (*Jer* 1:5). The genealogy of the person is thus united with the eternity of God, and only then with human fatherhood and motherhood, which are realized in time. At the moment of conception itself, man is already destined to eternity in God.

The common good of marriage and the family

---

[19] *Ibid.*

[20] *Confessiones*, I, 1: *CCL* 27, 1.

[21] Cf. Pastoral Constitution on the Church in the Modern World *Gaudium et spes*, 50.

10. Marital consent defines and consolidates *the good common to marriage and to the family*. "I, N., take you, N., to be my wife/husband. I promise to be true to you in good times and in bad, in sickness and in health. I will love you and honour you all the days of my life."[22] Marriage is a unique communion of persons, and it is on the basis of this communion that the family is called to become a community of persons. This is a commitment which the bride and groom undertake "before God and his Church," as the celebrant reminds them before they exchange their consent.[23] Those who take part in the rite are witnesses of this commitment, for in a certain sense they represent the Church and society, the settings in which the new family will live and grow.

The words of consent define the common good of the *couple and of the family*. First, the common good of the spouses: love, fidelity, honour, the permanence of their union until death — "all the days of my life." The good of both, which is at the same time the good of each, must then become the good of the children. The common good, by its very nature, both unites individual persons and ensures the true good of each. If the Church (and the State for that matter) receives the consent which the spouses express in the words cited above, she does so because that consent is "written in their hearts" (*Rom* 2:15). It is the spouses who give their consent to each other by a solemn promise, that is by confirming the truth of that consent in the sight of God. As baptized Christians, they are the ministers of the Sacrament of Matrimony in the Church. Saint Paul teaches that this mutual commitment of theirs is a "great mystery" (*Eph* 5:32).

The words of consent, then, express what is essential to the common good of the spouses, and *they indicate what ought to be the common good of the future family*. In order to bring this out, the Church asks the spouses if they are prepared to accept the children God grants them and to raise the children as Christians. This question calls to mind the common good of the future family unit, evoking the genealogy of persons which is part of the constitution of marriage and of the family itself. The question about children and their education is profoundly linked to marital consent, with its solemn promise of love, conjugal respect, and fidelity until death. The acceptance and education of children — two of the primary ends of the family — are conditioned by how that commitment will be fulfilled. Fatherhood and motherhood represent a *responsibility which is not simply physical but*

---

[22] *Rituale Romanum, Ordo Celebrandi Matrimonium*, No. 62, ed. cit., p. 17.

[23] *Ibid.*, No. 61, ed. cit., p. 17.

spiritual in nature; indeed, through these realities there passes the genealogy of the person, which has its eternal beginning in God and which must lead back to him.

The Year of the Family, as a year of special prayer on the part of families, ought to renew and deepen each family's awareness of these truths. What a wealth of biblical reflections could nourish that prayer! Together with the words of Sacred Scripture, these prayerful reflections should always include the *personal memories of the spouses-parents,* the children and grandchildren. Through the genealogy of persons, conjugal communion *becomes a communion of generations.* The sacramental union of the two spouses, sealed in the covenant which they enter into before God, endures and grows stronger as the generations pass. It must become a union in prayer. But for all this to become clearly apparent during the Year of the Family, prayer needs to become a regular habit in the daily life of each family. Prayer is thanksgiving, praise of God, asking for forgiveness, supplication and invocation. In all of these forms *the prayer of the family has much to say to God.* It also has much to say to others, beginning with the mutual communion of persons joined together by family ties.

The Psalmist asks: "What is man that you keep him in mind?" (*Ps* 8:4). Prayer is the place where, in a very simple way, the creative and fatherly remembrance of God is made manifest: not only man's remembrance of God, but also and especially *God's remembrance of man.* In this way, the prayer of the family as a community can become a place of common and mutual remembrance: the family is in fact a community of generations. In prayer everyone should be present: the living and those who have died, and also those yet to come into the world. Families should pray for all of their members, in view of the good which the family is for each individual and which each individual is for the whole family. Prayer strengthens this good, precisely as the common good of the family. Moreover, it creates this good ever anew. In prayer, the family discovers itself as the first "us," in which each member is "*I*" and "*thou*"; each member is for the others either husband or wife, father or mother, son or daughter, brother or sister, grandparent or grandchild.

Are all the families to which this *Letter* is addressed like this? Certainly a good number are, but the times in which we are living tend to restrict family units to two generations. Often this is the case because available housing is too limited, especially in large cities. But it is not infrequently due to the belief that having several generations living together interferes with privacy and makes life too difficult. But is this not where the problem really lies? *Families today have too little "human" life.* There is a shortage of people with whom to create and share the common good; and yet that good, by its nature, demands to be created and shared with others: *bonum est diffusivum sui* "good is diffusive of itself" [24] The more *common* the good, the *more properly one's own* it will also be: mine - yours - ours. This is the logic behind living according to the good, living in truth and charity. If man is able to accept and follow this logic, his life truly becomes a "sincere gift."

The sincere gift of self

11. After affirming that man is the only creature on earth which God willed for itself, the Council immediately goes on to say that he cannot "*fully find himself except through a sincere gift of self.*"[25] This might appear to be a contradiction, but in fact it is not. Instead it is the magnificent paradox of human existence: an existence called *to serve the truth in love.* Love causes man to find fulfillment through the sincere gift of self. To love means to give and to receive something which can be neither bought nor sold, but only given freely and mutually.

By its very nature the gift of the person must be lasting and irrevocable. The indissolubility of marriage flows in the first place from the very essence of that gift: *the gift of one person to another person.* This reciprocal giving of self reveals the *spousal nature of love.* In their marital consent the bride and groom call each other by name: "I... *take you*... as my wife (as my husband) and I promise to be true to you... for all the days of my life." A gift such as this involves an obligation much more serious and profound than anything which might be "purchased" in any way and at any price. Kneeling before the Father, from whom all fatherhood and motherhood come, the future parents come to realize that they have been "redeemed." They have been purchased at great cost, *by the price* of the most sincere gift of all, *the blood of Christ* of which they partake through the Sacrament. The liturgical crowning of the marriage rite is the Eucharist, the sacrifice of that "Body which has been given up" and that "Blood which has been shed," which in a certain way finds expression in the consent of the spouses.

When a man and woman in marriage mutually give and receive each other in the unity of "one flesh," the logic of the sincere gift of self becomes

---

[24] SAINT THOMAS AQUINAS, *Summa Theologiae*, I, q. 5, a. 4, ad 2.

[25] Pastoral Constitution on the Church in the Modern World *Gaudium et spes,* 24.

a part of their life. Without this, marriage would be empty; whereas a communion of persons, built on this logic, becomes a communion of parents. When they transmit *life to the child, a new human "thou" becomes a part of the horizon of the "we" of the spouses,* a person whom they will call by a new name: "our son... our daughter... ." "I have gotten a man with the help of the Lord" (*Gen* 4:1), says Eve, the first woman of history: a human being, first expected for nine months and then "revealed" to parents, brothers and sisters. The process from conception and growth in the mother's womb to birth makes it possible to create a space within which the new creature can be revealed as a "gift": indeed this is what it is from the very beginning. Could this frail and helpless being, totally dependent upon its parents and completely entrusted to them, be seen in any other way? The newborn child gives itself to its parents by the very fact of its coming into existence. *Its existence is already a gift, the first gift of the Creator to the creature.*

In the newborn child is realized the common good of the family. Just as the common good of spouses is fulfilled in conjugal love, ever ready to give and receive new life, so too the common good of the family is fulfilled through that same spousal love, as embodied in the newborn child. Part of the genealogy of the person is the genealogy of the family, preserved for posterity by the annotations in the Church's baptismal registers, even though these are merely the social consequence of the fact that "a man has been born into the world" (cf. *Jn* 16:21).

But is it really true that the new human being is a gift for his parents? A gift for society? Apparently nothing seems to indicate this. On occasion the birth of a child appears to be a simple statistical fact, registered like so many other data in demographic records. It is true that for the parents the birth of a child means more work, new financial burdens and further inconveniences, all of which can lead to the temptation not to want another birth.[26] In some social and cultural contexts this temptation can become very strong. Does this mean that a child is not a gift? That it comes into the world only to take and not to give? These are some of the disturbing questions which men and women today find hard to escape. *A child comes to take up room, when it seems that there is less and less room in the world.* But is it really true that a child brings nothing to the family and society? Is not every child a "particle" of that common good without which human communities break down and risk extinction? Could this ever really be denied? The child becomes a gift to its brothers, sisters, parents and entire family. *Its life becomes a gift for the very people who were givers of life* and

---

[26] Cf . Encyclical Letter *Sollicitudo rei socialis* (30 December 1987), 25: *AAS* 80 (1988), 543-544.

who cannot help but feel its presence, its sharing in their life and its contribution to their common good and to that of the community of the family. This truth is obvious in its simplicity and profundity, whatever the complexity and even the possible pathology of the psychological make-up of certain persons. *The common good of the whole of society dwells in man;* he is, as we recalled, "the way of the Church."[27] Man is first of all the "glory of God": "*Gloria Dei vivens homo,*" in the celebrated words of Saint Irenaeus,[28] which might also be translated: "the glory of God is for man to be alive." It could be said that here we encounter the loftiest definition of man: *the glory of God is the common good of all that exists;* the common good of the human race.

Yes! *Man is a common good:* a common good of the family and of humanity, of individual groups and of different communities. But there are significant distinctions of degree and modality in this regard. Man is a common good, for example, of the Nation to which he belongs and of the State of which he is a citizen; but in a much more concrete, unique and unrepeatable way he is a common good of his family. He is such not only as an individual who is part of the multitude of humanity, but rather as "*this individual.*" God the Creator calls him into existence "for himself"; and in coming into the world he begins, in the family, his "great adventure," the adventure of human life. "This man" has, in every instance, *the right to fulfill himself on the basis of his human dignity.* It is precisely this dignity which establishes a person's place among others, and above all, in the family. The family is indeed — more than any other human reality — the place where an individual can exist "for himself" through the sincere gift of self. This is why it remains a social institution which neither can nor should be replaced: it is the "sanctuary of life."[29]

The fact that a child is being born, that "a child is born into the world" (*Jn* 16:21) is a *paschal sign.* As we read in the Gospel of John, Jesus himself speaks of this to the disciples before his passion and death, comparing their sadness at his departure with the pains of a woman in labour: "*When a woman is in travail she has sorrow* (that is, she suffers), because *her hour* has come; but when she is delivered of the child, she no longer remembers the anguish, for *joy that a child is born into the world*" (*Jn*

---

[27] Encyclical Letter *Redemptor hominis* (4 March 1979), 14: *AAS* 71 (1979), 884-885; cf. Encyclical Letter *Centesimus annus* (1 May 1991), 53: *AAS* 83 (1991), 859.

[28] *Adversus haereses* IV, 20, 7: *PG* 7, 1057; *Sch* 100/2, 648-649.

[29] Encyclical Letter *Centesimus annus* (1 May 1991) 39: *AAS* 83 (1991), 842.

16:21). The "hour" of Christ's death (cf. *Jn* 13:1) is compared here to the "hour" of the woman in birth pangs; the birth of a new child fully reflects the victory of life over death brought about by the Lord's Resurrection. This comparison can provide us with material for reflection. Just as the Resurrection of Christ is the manifestation of *Life* beyond the threshold of death, so too the birth of an infant is a manifestation of life, which is always destined, through Christ, for that *"fullness of life" which is in God himself*: "I came that they may have life, and have it abundantly" (*Jn* 10:10). Here we see revealed the deepest meaning of Saint Irenaeus's expression: "*Gloria Dei vivens homo.*"

It is the Gospel truth concerning the gift of self, without which the person cannot "fully find himself," which makes possible an appreciation of how profoundly this "sincere gift" is rooted in the gift of God, Creator and Redeemer, and in the "grace of the Holy Spirit" which the celebrant during the Rite of Marriage prays will be "poured out" on the spouses. Without such an "outpouring," it would be very difficult to understand all this and to carry it out as man's vocation. Yet how many people understand this intuitively! Many men and women make this truth their own, coming to discern that only in this truth do they encounter "the Truth and the Life" (*Jn* 14:6). Without this truth, the life of the spouses and of the family will not succeed in attaining a fully human meaning.

This is why the Church never tires of teaching and of bearing witness to this truth. While certainly showing maternal understanding for the many complex crisis situations in which families are involved, as well as for the moral frailty of every human being, the Church is convinced that she must remain absolutely faithful to the truth about human love. Otherwise she would betray herself. To move away from this saving truth would be to close "the eyes of our hearts" (cf *Eph* 1:18), which instead should always stay open to the light which the Gospel sheds on human affairs (cf. 2 *Tim* 1:10). An awareness of that sincere gift of self whereby man "finds himself" must be constantly renewed and safeguarded in the face of the serious opposition which the Church meets on the part of those who advocate a false civilization of progress.[30] The family always expresses a new dimension of good for mankind, and it thus creates a new responsibility. We are speaking of the *responsibility for that particular common good* in which is included the good of the person, of every member of the family community. While certainly a "difficult" good ("*bonum arduum*"), it is also an attractive one.

---

[30] Cf. Encyclical Letter *Sollicitudo rei socialis* (30 December 1987), 25: *AAS* 80 (1988), 543-544.

Responsible fatherhood and motherhood

12. It is now time, in this *Letter to Families*, to bring up two closely related questions. The first, more general, concerns the *civilization of love,* the other, more specific, deals with *responsible fatherhood and motherhood*.

We have already said that marriage engenders a particular responsibility for the common good, first of the spouses and then of the family. This common good is constituted by man, by the *worth of the person* and by everything which represents the *measure of his dignity*. This reality is part of man in every social, economic and political system. In the area of marriage and the family, this responsibility becomes, for a variety of reasons, even more "demanding." The Pastoral Constitution *Gaudium et spes* rightly speaks of "*promoting the dignity of marriage and the family*." The Council sees this "promotion" as a duty incumbent upon both the Church and the State. Nevertheless, in every culture this duty remains primarily that of the persons who, united in marriage, form a particular family. "Responsible fatherhood and motherhood" express a concrete commitment to carry out this duty, which has taken on new characteristics in the contemporary world.

In particular, responsible fatherhood and motherhood directly concern the moment in which a man and a woman, uniting themselves "in one flesh," can become parents. This is a moment of special value both for their interpersonal relationship and for their service to life: they can become parents — father and mother — by communicating life to a new human being. *The two dimensions of conjugal union,* the unitive and the procreative, *cannot be artificially separated* without damaging the deepest truth of the conjugal act itself.[31]

This is the constant teaching of the Church, and the "signs of the times" which we see today are providing new reasons for forcefully reaffirming that teaching. Saint Paul, himself so attentive to the pastoral demands of his day, clearly and firmly indicated the need to be "urgent in season and out of season" (cf. *2 Tim 4:2),* and not to be daunted by the fact that "sound teaching is no longer endured" (cf. *2 Tim* 4:3). His words are well known to those who with deep insight into the events of the present time, expect that the Church will not only not abandon "sound doctrine," but will proclaim it with renewed vigour, seeking in today's "signs of the times" the incentive and insights which can lead to a deeper understanding of her teaching.

---

[31] Cf. POPE PAUL VI, Encyclical Letter *Humanae vitae* (25 July 1968), 12: *AAS* 60 (1968), 488-489; *Catechism of the Catholic Church,* No. 2366.

Some of these insights can be taken from the very sciences which have evolved from the earlier study of anthropology into *various specialized sciences* such as biology, psychology, sociology and their branches. *In some sense all these sciences revolve around medicine,* which is both a science and an art (*ars medica*), at the service of man's life and health. But the insights in question come first of all from human experience, which, in all its complexity, in some sense both precedes science and follows it.

Through their own experience spouses come to learn the meaning of responsible fatherhood and motherhood. They learn it also from the experience of other couples in similar situations and as they become more open to the findings of the various sciences. One could say that "experts" learn in a certain sense from "spouses," so that they in turn will then be in a better position to teach married couples the meaning of responsible procreation and the ways to achieve it.

This subject has been extensively treated in the documents of the Second Vatican Council, the Encyclical *Humanae vitae,* the "Propositiones" of the 1980 Synod of Bishops, the Apostolic Exhortation *Familiaris consortio,* and in other statements, up to the Instruction *Donum vitae* of the Congregation for the Doctrine of the Faith. The Church both teaches the moral truth about responsible fatherhood and motherhood and *protects it from the erroneous views and tendencies which are widespread today.* Why does the Church continue to do this? Is she unaware of the problems raised by those who counsel her to make concessions in this area and who even attempt to persuade her by undue pressures if not even threats? The Church's Magisterium is often chided for being behind the times and closed to the promptings of the spirit of modern times, and for promoting a course of action which is harmful to humanity, and indeed to the Church herself. By obstinately holding to her own positions, it is said, the Church will end up losing popularity, and more and more believers will turn away from her.

But how can it be maintained that *the Church,* especially the College of Bishops in communion with the Pope, is *insensitive to such grave and pressing questions?* It was precisely these extremely important questions which led Pope Paul VI to publish the Encyclical *Humanae vitae.* The foundations of the Church's doctrine concerning responsible fatherhood and motherhood are exceptionally broad and secure. *The Council demonstrates this above all in its teaching on man,* when it affirms that he is "the only creature on earth which God willed for itself," and that he cannot "fully find himself except through a sincere gift of himself."³² This is so because he has been created in the image and likeness of God and redeemed by the only-begotten Son of the Father, who became man for us and for our salvation.

The Second Vatican Council, particularly conscious of the problem of man and his calling, states that the conjugal union, the biblical *"una caro,"* can be understood and fully explained *only by recourse to the values of the "person" and of "gift."* Every man and every woman fully realizes himself or herself through the sincere gift of self. For spouses, the moment of conjugal union constitutes a very particular expression of this. It is then that a man and woman, in the "truth" of their masculinity and femininity, become a mutual gift to each other. All married life is a gift; but this becomes most evident when the spouses, in giving themselves to each other in love, bring about that encounter which makes them "one flesh" (*Gen* 2:24).

They then experience a moment of special responsibility, which is also the result of the procreative potential linked to the conjugal act. At that moment, the spouses can become father and mother, initiating the process of a new human life, which will then develop in the woman's womb. If the wife is the first to realize that she has become a mother, the husband, to whom she has been united in "one flesh," then learns this when she tells him that he has become a father. Both are responsible for their potential and later actual fatherhood and motherhood. The husband cannot fail to acknowledge and accept the result of a decision which has also been his own. He cannot hide behind expressions such as: "I don't know," "I didn't want it," or "you're the one who wanted it." In every case conjugal union involves *the responsibility of the man and of the woman,* a potential responsibility which becomes actual when the circumstances dictate. This is true especially for the man. Although he, too, is involved in the beginning of the generative process, he is left biologically distant from it; it is within the woman that the process develops. How can the man fail to assume responsibility? The man and the woman must assume together, before themselves and before others, the responsibility for the new life which they have brought into existence.

This conclusion is shared by the human sciences themselves. There is however a need for more in-depth study, analyzing the meaning of the conjugal act in view of the values of the "person" and of the "gift" mentioned above. This is what the Church has done in her constant teaching, and in a particular way at the Second Vatican Council.

---

³² Pastoral Constitution on the Church in the Modern World *Gaudium et spes,* 24.

In the conjugal act, husband and wife are called to confirm in a responsible way *the mutual gift* of self which they have made to each other in the marriage covenant. The logic of the *total gift of self to the other* involves a potential openness to procreation: in this way the marriage is called to even greater fulfillment as a family. Certainly the mutual gift of husband and wife does not have the begetting of children as its only end, but is in itself a mutual communion of love and of life. *The intimate truth of this gift* must always be *safeguarded*. "Intimate" is not here synonymous with "subjective." Rather, it means essentially in conformity with the objective truth of the man and woman who give themselves. The person can never be considered a means to an end; above all never a means of "pleasure." The person is and must be nothing other than the end of every act. Only then does the action correspond to the true dignity of the person.

In concluding our reflection on this important and sensitive subject, I wish to offer special encouragement above all to you, dear married couples, and to all who assist you in understanding and putting into practice the Church's teaching on marriage and on responsible motherhood and fatherhood. I am thinking in particular about pastors and the many scholars, theologians, philosophers, writers and journalists who have resisted the powerful trend to cultural conformity and are courageously ready to "swim against the tide." This encouragement also goes to an increasing number of experts, physicians and educators who are authentic lay apostles for whom the promotion of the dignity of marriage and the family has become an important task in their lives. In the name of the Church I express my gratitude to all! What would priests, Bishops and even the Successor of Peter be able to do without you? From the first years of my priesthood I have become increasingly convinced of this, from when I began to sit in the *confessional* to share the concerns, fears and hopes of many married couples. I met difficult cases of rebellion and refusal, but at the same time so many marvelously responsible and generous persons! In writing this *Letter* I have all those married couples in mind, and I embrace them with my affection and my prayer.

The two civilizations

13. Dear families, the question of responsible fatherhood and motherhood is an integral part of the "civilization of love," which I now wish to discuss with you. From what has already been said it is clear that *the family is*

fundamental to what Pope Paul VI called the "civilization of love,"[33] an expression which has entered the teaching of the Church and by now has become familiar. Today it is difficult to imagine a statement by the Church, or about the Church, which does not mention the civilization of love. The phrase *is linked to the tradition of the "domestic church" in early Christianity,* but it has a particular significance for the present time. Etymologically the word "civilization" is derived from "*civis*" — "citizen," and it emphasizes the civic or political dimension of the life of every individual. But the most profound meaning of the term "civilization" is not merely political, but rather pertains to human culture. Civilization belongs to human history because it answers man's spiritual and moral needs. Created in the image and likeness of God, man has received the world from the hands of the Creator, together with the task of shaping it in his own image and likeness. The fulfillment of this task gives rise to civilization, which in the final analysis is nothing else than the "humanization of the world."

In a certain sense civilization means the same thing as "culture." And so one could also speak of the "*culture of love,*" even though it is preferable to keep to the now familiar expression. The civilization of love, in its current meaning, is inspired by the words of the Conciliar Constitution *Gaudium et spes:* "*Christ... fully discloses man to himself and unfolds his noble calling.*"[34] And so we can say that the civilization of love originates in the revelation of the God who "is love," as John writes (1 *Jn* 4:8, 16); it is effectively described by Paul in the hymn of charity found in his *First Letter to the Corinthians* (13 : 1-13). This civilization is intimately linked to the love "poured into our hearts through the Holy Spirit which has been given to us" (*Rom* 5:5), and it grows as a result of the *constant cultivation* which the Gospel allegory of the vine and the branches describes in such a direct way: "I am the true vine, and my Father is the vinedresser. Every branch of mine that bears no fruit, he takes away, and every branch that does bear fruit he prunes, that it may bear more fruit" (*Jn* 15:1-2).

In the light of these and other texts of the New Testament it is possible to understand what is meant by the "civilization of love," and why the *family is organically linked to this civilization.* If the first "way of the Church" is the family, it should also be said that the civilization of love is also the "way of the Church," which journeys through the world and summons families to this way; it summons also other social, national and

---

[33] Cf. Homily for the Closing of the Holy Year (25 December 1975): *AAS* 68 (1976), 145.

[34] Pastoral Constitution on the Church in the Modern World *Gaudium et spes,* 22.

international institutions, because of families and through families. *The family in fact depends* for several reasons *on the civilization of love,* and finds therein the reasons for its existence as family. And at the same time *the family is the centre and the heart of the civilization of love.*

Yet there is no true love without an awareness that God "is Love" — and that man is the only creature on earth which God has called into existence "for its own sake." Created in the image and likeness of God, man cannot fully "find himself" except through the sincere gift of self. Without such a concept of man, of the person and the "communion of persons" in the family, there can be no civilization of love; similarly, without the civilization of love it is impossible to have *such a concept of person and of the communion of persons.* The family constitutes the fundamental "cell" of society. But Christ — the "vine" from which the "branches" draw nourishment — is needed so that this cell will not be exposed to the threat of a kind of *cultural uprooting* which can come both from within and from without. Indeed, although there is on the one hand the "civilization of love," there continues to exist on the other hand *the possibility of a destructive "anti-civilization,"* as so many present trends and situations confirm.

Who can deny that our age is one marked by a great crisis, which appears above all as a profound "*crisis of truth?*" A crisis of truth means, in the first place, a *crisis of concepts.* Do the words "love," "freedom," "sincere gift," and even "person" and "rights of the person," really convey their essential meaning? This is why the Encyclical on the "splendour of truth" (*Veritatis splendor*) has proved so meaningful and important for the Church and for the world — especially in the West. Only if the truth about freedom and the communion of persons in marriage and in the family can regain its splendour, will the building of the civilization of love truly begin and will it then be possible to speak concretely — as the Council did — about "promoting the dignity of marriage and the family."[35]

Why is the "splendour of truth" so important? First of all, by way of contrast: the development of contemporary civilization is linked to a scientific and technological progress which is often achieved in a one-sided way, and thus appears purely positivistic. Positivism, as we know, results in agnosticism in theory and utilitarianism in practice and in ethics. In our own day, history is in a way repeating itself. *Utilitarianism* is a civilization of production and of use, a civilization of "things" and not of "persons," a civilization in which persons are used in the same way as things are used. In the context of a civilization of use, woman can become an object for man,

---

[35] Cf. *ibid.*, 47.

children a hindrance to parents, the family an institution obstructing the freedom of its members. To be convinced that this is the case, one need only look at *certain sexual education programmes* introduced into the schools, often notwithstanding the disagreement and even the protests of many parents; or *pro-abortion tendencies* which vainly try to hide behind the so-called "right to choose" ("*pro-choice*") on the part of both spouses, and in particular on the part of the woman. These are only two examples; many more could be mentioned.

It is evident that in this sort of a cultural situation the family cannot fail to feel threatened, since it is endangered at its very foundations. Everything *contrary to the civilization of love is* contrary to the whole truth about man and becomes a threat to him: it does not allow him to find himself and to feel secure, as spouse, parent, or child. So-called "safe sex" which is touted by the "civilization of technology," is actually, in view of the overall requirements of the person, radically *not safe,* indeed it is extremely dangerous. It endangers both the person and the family. And what is this danger? It is *the loss of the truth about one's own self and about the family,* together with the risk of a loss of *freedom* and consequently of a loss of *love* itself. "You will know the truth," Jesus says, "and the truth will make you free" (*Jn* 8:32): the truth, and only the truth, will prepare you for a love which can be called "fairest love" (cf. *Sir* 24:24, Vulg.).

The contemporary family, like families in every age, is *searching for "fairest love."* A love which is not "fairest," but reduced only to the satisfaction of concupiscence (cf. 1 *Jn* 2:16), or to a man's and a woman's mutual "use" of each other, makes persons *slaves to their weaknesses.* Do not certain modern "cultural agendas" lead to this enslavement? There are agendas which "play" on man's weaknesses, and thus make him increasingly weak and defenceless.

The civilization of love evokes joy: joy, among other things, for the fact that a man has come into the world (cf. *Jn* 16:21), and consequently because spouses have become parents. The civilization of love means "rejoicing in the right" (cf. 1 *Cor* 13:6). But a civilization inspired by a consumerist, anti-birth mentality is not and cannot ever be a civilization of love. If the family is so important for the civilization of love, it is because of the particular *closeness and intensity of the bonds* which come to be between persons and generations within the family. However, the family remains *vulnerable* and can easily fall prey to dangers which weaken it or actually destroy its unity and stability. As a result of these dangers families cease to be witnesses of the civilization of love and can even become a negation of it, a kind of *counter-sign.* A broken family can, for its part, consolidate a specific form of "anti-civilization," destroying love in its

Love is demanding

14. The love which the Apostle Paul celebrates in the *First Letter to the Corinthians* — the love which is "*patient*" and "*kind,*" and *"endures all things"* (1 *Cor* 13:4, 7) — is certainly *a demanding love*. But this is precisely the source of its beauty: by the very fact that it is demanding, it builds up the true good of man and allows it to radiate to others. The good, says Saint Thomas, is by its nature "diffusive."[36] Love is true when *it creates the good of persons and of communities*; it creates that good and *gives it* to others. Only the one who is able to be demanding with himself in the name of love can also demand love from others. Love is demanding. It makes demands in all human situations; it is even more demanding in the case of those who are open to the Gospel. Is this not what Christ proclaims in "his" commandment? Nowadays people need to rediscover this demanding love, for it is the truly firm foundation of the family, a foundation able to "endure all things." According to the Apostle, love is not able to "endure all things" if it yields to "jealousies," or if it is "boastful... arrogant or rude" (cf. 1 *Cor* 13:5-6). True love, Saint Paul teaches, is different: "Love believes all things, hopes all things, endures all things" (1 *Cor* 13:7). This is the very love which "endures all things." At work within it is the power and strength of God himself, who "is love" (1 *Jn* 4:8, 16). At work within it is also the power and strength of Christ, the Redeemer of man and Saviour of the world.

Meditating on the thirteenth chapter of the *First Letter of Paul to the Corinthians*, we set out on a path which leads us to understand quickly and clearly the full truth about the civilization of love. No other biblical text expresses this truth so simply and so profoundly as the *hymn to love.*

The dangers faced by love are also dangers for the civilization of love, because they promote everything capable of effectively opposing it. Here one thinks first of all of *selfishness,* not only the selfishness of individuals, but also of couples or, even more broadly, of social selfishness, that for example of a class or nation (nationalism). Selfishness in all its forms is directly and radically opposed to the civilization of love. But is love to be defined simply as "anti-selfishness?" This would be a very impoverished and ultimately a purely negative definition, even though it is true that different forms of selfishness must be overcome in order to realize love and the

---

[36] *Summa Theologiae,* I, q. 5, a. 4, ad 2.

civilization of love. It would be more correct to speak of "altruism," which is the opposite of selfishness. But far richer and more complete is the concept of love illustrated by Saint Paul. The hymn to love in the First Letter to the Corinthians remains the *Magna Charta* of the civilization of love. In this concept, what is important is not so much individual actions (whether selfish or altruistic), so much as the radical acceptance of the understanding of man as a person who "finds himself" by making a sincere gift of self. A gift is, obviously, "for others": this is *the most important dimension* of the civilization of love.

We thus come to the very heart of the Gospel truth about *freedom*. The person realizes himself by the exercise of freedom in truth. Freedom cannot be understood as a license to do *absolutely anything:* it means a *gift of self.* Even more: it means an *interior discipline of the gift.* The idea of gift contains not only the free initiative of the subject, but also the aspect of *duty.* All this is made real in the "communion of persons." We find ourselves again at the very heart of each family.

Continuing this line of thought, we also *come upon the antithesis between individualism and personalism.* Love, the civilization of love, is bound up with personalism. Why with personalism? And *why does individualism threaten the civilization of love?* We find a key to answering this in the Council's expression, a "sincere gift." Individualism presupposes a use of freedom in which the subject does what he wants, in which he himself is the one to "establish the truth" of whatever he finds pleasing or useful. He does not tolerate the fact that someone else "wants" or demands something from him in the name of an objective truth. He does not want to "give" to another on the basis of truth; he does not want to become a "sincere gift." Individualism thus remains egocentric and selfish. The real antithesis between individualism and personalism emerges not only on the level of theory, but even more *on that of "ethos."* The "ethos" of personalism is altruistic: it moves the person to become a gift for others and to discover joy in giving himself. This is the joy about which Christ speaks (cf. *Jn* 15:11; 16:20, 22).

What is needed then is for human societies, and the families who live within them, often in a context of struggle between the civilization of love and its opposites, to seek their solid foundation in a correct vision of man and of everything which determines the full "realization" of his humanity. *Opposed to the civilization of love is* certainly the phenomenon of so-called "*free love*"; this is particularly dangerous because it is usually suggested as a way of following one's "real" feelings, but it is in fact destructive of love. How many families have been ruined because of "free love!" To follow in every instance a "real" emotional impulse by invoking a love "liberated" from all conditionings, means nothing more than to make the individual a slave to those human instincts which Saint Thomas calls "passions of the soul."[37] "Free love" exploits human weaknesses; it gives them a certain "veneer" of respectability with the help of seduction and the blessing of public opinion. In this way there is an attempt to "soothe" consciences by creating a "moral alibi." But not all of the consequences are taken into consideration, especially when the ones who end up paying are, apart from the other spouse, the children, deprived of a father or mother and condemned to be in fact *orphans of living parents.*

As we know, at the foundation of ethical utilitarianism there is the continual quest for "maximum" happiness. But this is a *"utilitarian happiness,"* seen only as pleasure, as immediate gratification for the exclusive benefit of the individual, apart from or opposed to the objective demands of the true good.

The programme of utilitarianism, based on an individualistic understanding of freedom — a *freedom without responsibilities* — is the opposite of love, even as an expression of human civilization considered as a whole. When this concept of freedom is embraced by society, and quickly allies itself with varied forms of human weakness, it soon proves a systematic and permanent threat to the family. In this regard, one could mention many dire consequences, which can be statistically verified, even though a great number of them are hidden in the hearts of men and women like painful, fresh wounds.

The love of spouses and parents has the capacity to cure these kinds of wounds, provided the dangers alluded to do not deprive it of its regenerative force, which is so beneficial and wholesome a thing for human communities. This capacity depends on the divine grace of forgiveness and reconciliation, which always ensures the spiritual energy to begin anew. For this very reason family members need to encounter Christ in the Church through the wonderful Sacrament of Penance and Reconciliation.

In this context, we can realize how important *prayer is* with families and for families, in particular for those threatened by division. We need to pray that married couples *will love their vocation,* even when the road becomes difficult, or the paths become narrow, uphill and seemingly insuperable; we need to pray that, even then, they will be faithful to their covenant with God.

---

[37] *Ibid.* I-II, q. 22.

"The family is the way of the Church." In this *Letter* we wish both to profess and to proclaim *this way,* which leads to the kingdom of heaven (cf. *Mt* 7:14) through conjugal and family life. It is important that the "communion of persons" in the family should become a preparation for the "communion of Saints." This is why the Church both believes and proclaims the love which "endures all things" (1 *Cor* 13:7); with Saint Paul she sees in it "*the greatest*" virtue of all (cf. 1 *Cor* 13:13). The Apostle puts no limits on anyone. Everyone is called to love, including spouses and families. In the Church everyone is called equally to perfect holiness (cf. *Mt* 5:48)[38]

The fourth commandment: "Honour your father and your mother"

15. The fourth commandment of the Decalogue deals with the family and its interior unity — its solidarity, we could say.

In its formulation, the fourth commandment does not explicitly mention the family. In fact, however, this is its real subject matter. In order to bring out the communion between generations, *the divine Legislator could find no more appropriate word than this:* "Honour..." (*Ex* 20:12). Here we meet another way of expressing what the family is. This formulation does not exalt the family in some "artificial" way, but emphasizes its subjectivity and the rights flowing from it. The family is a community of particularly intense interpersonal relationships: between spouses, between parents and children, between generations. It is a community which must be safeguarded in a special way. And God cannot find a better safeguard than this: "Honour."

"Honour your father and your mother, that your days may be long in the land which the Lord your God gives to you" (*Ex* 20:12). This commandment comes after the three basic precepts which concern the relation of the individual and the people of Israel with God: "*Shema, Izrael...,*" "Hear, O Israel: the Lord our God is one Lord" (*Dt* 6:4). "You will have no other gods before me" (*Ex* 20:3). This is the first and greatest commandment, the commandment of love for God "above all else": God is to be loved "with all your heart, and with all your soul, and with all your might" (*Dt* 6:5; cf. *Mt* 22:37). It is significant that the fourth commandment is placed in this particular context. "Honour your father and your mother," because for you they are in a certain sense representatives of the Lord; they are the ones who gave you life, who introduced you to human existence in a

---

[38] Cf. SECOND VATICAN ECUMENICAL COUNCIL, Dogmatic Constitution on the Church *Lumen gentium*, 11, 40 and 41.

particular family line, nation and culture. After God, they are your first benefactors. While God alone is good, indeed the Good itself, parents participate in this supreme goodness in a unique way. And so, honour your parents! *There is a certain analogy* here *with the worship owed to God.*

The fourth commandment is closely linked to the *commandment of love.* The bond between "honour" and "love" is a deep one. Honour, at its very centre, is connected with the virtue of justice, but the latter, for its part, cannot be explained fully without reference to love: the love of God and of one's neighbour. And who is more of a neighbour than one's own family members, parents and children?

Is the system of interpersonal relations indicated by the fourth commandment one-sided? Does it bind us only to honour our parents? Taken literally, it does. But indirectly we can speak of the "*honour*" *owed to children by their parents.* "To honour" means to acknowledge! We could put it this way: "let yourself be guided by the firm acknowledgment of the person, first of all that of your father and mother, and then that of the other members of the family." Honour is essentially an attitude of unselfishness. It could be said that it is "a sincere gift of person to person," and in that sense honour converges with love. If the fourth commandment demands that honour should be shown to our father and mother, it also makes this demand out of concern for the good of the family. Precisely for this reason, however, it makes demands of the parents themselves. You parents, the divine precept seems to say, should act in such a way that your life *will merit the honour* (and the love) of your children! Do not let the divine command that you be honoured fall into a moral vacuum! Ultimately then we are speaking of *mutual honour.* The commandment "honour your father and your mother" indirectly tells parents: Honour your sons and your daughters. They deserve this because they are alive, because they are who they are, and this is true from the first moment of their conception. The fourth commandment then, by expressing the intimate bonds uniting the family, highlights the basis of its inner unity.

The commandment goes on to say: "*that your days may be long in the land* which the Lord your God gives you." The conjunction "that" might give the impression of an almost utilitarian calculation: honour them so that you will have a long life. In any event, this does not lessen the fundamental meaning of the imperative "*honour,*" which by its nature suggests an *attitude of unselfishness.* To honour never means: "calculate the benefits." It is difficult, on the other hand, not to acknowledge the fact that an attitude of mutual honour among members of the family community also brings certain advantages. "*Honour*" *is certainly something useful,* just as every true good is "useful."

In the first place, the family achieves the good of "being together." This is the good par excellence of marriage (hence its indissolubility) and of the family community. It could also be defined as a good of the subject as such. Just as the person is a subject, so too is the family, since it is made up of persons, who, joined together by a profound bond of communion, form a single *communal subject*. Indeed, the family is more a subject than any other social institution: more so than the nation or the State, more so than society and international organizations. These societies, especially nations, possess a proper subjectivity to the extent that they receive it from persons and their families. Are all these merely "theoretical" observations, formulated for the purpose of "exalting" the family before public opinion? No, but they are another way of expressing what the family is. And this, too, can be deduced from the fourth commandment.

This truth deserves to be emphasized and more deeply understood: indeed it brings out the importance of the fourth commandment for the modern system of *human rights*. Institutions and legal systems employ juridical language. But God says: "honour." All "human rights" are ultimately fragile and ineffective, if at their root they lack the command to "honour"; in other words, if they lack *an acknowledgment of the individual* simply because he is an individual, "this" individual. *Of themselves, rights are not enough.*

It is not an exaggeration to reaffirm that the life of nations, of States, and of international organizations "passes" through the family and "is based" on the fourth commandment of the Decalogue. The age in which we live, notwithstanding the many juridical Declarations which have been drafted, *is still threatened to a great extent by "alienation."* This is the result of "Enlightenment" premises according to which a man is "more" human if he is "only" human. It is not difficult to notice how alienation from everything belonging in various ways to the full richness of man threatens our times. And this affects the family. Indeed, *the affirmation of the person* is in great measure to be referred back *to the family* and consequently to the fourth commandment. In God's plan the family is in many ways the first school of how to be human. *Be human!* This is the imperative passed on in the family — human as the son or daughter of one's country, a citizen of the State, and, we would say today, a citizen of the world. The God who gave humanity the fourth commandment is "benevolent" towards man (*philanthropos*, as the Greeks said). The Creator of the universe is *the God of love and of life:* he wants man to have life and have it abundantly, as Christ proclaims (cf. *Jn* 10:10); that he may have life, first of all thanks to the family.

At this point it seems clear that the "civilization of love" is strictly bound up with the family. *For many people the civilization of love is still a pure utopia.* Indeed, there are those who think that love cannot be demanded from anyone and that it cannot be imposed: love should be a free choice which people can take or leave.

There is some truth in all this. And yet there is always the fact that Jesus Christ left us the commandment of love, just as God on Mount Sinai ordered: "Honour your father and your mother." Love then is not a utopia: it is given to mankind as a task to be carried out with the help of divine grace. It is entrusted to man and woman, in the Sacrament of Matrimony, as the basic principle of their "duty," and it becomes the foundation of their mutual responsibility: first as spouses, then as father and mother. In the celebration of the Sacrament, the spouses give and receive each other, declaring their willingness to welcome children and to educate them. On this hinges human civilization, which cannot be defined as anything other than a "civilization of love."

The family is an expression and source of this love. *Through the family passes the primary current of the civilization of love,* which finds therein its "social foundations."

The Fathers of the Church, in the Christian tradition, have spoken of the family as a "domestic church," a "little church." They thus referred to the civilization of love as a possible system of human life and coexistence: "to be together" as a family, to be for one another, to make room in a community for affirming each person as such, for affirming "this" individual person. At times it is a matter of people with physical or psychological handicaps, of whom the so-called "progressive" society would prefer to be free. Even the family can end up like this kind of society. It does so when it hastily rids itself of people who are aged, disabled or sick. This happens when there is a loss of faith in that *God for whom "all live"* (cf. *Lk* 20:38) and are called to the fullness of Life.

Yes, *the civilization of love is possible; it is not a utopia.* But it is only possible by a constant and ready reference to the "Father from whom all fatherhood [and motherhood] on earth is named" (cf. *Eph* 3:14-15), from whom every human family comes.

Education

16. *What is involved in raising children?* In answering this question two fundamental truths should be kept in mind: first, that man is called to live in truth and love; and second, that everyone finds fulfillment through the sincere gift of self. This is true both for the educator and for the one being educated.

Education is thus a unique process for which the mutual communion of persons has immense importance. *The educator is* a person who *"begets" in a spiritual sense.* From this point of view, *raising children can be considered a genuine apostolate.* It is a living means of communication, which not only creates a profound relationship between the educator and the one being educated, but also makes them both sharers in truth and love, that final goal to which everyone is called by God the Father, Son and Holy Spirit.

Fatherhood and motherhood presume the coexistence and interaction of autonomous subjects. This is quite evident in the case of the mother when she conceives a new human being. The first months of the child's presence in the mother's womb bring about a particular bond which already possesses an educational significance of its own. The *mother, even before giving birth, does not only give shape to the child's body, but also, in an indirect way, to the child's whole personality.* Even though we are speaking about a process in which the mother primarily affects the child, we should not overlook the unique influence that the unborn child has on its mother. In this *mutual influence* which will be revealed to the outside world following the birth of the child, the father does not have a direct part to play. But he should be responsibly committed to providing attention and support throughout the pregnancy and, if possible, at the moment of birth.

For the "civilization of love" it is essential that *the husband should recognize that the motherhood of his wife is a gift:* this is enormously important for the entire process of raising children. Much will depend on his willingness to take his own part in this first stage of the gift of humanity, and to become willingly involved as a husband and father in the motherhood of his wife.

Education then is before all else *a reciprocal "offering" on the part of both parents:* together they communicate their own mature humanity to the newborn child, who gives them in turn the newness and freshness of the humanity which it has brought into the world. This is the case even when children are born with mental or physical disabilities. Here, the situation of the children can enhance the very special courage needed to raise them.

With good reason, then, the Church asks during the Rite of Marriage: "Will you accept children lovingly from God, and bring them up according to the law of Christ and his Church"?[39] In the raising of children conjugal love is expressed as authentic parental love. The "communion of persons,"

---

[39]*Rituale Romanum, Ordo Celebrandi Matrimonium,* No. 60, ed. cit., p. 17.

expressed as conjugal love at the beginning of the family, is thus completed and brought to fulfillment in the raising of children. Every individual born and raised in a family constitutes a potential treasure which must be responsibly accepted, so that it will not be diminished or lost, but will rather come to an ever more mature humanity. This, too, is a *process of exchange* in which the parents-educators are in turn to a certain degree educated themselves. While they are teachers of humanity for their own children, they learn humanity from them. All this clearly brings out the *organic structure of the family,* and reveals the fundamental meaning of the fourth commandment.

In rearing children, the "*we*" *of the parents,* of husband and wife, develops into the "*we*" *of the family,* which is grafted onto earlier generations, and is open to gradual expansion. In this regard both grandparents and grandchildren play their own individual roles.

If it is true that by giving life *parents* share in God's creative work, it is also true that by raising their children they *become sharers in his paternal and at the same time maternal way of teaching.* According to Saint Paul, God's fatherhood is the primordial model of all fatherhood and motherhood in the universe (cf. *Eph* 3:14-15), and of human motherhood and fatherhood in particular. We have been completely instructed in God's own way of teaching by the eternal Word of the Father who, by becoming man, revealed to man the authentic and integral greatness of his humanity, that is, being a child of God. In this way he also revealed the true meaning of human education. *Through Christ* all education, within the family and outside of it, *becomes part of God's own saving pedagogy,* which is addressed to individuals and families and culminates in the Paschal Mystery of the Lord's Death and Resurrection. The "heart" of our redemption is the starting-point of every process of Christian education, which is likewise always an education to a full humanity.

Parents are *the first and most important educators* of their own children, and they also possess a *fundamental competence* in this area: they are *educators because they are parents.* They share their educational mission with other individuals or institutions, such as the Church and the State. But the mission of education must always be carried out in accordance with a proper application of the *principle of subsidiarity.* This implies the legitimacy and indeed the need of giving assistance to the parents, but finds its intrinsic and absolute limit in their prevailing right and their actual capabilities. The principle of subsidiarity is thus at the service of parental love meeting the good of the family unit. For parents by themselves are not capable of satisfying every requirement of the whole process of raising children, especially in matters concerning their schooling and the entire gamut of socialization. Subsidiarity thus complements paternal and maternal love and confirms its fundamental nature, inasmuch as all other participants in the process of education are only able to carry out their responsibilities *in the name of the parents, with their consent* and, to a certain degree, *with their authorization.*

The process of education ultimately leads to the phase of *self-education,* which occurs when the individual, after attaining an appropriate level of psycho-physical maturity, *begins to "educate himself on his own."* In time, self-education goes beyond the earlier results achieved by the educational process, in which it continues to be rooted. An adolescent is exposed to new people and new surroundings, particularly teachers and classmates, who exercise an influence over his life which can be either helpful or harmful. At this stage he distances himself somewhat from the education received in the family, assuming at times a critical attitude with regard to his parents. Even so, the process of self-education cannot fail to be marked by the educational influence which the family and school have on children and adolescents. Even when they grow up and set out on their own path, young people remain intimately linked to their *existential roots.*

Against this background, we can see the meaning of the fourth commandment, "*Honour your father and your mother*" (*Ex* 20:12) in a new way. It is closely linked to the whole process of education. Fatherhood and motherhood, this first and basic fact in the *gift of humanity,* open up before both parents and children new and profound perspectives. To give birth according to the flesh means to set in motion a further "birth," one which is gradual and complex and which continues in the whole process of education. The commandment of the Decalogue calls for a child to honour its father and mother. But, as we saw above, that same commandment enjoins upon parents a kind of corresponding or "symmetrical" duty. Parents are also called to "honour" their children, whether they are young or old. This attitude is needed throughout the process of their education, including the time of their schooling. The *"principle of giving honour,"* the recognition and respect due to man precisely because he is a man, is the basic condition for every authentic educational process.

In the sphere of education *the Church* has a specific role to play. In the light of Tradition and the teaching of the Council, it can be said that it is not only a matter of *entrusting the Church* with the person's religious and moral education, but of promoting the entire process of the person's education "*together with*" *the Church.* The family is called to carry out its task of education *in the Church,* thus sharing in her life and mission. The Church wishes to carry out her educational mission above all *through families* who are made capable of undertaking this task by the Sacrament of

Matrimony, through the "grace of state" which follows from it and the specific "charism" proper to the entire family community.

Certainly one area in which the family has an irreplaceable role is that of *religious education,* which enables the family to grow as a "domestic church." Religious education and the catechesis of children make the family a true *subject of evangelization and the apostolate* within the Church. We are speaking of a right intrinsically linked to the *principle of religious liberty.* Families, and more specifically parents, are free to choose for their children a particular kind of religious and moral education consonant with their own convictions. Even when they entrust these responsibilities to ecclesiastical institutions or to schools administered by religious personnel, their educational presence ought to continue to be *constant and active.*

Within the context of education, due attention must be paid to the essential question of *choosing a vocation,* and here in particular that of *preparing for marriage.* The Church has made notable efforts to promote marriage preparation, for example by offering courses for engaged couples. All this is worthwhile and necessary. But it must not be forgotten that preparing for future life as a couple is *above all the task of the family.* To be sure, only spiritually mature families can adequately assume that responsibility. Hence we should point out the need for a special *solidarity among families.* This can be expressed in various practical ways, as for example by associations of families for families. The institution of the family is strengthened by such expressions of solidarity, which bring together not only individuals but also communities, with a commitment to pray together and to seek together the answers to life's essential questions. Is this not an invaluable expression of the *apostolate of families* to one another? It is important that families attempt to build bonds of solidarity among themselves This allows them to assist each other in the educational enterprise: parents are educated by other parents, and children by other children. Thus, a particular tradition of education is created, which draws strength from the character of the "domestic church" proper to the family.

The *gospel of love* is the inexhaustible source of all that nourishes the human family as a "communion of persons." In love the whole educational process finds its support and definitive meaning as the mature fruit of the parents' mutual gift. Through the efforts, sufferings and disappointments which are part of every person's education, love is constantly being put to the test. To pass the test, a source of spiritual strength is necessary. This is only found in the One who "loved to the end" (*Jn* 13:1). Thus, *education is fully a part of the "civilization of love."* It depends on the civilization of love and, in great measure, contributes to its up-building.

The Church's constant and trusting prayer during the Year of the Family is *for the education of man,* so that families will persevere in their task of education with courage, trust and hope, in spite of difficulties occasionally so serious as to appear insuperable. The Church prays that the forces of the "civilization of love," which have their source in the love of God, will be triumphant. These are forces which the Church ceaselessly expends for the good of the whole human family.

Family and society

17. The family is a community of persons and the smallest social unit. As such it is an *institution* fundamental to the life of every society.

What does the family as an institution expect from society? First of all, it expects *a recognition of its identity* and an acceptance of its *status as a subject in society.* This "social subjectivity" is bound up with the proper identity of marriage and the family. Marriage, which undergirds the institution of the family, is constituted by the covenant whereby "a man and a woman establish between themselves a partnership of their whole life," and which "of its own very nature is ordered to the well-being of the spouses and to the procreation and upbringing of children."[40] Only such a union can be recognized and ratified as a "marriage" in society. Other interpersonal unions which do not fulfill the above conditions cannot be recognized, despite certain growing trends which represent a serious threat to the future of the family and of society itself.

No human society can run the risk of permissiveness in fundamental issues regarding the nature of marriage and the family! Such moral permissiveness cannot fail to damage the authentic requirements of peace and communion among people. It is thus quite understandable why the Church vigorously defends the identity of the family and encourages responsible individuals and institutions, especially political leaders and international organizations, not to yield to the temptation of a superficial and false modernity.

As a community of love and life, the family is a firmly grounded social reality. It is also, in a way entirely its own, a *sovereign society,* albeit conditioned in certain ways. This affirmation of the family's sovereignty as an institution and the recognition of the various ways in which it is

---

[40]*Code of Canon Law,* Canon 1055, § 1; *Catechism of the Catholic Church,* No. 1601.

conditioned naturally leads to the subject of *family rights*. In this regard, the Holy See published in 1983 the *Charter of the Rights of the Family,* even today this document has lost none of its relevance.

The rights of the family are closely *linked to the rights of the person:* if in fact the family is a communion of persons its self-realization will depend in large part on the correct application of the rights of its members. Some of these rights concern the family in an immediate way, such as the right of parents to responsible procreation and the education of children. Other rights, however, touch the family unit only indirectly: among these, the right to property, especially to what is called family property, and the right to work are of special importance.

But the rights of the family *are not simply the sum total* of the rights of the person, since the family is *much more* than the sum of its individual members. It is a community of parents and children, and at times a community of several generations. For this reason its "status as a subject," which is grounded in God's plan, gives rise to and calls for certain proper and specific rights. The *Charter of the Rights of the Family,* on the basis of the moral principles mentioned above, consolidates the existence of the institution of the family in the social and juridical order of the "greater" society — those of the nation, of the State and of international communities. Each of these "greater" societies is at least indirectly conditioned by the existence of the family. As a result, the definition of the rights and duties of the "greater" society with regard to the family is an extremely important and even essential issue.

In the first place there is the almost organic link existing between *the family and the nation.* Naturally we cannot speak in all cases about a nation in the proper sense. Ethnic groups still exist which, without being able to be considered true nations, do fulfill to some extent the function of a "greater" society. In both cases, the link of the family with the ethnic group or the nation is founded above all on *a participation in its culture.* In one sense, parents also give birth to children for the nation, so that they can be members of it and can share in its historic and cultural heritage. From the very outset the identity of the family is to some extent shaped by the identity of the nation to which it belongs.

By sharing in the nation's cultural heritage, the family contributes to that *specific sovereignty,* which has its origin in a distinct culture and language. I addressed this subject at the UNESCO Conference meeting in Paris in 1980, and, given its unquestionable importance, I have often returned to it. Not only the nations, but every family realizes its *spiritual sovereignty* through culture and language. Were this not true, it would be very difficult to explain many events in the history of peoples, especially in Europe. From these events, ancient and modern, inspiring and painful, glorious and humiliating, it becomes clear how much the family is an organic part of the nation, and the nation of the family.

In regard to the *State,* the link with the family is somewhat similar and at the same time somewhat dissimilar. The State, in fact, is distinct from the nation; it has a less "family-like" structure, since it is organized in accordance with a political system and in a more "bureaucratic" fashion. Nonetheless, the apparatus of the State also has, in some sense, a "soul" of its own, to the extent that it lives up to its nature as a "political community" juridically ordered towards the common good.[41] Closely linked to this "soul" is the family, which is connected with the State precisely by reason of the *principle of subsidiarity.* Indeed, the family is a social reality which does not have readily available all the means necessary to carry out its proper ends, also in matters regarding schooling and the rearing of children. The State is thus called upon to play a role in accordance with the principle mentioned above. Whenever the family is self-sufficient, it should be left to act on its own; an excessive intrusiveness on the part of the State would prove detrimental, to say nothing of lacking due respect, and would constitute an open violation of the rights of the family. Only in those situations where the family is not really self-sufficient does the State have the authority and duty to intervene.

Beyond child-rearing and schooling at all levels, State assistance, while not excluding private initiatives, can find expression in institutions such as those founded to safeguard the life and health of citizens, and in particular to provide social benefits for workers. *Unemployment* is today one of the most serious threats to family life and a rightful cause of concern to every society. It represents a challenge for the political life of individual States and an area for careful study in the Church's social doctrine. It is urgently necessary, therefore, to come up with courageous solutions capable of looking beyond the confines of one's own nation and taking into consideration the many families for whom lack of employment means living in situations of tragic poverty.[42]

While speaking about employment in reference to the family, it is appropriate to emphasize how important and burdensome is *the work women*

---

[41] Cf. Pastoral Constitution on the Church in the Modern World *Gaudium et Spes,* 74.

[42] Cf. Encyclical Letter *Centesimus annus* (1 May 1991), 57: *AAS* 83 (1991), 862-863.

do within the family unit:[43] *that work should be acknowledged and deeply appreciated.* The "toil" of a woman who, having given birth to a child, nourishes and cares for that child and devotes herself to its upbringing, particularly in the early years, is so great as to be comparable to any professional work. This ought to be clearly stated and upheld, no less than any other labour right. Motherhood, because of all the hard work it entails, should be recognized as giving the right to financial benefits at least equal to those of other kinds of work undertaken in order to support the family during such a delicate phase of its life.

Every effort should be made so that the family will be recognized as the *primordial* and, in a certain sense "sovereign" *society!* The "sovereignty" of the family is essential for the good of society. A truly sovereign and spiritually vigorous nation is always made up of strong families who are aware of their vocation and mission in history. *The family is at the heart* of all these problems and tasks. To relegate it to a subordinate or secondary role, excluding it from its rightful position in society, would be to inflict grave harm on the authentic growth of society as a whole.

---

[43]Cf. Encyclical Letter *Laborem exercens* (14 September 1981), 19: *AAS* 73 (1981), 625-629.

II

THE BRIDEGROOM IS WITH YOU

At Cana in Galilee

18.   Engaged in conversation with John's disciples one day, Jesus speaks of a wedding invitation and the presence of the bridegroom among the guests: "the Bridegroom is with them" (*Mt* 9:15). In this way he indicated the fulfillment in his own person of the image of God the Bridegroom, which had already been used in the Old Testament, in order to reveal fully the mystery of God as the mystery of Love.

By describing himself as a "Bridegroom," Jesus reveals the essence of God and confirms his immense love for mankind. But the choice of this image also throws light indirectly on the profound truth of spousal love. Indeed by using this image in order to speak about God, Jesus shows to what extent the fatherhood and the love of God are reflected in the love of a man and a woman united in marriage. Hence, at the beginning of his mission, we find Jesus at *Cana in Galilee* taking part in a wedding banquet, together with Mary and with the first disciples (cf. *Jn* 2:1-11). He thus wishes to make clear *to what extent the truth about the family is part of God's Revelation and the history of salvation.* In the Old Testament, and particularly in the Prophets, we find many beautiful expressions about the *love of God.* It is a gentle love like that of a mother for her child, a tender love like that of the bridegroom for his bride, but at the same time an equally and intensely jealous love. It is not in the first place a love which chastises but one which forgives; a love which deigns to meet man just as the father does in the case of the prodigal son; a love which raises him up and gives him a share in divine life. It is an amazing love: something entirely new and previously unknown to the whole pagan world.

At Cana in Galilee Jesus is, as it were, the *herald of the divine truth about marriage,* that truth on which the human family can rely, gaining reassurance amid all the trials of life. Jesus proclaims this truth by his presence at the wedding in Cana and by working his first "sign": water changed into wine.

Jesus proclaims the truth about marriage again when, speaking to the Pharisees, he explains how the love which comes from God, a tender and spousal love, *gives rise to profound and radical demands.* Moses, by allowing a certificate of divorce to be drawn up, had been less demanding. When in their lively argument the Pharisees appealed to Moses, Jesus' answer was categorical: "from the beginning it was not so" (*Mt* 19:8). And he reminds them that the One who created man created him male and female, and ordained that "a man leaves his father and his mother and cleaves to his wife, and they become one flesh" (*Gen* 2:24). With logical consistency Jesus concludes: "So they are no longer two but one flesh. What therefore God has joined together, let no man put asunder" (*Mt* 19:6). To the objection of the Pharisees who vaunt the Law of Moses he replies: "For your hardness of heart Moses allowed you to divorce your wives, but from the beginning it was not so" (*Mt* 19:8).

Jesus appeals to "the beginning," seeing at the very origins of creation God's plan, on which the family is based, and, through the family, the entire history of humanity. What marriage is in nature becomes, by the will of Christ, a true sacrament of the New Covenant, sealed by the blood of Christ the Redeemer. *Spouses and families, remember at what price you have been "bought!"* (cf. 1 *Cor* 6:20).

But it is *humanly difficult* to accept and to live this marvelous truth. Should we be surprised that Moses relented before the insistent demands of his fellow Israelites, if the Apostles themselves, upon hearing the words of the Master, reply by saying: "If such is the case of a man with his wife, it is not expedient to marry" (*Mt* 19:10)! Nonetheless, in view of the good of man and woman, of the family and the whole of society, Jesus confirms the demand which God laid down from the beginning. At the same time, however, he takes the opportunity to affirm the value of a decision not to marry for the sake of the Kingdom of God. This choice, too, enables one to "beget," albeit in a different way. In this choice we find the origin of the consecrated life, of the Religious Orders and Religious Congregations of East and West, and also of the discipline of priestly celibacy, as found in the tradition of the Latin Church. Hence it is untrue that "it is not expedient to marry"; however, love for the kingdom of heaven can lead a person to choose not to marry (cf. *Mt* 19:12).

Marriage however remains *the usual human vocation,* which is embraced by the great majority of the people of God. It is in the family where living stones are formed for that spiritual house spoken of by the Apostle Peter (cf. 1 *Pet* 2:5). The bodies of the husband and wife are the dwelling-place of the Holy Spirit (cf. 1 *Cor* 6:19). Because the transmission of divine life presumes the transmission of human life, marriage not only brings about the birth of human children, but also, through the power of Baptism, the birth of adopted children of God, who live the new life received from Christ through his Spirit.

Dear brothers and sisters, spouses and parents, this is how the

Bridegroom is with you. You know that he is the Good Shepherd. You know who he is, and you know his voice. You know where he is leading you, and how he strives to give you pastures where you can find life and find it in abundance. You know how he withstands the marauding wolves, and is ever ready to rescue his sheep: every husband and wife, every son and daughter, every member of your families. You know that he, as the Good Shepherd, is prepared to lay down his own life for his flock (cf. *Jn* 10:11). He leads you by paths which are not the steep and treacherous paths of many of today's ideologies, and he repeats to today's world the fullness of truth, even as he did in his conversation with the Pharisees or when he announced it to the Apostles, who then proclaimed it to all the ends of the earth and to all the people of their day, to Jews and Greeks alike. The disciples were fully conscious that Christ had made all things new. They knew that man had been made a "new creation": no longer Jew or Greek, no longer slave or free, no longer male or female, but "one" in Christ (cf. *Gal* 3:28) and endowed with the dignity of an adopted child of God. On the day of Pentecost man received the Spirit, the Comforter, the Spirit of truth. This was the beginning of the new People of God, the Church, the foreshadowing of new heavens and a new earth (cf. *Rev* 21:1).

The Apostles, overcoming their initial fears even about marriage and the family, grew in courage. They came to understand that marriage and family are a true vocation which comes from God himself and is an apostolate: the apostolate of the laity. Families are meant to contribute to the transformation of the earth and the renewal of the world, of creation and of all humanity.

Dear families, you too should be fearless, ever ready to give witness to the hope that is in you (cf. 1 *Pet* 3:15), since the Good Shepherd has put that hope in your hearts through the Gospel. You should be ready to follow Christ towards the pastures of life, which he himself has prepared through the Paschal Mystery of his Death and Resurrection.

Do not be afraid of the risks! God's strength is always far more powerful than your difficulties! Immeasurably greater than the evil at work in the world is the power of the *Sacrament of Reconciliation,* which the Fathers of the Church rightly called a "second Baptism." Much more influential than the corruption present in the world is the divine power of the Sacrament of *Confirmation,* which brings Baptism to its maturity. And incomparably greater than all is the power of the Eucharist.

The *Eucharist* is truly a wondrous sacrament. In it Christ has given us himself as food and drink, as a source of saving power. He has left himself to us that we might have life and have it in abundance (cf. *Jn* 10:10):

the life which is in him and which he has shared with us by the gift of the Spirit in rising from the dead on the third day. The life that comes from Christ is a life for us. *It is for you, dear husbands and wives, parents and families!* Did Jesus not institute the Eucharist in a family-like setting during the Last Supper? When you meet for meals and are together in harmony, *Christ is close to you.* And he is Emmanuel, God with us, in an even greater way whenever you approach the table of the Eucharist. It can happen, as it did at Emmaus, that he is recognized only in "the breaking of the bread" (cf. *Lk* 24:35). It may well be that he is knocking at the door for a long time, waiting for it to be opened so that he can enter and eat with us (cf. *Rev* 3:20). The Last Supper and the words he spoke there contain all the power and wisdom of the sacrifice of the Cross. No other power and wisdom exist by which we can be saved and through which we can help to save others. There is no other power and no other wisdom by which you, parents, can educate both your children and yourselves. The *educational power of the Eucharist* has been proved down the generations and centuries.

Everywhere the Good Shepherd is with us. Even as he was at Cana in Galilee, *the Bridegroom in the midst of the bride and groom* as they entrusted themselves to each other for their whole life, so the Good Shepherd is also with us today as the reason for our hope, the source of strength for our hearts, the wellspring of ever new enthusiasm and the sign of the triumph of the "civilization of love." Jesus, the Good Shepherd, continues to say to us: *Do not be afraid. I am with you.* "I am with you always, to the close of the age" (*Mt* 28:20). What is the source of this strength? What is the reason for our certainty that you are with us, even though they put you to death, O Son of God, and you died like any other human being? What is the reason for this certainty? The Evangelist says: "He loved them to the end" (*Jn* 13:1). Thus do you love us, you who are the First and the Last, the Living One; you who died and are alive forevermore (cf. *Rev* 1:17-18).

The great mystery

19. Saint Paul uses a concise phrase in referring to family life: it is a "*great mystery*" (*Eph* 5:32). What he writes in the *Letter to the Ephesians* about that "great mystery," although deeply rooted in the *Book of Genesis* and in the whole Old Testament tradition, nonetheless represents a new approach which will later find expression in the Church's Magisterium.

The Church professes that Marriage, as the Sacrament of the covenant between husband and wife, is a "great mystery," because it expresses *the spousal love of Christ for his Church.* Saint Paul writes: "Husbands, love your wives, as Christ loved the Church and gave himself up for her, that he might sanctify her, having cleansed her by the washing of water with the word" (*Eph* 5:25-26). The Apostle is speaking here about Baptism, which he discusses at length in the *Letter to the Romans*, where he presents it as a sharing in the death of Christ leading to a sharing in his life (cf. *Rom* 6:3-4). In this Sacrament the believer *is born* as a new man, for Baptism has the power to communicate new life, the very life of God. The mystery of the God-man is in some way recapitulated in the event of Baptism. As Saint Irenaeus would later say, along with many other Fathers of the Church of both East and West: "Christ Jesus, our Lord, the Son of God, became the son of man so that man could become a son of God."[44]

The Bridegroom then is the very same God who became man. In the Old Covenant Yahweh appears as the Bridegroom of Israel, the chosen people — a Bridegroom who is both affectionate and demanding, jealous and faithful. Israel's moments of betrayal, desertion and idolatry, described in such powerful and evocative terms by the Prophets, can never extinguish the love with which *God-the Bridegroom* "loves to the end" (cf. *Jn* 13:1).

The confirmation and fulfillment of the spousal relationship between God and his people are realized in Christ, in the New Covenant. Christ assures us that the Bridegroom is with us (cf. *Mt* 9:15). He is with all of us; he is with the Church. *The Church becomes a Bride,* the Bride of Christ. This Bride, of whom the Letter to the Ephesians speaks, is present in each of the baptized and is like one who presents herself before her Bridegroom. "Christ loved the Church and gave himself up for her..., that he might present the Church to himself in splendour, without spot or wrinkle or any such thing, that she might be holy and without blemish" (*Eph* 5:25-27). The love with which the Bridegroom "has loved" the Church "to the end" continuously renews her holiness in her saints, even though she remains a Church of sinners. Even sinners, "tax collectors and harlots," are called to holiness, as Christ himself affirms in the Gospel (cf. *Mt* 21:31). All are called to become a glorious Church, holy and without blemish. "Be holy," says the Lord, "for I am holy" (*Lev* 11:44; cf. 1 *Pet* 1:16).

This is the deepest significance of the "great mystery," the inner meaning of the *sacramental gift* in the Church, the most profound meaning of Baptism and the Eucharist. They are fruits of the love with which the Bridegroom has loved us to the end, a love which continually expands and lavishes on people an ever greater sharing in the supernatural life.

---

[44]Cf. *Adversus Haereses,* III, 10, 2: PG 7, 873; SCh 211, 116-119; SAINT AUGUSTINE, *De Incarnatione Verbi,* 54: PG 25, 191-192; SAINT AUGUSTINE, *Sermo* 185, 3: PL 38, 999; *Sermo* 194, 3, 3: PL 38, 1016.

Saint Paul, after having said: "Husbands, love your wives" (*Eph* 5:25), emphatically adds: "Even so husbands should love their wives as their own bodies. He who loves his wife loves himself. For no man ever hates his own flesh, but nourishes and cherishes it, as Christ does the Church, because we are members of his body" (*Eph* 5:28-30). And he encourages spouses with the words: "Be subject to one another out of reverence for Christ" (*Eph* 5:21).

This is unquestionably a new presentation of the eternal truth about marriage and the family in the light of the New Covenant. Christ has revealed this truth in the Gospel by his presence at Cana in Galilee, by the sacrifice of the Cross and the Sacraments of his Church. Husbands and wives thus discover in Christ *the point of reference for their spousal love*. In speaking of Christ as the Bridegroom of the Church, Saint Paul uses the analogy of spousal love, referring back to the *Book of Genesis*: "A man leaves his father and his mother and cleaves to his wife, and they become one flesh" (*Gen* 2:24). This is the "great mystery" of that eternal love already present in creation, revealed in Christ and entrusted to the Church. "This mystery is a profound one," the Apostle repeats, "and I am saying that it refers to Christ and the Church" (*Eph* 5:32). The Church cannot therefore be understood as the Mystical Body of Christ, as the sign of man's Covenant with God in Christ, or as the universal sacrament of salvation, unless we keep in mind the "great mystery" involved in the creation of man as male and female and the vocation of both to conjugal love, to fatherhood and to motherhood. The "great mystery," which is the Church and humanity in Christ, does not exist apart from the "great mystery" expressed in the "one flesh" (cf. *Gen* 2:24; *Eph* 5:31-32), that is, in the reality of marriage and the family.

The family itself is the great mystery of God. As the "domestic church," it is the *bride of Christ*. The universal Church, and every particular Church in her, is most immediately revealed as the bride of Christ in the "domestic church" and in its experience of love: conjugal love, paternal and maternal love, fraternal love, the love of a community of persons and of generations. Could we even imagine human love without the Bridegroom and the love with which he first loved to the end? Only if husbands and wives share in that love and in that "great mystery" can they love "to the end." Unless they share in it, they do not know "to the end" what love truly is and how radical are its demands. And this is undoubtedly very dangerous for them.

The teaching of the Letter to the Ephesians amazes us with its depth and the *authority of its ethical teaching*. Pointing to marriage, and indirectly to the family, as the "great mystery" which refers to Christ and the Church, the Apostle Paul is able to reaffirm what he had earlier said to husbands: "Let each one of you love his wife as himself." He goes on to say: "And let the wife see that she respects her husband" (*Eph* 5:33). Respect, because she loves and knows that she is loved in return It is because of this love that husband and wife *become a mutual gift.* Love contains the acknowledgment of the personal dignity of the other, and of his or her absolute uniqueness. Indeed, each of the spouses, as a human being, has been willed by God from among all the creatures of the earth for his or her own sake.[45] Each of them, however, by a conscious and responsible act, makes a free gift of self to the other and to the children received from the Lord. It is significant that Saint Paul continues his exhortation by echoing the fourth commandment: "Children, obey your parents in the Lord, for this is right. 'Honour your father and mother' (this is the first commandment with a promise), 'that it may be well with you and that you may live long on the earth'. Fathers, do not provoke your children to anger, but bring them up in the discipline and instruction of the Lord" (*Eph* 6:1-4). The Apostle thus sees in the fourth commandment the implicit commitment of mutual respect between husband and wife, between parents and children, and he recognizes in it the *principle of family stability.*

Saint Paul's magnificent synthesis concerning the "great mystery" appears as the compendium or *summa,* in some sense, *of the teaching about God and man* which was brought to fulfillment by Christ. Unfortunately, Western thought, with the development of *modern rationalism,* has been gradually moving away from this teaching. The philosopher who formulated the principle of "*Cogito, ergo sum,*" "I think, therefore I am," also gave the modern concept of man its distinctive dualistic character. It is typical of rationalism to make a radical contrast in man between spirit and body, between body and spirit. But man is a person in the unity of his body and his spirit.[46] The body can never be reduced to mere matter: it is a *spiritualized body,* just as man's spirit is so closely united to the body that he can be described as *an embodied spirit.* The richest source for knowledge of the body is the Word made flesh. *Christ reveals man to himself.*[47] In a certain sense this statement of the Second Vatican Council is the reply, so long awaited, which the Church has given to modern rationalism.

---

[45] Cf. SECOND VATICAN ECUMENICAL COUNCIL, Pastoral Constitution on the Church in the Modern World *Gaudium et spes,* 24.

[46] "Corpore et anima unus," as the Council so clearly and felicitously stated: *ibid,* 14.

[47] *Ibid,* 22.

This reply is of fundamental importance for understanding the family, especially against the background of today's civilization, which, as has been said, seems in so many cases to have given up the attempt to be a "civilization of love." The modern age has made great progress in understanding both the material world and human psychology, but with regard to his deepest, metaphysical dimension contemporary man remains to a great extent a *being unknown* to himself. Consequently the family too remains an *unknown reality*. Such is the result of estrangement from that "great mystery" spoken of by the Apostle.

The separation of spirit and body in man has led to a growing tendency to consider the human body, not in accordance with the categories of its specific likeness to God, but rather on the basis of its similarity to all the other bodies present in the world of nature, bodies which man uses as raw material in his efforts to produce goods for consumption. But everyone can immediately realize what enormous dangers lurk behind the application of such criteria to man. When the human body, considered apart from spirit and thought, comes to be used as *raw material* in the same way that the bodies of animals are used — and this actually occurs for example in experimentation on embryos and fetuses — we will inevitably arrive at a dreadful ethical defeat.

Within a similar anthropological perspective, the human family is facing the challenge of a *new Manichaeanism,* in which body and spirit are put in radical opposition; the body does not receive life from the spirit, and the spirit does not give life to the body. Man thus *ceases to live as a person and a subject.* Regardless of all intentions and declarations to the contrary, he becomes merely an *object*. This neo-Manichaean culture has led, for example, to human sexuality being regarded more as a area *for manipulation and exploitation* than as the basis of that *primordial wonder* which led Adam on the morning of creation to exclaim before Eve: "This at last is bone of my bones and flesh of my flesh" (*Gen* 2:23). This same wonder is echoed in the words of the Song of Solomon: "You have ravished my heart, my sister, my bride, you have ravished my heart with a glance of your eyes" (*Song* 4:9). How far removed are some modern ideas from the profound understanding of masculinity and femininity found in Divine Revelation! Revelation leads us to discover in *human sexuality* a *treasure proper to the person,* who finds true fulfillment in the family but who can likewise express his profound calling in virginity and in celibacy for the sake of the Kingdom of God.

Modern rationalism *does not tolerate mystery*. It does not accept the mystery of man as male and female, nor is it willing to admit that the full truth about man has been revealed in Jesus Christ. In particular, it does not accept the "great mystery" proclaimed in the Letter to the Ephesians, but radically opposes it. It may well acknowledge, in the context of a vague deism, the possibility and even the need for a supreme or divine Being, but it firmly rejects the idea of a God who became man in order to save man. For rationalism it is unthinkable that God should be the Redeemer, much less *that he should be "the Bridegroom,"* the primordial and unique source of the human love between spouses. Rationalism provides a radically different way of looking at creation and the meaning of human existence. But once man begins to lose sight of a God who loves him, a God who calls man through Christ to live in him and with him, and once the family no longer has the possibility of sharing in the "great mystery," what is left except the mere *temporal dimension of life?* Earthly life becomes nothing more than the scenario of a battle for existence, of a desperate search for gain, and financial gain before all else.

The deep-seated roots of the "great mystery," the sacrament of love and life which began with Creation and Redemption and which *has Christ the Bridegroom as its ultimate surety,* have been lost in the modern way of looking at things. The "great mystery" is threatened in us and all around us. May the Church's celebration of the Year of the Family be a fruitful opportunity for husbands and wives to rediscover that mystery and recommit themselves to it with strength, courage and enthusiasm.

Mother of fairest love

20. The history of "fairest love" begins at the Annunciation, in those wondrous words which the angel spoke to Mary, called to become the Mother of the Son of God. With Mary's "yes," the One who is "God from God and Light from Light" becomes a son of man. Mary is his Mother; while continuing to be the Virgin who "knows not man" (cf. *Lk* 1:34). As Mother and Virgin, *Mary* becomes the *Mother of Fairest Love.* This truth is already revealed in the words of the Archangel Gabriel, but its full significance will gradually become clearer and more evident as Mary follows her Son in the pilgrimage of faith.[48]

The "Mother of Fairest Love" was accepted by the one who, according to Israel's tradition, was already her earthly husband: *Joseph, of the house of David.* Joseph would have had the right to consider his promised bride as his wife and the mother of his children. But God takes it upon himself to intervene in this spousal covenant: "Joseph, son of David, do

---

[48] Cf. SECOND VATICAN ECUMENICAL COUNCIL, Dogmatic Constitution on the Church *Lumen gentium,* 56-59.

not fear to take Mary as your wife, for that which is conceived in her is of the Holy Spirit" (*Mt* 1:20). Joseph is aware, having seen it with his own eyes, that a new life with which he has had nothing to do has been conceived in Mary. Being a just man, and observing the Old Law, which in his situation imposed the obligation of divorce, he wishes to dissolve his marriage in a loving way (cf. *Mt* 1:19). The angel of the Lord tells him that this would not be consistent with his vocation; indeed it would be contrary to the spousal love uniting him to Mary. This mutual spousal love, to be completely "fairest love," requires that he should take Mary and her Son into his own house in Nazareth. Joseph obeys the divine message and does all that he had been commanded (cf. *Mt* 1:24). And so, thanks also to Joseph, the *mystery of the Incarnation* and, together with it, the mystery of the Holy Family, *come to be profoundly inscribed in the spousal love of husband and wife* and, in an indirect way, in the genealogy of every human family. What Saint Paul will call the "great mystery" found its most lofty expression in the Holy Family. Thus the *family* truly takes its place *at the very heart of the New Covenant*.

It can also be said that the history of "fairest love" began, in a certain way, with the *first human couple:* Adam and Eve. The temptation to which they yielded and the original sin which resulted did not completely deprive them of the capacity for "fairest love." This becomes clear when we read, for example, in the Book of Tobit that the spouses Tobias and Sarah, in defining the meaning of their union, appealed to their first parents, Adam and Eve (cf. *Tob* 8:6). In the New Covenant, Saint Paul also bears witness to this, speaking of Christ as a new Adam (cf. 1 *Cor* 15:45). Christ does not come to condemn the first Adam and the first Eve, but to save them. He comes to renew everything that is God's gift in man, everything in him that is eternally good and beautiful, everything that forms the basis of "fairest love." The *history of "fairest love"* is, in one sense, the *history of man's salvation*.

"Fairest love" always *begins with the self-revelation of the person*. At creation Eve reveals herself to Adam, just as Adam reveals himself to Eve. In the course of history newly-married couples tell each other: "We shall walk the path of life together." The family thus begins as a union of the two and, through the Sacrament, as a new community in Christ. *For love to be truly "fairest," it must be a gift of God,* grafted by the Holy Spirit on to human hearts and continually nourished in them (cf. *Rom* 5:5). Fully conscious of this, the Church in the Sacrament of Marriage asks the Holy Spirit to visit human hearts. If love is truly to be "fairest love," a gift of one person to another, it must come from the One who is himself a gift and the source of every gift.

Such was the case, as the Gospel recounts, with Mary and Joseph who, at the threshold of the New Covenant, renewed the experience of "fairest love" described in the Song of Solomon. Joseph thinks of Mary in the words: "My sister my bride" (*Song* 4:9). Mary, the Mother of God, conceives by the power of the Holy Spirit, who is the origin of the "fairest love," which the Gospel delicately places in the context of the "great mystery."

When we speak about "fairest love," we are also speaking about *beauty:* the beauty of love and the beauty of the human being who, by the power of the Holy Spirit, is capable of such love. We are speaking of the beauty of man and woman: their beauty as brother or sister, as a couple about to be married, as husband and wife. The Gospel sheds light not only on the mystery of "fairest love," but also on the equally profound mystery of beauty, which, like love, is from God. Man and woman are from God, two persons called to become a mutual gift. From the primordial gift of the Spirit, the "giver of life," there arises the reciprocal gift of being husband or wife, no less than that of being brother or sister.

All this is confirmed by the mystery of the Incarnation, a mystery which has been *the source of a new beauty* in the history of humanity and has inspired countless masterpieces of art. After the strict prohibition against portraying the invisible God by graven images (cf. *Dt* 4:15-20), the Christian era began instead to portray in art the God who became man, Mary his Mother, Saint Joseph, the Saints of the Old and New Covenant and the entire created world redeemed by Christ. In this way it began a new relationship with the world of culture and of art. It can be said that this *new artistic canon,* attentive to the deepest dimension of man and his future, originates in the mystery of Christ's Incarnation and draws inspiration from the mysteries of his life: his birth in Bethlehem, his hidden life in Nazareth, his public ministry, Golgotha, the Resurrection and his final return in glory. The Church is conscious that her presence in the contemporary world, and in particular the contribution and support she offers to the promotion of the dignity of marriage and the family, are intimately linked to the development of culture, and she is rightly concerned for this. This is precisely why the Church is so concerned with the direction taken by the means of social communication, which have the duty of *forming* as well as *informing* their vast audience.[49] Knowing the vast and powerful impact of the media, she never tires of reminding communications workers of the dangers arising from the manipulation of truth. Indeed, what truth can there be in films, shows

---

[49]Cf. PONTIFICAL COUNCIL FOR SOCIAL COMMUNICATIONS, Pastoral Instruction *Aetatis novae* (22 February 1992), 7.

and radio and television programmes dominated by pornography and violence? Do these really serve the *truth about man?* Such questions are unavoidable for those who work in the field of communications and those who have responsibility for creating and marketing media products.

This kind of critical reflection should lead our society, which certainly contains many positive aspects on the material and cultural level, to realize that, from various points of view, it is a *society which is sick* and is creating profound distortions in man. Why is this happening? The reason is that our society has broken away from the full truth about man, from the truth about what man and woman really are as persons. Thus it cannot adequately comprehend the real meaning of the gift of persons in marriage, responsible love at the service of fatherhood and motherhood, and the true grandeur of procreation and education. Is it an exaggeration to say that the *mass media,* if they are not guided by sound ethical principles, fail to serve the truth in its fundamental dimension? This is the real drama: the modern means of social communication are tempted to manipulate the message, *thereby falsifying the truth about man.* Human beings are not the same thing as the images proposed in advertising and shown by the modern mass media. *They are much more,* in their physical and psychic unity, as composites of soul and body, as persons. They are much more because of their vocation to love, which introduces them as male and female into the realm of the "great mystery."

Mary was the first to enter this realm, and she introduced her husband Joseph into it. Thus they became the *first models* of that "fairest love" which the Church continually implores for young people, husbands and wives and families. Young people, spouses and families themselves should never cease to pray for this. How can we not think about the crowds of pilgrims, old and young, who visit Marian shrines and gaze upon the face of the Mother of God, on the faces of the Holy Family, where they find reflected the full beauty of the love which God has given to mankind?

In the Sermon on the Mount, recalling the sixth commandment, Christ proclaims: "You have heard that it was said, 'You shall not commit adultery.' But I say to you that every one who looks at a woman lustfully has already committed adultery with her in his heart" (*Mt* 5:27-28). With regard to the Decalogue and its purpose of defending the traditional solidity of marriage and the family, these words represent a great step forward. Jesus goes to the very source of the sin of adultery, which dwells in the innermost heart of man and is revealed in a way of looking and thinking dominated by *concupiscence.* Through concupiscence *man tends to treat as his own possession another human being,* one who does not belong to him but to God. In speaking to his contemporaries, Christ is also speaking to men and women in every age and generation. He is speaking in particular to our own generation, living as it is in a society marked by consumerism and hedonism.

Why does Christ speak out in so forceful and demanding a way in the Sermon on the Mount? The reason is quite clear: Christ wants to safeguard *the holiness of marriage and of the family*. He wants to defend the full truth about the human person and his dignity.

Only in the light of this truth can the family be "to the end" the great "revelation," the *first discovery of the other:* the mutual discovery of husband and wife and then of each son and daughter born to them. All that a husband and a wife promise to each other — to be "true in good times and in bad, and to love and honour each other all the days of their life" — is possible only when "fairest love" is present. Man today cannot learn this from what modern mass culture has to say. "Fairest love" is learned above all in prayer. *Prayer,* in fact, always brings with it, to use an expression of Saint Paul, a type of *interior hiddenness with Christ in God; "your life is hid with Christ in God"* (*Col* 3:3). Only in this hiddenness do we see the workings of the Holy Spirit, the source of "fairest love." He has poured forth this love not only in the hearts of Mary and Joseph but also in the hearts of all married couples who are open to hearing the word of God and keeping it (cf. *Lk* 8:15). The future of each family unit depends upon this "fairest love": the mutual love of husband and wife, of parents and children, a love embracing all generations. Love is the true *source of the unity and strength of the family*.

Birth and danger

21. It is significant that the brief account of the infancy of Jesus mentions, practically at the same time, his *birth* and the *danger* which he immediately had to confront. Luke records the prophetic words uttered by the aged Simeon when the Child was presented to the Lord in the Temple forty days after his birth. Simeon speaks of "light" and of a "sign of contradiction." He goes on to predict of Mary: "And a sword will pierce through your own soul also" (cf. *Lk* 2:32-35). Matthew, for his part, tells of the plot of Herod against Jesus. Informed by the Magi who came from the East to see the new king who was to be born (cf. *Mt* 2:2), Herod senses a threat to his power, and after their departure he orders the death of all male children aged two years or under in Bethlehem and the surrounding towns. Jesus escapes from the hands of Herod thanks to a special divine intervention and the fatherly care of Joseph, who takes him with his mother into Egypt, where they remain until Herod's death. The Holy Family then returns to Nazareth, their home town, and begins what for many years would be a

hidden life, marked by the carrying out of daily tasks with fidelity and generosity (cf. *Mt* 2:1-23; *Lk* 2:39-52).

The fact that Jesus, from his very birth, had to face threats and dangers has a certain *prophetic eloquence*. Even as a Child, Jesus is a "sign of contradiction." Prophetically eloquent also is the tragedy of the innocent children of Bethlehem, slaughtered at Herod's command.[50] According to the Church's ancient liturgy, they shared in the birth and saving passion of Christ. Through their own "passion," they complete "what is lacking in Christ's afflictions for the sake of his body, that is, the Church" (*Col* 1:24).

In the infancy Gospel, *the proclamation of life,* which comes about in a wondrous way in the birth of the Redeemer, is thus put in sharp contrast with the *threat to life,* a life which embraces the mystery of the Incarnation and of the divine-human reality of Christ in its entirety. The Word was made flesh (cf. *Jn* 1:14): God became man. The Fathers of the Church frequently call attention to this sublime mystery: "God became man, so that we might become gods."[51] This truth of faith is likewise the truth about the human being. It clearly indicates the gravity of all attempts on the life of a child in the womb of its mother. Precisely in this situation we encounter *everything which is diametrically opposed* to "fairest love." If an individual is exclusively concerned with "use," he can reach the point of killing love by killing the fruit of love. For the culture of use, the "blessed fruit of your womb" (*Lk* 1:42) becomes in a certain sense an "accursed fruit."

How can we not recall, in this regard, the aberrations that the so-called *constitutional State* has tolerated in so many countries? The law of God is univocal and categorical with respect to human life. God commands: "You shall not kill" (*Ex* 20:13). *No human lawgiver can therefore assert: it is permissible for you to kill, you have the right to kill, or you should kill.* Tragically, in the history of our century, this has actually occurred when certain political forces have come to power, even by democratic means, and have passed laws contrary to the right to life of every human being, in the name of eugenic, ethnic or other reasons, as unfounded as they are mistaken. A no less serious phenomenon, also because it meets with widespread acquiescence or consensus in public opinion, is that of laws which fail to respect the right to life from the moment of conception. How can one

---

[50] In the liturgy of their Feast, which has its origins in the fifth century, the Church turns to the Holy Innocents, invoking them with the words of the poet Prudentius (✝ c. 405) as "the flowers of the martyrs whom, at the very threshold of their lives, the persecutor of Christ cut down as the whirlwind does to roses still in bud."

[51] SAINT ATHANASIUS, *De Incarnatione Verbi,* 54: PG 25, 191-192.

morally accept laws that permit the killing of a human being not yet born, but already alive in the mother's womb? The right to life becomes an exclusive prerogative of adults who even manipulate legislatures in order to carry out their own plans and pursue their own interests.

We are facing an immense threat to life: not only to the life of individuals but also to that of civilization itself. The statement that civilization has become, in some areas, a "civilization of death" is being confirmed in disturbing ways. Was it not a *prophetic event* that the birth of Christ was accompanied by danger to his life? Yes, even the life of the One who is at the same time Son of Man and Son of God was threatened. It was endangered from the very beginning, and only by a miracle did he escape death.

Nevertheless, in the last few decades some consoling signs of a *reawakening of conscience* have appeared: both among intellectuals and in public opinion itself. There is a new and growing sense of respect for life from the first moment of conception, especially among young people. "Pro-life" movements are beginning to spread. This is a leaven of hope for the future of the family and of all humanity.

"You welcomed me"

22. Married couples and families of all the world: *the Bridegroom is with you!* This is what the Pope wishes to say to you above all else during this Year which the United Nations and the Church have dedicated to the family. "God so loved the world that he gave his only Son, that whoever believes in him should not perish but have eternal life. For God sent his Son into the world, not to condemn the world, but that the world might be saved through him" (*Jn* 3:16-17). "That which is born of the flesh is flesh, and that which is born of the Spirit is spirit... You must be born anew" (*Jn* 3:6-7). You must be born "of water and the Spirit" (*Jn* 3:5). You yourselves, dear fathers and mothers, are the *first witnesses and servants* of this *rebirth* in the Holy Spirit. As you beget children on earth, never forget that *you are also begetting them for God.* God wants their birth in the Holy Spirit. He wants them to be adopted children in the Only-begotten Son, who gives us "power to become children of God" (*Jn* 1:12). The work of salvation continues in the world and is carried out through the Church. All this is the work of the Son of God, the Divine Bridegroom, who has given to us the Kingdom of his Father and who reminds us, his disciples, that "the Kingdom of God is in the midst of you" (*Lk* 17:21).

Our faith tells us that Jesus Christ, who "is seated at the right hand of the Father," will come to judge the living and the dead. On the other hand, the Gospel of John assures us that Christ was sent "into the world, not to condemn the world, but that the world might be saved through him" (*Jn* 3:17). In what then does judgment consist? Christ himself gives the answer: "And this is the judgment, that the light has come into the world... But he who does what is true comes into the light, that it may be clearly seen that his deeds have been wrought by God" (*Jn* 3:19, 21). Recently, the Encyclical *Veritatis splendor* also reminded us of this.[52] Is Christ then a judge? *Your own actions will Judge you in the light of the truth which you know.* Fathers and mothers, sons and daughters, will be judged by their actions. Each one of us will be judged according to the Commandments, including those we have discussed in this *Letter*: the Fourth, Fifth, Sixth and Ninth Commandments. But ultimately everyone will be judged *on love,* which is the deepest meaning and the summing-up of the Commandments. As Saint John of the Cross wrote: "In the evening of life we shall be judged on love."[53] Christ, the Redeemer and Bridegroom of mankind, "was born for this and came into the world for this, to bear witness to the truth. Everyone who is of truth hears his voice" (cf. *Jn* 18:37). Christ will be the judge, but in the way that he himself indicated in speaking of the Last Judgment (cf. *Mt* 25:31-46). His will be a *judgment on love,* a judgment which will definitively confirm the truth that the Bridegroom was with us, without perhaps our having been aware of it.

The judge is the *Bridegroom of the Church and of humanity*. This is why he says, in passing his sentence: "Come, O blessed of my Father... for I was hungry and you gave me food, I was thirsty and you gave me drink, I was a stranger and you welcomed me, I was naked and you clothed me" (*Mt* 25:34-36). This list could of course be lengthened, and countless other problems relevant to married and family life could be added. There we might very well find statements like: "I was an unborn child, and you welcomed me by letting me be born"; "I was an abandoned child, and you became my family"; "I was an orphan, and you adopted me and raised me as one of your own children." Or again: "You helped mothers filled with uncertainty and exposed to wrongful pressure to welcome their unborn child and let it be born," and "You helped large families and families in difficulty to look after and educate the children God gave them." We could continue with a long and detailed list, including all those kinds of true moral and human good in which love is expressed. This is *the great harvest* which the Redeemer of the world, to whom the Father has entrusted judgment, will come to reap. It is

---

[52] Cf. *Veritatis splendor* (6 August 1993), 84.

[53] *Words of Light and Love,* 59.

the *harvest of grace and of good works,* ripened by the breath of the Bridegroom in the Holy Spirit, who is ever at work in the world and in the Church. For all of this, let us give thanks to the Giver of every good gift.

We also know however that according to the Gospel of Matthew the Final Judgment will contain another list, solemn and terrifying: "Depart from me... for I was hungry and you gave me no food, I was thirsty and you gave me no drink, I was a stranger and you did not welcome me, naked and you did not clothe me" (*Mt* 25:41-43). To this list also we could add other ways of acting, in which Jesus is present in each case as the *one who has been rejected.* In this way he would identify with the abandoned wife or husband, or with the child conceived and then rejected: "You did not welcome me!" This judgment is also to be found throughout the history of our families; it is to be found throughout the history of our nations and all humanity. Christ's words, "You did not welcome me," also touch social institutions, governments and international organizations.

Pascal wrote that "Jesus will be in agony until the end of the world."[54] The agony of Gethsemane and the agony of Golgotha are *the summit of the revelation of love.* Both scenes reveal the Bridegroom who is with us, who loves us ever anew, and "loves us to the end" (cf. *Jn* 13:1). The love which is in Christ, and which from him flows beyond the limits of individual or family histories, flows beyond the limits of all human history.

At the end of these reflections, dear Brothers and Sisters, in view of what will be proclaimed from various platforms during the Year of the Family, I would like to renew with you the profession of faith which Peter addressed to Christ: "You have the words of eternal life" (*Jn* 6:68). Together let us say: "Your words, O Lord, will not pass away!" (cf. *Mk* 13:31). What then is the Pope's wish for you at the end of this lengthy *meditation on the Year of the Family?* It is his prayer that all of you will be in agreement with these words, which are "spirit and life" (*Jn* 6:63).

"Strengthened in the inner man"

23. I bow my knees before the Father, from whom every fatherhood and motherhood is named, "that he may grant you to be strengthened with might through his Spirit in the inner man" (*Eph* 3:16). I willingly return to these words of the Apostle, which I mentioned in the first part of this *Letter.* In a certain sense they are pivotal words. *The family, fatherhood and motherhood*

---

[54]B. PASCAL, *Pensées, Le mystère de Jésus,* 553 (ed. Br.).

all go together. The family is the first human setting in which is formed that "inner man" of which the Apostle speaks. The growth of the inner man in strength and vigour is a gift of the Father and the Son in the Holy Spirit.

The Year of the Family sets before us in the Church an immense task, no different from the task which families face every year and every day. In the context of this Year, however, that task takes on particular meaning and importance. We began the Year of the Family in Nazareth on the *Solemnity of the Holy Family.* Throughout this Year we wish to make our pilgrim way towards that place of grace which has become the *Shrine of the Holy Family* in the history of humanity. We want to make this pilgrimage in order to become aware once again of that heritage of truth about the family which from the beginning has been *a treasure for the Church.* It is a treasure which grows out of the rich tradition of the Old Covenant, is completed in the New and finds its fullest symbolic expression in the mystery of the Holy Family in which the divine Bridegroom brings about the redemption of all families. From there Jesus proclaims the *"gospel of the family."* All generations of Christ's disciples have drawn upon this treasure of truth, beginning with the Apostles, on whose teaching we have so frequently drawn in this *Letter.*

In our own times this treasure has been examined in depth in the documents of the Second Vatican Council.[55] Perceptive analyses were developed in the many addresses given by Pope Pius XII to newlyweds,[56] in the Encyclical *Humanae vitae* of Pope Paul VI, in the speeches delivered at the Synod of Bishops on the Family (1980) and in the Apostolic Exhortation *Familiaris consortio.* I have already spoken of these statements of the Magisterium. If I return to them now, it is in order to emphasize how vast and rich is the *treasure of Christian truth about the family.* *Written testimonies* alone, however, will not suffice. Much more important are *living testimonies.* As Pope Paul VI observed, "contemporary man listens more willingly to witnesses than to teachers, and if he listens to teachers it is because they are witnesses."[57] In the Church, the treasure of the family has been entrusted first and foremost to witnesses: to those fathers and mothers,

---

[55] Cf. in particular Pastoral Constitution on the Church *Gaudium et spes,* 47-52.

[56] Of particular interest is the Address to those taking part in the Convention of the Italian Catholic Union of Midwives (29 October 1951), in *Discorsi e Radiomessaggi, XIII, 333-353.*

[57] Cf. Address to the members of the "Consilium de Laicis" (2 October 1974) in *AAS* 66 (1974), 568.

sons and daughters who through the family have discovered the path of their human and Christian vocation, the dimension of the "inner man" (*Eph* 3:16) of which the Apostle speaks, and thus have attained holiness. *The Holy Family is the beginning of countless other holy families.* The Council recalled that holiness is the vocation of all the baptized.[58] In our age, as in the past, there is no lack of witnesses to the "gospel of the family," even if they are not well known or have not been proclaimed saints by the Church. The Year of the Family is the appropriate occasion to bring about an increased awareness of their existence and their great number.

The history of mankind, the history of salvation, passes by way of the family. In these pages I have tried to show how the family is placed at the centre of the great struggle between good and evil, between life and death, between love and all that is opposed to love. To the family is entrusted the task of striving, first and foremost, *to unleash the forces of good,* the source of which is found in Christ the Redeemer of man. *Every family unit needs to make these forces their own so that,* to use a phrase spoken on the occasion of the Millennium of Christianity in Poland, the family will be "*strong with the strength of God.*"[59] This is why the present *Letter* has sought to draw inspiration from the apostolic exhortations found in the writings of Paul (cf. 1 *Cor* 7:1-40; *Eph* 5:21-6:9; *Col* 3:25) and the Letters of Peter and John (cf. 1 *Pet* 3:1-7; 1 *Jn* 2:12-17). Despite the differences in their historical and cultural contexts, how similar are the experiences of Christians and families then and now!

What I offer, then, is *an invitation:* an invitation addressed especially to you, dearly beloved husbands and wives, fathers and mothers, sons and daughters. It is an invitation to all the particular Churches to remain united in the teaching of the apostolic truth. It is addressed to my Brothers in the Episcopate, and to priests, religious families and consecrated persons, to movements and associations of the lay faithful; to our brothers and sisters united by common faith in Jesus Christ, even while not yet sharing the full communion willed by the Saviour;[60] to all who by sharing in the faith of Abraham belong, like us, to the great community of believers in the one God;[61] to those who are the heirs of other spiritual and religious traditions;

---

[58] Cf. Dogmatic Constitution on the Church *Lumen gentium,* 40.

[59] Cf. CARDINAL STEFAN WYSZYŃSKI, *Rodzina Bogiem silna,* Homily delivered at Jasna Góra (26 August 1961).

[60] Cf. Dogmatic Constitution on the Church *Lumen gentium,* 15.

[61] Cf. *ibid.,* 16.

and to all men and women of good will.

May Christ, who is the same "yesterday and today and for ever" (*Heb* 13:8), be with us as we bow the knee before the Father, from whom all fatherhood and motherhood and every human family is named (cf. *Eph* 3:14-15). In the words of the prayer to the Father which Christ himself taught us, may he once again offer testimony of that love with which he loved us "to the end!" (*Jn* 13:1).

I speak with the power of his truth to all people of our day, so that they will come to appreciate the grandeur of the goods of marriage, family and life; so that they will come to appreciate the great danger which follows when these realities are not respected, or when the supreme values which lie at the foundation of the family and of human dignity are disregarded.

May the Lord Jesus repeat these truths to us *with the power and the wisdom of the Cross,* so that humanity will not yield to the temptation of the "father of lies" (*Jn* 8:44), who constantly seeks to draw people to broad and easy ways, ways apparently smooth and pleasant, but in reality full of snares and dangers. May we always be enabled to follow the One who is "the way, and the truth, and the life" (*Jn* 14:6).

Dear Brothers and Sisters: Let all of this be the task of Christian families and the object of the Church's missionary concern throughout this Year, so rich in singular divine graces. May the Holy Family, icon and model of every human family, help each individual to walk in the spirit of Nazareth. May it help each family unit to grow in understanding of its particular mission in society and the Church by hearing the Word of God, by prayer and by a fraternal sharing of life. May Mary, Mother of "Fairest Love," and Joseph, Guardian of the Redeemer, accompany us all with their constant protection.

With these sentiments I bless every family in the name of the Most Holy Trinity: Father, Son and Holy Spirit.

Given in Rome, at Saint Peter's, on 2 February, the Feast of the Presentation of the Lord, in the year 1994, the sixteenth of my Pontificate.

Address of His Holiness Pope John Paul II to a Gathering of Families from Around the World Attending the World Meeting with Families
Saint Peter's Square, 8 October 1994

On Saturday, 8 October 1994, the Holy Father spoke in St. Peter's Square to a gathering of families who had come from around the world to attend the World Meeting with Families. Here is a translation of his address, which was given in Italian.

1. *Familia, quid dicis de te ipsa?* I heard the similar words for the first time in the Council hall, at the beginning of the Second Vatican Council. But the Cardinal who pronounced them, said *"Ecclesia, quid dicis de te ipsa?"* instead of *"familia."*

There is a parallel here. When I reflected and prayed prior to this meeting, this parallel between the two questions became impressed upon my heart and mind: *Familia, quid dicis de te ipsa?* A question, a question that expects an answer.

We can say that this Year of the Family is a great response precisely to this question. *Quid dicis de te ipsa?* Family, Christian family: what are you? We already find an answer in the early Christian times. In the post-apostolic period: "I am the domestic Church." In other words, I am an *Ecclesiola*, a domestic Church. And again we see the same parallelism: Family-Church; the apostolic and universal dimension of the Church on the one hand, the family dimension, the domestic dimension of the Church on the other.

Both are nourished by the same sources. They have the same genealogy in God: in God, Father, Son and Holy Spirit. With this genealogy they come into being through the great mystery of divine love. This mystery is called *Deus homo*, the Incarnation of God who so loved the world that he gave his only begotten Son, so that none of those who followed him might perish. God the Father, God the Son, God the Holy Spirit. A single God, three Persons: an unfathomable mystery. The Church, and the family, the domestic Church, find their source in this mystery.

Year of the Family goes back to Vatican II

2. Beloved brothers and sisters who have come from 100 different countries for this important appointment on the occasion of the Year of the Family, "grace to you, and peace from God our Father!" (Col 1:2).

I have listened with great attention to the *testimonies* and *reflections* which have just been presented. I am grateful to Cardinal López Trujillo for his words and for the work which he and his co-workers have done in order to make this celebration, and many others, a reality in this Year of the Family. I greet you together with all those who are present here, Cardinals and Bishops, members of the Synod now working on a most important theme: that of consecration, of consecrated persons and communities in the Church. One could have thought of a different topic, but these two themes are very closely related. Because in the mystery of the Church, family and consecration go together. Did not the Second Vatican Council also say that married couples are consecrated as it were to God in the sacrament of marriage? They are consecrated to create an environment of love and an environment of life. Love and life. This is your vocation, beloved brothers and sisters; your vocation, beloved families. This is your vocation, which runs through all generations, starting with your ancestors, your grandparents, down to the grandchildren and great-grandchildren; a family of generations. In the same family there is this pilgrimage of generations through earthly life, to reach the Father's house.

On this occasion when everyone is offering their witness, I would also like to give testimony on behalf of the Church in Rome and the Petrine Office about what we have tried to do for families in our time. We can start with the Second Vatican Council: *"Familia, quid dicis de te ipsa?"* "Church, what do you say about yourself?"

With regard to the family, in *Gaudium et spes* there is a separate chapter which discusses the promotion of the family, "fostering the dignity of the family." This is the proper point of view. The title itself is sufficient for a deep reflection on what it means to be family, bride and bridegroom, husband and wife, on what it means to be father and mother, and also son and daughter and even grandchildren. All this is found definitively in the dimension of a common dignity, family dignity, promotion of family dignity. This promotion of family dignity is precisely the beacon, we could say, with which the Second Vatican Council opened the Year of the Family.

This Year of the Family, as you well know, was opened in Nazareth. But it was inaugurated in more distant times, during the Second Vatican Council, in that amazing document: *Gaudium et spes*, where fostering the dignity of the family is discussed.

And then I must cite Paul VI. One of the unfading merits of Paul VI is that of having given the Church the Encyclical *Humanae vitae* (1968), which in its day was not understood in all its importance but which, with the passage of time, has come to reveal all its prophetic content. In *Humanae vitae* Paul VI, the great Pontiff, indicated the criteria for preserving the love of a couple from the danger of hedonistic selfishness which, in not a few parts of the world, is tending to lessen the vitality of families and render marriages almost sterile. In his other historic Encyclical *Populorum progressio*, Pope Paul spoke for the developing peoples of the world, inviting the richer countries to follow a policy of true solidarity, a far cry from the deceptive form of neo-colonialism which imposes projects of the systematic limitation of births.

Church has created new structures to serve the family

The family was also dealt with by the 1980 Synod of Bishops, from which came the Apostolic Exhortation *Familiaris consortio*, which introduced an organized context for the pastoral care of the family as a priority and the basis of the new evangelization. There is also a logical connection between that synod and that Post-Synodal Exhortation and the 1983 *Charter of the Rights of the Family*.

I would also like to recall here my own *catecheses* on this subject, developed in a series of Wednesday General Audiences and collected in a book called *Male and Female He Created Them*. In addition, there have been many other statements on various occasions, and most recently the *Letter to Families*, with which I knocked on the door of every home to proclaim the "Gospel of the family," well aware that *the family is the first and most important way of the Church* (n. 1).

3. The attention given to the institution of the family has caused the Church in recent years to create *new structures to serve the family*. Thus not only documents, but also structures, accomplishments.

On 13 May 1981, a very significant date, the Pontifical Council for the Family was created, and then, on the academic level, the Institute for Studies on Marriage and Family. I have been encouraged to promote such institutions also by the experiences which formerly marked *my activity as priest and Bishop in my country*, where I always gave special attention to youth and to families. It is precisely from those experiences that I realized the indispensable need for a profound intellectual and theological formation in this area, in order to develop an adequate ethical approach to the value of our bodily reality, to the meaning of marriage and family, and to the question of responsible parenthood.

How important this is has come to light especially in the current year 1994, which, at the initiative of the United Nations Organization, has been dedicated to the family. A certain tendency which emerged at the recent Cairo Conference on "Population and Development" and at other meetings held in recent months, as well as certain attempts in seats of government to distort the meaning of the family by depriving it of its natural reference to marriage, have demonstrated how necessary the steps taken by the Church are in support of the family and its indispensable role in society.

Society cannot do without the family

4. Thanks to the concerted action of Bishops and informed lay people, we have faced numerous obstacles and misunderstandings, if only to offer this *witness of love*, which has emphasized the unbreakable bond of solidarity which exists between Church and family. But the task which awaits us is certainly still great. And you, dear families, are here also in order to take on this further commitment, in this decisive area which requires the vigilant and responsible participation not only of Christians but of the whole of society.

We are in fact convinced that *society cannot do without the institution of the family* for the simple reason that society itself arises from families and draws its solidity from families.

Faced with the cultural and social decay presently taking place, in the presence of the spread of ills such as violence, drugs and organized crime, what better guarantee of prevention and liberation is there than a united family, morally healthy and socially involved? It is in families like these that people are trained in the virtues and in the social values of solidarity, openness, loyalty, respect for others and their dignity.

5. Returning to the importance of this Year, I would again like to recall that we are preparing for the Year 2000, the Great Jubilee of Christ's

coming, of the Incarnation. For this date, for the celebration of these 2,000 years, we are preparing in different stages: the Year of the Redemption (1983) and the Marian Year (1987-1988), and now this Year of the Family which certainly represents *an important stage* in the preparation for the Great Jubilee of the Year 2000. God willing, at the end of this Year of the Family, as one of its most valuable results and as a programme for the future, I will endeavour to publish the already announced Encyclical on life.

This Encyclical had been requested by the Cardinals two years ago. I think that we now have the right circumstance for the preparation and publication of this Encyclical on life, on human life, on holiness of life. And it would be in perfect harmony as it were with the first Encyclical of this period, which also concerns life, for it begins with the words *Humanae vitae*....

I must say that they allowed me 25 minutes, and I do not know whether or not I have already exceeded these 25 minutes! ... There, you see, the Pope is kept under rigorous restrictions, extremely rigorous, but I would not like to go on too long....

Family is eloquent image of the Blessed Trinity

6.   So, beloved, these lights we see are lights that come from all over the world. Each family bears a light, and each family is a light! It is a light, a beacon which must illumine the way of the Church and of the world in the future, to the end of this millennium and even beyond, as long as God permits this world to exist.

Dear married couples! Dear parents! The communion of man and woman in marriage *corresponds to the specific requirements of human nature*. At the same time, it is a reflection of God's goodness, which becomes fatherhood and motherhood. Sacramental grace — first in Baptism and Confirmation, then later in Matrimony — has poured a fresh and powerful wave of supernatural love into your hearts. It is love which flows from the inner depths of the Blessed Trinity, of which the human family is an eloquent and living image.

This is a supernatural reality which helps you to sanctify your joys, to face hardships and sufferings, and to triumph over difficulties and moments of fatigue. In a word, it is a source of sanctification for you, and a source of strength for selfgiving.

It grows by constant prayer and above all by your sharing in the sacraments of Reconciliation and of the Eucharist.

Strengthened by this supernatural help, be ever ready, dear families, to account for the hope that is within you (cf. 1 Peter 3:15).

May you always *be examples of openness, dedication and generosity. Preserve, assist* and *promote* the life of every person, especially the weak, the sick and the handicapped. *Bear witness* to love for life, and sow that love abundantly. *Be builders of the culture of life and the civilization of love.*

In the Church and in society, *now is the hour of the family*. Families are called to play a primary role in the task of the new evangelization. From the heart of families devoted to prayer, to the apostolate and to the Church's life there will develop genuine vocations not only for the formation of other families, but also for the life of special consecration, whose beauty and mission is being described during these very days by the Synod of Bishops.

God has given the family the right to exist

7. Finally, I will return to what I said at the very beginning. *Familia, quid dicis de te ipsa?* Here at our gathering in St. Peter's Square, the family has tried to answer this question: *Quid dicis de te ipsa*? So: "I am," says the family. "Why do you exist"? I exist because he who said of himself: "I alone am what I am," has given me the right and the strength to exist. I am, I am the family, I am the environment of love; I am the environment of life; I exist. *What do you say about yourself? Quid dicis de te ipsa?* I am *gaudium et spes!* And thus we may end this improvisation, because .... There are papers, it is true, but half my speech has been improvised, dictated by my heart and sought in prayer over many days.

ADDRESS (EXCERPTS) OF
HIS HOLINESS POPE JOHN PAUL II
TO THE DIPLOMATIC CORPS ACCREDITED TO THE HOLY SEE
VATICAN, 9 JANUARY 1995

His Holiness Pope John Paul II spoke on the occasion of the traditional exchange of New Year greetings with the Ambassadors on 9 January 1995. The final segment of the address (No. 9 - 11) concerned the International Conference on Population and Development, held in Cairo. Below is a translation of that portion. The original was given in French.

Holy See seeks to be voice of human conscience

9.	In a few months we are going to celebrate the 50th anniversary of the foundation of the *United Nations Organization*: how could we fail to want the Organization to become ever more the instrument par excellence for promoting and safeguarding peace? In recent years it has increased the number of its peace-keeping operations, as also its interventions aimed at easing the transition to democracy in States rejecting a single-party regime. It has set up tribunals for trying those held to be responsible for war crimes.

These are significant developments which foster hope that the Organization will provide itself with means ever more suitable and effective, capable of sustaining its ambitions. In the end, the achievements of an Organization like the United Nations clearly demonstrate that *respect for human rights, the demands of democracy and observance of the law are the foundations upon which must rest an infinitely complex world, the survival of which depends upon the place attributed to man as the true goal of all political activity.*

10.	It is in this spirit that the Holy See acted on the occasion of the recent *Conference on Population and Development* held in Cairo in September 1994. In the face of an attempt to demote the person and his motivations, in a sphere as serious as that of human life and solidarity, the Holy See considered that it was its duty to remind the leaders of the nations of their responsibilities, and to make them realize the risk that there could be forced on humanity a vision of things and a style of living belonging to a minority. In doing so, the Holy See considers that it has defended man. Allow me to quote to you in this regard the unforgettable words of my predecessor Pope Paul VI, in his *Christmas Message* of 1973: "Woe to the person who lays his hand on man: for man is born sacred in this life, from his mother's womb. He is born ever endowed with the perilous but divine prerogative of freedom. This freedom can be trained but is inviolable. Man is born as a person sufficient in himself, yet needing social companionship; he is born a thinking being, a willing being, a being destined for good but capable of error and sin. He is born for truth and he is born for love."

Many of those taking part in the Cairo Conference were expecting this statement and this witness from the Holy See. Such in fact is the reason why the Holy See has a place in the midst of the community of nations: to be the voice which the human conscience is waiting for, without thereby minimizing the contribution of other religious traditions. Being a spiritual and worldwide authority, the Apostolic See will continue to provide this service to humanity, with no other aim than tirelessly to recall the demands of the common good, respect for the human person, and the promotion of the highest spiritual values.

What is at stake is the transcendent dimension of man: this can never be made subject to the whims of statesmen or ideologies. It is equally the service of man that must concern the leaders of societies: their fellow-citizens, by giving them their trust, expect from them an indefectible attachment to what is good, persevering effort, honesty in the conduct of government, and the ability to listen to everyone, without any discrimination. There is a *morality of service to the earthly city* which excludes not only corruption but, even more, ambiguity and the surrender of principles. The Holy See considers itself at the service of this reawakening of conscience, without the least temporal ambition, the small Vatican City State being merely the minimum support necessary for the exercise of a spiritual authority which is independent and internationally recognized. Your presence here, ladies and Gentlemen, bears witness to the fact that it is precisely thus that your leaders regard the Holy See.

11. It only remains for me to express to you my gratitude for the wisdom with which you carry out your duties, Ladies and Gentlemen, and to express to you once more my affectionate good wishes for yourselves, your families and the peoples whom you represent. With all my heart I hope that we shall cooperate ever more closely in the creation of a climate of brotherhood and trust between individuals and peoples, in order to prepare a world more

worthy of humanity in the eyes of God. May God bless you and your fellow-citizens, he "who by the power at work within us is able to do far more abundantly than all we ask or think" (*Ephesians* 3:20)!

CHARTER
OF THE RIGHTS OF THE FAMILY

PRESENTED BY THE HOLY SEE
TO ALL PERSONS, INSTITUTIONS
AND AUTHORITIES
CONCERNED WITH THE MISSION
OF THE FAMILY IN TODAY'S WORLD

22 OCTOBER 1983

INTRODUCTION

The *"Charter of the Rights of the Family"* has its origins in the request formulated by the Synod of Bishops held in Rome in 1980 on the theme "The Role of the Christian Family in the Modern World" (cf. *Propositio* 42). His Holiness Pope John Paul II, in the Apostolic Exhortation *Familiaris consortio* (no. 46), acceded to the Synod's request and committed the Holy See to prepare a *Charter of the Rights of the Family* to be presented to the quarters and authorities concerned.

It is important to understand correctly the nature and style of the *Charter* as it is now presented. The document is not an exposition of the dogmatic or moral theology of marriage and the family, although it reflects the Church's thinking in the matter. Nor is it a code of conduct for persons or institutions concerned with the question. The *Charter* is also different from a simple declaration of theoretical principles concerning the family. It aims, rather, at presenting to all our contemporaries, be they Christian or not, a formulation — as complete and ordered as possible — of the fundamental rights that are inherent in the natural and universal society which is the family.

The rights enunciated in the *Charter* are expressed in the conscience of the human being and in the common values of all humanity. The Christian vision is present in this *Charter* as the light of divine revelation which enlightens the natural reality of the family. These rights arise, in the ultimate analysis, from that law which is inscribed by the Creator in the heart of every human being. Society is called to defend these rights against all violations and to respect and promote them in the entirety of their content.

The rights that are proposed must be understood according to the specific character of a *"Charter."* In some cases they recall true and proper juridically binding norms; in other cases, they express fundamental postulates and principles for legislation to be implemented and for the development of family policy. In all cases they are a prophetic call in favour of the family institution, which must be respected and defended against all usurpation.

Almost all of these rights are already to be found in other documents of both the Church and the international community. The present *Charter* attempts to elaborate them further, to define them with greater clarity and to bring them together in an organic, ordered and systematic presentation. Annexed to the text are indications of "Sources and References" from which some of the formulations have been drawn.

The *Charter of the Rights of the Family* is now presented by the Holy See, the central and supreme organ of government of the Catholic Church. The document is enriched by a wealth of observations and insights received in response to a wide consultation of the Bishops' Conferences of the entire Church as well as of experts in the matter from various cultures.

The *Charter* is addressed principally to governments. In reaffirming, for the good of society, the common awareness of the essential rights of the family, the Charter offers to all who share responsibility for the common good a model and a point of reference for the drawing up of legislation and family policy, and guidance for action programmes.

At the same time the Holy See confidently proposes this document to the attention of intergovernmental international organizations which, in their competence and care for the defence and promotion of human rights, cannot ignore or permit violations of the fundamental rights of the family.

The *Charter* is of course also directed to the families themselves: it aims at reinforcing among families an awareness of the irreplaceable role and position of the family; it wishes to inspire families to unite in the defence and promotion of their rights; it encourages families to fulfill their duties in such a way that the role of the family will become more clearly appreciated and recognized in today's world.

The *Charter* is directed, finally, to all men and women, and especially to Christians, that they will commit themselves to do everything possible to ensure that the rights of the family are protected and that the family institution is strengthened for the good of all mankind, today and in the future.

The Holy See, in presenting this *Charter*, desired by the representatives of the World Episcopate, makes a special appeal to all the Church's members and institutions, to bear clear witness to Christian convictions concerning the irreplaceable mission of the family, and to see that families and parents receive the necessary support and encouragement to carry out their God-given task.

CHARTER OF THE RIGHTS OF THE FAMILY

Preamble

Considering that:

A. the rights of the person, even though they are expressed as rights of the individual, have a fundamental social dimension which finds an innate and vital expression in the family;

B. the family is based on marriage, that intimate union of life in complementarity between a man and a woman which is constituted in the freely contracted and publicly expressed indissoluble bond of matrimony, and is open to the transmission of life;

C. marriage is the natural institution to which the mission of transmitting life is exclusively entrusted;

D. the family, a natural society, exists prior to the State or any other community, and possesses inherent rights which are inalienable;

E. the family constitutes, much more than a mere juridical, social and economic unit, a community of love and solidarity, which is uniquely suited to teach and transmit cultural, ethical, social, spiritual and religious values, essential for the development and well-being of its own members and of society;

F. the family is the place where different generations come together and help one another to grow in human wisdom and to harmonize the rights of individuals with other demands of social life;

G. the family and society, which are mutually linked by vital and organic bonds, have a complementary function in the defence and advancement of the good of every person and of humanity;

H. the experience of different cultures throughout history has shown the need for society to recognize and defend the institution of the family;

I. society, and in a particular manner the State and International Organizations, must protect the family through measures of a political, economic, social and juridical character, which aim at consolidating the unity and stability of the family so that it can exercise its specific function;

J. the rights, the fundamental needs, the well-being and the values of the family, even though they are progressively safeguarded in some cases, are often ignored and not rarely undermined by laws, institutions and socio-economic programmes;

K. many families are forced to live in situations of poverty which prevent them from carrying out their role with dignity;

L. the Catholic Church, aware that the good of the person, of society and of the Church herself passes by way of the family, has always held it part of her mission to proclaim to all the plan of God instilled in human nature concerning marriage and the family, to promote these two institutions and to defend them against all those who attack them;

M. the Synod of Bishops celebrated in 1980 explicitly recommended that a Charter of the Rights of the Family be drawn up and circulated to all concerned;

the Holy See, having consulted the Bishops' Conferences, now presents this

CHARTER OF THE RIGHTS OF THE FAMILY

and urges all States, International Organizations, and all interested Institutions and persons to promote respect for these rights, and to secure their effective recognition and observance.

ARTICLE 1

All persons have the right to the free choice of their state of life and thus to marry and establish a family or to remain single.

a) Every man and every woman, having reached marriage age and having the necessary capacity, has the right to marry and establish a family without any discrimination whatsoever; legal restrictions to the exercise of this right, whether they be of a permanent or temporary nature, can be introduced only when they are required by grave and objective demands of the institution of marriage itself and its social and public significance; they must respect in all cases the dignity and the fundamental rights of the person.

b) Those who wish to marry and establish a family have the right to expect from society the moral, educational, social and economic conditions which will enable them to exercise their right to marry in all maturity and responsibility.

c) The institutional value of marriage should be upheld by the public authorities; the situation of non-married couples must not be placed on the same level as marriage duly contracted.

ARTICLE 2

Marriage cannot be contracted except by the free and full consent of the spouses duly expressed.

a) With due respect for the traditional role of the families in certain cultures in guiding the decision of their children, all pressure which would impede the choice of a specific person as spouse is to be avoided.

b) The future spouses have the right to their religious liberty. Therefore to impose as a prior condition for marriage a denial of faith or a profession of faith which is contrary to conscience, constitutes a violation of this right.

c) The spouses, in the natural complementarity which exists between man and woman, enjoy the same dignity and equal rights regarding the marriage.

ARTICLE 3

The spouses have the inalienable right to found a family and to decide on the spacing of births and the number of children to be born, taking into full consideration their duties towards themselves, their children already born, the family and society, in a just hierarchy of values and in accordance with the objective moral order which excludes recourse to contraception, sterilization and abortion.

a) The activities of public authorities and private organizations which attempt in any way to limit the freedom of couples in deciding about their children constitute a grave offence against human dignity and justice.

b) In international relations, economic aid for the advancement of peoples must not be conditioned on acceptance of programmes of contraception, sterilization or abortion.

c) The family has a right to assistance by society in the bearing and rearing of children. Those married couples who have a large family have a right to adequate aid and should not be subjected to discrimination.

ARTICLE 4

Human life must be respected and protected absolutely from the moment of conception.

a) Abortion is a direct violation of the fundamental right to the life of the human being.

b) Respect of the dignity of the human being excludes all experimental manipulation or exploitation of the human embryo.

c) All interventions on the genetic heritage of the human person that are not aimed to the correcting anomalies constitute a violation of the right to bodily integrity and contradict the good of the family.

d) Children, both before and after birth, have the right to special protection and assistance, as do their mothers during pregnancy and for a reasonable period of time after childbirth.

e) All children, whether born in or out or wedlock, enjoy the same right to social protection, with a view to their integral personal development.

f) Orphans or children who are deprived of the assistance of their parents or guardians must receive particular protection on the part of the society. The State, with regard to foster-care or adoption, must provide legislation which assists suitable families to welcome into their home children who are in need of permanent or temporary care. This legislation must, at the same time, respect the natural rights of the parents.

g) Children who are handicapped have the right to find in the home and the school an environment suitable to their human development.

ARTICLE 5

Since they have conferred life on their children, parents have the original, primary and inalienable right to educate them; hence they must be acknowledged as the first and foremost educators of their children.

a) Parents have the right to educate their children in conformity with their moral and religious convictions, taking into account the cultural traditions of the family which favour the good and the dignity of the child; they should also receive from society the necessary aid and assistance to perform their educational role properly.

b) Parents have the right to choose freely schools or other means necessary to educate their children in keeping with their convictions. Public authorities must ensure that public subsidies are so allocated that parents are truly free to exercise this right without incurring unjust burdens. Parents should not have to sustain, directly or indirectly, extra charges which would deny or unjustly limit the exercise of this freedom.

c) Parents have the right to ensure that their children are not compelled to attend classes which are not in agreement with their own moral and religious convictions. In particular, sex education is a basic right of the parents and must always be carried out under their close supervision, whether at home or in educational centres chosen and controlled by them.

d) The rights of parents are violated when a compulsory system of education is imposed by the State from which all religious formation is excluded.

e) The primary right of parents to educate their children must be upheld in all forms of collaboration between parents, teachers and school authorities, and particularly in forms of participation designed to give citizens a voice in the functioning of schools and in the formulation and implementation of educational policies.

f) The family has the right to expect that the means of social communication will be positive instruments for the building up of society, and will reinforce the fundamental values of the family. At the same time the family has the right to be adequately protected, especially with regard to its youngest members, from the negative effects and misuse of the mass media.

ARTICLE 6

The family has the right to exist and to progress as a family.

a) Public authorities must respect and foster the dignity, lawful independence, privacy, integrity and stability of every family.

b) Divorce attacks the very institution of marriage and of the family.

c) The extended family system, where it exists, should be held in esteem and helped to carry out better its traditional role of solidarity and mutual assistance, while at the same time respecting the rights of the nuclear family and the personal dignity of each member.

ARTICLE 7

Every family has the right to live freely its own domestic religious life under the guidance of the parents, as well as the right to profess publicly and to propagate the faith, to take part in public worship and in freely chosen programmes of religious instruction, without suffering discrimination.

ARTICLE 8

The family has the right to exercise its social and political function in the construction of society.

a) Families have the right to form associations with other families and institutions, in order to fulfill the family's role suitable and effectively, as well as to protect the rights, foster the good and represent the interests of the family.

b) On the economic, social, juridical and cultural levels, the rightful role of families and family associations must be recognized in the planning and development of programmes which touch on family life.

ARTICLE 9

Families have the right to be able to rely on an adequate family policy on the part of public authorities in the juridical, economic, social and fiscal domains, without any discrimination whatsoever.

a) Families have the right to economic conditions which assure them a standard of living appropriate to their dignity and full development. They should not be impeded from acquiring and maintaining private possessions which would favour stable family life; the laws concerning inheritance or transmission of property must respect the needs and rights of family members.

b) Families have the right to measures in the social domain which take into account their needs, especially in the event of the premature death of one or both parents, of the abandonment of one of the spouses, of accident, or sickness or invalidity, in the case of unemployment, or whenever the family has to bear extra burdens on behalf of its members for reasons of old age, physical or mental handicaps or the education of children.

c) The elderly have the right to find within their own family or, when this is not possible, in suitable institutions, an environment which will enable them to live their later years of life in serenity while pursuing those activities which are compatible with their age and which enable them to participate in social life.

d) The rights and necessities of the family, and especially the value of family unity, must be taken into consideration in penal legislation and policy, in such a way that a detainee remains in contact with his or her family and that the family is adequately sustained during the period of detention.

Article 10

Families have a right to a social and economic order in which the organization of work permits the members to live together, and does not hinder the unity, well-being, health and the stability of the family, while offering also the possibility of wholesome recreation.

a) Remuneration for work must be sufficient for establishing and maintaining a family with dignity, either through a suitable salary, called a "family wage," or through other social measures such as family allowances or the remuneration of the work in the home of one of the parents; it should be such that mothers will not be obliged to work outside the home to the detriment of family life and especially of the education of the children.

b) The work of the mother in the home must be recognized and respected because of its value for the family and for society.

Article 11

The family has the right to decent housing, fitting for family life and commensurate to the number of the members, in a physical environment that provides the basic services for the life of the family and the community.

ARTICLE 12

The families of migrants have the right to the same protection as that accorded other families.

a) the families of immigrants have the right to respect for their own culture and to receive support and assistance towards their integration into the community to which they contribute.

b) Emigrant workers have the right to see their family united as soon as possible.

c) Refugees have the right to the assistance of public authorities and International Organizations in facilitating the reunion of their families.

SOURCES AND REFERENCES

Preamble

A. *Rerum novarum*, 9; *Gaudium et spes*, 24.
B. *Pacem in terris*, Part 1; *Gaudium et spes*, 48 and 50; *Familiaris consortio*, 19; *Codex Iuris Canonici*, 1056.
C. *Gaudium et spes*, 50; *Humanae vitae*, 12; *Familiaris consortio*, 28.
D. *Rerum novarum*, 9 and 10; *Familiaris consortio*, 45.
E. *Familiaris consortio*, 43.
F. *Gaudium et spes*, 52; *Familiaris consortio*, 21.
G. *Gaudium et spes*, 52; *Familiaris consortio*, 42 and 45.
I. *Familiaris consortio*, 45.
J. *Familiaris consortio*, 46.
K. *Familiaris consortio*, 6 and 77.
L. *Familiaris consortio*, 3 and 46.
M. *Familiaris consortio*, 46.

Article 1

Rerum novarum, 9; *Pacem in terris*, Part 1; *Gaudium et spes*, 26; *Universal Declaration of Human Rights*, 16,1.
a) *Codex Iuris Canonici*, 1058 and 1077; *Universal Declaration*, 16, 1.
b) *Gaudium et spes*, 52; *Familiaris consortio*, 81.
c) *Gaudium et spes*, 52; *Familiaris consortio*, 81 and 82.

Article 2

Gaudium et spes, 52; *Codex Iuris Canonici*, 1057; *Universal Declaration*, 16, 2.
a) *Gaudium et spes*, 52.
b) *Dignitatis humanae*, 6.
c) *Gaudium et spes*, 49; *Familiaris consortio*, 19 and 22; *Codex Iuris Canonici*, 1135; *Universal Declaration*, 16, 1.

Article 3

Populorum progressio, 37; *Gaudium et spes*, 50 and 87; *Humanae vitae*, 10; *Familiaris consortio*, 30 and 46.
a) *Familiaris consortio*, 30.
b) *Familiaris consortio*, 30.
c) *Gaudium et spes*, 50.

ARTICLE 4

Gaudium et spes, 51; Familiaris consortio, 26.
a) Humanae vitae, 14; Sacred Congregation for the Doctrine of the Faith, Declaration on Procured Abortion, 18 November 1974; Familiaris consortio, 30.
b) Pope John Paul II, Address to the Pontifical Academy of Sciences, 23 October 1982.
d) Universal Declaration, 25, 2; Convention on the Rights of the Child, Preamble and 4.
e) Universal Declaration, 25, 2.
f) Familiaris consortio, 41.
g) Familiaris consortio, 77.

ARTICLE 5

Divini illius magistri, 27-34; Gravissimum educationis, 3; Familiaris consortio, 36; Codex Iuris Canonici, 793 and 1136.
a) Familiaris consortio, 46.
b) Gravissimum educationis, 7; Dignitatis humanae, 5; Pope John Paul II, Religious Freedom and the Helsinki Final Act (Letter to the Heads of State of the nations which signed the Helsinki Final Act), 4b; Familiaris consortio, 40; Codex Iuris Canonici, 797.
c) Dignitatis humanae, 5; Familiaris consortio, 37 and 40.
d) Dignitatis humanae, 5; Familiaris consortio, 40.
e) Familiaris consortio, 40; Codex Iuris Canonici, 796.
f) Pope Paul VI, Message for the Third World Communications Day, 1969; Familiaris consortio, 76.

ARTICLE 6

Familiaris consortio, 46.
a) Rerum novarum, 10; Familiaris consortio, 46; International Covenant on Civil and Political Rights, 17.
b) Gaudium et spes, 48 and 50.

* * *

ETHICAL AND PASTORAL DIMENSIONS OF POPULATION TRENDS ISSUED BY THE PONTIFICAL COUNCIL FOR THE FAMILY

INSTRUMENTUM LABORIS

Vatican, 25 March 1994

Contents

Introduction

Part One
Demographic Realities Today

Chapter I: Different Trends

1. Population growth and population geography
2. A "second demographic revolution"
3. The developing continents

Chapter II: Populations and Societies

1. Demographic growth and standards of living
2. Food, resources and population
3. Environment and population

Part Two
Attitudes Towards Demographic Realities

Chapter I: Population Control and Development

Chapter II: Methods of Population Control

1. Hormonal contraception
2. Sterilization
3. Abortion
4. Infanticide

Part Three
The Ethical And Pastoral Position of the Catholic Church

Chapter I: Papal Teachings

1. From John XXIII to Paul VI
2. John Paul II
3. The dignity of man and justice

Chapter II: Ethical Principles for a Pastoral Position

1. The contribution of the social teaching of the church
2. For life and the family
3. Responsible choice

Chapter III: Guidelines for Action

1. Correct knowledge of realities
2. Family policy
3. Justice for women
4. No possible compromise

Conclusion

1. Development, resources and population
2. Solidarity with the family

ETHICAL AND PASTORAL DIMENSIONS OF POPULATION TRENDS
ISSUED BY THE PONTIFICAL COUNCIL FOR THE FAMILY
INSTRUMENTUM LABORIS
VATICAN, 25 MARCH 1994

INTRODUCTION

1. In publishing this text, the Pontifical Council for the Family wishes to present points for consideration concerning population realities. The first part of this document examines populations *trends*. The second part describes *attitudes* regarding demographic realities. The third part sets out *ethical principles* in the light of which the Church analyzes these realities. This examination forms the basis for proposing *pastoral guidelines*.

2. In order to understand concrete situations better, population trends are currently the object of reflection, studies and meetings at international, national and regional levels. This document will help Episcopal Conferences and Catholic organizations to be well-informed on these realities, to draw up guidelines for pastoral action.

3. This working document prepared by the Pontifical Council for the Family is the fruit of patient work, after consultation and dialogue with specialists such as theologians, pastoral workers and demographers. Its scope is to make persons aware of the values upon which a truly human understanding of demographic realities is founded. These values are the dignity and transcendence of the human person; the importance of the family as the basic cell of society, solidarity between peoples and nations, and that humanity is called to salvation.

Given the Pontifical Council for the Family's competence in ethical and pastoral fields involving demography, it proposes the present document to help form guidelines for the Church's *pastoral work*.

Ethical principles must particularly guide pastoral work in the area of demography because population questions affect the family with regard to the freedom and responsibility of married couples in their task of transmitting life. With realism, the Church recognizes the serious problems linked to population growth, in the forms these take in various parts of the world, with attendant moral implications.[1] At the same time, the pastoral work of the Church must take into account different current and future effects of the declining birth rate in many countries. Therefore, one must begin by examining different demographic trends in an objective and dispassionate way.

---

[1] Cf. POPE JOHN PAUL II, Apostolic Exhortation *Familiaris consortio* (22 November 1981), 31; *AAS* 74 (1982), p. 117.

PART ONE

DEMOGRAPHIC REALITIES TODAY

Chapter I

DIFFERENT TRENDS

4.   During this century the world population has grown steadily. It has been estimated for 1993 at 5,506,000,000.[2] Population increase must be interpreted in the light of well identified and thoroughly understood factors. The most important of these factors is completely new in human history: the *increase of the average life-span.* In many countries the average life-span has more than doubled in a century. This increase results from improved health care conditions and standards of living, from better food production and more efficient policies. In less than two centuries, we have witnessed an almost general lowering of the infant mortality rate, by more than 90% in many countries. At the same time the maternal mortality rate has also fallen in unprecedented proportions.

1. Population growth and population geography

5.   The world population has doubled between 1950 and 1991. Nonetheless, the demographic growth rate decreased after reaching a maximum during the years 1965-1970.[3] This slowing down in the evolution of world population is in harmony with what population science calls the "demographic transition." This term signifies the lowering of the mortality-rate and birth-rate while countries benefit from improved health care and/or economic conditions. However, *depending upon the country,* it must be kept in mind that population trends are *very different.* The so-called developed countries have experienced a very significant lowering of the synthetic fertility indices.[4] In almost all these countries, this index is at a lower level than is actually needed simply to ensure that generations be replaced On the other hand, in so-called developing countries, these same

---

[2] Cf. Population Reference Bureau, *World Population Data Sheet, 1993.*

[3] DANIEL NOIN, *Atlas de la population mondiale,* Paris, Reclus, La Documentation française, 1991, p. 22.

[4] The synthetic fertility index, calculated by adding up the fertility-rate according to age, allows a comparison in time and space of fertility behaviour because it practically eliminates the effects linked to the differences of age groups in the population.

indices are at a level which allows for the replacement of generations, taking into account their healthcare conditions and mortality rate.

But even if there is a great contrast between the trends from the 1960's to the present, the *fall of fertility,* very significant in almost all parts of the world, is *irrefutable* and *evident* from the facts published by specialized organizations. It is, nonetheless, frequently *disregarded.*

6. Another important trend is *population geography.* There is a *growing urbanization,* above all in developing countries, as an effect of rural emigration and international migrations, almost always directed towards urban regions. It is true that certain policies, notably in the area of finance and/or agriculture, arising from national and/or international pressure, have the effect of discouraging rural development. Urbanization is further explained by the evolution of structures of production and by the desire to have access to the greatest possibilities for employment, to manufacturing markets, shopping, educational institutions, health facilities, recreational activities and the other advantages offered by the city.

7. Understanding population trends also requires the study of *migrations.* Various factors help understand their importance. Unfortunately each day brings the news that people are forced to move to escape wars or massacres. These sometimes cause massive exoduses.[5] Other persons, hoping to better their living conditions, leave their homes for economic reasons: to avoid unemployment and find better paying work. Because of structural changes in methods of production, economic situations also bring about significant migrations: rural emigration, emigration from once-industrialized regions, emigration toward regions considered to have a future. Migrations have effects on the physiognomy of countries, their evolution, the geography of their population. This is true for both the countries of emigration and the countries of immigration.

2. A "second demographic revolution"

8. How are behavioral trends regarding the birth-rate in "developed" societies to be understood? The importance of the *fall in fertility* leads some to claim that there is a "second demographic revolution." Here one deals with as considerable a change as in the "first demographic revolution," even if in a different sense. This first revolution in some way helped to "*curb*" the

---

[5] Cf. Pontifical Council "Cor Unum," Pontifical Council for the Pastoral Care of Migrants and Itinerant People, *Refugees: A Challenge to Solidarity,* Libreria Editrice Vaticana, Vatican City, 1992.

mortality rate, and especially the three rates which previously controlled demographic patterns: birth, infant and adolescent mortality.

9.   This second demographic revolution has different causes which belong primarily to the moral and cultural order: materialism, individualism and secularization. Consequently, many women are forced to work more and more outside the home.[6] This results in unbalanced structures according to age. This imbalance brings about present political, economic and social problems. However, there is a risk that these problems are only perceived clearly when they have run their course because population trends are long-term. For example, a greater number of aged persons will find themselves depending upon pensions which could only be assured by the work of an active population, which is certainly decreasing according to demographic projections. In various advanced countries there is a "demographic winter" which is becoming more and more severe. The authorities are beginning to be concerned: today there are more coffins than cradles, more elderly persons than children.

10.   One of the more serious consequences of the ageing of the population is the risk of *damage to solidarity* between generations. This could lead to real struggles between the generations for a share in economic resources. Perhaps discussions about *euthanasia* are not extraneous to these conflicting trends.

11.   This "second demographic revolution" is often misunderstood for three reasons. The first reason is that these societies, living on advantages gained during periods of sufficient fertility, benefit from the *age-rated structures* which up to now *favour their active population.* This is one of the reasons which still makes high productivity possible. The negative effects which the falling birthrate will produce in the economic and social domains are just beginning to be felt. Following upon this, the presence in these societies of the *immigrant* workforce also helps delay the recognition of this falling fertility and its possible consequences. Finally, translated into less investments in human resources, hence in education, the fall in the birthrate releases financial means in the short term. These are seen as advantageous but they benefit present generations *to the detriment of the future.*[7]

12.   What happened to *Eastern Europe* after the collapse of the

---

[6] Cf. JOHN PAUL II, Encyclical Letter *Laborem exercens* (14 September 1981), 19; *AAS* 73 (1981), p. 625.

[7] This phenomenon can be seen in the various European countries, in particular: Italy, France, Germany and Spain.

Communist system? A widespread and significant lowering of the birthrate took place in certain countries, leading to a trend similar to that in some regions of Western Europe — less births than deaths. For decades, the people of Eastern Europe suffered from different demographic policies. Often these did not respect the human person; they were very authoritarian, inspired by the *a priori* requirements of the Marxist-Leninist ideology and the imperatives attributed to the "necessities" of history. The present demographic behaviour of the countries of Eastern Europe cannot be understood without taking into account the lingering effect of the situation into which they were plunged. Moreover, these countries are exposed to the influence of consumer models coming from Western Europe.

3. The developing continents

13. According to most recent estimates, *Africa* is a continent with a high fertility. However, it is also underpopulated, with weak population densities in the greater part of its territory. Moreover, the uncertainty of specific demographic data has been particularly evident in this continent.[8] Poor healthcare conditions and policies often limit in some countries and even stop the expected fall of the mortality-rate.[9] Attention must also be given to the future demographic effects of AIDS, effects which could prove quite disastrous in certain regions.

In Northern Africa a lowering of the fertility-rate seems to be an established phenomenon from now on, even if, with a very young population structure, the play of inertia common to all demographic phenomena has a potential for population growth.

14. If one considers *Latin America* in relation to other developing continents, a first characteristic is to be found in weaker mortality-rates with birthrates less high in temperate South America than in tropical South America and Central America. A second specific feature of some of these countries is the lower proportion of married women than in Asia and Africa. The specific consequence of this is a high number of births outside

---

[8] Considered by observers as reliable, the census of November 1991 in Nigeria, the most populated country in Africa, registered 88.5 million inhabitants. The previous official estimate indicated 122.5 million inhabitants, that is, an over-estimation of 34 million people!

[9] This phenomenon can be seen in various countries. However, in Rwanda, a small country, there is a very strong concentration of population caused by immigration to a fertile region and maintained by a high rate of procreation.

marriage.[10]

The lowering of fertility, largely correlated with the lower mortality mentioned above, leads to a population growth inferior to Asia (ex-USSR not included) and Africa.

15. The immense continent of Asia contains the major part of the Russian Federation and two of the most populated countries on earth: China and India. While the demographic evolution of Russia seems somewhat comparable to that of Eastern Europe, the other Asian countries present very different situations, not only between but even within the nations themselves. The Asian countries which are among those known as "the new industrial nations" seem to be entering the "second demographic revolution." Other nations have not yet completed the phase of the "first demographic revolution" and combine rather high fertility with equally high mortality. Thus, in a world trend marked by a lowering of fertility following a lowering of mortality, Asia experiences very great demographic differences. Even within China and India, fertility can vary twofold, or even more, whereas the urbanization-rates are twice as low as Europe.

16. Therefore, the evolution of world population cannot be examined without taking into account an almost general fact: *the relationship between fertility and mortality rates,*[11] and the *very strong demographic contrasts,* not only between continents, but even within continents and countries where very great regional differences are at times recorded. Thinking globally in terms of world population tends to gloss over the diversity of mortality rates, the different phenomena of migration, the difference in population growth rates, which are even negative in certain regions. Without a knowledge of these differences, one can only misunderstand the reality of population trends.

Chapter II

POPULATIONS AND SOCIETIES

17. Bearing in mind the quantitative data provided by major statistical

---

[10] The importance of the relationship between fertility and distribution of the population seems to be illustrated by Bolivia which has the most significant fertility index in Latin America, but also one of the weakest population densities.

[11] In the "first demographic revolution" in developing countries, medical progress reduced general mortality and births increased (inverse relationship). In the "second demographic revolution," for example in Europe today, medical science has reduced mortality even more, but births are decreasing.

institutions and the causality of calculated trends, the demographic realities are in fact very different according to regions. Moreover, they are very complex.[12] Every population study should take into account the history of the peoples under consideration, the changes which took place in the demographic pattern, as well as the sometimes considerable difference between regions. However, many people are led to believe there will be a "world population crisis," especially those whose experience is limited to living in cities. To justify "population control," they have talked about a "population bomb," a "population explosion," an "over-populated world" with irremediably limited resources. They say that there is a "world consensus" about the urgency of the situation. However, the slogans spread about these matters cannot stand up to analysis because the history of human development shows that it is simplistic to affirm that controlling population growth is necessary to achieve or maintain a certain level of prosperity. Therefore, a serious and lucid examination of demographic trends is in order.

1. Demographic growth and standards of living

18.   Development problems in the relevant countries are not only to be sought in the increase of the number of their inhabitants. Many of these countries have considerable natural resources which would often be able to sustain populations larger than the ones they currently have. Unfortunately, too often this potential is presently either not sufficiently exploited or badly exploited. More often than not, the earth possesses materials which, thanks to man's inventiveness, have been shown throughout history to be decisive resources for human progress. In the first place, the source of the difficulties of so-called Third World countries is to be sought in *international relations*. These difficulties have often been examined and even denounced by the Church.[13] With regard to these causes which have bearing on the problem of development, *solidarity is shown to be necessary,* but *this presupposes a change in the policies of developed nations.*

There are also other *internal causes* in developing countries. The low standards of living and the scarcity of food, even to the point of famine, can

---

[12] See, for example, *World Population Monitoring, 1991,* Population Studies, No. 126, United Nations, New York, 1992; *The Sex and Age Distributions of Population, The 1990 Revision of the United Nations Global Population Estimates and Projections,* Population Studies, No. 122, United Nations, New York 1991, and *1991 Demographic Year Book,* United Nations, New York 1993.

[13] Cf. POPE JOHN PAUL II, Encyclical Letter *Sollicitudo rei socialis* (30 December 1987), 11-26; *AAS* 80 (1988), pp. 525-547.

be the result of bad political and economic administration, often accompanied by corruption. To this must be added: exaggerated military budgets, in contrast to the small amount set aside for education; wars — sometimes instigated by other nations — or fratricidal conflicts; glaring injustices in the allocation of revenues; the concentration of the means of production for the profit of a privileged group; discrimination against minorities; the paralysizing burden of foreign debt accompanied by the flight of capital; the weight of certain negative cultural practices; unequal access to property; bureaucracies blocking initiative and innovation, etc. In reality, if objective conditions explain under-development in certain regions of the planet, *a lack of development is not inevitable since all these causes can be overcome* when suitable measures are applied, even if this is difficult.

2. Food, resources and population

19. According to those who assert that world food and other resources are limited, would an increase in population inevitably result in poverty and want? It must be kept in mind that *the amount of resources at the planet's disposal is neither pre-defined nor unchangeable.* The history of societies and civilizations shows that during certain periods some peoples were able to exploit hidden resources or resources neglected by previous generations. Thus, throughout the centuries, humanity's resources have neither stagnated nor diminished. Instead, they have increased and become more diversified. People have augmented resources; some examples of this would be: the cultivation of new crops such as the potato, which really revolutionized nutrition; the use of new techniques such as irrigating rice fields or greenhouse cultivation; the ability to utilize resources which before had been neglected, such as coal, petroleum, fertilizers, the atom, and sand. Such progress can also be seen in the fields of agriculture and breeding where modern methods increase possibilities.

People still have great potential at their disposal for the development of the planet; from solar energy — largely under utilized today — to underwater capsules, not to mention the centres of the "green revolution" announced by agronomists, also taking particular note of the progress made in animal and vegetable genetic engineering.[14]

20. Moreover, if the use of agricultural technologies in the most advanced countries is studied, it is apparent that *from now on* people are able to

---

[14] In 1991 the Pontifical Academy of Sciences studied the relationship between resources and population, see below 56, 57.

produce sufficient food for the world's population — even if the hypotheses of international organizations were to be verified according to their highest projections. All this does not even take into account the technical progress yet to come.[15]

This confirms the fact that the most critical food shortages are *remediable* as long as people are equipped to confront them and are animated by solidarity.[16]

The food shortages publicized by the mass media in recent years resulted from wars, fratricidal conflicts, seen today in different countries, or from poor public or private administration, far more than from adverse climatic conditions or other natural causes.

3. Environment and population

21. According to a frequently repeated affirmation, the number of earth's inhabitants will cause growing pollution or the *degradation of the environment*. Environmental concern was raised during the World Conference of the United Nations on Population of 1974.[17] It was addressed again at the World Conference on Population in Mexico in 1984,[18] and at the Conference on Environment and Development in Rio de Janeiro in 1992.[19] However, no one has ever shown any direct cause and effect relationship between population growth and the degradation of the environment. On the other hand, the developed countries with great population density have less signs

---

[15] To speak of an agricultural "crisis" in the United States or in the European Community, is to speak of a crisis of over-production rather than under-production.

[16] Cf. *World Declaration on Nutrition,* International Conference on Nutrition, Food and Agricultural Organization of the United Nations, World Health Organization, 12 December 1992.

[17] Cf. *Report of the United Nations World Population Conference,* Bucharest, 19-30 August 1974, United Nations, New York, 1975 Resolution 9, pp. 50, 95-106.

[18] *Mexico City Declaration on Population and Development, Recommendation 4,* in *Report on the International Conference on Population 1984,* United Nations, Department for Technical Cooperation for Development, 1984, p. 16.

[19] Cf. *Rio Declaration on Environment and Development, Report of the United Nations Conference on Environment and Development,* Rio de Janeiro, 3-14 June 1992, United Nations, New York 1992, Vol. I, pp. 8-12.

of pollution than the very elevated ones verified not long ago in countries formerly under Communist regimes.[20] In these countries, the system of production proved to be extremely polluting. These models of production and consumption, as well as the kind of economic activities, determine environmental quality. The degradation of the environment is often due to mistaken policies which can and should be corrected by reasonable and joint efforts on the part of public and private sectors.

22.   It is no less true that certain patterns of consumption should be corrected in developed societies. These patterns do not respect the environment nor do they take into account the responsibilities of people today towards the generations which are yet to come.

23.   The problem of the environment should always be seen in the light of human development, taking into account its economic and social aspects. For this reason all these matters have ethical implications. Facts confirm that industrialized countries are making, and are willing to make, a real effort to protect their environment. This requires using nonpolluting techniques of production and having a deeper sense of the responsibilities of these countries. The environmental problem also exists in developing countries. In this case, the greatest problems arise from the badly controlled exploitation of natural resources, recourse to antiquated agricultural methods which exhaust the soil, or the disorderly introduction of industries, often foreign, which are highly polluting. In these regions, the adoption of appropriate technologies could prevent the degradation of the immediate environment. In any case, it would be simplistic to accuse the populations of these regions of being responsible for the acid rain or the fears raised at times about the ecological balance of the planet.

---

[20] For example, the disaster of Chernobyl in 1986.

PART TWO

ATTITUDES TOWARDS DEMOGRAPHIC REALITIES

Chapter I

POPULATION CONTROL AND DEVELOPMENT

24.   Citing the rates at which population trends occur often causes a strong reaction. Raw statistics are brought up to explain the relationship between demographic growth and births. According to this kind of thinking, birth control is the indispensable pre-condition for the "sustainable development" of poor countries. By "sustainable development" is meant a development where the different factors involved (food, health, education, technology, population, environment, etc.) are brought into harmony so as to avoid unbalanced growth and the waste of resources. The developed countries define for other countries what must be, from their point of view, "sustainable development." This explains why certain rich countries and major international organizations are willing to help these countries, but on one condition — that they accept programmes for the systematic control of their births.

Those who react in this manner have generally not understood the logic of demographic processes, and particularly the phenomenon of self-regulation evidenced in data. They consequently ignore or underestimate both the importance of the lowering of fertility in the developing countries as well as the demographic decline seen in industrialized countries.

25.   It would be difficult to find an example in history of a country which underwent a prolonged trend (more than twenty-five years) of falling population and enjoyed substantial economic development at the same time. It has even been shown that population growth has often *preceded* economic growth. Attentive to current facts and the lessons of history, the Church cannot accept that the poorest populations be treated as "scapegoats" for under-development. The Church regards this attitude as particularly unjust considering that some countries are undergoing grave economic difficulties when, at the same time, they have a low population density and abundant exploitable resources. Furthermore, the Church can no longer ignore the *negative* demographic trends of industrial countries, all the more because the effects of these trends cannot be neutral. At the same time, the Church wishes to maintain a constructive dialogue with those who remain convinced of the necessity of setting up imperative population control, and with governments and institutions concerned with population policies. There are

real demographic problems, even though they are often envisaged from an erroneous point of view and perverse solutions to them are often proposed.

26. It is now useful to explain the principal methods of those who promote limiting population growth as one of the first conditions for economic and social development. Special attention will be given to the problem of abortion.

Chapter II

METHODS OF POPULATION CONTROL

27. It is well known that there is a *vast international network* of wealthy organizations which direct their efforts towards reducing population. In different degrees, these organizations share a similar perspective and they publicly commend anti-natalist policies. Certain of these organizations often collaborate with companies which experiment with, produce and distribute contraceptive substances or devices (such as the intra-uterine device) or which recommend sterilization or even abortion. These organizations counsel, promote and often impose this variety of methods for reducing population.

28. The Holy Father himself has denounced these "systematic campaigns against birth."[21] In fact, certain campaigns are developed and financed by international organizations (public or private), which, in turn, are often controlled by governments. These campaigns are frequently made in the name of the *health and well-being of women* and are also directed at young people under the forms of *anti-birth sex education programmes*. It should be noted, in passing, that in many countries there is a factor which controls population and, although indirect, is no less significant: a *lack of adequate housing for families*. Nevertheless, *methods developed for directly controlling births* are actually the principal means employed for population control.

Recently-developed methods of birth control will be presented here, noting, however, that "traditional" methods (mechanical and *coïtus interruptus*) are still largely used. All of these artificial methods raise important ethical problems regarding both human life and the rights of the person and the family.

---

[21] POPE JOHN PAUL II, Encyclical Letter *Sollicitudo rei socialis, 25; AAS* 80 (1988), p. 543.

1. Hormonal contraception

29. Hormonal contraception is one of the modern methods for limiting population which has been widely diffused at the international level. Certain reports of international organizations regularly publish statistics on the number of women having access to this type of contraception. Other reports also speak of initiatives taken by some of these organizations to encourage and finance research on these products and their promotion on a wide scale.

30. In certain recent applications, hormonal contraception poses *new problems*. It is known that the first generation of these pills — oestroprogestitives — have essentially a contraceptive effect: they make conception impossible by blocking oocyte release. However, among the pills presented today as contraceptives, there are some which have several different effects.[22] The pill acts either to impede conception or to prevent the implantation of the fertilized egg, that is, of an individual of the human species. In this latter case, notwithstanding the euphemisms used, these pills bring about an abortion of the fertilized egg. Thus, the woman who uses this kind of pill, or certain other new methods of hormonal contraception,[23] is never able to know exactly what has happened and, particularly, whether she has aborted.

2. Sterilization

31. Another method of population control which is also widely encouraged in many countries is male or female *sterilization*. The way in which it is promoted raises serious questions concerning human rights and respect for persons. In particular, these questions have bearing on the

---

[22] 1. They modify the structure of the cervical mucus making it impenetrable to spermatozoids. 2. They modify the motility of the Fallopian tube, impeding the passage of the fertilized egg from it to the uterine cavity. 3. They alter the normal development of the endometrium, making it unfit for the implantation of the embryo. These last two effects are *abortive* and are prevalent when the oestro-progestatin pill does not block ovulation and cannot consequently work as a contraceptive.

[23] Besides the oestroprogestitive pill, other hormonal products, wrongly defined as contraceptives, are sold. In reality, they work by impeding the continuation of pregnancy, which terminates in abortion. These are pills or injectable or implantable substances (such as Norplant) which alter the endometrium and the motility of the tubes, without stopping ovulation and, therefore, act as abortifacients. These substances may be administered to the woman in a continuous fashion, or in the case of presumably fertile relationships ("the morning-after pill").

honesty and quality of information given about sterilization and its consequences, as well as the degree of informed and free consent obtained from the persons concerned. The question of *competent consent is* often posed when dealing with persons with little formal education. Here, as in other cases, euphemisms are often used: for example, describing tubal ligation as "voluntary surgical contraception for women."

On the moral level, because sterilization is a *deliberate suppression of the procreative function,* it violates not only human dignity, but also removes all responsibility from sexuality and procreation. Sterilization programs have already provoked many strong protests, with direct political repercussions in certain cases. Because surgical sterilization is usually irreversible, it can have more serious long-term demographic effects than contraception and abortion.

3. Abortion

32. Despite certain denials, *abortion* (surgical and pharmaceutical) is being promoted more and more, openly or in a hidden way, *as a method of population control.* This tendency is true even of institutions which, when they began, did not have abortion as part of their programme. After the International Conference on Population held at Mexico City in 1984, one is bound to ask to what extent an agreed Recommendation — approved by the Conference — has been honoured which rejects using abortion as a method of population control.

33. Recommendation 18 of this Conference states that: "All efforts should be made to reduce maternal morbidity and mortality"; and with precise reference to women's health: "Governments are urged... to take appropriate steps to help women avoid abortion, which in no case should be promoted as a method of family planning, and whenever possible, provide for the humane treatment and counselling of women who have had recourse to abortion."[24]

34. This Recommendation was accepted by the general consensus of the nations participating in the Conference. The Recommendation was addressed to governments, some of which provide funds for population control organizations. However, the activities and research of a number of these organizations indicate that in practice they do not apply Recommendation 18. Many of these organizations include abortion, at least *de facto,* among

---

[24] *Report on the International Conference on Population 1984, op. cit., Recommendation 18,* pp. 20, 21. In the French text the following phrase is missing: "which in no case should be promoted as a method of family planning."

methods of family planning.

35. In developed countries, some women consider abortion as a fall-back solution in the case of contraception failure. In developing countries, there is a tendency to facilitate easier access to abortion as an effective method of population control, especially among the poorest sectors of the population.

36. Besides different surgical methods, *chemical methods* have also been developed to bring about abortion. Among these are the anti-pregnancy vaccines,[25] injections based upon progestogens such as Depo-Provera or Noristerat,[26] the prostoglandins, or high dosages of oestro-progesterone (commonly called the "morning-after" pill) or the abortion pill RU486, developed by the Roussel-Uclaff Laboratory, a subsidiary of Hoechst. Moreover, the intra-uterine device (IUD) can be included in the context of early abortion.

4. Infanticide

37. Finally, it should be recalled that infanticide is still practised in certain countries as a method of population control. Girls are more frequently the innocent victims.

---

[25] Anti hCG (human Chorionic Gonadotropin) vaccines.

[26] Depo-Provera = Depot-medroxyprogesterone acetate; Noristerat = Norethisterone enantate.

PART THREE

THE ETHICAL AND PASTORAL POSITION OF THE CATHOLIC CHURCH

38. Far from being indifferent to various population trends, the Church closely evaluates their significance and complexity. Nevertheless she proclaims that *among the attitudes which are envisaged, all are not morally acceptable.* The Church's position in this matter can never be dictated by simple quantitative considerations. Her stand begins with the truth about man,[27] with a specific concept of the human person and society.

39. The main lines of the Church's position will be set out here. In the first place, papal teachings on this matter will be summarized. Then the principles will be enunciated which the Church uses to make her contribution to understanding the data relative to population. Finally, timely courses of action will be presented which should be encouraged.

Chapter I

PAPAL TEACHINGS

40. The teaching of the Popes on moral questions relative to population is written in a *body of doctrine comprising several sections:* teaching relating to sexuality and the family, and also teaching relating to society and public authorities. This body of doctrine is itself under-pinned by the total vision of the human person as the centre of creation and called to salvation.

The Church has always considered that the *systematic control of births,* using directly or indirectly coercive means to limit population size, *does not contribute to authentic human development.* Moreover, anticipating certain contemporary criticisms of population control theories and practices, the Popes have regarded what is sometimes called the "population crisis" *only with great prudence.* However, it should be noted that the Supreme Pontiffs have closely followed the different population trends, paying the same attention to the population growth observed in some countries as to the declining population observed in other places. At the same time they have vigorously striven to promote justice, peace and development. By *attacking the problems of poverty and hunger at their source,* they wished to help

---

[27] Cf. POPE JOHN PAUL II, Encyclical Letter *Centesimus annus,* (1 May 1991) 25, 29; *AAS* 83 (1991), pp. 822-824, 829, where the Holy Father presents the truth about man in the context of the collapse of the Communist regimes.

732   *Appendix*

resolve these problems. This papal teaching is set out in different documents. The most prominent will be mentioned here, but limited to the teachings of the most recent Popes and the Second Vatican Council.

1. From John XXIII to Paul VI

41.   In his Encyclical Letter *Mater et magistra,* Pope John XXIII referred in 1961 to the problems of food and demographic trends. He stated: "But whatever be the situation, we clearly affirm that these problems should be posed and resolved in such a way that man does not have recourse to methods and means contrary to his dignity, which are proposed by those persons who think of man and his life solely in material terms."[28]

42.   Referring to population trends, in the Pastoral Constitution *Gaudium et spes* (1965), the Fathers of the Second Vatican Council reaffirmed the rights of the family and rejected dishonorable solutions, including abortion and infanticide.[29] They also advocated the right and duty of "responsible parenthood," which is licit only within the context of marriage. "Married couples should regard it as their proper mission to transmit human life and to educate their children; they should realize that they are thereby cooperating with the love of God the Creator and are, in a certain sense, its interpreters. This involves the fulfillment of their role with a sense of human and Christian responsibility and the formation of correct judgments through docile respect for God and common reflection and effort; it also involves a consideration of their own good and the good of their children already born or yet to come, an ability to read the signs of the times and of their own situation on the material and spiritual level, and finally, an estimation of the good of the family, of society, and of the Church. It is the married couple themselves who must in the last analysis arrive at these judgments before God."[30]

43.   This same conciliar document devotes an important paragraph to the population growth of certain nations. The Council Fathers affirm: "International cooperation is vitally necessary in the case of those peoples who... are faced with the special problems arising out of rapid increases in population. There is a pressing need to harness the full and eager cooperation of all, particularly of the richer countries, in order to explore

---

[28] POPE JOHN XXIII, Encyclical Letter *Mater et magistra* (15 May 1961) 191; *AAS* 53 (1961), p. 447.

[29] Cf. VATICAN COUNCIL II, *Gaudium et spes,* (1965), 5, 8, 47, 51.

[30] Cf. *ibid.,* 50.

how the human necessities of food and suitable education can be furnished and shared with the entire human community."

Finally the Council recalls the limits of the intervention of "public authority" and "exhorts all men to beware of all solutions, whether uttered in public or in private or imposed at any time, which transgress the natural law."[31]

44. In his historic address to the United Nations General Assembly in 1965, Pope Paul VI said: "You proclaim here the fundamental rights and duties of man, his dignity, freedom — and above all his religious freedom. We feel that you thus interpret the highest sphere of human wisdom and, we might add, its sacred character. For you deal here above all with human life and the life of man is sacred; no one may dare offend it. Respect for life, even with regard to the great problem of birth, must find here in your assembly its highest affirmation and its most reasoned defence. You must strive to multiply bread so that it suffices for the tables of mankind, and not rather favour an artificial control of birth, which would be irrational, in order to diminish the number of guests at the banquet of life."[32]

45. In 1967, in his Encyclical *Populorum progressio,* Pope Paul VI again wrote about demographic realities: "It is certain that public authorities can intervene, within the limits of their competence, by favouring the availability of appropriate information and by adopting suitable measures, provided that these are in conformity with the moral law and that they respect the rightful freedom of married couples. Where the inalienable right to marriage and procreation is lacking, human dignity has ceased to exist.

"Finally, it is for parents to take a thorough look at the matter and decide upon the number of their children. This is an obligation they take upon themselves, before their children already born, and before the community to which they belong —following the dictates of their own consciences informed by God's law authentically interpreted, and bolstered by their trust in Him."[33]

---

[31] Cf. *ibid.,* 87.

[32] POPE PAUL VI, *Address to the United Nations General Assembly* (4 October 1965), 6; *AAS* 57 (1965), p. 883.

[33] POPE PAUL VI Encyclical Letter *Populorum progressio* (26 March 1967), 37; *AAS* 59 (1967), P. 276.

46. In his Encyclical *Humanae vitae* (1968), Pope Paul VI confirmed these teachings. He explained "responsible parenthood": "Hence conjugal love requires in husband and wife an awareness of their mission of 'responsible parenthood,' which today is rightly much insisted upon, and which also must be exactly understood. Consequently it is to be considered under different aspects which are legitimate and connected with one another.

"In relation to the biological processes, responsible parenthood means the knowledge and respect of their functions; human intellect discovers in the power of giving life biological laws which are part of the human person.

"In relation to the tendencies of instinct or passion, responsible parenthood means that necessary dominion which reason and will must exercise over them.

"In relation to physical, economic, psychological and social conditions, responsible parenthood is exercised, either by the deliberate and generous decision to raise a numerous family, or by the decision, made for grave motives and with due respect for the moral law, to avoid for the time being, or even for an indeterminate period, a new birth.

"Responsible parenthood also and above all implies a more profound relationship to the objective moral order established by God, of which a right conscience is the faithful interpreter. The responsible exercise of parenthood implies, therefore, that husband and wife recognize fully their own duties towards God, towards themselves, towards the family and towards society, in a correct hierarchy of values.

"In the task of transmitting life, therefore, they are not free to proceed completely at will, as if they could determine in a wholly autonomous way the honest path to follow; but they must conform their activity to the creative intention of God, expressed in the very nature of marriage and of its acts, and manifested by the constant teaching of the Church."[34]

Responsible fatherhood and motherhood include not only the couple's prudent decisions but also the refusal of artificial methods of birth control and, when there are serious reasons, the choice of the natural regulation of fertility.[35]

---

[34] Cf. POPE PAUL VI, Encyclical Letter *Humanae vitae* (25 July 1968), 10; *AAS* 60 (1968), pp. 487, 488.

[35] Cf. *ibid*, 11-16, *AAS* 60 (1968), pp. 488-492; see below 76.

47. In *Humanae vitae,* Pope Paul VI called attention to the fact that public authorities might be tempted to impose artificial methods of birth control.[36] For this reason he appealed to these authorities: "To rulers, who are those principally responsible for the common good, and who can do so much to safeguard moral values, We say: Do not allow the morality of your peoples to be degraded; do not permit that by legal means practices contrary to the natural and divine law be introduced into the fundamental cell, the family. Quite other is the way in which public Authorities can and must contribute to the solution of the demographic problem: namely, the way of a provident policy for the family, of a wise education of peoples in respect of the moral law and the liberty of citizens."[37]

48. In 1971, in his Apostolic Letter *Octogesima adveniens,* Pope Paul VI examined the phenomenon of urbanization.[38] Regarding demographic growth he wrote: "It is disquieting in this regard to note a kind of fatalism which is gaining a hold even on people in positions of responsibility. This feeling often leads to Malthusian solutions inculcated by active propaganda for contraception and abortion. In this critical situation, it must on the contrary be affirmed that the family, without which no society can stand, has a right to the assistance which will assure it of the conditions for a healthy development."[39]

49. In the sixties, it was evident that rich nations thought population control was the indispensable tool for development. On 9 November 1974, Paul VI addressed the participants of the World Conference of the Food and Agriculture Organization (FAO). He denounced "an irrational and one-sided campaign against demographic growth." He forcefully added: "It is inadmissable that those who have control of the wealth and resources of mankind should try to resolve the problem of hunger by forbidding the poor to be born, or by leaving to die of hunger children whose parents do not fit into the framework of theoretical plans based on pure hypotheses about the future of mankind. In times gone by, in a past that we hope is now finished with, nations used to make war to seize their neighbours' riches. But is it not a new form of warfare to impose a restrictive demographic policy on nations,

---

[36] Cf. *ibid,* 17, *AAS* 60 (1968), p. 493.

[37] *Ibid.,* 23, *AAS* 60 (1968), p. 497.

[38] Cf. POPE PAUL VI, Apostolic Letter *Octogesima adveniens* (14 May 1971), 10-12; *AAS* 63 (1971), pp. 414, 415.

[39] *Ibid,* 18; *AAS* 63 (1971), pp. 414, 415.

to ensure that they will not claim their just share of the earth's goods?".[40]

2. John Paul II

50. This papal teaching can be linked with the *Message to Christian Families in the Modern World* given by the Bishops at the close of the Synod on the Family, held in Rome in 1980. In this message, among other things, they said: "Often certain governments and some international organizations do violence to families... Families are compelled — and this we oppose vehemently — to use such immoral means for the solution of social, economic and demographic problems as contraception or, even worse, sterilization, abortion and euthanasia. The Synod therefore urges a charter of family rights to safeguard these rights everywhere."[41]

51. In 1982, in his Apostolic Exhortation on the Family *Familiaris consortio,* Pope John Paul II analyzed the birth of a secularist anti-life mentality: "One thinks, for example of a certain panic deriving from the studies of ecologists and futurologists on population growth, which sometimes exaggerates the danger of demographic increase to the quality of life. But the Church firmly believes that human life, even if weak and suffering is always a splendid gift of God's goodness. Against the pessimism and selfishness which cast a shadow over the world, the Church stands for life... Thus the Church condemns as a grave offence against human dignity and justice all those activities of governments or other public authorities which attempt to limit in any way the freedom of couples in deciding about children. Consequently any violence applied by such authorities in favour of contraception or, still worse, of sterilization and procured abortion, must be altogether condemned and forcefully rejected. Likewise to be denounced as gravely unjust are cases where, in international relations, economic help given for the advancement of peoples is made conditional on programmes of contraception, sterilization and abortion.

"The Church is certainly aware of the many complex problems which couples in many countries face today in their task of transmitting life — in a responsible way. She also recognizes the serious problem of population growth in the form it has taken in many parts of the world and its moral

---

[40] POPE PAUL VI, *Address to the Participants of the World Food Conference,* 9 November 1974, 6; *AAS* 66 (1974), p. 649.

[41] *Message of Sixth Synod of Bishops to Christian Families in the Modern World, 24* October 1980, 5.

implications.

"However, she holds that consideration in depth of all the aspects of these problems offers a new and stronger confirmation of the importance of the authentic teaching on birth regulation reproposed in the Second Vatican Council and in the Encyclical *Humanae vitae*."[42]

52. The Pope again spoke on this theme in 1984, in an address to the Secretary of the World Population Conference held in Mexico City. He defended the rights of the individual, the family, women and young people: "The experience and trends of recent years clearly emphasize the profoundly negative effects of contraceptive programmes. These programmes have increased sexual permissiveness and promoted irresponsible conduct, with grave consequences especially for the education of youth and the dignity of women. The very notion of *"responsible* parenthood" and *"family* planning" has been violated by the distribution of contraceptives to adolescents. Moreover, from contraceptive programmes a transition has in fact often been made to the practice of sterilization and abortion, financed by governments and international organizations."[43]

The Delegation of the Holy See at this Conference proposed a resolution which was adopted. This resolution asked governments "to take appropriate steps to help women avoid abortion, which in no case should be promoted as a method of family planning."[44]

53. With the explicit approval of Pope John Paul II, the Instruction *Donum vitae* appeared in 1987. The study of problems raised by new bio-medical practices provided an occasion to re-examine the right of society to intervene in the transmission of human life. Life must be transmitted in a context of interpersonal love. It is therefore necessary to protect the family cell. In the light of the principle of subsidiarity, it must also be reaffirmed that public authorities have the duty to protect the family. Far from intervening in an abusive way to control the transmission of life, they must,

---

[42] POPE JOHN PAUL II, *Familiaris consortio*, 30, 31, *AAS* 74 (1982) pp. 116, 117.

[43] Cf. POPE JOHN PAUL II, *Address to Dr. Rafael M. Salas, Secretary General of the 1984 International Conference on Population and Executive Director of the United Nations Fund for Population Activities, 7 June 1984; Insegnamenti di Giovanni Paolo II*, VII. 1, 1984, p. 1628.

[44] *Report on the International Conference on Population 1984, op. cit., Recommendation* 18, pp. 20, 21. See above 32 and 34.

on the contrary, apply themselves to see that life is respected from its very beginning.⁴⁵

54. In his Encyclical Letter of 1987, *Sollicitudo rei socialis,* Pope John Paul II wrote: "One cannot deny the existence especially in the southern hemisphere, of a demographic problem which creates difficulties for development. One must immediately add that in the northern hemisphere the nature of this problem is reversed; here the cause for concern is the *drop in the birthrate,* with repercussions on the ageing of the population, unable even to renew itself biologically. Just as it is incorrect to say that such difficulties stem solely from demographic growth, neither is it proved that *all* demographic growth is incompatible with orderly development. On the other hand, it is very alarming to see governments in many countries launching *systematic campaigns* against birth, contrary not only to the cultural and religious identity of the countries themselves, but also contrary to true development. It often happens that these campaigns are the result of pressure coming from abroad, and in some cases they are made a condition for the granting of financial and economic aid and assistance. In any event, there is an absolute lack of respect for the freedom of choice of the parties involved, men and women often subjected to intolerable pressures, including economic ones, in order to force them to submit to this new form of oppression. It is the poorest populations which suffer such mistreatment, and this sometimes leads to a tendency towards a form of racism, or the promotion of equally racist forms of eugenics. This fact too, which deserves the most forceful condemnation, is a *sign* of an erroneous and perverse idea of true human development."⁴⁶

55. In his Encyclical Letter *Centesimus annus,* marking the centenary of *Rerum novarum* in 1991, Pope John Paul II wrote on population: "Human ingenuity seems to be directed towards limiting, suppressing or destroying the sources of life — including recourse to abortion, which unfortunately is so widespread in the world — than towards defending and opening up the possibilities of life. The Encyclical *Sollicitudo rei socialis* denounced systematic anti-childbearing campaigns which, on the basis of a distorted view of the demographic problem and in a climate of 'absolute lack of respect for the freedom of choice of the parties involved,' often subject them to 'intolerable pressures... in order to force them to submit to this new form of

---

⁴⁵ Cf. Congregation for the Doctrine of the Faith, *Instruction on Respect for Human Life in its Origin and on the Dignity of Procreation, Donum vitae (22* February 1987), Chapter III; *AAS* 80 (1988), pp. 98-100.

⁴⁶POPE JOHN PAUL II, *Sollicitudo rei socialis, 25; AAS* 80 (1988), pp. 543, 544.

oppression'. These policies are extending their field of action by the use of new techniques, to the point of poisoning the lives of millions of defenceless human beings, as if in a form of 'chemical warfare.'"[47]

56.   The address of the Holy Father on 22 November 1991, should not be forgotten. It was delivered at an audience granted to the Pontifical Academy of Sciences. The Academy had just spent a week studying the relationship between "resources and population." The Pope said: "There is a widespread opinion that population control is the easiest method of solving the underlying problem, given that a worldwide reorganization of the processes of production and a redistribution of resources would require an enormous amount of time and would immediately give rise to economic complications.

"The Church is aware of the complexity of the problem. It is one that must be faced without delay; but account must also be taken of the differing regional situations, some of which are the complete opposite of others: some countries show a massive population increase while others are heading towards a dwindling, ageing population. And often it is precisely the latter countries, with their high level of consumption, which are most responsible for the pollution of the environment.

"The urgency of the situation must not lead into error in proposing ways of intervening. To apply methods which are not in accord with the true nature of man actually ends up by causing tragic harm. For this reason the Church, as an 'expert in humanity' (Cf. Paul VI), upholds the principle of responsible parenthood and considers it her chief duty to draw urgent attention to the morality of the methods employed. These must always respect the person and the person's inalienable rights.

"The increase or the forced decrease of population is partly the result of deficiencies in social institutions. Damage to the environment and the increasing scarcity of natural resources are often the result of human errors. Despite the fact that the world produces enough food for everyone, hundreds of millions of people are suffering from hunger, while elsewhere enormous quantities of food go to waste.

"In view of these many different mistaken human attitudes, it is necessary to address first of all the people who are responsible for them.

"Population growth has to be faced not only by the exercise of a

---

[47] POPE JOHN PAUL II, *Centesimus annus*, 39; *AAS* 83 (1991), p. 842. In his words "chemical warfare," the Holy Father again uses the strong expression of Paul VI, *Address to the Participants of the World Food Conference,* see above 49.

responsible parenthood which respects the divine law, but also by economic means which have a profound effect on social institutions. Particularly in the developing countries, where young people represent a high percentage of the population, it is necessary to eliminate the grave shortage of adequate structures for ensuring education, the spread of culture and professional training. The condition of women must also be improved as an integral part of the modernization of society."[48]

57. Calling for a responsible attitude regarding procreation, the Holy Father declared: "Thanks to advances in medicine which have reduced infant mortality and increased the average life expectancy, and thanks also to the development of technology, there has been a real change in living conditions. These new conditions must be met not only with scientific reasoning, but, more importantly, with recourse to all available intellectual and spiritual energies. People need to rediscover the moral significance of respecting limits; they must grow and mature in the sense of responsibility with regard to every aspect of life. (Cf. *Mater et magistra,* 195; *Humanae vitae, passim; Gaudium et spes,* 51-52).

"By not taking steps in this direction, the human family could well fall victim of a devastating tyranny which would infringe upon a fundamental aspect of what it means to be human, namely giving life to new human beings and leading them to maturity.

"It is the responsibility of the public authorities, within the limits of their legitimate competence, to issue directives which reconcile the containment of births and respect for the free and personal assumption of responsibility by individuals (Cf. *Gaudium et spes,* 87). A political programme which respects the nature of the human person can influence demographic developments, but it should be accompanied by a redistribution of economic resources among the citizens. Otherwise such provisions can risk placing the heaviest burden on the poorest and weakest sectors of society, thus adding injustice to injustice."

The Pope concluded: "Man, 'the only creature on earth whom God willed for its own sake' (*Gaudium et spes,* 24), is the subject of primordial rights and duties, which are antecedent to those deriving from social and political life (Cf. *Pacem in terris,* 5, 35). The human person is 'the origin, the subject and the purpose of all social institutions' (*Gaudium et spes,* 25), and for this reason authorities must keep in mind the limits of their own

---

[48] POPE JOHN PAUL II, *Address to the Pontifical Academy of Sciences,* 22 November 1991, 4-6; *L'Osservatore Romano,* English edition, N. 48, 2 December 1991, p. 6.

competence. For her part, the Church invites the human family to plan its future, impelled not just by material concerns but also and especially by respect for the order which God has placed within creation."[49]

58. In 1992, the United Nations Conference on Environment and Development took place in Rio de Janeiro. In his discourse on June 13, the Secretary of State, Cardinal Angelo Sodano, declared: "It is not possible, from the moral point of view, to justify the attitude of that part of the world which highlights human rights but attempts to deny the rights of those in less fortunate circumstances by deciding in a 'devastating tyranny' (John Paul II, *Speech to the Pontifical Academy of Sciences*, 22 November 1991, n. 6), how many children they can have, and by threatening to link aid for development to that dictate."[50]

59. In 1992, the Bishops of Latin America applied the teachings of John Paul II to the current situations in their countries. During the work of the Fourth General Conference of the Latin American Episcopate, held at Santo Domingo, some two hundred participating Bishops sent a message in defence of human life to the United Nations Organization and to its various bodies. In particular the message denounced systematic campaigns against birth, conducted by international institutions and Governments.[51]

3. The dignity of man and justice

60. When examining demographic trends, the Magisterium of the Church reaffirms the sacred nature of human life, responsibility for the transmission

---

[49] *Ibid.*, 6.

[50] CARDINAL ANGELO SODANO, *Environment and Development in the Christian Vision, L'Osservatore Romano,* English edition, N. 25, 24 June 1992, p. 5.

[51] Cf. *Message of the Latin American Episcopate to the United Nations Organization, L'Osservatore Romano,* English edition, N. 50, 16 December 1992, p 10. "It is necessary to strengthen the culture of life against the culture of death which is claiming so many victims among our peoples. True progress, one worthy of the human person, is never made by offending the human being. It is urgent to say this to humanity in an unequivocal cry: Let us respect the sacred gift of life! This cry rises with new force from the heart of our people who received the Gospel of Jesus Christ 500 years ago. It is essential to have a clear awareness of the urgency of the ethical dimension for true human progress, safeguarding 'the moral conditions for an authentic human ecology' *(Centesimus annus,* n. 38). It is tragic that people are seeking an economic development which results in drying up the sources of life thus changing it into a culture of death."

of life, the inherent rights of fatherhood and motherhood, the values of marriage and family life, in the context of which children are the gift of God the Creator.[52] In answer to the supporters of population control and without denying realities, the Church takes the part of justice by defending the rights of women and men, of families and young people and those called with the beautiful term *nascituri*, i.e. babies who have been conceived and are yet to be born and have the right to be born. Noting how population control can in no way be a substitute for true development, the Popes affirm the right of all people to profit from the abundant resources of the earth and human intelligence.

61. The Popes cannot subscribe to alarmist views concerning the different world population trends. With the passing of the years the facts show the necessity *of completely re-examining this alarmist interpretation*. Ideologies which deny the possibility of teaching people a responsible management of their fertility and which maintain a sense of insecurity and fear, ideologies which base themselves on threatening "want" and/or the destruction of the environment, seem to ignore the diversity and the complexity of the different aspects of demographic realities. These ideologies underestimate not only natural resources, but, above all, the capacity of the human person to exploit these resources more judiciously — beginning with human resources. They underestimate the capacity of the human person to distribute resources better and to provide institutions for *human* society which can be both efficient and respectful of the demands of justice.

Chapter II

ETHICAL PRINCIPLES FOR A PASTORAL POSITION

62. The anxiety of those who always speak about a "world population crisis" *does not seem justified by the diversified trends* actually found among populations in the different countries of the world. This anxiety really expresses a kind of *ideology of fear of the future and mistrust of man*. This security-minded attitude is found in different periods of history under different but basically converging forms. It undermines solidarity between generations and between nations. The Church must guide and help people to reflect upon this ideology which is so often presented by the mass media.

---

[52] Cf. VATICAN COUNCIL II, *Gaudium et spes*, 50.

1. The contribution of the social teaching of the church

63.   First of all, the Church forcefully calls attention to the covert appearance of a *new form of poverty*. It is expressed precisely In negative attitudes regarding life and family. These attitudes lead to forgetting solidarity; they drive man back into solitude, they are not sufficiently open to future generations nor are they sensitive enough to what the lack of people involves. These attitudes reveal the worst kind of poverty: *moral poverty*.

64.   The positive experiences acquired from past generations risk being compromised, if not partly lost, because of a lack of persons capable of passing them on. *The transmission of the common patrimony of humanity is in peril*. This patrimony is made up of moral and religious values, cultural assets, the arts, sciences and skills. It can only be transmitted and enriched with the cooperation of new generations. Because the rich but ageing societies risk sinking into extreme selfishness, the first to suffer from this impoverishment and decline will be precisely the most defenseless people. Therefore the Church cannot cease to show her preferential, but not exclusive, option for the most vulnerable.[53]

65.   The Church is also aware of the reality of population changes in developing nations. She affirms the vocation of *every person and nation to development*. The inequalities in living conditions, in possessions, in knowledge and professional competence can be remedied. Underdevelopment is not inevitable. Forces can be put into motion which allow each person and country to develop their potentialities and thus overcome underdevelopment. Among others, universal access to knowledge is an absolute priority, so that all people and all nations themselves find a satisfactory solution to the basic problems of subsistance and development, within the framework of international solidarity.[54]

66.   With regard to demographic realities, the search for a truly human response is clarified by the Church's teaching on the common good, on what is surplus and on the universal destination of goods.[55] Seeing the universal common good as requiring effective solidarity among peoples could guide the efforts of each to the benefit of all. No one — whether individual or nation — is justified in putting his particular good over the demands of the *common*

---

[53] Cf. POPE JOHN PAUL II, *Centesimus annus,* 38-40, 49, 51; *AAS* 83 (1991), pp. 840-843, 854-857.

[54] Cf. *ibid.* 32-34; *AAS* 83 (1991), pp. 832-836.

[55] Cf. *ibid.* 30; *AAS* 83 (1991), pp. 830, 831.

good of the human family.

67. The Church also teaches that justice requires that the most favoured should share their *surplus goods* with those who lack the necessities of life.[56]

68. In its teaching on the *universal destination of goods,* the Church recalls that, according to the Creator's plan, the whole of humanity's goods — spiritual and intellectual included — are at the disposal of the human community, both present and future, and each generation should act as its responsible stewards.[57]

69. The *principle of subsidiarity* also applies to the demographic domain. As recent Popes have indicated, the Church recognizes a right of public authorities, within the limit of their competence, to intervene regarding population matters, but she also affirms that in this area the State is not to arrogate to itself the responsibilities of which couples ought not to be deprived. All the more so, the State cannot use extortion, coercion or violence to make couples submit to its directives in this matter.[58] Whether it is concealed or obvious, any type of authoritarian demographic policy is unacceptable. On the contrary, the duty of the State is to protect the family and the freedom of couples, to guarantee the life of the innocent, and to see that the woman is respected, especially in her dignity as a mother.[59] To carry out these basic tasks, the State and public authorities in general must establish essential policies, notably in the areas of finance and education.

70. This same principle of subsidiarity applies equally to *public international institutions.* Nothing can justify their pressuring States or national communities to impose policies incompatible with respect for persons, families or national independence. These institutions were born out of a desire to bring together freely the efforts of all nations for a more just

---

[56] Cf. VATICAN COUNCIL II, *Gudium et spes,* 69; Pope JOHN PAUL II, *Sollicitudo rei socialis,* 28, 31; *AAS* 80 (1988), pp. 548-550, 553-556; *Centesimus annus,* 58; *AAS* 83 (1991), pp. 863, 864.

[57] Cf. POPE JOHN PAUL II, *Centesimus annus,* 31; *AAS* 83 (1991), pp. 831, 832.

[58] Cf. POPE JOHN PAUL II, *Address to Dr. Rafael M. Salas, Secretary General of the International Conference on Population 1984 and Executive Director of the United Nations Fund for Population Activities,* 2; *Insegnamenti di Giovanni Paolo II,* VII. 1, 1984, pp. 1626-1628; and see above 45-49, 51, 54, 55, 57, 58.

[59] Cf. POPE JOHN PAUL II, *Centesimus annus,* 39, 47, 49; *AAS* 83 (1991), pp. 841-843, 851, 852, 854-856.

society. Therefore they must respect the legitimate sovereignty of nations as well as the just autonomy of couples. It follows that these institutions would go beyond their competence if they were to encourage States to adopt population policies which they themselves define and if they were to apply pressure so that these policies might be more easily carried out.

71. Care must also be taken lest these institutions serve powerful nations. There is the risk of arousing suspicion among poor nations that certain nations might be seeking to exercise power on a worldwide level, through the methods which these institutions use. Therefore the Church reaffirms that international solidarity is a duty and that aid for the world's poor is an obligation of justice for the rich. The Church also affirms that it would be scandalous to link the granting of this aid with immoral conditions involving the control of human life. She again affirms that it would be a *grave abuse of intellectual, moral and political power* to present anti-childbearing campaigns — sometimes associated with moral or physical violence — as the most appropriate expressions of aid by rich populations to disadvantaged ones.[60]

72. Similar warnings apply to *private international institutions*. These should not make the particular interests of private groups prevail over the inalienable rights of every human being to life, physical integrity, education, personal freedom, and the right of all peoples to autonomy and to human development in solidarity.

2. For life and the family

73. Two other ethical principles must be recalled, because the Church begins with these when she speaks out on population trends. The first is concerned with *the sacred nature of human life and the responsibility of couples for the transmission of life.* Created in the image and likeness of God, the origin of all life, men and women are called to be partners with the Creator in transmitting the sacred gift of human life. Within the communion of life and love which is marriage, they form the family which is the basic

---

[60] One may also cite again the message sent to the United Nations Organization by the Bishops of Latin America (see above 59): "We are aware of the population problem existing in some of our countries, but it is not licit to deal with that problem by using methods which are unethical. No one can accept the systematic anti-childbearing campaigns organized by international institutions or by governments, many times accompanied by pressure, which are against the cultural and religious identity of our nations."

cell of society.⁶¹ It is not in conformity with God's design that couples should neutralize or destroy their fertility by artificial contraception or sterilization, and still less that they have recourse to abortion to kill their offspring before birth.⁶² A truly responsible fatherhood and motherhood begins with the couple's responsibility before the Author and Lord of Life. Such fatherhood and motherhood is based upon generosity within marriage and the respect of the unborn child's right to life.

74. The second principle regards the *inherent right of parenthood*. In the *Charter of the Rights of the Family,* the Church affirms: "The spouses have the inalienable right to found a family and to decide on the spacing of births and the number of children to be born, taking into full consideration their duties towards themselves, their children already born, the family and society, in a just hierarchy of values and in accordance with the objective moral order which excludes recourse to contraception, sterilization and abortion."⁶³

75. For this reason, in the measure in which international agencies use coercion or deceit, they violate not only *the rights of men and women as individuals,* but also *the rights of the family*. Moreover, the *Charter of the Rights of the Family* affirms: "a) The activities of public authorities and private organizations which attempt in any way to limit the freedom of couples in deciding about their children constitute a grave offence against human dignity and justice; b) In international relations, economic aid for the advancement of peoples must not be conditioned on acceptance of programmes of contraception, sterilization and abortion; c) The family has a right to assistance by society in the bearing and rearing of children. Those married couples who have a large family have a right to adequate aid and should not be subjected to discrimination."⁶⁴

More precisely, however morally licit the population policies which they pursue may be, governments have no right to decide for couples the

---

[61] Cf. POPE JOHN PAUL II, *Familiaris consortio,* 11, 14, 28; *AAS* 74 (1982), pp. 91-93, 96, 97, 114.

[62] Cf. VATICAN COUNCIL II, *Gaudium et spes,* 51; POPE PAUL VI, *Humanae vitae,* 12-14; *AAS* 60 (1968), pp. 488-491; POPE JOHN PAUL II, *Familiaris consortio,* 29-31; *AAS* 74 (1982), pp. 114-120.

[63] HOLY SEE, *Charter of the Rights of the Family,* 22 October 1983, Article 3.

[64] *Ibid.,* Article 3 a), b), c). A Charter of Family Rights published by the United Nations would be useful.

number of children they can or should have. Only the discovery of the inherent value of the human person, of marriage and of the family can encourage people to be receptive to children in view of the world of the future.

3. Responsible choice

76. Free to choose the number of children they desire, the couple must be equally free to use natural methods for the responsible regulation of their fertility, for serious reasons and in conformity with the teaching of the Church. These various methods deserve to be known and spread widely.[65] Couples must be offered *the means* to freely exercise their responsible motherhood and fatherhood. The artificial methods of birth control as well as sterilization do not respect the human person of a woman and man because they eliminate or impede fertility which is an integral part of the person.

This is why in his *Letter to Families* for the International Year of the Family in 1994, the Holy Father John Paul II, explained the couple's responsible motherhood and fatherhood: *"They then experienced a moment of special responsibility,* which is also the result of the procreative potential linked to the conjugal act. At that moment, the spouses can become father and mother, initiating the process of a new human life, which will then develop in the woman's womb. If the wife is the first to realize that she has become a mother, the husband, to whom she has been united in 'one flesh,' then learns this when she tells him that he has become a father. Both are responsible for their potential and later actual fatherhood and motherhood."[66]

Chapter III

---

[65] Cf. POPE JOHN PAUL II, *Familiaris consortio,* 35; *AAS* 74 (1982), pp. 125, 126; and see the *Final Declaration of the Meeting on the Natural Methods of Regulating Fertility, L'Osservatore Romano,* English edition, N. 2, 12 January 1993, pp. 7, 8. The experts attending this meeting said: "The natural methods are easy to teach and understand. They can be used in any social context and do not require literacy. The health of mothers and infants is furthered through spacing childbirth in a natural way which harms neither the mother nor her baby. Natural methods do not harm the health of couples. The freedom and rights of the wife and husband are respected through these methods which center around the woman and are based on the integrity of her body."

[66] POPE JOHN PAUL II, *Letter to Families,* 2 February 1994, 12, and *Catechism of the Catholic Church.* nn. 2366-2379.

GUIDELINES FOR ACTION

77. Much of the information published about demographic facts is open to question and is erroneous at times. Confronted by the caution this information requires and the moral inadmissability of population control programmes, the Church cannot remain silent or passive. She does not limit herself merely to stating principles about these abuses. Rather, she responds in a practical and positive way in accord with her mission of service to the family, the "sanctuary of life." *Christians must first of all promote the truth,* especially when it is *concealed* by widely disseminated, but groundless, cliches.

78. All are called to be vigilant about practices which do not respect *the human person.* In each concrete situation, how is the subject of the *environment* used to justify coercive population control? What about *family policy?* Does this policy assure true *freedom for couples?* Does anyone *denounce* cases where public or private international or national organizations violate the rights of individuals or the family under the pretext of fallacious "population imperatives"? To what extent do international organizations put *pressure* on nations to influence them to subscribe to demographic "containment" policies, incompatible with the just sovereignty of nations?

79. Without question, there are certain necessary *priorities.* The following require rapid action:

- many attempts on the part of the "population crisis ideology" to influence international agencies and governments;
- invoking so-called new "women's rights" while underestimating the woman's vocation to give life;
- invoking environmental questions in an excessive or improper way to justify coercive population control;
- attempts to spread abortifacient products such as RU486 in the developed countries and, above all, in poor countries;
- spreading sterilization everywhere;
- making devices against life such as the intra-uterine device (IUD) commonplace and distributing them;
- violations of the absolute and inalienable rights of individuals and families;
- and more generally: the abuse of moral, intellectual and political power.

Moreover, the Church recalls the necessity of priority action when confronted by disastrous practices — challenges to life such as drugs, pornography, violence, etc.

1. Correct knowledge of realities

80.   Christians and all people of good will should *be informed* so as to understand how populations differ in conditions and evolution. They should develop a *critical spirit* regarding the "population crisis ideology." In the face of constant hammering by the media, which is used by many movements in favor of coercive population control, Christians and all people of good will are urged to become aware of the fact that the tactics employed always make use of simplistic economic and demographic information and approximate, that is, inexact, projections.[67]

81.   The Church vigorously encourages *the relevant experts,* especially demographers, economists and political experts, to carry out deeper scientific research on demographic realities. All associations and organizations committed to respect for the human person and the family must *make provision for a correct knowledge of facts and demographic diversity* in their reflection and activities. They should provide a reasoned rejection of the ideology which is expressed as a fear of life and the future. This task also involves organizations working for justice and peace in solidarity.

On their part, all educational institutions are asked to include systematic and critical reflection on demographic realities in their programme. All these efforts should be crowned with the resolve to provide objective information for opinion makers and the mass media, as well as public opinion.

2. Family policy

82.   Every governing authority, whether national, regional or local, owes it to itself to have a family policy which enables families freely to assume their responsibilities in contemporary society and in the chain which links the generations. These family policies must deploy various means for regulating work, adapting taxation, providing access to housing and education, etc.

Furthermore, *family politics* should include the struggle against "contraceptive imperialism" which the Delegation of the Holy See already

---

[67] This information is often provisional. Therefore, it must be verified and kept up to date, taking into account the diversity of the current situations in different countries and regions. One must also be aware of the inaccuracy of demographic projections which tolerate, for example, an imprecision of 660 million inhabitants in the world population projections for the next twenty years.

denounced in 1974 during the International Conference on Population held in Bucharest. This "contraceptive imperialism," which violates the religious and cultural traditions of family life, does violence to the freedom of persons and couples and, through them, harms families and nations.

83. Associations and organizations — national or international, public or private — also have their responsibilities to promote a just family policy. In the interest of the expansion of interdependent human communities, family politics are indispensable to allow those basic cells, the families, to contribute to the development of the whole human community. The agents and protagonists of true family politics are not only the politicians and legislators, but in a special way, parents and families themselves.[68]

3. Justice for women

84. The Church also recommends the setting up of policies which assure respect of the *woman's specifically human character as a person, as a wife and as a mother*. Women are the first to suffer psychologically and physically from campaigns inspired by the ideology of population fear. In these campaigns a false concept of the woman's "reproductive health" is used to promote different methods of contraception or abortion. These methods not only can suppress the unborn child's life, but also have grave repercussions on women's health, even risking their lives.

This ideology of population fear puts the blame on the woman for being a mother, concealing the fact that *through this maternal dimension she makes her essential and irreplaceable contribution to society*. The quality of a society is expressed in the respect it shows with regard to the woman. A society which shows contempt for welcoming the child and human life, holds the woman in contempt. For this reason everything must be done to help women fulfill their responsibilities and reconcile their family, professional, associative and social duties as they see fit. This is possible only if in practice the equal dignity of man and woman is recognized. In particular, women must be able to express themselves and set up movements which help them take their place in society and make it better recognized.[69]

---

[68] Cf. POPE JOHN PAUL II, *Familiaris consortio,* 47, 48; *AAS* 74 (1982), pp. 139, 140.

[69] Cf. POPE JOHN PAUL II, *Laborem exercens,* 19; *AAS* 73 (1981) p. 625, *Familiaris consortio,* 22-24; *AAS* 74 (1982) pp. 106-110; Apostolic Letter *Mulieris dignitatem (*15 August 1988), 19, 30; *AAS* 80 (1988), pp. 1693-1697, 1724-1727.

4. No possible compromise

85. It so happens that organizations favourable to controlling population by illicit means deliberately *compromise* Christians in their activities. Thus, Christians may be invited to take part in projects or programmes of action with rather general objectives, such as development or environment, while, in fact, the real aim of these initiatives is to promote the ideology of the fear of life (anti-life mentality) and to involve Christians by leading them into "mismatched partnerships."[70] Christians must prove themselves to be watchful, prudent and courageous. They should be ready to bear witness, even if necessary by martyrdom, to the worth of each person in God's eyes.[71]

Pastoral letters could help the faithful discern the moral problems raised in this context by population trends as well as helping them organize appropriate action.

---

[70] Cf. 2 *Corinthians* 6:14.

[71] Cf. POPE JOHN PAUL II, Encyclical Letter *Veritatis splendor* (6 August 1993), 90-94; *AAS* 85 (1993), pp. 1205-1208.

CONCLUSION

1. Development, resources and populations

86. The diversity and complexity of the population trends of the different peoples of the earth cannot be summed up in catchy but superficial formulas, as is so often the case. Furthermore, the growth-rate of population (an *average* which by its very nature does not take into account the variety of situations) *is decreasing* after having reached a maximum between 1965-1970. On the other hand, taking into account all the populations of different countries, the average projections of specialist organizations for the twenty-first century refer to an increase three times inferior to that verified during the twentieth century. All this indicates that *the world's potentialities are largely sufficient* to satisfy humanity's needs. As Pope John Paul II forcefully emphasized: "Indeed, besides the earth, man's principal resource is *man himself.* His intelligence enables him to discover the earth's productive potential and the many different ways in which human needs can be satisfied."[72] The Holy Father specifies and summarizes his thought: "Man... is God's gift to man."[73] Therefore, it is man's duty to be a responsible and inventive steward of the goods which the Creator has placed at his disposal.

87. In her teaching, the Church takes into consideration the fact of population trends. However, she is challenged by campaigns which create a fear for the future. Those promoting these campaigns have not understood the logic of long-term demographic mechanisms, and notably what population science calls the "demographic transition."[74] Confronted by these campaigns, the Church is above all deeply concerned about promoting justice for the weakest. Certain groups encourage coercive population control by contraception, sterilization and even abortion. They believe that they see in these practices "the solution" to problems raised by the different forms of underdevelopment. When this recommendation comes from prosperous nations, it seems to express *a refusal on the part of the rich to face the true causes of underdevelopment.* Even more, the methods promoted to reduce births cause more damaging effects than the evils which they claim to remedy. This damage is seen particularly at the level of human rights and

---

[72] POPE JOHN PAUL II, *Centesimus annus,* 32; *AAS* 83 (1991), p. 833.

[73] *Ibid,* 38; *AAS* 83 (1991), p. 841.

[74] Cf. *above* 5.

family rights.

2. Solidarity with the family

88. Only when the rights of the family are recognized and promoted can there exist an authentic development which respects women and children and gives attention to the rich diversity of cultures. In the context of this authentic human development, there is a fundamental moral truth which cannot be changed either by laws or population policies, whether these be evident or hidden. This fundamental truth is that *human life must be respected from conception until natural death.* The quality of a society is not only shown by the respect it has for the woman. Its quality is also shown by the respect or contempt a society has for life and human dignity.

In *Centesimus annus,* Pope John Paul II specifies that respect for life must be upheld in the *family.* It is necessary to see "the family as the *sanctuary of life.* The family is indeed sacred: it is the place in which life — the gift of God — can be properly welcomed and protected against the many attacks to which it is exposed, and can develop in accordance with what constitutes authentic human growth. In the face of the so-called culture of death, the family is the heart of the culture of life."[75]

89. In discovering the family as the *"sanctuary of life"* and the *"heart of the culture of life,"* men and women can be freed from the "culture of death." This latter culture begins with the *"anti-baby mentality,"* so widely developed in the ideology of coercive population control. In each child, couples and society must recognize a gift coming to them from the Creator, a precious gift which must be loved and welcomed with joy.[76]

Together with efforts aimed at establishing family policies, the inherent value of each child as a human being must be proclaimed. In the face of population trends, everyone is invited to put to good use the talents given by the Creator to realize personal development and to contribute in an original way to the development of the community. In the final analysis, God created man only to make him a partner in his plan of life and love.

The words of the Holy Father, Paul VI, cited above, must continue to challenge those responsible for the nations of the world: "... You must

---

[75] POPE JOHN PAUL II, *Centesimus annus*, 39; *AAS* 83 (1991), p. 842.

[76] Cf. VATICAN COUNCIL II, *Gaudium et spes,* 50.

strive to multiply bread so that it suffices for the tables of mankind, and not rather favour an artificial control of birth, which would be irrational, in order to diminish the number of guests at the banquet of life."[77]

Vatican City, 25 March 1994

✠ ALFONSO Card. LOPEZ TRUJILLO
President of the Pontifical Council for the Family

✠ ELIO SGRECCIA
Titular Bishop of Zama Minor
Secretary of the Pontifical Council for the Family

---

[77] POPE PAUL VI, *Address to the United Nations Assembly*, 6; *AAS* 57 (1965), p. 883.

Declaration of the Pontifical Academy for Life
Issued by the Executive Board at their First Meeting
Vatican, 19 June 1994

The issue of human life is today recognized as a primary, fundamental value in all human rights charters. However, this recognition becomes effective only when the life of every human being — from conception to natural death — is welcomed, defended and supported with respect for its inviolable dignity. What applies to the individual human being also applies to the world population. All men, in fact, have the same inviolable right to life, since the subject of this inalienable right is the human person as such.

In view of the alarmist campaigns underway, we consider it our duty to state that one cannot maintain that the world is experiencing such a growth in population as to make a future of insecurity and poverty imminent. Hence it is false and contrary to natural and Hippocratic ethics to assert that the birth rate must be drastically curbed, using any means whatever, so long as they can control demographic growth: contraception, sterilization, abortion, euthanasia.

The so-called "demographic explosion" is actually subsiding: the most recent statistical indices confirm that in various parts of the world not only is the population no longer increasing, but a worrying trend in the opposite direction has been observed. Wealthier countries should undertake to provide economic and social aid to developing countries, rather than impose birth-control policies.

From the ethical standpoint, two extremely serious facts that challenge the reason and conscience of every upright person of whatever people must be pointed out: first, the attempt to impose on society, particularly in developing countries and on individual families, a birth-control programme based on a merely economic and utilitarian vision, and for that reason, one that disregards the demands of justice and, consequently, gravely violates the right of parents to responsible procreation under conditions of real freedom; second, in order to achieve this aim, the recourse to means and methods offensive to life and the dignity of the human person.

As servants of life, we subscribe to the following: We affirm that every member of the human species is a person. The care owed to every individual does not depend on either his age or the infirmity he may suffer. From conception to the last moment of life, it is the same human being that develops and dies.

Personal rights are *absolutely inalienable*. The fertilized human egg, the embryo, the foetus can be neither donated nor sold. It cannot be denied the right to progressive development in its own mother's womb.

No one can subject it to any kind of exploitation. No authority, not even that of the father or mother, can threaten its life.

The manipulation and dissection of the embryo and foetus, abortion and euthanasia cannot be appropriate for a servant of life.

We also affirm that the human seeds of life must always be protected. The human genome, of which each generation is merely the custodian, cannot be the object of ideological and commercial speculation. The composition of this genome is the patrimony of all humanity and, therefore, can never be patented.

Wishing to continue the tradition of Hippocrates and to conform our practice to the teaching of the Catholic Church, we reject all deliberate damage to the genome, all exploitation of gametes and any induced alteration of the reproductive functions.

Relieving suffering and healing illness, preserving health and correcting hereditary defects are the goal of our efforts, with constant respect for the dignity and sacredness of the person.

Consequently, we consider it urgently necessary for all humanity, through the United Nations Organization which represents it, to deal with the problem of population and the distribution of resources in a genuinely scientific manner, in harmony with natural and Hippocratic ethics. This harmonious agreement between scientific endeavour and the ethical requirements of safeguarding the value of life will promote that responsible birth regulation which is set forth and defended by the moral teaching of the Catholic Church as a true human ecology and which will allow for a stance respectful of the couple's freedom of conscience before God, whose will man comes to know through the true, upright and certain judgment of conscience.

ADDRESS OF
HIS EMINENCE ALFONSO CARDINAL LÓPEZ TRUJILLO
PRESIDENT OF THE PONTIFICAL COUNCIL FOR THE FAMILY
AT THE PRESS CONFERENCE PRESENTING THE PROCEEDINGS OF
A STUDY CONFERENCE ON NATURAL FAMILY PLANNING METHODS
VATICAN, 7 JULY 1994

This volume contains the *Proceedings* (Atti) of the study conference organized by the Pontifical Council for the Family on 9-11 December 1992, for the purpose of hearing the world's principal researchers, promoters and representatives on methods for the diagnosis and natural regulation of human fertility.

The conference's aim was not to defend the right of the natural methods to be accepted in the area of science and social welfare, because they had already been recognized by the World Health Organization at the end of 1982. It is obvious that during the sessions of this important meeting the following was also confirmed: there is a scientific basis for the best-known of the so-called "natural" methods — the temperature method, the sympto-thermal method, the ovulation or Billings method — there are results concerning their practicability and viability with regard both to the well-motivated and ethically justifiable spacing of births and to seeking a child when conception is difficult.

Some researchers, as can be read in the Proceedings, also updated the participants on the latest advances in further research and the results of what now seems a new and different strategy as compared to the repeated attempts over the past 30 years or so to intervene in the fertilization process. The new strategy is based on knowledge of and respect for the fertility cycle.

Natural methods promote integral view of sexuality

From the direction this research has taken, what was hoped for in *Humanae vitae,* n. 24, regarding science's contribution to the solution of the problem of the couple in terms of fertility control, now appears to have been achieved.

Even if the conference's main goal was not a scientific verification, this aspect was most interesting to the participants, who exchanged useful information. Following the progress of the biomedical sciences in relation to the defence and promotion of human life is, in fact, the essential task of the Pontifical Council for the Family, which "supports and coordinates initiatives to safeguard life from the moment of conception, and encourages responsible procreation" (Apostolic Constitution *Pastor bonus,* 1988, art. 141, 3).

There was also a desire to examine in greater detail the philosophical and theological aspects implicit in proposing natural methods, and to set aside enough time to verify their application in pastoral work where worthwhile techniques have been developed.

The various centres in the world, with their organizations which have now become international, have for many years spread a new culture and made people aware of it, a culture based on personalization and on procreative responsibility within the framework of human ecology; these efforts and activities are notably increasing, more or less everywhere in the Church. It was necessary to compare the methodology, the cultural support in the context of a "culture of life," the level of acceptability, the ethical and pastoral conditions.

The picture that emerged was more than positive, even in the variety of experiences and methodologies. The so-called natural methods now appear not only as an aid, or indeed, a "method" for solving, from the technical point of view, some of the problems in married life, but their use implies an integral view of sexuality and human love, a view that is fulfilled in marriage, but implies an overall plan of life that is prepared right from adolescence.

Thus what emerges is an integral anthropology for living conjugal love fully and responsibly (*Humanae vitae*, n. 9). On this basic point, the theological and moral reports provided a satisfactory doctrinal framework.

In fact, these methods require and imply a creationist view of man, woman, marriage and the family. At the same time they sensitize people to discovering and interpreting God's plan inherent in the human corporeity of man and woman, and therefore in conjugal sexual activity. The person is viewed not as a subjectivity that considers sex as an object and demands its free availability, but in its existential and ontological totality, in which the body is also the subject and requires the same respect due to personhood itself. It carries a message and a plan of which the consciences of the spouses are the responsible stewards, not the arbiters. The gift of the body in sexuality is a gift of the person in his totality: the body is an essential and subjectively binding epiphany, a sign and expression.

Therefore knowledge of corporeity in relation to fertility implies the interpretation of God's plan, of all the meaningful and expressive ways of loving and the conditions of fertility.

All the speakers concurred in noting that these methods both imply and encourage couples to have a new vision and a new feeling about themselves.

The ethical requirements for using the natural methods thus consist in overcoming dualism: free-subject/sex-object, the overcoming of aggressiveness and the exploitation of depersonalized sexuality. The ethic which sustains and accompanies the use of the natural methods is thus marked by respect, responsibility, shared decision-making, the spouses' reciprocal acceptance as a mutual and total gift, conscious justification of the reasons for seeking a new birth or recommending its postponement, with constant respect for life and the human person.

Ethical and political values cannot be ignored

Experts unanimously observe the aspect of communion which is encouraged in couples by the obvious need to know themselves and to communicate or share the most important decisions of their life, those of procreation and the gift of self.

This anthropological, ethical and cultural view, implied in proposing the natural methods, includes a sound ecological and political element. The de-medicalization of sexuality, its liberation from financial exploitation by the contraceptive drug market and respect for the normal physiology of sexuality in its delicate and complex mechanisms, are reasons based on the ecology of the body to which contemporary society is justly sensitive.

It is indeed paradoxical that respect for nature external to man is demanded for the serious and urgent reasons, with which we are all familiar, regarding health and the very survival of the human race, while the reasons for protecting and respecting the body, which are just as urgent, are forgotten — or deliberately concealed for reasons of financial gain.

The natural methods have this very important feature in that they allow the normal physiological functions of human reproduction to be respected.

Some object that many drugs interfere with the normal physiological functions but that not all drug treatments can be condemned in the name of the ecology of the body. This objection is not applicable here because contraceptives are not medicine for treating an illness and pregnancy is not an illness. When it is a question of using therapeutic means in the strict sense for treating true and proper dysfunctions, the Encyclical *Humanae vitae* itself allows the use of these substances, which in this case do not have a contraceptive purpose.

The ethical and political value of proposing natural methods cannot be ignored. It is known that over the past 25 years contraception, together with abortion and sterilization, has formed the main basis for family planning programmes developed by immensely powerful international, private and public institutions, able to influence the policies of individual States. Sometimes developing countries are blackmailed into accepting these family planning programmes in order to receive economic and financial aid, and are in any case persuaded by a mass propaganda that spares no corner of the world from alarm about the population explosion.

The negative aspects of such policies stem particularly from the fact that they use means and methods detrimental to life, health and human dignity, precisely because they are based on mass contraception, sterilization and abortion, including these practices as indicative of progress and mutual benefit. Moreover, since the "induction" is compulsory and without adequate information, it eliminates the appeal to exercise authentic procreative responsibility. From this angle, there is no room for responsible procreation in the true sense of the word, nor in the political sense of the term.

The proposal of natural methods thus has an inherent value, that of bringing liberation from one of the most insidious forms of political domination: "biological colonialism," targeted at procreation.

Should we not recognize that this fact, plus the fact that the natural methods thwart powerful industrial, economic and financial interests, could be the reason for the opposition from so many sides against the dissemination of natural methods?

To save couples from economic intimidation and from politically and economically imposed family planning is not a secondary aspect of the strategy of ethical and responsible self-control of procreation.

The discussion, expressed positively in this way, should not overlook the negative moral-theological significance of a different type of contraception — mechanical, behavioural and chemical — for the important topics present in the doctrine of *Humanae vitae:* the separation of the unitive and procreative meanings of sexuality, the degradation of sexuality into consumerism (*Humanae vitae*, nn. 11 and 12).

Today perhaps we must talk about the commercialization of the woman's body, something that is happening not only in the area of artificial procreation (surrogate motherhood, the sale of gametes), but also in the simple and repeated suppression of procreation with products specifically designed for this.

Several national bioethics committees in Europe have sounded the alarm, which has also been taken up by humanist-Marxist ethical thought, on the subject of the commercialization of the human body. We maintain, and the conference has given us the proof, that the greatest and most serious commercialization of the body and of sexuality has taken place as a result of contraception, which is being more and more frequently associated with sterilization or abortion.

Precisely in order to define more clearly the urgent anthropological and cultural need for using the natural methods, it is appropriate to recall, even briefly, how contraception today is increasingly similar to chemical abortion, through a whole series of pharmacological inventions of an interceptive and counter gestational type, aimed at preventing the definitive implantation of the fertilized egg when it contains a new, living, human being.

Serious motives needed for postponing conception

The relationship, even chemical, between contraception and abortion is thus ever more clearly the object of internationally financed research with a wide range of low dosage pills, vaccines, subcutaneous implants, coils and vaginal rings of various kinds, introduced with such an extensive international organization that it reminds one of the black slave trade and that of other eras, down to the notorious RU 486 pill.

The participants certainly did not forget to make a theological assessment of the use of the natural methods in comparison with reliance on contraception (apart from the differences already mentioned), whenever the natural methods themselves are used with a contraceptive mentality, in other words, for the mere purpose of avoiding childbirth.

The conditions of biological and physical respect for the integral nature of the act and of the self-gift certainly do not dispense one from seeking — indeed they require — that motivational prerequisite of respect for the individual and the Creator, just as serious motives are also required for spacing or postponing conception.

Discussion of these pastoral and ethical topics were foreseen by the conference, and the conference made it possible to compare the different schools activities and strategies that present the natural methods. It confirmed their validity and the fact that they are increasingly part of catechetical programmes for marriage preparation.

It was impossible during the sessions to introduce the delicate subject of the relationship of centres promoting the natural methods with national and international public authorities in regard to possible financing and conditions for this funding that financing institutions could require of centres offering natural methods. This is a sensitive issue, which is why it was agreed that the subject be further studied in conjunction with the Congregation for the Doctrine of the Faith.[1]

The work of these past few years has made it possible to describe and to recommend the natural methods as a "true alternative" to replace contraception and "family planning," since the alternative expression highlights the ethical anthropological and cultural difference for responsible procreation in comparison with the contraceptive and anti-birth strategies widespread throughout the world.

The Holy Father's address clearly emphasized the value of this perspective connected with the natural methods and recognized its moral legitimacy for the concrete situations of families in the world when he stated: "Because of the generous contribution of scientists, educators and married couples, one can speak of a turning-point in the defence and promotion of the dignity of conjugal life. There is a growing awareness of the true nature of married love, which is capable of bringing about an authentic liberation from so many abuses of power against women and the family both in industrialized countries and, to an even greater degree, in the developing ones. The results of scientific studies, the experience gained in teaching programmes in Dioceses in different parts of the world, in associations and movements, and

---

[1] It is known that family planning organizations consider the natural methods in the same light as contraception: a way to limit and plan births as necessary, and as a result these organizations believe that centres promoting natural methods can apply for the government funding allocated to all centres that come under the family planning category.

The granting of this financial aid however, apart from the mistaken presumption that the natural methods are contraceptive methods (obviously a misleading opinion from the conceptual point of view), is nevertheless conditioned by certain commitments such as the obligation for those proposing the natural methods to supply additional information on other contraceptive methods or even to encourage possible access to hormonal or mechanical contraception, providing comprehensive information about them. This is the delicate question of so-called "referrals."

especially the testimony of couples themselves, show the validity, the advantages and the ethical value of methods based upon periodic continence. These methods, with their corresponding way of living, free couples from the cultural, economic and political conditioning imposed by programmes of family planning. They liberate the person, above all women, from recourse to pharmaceutical or other forms of interference in the natural processes connected with the transmission of life. They have proved to be practicable not only for elite groups but for couples everywhere, including the poorest and least economically developed peoples. I wish to assure you of the importance of your specific contribution to the welfare of marriage and the family, and to encourage you in your work" (Pope John Paul II, *Address* to Experts Participating in a Study Conference on Natural Family Planning Methods, *L'Osservatore Romano* English edition, 16 December 1992, p. 6).

STATEMENT BY
HIS EMINENCE ALFONSO CARDINAL LÓPEZ TRUJILLO
PRESIDENT OF THE PONTIFICAL COUNCIL FOR THE FAMILY,
TO THE UNITED NATIONS GENERAL ASSEMBLY
ON THE OCCASION OF
THE INTERNATIONAL CONFERENCE ON FAMILIES
NEW YORK, 19 OCTOBER 1994

Mr. Chairman,

This session is taking place in the International Year of the Family, convened by the United Nations and celebrated by the Catholic Church in the different nations of the world with particular enthusiasm.

In Rome, on October 8th and 9th, two significant events have just taken place: the World Meeting of Families with Pope John Paul II: An immense multitude — like a sea into which abundant tributaries flowed — of nearly 200,000 pilgrims from almost every country in the world filled St. Peter's Square.

This celebration was preceded by numerous initiatives carried out in all the countries that showed the vitality of the family. In this way, the Rome Meeting with the Pope was a demonstration of hope in the energies of the Family, based on marriage, as a community of life and love, characterized by the reciprocal self-giving of a man and a woman, a husband and wife, in a free, stable — until death — responsible way that is open to life. Indeed, children are God's most precious gift to marriage.[1]

In the Catholic Church, the *Charter of the Rights of the Family* prepared by the Holy See, has been used as the instrument for work and dialogue. It synthesized the principal aspects and points, based on a rich conception of fundamental human rights, because the rights of the family are a systematic manifestation and application of the natural law in reference to the family community, the vital foundation of society.

During this Year it has been possible to study in depth what the Family entails as the vital basis and foundation of society,[2] and to draw the

---

[1] Cf. Pastoral Constitution *Gaudium et spes*, No. 50.

[2] Cf. HOLY SEE, *Charter of the Rights of the Family*, 22 October 1993, Preamble.

consequences both for the personal and social spheres and for the life of humanity in the network of the human family. It would not be logical or coherent to state and recognize that the family is the basic cell of the social fabric and then deny or weaken its status as a real *social subject* with its own peculiar *sovereignty*,[3] rights and duties.

Pope John Paul II makes reference to these vital themes in his rich *Letter to Families*, his gift to the human family on the occasion of the Year of the Family.

In a recent meeting in Rome with many families from all around the world,[4] we were able to verify the deep convergence that exists among the most varied religions regarding the fundamental values of the family. It could not be otherwise because the family is humanity's heritage through which necessarily the future of society on our planet passes.[5]

It is very significant to bring together similar manifestations in the cultural heritage of our peoples. In *Nichomachaen Ethics*, we can read these reflections: "Friendship between husband and wife is recognized, it is natural: in fact, by nature, man is more inclined to live as a couple than to associate politically because the family is something prior to, and more necessary than the State."[6] This text was written 350 years before Christ.

Throughout history attempts have been made to defend and help the family community in which the good of the spouses, the children and society is ensured. I do not wish to dwell on this aspect too long, but what would be the future of children, their harmonious development, their up-bringing in the sense of integral formation, and their dynamic and positive incorporation into society, if they were not born and raised in a family, a responsible union of hearts under one roof, as we see it in the United Nations' symbol for the International Year of the Family? Are not the strength of the family and its protection the best guarantee for respecting children in agreement with the

---

[3] Cf. JOHN PAUL II, *Letter to Families*, No. 17.

[4] From September 21-26, 1994 in Rome, a meeting took place with families representing the major religions of the world organized by the Pontifical Council for Inter-religious Dialogue and the Pontifical Council for the Family.

[5] Cf. Apostolic Exhortation *Familiaris consortio*, No. 75.

[6] ARISTOTLE, *Nichomachaen Ethics*, VIII, 15-20.

Convention on the Rights of Child?[7]

Children are the first victims of instability and erosion. They are innocent victims who have the right to their parents' generous and sacrificial love, their example, and to a formation of which their parents' behavior is a condition.

Today very high social costs of all sorts are paid either because millions of children do not have families or — as the Pope says — because they are orphans with living parents.[8]

Mr. Chairman, this International Year is urging us to confirm and give appropriate and necessary application to one fundamental principle: the family based on marriage is a value proper to this *Natural Institution*, willed by God, inscribed in the depths of human nature. It is a *value*, I repeat, as the Second Vatican Council notes, for the spouses, the children and society.[9] It is a *value* which must be recognized, defended and placed as the pillar of authentic family policies.

The family is not a private matter and situation: it has social importance which is not derived from any concessions or the generosity of the State.

It has been possible to observe, on the one hand, what some nations have achieved, and, on the other, a symptomatic hollowing of family policies and legislation worthy only of the name in many countries. Some documents of the International Year make reference to this requirement.[10]

An adequate family policy requires that the family be recognized and helped as a social subject, one that *integrates* each and every one of its members, the man and woman, the husband and wife, sons and daughters, babies, youth, the elderly, the healthy and the sick.

---

[7] Cf. *United Nations Convention on the Rights of Children*, 20 November 1989, Preamble.

[8] Cf. JOHN PAUL II, *Letter to Families*, No. 14.

[9] Cf. Pastoral Constitution *Gaudium et spes*, No. 50.

[10] Cf. United Nations 1994 International Year of the Family *"Building the Smallest Democracy in the Heart of Society."*

We have been able to work more vigorously for the members of the family who also deserve appropriate assistance of a social nature that is in harmony and not in opposition to the family as an integrating body or community.

Lastly, Mr. Chairman, together with the repeated desire for real recognition of the rights of the family and necessary, positive family legislation, to which Pope John Paul II and the Catholic Church are very committed, I would like to express the hope for a decisive, enthusiastic and universal defense of the family on the part of those who govern. If they act in this way, they are in encouraging syntony with the good of the family, of society and the common good which must be ensured for all humanity.

Finally, during the preparatory process leading up to the International Conference on Population and Development in Cairo, His Holiness Pope John Paul II expressed concern regarding the treatment of the traditional form of the family. The Holy See is pleased to note that in the Principles of the Cairo Document, the basis for interpreting and understanding the text in its entirety, it is clearly stated that "the family is the basic unit of society and as such should be strengthened. It is entitled to receive comprehensive protection and support" (Principle 9). This same principle goes on to say that "Marriage must be entered into with the free consent of the intending spouses, and husband and wife should be equal partners." This principle must inspire all family policy and any true demographic policy.

I would like to convey paternal, warm and hopeful greetings to all of you and your families from Pope John Paul II, the Pope of the Family, the Pope of Life.

Thank you very much.

REPORT OF
HIS EMINENCE ALFONSO CARDINAL LÓPEZ TRUJILLO
PRESIDENT OF THE PONTIFICAL COUNCIL FOR THE FAMILY,
TO THE TWENTY-SEVENTH GENERAL CONGREGATION OF THE
SYNOD OF BISHOPS
ON THE YEAR OF THE FAMILY AND THE CAIRO CONFERENCE
VATICAN, 28 OCTOBER 1994

I am very grateful for this valued opportunity once again offered to our Dicastery, to provide information on some aspects of the Year of the Family, on the recent celebration which took place in the General Assembly of the United Nations. This is the living experience of the Church, bearing many consequences in the midst of converging international events: the *Conference on the Environment at Rio de Janeiro* (1-12 June 1992), the *Cairo Conference on Population and Development* (5-13 September 1994) and the *International Conference on Women* which will be held in Beijing, 4-15 September 1995. Less well known, but no less important, is the *World Summit for Social Development*, to be held at Copenhagen, 11-12 April 1995.

I want to emphasize that we also received detailed information on these themes during the Special Synod of the Bishops of Africa (10 April to 8 May 1994) and during the Extraordinary Consistory of Cardinals (13-14 June 1994). In fact, the African Synod Fathers also had accurate and timely information on the preparation for the Cairo Conference from the Secretary of State, Cardinal Angelo Sodano. Moreover, during the same Synod, Monsignor Diarmuid Martin, Secretary of the Pontifical Council for Justice and Peace, provided useful precisions on the work of the Preparatory Committee meeting on the Cairo Document, held in New York, 5 - 22 April 1994.

In these circumstances, I must limit myself to a general overview and perhaps some suggestions, given the role of the participants of this Synod, with Fathers coming from all nations and Episcopal Conferences, and representatives of so many religious families. Some have requested general information.

The International Year of the Family

Concerning the *International Year of the Family*, it can be said that a great mobilization was set in train within the Church after Pope John Paul II announced the Year, on 6 June 1993, and after the inauguration celebrated on the liturgical feast of the Holy Family at Nazareth, a stimulating and significant celebration.

Thanks particularly to the guidance and impetus of the Successor of Peter, this year has been a great grace of the Lord and so many energies have been aroused on the part of Episcopal Conferences, Dioceses, parishes, movements, associations, apostolic groups. It would be very interesting to be able to put together a synthesis of such intense and encouraging activity, bearing the riches which spring up from families, and which abundantly surpassed what we had foreseen. A striking example is the publication of major activities carried out in each of the nations of Latin American and edited by CELAM (Episcopal Council of Latin America).

In various continents and nations, in different societies and internationally, the opportunity of this gathering (a celebration still not over and which should continue in some adequate way) was positively recognized to affirm the decisive importance of the family and its rights, specifically defended by the Church in the *Charter of the Rights of the Family*, prepared by the Holy See. Many Episcopal Conferences once again will publish this document, which is so synthetic, solid and current. It is a necessary means for dialogue to give stimulus to the recognition of the rights of the family as such, that is, as a social subject, capable of integrating its members who thus should not be considered separately, also in terms of the urgent need to make society and the State aware that their own future is at stake in terms of support given, or not given, to the identity and reality of the family, founded on marriage, because it is the primordial and vital basis of society. As was also emphasized at the United Nations Assembly, one of the most incisive effects of this work of sensibilization is the rediscovery, as it were, of the necessity for genuine family policies, through which kind of orientation the Church can collaborate and contribute much.

The family in fact is not a private matter, nor is it marginal, rather it is of serious, necessary and intense interest for all people.

Without united and stable families, a community of life and love, open to life, the social costs are immense, to the point of risking the weakening and tearing apart of the very fabric of society.

This is a central and fundamental point which the Holy Father has firmly recalled in a timely way, in so many circumstances during this Year, with such enthusiasm in his different Messages, such as those for Christmas and Easter, on the occasions of various days and celebrations and, with particular importance, in the *Letters* personally addressed to all the Heads of State.

We know that many of you have expressed your own gratitude, even publicly, for this truly prophetic service of the Successor of Peter.

The Year of the Family thus took shape and, by arousing concern, it took on some stimulating concrete features. The importance of these valued concerns can be verified today more clearly than ever.

With regard to the *Cairo Conference*, it was the family above all that was put on trial, as the Holy Father said in his *Letter to the Heads of State*. The challenges of the integral development of the person and society are reduced to "a *life-style* the consequences of which, were it accepted as a model and plan of action for the future, could prove particularly negative." The Pope warned that in the Document, "the idea of sexuality underlying the text is totally individualistic, to such an extent that marriage now appears as something outmoded." He also affirmed, "An institution as natural, fundamental and universal as the family cannot be manipulated by anyone!"

Following up the indications of the Holy Father, the positions and replies of various Episcopal Conferences and Pastors have had a positive impact on public opinion and given ecclesial communities clarity and certainty in this particular struggle. For example, how could we fail to make reference to the Declaration of all the Presidents of the Episcopal Conference of Latin America, the fruit of the three-day meeting at Santo Domingo (16-18 June 1994), a Declaration which was also sent to Governments which, for the great part, sent Delegations to Cairo with very positive indications? Also in Europe there was the Declaration of the Presidents of Episcopal Commissions for the Family, gathered in Rome (4-5 July 1994).

The African Synod sent a clear and penetrating letter to the Secretary-General of the United Nations on the Cairo Conference and the defence of the family.

In Europe, the Declaration of the Episcopal Conference of Europe is known and, in the United States, some days before the visit of President Clinton to the Holy Father, the forcible position of the President of the Episcopal Conference and the Cardinals of that nation on the Cairo Conference was made public.

The dynamic presence of the Secretariat of State was very useful, with recommendations and information offered to Episcopal Conferences and all referred to it again and again.

With this vigorous demonstration of unity in the cause of the family, the Church had strong influence in the Cairo Conference, and that fact cannot but fail to impress!

This was so not only in the political ambit, so to say, but also in the religious field, beginning with non-Christian religions. I would like to refer to a very significant meeting which the Dicastery for Interreligious Dialogue, together with our Pontifical Council, organized in Rome (21-25 September 1994). Presided over by His Eminence Cardinal Francis Arinze, this was an International Colloquium on marriage and the family in today's world, with the participation of delegate couples from various religions. It showed well, it seems to me, the profound agreement — and we can put in no other way — on the reality of the family as a natural institution willed by God, in the original plan of creation (*ab initio*!) and on the value of marriage as the foundation of the family. There was great convergence concerning the actual state of the family in defence of its identity as well as concerning concerns and challenges which were revealed. It was good to discover how this cause is so central for different religions! There is no time to go more deeply into the significant and decisive convergence (not a coalition, and still less a conspiracy) with Islam before and during the Cairo Conference.

The *Letter of the Holy Father to Families* was received everywhere as a precious gift. Addressed, as you know, to all families, even non-Catholic and non-Christian families (cf. N. 23), it constitutes a rich instrument for a serious and systematic study of the most important themes along the lines set out in the Apostolic Exhortation *Familiaris consortio*, but with so many points for deeper study. The World Council of Churches expressed its thanks for this *Letter* and we have news of a positive welcome in various Churches. Although planned, an Ecumenical Meeting on the Family did not take place as was the wish we shared with the Dicastery for the Unity of Christians. We hope that next year it will be possible to hold a meeting on the Family and Life, especially with our Orthodox brethren, according to projects for which I have made contacts in some Eastern European nations. An excellent opportunity is raised by the Holy Father's Encyclical *Evangelium vitae*.

Last week I took part in the General Assembly of the United Nations, in New York. In those days, 18-19 October, in the Plenary Session of the 49th General Assembly of the U.N., what was called a *"Conference on Families"* took place, to gather the fruits of this International Year of the Family. About 50 States asked to speak, but there was not sufficient time for all interventions. The Secretary-General of the United Nations, Mr. Boutros Boutros-Ghali, stated that families provided an integrating focus for many development problems and a mechanism for coherent action at the basic level of human life. Families, he continued, should receive the full support of society and the State, with tangible assistance through need-based and participatory policies, programmes and services.

In many interventions one could see how many nations find themselves *under stress* on account of so many serious problems which the family undergoes in the world. For the greater part, as often happens, the spirit was rather pragmatic but, before so many great challenges, always the importance of the family as the basic cell of society was recognized. In reality, because of this, many States judged this Year as representing only an initial stage in developing awareness of the problems in all their globality and gravity, with all the threats and the possible solutions.

Some Delegations spoke of the difficulties in dealing with the subject with a unitary vision at the Conference, given the plurality of family structures, and this is the reason for defending the plural, "families." One delegate (who was the exception) came to put forward his fear over a debate at a particular and global level which could be used to promote discrimination against "other forms of house-hold" apart from the traditional nuclear family. These other households were defined as single-parent families or unmarried individuals who have a common life, even of the same sex. This intervention expressly warned Governments not to pass judgments on this, but only see to the growth and education of children who live in a variety of circumstances.

The Delegations reported on their Governments' various activities and priorities. Part of the time was dedicated also to some Non-Governmental Organizations.

The papers presented will serve as the basis for a preparatory plan of action which the Secretary General will put before the 50th Assembly next year.

One cannot say, therefore, that the main problems which have been raised by our Dicastery at various times ought not to continue to be presented. The idea of the *impossibility of defining* the family is widespread, and the propensity towards a vague concept of the family is well known, together with the symptomatic attitude of not adopting, even rejecting, the use of the term *marriage* in various international meetings.

The regrettable logical consequences of such a position are the propensity to make free unions equal to marriage, putting them on the same level, or to consider the family or marriage as a private fact, virtually the refuge of affections and emotions, without social relevance — and this constitutes a trap! Very symptomatic of moral erosion and confusion about fundamental concepts (a most serious social malady, as the Pope puts it; cf.

Letter to Families, nn. 13, 20), another consequence of the non-definition of the family was the *Declaration of the Parliament of Europe* on homosexual unions and their presumed rights, including the right to adoption. The risk of accepting that recommendation lacking morals or ethics can be observed in some European nations. While this divisive position and a certain lack of trust in the family retains its full force in the ambit of the United Nations, because of these alarming aspects, nevertheless it is possible to say that the atmosphere was much more positive and reassuring in the various interventions in the Assembly. Some cited texts of the Holy Father, whose presence, as you know, was strongly desired there.

On 7 December 1993, at the Inauguration of the International Year, there was clear opposition, for example, between a coherent vision of the family and the statement actually made in that inaugural session by the lady Delegate of the United States, who announced the return to pro-abortion policies and financial assistance to institutions such as IPPF (International Planned Parenthood Federation). On that occasion I had the honour to hand over the message of the Holy Father to the President of the Assembly, who referred to it, and which was distributed to the Delegations but not read in the auditorium. No other alternative was offered because of limited time. On the other hand, now it is possible in an ample paper to recall and set out the thought of the Church in the Magisterium of the Holy Father, which was very well received. The text was published by *L'Osservatore Romano*.

Certainly, this was in the context of the so-called battle of Cairo. In my text, read at the United Nations, I referred to principle *nine* in the Cairo Document: "The Holy See is pleased to note that in the Principles of the Cairo Document, the basis for interpreting and understanding the text in its entirety, it is clearly stated that 'the family is the basic unit of society and as such should be strengthened. It is entitled to receive comprehensive protection and support'. This same principle goes on to say that 'Marriage must be entered into with the free consent of the intending spouses, and husband and wife should be equal partners' (Principle 9). This Principle must inspire all family policy and any true demographic policy."

Notwithstanding the tensions and the hard struggle, this is one of the positive points of the results obtained.

In recognition of this, after taking part in the World Meeting of the Holy Father with Families, the Coordinator of the International Year, Dr. Sokalski offered our Dicastery the *Patron's* Diploma of the International Year.

Some words about Cairo

Before offering more detailed information, I wish to put forward some general impressions.

Carefully reading an immense mountain of literature, the first impression is this: all the concerns of the Holy Father, expressed to the Heads of State and in the message handed to Mrs. Nafis Sadik, Secretary General of the Conference, came up at Cairo, not only in the Document, but in the attitudes and pressures of well-coordinated groups.

In this sense Cairo was an expression of all that was strategically seeded by political pressures in recent years, pressures which drain and batter the heart of society and humanity, the *vital centre* of the family and life. Only in this way can we understand the totality, the historic, prophetic and providential struggle which the Holy Father personally thought through and guided, aware that he was doing the will of God, to whom we must render obedience rather than to men (cf. *Acts* 5:29).

Another aspect: what would the Cairo Conference have been had the Pope not acted as he did, and with him and following him, the Holy See, in the first place the Secretariat of State and various Dicasteries, then the Episcopal Conferences and the various organizations and institutions? There was this chain-reaction, hence a strong presence which decisively helped to *open eyes*. An alarm was sounded and a kind of worldwide outcry went up. Under other circumstances, the Cairo Document would have been imposed and passed by unknowing delegates, unaware, even manipulated by language full of ambiguity. In that language they wanted to pass, as worthwhile and necessary objective thinking, what was in effect the most concerted attack against the rights of the family and the right to life. Let us just recall such difficult concepts to interpret as "reproductive health," "sexual rights," "quality of life," "family planning." New politically significant concepts were also employed, such as "rare abortion" and "safe abortion," with an "intended" confusion of concepts, like that denounced by the Holy Father when he spoke of "pro-choice," which presents what is nothing but the elimination of a human being, a human person, poor and innocent and also the systematic negation of the fundamental right to life as a noble exercise of freedom and a human decision (cf. *Letter to Families*, n. 13).

"Rare" abortion, when there are more than 50 million procured abortions every year in the world; "safe" abortion, in relation only to the dangers of infection and complications to the mother, after the elimination of the unborn, the conceived baby. The unborn are the sure and certain victims.

One can speak of a certain *victory* at Cairo on the part of the Church on some points, such as the statement that condemned recourse to abortion willed as a *real* demographic policy and as "family planning," which previously could and would be clearly concluded from the whole of the Document.

The bitter protest of some who had other hopes is very symptomatic, such as that of the parliament of Europe itself, in a curious Declaration obtained with a slight majority.

The Delegation of the Holy See, which carried out such a great task, approved the Document in its positive aspects, but with many *reservations* which should be well known, referring to themes and points which might become a grave wound to the truth about man, the family, the truth about sex, etc.

I may be permitted to say that, in a certain sense, everything does not finish with Cairo, but rather a new process begins in a stronger form, or the point of a gigantic iceberg shows itself more clearly, or a vast inundation advances, which must be stopped with all the energies of the Gospel, armed with the truth (cf. *Ephesians* 4:21).

In some aspects a battle has been won, but a much greater war is going on and it has historical significance. A door to abortion has been closed, restoring to the family its right as the Sanctuary of Life, but they are trying to come in through the window. Abortion in fact is permitted as a course of safety in medical services, social services, basic services.

Here is a synthesis of some points for which I have had the valued collaboration of His Excellency Archbishop Renato Martino, who excellently guided the Delegation of the Holy See at Cairo, and of Monsignor Diarmuid Martin.

The fact that the Conference was held in Cairo, in a nation where religious values are very deeply felt, facilitated including significant references in the text to the importance of respect for religious and cultural values in the preparation and application of demographic policies. This is particularly evident in the preamble to the chapter on principles.

In order to make an evaluation of what was accomplished by the Holy See in the context of the International Conference on "Population and Development," first a *comparison must be drawn* between the *text presented* at the beginning of the Preparatory Committee Meeting in New York last April, and the *text accepted* by consensus at the conclusion of the Cairo

Conference itself in September.

The commitment was immense, demonstrated by the Holy Father's vigorous inspiration and guidance, and concentrated intensely over a period of a few months. This succeeded in encouraging reflection by governments and religious leaders, the international press and many movements in so many parts of the world.

The Cairo Document contains some noteworthy improvements although it still includes aspects that cause concern for international life. In fact, the Holy See *adhered only partially to the final "consensus"* of the Conference and *abstained from those parts* or sections which are not in harmony with its mission.

Let us first examine the sections where it was possible to obtain some improvement in the text. A new chapter on Principles was inserted into the Document which is referred to at various points in the subsequent chapters. In this way, all the other chapters have to be interpreted in the sense expressed in the chapter on Principles.

Principle 9, for example, as I have already noted, states that the family is the fundamental cell of society. Husband and wife, who enjoy equal rights, must be able to contract marriage freely.

Some references to different concepts of the Family were removed from the Document as well as references to *"other unions."*

In this way, it was possible to eliminate the more ambiguous texts which threatened to deviate reflections on the nature of the Family throughout the whole Document.

The theme of the family was also dealt with in some paragraphs regarding *parents' rights*, especially concerning *adolescents*. In the various drafts, a right of adolescents was mentioned — protected by strict confidentiality — to family planning, formation and consultation services without any reference to or knowledge of parents. Some Delegations would have liked to extend this right to confidentiality even to children.

The approved text points out both parents' rights and responsibilities clearly, and respect for the religious and cultural values of the various societies.

It should be noted that the Representative of the European Union, at the conclusion of the Conference, expressed the disappointment of the countries in the Union regarding the affirmation of parents' rights. According to the European Union, an autonomous right of adolescents to establish any type of relationship, including sexual relationships, should be recognized.

The common language of the United Nations, since the 1974 Bucharest Conference, attributes a right to "individuals and couples" to decide regarding the number of children and the spacing of births. This reference to "individuals and couples" has been defined by some delegates as "one of the most sacred texts of the United Nations!"

As to the theme of abortion, the document stresses in various places that abortion must not be promoted as a method of family planning. Furthermore, it states that the Conference did not intend to promulgate any new, recognized international rights. This was to avoid any possibility of supporting the concept of a right to abortion.

Nonetheless, the theme of abortion does find its place in the Document. In the Bucharest Documents, the word "abortion" does not appear. The Conference in Mexico City limited itself to stating that abortion must not be promoted as a method of family planning.

In the Cairo Document, abortion is spoken about in a generally negative context. Recourse to abortion must be avoided and the number of abortions must be reduced. However, it states that where abortion is not against the law, it must be "safe."

With this paragraph, which would only seem to deal with the question of risks for a woman's health or life, a *new situation is opened up. For the first time:*

— abortion is recognized as a dimension of demographic policies;

— abortion is recognized as a dimension of development policies and programmes;

— Governments of developed countries could, in development programmes for poor countries, designate funds for "making abortion 'safe' where it is not against the law."

However, this could easily lead to the promotion of abortion. In other cases, where legislation currently prohibits earmarking development funds for abortion, the Cairo Document could become a means for exerting pressure to change those laws. It is well known today that the "population control" institutions have more than 6 billion dollars annually and that before the year 2000 this will reach 13 billion dollars.

— Abortion is listed as one of the dimensions of *"primary health care."*

It should be recalled that there are approximately 96,000 centres of "primary health care" around the world which depend on Catholic institutions. Any possible pressure on these centres must be avoided or prevented which would require them either to practice abortion, or to collaborate with organisms that practice it.

It is important to recall how much the Church does through her network of schools, health and social services for women's promotion, and here there are so many religious families working with exemplary generosity. It is important to recall what the Church is doing and has done for generations by now in the developing countries for the sake of entire peoples, without any discrimination or personal interest. In this way, she has anticipated many of the proposals of the Cairo Conference in this regard.

The period between the April Preparatory Committee and the Conference last September was one of the great mobilization by the *defenders of Life and the Family in the Catholic Church* and in the other Religions, as well as by very many persons of good will.

However, the negative effects cannot be overlooked of the activities of some groups who intend to use the name "Catholic," whereas their real aim is to damage the Church's image and benefit from huge financial assistance from international foundations.

It is well known that the Holy See has expressed its overall position regarding the results of the Conference in an intervention by the Head of its Delegation. This intervention is inseparable from its reservations on some points in the Document which do not exclude those regarding reproductive rights.

The Cairo Conference was the reason for intense commitment by Catholics who were able to see important principles reaffirmed there, such as those regarding the defence of life and the family. However, we cannot rest on our laurels because this is only one step. The "missionaries" of the culture of death are at prey to nullify the success obtained, and they will make efforts at every international meeting to impose their theses and principles once again. Therefore, the mobilization of Catholics must take on an ongoing character if we truly want the world to be converted to respect for the precious gift of life, in the family, the sanctuary of life.

Finally, because it is carried out in the name of God and his truth, in the name of the Lord who is *Veritatis splendor*, this truly paschal struggle involves everyone. To defend the family and life might seem a negative limited attitude, but it is an ecclesial and human task, a most positive and necessary task before all forms of poverty. It is at the very root of God's plan, of the Gospel of the Family and Life, at the heart of that which is most precious and decisive for humanity and the future, *the family and life*. There, for the greater part, the future of evangelization, the transmission of the faith and moral values is at stake. Cairo is not only a question of population, a serious question to consider in the ambit of demography (our Dicastery has published as a working document *Ethical and Pastoral Dimensions of Population Trends*), but it is a question which also touches on *development*, which the Church wants to be true, integral, for the whole man and for all people, in active and dynamic human solidarity, dealing with the central and most critical aspects of human existence. This whole question concerns the type of man and humanity that we want, building the style of life and type of family, the heart of the civilization of love.

In a very special way, all religious families in turn are involved and engaged in this struggle. Part of their future (e.g. vocations) is also at stake here, the very meaning of educational values, moral values, respect for people and families who are poor, but who love life and, in the sight of God, have the right to grow in their specific noble vocation. This is a difficult struggle, full of dangers. Humanly speaking, it is an unequal struggle, when one considers the means at our disposal, but the new Goliaths will be defeated by David: *Dux vitae regnat vivus!*

Selected Statements by Bishops' Conferences and Pro-Life Leaders and Organizations with Regard to the International Conference on Population and Development

Below are selected statements, published by L'Osservatore Romano, with regard to the International Conference on Population and Development.

Letter of the Latin-American Episcopal Council (CELAM) to Mrs. Nafis Sadik, Secretary-General of the International Conference on Population and Development
Santafé de Bogotá, 14 March 1994

Dr. Nafis Sadik
Secretary-General
International Conference on Population and Development
United Nations, New York

Honorable Secretary General,

We, the Presidency of the Latin American Episcopal Council (CELAM), under the Directors and the Presidents of the Episcopal Conferences of Latin America, representing the Bishops of this Continent whose population surpasses 460 million inhabitants, of whom the majority is Catholic, address ourselves to you in your capacity of Secretary General of the Conference on Population and Development, which will be held in Cairo in September of 1994, to express to you, and through you to all the delegates of that Conference, our grave concerns and reservations about the well-known goals and the principal objectives of that Conference.

Be assured that we are not moved to write this letter by any other motive than the sacredness and absolute value of life, the fundamental gift of God to humanity, as well as the innate dignity of the human being, which precedes and is superior to every right of society, and to every reason for the existence of the State.

We are moved, on the other hand, to write to you because of your nationality, your status as a woman and your noble calling as a doctor.

1. **The documents**

The Documents, the result of the work and preparatory meetings of the Conference, are very troubling to us. They clearly reveal a marked disregard for the basic human right: the right to life. This disregard appears in various Reports emanating from international organizations, both public and private. These Documents confirm the pressure placed by the UNFPA on the programs for the control and the destruction of human life in those countries which are said to be in the "Third World." What is clear in those Documents is the unquestionable will to spread, promote, establish and impose, on a universal scale, all the means to contain the growth of the world's population. In the name of "sustainable development" considerable sums are dedicated to campaigns through which the world's populations "must" be "stabilized." Today, in many countries on the path to development, more than half of the international economic assistance is linked to antinatal activities. Man is increasingly presented as one product among many, subject to quotas, including criteria of selection, defined according to the "needs" of the "new world order." In the name of the "need to integrate population and development," the existence of man ends up being subordinated to environmental and economic imperatives. In short, it has been forgotten that economic and technical development is carried out for mankind. Mankind does not exist to serve development. In particular, it has been forgotten that the moral component must be integrated into the concept of development whose promotion is sought.

2. The incontrovertible facts

Distressing facts testify to the implacable decision of the authors of these programs. The *Inventory of Population Projects in Developing Countries Around the World* enumerates without reservation the project programs, the resources destined for its effects, the agencies that carry them out and the countries which are its victims. Campaigns to legalize abortion are launched with regularity in our countries. The preparatory Documents recommend that "legal obstacles" be removed and that countries should undertake "structural" adaptations to allow for better control of life.

In some countries, unacceptable programs of sex education are imposed and financed by the world banking organizations of great prestige. And through International Planned Parenthood, they are spread throughout our youth.

The indicators of fertility in our countries are on the decline almost everywhere. And taking into account the levels of infant mortality and the life expectancy at one year of age, the populations of our continent are tending toward a greater ageing, and they will be renewed only with difficulty. The situation in countries like Bolivia, Colombia, the Dominican Republic, Honduras, Brazil and Mexico are particularly worrisome, and the proportion of sterilized women, especially among the poor, is alarming.

3. Our objections

Confronted with this reality, we are obliged to protest publicly against this violation of human rights on a large scale. Each and every man and woman has an inalienable right to physical integrity. It is incumbent upon the legislation of each country to protect this right against all those who seek to violate it, including international organizations and even the State itself, as well as organizations and bilateral assistance agencies and non-governmental organizations. Every person has a right to life and the unborn child in particular has the right to special protection. The right to life of human beings, beginning at the moment of conception, is further recognized and proclaimed in the majority of Latin-American constitutions and it must become the reality. Nor can we admit the violation of the sovereignty of our States — even less when such a violation is the work of international agencies whose reason for existing is to be at the service of States, and not that of exercising over them in an abusive way some sort of supernational power.

In view of these facts, we cannot remain silent, especially when we receive information according to which the granting of loans to our countries will, at times, be conditioned upon the acceptance by those "beneficiary" States of programs of demographic control. Finally, we denounce the complicity of certain leaders of our own countries who, failing to recognize the dignity of the powers entrusted to them, place their mandate or their authority at the service of imperialistic interests of the rich societies.

4. False premises

These campaigns are supported by certain false premises: the earth is already "overpopulated"; its resources are "limited" and its "carrying capacity" has already been reached.

We believe that a minimum of responsibility requires that consideration be given to those scientific works which disagree with these "pseudo-proofs." These notions or premises are, in effect, all *relative*. On one hand, they refer to the capacity which the people in a given society have to resolve their problems of subsistence, and on the other hand, to the ingenuity which they demonstrate to transform the available elements of the earth into useable wealth.

The wind, petroleum, titanium, sand, sun and other elements have been transformed into resources thanks to human intervention.

In the face of the demographic problem — which is real — there are two solutions: drastic control of births, or *"jointly shared economic development and social progress."* By means of this latter concept, efforts are made so that production would grow at the same pace as the growth of the population, and the newly created wealth would be distributed equitably among the world's people. In other words, it proposes to increase the size of the meal and distribute it better, instead of reducing the number of people who come to the table to eat.

5. The ideology which underlies these premises

We find it impossible to accept the materialistic, hedonistic and selfish ideology which inspires these campaigns, according to which the security (the comfort and luxury!) of the rich countries would be the basis for their right to control the poor population, their resources, as well as the knowledge and technology to which these people would have access. We cannot admit any kind of "contraceptive imperialism" which rules, under this aspect, the relations between the "North" and the "South."

6. What our countries need

Instead of being victims of unacceptable campaigns of demographic control, our countries need family and education policies which are truly constructive and effective.

It is the task of the State to strengthen the family, this union between a man and a woman which is free and lasting, loving and life-giving. The family is the basic cell of society; it is the place of personalization and of socialization. Public authorities can and must help couples to exercise their paternal responsibilities, but they must do so with respect for the dignity of women, men and the child. Any psychological pressure and/or physical mutilation, must be absolutely rejected as a direct assault against this dignity of the human person and against his rights.

In particular, education of the woman must be the object of special care adapted to the condition which maternity brings to her, along with her family dimension — a fundamental policy dimension. In essence, when she receives a child, a mother associates herself to and collaborates with the foundational act of a democratic society. She proclaims, by this acceptance, that every human being, no matter how small, has the right to life and the same dignity as those who are stronger than he [the child].

Nevertheless, it is the right of a responsible fatherhood and motherhood to decide about the number of children which they shall bring into the world, taking into account the personal good of the spouses, of the children and of the human community.

It is the duty of public authorities to protect the child since he is, at one and the same time, the future of the family and of society. With this double function, he must be protected and educated. This is a criterion which has been left aside, in order to respond to a Malthusian vision of the world, and so to consider the child as a mere consumer, or even a parasite, when we know that it is precisely in him that sooner or later will reside the fate of the adult population when it grows old. We once again call attention to the thousands upon thousands of children, especially in the Third World, who walk the streets without a home, pursued and even exterminated by the police, while they are exposed or even incorporated into every kind of crime.

For these reasons, we feel that the human resources and the considerable sums of money which are designated for the limitation of births would have much different results if they were utilized for the intellectual and moral education of men and women, as well as for the establishment of more just social structures. A world of human solidarity cannot exist when the strongest impose cruel principles of discrimination by means of deed and laws.

7. Conclusion

We know that every totalitarian regime has sought to destroy the family, make procreation an object of State control, and to regulate human sexuality. In its contemporary forms, the proponents of totalitarianism have arrived at times at the extreme of legalizing the destruction of the child, the weakest and most defenseless member of the family community.

– We vigorously denounce this totalitarian practice which appears in the ongoing campaigns which serve as an attack, in the first place, against those who are defenseless.

– We categorically affirm that the exercise of liberty requires respect for the right to life.

– We affirm that respect for the equality between men and women requires respect for their physical and psychic integrity.

– We reject the efforts of foreign powers and institutions to launch upon us a "demographic winter," into which many of the rich countries have already fallen.

Honorable Secretary-General: In the name of the countries of Latin America and the Caribbean, we ask you to overturn the dynamic which appears in the preparatory work of the Cairo Conference, by listening to the voice of the poor and by respecting their dignity, their integrity and their rights.

Imagining how you yourself worry about these problems, we ask you to protect the poor of our continent and of the whole world against the maneuvering of those who, by abusing their power or making unwarranted use of their positions, reinforce to the benefit of the rich, the means of domination and exploitation.

With our sincerest expression of consideration and esteem, we avail ourselves of this opportunity to greet you deferentially, thanking you in advance for your attention which you shall grant to this letter.

* * *

Letter on behalf of the African Bishops during the Special Synod for Africa, to Secretary-General Boutros Boutros-Ghali, concerning the International Conference on Population and Development; Rome, 23 April 1994

To His Excellency,
The Secretary-General of the United Nations
Mr. Boutros Boutros-Ghali
United Nations, New York

Your Excellency,

We, the 242 Cardinals, Bishops and Priests, coming from all the nations of Africa and elsewhere, gathered in Rome in a Special Synod presided over by His Holiness Pope John Paul II, are striving to find the means to better fulfill the will of God and to work for the good of the people whom we serve.

This has brought us to turn our special attention to the basic institution of the family. It is true that the family, in the world and especially in Africa, has need of measures which defend it and give it greater protection. It is necessary to create the conditions which assist it to fulfill the mission which is properly its own. Does not the *Universal Declaration of Human Rights* affirm that "the family is the natural and fundamental group unit of society?"

The United Nations has proclaimed this year as the "Year of the Family" and the Catholic Church has gladly welcomed this initiative. In the sphere which is proper to it, and with the means which are at its disposition, the Church offers her collaboration. Of course, this celebration of the "Year of the Family" will achieve a positive result to the extent that it responds to the efforts put forth by families themselves, and in this way all of humanity will be the beneficiary.

We are informed, Mr. Secretary-General, that the United Nations has convoked an International Conference on Population and Development, which is soon to be held in Cairo. We hope that the propositions, which will be adopted there, truly correspond to the needs of the family in these troubled times. It is necessary to recognize the irreplaceable role of the family, today more than ever, at the heart of society.

Nevertheless, we fear, not without reason it seems, that this Conference will not attain its desired result. The Conference on Population and Development risks becoming a disappointment in the context of the hopes that were aroused by the announcement of that "Year of the Family."

We know, Mr. Secretary-General, of all the efforts and initiatives that you have undertaken to bring peace back to our continent. We are grateful to you for this, and we are making our own efforts as well so that a time of peace and progress might finally reign in Africa. For this reason, we are making a special appeal to the strength and creative enthusiasm of our young people. And for this reason, we ask ourselves about what kind of youth will be prepared for us by the final draft of the Conference on Population and Development. In that draft, a permissive morality is openly proposed. Pleasure and material well-being seem to be presented there as the ideals of life. And this, for example, is how sexual activity is mentioned, especially among young people.

Mr. Secretary-General, you know very well that in our cultural tradition, the sexual act is not given over to the whim of the individual, and even less to that of adolescents since the resulting implications for the nature of our communities are very serious.

The role that the above-mentioned draft attributes to abortion in the life of a couple or of a woman is also foreign to our traditional culture.

We continue to hope that the more technically advanced countries might assist Africa, not to deny its most authentic cultural values, but rather to integrate them harmoniously with a respect for the human person.

We are aware that there are serious challenges to be taken up in the area of demographics. However, we think that it is possible to respond to them in a satisfactory way without violating the moral laws which protect human life, marriage and the dignity which is owed to women. We are also convinced that the natural methods of the regulation of birth constitute a valid solution. We wish to insist upon the dignity of women and men since it would be intolerable for us to see, in our day, the institution of marriage born along a path whereon it would be undermined or torn apart.

Please be assured, Mr. Secretary-General, of our most cordial best wishes.

Written in Rome, 23 April 1994.

The Delegated Presidents

✠ His Eminence Cardinal Francis Arinze
President of the Pontifical Council for Inter-religious Dialogue

✠ His Eminence Cardinal Christian Wiyghan Tumi
Archbishop of Douala (Cameroon)

✠ His Eminence Cardinal Paulos Tzadua
Archbishop of Addis Ababa (Ethiopia)

* * *

United States Cardinals and Conference President's Letter to President William Clinton on the Cairo Conference

The draft final document for September's U.N. Conference on Population and Development in Cairo, Egypt, "continues to advocate abortion as a way of controlling population growth and promiscuity" — however cleverly it may be crafted, the six active U.S. Cardinals and the President of the National Bishops' Conference, Archbishop William Keeler of Baltimore, said in a letter to President Clinton that was delivered to the White House on 29 May 1994. The six Cardinals who signed the letter were: Cardinals James Hickey of Washington, Joseph Bernardin of Chicago, Bernard Law of Boston, John O'Connor of New York, Anthony Bevilacqua of Philadelphia and Roger Mahony of Los Angeles. The letter follows.

As plans proceed for the International Conference on Population and Development at Cairo in September, we write with great urgency as leaders of the Catholic Church in our nation concerning your administration's promotion of abortion, contraception, sterilization and the redefinition of the family.

We speak, Mr. President, not only for Catholics throughout the United States but also for many other people of good will. We are looking for leadership that truly respects the dignity of innocent of human life and recognizes the fundamental importance of the family for the development of nations and individual persons. We are calling for policies which promote sound economic and social development throughout the world precisely because they recognize the indispensable role of the family and respect the innate dignity and rights of each person.

There is a broad consensus in our country that abortion on demand is morally repugnant. With millions of people representing all faiths, we recognize that abortion destroys not only the child in the womb but also creates untold conflict in the lives of millions of women. Abortion cheapens human life, tears apart families and contributes to the violence that plagues our culture. However cleverly the current Cairo Document may be crafted, in fact it continues to advocate abortion as a way of controlling population growth and promiscuity.

Mr. President, we urge you to shun the advice of those who would apply pressure on developing nations to mandate abortion as a condition for receiving aid from other countries. Do not allow our country to participate in trampling the rights and religious values of people around the world. Please recognize that abortion is not a legitimate way to control population and that it does not improve women's lives. There is no such thing as a "safe" abortion: Whether legal or not, abortion is lethal for the child and destructive of the mother and society.

The draft final document of the Cairo Conference, with the support of the United States, also advocates the worldwide distribution of artificial contraceptives and the increased practice of sterilization which will have the effect of promoting a self-centered and casual view of human sexuality, an approach so destructive of family life and the moral fiber of society. When the United States supports such measures for unmarried adolescents as well as adults, what ideals are we holding up to young people? How are we helping them develop authentic values and that mastery of self which is the calling of every human being? As we prepare for tomorrow, we dare not take the course of least resistance today!

So also, when our government advocates population control through abortion, contraception and sterilization, it is not a force for freedom but an agent of coercion. Sadly it appears that the United States is urging developing countries to adopt population control programs that will interfere with the rights of couples to make responsible and moral family planning decisions. Couples in poor countries will find themselves at the mercy of government officials and programs that have no real regard for the dignity of the human person. They will face the prospect of government agencies providing abortion and contraceptives for their adolescent children with utterly no regard for parental authority and responsibility. At the same time, such policies could be insensitive to the existing realities of strong family life in many of those countries. As you have stated, Mr. President, "families raise children, not governments."

Even if such coercive population control measures would lead to economic growth and development, they would still be morally objectionable. In fact, however, there is no proof that enforced population control will bring about economic development in the Third World. What will help poor nations develop their full potential is not pressure from the First World for population control, but rather a greater commitment on the part of wealthy nations to foster sustainable economic growth in the Third World countries. That is the kind of constructive leadership we should expect from our country!

The Cairo Conference represents a golden opportunity for nations to come together to improve the lives of people throughout the world. That improvement will come only if the participants have the vision and moral courage to recognize that the future of humanity lies in strong, stable families. Time and time again, the bishops of the United States have shared with you our alarm over administration policies and statements that place nonmarital sexual relationships on a par with marriage and family. Archbishop Keeler, president of the National Conference of Catholic Bishops, has pointed out the dangers in such positions in a personal letter to Secretary of State Christopher. Sadly, however, the U.S. participation in the preparatory meeting of the Cairo Conference mirrored administration policies and positions by advocating "a plurality of family forms."

The United States is doing the world no favor by exporting a false ideology which claims that any type of union, permanent or temporary, is as good as the traditional family. There is mounting evidence that being part of an intact, traditional family or an extended family helps children grow into emotionally well-adjusted and productive citizens. While it is true that many single parents do an admirable job of raising their children, nonetheless we owe it to the children of our country and of the world to encourage stable, intact two-parent families. Mr. President, we wholeheartedly agree with what you said in your 1994 State of the Union address: "We cannot renew our country when, within a decade, more than half of the children will be born into families where there is no marriage." We hasten to add that we will never develop and renew our world by encouraging substitutes for marriage and family life.

Mr. President, the U.S. Delegation to the Cairo Conference will have enormous influence; it will represent the power, prestige and influence of the United States among the family of nations. We ask you, as the leader of our country, to steer our nation away from promoting an agenda so destructive of our own society and of the nations of the world. We thank you for your attention to the pressing concerns we have shared with you in loyalty to our country and to the many citizens whom we serve.

I sign, Mr. President, for myself and for the following Cardinal-Archbishops of the United States listed below, who, together with the President of the U.S. Conference of Catholic Bishops, have explicitly authorized this letter.

* * *

Statement of the United States Bishops

At their June 1994 meeting in San Diego, the National Conference of Catholic Bishops (USA) unanimously approved the following Statement regarding the Cairo Conference on Population and Development.

In recent months we Bishops of the United States have followed reports on the forthcoming International Conference on Population and Development with deep concern. We also have welcomed the powerful leadership and insightful statements of Pope John Paul II. We stand firmly united with the Holy Father and with the Holy See's Delegation to the Cairo Conference. We see population issues as but one dimension of the Church's teaching on social justice and development.

The Conference, which will take place in Cairo in September, is intended to give the world's nations an opportunity to discuss and respond to the complex and interrelated realities of population and development.

True development must be based on the social, cultural and spiritual dimensions of the human person, as well as on the common good. Its goals must be to protect and enhance the life and dignity of every person, especially the poor. Genuine support for development must be an exercise of justice and solidarity, not domination and control. Every precaution must be taken not to impose on individuals or societies methods of population control that are ethically objectionable or a threat to human rights as a substitute for development assistance.

We call attention to the Cairo Conference's Draft Plan of Action, a document intended to set global development policies well into the next century. Unfortunately, in several aspects, this proposed plan is devoted less to population and development concerns and more to the advocacy of policies in conflict with fundamental moral values.

The United States Government's approach also tends to focus too often on population at the expense of development rather than on the links between the two. Authentic and sustainable development not only offers hope and opportunity for the poor but can ease the strains of population growth. Unfortunately, the United States falls well behind other developed nations in its per capita support for development. Rather than simply focusing on what the poor nations should do, perhaps our nation should re-examine its responsibilities in areas of aid, trade and development. In particular, we should curb our global leadership in the arms trade with its deadly human consequences and serious economic impact in poor nations. The United States, as one of the wealthiest and most scientifically and technologically advanced countries in the world, should provide international leadership in helping developing countries overcome their financial problems, build their productive capacity and find access to world markets for their goods. These nations need modern technology, new capital and workable partnerships to achieve their development goals.

The family

In 1994, which the United Nations has identified as the Year of the Family, the international community should unite to defend and protect the family. As Pope John Paul II said in his Message to the Secretary General of the Cairo Conference, "anything less would be a betrayal of the noblest ideals of the United Nations."

Instead, in a decisive shift from past U.N. documents, the Draft Plan of Action seeks to redefine the family and its importance to individual societies and to the global community. It virtually ignores the institution of marriage, and in so doing devalues marriage between a man and a woman, the institution through which children are given an appropriate welcome.

We urge the United States Government to uphold the importance of the family, support its fundamental role in the lives of individuals and society, and pursue economic and social policies which support families, rather than undermine them.

Adolescents

The Plan also treats all sexual behaviour as acceptable, even for unmarried adolescents. It urges that contraceptives and abortion be provided to unmarried minors without parental knowledge or support, and envisions the widest possible distribution of condoms. In an age when young people thirst for self-esteem, a sense of values and the courage to live them out, technological fixes deprive them of incentives to genuine moral growth. At a time when AIDS threatens so many populations, to offer young people an invitation to sexual license, condoms and pills, promotes only a false sense of security — physically, emotionally and spiritually. Technology, as we have learned in our own country, cannot substitute for moral formation.

We urge our Government to do nothing which would lead young people to be isolated and alienated from their families and guardians.

Human life

The Draft Plan of Action advocates abortion as part of reproductive health care, and ignores the fact that abortion takes the life of the child before birth.

As religious leaders, and as U.S. citizens, we are outraged that our Government is leading the effort to foster global acceptance of abortion. The U.S. Department of State has informed diplomats around the world that the Administration believes that "safe, legal and voluntary abortion is a fundamental right of all women," and that it would be "working for stronger language on the importance of access to abortion services." And it has done so. It has urged other Delegations to accept abortion, as if there were an international consensus that abortion is an appropriate method of family planning, which is certainly not the case. In fact, the policy of the United Nations set forth in 1984 is that "Governments are urged to help women avoid abortion, which in no case should be promoted as a method of family planning..." In addition, the constitutions and laws of a number of nations specifically reject abortion and affirm the right of a child, once conceived, not to be directly killed.

We urge the United States Government to reverse its efforts in this regard. We urge instead that our nation exercise leadership to bring about global agreement on a document that respects the life and dignity of every innocent human being, born and unborn, that recognizes and supports the fundamental and indispensable role of the family for the good of humankind, and that identifies the genuine needs of developing nations and commits resources essential for their true development.

Together, through international efforts that support the integral development of the person and society, we can respond to problems of population and development in a manner that respects the inherent dignity of the human person. To do otherwise, risks reducing less developed nations to mere objects of the ideological policies of wealthier nations. The United States should work for the development of nations, with full regard for those nations' cultural traditions and values. Genuine development, not moral and social confusion, should be our Government's major contribution to the developing world.

* * *

European Bishops Declaration
(President and Vice-Presidents of the
Council of European Episcopal Conferences)

The following is the text of the 4 June 1994 Declaration issued by the President and two Vice-Presidents of the Council of European Episcopal Conferences on the United Nations International Conference on Population and Development.

During the month of September 1994, an "International Conference on Population and Development" organized by the United Nations will be held in Cairo. The intense discussions and negotiations that are taking place in preparation for this Conference cannot leave the Council of European Episcopal Conferences (CCEE) indifferent: the challenge that many countries and humanity as such are facing in view of the surge of demographic growth is too great, and certain tendencies expressed in the demographic plan of action under discussion at the moment are too ambiguous. Rightly, the Holy Father has warned the community of States against taking steps that could lead to a "serious setback for humanity, one in which man himself would be the first victim."

1. The rapid demographic growth in some regions of the world and consequently on the global level is giving rise in many States to serious problems that cannot be ignored. The number of people living on this earth will be doubled in the course of the next few decades. Nor can an objective analysis conceal the fact that the number of births per childbearing woman is considerably decreasing, even in most of the developing countries: in the long term, then, it is possible to forecast that population figures will reach a stable level.

2. To counter the strong demographic increase in developing countries, birth control policies that subject parents to direct or indirect coercion are

absolutely out of the question. The internationally recognized right of the couple to decide freely, with full knowledge of the facts and responsibly on the number of children and the space between births cannot be debated. We approve of the fact that the preliminary draft of the final document of the Cairo Conference focuses greater attention on the rights and needs of the couple regarding the number of children, and is opposed to all restrictive policies.

We likewise support the efforts being made to allow women full equality of rights in all social structures.

3. Although we recognize these positive aspects outlined in the process preparatory to the International Population Conference, we cannot fail to voice several serious reservations. In general, the draft document to be discussed in Cairo involves a very individualistic image of man. The individual is mentioned almost exclusively as the reference point of national and international policies. The importance of the family is referred to occasionally, but its rights and interests are largely marginalized: notwithstanding, the family is the basic unit of society and "is part of the heritage of humanity" (ibid.). Therefore the global policy and the individual measures directly and indirectly concerning birth and conception issues, family planning and sex education, should constantly focus on the high dignity of the family and take into account the basic rights of parents, particularly in the area of their children's education.

4. The present draft document speaks of abortion in an ethically unacceptable way. The tendency to declare a kind of right to abortion is clearly apparent. Together with the Holy Father, we must express our open disapproval of such attempts. In no case may human life be submitted to the discretional authority of a third party. Its protection, from conception to natural death, is included in the duties of State authorities and of social forces.

5. The coming International Conference in Cairo claims to be a conference "on population and development." Nevertheless, it gives no importance to urgent developmental issues. Not only the Holy See, but indeed a great many experts have vigorously criticized this fact. Only with greater efforts for a development understood in its global sense will humanity be able to meet the challenge of demographic growth. The cooperation of the developing nations is needed, but also the willingness of wealthy nations to take responsibility and bear the burdens.

6. In most of Western society precise demographic problems are appearing that — contrary to what is happening in the developing societies —

are caused by an extremely low birth rate. This trend can cause in our countries, over and above economic and social effects, other significant negative consequences: an ageing Europe could lack the courage to face the future. This is also why States and organizations must join forces and increase their efforts to build a society sensitive to the values of the family and the child. The Catholic Churches in Europe are not shirking this challenge.

Saint-Gall, Switzerland, 4 June 1994

✠ Most Reverend Miloslav Vlk
Archbishop of Prague, President

✠ Most Reverend Karl Lehmann
Bishop of Mainz, Vice-President

✠ Most Reverend István Seregély
Archbishop of Eger, Vice-President

* * *

Message of the Presidents of the Latin American Bishops' Conferences to the Leaders of the Region
Santo Domingo, Dominican Republic; 18 June 1994

Convoked by the Pontifical Council for the Family, in collaboration with the Pontifical Commission for Latin America and the Latin American Episcopal Council (CELAM), the Presidents of the Bishops' Conferences of Latin America and the Caribbean met on 16-18 June 1994, in Santo Domingo, Dominican Republic. The meeting had, as its objective reflection, study and analysis of various themes connected to the family and life on the Latin American Continent. The central point of discussion was the International Conference on Population and Development, to be held in Cairo, Egypt, in September 1994. At the conclusion of the meeting, the participants issued a concluding message, addressed to the faithful, the text of which follows.

Introduction

1. Two years ago the Latin American and Caribbean Bishops met in this Antillean city for the IV General Episcopal Conference, presided over by Pope John Paul II, from which resulted the Document of Santo Domingo.

Midway in the International Year of the Family, we, the Presidents of the Bishops' Conferences of this Region have assembled, at the invitation of the Pontifical Commission for Latin America, the Pontifical Council for the Family and the Latin American Bishops' Council (CELAM). The scope of the meeting has been the upcoming International Conference on Population and Development, organized by the United Nations Organization, to be held in Cairo, and whose Preparatory Document as well as the perspectives it opens present serious concerns with regard to the topic of the family as well as the integral development of persons and peoples. The Holy Father has expressed himself in this regard, especially in his recent *Letter to the Heads of State*. We bishops share his concerns and make ours his orientations.

2. The importance and transcendence of the Conference's theme, as well as the fact that fundamental values of persons, families and society are at stake, impel us to share with our brothers in faith and with men of good will the fruit of our work. This message which we wish to address to the leaders of our countries and to the Delegations to the Cairo Conference seeks to recall basic human rights and obligations and to promote the choice for a culture of family and of life, of love and of solidarity.

I. Marriage, freedom and love

3. The family is a wealth which belongs to the patrimony of humanity. "The family is based on marriage, that intimate union of life in complementarity between a man and a woman, which is constituted in the freely contracted and publicly expressed indissoluble bond of matrimony, and is open to the transmission of life" (*Charter of the Rights of the Family,* Holy See, 1983, Preamble, B).

The draft of the final document of Cairo provokes a "disturbing surprise" because it contains "on the level of both concepts and wordings" such innovations which, not respecting the nature of the family, could cause a "moral decline resulting in a serious setback for humanity, one in which man himself would be the first victim" (John Paul II, *Letter to the World's Heads of State,* 19 March 1994).

The Church struggles always, as is her mission, for the integral salvation of man. For this it is necessary to save the family, the primary and vital cell of society, the school of social virtues, the sanctuary of life, the educator of persons, the creator of culture, the springing source of humanity and, according to our faith, the Domestic Church.

4. The family is made the victim of assaults, often programmed, of multiple forces caused by those who have taken upon themselves the mission

of "liberating" man from all his transcendence in order to confine him in the range of his own power. Here lies a false anthropology, particularly affected by the corruption of the idea of freedom, "conceived not as a capacity for realizing the truth of God's plan for matrimony and the family, but as an autonomous power of self-affirmation, often against others, for one's own selfish well-being" (*Familiaris consortio*, no. 6).

Many would think that man should enjoy an uncontrolled freedom which alienates him from every transcendence. Thus he pretends to make himself into his own absolute creator and sees to it that nothing holds him back. By consequence, manipulations are permitted in all fields, especially in the biological. Freedom, thus, would be nothing more than an uncontrolled search for happiness, which is confounded with the utilization of material goods and pleasures, especially those that are sexual. Morality, since it speaks of responsibility and consequently of sin, would be rejected as something already outdated.

On the contrary, it is necessary to teach that freedom has to be confronted with the truth about man, with his authentic reality. Man cannot be his own law because he is a creature and not God. He experiences his own limitations and feels in his conscience the call to live in just relationship with his Creator and with other creatures. Freedom, true freedom, is man's capacity to realize himself according to his "original truth," which means, according to the divine plan.

5. The family should not fear this freedom. Rather, it constitutes itself and grows through it. In freedom the spouses choose mutual love, fruitful and faithful. Without such freedom, the family is sick and threatened. In order to save the family, we need to rescue man in his integrity, preserving his dominion over his freedom which is destined towards truth and love.

Truly, family is the foundation and, par excellence, the "centre and the heart of the civilization of love" (John Paul II, *Letter to Families*, n. 13), as opposed to a civilization of hatred and violence which tears apart the world with its criminalities and wars.

The family is the social subject of law, existing prior to the State, and consequently should be protected by it. It is neither a simple private affair ruled by that which the spouses arbitrarily establish, nor should it be left to the mercy of an abusive legislation of Parliaments, but possesses its own law proceeding from its nature, law which guarantees the rights and points out the obligations of all its members. "Family, as a community of love and life ..., is in a way, entirely its own, a sovereign society, albeit conditioned in certain ways" (*Letter to Families*, n. 17). Therefore one can speak of the rights of the family.

II. The good of life

6. Life is the fundamental good which sustains all the rights of man. Love, which unites the spouses in matrimony, makes them fruitful agents of the transmission of life. A child is the most precious gift of God (cf. *Gaudium et spes*, n. 50), an immense gift which should be received with joy, gratitude and responsibility. The sexuality of man and woman, by its very nature, is ordered to the communion of life of the spouses and for the procreation of the new life of children. It is necessarily an interpersonal happening which does not exhaust itself in one individual alone.

7. "The Massacre of Abortion" (Santo Domingo, 219) which threatens to pervade Latin America, carries the crime to the source of life, to the maternal womb which should be treated with respect and veneration. The moment of conception begins the story of a person, unique and unrepeatable, promising to enrich humanity in the fulfillment of its mission. Moreover, it enriches it already with the hope of its new life. The projects of abortion install the culture of death at the very beginning stages of the innocent and undefended life of the unborn. Sadly, in the Preparatory Document of Cairo, expressions such as "quality of life" and "family planning" have been introduced with a meaning to accept abortion as one of its methods.

8. God alone is the author of life, and therefore life is sacred. No motive could justify the killing of an innocent life. No one, neither the parents nor the State nor any international entity can consider themselves the owners of human existence.

The "quality of life" which the projects of contraception and abortion pretend to attain, is often understood from a consumerist and hedonist viewpoint. We proclaim once again that man is to be valued to what he is and not for what he has, for his capacity to enjoy true and generous love, not cheap egoism.

9. The family, by its nature, is the principal source of humanity and the center of the culture of life. But today it is confronted with the culture of death which has at its service powerful forces and enormous structures, which are partially based on error but fundamentally in egoism of individuals and of nations. We must become conscious of the magnitude of this challenge.

III. Responsible fatherhood and motherhood

10. The dignity of the human person confers a high value on the

procreative capacity and mission of the spouses, because human procreation presupposes a responsible collaboration with the fruitful love of God. It is understood as the fruit and sign of mutual donation of the spouses, of their love and fidelity. They are capable of producing a new human life and have the possibility of becoming father or mother only through the cooperation of the other. "The child has the right to be conceived, to be carried in the womb of the mother, to be brought into the world and to be educated within the context of matrimony" (*Donum vitae*), in the stable and mutually faithful love of his parents. Responsible fatherhood and motherhood know how to respect and promote the rights of the spouse and of the children. Sexuality, an attribute of the individual, is a responsibility to be fulfilled by two: the couple, husband and wife. To separate sex, love and fecundity is to misinterpret the nature of human sexuality.

11. Speaking of family planning, the primary and fundamental responsibility of the spouses not to be subjected to external pressures or determinations with regard to the number of children and the moment of having them should be respected. This responsible fatherhood or motherhood is assumed before God, between themselves, before their children and society.

12. Sexual conduct should be guided by laws which God has inscribed in the nature and in the heart of the human person. Natural methods of family planning show more and more their scientific seriousness and efficacy as compared to artificial methods. The latter are often presented as modern but, in fact, are surpassed in their "modernity" by natural methods which are in conformity with human ecology and neither violate nor deteriorate the nature of the person.

13. Abortion can never be a licit means for regulating birthrate, since it violates the rights of the child who is alive and waits to be born. On the other hand, sterilization goes against the right and the obligation to conserve the physical integrity of the mother or of the father, taking from them the capability of transmitting life.

14. "Reproductive rights" — an expression used in the Preparatory Document — is an ambiguous formulation requiring clarification. If it refers to the rights which help the spouses to exercise their parenthood responsibly, it would be an ethically acceptable concept. But this expression should not be applied to individuals considered separately or for any other type of union among them.

If "reproductive health" — another ambiguous term in the mentioned document — is intended for promoting and ensuring good and preventive health conditions and for assisting in preventing infectious and contagious diseases or for controlling the deterioration of the health of the spouses or of the child, it could validly be used. However, if under the pretext of defending the health of the mother, "reproductive health" is used for accepting or promoting, even in concealed form, intentions of abortion, it deserves to be rejected absolutely.

"Safe sex" is another ambiguous expression of the same document which deserves to receive a valid consideration only if it takes into account all pertinent ethical considerations. Sexuality, created by God, cannot be exercised arbitrarily.

IV. Population and development

15. The Preparatory Document for the Cairo Conference seems to make a strong connection between population growth and poverty; conservation of the environment and control of population growth; development and low birthrate.

These affirmations, because of their repeated use in meetings prior to this Conference, and their defusion in the media, have become alarming premises: a greater population would mean more misery, deterioration of the environment and difficult access to development.

Far from defining the problem of development in all its dimensions, above all in its economic and political dimensions, and instead of considering how to offer urgent help to those parts of the world which are less favoured and to create a healthy world economy, the Preparatory Document dwells completely on certain gloomy and frightening forecasts, true modern myths which would terrify the most needy people of the world.

16. Starting from these myths, the industrialized countries and the international organizations affirm that if there is no control on population there will be no economic or technical aid, and consequently there will be no development and the misery will continue to grow. Numerous Non-Governmental Organizations (NGOs) associate themselves with this campaign, following the style of some governments of developed countries, that are more disposed to funding birth control programmes than authentic plans of development. They prefer to reduce the number of invitees to the banquet of humanity, rather than to multiply the bread.

This systematic defusion has a colonialist character, and the Preparatory Document itself is not free from that trend. Our continent suffers from "the contraceptive imperialism which consists in imposing upon peoples and cultures all forms of contraception, sterilization and abortion, which are considered effective, without respecting the religious, ethnic and family traditions of a people or culture" (*Letter of the Holy See to the WHO Meeting in Bangkok*).

17. Once such myths are established which instill fear of overpopulation that might exhaust the resources of the earth, it would seem to be easy to propose the method to liberate people from this terrible scourge: birth control in all its forms, condoms, contraceptives, sterilization, abortion, etc. For that there is a total readiness to render economic aid, propaganda facilities and technical training. The poorest among peoples are the destined recipients of these birth control plans.

18. Oftentimes, poverty is equated with the indigenous ethnic population of the continent. Thus a racist dimension is added to these plans which already rest on false arguments. In this context it is worthy to note that according to a good many experts, it is not scientifically certain that the earth does not have enough resources to feed a larger population. In this argumentation an evident collective egoism of rich countries is reflected, who are determined to defend their consumeristic lifestyle, which is a threat to the poor, who are appealing to them asking for solidarity. It is not by accident that a wave of xenophobia is today permeating some of these countries.

Conclusions

19. We Bishops would like to raise our voices before the leaders of the region and before all politicians, economists and experts in population issues, who have responsibilities in the governing of peoples, including those who work with the United Nations, so that the Latin American peoples are respected in their proper cultural identity, which includes a high appreciation of religious faith as the source of family and social values and which manifests itself, especially among its indigenous people, in an eminent appreciation for the family. We encourage those leaders of society who work for a culture of family and of life so that they do not lose heart. Likewise, from this continental meeting we wish to encourage the Latin American people as a whole so that they may not be deceived by half truths, false fears and appearances of progress which could erroneously justify anti-birth campaigns without respect for life and for the dignity of man and woman. Our peoples have the right and duty to defend their values without being manipulated by centers of power who want to impose their own criteria, especially when those criteria are not based on full truth.

20. In sharing the fruits of our work, we thought of recalling and reaffirming the fundamental principles regarding life, family and development

and to offer in this way a positive contribution toward the construction of a truly human society. The Cairo Conference and the path it opens constitutes a challenge to the responsibility of all, especially the leaders of our people.

The Church at this moment is called upon to deepen the new evangelization which includes, as underlined in the document of Santo Domingo, "an integral promotion of the Latin American and Caribbean people from an evangelical and renewed preferential option for the poor toward a service to life and to the family" (n. 302).

We invite our brothers in the episcopate so that all of us, united, will promote in our local Churches a campaign of prayer for the family in the light of the Cairo Conference and a family ministry which announces "with joy and conviction the Good News about the family" (*Familiaris consortio*, n. 86).

We entrust to the Holy Family of Nazareth, in which Jesus Christ, Son of God and Redeemer of the Family was born and raised, all families of our countries and of the entire world, with their sorrows and hopes, so that from her bosom may sprout the new generations which constitute in the third millennium the culture of life and love, of freedom and peace.

Santo Domingo, Dominican Republic
18 June 1994

* * *

European Bishops Issue Final Declaration

On 4-5 July 1994, a meeting of the Presidents of the European Episcopal Commissions for the Family was held in Rome, organized by the Pontifical Council for the Family, which was represented by: Cardinal Alfonso López Trujillo (President), Bishop Elio Sgreccia (Secretary) and Mons. Francisco Gil Hellín (Undersecretary). Mons. Claudio Celli of the Secretariat of State was also present. Here is a translation of the Italian-language text of the Final Declaration.

Convened in Rome by the Pontifical Council for the Family to study the state of the family, we Bishops, Presidents of the European Commissions for the Family, particularly from Western European countries, would like to state that we fully share the anxieties of the Holy Father John Paul II regarding the prospects of the forthcoming World Conference on Population and Development.

We are well aware of the importance of the Cairo Conference's theme. It is true that the well-being of peoples is closely linked to the possibilities for integral development of individuals. These possibilities are in turn conditioned by a just distribution of the world's economic resources. Many resources are not utilized yet and a few well-to-do people benefit from many of them.

However, man's happiness does not only stem from economic prosperity; it also depends on the full development of the human person's potential. This is expressed through marriage, lived in accordance with its dignity, with respect for life and the fulfillment of young people's hopes.

1. The dignity of marriage

We make our own the words of the Holy Father in his *Letter to Heads of State*. "An institution as natural, fundamental and universal as the family cannot be manipulated by anyone."

Indeed, according to Art. 16 of the *Declaration of Human Rights*, the family cannot be a temporary union but is based on marriage, that is, on a recognized stable union characterized by a full communion and openness to life and to society.

If this human reality, which is the family based on marriage, is lacking, society loses its natural basis and its stability.

We therefore appeal to all Catholics and to men and women of goodwill, to reject every attempt to manipulate the family.

To neglect the family, to empty marriage of its meaning or even to promote other kinds of relationships between individuals with the intention of making them equal or equivalent to marriage, would be to damage and destroy society itself.

2. Respect for human life

We are concerned that the Final Document of the Cairo Conference expresses an intention to introduce legal abortion, under the guise of so-called "reproductive rights" and in the promotion of "reproductive health," "fertility control" and "safe motherhood." These proposals imply a denial of the dignity and spiritual nature of man and pave the way to a culture of death. In this way not only will millions of women personally suffer the negative consequences of procured abortion, but millions of babies, who have the basic right to live, will be the victims of this even more widespread "abominable crime" (*Gaudium et spes*, n. 51).

As Pastors of the Church, we are of course sensitive to women's problems, but this is precisely why for their sake we wish to avert the sad experience of procured abortion, and with them to assert human sensitivity and deep love for so many babies who, once conceived, should be allowed to be born and to live.

We address the leaders of European nations, so that at the Cairo Conference they may show the necessary courage in their defence of the family and human life from the very moment of conception.

We are particularly worried about the possibility that after the Cairo Conference even more widescale and pressing campaigns will be developed and legislation passed that more directly denies or does not take into account the conscience and freedom of parents to decide, responsibly before God and according to their own family and living conditions, on how many children they should have.

With the Holy Father, we affirm the right of every man and every woman to responsible parenthood, freely assumed and exercised, without coercion by the State, even in the case of particular conditions of economic poverty, which should be remedied by greater social justice.

3. Hope for our parents

The particularly serious phenomenon for Europe of the declining birthrate and the disproportionate increase in the elderly population is well known. It is sad to see how the arrival of a baby is felt as a burden rather than as a gift from God. From this fact, which leads to grave imbalances, many other social and economic problems will arise that will be hard to solve.

European countries should not assume the serious moral responsibility of exporting their own model of life, characterized by the "demographic winter," to developing countries by adopting policies based on the drastic reduction of the world population.

We appeal to spouses to accept willingly every child as a *precious gift* of God (cf. *Gaudium et spes*, n. 50), who is capable of enriching their lives and their families with love and joy, and thus to guarantee, by their commitment to education, a better future for Europe and for the world.

Nevertheless, the most recent surveys taken in Europe show that young people are attached to families and to family values, but this basic sentiment is often overpowered by a cultural environment saturated with individualism and materialism. States ought to help young people preserve their sense of beauty and the values of life, not in selfishly claiming rights to sexual anarchy, but in building a stable family.

We address young people in particular, so that they will reject the utilitarian vision of the social planners and will struggle to assert their creative capacity, their faith and the values that can give the world hope.

Conclusion

While the Cairo Conference declares its desire to reflect on lifestyles, it actually seems to be influenced by a dim, pessimistic view of man's life and society's future which ultimately denies the true dignity of the human person: "the only creature on earth that God has wanted for its own sake" (*Gaudium et spes*. n. 24).

* * *

**Canadian Bishops' Conference on Cairo Conference
Letter to Prime Minister Jean Chrétien
18 July 1994**
(*from L'Osservatore Romano English edition, N. 31, p. 8*)

Catholic Bishops are so concerned about the positions Canada might take at the upcoming Cairo Conference on Population and Development that they have written directly to Prime Minister Jean Chrétien. The Conference, sponsored by the United Nations, will occur 5-11 September.

Bishop Jean-Guy Hamelin, President of the Canadian Conference of Catholic Bishops, wrote to the Prime Minister on 18 July, urging him to help ensure that Canada's interventions at the Conference "truly reflect a vision of integral development for all peoples."

Bishop Hamelin told the Prime Minister that as the Cairo Conference approaches, "two visions of people and their development have been vying for international attention and approval."

One of those visions, Bishop Hamelin said, is that the number of people is growing too rapidly, particularly in the developing nations. "The main way to avoid this risk, it is proposed, is a massive effort with our aid to reduce and control population growth in developing countries, including greater access to abortion. To make this dire formula seem acceptable, it is presented as a way to enhance the reproductive rights and freedom of individuals in the threatened countries."

In this regard, Bishop Hamelin recalled that a resolution adopted by consensus at the 1984 Population Conference in Mexico affirmed that "in no case should abortion be promoted as a method of family planning."

Bishop Hamelin said there is another vision regarding population and development that "sees underdevelopment in some areas and overdevelopment in others as the principal problem to be resolved."

"This perspective acknowledges that as human numbers increase, human needs also mount, and can become acute," Bishop Hamelin said. "It pays attention, however, to the fact that wherever human needs have been met and human rights enhanced, people have learned to match their numbers to their resources."

In his letter to the Prime Minister, Bishop Hamelin said that the task for governments "is not to try to influence directly the choices wives and husbands may make about having families. Rather, the challenge is to change the international systems that control resource development, commodity prices, terms of trade, monetary and fiscal policies, debt and debt service costs, and the development and transfer of technology."

* * *

German Bishops' Statement

The following is a translation of the statement released on 4 August 1994 by Bishop Karl Lehmann of Mainz, Germany, President of the German Bishops' Conference, regarding the debate on the International Conference on Population and Development.

The impression has been given in several recent publications that the German Bishops Conference's views with regard to the forthcoming World Conference on Population and Development to be held in Cairo diverge from the stand taken by the Holy See. However, these rumours have no basis in the statements released. Indeed, the Catholic Church throughout the world is critical of those who want to use the Cairo Conference — under any pretext — to impoverish values even further.

Together with the Pope, over the past few months the German

Bishops have constantly opposed dangerous tendencies in the draft final document of the World Conference on Population and Development. The Catholic Church unanimously rejects the political concept expressed in that draft, which does not grant the right to unborn life the dignity it deserves. She criticizes a concept of society which is extremely individualistic, does not pay sufficient attention either to the central importance of the family for society, nor to parental rights, especially in the area of sex education.

Likewise it should be noted that the orientation of the current draft of the Cairo document, despite the close connection between development and population problems, is very one-sided with regard to procreation issues. In harmony with the entire universal Catholic Church, the German Bishops have always asked, in addition, that the implementation of family planning programmes should never be considered a condition for the allocation of development aid.

These are the main points of the Holy See's criticism in the current debate on the international population policy, which it will also be maintaining in the future. The German Bishops have already backed this stance in their statement published in December 1993: *Bevölkerungswachstum und Entwicklungsförderung* (Population Growth and Promoting Development).

* * *

European Pro-Life Leaders Issue Declaration

The leaders of European pro-life movements gathered in Frascati, Italy, on 8-9 July 1994, at a meeting organized by the Pontifical Council for the Family. Here is the English text of their Final Declaration issued at the end of their session.

The leaders of European Pro-Life Movements have been greatly encouraged by our meeting in Rome, convened by the Pontifical Council for the Family. We particularly welcomed reports of the tremendous and rapid growth of pro-life activities, especially in the Eastern European nations, such as Russia which participated in an international pro-life leaders' meeting for the first time.

The family — sanctuary of life

Millions of families are living together out of freely chosen, mutual, permanent and mature love. They welcome their children as a gift of God, in the context of their truly responsible fatherhood and motherhood. They cherish their children with love. They live without temporary or permanent sterilization and without terminating the life of any of their unborn children. They take care of their aged or ill relatives until natural death.

This is the way of life we want to see protected and promoted by all persons and by all associations, as well as by all State or international health authorities.

Justice, honesty, kindness and compassion demand such a way of life and such humane behaviour. Therefore, to defend this way of life we express our concerns and our hopes.

The challenge of Cairo

We warmly welcome Pope John Paul II's vigorous and prophetic denunciation of the Draft Final Document of the United Nations Conference on Population and Development, to be held in Cairo. We share his concern because that draft text proposes the repression of developing countries by rich countries through the "contraceptive colonialism" of inhumane population-control measures. These include universal access to abortion in the name of "reproductive and sexual rights" and "reproductive health." Such policies are an unjust and scandalous substitute for true human development and international solidarity, to which the nations of Europe should be committed.

New methods of abortion

We warn of the spread of methods of early abortion, whether in the form of the abortion pill RU 486 or as the intrauterine devices (IUD) or as implants or "vaccines" against pregnancy and the various pills that have an abortifacient effect. Men and women have the right to be informed about these new attacks on innocent human life. These methods of abortion are part of population-control campaigns and have direct impact on the family.

However, contrary to the arguments for liberalized abortion law based on maternal mortality, in Ireland, where abortion has never been available, maternal mortality is the lowest in the world. Also in Ireland, the rates of infant mortality and child murder are among the lowest worldwide.

Euthanasia

We are concerned about new efforts to justify and legalize euthanasia, whether of aged and infirm people or of disabled adults and infants. We affirm that the disabled are playing a more important role in pro-life work —

speaking out courageously for their right to life, which is threatened by abortion and euthanasia. We call on them to increase their activities in the face of new and subtle attempts to revive the unspeakable crimes of a past era.

Justice for women

We will strive to renew our efforts to support pregnant women who are tempted to choose abortion. We welcome the continuing growth of pro-life caring and educational groups which give loving and practical support to mothers-to-be. At the same time we call for renewed efforts to care for women who have had abortions and who suffer the profound and long-term personal consequences. After the unborn child, the woman is the second victim of this crime.

The pro-life future

We renew our commitment to promoting wider programmes of pro-life education and stronger social and political action at every level in Europe. We are convinced that the future of a united Europe will only be assured if human life enjoys the full protection of law at the level of the Parliament of Europe and through every national legislature. In this common enterprise, we resolve to work together with Christians of all denominations, with other religions, especially our Moslem brethren, and with all men and women of goodwill. We rejoice to see the growing number of dedicated young people working in the various European pro-life movements.

Finally, we thank Pope John Paul II for his unswerving defence of the sanctity of human life and the integrity of the family, especially in his *Letter to Families* which was so warmly received by many leaders of different religious traditions. We look forward with hope and expectation to his forthcoming Encyclical Letter on Human Life, which we believe will renew the faith of men and women of goodwill in the struggle to protect the sanctity of human life and to maintain the basic inalienable human right — to life itself.

* * *

Knights of Columbus Statement

The following is the text of a statement on the Cairo Conference on Population and Development, issued by Supreme Knight Virgil C. Dechant on 13 September 1994, the day before the Conference was scheduled to end.

The close of the Cairo Conference on Population and Development will mark the end of only one chapter in an ongoing story — the struggle to defend human life and human dignity in our times.

Pope John Paul II is at the forefront of this effort, but he is not alone.

In recent days, nevertheless, the media have frequently chosen to depict the Pope as if he were isolated, a lone voice, in his opposition to abortion and his defence of traditional moral values regarding marriage, family and the sanctity of life.

This may be an ideologically convenient stereotype, but it is not true.

Pope John Paul II does not stand alone on these matters. He has the wholehearted support of many millions of people, including the Knights of Columbus.

His values are our values, his message is ours: Human life is sacred and inviolable from conception to natural death. With Pope John Paul II we stand for life, not death, in this great conflict of our day.

* * *

SPEECH BY MR. JOHN M. KLINK
ADVISOR, PERMANENT OBSERVER MISSION OF THE HOLY SEE TO THE UNITED NATIONS
TO THE ORGANIZATION "WOMEN AFFIRMING LIFE"
WASHINGTON, D.C., 24 SEPTEMBER 1994

Ladies and Gentlemen,

It is a pleasure for me to be with you this morning and I am especially appreciative to Mrs. Bork for extending the invitation to address this distinguished group whose respect-for-life cause, despite many press reports to the contrary, was shared by many Delegations and individuals participating at the International Conference on Population and Development in Cairo, not to mention by many millions of people throughout the world.

For the purposes of our discussion today, I would like to concentrate on three aspects of the Cairo Conference and its outcome: the first is what I would term as "the clarion call," the Holy See's efforts to focus the world's attention on the vital issues addressed in the Conference's Programme of Action; the second is a brief comparison of some of the language of the first draft vs. the final document; and lastly, on the meaning and importance of consensus within and outside the United Nations.

While a significant amount of attention had been addressed over the course of the past two years to the Cairo Conference, and in particular to the Draft Plan of Action of the Conference, one significant reading of the Document was to result in a greatly intensified worldwide focus on its meaning and relevancy. Pope John Paul II deemed that a document which dealt so intimately with the human family deserved his personal attention. As a result of his own reading of the document, his clarion call began.

Following his analysis of the draft document, the Holy Father received in private audience Dr. Nafis Sadik, the Executive Director of the United Nations Fund for Population Activities, who was the Secretary General of the Cairo Conference. Immediately thereafter the substance of the Pope's observations made to her at that time was published.

His major concern that he expressed was that "proper attention should be given to the ethical principles determining actions taken in response to the demographic, sociological and public policy analyses of the data on population trends." That is, that far more than about numbers, issues of population are about people, and as such, attention should be focused on basic truths: "that each and every person — regardless of age, sex, religion or national background — has a dignity and worth that is unconditional and inalienable; that human life itself from conception to natural death is sacred; that human rights are innate and transcend any constitutional order; and that the fundamental unity of the human race demands that everyone be committed to building a community which is free from injustice and which strives to promote and protect the common good."

Some of the Pope's major concerns hinged on the Draft Document's short shrift of development; its ambiguous references to, and relative unimportance given to the family, as well as to the rights, duties and responsibilities of parents for their offspring; the danger of even inadvertent encouraging of sexual activity amongst adolescents; its relative over-emphasis on the impact of developing countries' population growth on the environment compared with the impact of over-consumption and waste in developed countries; the needs of the elderly over their reproductive health needs, which were the singular focus of earlier drafts; and the relative sidelining of the importance of the responsibilities of States towards migrant families.

What was unparalleled, however, was the continued possibility that abortion might explicitly or implicitly be accepted as a method of family planning — something which had been specifically precluded in the language of the previous Population Conference in Mexico City in 1984. In the words of the Holy Father: "What is at stake here is the very future of humanity. Fundamental questions like the transmission of life, the family, and the material and moral development of society, need very serious consideration."

As a further concrete expression of his concern, the Pope gave instructions that the Diplomatic Corps accredited to the Holy See be convoked in order to have his viewpoint communicated directly to their governments. At that time, Archbishop Jean-Louis Tauran noted that Holy See Delegations had participated in regional preparatory meetings for the Cairo Conference which had been held in Bali, (Indonesia), Dakar, (Senegal) Geneva, (Switzerland), Aman, (Jordan) and Mexico City, (Mexico). Such interest, he noted, was not "just an interest of the moment," but was characteristic of the concern of the Holy See for the human person and since the theme of population touches the most important issues of life, it thus "touches the dignity of the human person in a special way." The Diplomatic Corps was asked to convey to their governments the invitation to "reflect on the consequences, both for your own country and for society on the world level, of what is involved in many of the recommendations contained in the Draft Final Document."

Finally, as an unprecedented expression of his concern, the Holy Father wrote personally to each Head of State, including President Clinton, inviting them to take a personal interest in the Document. The Pope stated in his letters that he was appealing to them "who are concerned for the good of [their] own people and of all humanity... not to weaken man, his sense of the sacredness of life, his capacity for love and self-sacrifice." In his words, the issues touched upon in the Document are "sensitive issues, issues upon which our societies stand or fall."

Throughout the course of the summer months, each Sunday Angelus prayer of the Holy Father addressed an aspect of the Holy See's teachings regarding the major issues addressed or which should have been addressed in the Draft Document. These issues included "The Authentic Emancipation of Women," "Natural Law Must be the Measure of All Human Legislation," "Parents Are God's Co-Workers," "Children Have the Right to Be Born From An Act of True Love" and "The State Must Ensure the Right to Life."

In continuing to keep the Cairo Conference in the public eye, the Holy Father's remarks did not go unheaded by other religious groups and leaders. While many joined in expressing views similar to the Pope's, one of the most significant was certainly that of the Islamic community. Of particular note was the decision by the Al Azhar University in Cairo, (one of, if not the most prestigious institution of Islamic learning) to condemn the draft's perceived condoning of extramarital sex and unrestricted access to abortion. One by one, other Islamic leaders began to publicly examine and question the text of the Document, asking the important question as to how such language could have been allowed to remain in the Document through the various preparatory committees at which most Islamic countries were represented.

In recognition of such criticism, several Islamic countries stated their intention to withdraw from participation in the Conference so as not to be perceived as being supportive of it. Seeking to preclude a developing crisis for the Conference, Egypt as the host country, was quick to prescribe to one and all that the surest way of achieving an ameliorated text was for all countries critical of the Draft Document's wording to participate in the Conference and seek appropriate revisions. In keeping with this philosophy, Egypt took upon itself the important task of ensuring that language regarding "other unions" in addition to marriage be removed. While unsuccessful in changing the minds of boycotting countries to attend, nevertheless throughout the Cairo negotiations, the attending Islamic countries held joint consultations to arrive at common positions to introduce or revise language so as to highlight the importance of religious viewpoints, of the family and of marriage.

In this way, far from being isolated, the Holy See's position, already shared by many of the Latin American countries amongst others from Africa, Europe and Asia, was greatly reinforced by the very plurality of the viewpoints which stressed a common theme — respect for cultural and family values and the dignity of the person. Whether without the Holy Father's clarion call such support would have been forthcoming can only be a matter for speculation. What is clear is that a change in the chemistry of viewpoints took place between the last Preparatory Meeting in New York in May and the actual Conference in Cairo. Principles for which the Holy See had been publicly ridiculed for proposing in a highly irregular fashion by none other than the Conference Secretariat, now became part and parcel of the final Document.

However, it is to be clearly noted that despite significant progress in the document, from the Holy See's position, despite its best efforts, much of the language of the Document remains flawed. For this reason the Holy See was able to join the consensus for some, but not all of the chapters of the document. It would thus be useful to spend some moments comparing the revisions of the Document's language in the course of the Cairo negotiations.

While the Preamble of the previous Document notes that there is a "growing awareness of the interlinkages among population issues, sustained economic growth and sustainable development," the final Document expands these issues to include "poverty, patterns of production and consumption" and notes that they are so closely interconnected that none of them can be considered in isolation." That is, in aiming at sustained development and environmental concern, *all* aspects must be taken into account in a more balanced approach which includes not only alarmist figures of world population growth and the Document's perceived urgency of quintupling world resource allocation for contraception, but the developed countries responsibilities to curb over-consumption and to assist significantly in overall human development efforts as well.

Similarly, in the Preamble, all previous references to abortion and "unsafe" abortion have been removed. Additionally, language highlighting the sovereignty of each country and the need to take into account the economic, social, and environmental diversity of conditions in each country has been greatly improved by the addition of the phrase "with full respect for the various religious and ethical values, cultural backgrounds and philosophical convictions of its people." Similar language is again repeated both in the Preamble and in a chapeau paragraph to the Principles, to the effect that the Programme of Action "will require the establishment of common ground, with full respect for the various religious and ethical values and cultural backgrounds."

Most importantly, the Preamble clearly notes that the Programme of Action of the Cairo Conference "does not create any new rights" — clearly a setback for those who sought by means of the Document to create an international right to abortion. Unfortunately, this was also a setback for the developing countries who wished to affirm a right to family reunification for migrants.

In the Principles chapter, perhaps the most significant change consistently advocated by the Holy See and other like-minded Delegations was to replace the phrase "everyone has the right to liberty and the security of person..." to "Everyone has the right to *life*, liberty and the security of person." Following a careful review of the text it became clear that the desire by the document's drafters to emphasize "security of person" was based on a desire to establish "code word" language connected with abortion rights both by emphasizing the woman's control over her own body, and simultaneously preclude reference to the right to life. Various efforts were made by the developed nations to form a connecting sentence to the effect that "All human beings are born free and equal in dignity and rights and have the right to life, liberty and security of person." In this formulation, the right to life would be implied as belonging only to those who are born. Thus, maintaining the separation of these ideas in two sentences was one of the major achievements of the overall Document.

The Holy See was pleased to see in Principle 2 the maintenance of the phrase "Human beings are at the center of concerns for sustainable development" which it had initiated in previous negotiations for the Agenda 21 Document from the 1992 World Summit on Environment and Development in Rio de Janeiro. It has long been the Holy See's position that rather than center the documents on the rights of States to make life decisions for their people, the primary focus should rather be on human beings as the center of God's creation whose rights it is the responsibility of States to protect.

Similarly, a long-term concern of the Holy See and of the Holy Father has been the right to development which is clearly enshrined in Principle 3: "The right to development is a universal and inalienable right and an integral part of fundamental human rights, and the human person is the central subject of development."

Far less satisfactory is the reference in Principle 4 to "ensuring women's ability to control their own fertility" as a cornerstone of population and development-related programmes. This phrase, which is ambiguous at best, is closely linked with one of the major battles within the Conference of the suggested replacement of "fertility regulation" with the term "family planning."

Already during Preparatory Committee negotiations in New York the Holy See indicated that it would take the brackets off of the text of "family planning" and take appropriate written reservations on the term as soon as language was inserted in any part of the Document to the effect of that which was agreed to in the 1984 Mexico City Population Conference: that "abortion is in no way to be promoted as a means of family planning." This offer was categorically refused at the time by the European Union with support from the United States and continued to serve as a major bone of contention up to the last days of the Cairo Conference.

When at last the Mexico City language was reinstated in the text, thereby closing the door on the issue of abortion as a means of family planning, a side door remained open in terms of the term "fertility regulation" which, according to the World Health Organization includes abortion and was thus to be another "code word" for abortion. The Holy See and several other Delegations insisted that the term "fertility regulation" be replaced by "family planning," which the developed countries determined to be unacceptable. This issue, which was one of the most contentious issues of the Conference, was finally rather unsatisfactorily resolved through changing the terminology from "fertility regulation" to "the regulation of fertility," thereby bypassing or skirting the abortion-inclusive definition provided by WHO.

As I previously mentioned, other problem areas in relation to abortion-related language remain. These include rather ambiguous terminology used throughout the text including: "sexual health," "sexual rights," "reproductive health," "reproductive rights" and "women's ability to control their own fertility." Most problematic of all are the references in Chapters 7 and 8 to abortion which, while stressing that abortion should not be promoted as a means of family planning and urging nations to find alternatives to abortion, unlike the language of the previous Population Conferences in Bucharest and Mexico City, it recognizes abortion as a dimension of population policy and indeed, of primary health care. For this reason the Holy See, in the end, could not join consensus on these chapters. As Archbishop Renato R. Martino, the Permanent Observer of the Holy See to the United Nations and the Head of the Holy See Delegation to the Cairo Conference explained in his final Statement at the conclusion of the Conference on 13 September 1994, these "chapters also contain references which could be seen as accepting extra-marital sexual activity, especially among adolescents." Further, he stated, "They would seem to assert that abortion services belong within primary health care as a method of choice."

To end the comparison on a more positive note, in regard to the Holy

Father's particular concerns regarding the family, one finds the text much improved. In previous texts the principle on the family read: "While various concepts of the family exist in different social, cultural and political systems, the family is the basic unit of society and as such is entitled to receive comprehensive protection and support." Following the Cairo negotiations Principle 9 now begins: "the family is the basic unit of society and as such should be strengthened. It is entitled to receive comprehensive protection and support." While it goes on to state that "In different cultural, political and social systems, various forms of the family exist," it is much clearer that the family is the center of society and other concepts offshoot therefrom rather than vice-versa.

Further, while the remaining language made reference to the fact that "marriage should be entered into with the free consent of the intending spouses," the new Principle 9 makes specific reference to "husband and wife" as "equal partners" effectively sidelining the desire on the part of certain parties to make the language as ambiguous as possible so as to allow for same-sex marriages.

Again, in Principle 10, language was negotiated which refers to the responsibility for education and guidance for children as lying "in the first place with parents," an acknowledgment which was sorely missing in original drafts.

In the final analysis, perhaps the most important achievement of the Document's negotiations is its new emphasis on the unacceptability of abortion as a solution for any population-related concerns. Examples of improved language include "all attempts should be made to eliminate the need for abortion" and "post-abortion counseling, education and family planning services should be offered promptly which will also help to avoid repeat abortions."

As can well be imagined, the stories of the negotiations could continue for nearly as long as the duration of the Conference itself. In my final comments I would like to concentrate on the attempts of certain Delegations or groups to subvert the consensus process and tradition of the United Nations. In the case of the Holy See, extraordinary efforts were taken to portray the Holy See as a singular, lonely hold-out, obstreperously blocking the unstoppable waves of "progress" and "modern" thought. Thus, those individual delegates who had participated in the various preparatory meetings and found themselves at variance with the forced agenda of the Conference would find themselves having to explain in their capitals that efforts really were afoot to seek, for example, unacceptable new "rights" to abortion and/or its synonyms.

Thus, surprisingly, the previously almost unspoken great divide of opinions was heard on the first day of the Plenary in Cairo prior to the Holy See's first formal intervention. Prime Minister Brundtland of Norway, who has long been publicly vocal in her desire to preclude the Holy See's influence in such international fora, used the opportunity as one of the keynote speakers to encourage the international legalization of abortion. The candor of her public remarks were extraordinarily effective in convincing many skeptics of her abortion legalization game plan and in mobilizing opposition to her desires.

The moment's drama was further increased a few moment's later when Mrs. Brundtland was followed by Prime Minister Bhutto of Pakistan who spoke vehemently against any legalization of abortion not allowed in the Koran. In a riveting speech in which she warned that what she was about to say would not be appreciated by many of the NGO community present, she quoted the Koran's admonishment for mothers not to kill their children since God is the giver of sustenance. Somehow, when least expected, truth wins out.

While all of those who are united in the affirmation of life over what Pope John Paul II has aptly termed "the culture of death" cannot often help but feel themselves to be voices crying in the desert, one cannot help but be encouraged by even small victories. In the last analysis it is difficult to determine whether Cairo was a victory in the true sense of the term. What is clear is that it certainly was not a defeat. The challenge, as always, lies ahead.

Even as we speak, Delegations are gathering in Mar del Plata, Argentina for the Latin America/Caribbean Regional Conference on the Integration of Women into the Economic and Social Development of Latin America and the Caribbean. The major focus of this Conference, as will be that of numerous other regional conferences throughout the world over the course of the next several months, will be to prepare for both the World Summit on Social Development and the Fourth World Conference on Women. Among the "strategic actions" proposed in the Draft Regional Programme of Action for the Mar del Plata Conference is, and I quote, "encouraging the adoption of measures to protect women's reproductive rights" and "abortion and its relationship to maternal mortality."

In the Cairo Conference, as was predictable, the vast majority of Delegations accepted the concept that abortion "should be safe in places where it is not illegal" since in most countries abortion is in fact legal in at least some restricted form. However, this ploy relies on a self assurance that the Trojan Horse of "safe abortion" will have to obey the local rules of procedure once inside the gate of Troy. However, the further game plan is already prepared. What is aimed at is nothing less than what Mrs. Brundtland had the candor to admit: an international "human right" to abortion. Unless extremely vigilant, unsuspecting countries will find the trap door of the Trojan Horse easily popped open with the magic word of human rights. As John Leo, in a recent article in *U.S. News and World Report* noted concerning this very prospect, "once international organizations accept abortion as a fundamental right, it can be cited to trump the laws, constitutions and sovereignty of any nation."

What can we do? Only what we can. Being forewarned helps. Forewarning various delegates was the laudable role performed by many at the Cairo Conference including many effective life-affirming NGO's. Each person must seek to build awareness, and build consensus in the context of his or her daily life. Each person must seek to build a consensus regarding the sacredness of the value of human life. As the Holy Father in prayerful reflection has so clearly indicated, on questions of such particular sensitivity as abortion and euthanasia, the continued existence of human civilization itself hangs in the balance. The reality is stark, but it is certainly not without hope. And as in all issues of such gravity, prayer is essential. Without it, the small David which was the Holy See Delegation to Cairo would never have been able to confront the forces of the Goliath of almost inexpressible power arrayed against the Holy See at the Cairo Conference. Pray fervently not only for our friends that they may remain stalwart in their convictions in favor of life, but also just as intently for our adversaries, as the Holy Father has encouraged all to do, that they may understand the perils which we commonly face with the advances of the culture of death.

On a personal level, I must acknowledge that one of the greatest gifts in my life is the knowledge that the birth mothers of my two adopted children had no great international role to play, and know little about the United Nations, but they made their own statement and bore their own witness more effectively than most international leaders can or do. Thinking of what the alternatives were for those two women and the bravery of their decisions gives me a particular strength as I witness in my children's eyes the magnificence of the power of day to day choices in favor of life.

Thank you.

Appendix

**MESSAGE OF
HIS HOLINESS POPE JOHN PAUL II
FOR THE CELEBRATION OF THE
WORLD DAY OF PEACE
VATICAN, 1 JANUARY 1995**

WOMEN: TEACHERS OF PEACE

1.   At the beginning of 1995, with my gaze fixed on the new millennium now fast approaching, I once again address to you, men and women of good will, a pressing appeal for peace in the world.

The violence which so many individuals and peoples continue to experience, the wars which still cause bloodshed in many areas of the world, and the injustice which burdens the life of whole continents can no longer be tolerated.

The time has come to move from words to deeds: may individual citizens and families, believers and Churches, States and International Organizations all recognize that they are called to renew their commitment to work for peace!

Everyone is aware of the difficulty of this task. If it is to be effective and long-lasting, work for peace cannot be concerned merely with the external conditions of coexistence; rather, it must affect people's hearts and appeal to a new awareness of human dignity. It must be forcefully repeated: authentic peace is only possible if the dignity of the human person is promoted at every level of society, and every individual is given the chance to live in accordance with this dignity. "Any human society, if it is to be well-ordered and productive, must lay down as a foundation this principle, namely, that *every human being is a person,* that is, his nature is endowed with intelligence and free will. Indeed, precisely because he is a person he has rights and obligations which flow directly and immediately from his very nature. And these rights and obligations are universal, inviolable and inalienable."[1]

The truth about man is the keystone in the resolution of all the problems involved in promoting peace. To teach people this truth is one of the most fruitful and lasting ways to affirm the value of peace.

Women and the teaching of peace

2. To educate in the ways of peace means to open minds and hearts to embrace the values which Pope John XXIII indicated in the Encyclical *Pacem in terris* as essential to a peaceful society: truth, justice, love and freedom.[2] This is an educational programme which involves every aspect of life and is lifelong. It trains individuals to be responsible for themselves and for others, capable of promoting, with boldness and wisdom, the welfare of the whole person and of all people, as Pope Paul VI emphasized in the Encyclical *Populorum progressio*.[3] The effectiveness of this education for peace will depend on the extent to which it involves the cooperation of those who, in different ways, are responsible for education and for the life of society. Time dedicated to education is time truly well spent, because it determines a person's future, and therefore the future of the family and of the whole of society.

In this context, I wish to direct my Message for this year's World Day of Peace especially to *women,* and to invite them to become *teachers of peace with their whole being and in all their actions.* May they be witnesses, messengers and teachers of peace in relations between individuals and between generations, in the family, in the cultural, social and political life of nations, and particularly in situations of conflict and war. May they continue to follow the path which leads to peace, a path which many courageous and far-sighted women have walked before them!

---

[1] JOHN XXIII, Encyclical Letter *Pacem in terris* (11 April 1963), I: *AAS* 55 (1963), 259.

[2] Cf. *loc. cit.,* 259-264.

[3] Cf. PAUL VI, Encyclical Letter *Populorum progressio* (26 March 1967), 14: *AAS* 59 (1967), 264.

In communion of love

3. This invitation to become teachers of peace, directed particularly to women, is based on a realization that to them God *"entrusts the human being in a special way."*[4] This is not however to be understood in an exclusive sense, but rather according to the logic of the complementary roles present in the common vocation to love, which calls men and women to seek peace with one accord and to work together in building it. Indeed, from the very first pages of the Bible God's plan is marvelously expressed: he willed that there should be a relationship of profound communion between man and woman, in a perfect reciprocity of knowledge and of the giving of self.[5] In woman, man finds a partner with whom he can dialogue in complete equality. This desire for dialogue, which was not satisfied by any other living creature, explains the man's spontaneous cry of wonder when the woman, according to the evocative symbolism of the Bible, was created from one of his ribs: "This at last is bone of my bones and flesh of my flesh" (*Gen* 2:23). This was the first cry of love to resound on the earth!

Even though man and woman are made for each other, this does not mean that God created them incomplete. God "created them to be a communion of persons, in which each can be a 'helpmate' to the other, for they are equal as persons ('bone of my bones...') and complementary as masculine and feminine."[6] Reciprocity and complementarity are the two fundamental characteristics of the human couple.

4. Sadly, a long history of sin has disturbed and continues to disturb God's original plan for the couple, for the male and the female, thus standing in the way of its complete fulfillment. We need to return to this plan, to proclaim it forcefully, so that women in particular — who have suffered more from its failure to be fulfilled — can finally give full expression to their womanhood and their dignity.

In our day women have made great strides in this direction, attaining a remarkable degree of self-expression in cultural, social, economic and political life, as well as, of course, in family life. The journey has been a difficult and complicated one and, at times, not without its share of mistakes. But it has been substantially a positive one, even if it is still unfinished, due

---

[4] JOHN PAUL II, Apostolic Letter *Mulieris dignitatem* (15 August 1988), 30: *AAS* 80 (1988), 1725.

[5] Cf. *Catechism of the Catholic Church*, No. 371. *Ibid.*, No. 372.

[6] *Ibid.*, No. 372.

to the many obstacles which, in various parts of the world, still prevent women from being acknowledged, respected, and appreciated in their own special dignity.[7] The work of building peace can hardly overlook the need to acknowledge and promote the dignity of women as persons, called to play a unique role in educating for peace. I urge everyone to reflect on the critical importance of the role of women in the family and in society, and to heed the yearning for peace which they express in words and deeds and, at times of greatest tragedy, by the silent eloquence of their grief.

Women of peace

5.   In order to be a teacher of peace, a woman must first of all nurture peace within herself. Inner peace comes from knowing that one is loved by God and from the desire to respond to his love. History is filled with marvelous examples of women who, sustained by this knowledge, have been able successfully to deal with difficult situations of exploitation, discrimination, violence and war.

Nevertheless, many women, especially as a result of social and cultural conditioning, do not become fully aware of their dignity. Others are victims of a materialistic and hedonistic outlook which views them as mere objects of pleasure, and does not hesitate to organize the exploitation of women, even of young girls, into a despicable trade. Special concern needs to be shown for these women, particularly by other women who, thanks to their own upbringing and sensitivity, are able to help them discover their own inner worth and resources. *Women need to help women,* and to find support in the valuable and effective contributions which associations, movements and groups, many of them of a religious character, have proved capable of making in this regard.

6.   In rearing children, mothers have a singularly important role. Through the special relationship uniting a mother and her child, particularly in its earliest years of life, she gives the child that sense of security and trust without which the child would find it difficult to develop properly its own personal identity and, subsequently, to establish positive and fruitful relationships with others. This primary relationship between mother and child also has a very particular educational significance in the religious sphere, for it can direct the mind and heart of the child to God long before

---

[7] Cf. JOHN PAUL II, Apostolic Letter *Mulieris dignitatem* (15 August 1988), 29: *AAS* 80 (1988), 1723.

any formal religious education begins.

In this decisive and sensitive task, no mother should be left alone. *Children need the presence and care of both parents,* who carry out their duty as educators above all through the influence of the way they live. The quality of the relationship between the spouses has profound psychological effects on children and greatly conditions both the way they relate to their surroundings and the other relationships which they will develop throughout life.

This primary education is extremely important. If relationships with parents and other family members are marked by affectionate and positive interaction, children come to learn from their own experience the values which promote peace: love of truth and justice, a sense of responsible freedom, esteem and respect for others. At the same time, as they grow up in a warm and accepting environment, they are able to perceive, reflected in their own family relationships, the love of God himself; this will enable them to mature in a spiritual atmosphere which can foster openness to others and to the gift of self to their neighbour. Education in the ways of peace naturally continues throughout every period of development; it needs particularly to be encouraged during the difficult time of adolescence, when the passage from childhood to adulthood is not without some risks for young people, who are called to make choices which will be decisive for life.

7. Faced with the challenge of education, the family becomes "the first and fundamental school of social living,"[8] the first and fundamental *school of peace.* And so it is not difficult to imagine the tragic consequences which occur when the family experiences profound crises which undermine or even destroy its inner equilibrium. Often, in these circumstances, women are left alone. It is then, however, that they most need to be assisted, not only by the practical solidarity of other families, of communities of a religious nature and of volunteer groups, but also by the State and by International Organizations through appropriate structures of human, social and economic support which will enable them to meet the needs of their children without being forced to deprive them unduly of their own indispensable presence.

8. Another serious problem is found in places where the intolerable custom still exists of discriminating, from the earliest years, between boys and girls. If, from the very beginning, girls are looked down upon or regarded as inferior, their sense of dignity will be gravely impaired and their

---

[8] JOHN PAUL II, Apostolic Exhortation *Familiaris consortio* (22 November 1981), 37: *AAS* 74 (1982), 127.

healthy development inevitably compromised. Discrimination in childhood will have lifelong effects and will prevent women from fully taking part in the life of society.

In this regard, how can we fail to acknowledge and encourage the invaluable efforts of so many women, including so many Congregations of women religious, who on different continents and in every cultural context make the education of girls and women the principal goal of their activity? Similarly, how can we fail to acknowledge with gratitude all those women who have worked and continue to work in providing health services, often in very precarious circumstances, and who are frequently responsible for the very survival of great numbers of female children?

Women, teachers of peace in society

9. When women are able fully to share their gifts with the whole community, the very way in which society understands and organizes itself is improved, and comes to reflect in a better way the substantial unity of the human family. Here we see the most important condition for the consolidation of authentic peace. The growing presence of women in social, economic and political life at the local, national and international levels is thus a very positive development. Women have a full right to become actively involved in all areas of public life, and this right must be affirmed and guaranteed, also, where necessary, through appropriate legislation.

This acknowledgment of the public role of women should not however detract from their unique role within the family. Here their contribution to the welfare and progress of society, even if its importance is not sufficiently appreciated, is truly incalculable. In this regard I will continue to ask that more decisive steps be taken in order to recognize and promote this very important reality.

10. With astonishment and concern we are witnessing today a dramatic increase in all kinds of violence. Not just individuals but whole groups seem to have lost any sense of respect for human life. Women and even children are unfortunately among the most frequent victims of this blind violence. We are speaking of outrageous and barbaric behaviour which is deeply abhorrent to the human conscience.

We are all called upon to do everything possible to banish from society not only the tragedy of war but also every violation of human rights, beginning with the indisputable right to life, which every person enjoys from the very moment of conception. The violation of the individual human being's right to life contains the seeds of the extreme violence of war. For this reason, I appeal to all women ever to take their place on the side of life. At the same time I urge everyone to help women who are suffering, and particularly children, in a special way those scarred by the painful trauma of having lived through war. Only loving and compassionate concern will enable them once again to look to the future with confidence and hope.

11. When my beloved predecessor Pope John XXIII indicated the participation of women in public life as one of the signs of our times, he also stated that, being aware of their dignity, they would no longer tolerate being exploited.[9]

Women have the right to insist that their dignity be respected. At the same time, they have the duty to work for the promotion of the dignity of all persons, men as well as women.

In view of this, I express the hope that the many international initiatives planned for 1995 — of which some will be devoted specifically to women, such as the Conference sponsored by the United Nations in Beijing on work for equality, development and peace — will provide a significant opportunity for making interpersonal and social relationships ever more human, under the banner of peace.

Mary, model of peace

12. Mary, Queen of Peace, is close to the women of our day because of her motherhood, her example of openness to others' needs and her witness of suffering. Mary lived with a deep sense of responsibility the plan which God willed to carry out in her for the salvation of all humanity. When she was made aware of the miracle which God had worked in her by making her the Mother of his Incarnate Son, her first thought was to visit her elderly kinswoman Elizabeth in order to help her. That meeting gave Mary the chance to express, in the marvelous canticle of the Magnificat (*Lk* 1:46-55), her gratitude to God who, with her and through her, had begun a new creation, a new history.

I implore the Most Holy Virgin Mary to sustain those men and women who, in the service of life, have committed themselves to building peace. With her help, may they bear witness before all people, especially

---

[9] Cf. JOHN XXIII, Encyclical Letter *Pacem in terris* (11 April 1963), I: *AAS 55* (1963), 267-268.

those who live in darkness and suffering and who hunger and thirst for justice, to the loving presence of the God of peace!

From the Vatican. 8 December 1994.

**LETTER OF
HIS HOLINESS POPE JOHN PAUL II
TO WOMEN
VATICAN, 29 JUNE 1995**

I greet you all most cordially, women throughout the world!

1. I AM WRITING THIS LETTER to each one of you as a sign of solidarity and gratitude on the eve of the Fourth World Conference on Women, to be held in Beijing this coming September.

Before all else, I wish to express my *deep appreciation* to the United Nations Organization for having sponsored this very significant event. The Church desires for her part to contribute to upholding the dignity, role and rights of women, not only by the specific work of the Holy See's official Delegation to the Conference in Beijing, but also by speaking directly to the heart and mind of every woman. Recently, when *Mrs. Gertrude Mongella,* the Secretary General of the Conference, visited me in connection with the Peking meeting, I gave her a written *Message* which stated some basic points of the Church's teaching with regard to women's issues. That message, apart from the specific circumstances of its origin, was concerned with a broader vision of the situation and problems of *women in general,* in an attempt to promote the *cause* of women in the Church and in today's world. For this reason, I arranged to have it forwarded to every Conference of Bishops, so that it could be circulated as widely as possible.

Taking up the themes I addressed in that document, I would now like to *speak directly to every woman,* to reflect with her on the problems and the prospects of what it means to be a woman in our time. In particular I wish to consider the essential issue of the *dignity* and *rights* of women, as seen in the light of the word of God.

This "dialogue" really needs to begin with a word of thanks. As I wrote in my Apostolic Letter *Mulieris dignitatem,* the Church "desires to give thanks to the Most Holy Trinity for the 'mystery of woman' and for every woman — for all that constitutes the eternal measure of her feminine dignity, for the 'great works of God,' which throughout human history have been accomplished in and through her" (No. 31).

2. This word of thanks to the Lord for his mysterious plan regarding the vocation and mission of women in the world is at the same time a concrete and direct word of thanks to women, to every woman, for all that they represent in the life of humanity.

Thank you, *women who are mothers!* You have sheltered human beings within yourselves in a unique experience of joy and travail. This experience makes you become God's own smile upon the newborn child, the one who guides your child's first steps, who helps it to grow, and who is the anchor as the child makes its way along the journey of life.

Thank you, *women who are wives!* You irrevocably join your future to that of your husbands, in a relationship of mutual giving, at the service of love and life.

Thank you, *women who are daughters* and *women who are sisters!* Into the heart of the family, and then of all society, you bring the richness of your sensitivity, your intuitiveness, your generosity and fidelity.

Thank you, *women who work!* You are present and active in every area of life — social, economic, cultural, artistic and political. In this way you make an indispensable contribution to the growth of a culture which unites reason and feeling, to a model of life ever open to the sense of "mystery," to the establishment of economic and political structures ever more worthy of humanity.

Thank you, *consecrated women!* Following the example of the greatest of women, the Mother of Jesus Christ, the Incarnate Word, you open yourselves with obedience and fidelity to the gift of God's love. You help the Church and all mankind to experience a "spousal" relationship to God, one which magnificently expresses the fellowship which God wishes to establish with his creatures.

Thank you, *every woman,* for the simple fact of being *a woman!* Through the insight which is so much a part of your womanhood you enrich the world's understanding and help to make human relations more honest and authentic.

3.   I know of course that simply saying thank you is not enough. Unfortunately, we are heirs to a history which has *conditioned* us to a remarkable extent. In every time and place, this conditioning has been an obstacle to the progress of women. Women's dignity has often been unacknowledged and their prerogatives misrepresented; they have often been relegated to the margins of society and even reduced to servitude. This has prevented women from truly being themselves and it has resulted in a spiritual impoverishment of humanity. Certainly it is no easy task to assign the blame for this, considering the many kinds of cultural conditioning which down the centuries have shaped ways of thinking and acting. And if objective blame, especially in particular historical contexts, has belonged to not just a few members of the Church, for this I am truly sorry. May this regret be transformed, on the part of the whole Church, into a renewed commitment of fidelity to the Gospel vision. When it comes to setting women free from every kind of exploitation and domination, the Gospel contains an ever relevant message which goes back to the *attitude of Jesus Christ himself.* Transcending the established norms of his own culture, Jesus treated women with openness, respect, acceptance and tenderness. In this way he honoured the dignity which women have always possessed according to God's plan and in his love. As we look to Christ at the end of this Second Millennium, it is natural to ask ourselves: how much of his message has been heard and acted upon?

        Yes, it is time to *examine the past with courage,* to assign responsibility where it is due in a review of the long history of humanity. Women have contributed to that history as much as men and, more often than not, they did so in much more difficult conditions. I think particularly of those women who loved culture and art, and devoted their lives to them in spite of the fact that they were frequently at a disadvantage from the start, excluded from equal educational opportunities, underestimated, ignored and not given credit for their intellectual contributions. Sadly, very little of women's achievements in history can be registered by the science of history. But even though time may have buried the documentary evidence of those achievements, their beneficent influence can be felt as a force which has shaped the lives of successive generations, right up to our own. To this great, immense feminine "tradition" humanity owes a debt which can never be repaid. Yet how many women have been and continue to be valued more for their physical appearance than for their skill, their professionalism, their intellectual abilities, their deep sensitivity; in a word, the very dignity of their being!

4.   And what shall we say of the obstacles which in so many parts of the world still keep women from being fully integrated into social, political and economic life? We need only think of how the gift of motherhood is often

penalized rather than rewarded, even though humanity owes its very survival to this gift. Certainly, much remains to be done to prevent discrimination against those who have chosen to be wives and mothers. As far as personal rights are concerned, there is an urgent need to achieve *real equality* in every area: equal pay for equal work, protection for working mothers, fairness in career advancements, equality of spouses with regard to family rights and the recognition of everything that is part of the rights and duties of citizens in a democratic State.

This is a matter of justice but also of necessity. Women will increasingly play a part in the solution of the serious problems of the future: leisure time, the quality of life, migration, social services, euthanasia, drugs, health care, the ecology, etc. In all these areas a greater presence of women in society will prove most valuable, for it will help to manifest the contradictions present when society is organized solely according to the criteria of efficiency and productivity, and it will force systems to be redesigned in a way which favours the processes of humanization which mark the "civilization of love."

5. Then too, when we look at one of the most sensitive aspects of the situation of women in the world, how can we not mention the long and degrading history, albeit often an "underground" history, of violence against women in the area of sexuality? At the threshold of the Third Millennium we cannot remain indifferent and resigned before this phenomenon. The time has come to condemn vigorously the types of *sexual violence* which frequently have women for their object and to pass laws which effectively defend them from such violence. Nor can we fail, in the name of the respect due to the human person, to condemn the widespread hedonistic and commercial culture which encourages the systematic exploitation of sexuality and corrupts even very young girls into letting their bodies be used for profit.

In contrast to these sorts of perversion, what great appreciation must be shown to those women who, with a heroic love for the child they have conceived, proceed with a pregnancy resulting from the injustice of rape. Here we are thinking of atrocities perpetrated not only in situations of war, still so common in the world, but also in societies which are blessed by prosperity and peace and yet are often corrupted by a culture of hedonistic permissiveness which aggravates tendencies to aggressive male behaviour. In these cases the choice to have an abortion always remains a grave sin. But before being something to blame on the woman, it is a crime for which guilt needs to be attributed to men and to the complicity of the general social environment.

6. My word of thanks to women thus becomes a *heartfelt appeal* that

everyone, and in a special way States and international institutions, should make every effort to ensure that women regain full respect for their dignity and role. Here I cannot fail to express my admiration for those women of good will who have devoted their lives to defending the dignity of womanhood by fighting for their basic social, economic and political rights, demonstrating courageous initiative at a time when this was considered extremely inappropriate, the sign of a lack of femininity, a manifestation of exhibitionism, and even a sin!

In this year's *World Day of Peace Message,* I noted that when one looks at the great process of women's liberation, "the journey has been a difficult and complicated one and, at times, not without its share of mistakes. But it has been substantially a positive one, even if it is still unfinished, due to the many obstacles which, in various parts of the world, still prevent women from being acknowledged, respected, and appreciated in their own special dignity" (No. 4).

This journey must go on! But I am convinced that the secret of making speedy progress in achieving full respect for women and their identity involves more than simply the condemnation of discrimination and injustices, necessary though this may be. Such respect must first and foremost be won through an effective and intelligent *campaign for the promotion of women,* concentrating on all areas of women's life and beginning with a *universal recognition of the dignity of women.* Our ability to recognize this dignity, in spite of historical conditioning, comes from the use of reason itself, which is able to understand the law of God written in the heart of every human being. More than anything else, the word of God enables us to grasp clearly the ultimate *anthropological basis* of the dignity of women, making it evident as a part of God's plan for humanity.

7. Dear sisters, together let us reflect anew on the magnificent passage in Scripture which describes the creation of the human race and which has so much to say about your dignity and mission in the world.

The Book of Genesis speaks of creation in summary fashion, in language which is poetic and symbolic, yet profoundly true: "God created man in his own image, in the image of God he created him; *male and female he created them*" (*Gen* 1:27). The creative act of God takes place according to a precise plan. First of all, we are told that the human being is created "in the image and likeness of God" (cf. *Gen* 1:26). This expression immediately makes clear what is distinct about the human being with regard to the rest of creation.

We are then told that, from the very beginning, man has been created "male and female" (*Gen* 1:27). Scripture itself provides the interpretation of this fact: even though man is surrounded by the innumerable creatures of the created world, he realizes that *he is alone* (cf. *Gen* 2:20). God intervenes in order to help him escape from this situation of solitude: *"It is not good that the man should be alone, I will make him a helper fit for him"* (*Gen* 2:18). The creation of woman is thus marked from the outset by *the principle of help:* a help which is not one-sided but *mutual.* Woman complements man, just as man complements woman: men and women are *complementary.* Womanhood expresses the "human" as much as manhood does, but in a different and complementary way.

When the Book of Genesis speaks of "help," it is not referring merely to *acting,* but also to *being.* Womanhood and manhood are complementary *not only from the physical and psychological points of view,* but also from the *ontological.* It is only through the duality of the "masculine" and the "feminine" that the "human" finds full realization.

8. After creating man male and female, God says to both: *"Fill the earth and subdue it"* (*Gen* 1:28). Not only does he give them the power to procreate as a means of perpetuating the human species throughout time, *he also gives them the earth, charging them with the responsible use of its resources.* As a rational and free being, man is called to transform the face of the earth. In this task, which is essentially that of culture, *man and woman alike* share equal responsibility from the start. In their fruitful relationship as husband and wife, in their common task of exercising dominion over the earth, woman and man are marked neither by a static and undifferentiated equality nor by an irreconcilable and inexorably conflictual difference. Their most natural relationship, which corresponds to the plan of God, is the "unity of the two," a relational "uni-duality," which enables each to experience their interpersonal and reciprocal relationship as a gift which enriches and which confers responsibility.

To this "unity of the two" God has entrusted not only the work of procreation and family life, but the creation of history itself. *While the 1994 International Year of the Family* focused attention on *women as mothers,* the Beijing Conference, which has as its theme "Action for Equality, Development and Peace," provides an auspicious occasion for heightening awareness of *the many contributions made by women to the life of whole societies and nations.* This contribution is primarily spiritual and cultural in nature, but socio-political and economic as well. The various sectors of society, nations and States, and the progress of all humanity, are certainly deeply indebted to the contribution of women!

9. Progress usually tends to be measured according to the criteria of

science and technology. Nor from this point of view has the contribution of women been negligible. Even so, this is not the only measure of progress, nor in fact is it the principal one. Much more important is *the social and ethical dimension,* which deals with human relations and spiritual values. In this area, which often develops in an inconspicuous way beginning with the daily relationships between people, especially within the family, society certainly owes much to the *"genius of women."*

Here I would like to express particular appreciation to those women who are involved in the various *areas of education* extending well beyond the family: nurseries, schools, universities, social service agencies, parishes, associations and movements. Wherever the work of education is called for, we can note that women are ever ready and willing to give themselves generously to others, especially in serving the weakest and most defenceless. In this work they exhibit a kind of *affective, cultural and spiritual motherhood* which has inestimable value for the development of individuals and the future of society. At this point how can I fail to mention the witness of so many Catholic women and Religious Congregations of women from every continent who have made education, particularly the education of boys and girls, their principal apostolate? How can I not think with gratitude of all the women who have worked and continue to work in the area of health care, not only in highly organized institutions, but also in very precarious circumstances, in the poorest countries of the world, thus demonstrating a spirit of service which not infrequently borders on martyrdom?

10. It is thus my hope, dear sisters, that you will reflect carefully on what it means to speak of the "*genius of women,*" not only in order to be able to see in this phrase a specific part of God's plan which needs to be accepted and appreciated, but also in order to let this genius be more fully expressed in the life of society as a whole, as well as in the life of the Church. This subject came up frequently during *the Marian Year* and I myself dwelt on it at length in my Apostolic Letter *Mulieris dignitatem* (1988). In addition, this year in the *Letter* which I customarily send to priests for Holy Thursday, I invited them to reread *Mulieris dignitatem* and reflect on the important roles which women have played in their lives as mothers, sisters and co-workers in the apostolate. This is another aspect — different from the conjugal aspect, but also important — of that "help" which women, according to the Book of Genesis, are called to give to men.

The Church sees in Mary the highest expression of the "feminine genius" and she finds in her a source of constant inspiration. Mary called herself the "handmaid of the Lord" (*Lk* 1:38). Through obedience to the Word of God she accepted her lofty yet not easy vocation as wife and mother in the family of Nazareth. Putting herself at God's service, she also put herself at the service of others: a *service of love.* Precisely through this service Mary was able to experience in her life a mysterious, but authentic "reign." It is not by chance that she is invoked as "Queen of heaven and earth." The entire community of believers thus invokes her; many nations and peoples call upon her as their "Queen." *For her, "to reign" is to serve! Her service is "to reign!"*

This is the way in which authority needs to be understood, both in the family and in society and the Church. Each person's fundamental vocation is revealed in this "reigning," for each person has been created in the "image" of the One who is Lord of heaven and earth and called to be his adopted son or daughter in Christ. Man is the only creature on earth "which God willed for its own sake," as the Second Vatican Council teaches; it significantly adds that man "cannot fully find himself except through a sincere gift of self" (*Gaudium et spes, 24*).

The maternal "reign" of Mary consists in this. She who was, in all her being, a gift for her Son, *has also become a gift for the sons and daughters of the whole human race,* awakening profound trust in those who seek her guidance along the difficult paths of life on the way to their definitive and transcendent destiny. Each one reaches this *final goal* by fidelity to his or her own vocation; this goal provides meaning and direction for the earthly labours of men and women alike.

11. In this perspective of "service — which, when it is carried out with freedom, reciprocity and love, expresses the truly "royal" nature of mankind — one can also appreciate that the presence of *a certain diversity of roles* is in no way prejudicial to women, provided that this diversity is not the result of an arbitrary imposition, but is rather an expression of what is specific to being male and female. This issue also has a particular application within the Church. If Christ — by his free and sovereign choice, clearly attested to by the Gospel and by the Church's constant Tradition — entrusted only to men the task of being an *"icon" of his countenance as "shepherd" and "bridegroom" of the Church through the exercise of the ministerial priesthood,* this in no way detracts from the role of women, or for that matter from the role of the other members of the Church who are not ordained to the sacred ministry, since *all* share equally in the dignity proper to the *"common priesthood"* based on Baptism. These role distinctions should not be viewed in accordance with the criteria of functionality typical in human societies. Rather they must be understood according to the particular criteria of the *sacramental economy,* i.e. the economy of "signs" which God freely chooses in order to become present in the midst of humanity.

Furthermore, precisely in line with this economy of signs, even if apart from the sacramental sphere, there is great significance to that "womanhood" which was lived in such a sublime way by Mary. In fact, there is present in the "womanhood" of a woman who believes, and especially in a woman who is "consecrated," a kind of inherent "prophecy" (cf. *Mulieris dignitatem,* 29), a powerfully evocative symbolism, a highly significant "iconic character," which finds its full realization in Mary and which also aptly expresses the very essence of the Church as a community consecrated with the integrity of a *"virgin"* heart to become the *"bride"* of Christ and *"mother"* of believers. When we consider the "iconic" complementarity of male and female roles, two of the Church's essential dimensions are seen in a clearer light: the "Marian" principle and the Apostolic-Petrine principle (cf. *ibid., 27).*

On the other hand — as I wrote to priests in this year's *Holy Thursday Letter* — the ministerial priesthood, according to Christ's plan, "is an expression not of domination but of service" (No. 7). The Church urgently needs, in her daily self-renewal in the light of the Word of God, to emphasize this fact ever more clearly, both by developing the spirit of communion and by carefully fostering all those means of participation which are properly hers, and also by showing respect for and promoting the diverse personal and communal charisms which the Spirit of God bestows for the building up of the Christian community and the service of humanity.

In this vast domain of service, the Church's two-thousand-year history, for all its historical conditioning, has truly experienced the "genius of woman"; from the heart of the Church there have emerged women of the highest calibre who have left an impressive and beneficial mark in history. I think of the great line of woman martyrs, saints and famous mystics. In a particular way I think of Saint Catherine of Siena and of Saint Teresa of Avila, whom Pope Paul VI of happy memory granted the title of Doctors of the Church. And how can we overlook the many women, inspired by faith, who were responsible for initiatives of extraordinary social importance, especially in serving the poorest of the poor? The life of the Church in the Third Millennium will certainly not be lacking in new and surprising manifestations of "the feminine genius."

12. You can see then, dear sisters, that the Church has many reasons for hoping that the forthcoming United Nations Conference in Beijing *will bring out the full truth about women.* Necessary emphasis should be placed on the *"genius of women*," not only by considering great and famous women of the past or present, but also those *ordinary* women who reveal the gift of their womanhood by placing themselves at the service of others in their everyday lives. For in giving themselves to others each day women fulfill their deepest vocation. Perhaps more than men, women *acknowledge the person,* because

they see persons with their hearts. They see them independently of various ideological or political systems. They see others in their greatness and limitations; they try to go out to them and *help them*. In this way the basic plan of the Creator takes flesh in the history of humanity and there is constantly revealed, in the variety of vocations, that beauty — not merely physical, but above all spiritual — which God bestowed from the very beginning on all, and in a particular way on women.

While I commend to the Lord in prayer the success of the important meeting in Beijing, I invite *Ecclesial Communities* to make this year an occasion of heartfelt thanksgiving to the Creator and Redeemer of the world for the gift of *this great treasure* which is womanhood. In all its expressions, womanhood is part of the essential heritage of mankind and of the Church herself.

May Mary, Queen of Love, watch over women and their mission in service of humanity, of peace, of the spread of God's Kingdom!

With my Blessing.

From the Vatican, 29 June 1995, the Solemnity of Saints Peter and Paul.

MESSAGE OF HIS HOLINESS POPE JOHN PAUL II FOR WORLD MIGRATION DAY
VATICAN, 10 AUGUST 1994

MAY YOU REACH THE GOALS YOU HAVE CHOSEN

Every year the individual churches are asked to observe World Migration Day, a special day in honour of migrants on a date chosen by the Episcopal Conferences. To commemorate this occasion, the Holy Father has issued a Message drawing attention to the plight of migrants. This year, influenced by the United Nations' proclamation of the International Year of the Woman to be celebrated in 1995, the Pope has focused in particular on emigrant women, and the additional burdens they must bear. Here is a translation of the Message given in Italian.

Dear Brothers,

The International Year of the Woman proclaimed by the United Nations for 1995 — an initiative which the Church cordially welcomes — has persuaded me to assume as the theme of the Message for next World Migration Day that of the woman involved in the migrant phenomenon. The increasing ground she is gaining in the world of work has resulted in her ever greater involvement in problems associated with migration. The extent of this involvement varies considerably within the different countries, but the overall number of migrating women tends to equal that of men.

This has echoes of great relevance on the female world. One thinks first and foremost of the women who are experiencing the heartbreak of having left their own family behind in their native country. This is often the immediate consequence of laws that delay or even refuse to recognize the right to family reunion. While one can understand a temporary delay in the reunion of families in order to favour their subsequent, better acceptance, one must reject the attitude of those who refuse it almost as though it were a claim with no juridical basis. On this subject, the teaching of the Second Vatican Council is explicit: "that in emigration regulations family life [should be] perfectly safeguarded" (*Apostolicam Actuositatem,* no. 11).

Then how can we possibly overlook that, in the case of emigration, a large part of the burden of the family often falls on the woman? For their own members, the most sophisticated societies, which mostly attract the flows of migrants, have already created an atmosphere where both spouses often feel obliged to work. Those who come among them as migrants are even more subject to this fate. They have to submit to a great pressure of work in order to provide for the family's daily sustenance, so as to achieve the goals for which they left their native country. Such a situation generally imposes the heaviest tasks on the woman who, in fact, is forced to do a double and an even more demanding job when there are children to care for.

Particular pastoral attention must be given to unmarried women, who are increasingly more numerous within the migratory phenomenon. Their condition demands from those in charge not only solidarity and acceptance, but also protection and defence from abuse and exploitation.

The Church recognizes that everyone has "the right to leave [their] native land for various motives...in order to seek better conditions of life in another country" (*Laborem exercens,* no. 23). Nevertheless, while she declares that "the more prosperous nations are obliged, to the extent they are able, to welcome the foreigner in search of the security and the means of livelihood which he cannot find in his country of origin" (*Catechism of the Catholic Church,* no. 2241), she does not deny public authorities the right to control and limit the flow of migrants when for the common good serious and objective reasons exist which affect the migrants' own interests.

Public authorities cannot forget the many and often grave reasons that force so many women to leave their native land. Their decision is not only based on the need for greater opportunities; they are frequently driven by the need to flee cultural, social, or religious conflicts, inveterate traditions of exploitation, unjust or discriminatory laws, to give only a few examples.

As is well known it is unfortunate that regular migration has always been accompanied, like an umbra, by that which is irregular, a growing phenomenon, with negative aspects which conspicuously affect women in particular. Not infrequently, elements of degeneration, such as the drug trade and the scourge of prostitution, filter in through the streams of clandestine immigration.

In this respect, proper vigilance should also be exercised in the countries of origin, since, profiting from the limited lawful emigration channels, unreliable organizations force young women onto the ways of clandestine emigration, enticing them with the prospects of success, not without previously despoiling them of their hard-earned savings. The fate many of them face is well-known and sad: turned back at the frontier, they are often dragged into the dishonour of prostitution, despite themselves.

The concerted action of the governments concerned to identify and penalise those responsible for such offences to human dignity of this kind is essential.

The recent phenomenon of a more widespread presence of women emigrants thus requires a change of perspective in the formulation of the relevant policies, and there emerges the urgent need to guarantee women equal treatment, both with regard to remuneration as well as to working conditions and security. Thus it will be easier to obviate the tendency to discriminate against migrants in general which might nevertheless continue to target women. It is also necessary to set up means to facilitate women's integration and cultural and professional training, as well as a fair share of the social benefits, such as the provision of housing, schooling for children, and adequate tax reductions.

I now address a pressing invitation to the Christian communities which migrants are joining. By a cordial and fraternal welcome they witness by deeds even more than words, that "the families of migrants ... should be able to find a homeland everywhere in the Church. This is a task stemming from the nature of the Church as being a sign of unity in diversity" (*Familiaris Consortio,* no. 77).

My affectionate wishes are addressed in a special way to you women, who courageously face your condition as emigrants.

I am thinking of you, mothers, who struggle with daily problems, sustained by love for your dear ones. I am thinking of you, young women, who are on your way to a new country, eager to improve your condition and that of your families by alleviating their financial difficulties. May you be supported by the assurance of leading your life in contexts where greater material, spiritual, and cultural resources enable you to implement your choices of life with greater freedom and responsibility.

My wish, accompanied by constant prayer, is that in carrying out the difficult and delicate role which falls to you, you may attain the goals you have set yourselves. The Church is close to you with the care and support that you need.

I am thinking of you, Christian women, who in emigration can do a great service to the cause of evangelisation. Continue with courage and trust what love and the sense of responsibility suggest to you, to acquire ever greater wisdom about your vocation as wives and mothers.

When you are entrusted with the task of looking after children in the families for whom you work, without forcing and in complete harmony of intention with the parents, make the most of the great opportunity that is given you to help the religious formation of these children. The common priesthood, rooted in baptism, expressed in you in the typical endowments of femininity, such as the capacity to serve life with a commitment which is deep, unconditional, and above all, inspired by love.

The history of salvation reminds us how divine providence acted within the unpredictable and mysterious interactions of peoples, religions, cultures, and different races. Among the many examples offered by the Bible, I like to recall one in particular which centers on the figure of a woman. It is the story of Ruth the Moabite, the wife of an Israelite who emigrated to the country of Moab because of the famine afflicting Israel. After she was widowed, she decided to go and live in Bethlehem, her husband's native city. To her mother-in-law, Naomi, who urged her to go back to her own mother in the land of Moab, she replied, "Do not ask me to abandon or forsake you! For wherever you go I will go, wherever you lodge I will lodge, your people shall be my people, and your God my God. Wherever you die I will die, and there be buried" (*Ru* 1:16-17). Thus Ruth followed Naomi to Bethlehem where she became the wife of Boaz, from whose descendants David was born and later Jesus.

In this perspective, the words the Lord addressed to his people exiled in Babylon through the mouth of the prophet Jeremiah are very appropriate and meaningful. "Build houses to dwell in; plant gardens, and eat their fruits. Take wives and beget sons and daughters, find wives for your sons and give your daughters husbands, so that they may bear sons and daughters. There you must increase in number, not decrease. Promote the welfare of the city to which I have exiled you; pray for it to the Lord, for upon its welfare depends your own" (*Jer* 29:5-7). This is an invitation addressed to people full of nostalgia for their own native land to which they were bound by memories of people and family events.

May Mary who, supported by faith in the fulfillment of the Lord's promises, was always careful to interpret events in the light of the fulfillment of the Lord's word, accompany and enlighten your journey as emigrant women, mothers, and wives.

May she, who in her pilgrimage of faith also experienced exile, fortify in you the desire for good, sustain your hope, and strengthen you in love. Entrusting your commitments and hopes to the Mother of God, the Virgin of the wayside, I bless you with all my heart, together with your families and all those who are working to promote a respectful and fraternal welcome for you.

From the Vatican, 10 August 1994, the sixteenth year of my Pontificate.

**MESSAGE OF
HIS HOLINESS POPE JOHN PAUL II
FOR THE 30TH WORLD COMMUNICATIONS DAY
VATICAN, 24 JANUARY 1996
"THE MEDIA: MODERN FORUM FOR PROMOTING THE ROLE OF
WOMEN IN SOCIETY"**

Dear Brothers and Sisters,

This year, the theme for World Communications Day, "The Media: Modern Forum for Promoting the Role of Women in Society," recognizes that the communications media play a crucial role not only in promoting justice and equality for women but in fostering appreciation for their specific feminine gifts, which elsewhere I have called the "genius" of women (cf. *Mulieris dignitatem*, n. 30; *Letter to Women*, n. 10).

Last year, in my *Letter to Women*, I sought to advance a dialogue, especially with women themselves, on what it means to be a woman in our time (cf. n. 1). I also pointed out some of "the obstacles which in so many parts of the world still keep women from being fully integrated into social, political and economic life" (n. 4). This is a dialogue which people in the communications media can, indeed have an obligation to, foster and support. People in the media often become advocates, and commendably so, of the voiceless and the marginalized. They are in a unique position also to stimulate public consciousness with regard to two serious issues concerning women in today's world.

First, as I noted in my *Letter*, motherhood is often penalized rather than rewarded, even though humanity owes its very survival to those women who have chosen to be wives and mothers (cf. n. 4). It is certainly an injustice that such women should be discriminated against, economically or socially, precisely for following that fundamental vocation. Likewise I pointed out that there is an urgent need to achieve real equality in every area:

equal pay for equal work, protection for working mothers, fairness in career advancement, equality of spouses with regard to *family rights*, and the recognition of everything that is part of the rights and duties of citizens in a democratic State (cf. n. 4).

Values of life and love must be radically affirmed

Secondly, the advancement of women's genuine emancipation is a matter of justice, which can no longer be overlooked; it is also a question of society's welfare. Fortunately, there is a growing awareness that women must be enabled to play their part in the solution of the serious problems of society and of society's future. In every area, "a greater presence of women in society will prove most valuable, for it will help to manifest the contradictions present when society is organized solely according to the criteria of efficiency and productivity, and it will force systems to be redesigned in a way which favours the processes of humanization which mark the 'civilization of love'" (ibid., n. 4).

The "civilization of love" consists, most particularly, in *a radical affirmation of the value of life and of the value of love*. Women are especially qualified and privileged in both of these areas. Regarding life, although not alone responsible for affirming its intrinsic value, women enjoy a unique capacity for doing so because of their intimate connection with the mystery of life's transmission. Regarding love, women can bring to every aspect of life, including the highest levels of decision-making, that essential quality of femininity which consists in objectivity of judgement, tempered by the capacity to understand in depth the demands of interpersonal relationships.

The communications media, including the press, the cinema, radio and television, the music industry and computer networks, represent the modern forum where information is received and transmitted rapidly to a global audience, where ideas are exchanged, where attitudes are formed — and, indeed, where a new culture is being shaped. The media are therefore destined to exercise a powerful influence in determining whether society fully recognizes and appreciates not only the rights but also the special gifts of women.

Sadly though, we often see not the exaltation but the exploitation of women in the media. How often are they treated not as persons with an inviolable dignity but as objects whose purpose is to satisfy others' appetite for pleasure or for power? How often is the role of woman as wife and mother undervalued or even ridiculed? How often is the role of women in business or professional life depicted as a masculine caricature, a denial of the specific gifts of feminine insight, compassion and understanding, which so greatly contribute to the "civilization of love"?

Media should focus on true heroines of society

Women themselves can do much to foster better treatment of women in the media: by promoting sound media education programmes, by teaching others, especially their families, to be discriminating consumers in the media market, by making known their views to production companies, publishers, broadcasting networks and advertisers with regard to programmes and publications which insult the dignity of women or debase their role in society. Moreover, women can and should prepare themselves for positions of responsibility and creativity in the media, not in conflict with or imitation of masculine roles but by impressing their own "genius" on their work and professional activity.

The media would do well to focus on the true heroines of society, including the saintly women of the Christian tradition, as role models for the young and for future generations. Nor can we forget, in this respect, the many consecrated women who have sacrificed all to follow Jesus and to dedicate themselves to prayer and to the service of the poor, the sick, the illiterate, the young, the old, the handicapped. Some of these women are themselves involved in the communications media — working so that "the poor have the Gospel preached to them" (cf. *Lk* 4:18).

"My soul proclaims the greatness of the Lord" (*Lk* 1:46). The Blessed Virgin Mary used these words in responding to the salutation of her cousin Elizabeth, thus acknowledging the "great things" that God had done in her. The image of women communicated by the media should include the recognition that every feminine gift proclaims the greatness of the Lord, the Lord who has communicated life and love, goodness and grace, the Lord who is the source of the dignity and equality of women, and of their special "genius."

My prayer is that this 30th World Communications Day will encourage all those involved in the media of social communication, especially the sons and daughters of the Church, to promote the genuine advancement of women's dignity and rights, by projecting a true and respectful image of their role in society, and by *bringing out "the full truth about women"* (*Letter to Women*, n.12).

From the Vatican, 24 January 1996

Statements Regarding "Catholics for a Free Choice"

President of NCCB/USCC: Opposing Catholics for a Free Choice Means Taking "Stand for Truth"
USCC Press Release, 16 March 1995

WASHINGTON — Cardinal William H. Keeler, President of the National Conference of Catholic Bishops/United States Catholic Conference, said those who oppose granting accreditation to Catholics For a Free Choice at the United Nations' Commission on the Status of Women in preparation for the U.N.'s Fourth World Conference on Women, to be held in Beijing, "take a stand for truth."

"Those who oppose the United Nations' granting accreditation to the group which calls itself 'Catholics for a Free Choice' take a stand for truth," Cardinal Keeler said. "One hopes that the United Nations will honor the position of those who oppose accrediting the group as a non-governmental organization accredited by the Commission on the Status of Women in preparation for the Fourth World Conference on Women to be held in Beijing," Cardinal Keeler said in a March 16 Statement.

"No group which promotes abortion can legitimately call itself Catholic," Cardinal Keeler said.

"To use the name Catholic to promote the taking of innocent life is offensive not only to the Catholic Church, but also to all who expect forthrightness in public discourse," he added. In his comment, Cardinal Keeler reiterated words of a 4 November 1993 Statement of the U.S. Bishops' Administrative Committee, noting that Catholics for a Free Choice "has no affiliation, formal or otherwise, with the Catholic Church."

"In fact Catholics For a Free Choice is associated with the pro-abortion lobby in Washington, D.C. It attracts public attention by its denunciations of basic principles of Catholic morality and teaching — denunciations given enhanced visibility by media outlets that portray CFFC as a reputable voice of Catholic dissent."

"CFFC can in no way speak for the Catholic Church and its 59 million members in the United States. Most of CFFC's funding is from secular foundations supporting legal abortion in this country and abroad."

Attachments: A) *Cardinal Keeler's Statement, 16 March 1995*
  B) *Administrative Committee Statement, 4 November 1993*

ATTACHMENT A:
STATEMENT BY
HIS EMINENCE WILLIAM CARDINAL KEELER
PRESIDENT, NATIONAL CONFERENCE OF CATHOLIC BISHOPS/
UNITED STATES CATHOLIC CONFERENCE
WASHINGTON, D.C., 16 MARCH 1995

Those who oppose the United Nations' granting accreditation to the group which calls itself "Catholics for a Free Choice" take a stand for truth. One hopes that the United Nations will honor the position of those who oppose accrediting the group as a non-governmental organization accredited by the Commission on the Status of Women in preparation for the Fourth World Conference on Women to be held in Beijing.

No group which promotes abortion can legitimately call itself Catholic.

To use the name Catholic to promote the taking of innocent life is offensive not only to the Catholic Church, but also to all who expect forthrightness in public discourse.

As the Administrative Committee of the U.S. Bishops said on 4 November 1993, of Catholics for a Free Choice:

"It has no affiliation, formal or otherwise, with the Catholic Church."

"In fact Catholics For a Free Choice is associated with the pro-abortion lobby in Washington, D.C. It attracts public attention by its denunciations of basic principles of Catholic morality and teaching — denunciations given enhanced visibility by media outlets that portray CFFC as a reputable voice of Catholic dissent."

"CFFC can in no way speak for the Catholic Church and its 59 million members in the United States. Most of CFFC's funding is from secular foundations supporting legal abortion in this country and abroad."

ATTACHMENT B:
**STATEMENT BY THE ADMINISTRATIVE COMMITTEE
OF THE NATIONAL CONFERENCE OF CATHOLIC BISHOPS
REGARDING "CATHOLICS FOR A FREE CHOICE"
WASHINGTON, D.C., 4 NOVEMBER 1993**

During Pope John Paul II's recent visit to this country, programs about dissent in the Catholic Church often included a spokesperson for a group calling itself "Catholics for a Free Choice" (CFFC). Both before and since World Youth Day, because of CFFC's presuming to speak for American Catholics, and because of the attention the media have paid to the group, many people, including Catholics, may be led to believe that it is an authentic Catholic organization. It is not. It has no affiliation, formal or otherwise, with the Catholic Church.

In fact Catholics for a Free Choice is associated with the pro-abortion lobby in Washington, D.C. It attracts public attention by its denunciations of basic principles of Catholic morality and teaching — denunciations given enhanced visibility by media outlets that portray CFFC as a reputable voice of Catholic dissent.

CFFC can in no way speak for the Catholic Church and its 59 million members in the United States. Most of CFFC's funding is from secular foundations supporting legal abortion in this country and abroad. It shares an address and funding sources with the National Abortion Federation, a trade association which seeks to advance the financial and professional interests of abortionists.

Therefore it is important to educate the public, especially Catholics, about CFFC's insistence on claiming a Catholic label. This group has rejected unity with the Church on important issues of longstanding and unchanging Church teaching. In fact there is no room for dissent by a Catholic from the Church's moral teaching that direct abortion is a grave wrong.

Our Catholic position embraces the truth regarding the sacredness of every human life, before as well as after birth. CFFC endorses the violent destruction of innocent unborn human beings and regularly issues legal briefs and other publications endorsing legalized abortion for all nine months of pregnancy and for any reason. Most Americans do not support its extreme agenda.

Because of its opposition to the human rights of some of the most defenseless members of the human race, and because its purposes and activities deliberately contradict essential teachings of the Catholic faith, we state once again that Catholics for a Free Choice merits no recognition or support as a Catholic organization.

Administrative Committee
National Conference of Catholic Bishops

Released in Washington, D.C., 4 November 1993

HOLY SEE MISSION PRESS RELEASE
HOLY SEE DELEGATION QUESTIONS
ACCREDITATION OF "CATHOLICS FOR A FREE CHOICE"
NEW YORK, 17 MARCH 1995

On 15 March 1995, the United Nations Commission on the Status of Women began preparations for the Fourth World Conference on Women. Due to erroneous public reports as to what occurred at that meeting, the Mission of the Holy See to the United Nations would like to make the following clarification:

> The Delegation of the Holy See to the 39th Session of the Commission on the Status of Women has questioned the accreditation of the non-governmental organization entitled "Catholics for a Free Choice." Even though the organization uses the word "Catholic" in its title, it publicly assumes and promotes positions totally contrary to those held by the Catholic Church. Such an organization cannot be recognized as Catholic.

The Mission of the Holy See to the United Nations will issue no further comment until this question of the accreditation of "Catholics for a Free Choice" has been officially resolved.

HOLY SEE MISSION PRESS RELEASE
HOLY SEE DELEGATION CHALLENGES NGO ACCREDITATION OF "CATHOLICS FOR A FREE CHOICE" TO UNITED NATIONS WOMEN'S CONFERENCE
NEW YORK, 21 MARCH 1995

On 15 March 1995 the Holy See Delegation disapproved the accreditation of the non-governmental organization "Catholics for a Free Choice" during the 39th Session of the Commission on the Status of Women in preparation for the Fourth World Conference on Women to be held in Beijing. Its disapproval lies in the organization's misleading use of the word "Catholic" in its title. Because the said NGO publicly promotes some fundamental positions contrary to those held by the Catholic Church, it cannot be recognized as Catholic.

In clarifying its position in this regard the Holy See referred to a 4 November 1993 statement by the Administrative Committee of the National Conference of Catholic Bishops asserting that Catholics For a Free Choice "has no affiliation, formal or otherwise, with the Catholic Church" and therefore merits no recognition as a Catholic organization. Cardinal William H. Keeler, President of the NCCB, issued a 16 March 1995 Statement stressing that "to use the name Catholic to promote the taking of innocent life is offensive not only to the Catholic Church, but also to all who expect forthrightness in public discourse."

The word "Catholic" means "universal," in the sense of "in keeping with the whole" and signifies union with Catholic Church teaching, the Pope and the Bishops. This organization promotes the killing of unborn children, which directly contradicts Church teaching, the Pope and the Bishops. Therefore, the Holy See cannot approve of the accreditation of a group which claims to be Catholic yet fails to recognize and uphold the dignity and value of every human being. Furthermore, it is within the jurisdiction of the Holy See and the Catholic hierarchy alone to determine what organizations use the title "Catholic."

The Holy See does not intend to disrupt the preparatory process of the Conference. It brought this matter to the fore as a full member of the Beijing Conference and also in response to numerous inquiries concerning "Catholics For A Free Choice." In doing so the Holy See has addressed its concerns. And Catholics, as well as all other persons are formally apprised that "Catholics For a Free Choice" holds absolutely no connection with the Holy See and the Catholic Church. As such, it can not be recognized as "Catholic."

ADDRESS OF
HIS HOLINESS POPE JOHN PAUL II
AT THE OPENING SESSION OF THE
INTERNATIONAL CONFERENCE ON NUTRITION
SPONSORED BY THE U.N. FOOD AND AGRICULTURE ORGANIZATION
(FAO) AND THE WORLD HEALTH ORGANIZATION (WHO)
FAO HEADQUARTERS, ROME; 5 DECEMBER 1992

On Saturday, 5 December, the Holy Father visited the headquarters of the U.N. Food and Agriculture Organization in Rome for the inauguration of the International Conference on Nutrition sponsored by FAO and WHO. The Pope addressed the officials and Delegations from U.N. Member Countries, speaking about the nutritional needs, especially of children, and the moral obligations of the international community in providing for their fulfillment. The following is a translation of the Address given by the Holy Father in French.

Mr. President,
Directors General,
Ministers,
Permanent Representatives,
Ladies and Gentlemen,

1.   It gives me great pleasure to accept your invitation to speak at the opening of the International Conference on Nutrition which brings together the highest world authorities in this most important sector. You come from very different countries and your cultures too are very different, but it is in essence the same service that motivates you each day in your struggle to ensure that every human being enjoys a standard of living compatible with his dignity as a person; in the present circumstances, I am sure that you will not fail to progress together towards this goal.

I would like to pay homage to the two great intergovernmental organizations which have taken this initiative and have brought it to fruition, thanks to their joint efforts and the experience they have gained in the service of humanity: the Food and Agriculture Organization of the United Nations and the World Health Organization. The personal commitment of their Directors-General, Mr. Saouma and Mr. Nakajima, shows their common desire not to make this Conference a formal event, but the starting point for a fresh, more vigorous action inspired by the mottoes of the two organizations: "Food for all" and "Health for all."

The dynamism of your organizations has made nutrition and health priorities for the international community, which is trying to ensure that nobody lacks them. The Church will always show her sympathy for these efforts, supporting them by word and deed, faithful to the teaching of her Founder, the one who, faced with a hungry multitude, showed generous understanding (cf. *Mt* 15:32).

Undernourished multitudes are counting on your work

2. The theme of your Conference reminds us that whether it is a question of food supply or health care, nutrition is a basic element in the life of each person, each group, each people on the earth. Your Conference, however, also shows that despite the efforts already made by the international community, there are frequently worsening obstacles and imbalances that prevent millions of men and women from providing adequately for their own nutrition. This is a serious warning for the common conscience of humanity.

The multitudes who are deprived of a suitable healthy diet, even to the point of death, are counting on your work today to decide on bold interventions to ward off the spectre of starvation and malnutrition that haunts humanity. These brothers and sisters ask you to consider as a duty of justice your determined commitment to the cause of an increasingly active solidarity, the only means by which everyone can have an equitable share in the benefits of creation. They expect from this Conference that the necessary ethical appeals will lead to resolutions that will be legally enforced, in conformity with international law.

Here you should listen to the cries of suffering millions faced with the scandal caused by the "paradox of abundance" that has become the main obstacle to serving humanity's nutritional problems. World food production — as you well know — is easily sufficient to satisfy the needs of an increasing population, on the condition that the resources which allow access to proper nutrition are shared according to real needs. I can only subscribe to the opening lines of your project for a *World Declaration on Nutrition:* "Hunger and malnutrition are unacceptable in a world with both the necessary knowledge and resources to put an end to this human catastrophe" (n. 1).

However, the paradox continues to yield dramatic consequences every day. On the one hand, we are stricken by the images of a part of humanity condemned to die of hunger because of natural calamities that are aggravated by manmade disasters, by obstacles put in the way of the distribution of food supplies, by restrictions imposed on the trade of local produce, depriving the poorest countries of their market benefits. Moreover, we are witnessing the disintegration of solidarity: the destruction of whole harvests, the selfish demands inherent in current economic models, the rejection of the exchange of technology and conditions imposed on the allocation of food aid, even in cases of obvious emergency.

The causes and effects of this paradox, with their multiple contradictory elements, are once again being brought to your attention in the framework of this Conference; it is enough here to recall the unacceptable facts: every day hunger causes the death of thousands of children, elderly people and members of the more vulnerable groups; a considerable part of the world population is unable to obtain its essential basic daily food ration; masses of people are heavily burdened by poverty, ignorance and political conditions which oblige them to leave their homes by the millions in search of a land where they can find enough to eat.

Every human person has right to nutrition

3.   Today, ladies and gentlemen, yours is a weighty responsibility. After thorough research, the International Conference on Nutrition will present a clear analysis of the situation of health and nutrition throughout the world, and will also propose a legal and political framework for necessary and viable interventions. Thanks to this Conference, all humanity will know what measures governments and international institutions have chosen on behalf of the neediest.

It is up to you to shed new light on the basic right to nutrition that properly belongs to each human person. The *Universal Declaration of Human Rights* has already declared the right to sufficient food. For the application of this right, we must now assure everyone access to nourishment, food security, a healthy diet, and training in nutrition techniques. Briefly, everyone should benefit from personal and community living conditions that allow the full development of every human being at every moment of his or her existence.

All too often, situations in which peace is lacking, where justice is not taken seriously, or where the natural environment is destroyed, dangerously threaten entire populations with the inability to satisfy their basic food needs.

Wars between nations and domestic conflicts should not sentence defenceless civilians to death from hunger for selfish or partisan motives. In these cases, food aid and health care must in all circumstances be guaranteed, and all obstacles must be removed, including those stemming from an arbitrary appeal to the principle of non-interference in a country's domestic affairs. The conscience of humanity, henceforth backed by measures of international humanitarian law, makes human involvement in situations that seriously jeopardize the survival of peoples and whole ethnic groups obligatory. This is a duty for nations and the international community, as we are reminded by the guidelines proposed at this Conference.

4. Humanity realizes today that the problem of hunger cannot be solved at the local level, but only by global development. Access to available resources should be guaranteed; the training of the most underprivileged and their participation in the responsibilities involved should be ensured. To achieve these goals, it is increasingly necessary to spread a concept of economic relations that goes beyond the existing boundaries between countries and which is based on true solidarity and the sharing of resources and goods produced.

As regards food resources, one should insist on the need not so much to increase their overall production, but rather to assure their effective distribution by giving priority to areas at risk. It is also important for the populations burdened by the effects of malnutrition and hunger to receive an education that prepares them to provide healthy and sufficient foodstuffs on their own.

The Declaration and the Plan of Action that your Conference is called to approve place the family nucleus at the heart of this programme for education and training. I note this with pleasure. Likewise, it is right to state that it is impossible to provide serious training in nutrition and more generally, to prepare a world free from divisions and suffering, without a common commitment to recognizing the proper rights of the family and its members, and without guaranteeing them the indispensable means to reinforce their essential role in society.

As regards nutrition, consideration will be focused on how to give better support to women because of the vital tasks they perform in rural areas at risk from the nutritional point of view: the woman is mother and teacher, breadwinner and primarily responsible for managing the household. Special attention will also be paid to children, so that their basic right to life and nutrition, a right that was recently proclaimed by the *"Convention on the Rights of the Child"* may be safeguarded. Nor can one fail to recognize the right of the couple to decide on procreation and the spacing of births. It is obvious that only living conditions that remove the extreme forms of poverty for millions of people will be able to foster responsible parenthood and guarantee the free exercise of this basic right of the couple.

We must answer to the Lord for our actions

5. As you know, when the Church fulfills her mission to proclaim the "Good News to all nations," she desires to be especially close to poor, suffering or hungry humanity. It is not up to her to suggest technical solutions but she is always ready to give wholehearted support to those who are working to reinforce international solidarity and to promote justice among peoples. On her part, the Church does so by proclaiming that the law of love of God and neighbour is the basis of social life. She is also well aware that her "social message will gain credibility more immediately from the witness of actions" (*Centesimus annus*, n.57). It is in seeking to act according to the law of love that her institutions and her various organizations take numerous initiatives to be of direct service to the poor, the hungry, the sick, these "lowly ones" who are the object of God's special favour. We cannot forget that at the end of history we shall have to answer, before the Lord, for our actions regarding the welfare of our brothers and sisters (cf. *Mt* 25:31-46).

This is why the Pope is asking you, the participants in the International Conference on Nutrition to strive to ensure that no person will be refused his or her daily bread and necessary health care. Individual calculations and interests must therefore be overcome; the initiatives of the Food and Agriculture Organization and the World Health Organization meant to guarantee a minimum level of nutrition to all the peoples of the world, must be supported and developed. By such a commitment, it will be possible to give this Conference the necessary authority for the principles of the *World Declaration on Nutrition* to be put into practice.

It is above all necessary that States, intergovernmental organizations, humanitarian institutions and private associations everywhere be convinced that no political criteria or economic law should harm man, his life, his dignity, or his freedom. All peoples should learn to share the lives of others and to see that the earth's resources which the Creator entrusted to humanity are shared.

In this spirit, I express my fervent best wishes for the success of your work, and I invoke the blessing of the Most High on you and on all the peoples of the earth.

ADDRESS OF
HIS HOLINESS POPE JOHN PAUL II
TO PARTICIPANTS IN THE 28TH CONFERENCE OF THE
UNITED NATIONS FOOD AND AGRICULTURE ORGANIZATION (FAO)
VATICAN, 23 OCTOBER 1995

Mr. Chairman,
Mr. Director-General,
Ladies and Gentlemen,

1. I gladly welcome the distinguished participants in the 28th Conference of the United Nations Food and Agriculture Organization, making your now traditional visit to the See of Peter. Because this year marks the 50th anniversary of FAO, I am especially pleased that, despite your busy schedule, you did not wish to miss this occasion — a custom which has been honoured at meetings of the Conference since FAO settled in Rome in 1951.

Through you, Mr. Chairman, I offer warm good wishes to the Delegates and representatives of the member States, and extend a special welcome to the new members of your Organization which more than ever reflects a world which, in spite of often painful divisions, has an increasing need to unite around common objectives.

I thank you, Mr. Director-General, and renew my esteem for your generous commitment during the first phase of your mandate, which also involves the difficult but necessary task of restructuring the Organization.

Underlying causes of poverty must be addressed

2. It is not by chance that the beginning of FAO coincided with the formation of that broader Organization, the United Nations, whose ideals inspired FAO and with whose activity it is associated. The establishment of FAO was thus intended to emphasize the complementarity of the principles

contained in the *Charter of the United Nations*: true peace and effective international security are achieved not only by preventing wars and conflicts, but also by promoting development and creating conditions which ensure that basic human rights are fully guaranteed.

3.   The 50th anniversary celebration of FAO offers a suitable occasion to reflect on the international community's commitment to a fundamental good and duty: the freeing of human beings from malnutrition and the threat of starvation. As you have pointed out in the recent *Quebec Declaration*, it cannot be forgotten that at the origins of FAO there was not only a desire to strengthen effective cooperation among States in a primary sector such as agriculture but also the intention *to find ways to guarantee sufficient food for the whole world*, through sharing the fruits of the earth in a rational way. By setting up FAO on 16 October 1945, the world community hoped to eradicate the scourge of famine and starvation. The enormous difficulties still involved in this task must not be allowed to diminish the firmness of your commitment.

Even today tragic situations are unfolding before our eyes: people are dying of starvation because peace and security have not been guaranteed. The social and economic situation of the contemporary world makes us all aware of the extent to which the hunger and malnutrition of millions of people are the result of evil mechanisms within economic structures, or are the consequence of unjust criteria in the distribution of resources and production, policies formulated in order to safeguard special interest groups, or different forms of protectionism. Furthermore, the precarious situation in which whole peoples find themselves has led to *a mobility of such alarming dimensions that it cannot be dealt with by traditional humanitarian assistance alone*. The question of refugees and displaced persons gives rise to dramatic consequences at the level of agricultural production and of food security, affecting the nutrition of millions of people. FAO's action in recent years has shown that the provision of emergency help for refugees is not enough; this kind of assistance does not bring a satisfactory solution as long as conditions of extreme poverty are allowed to continue and become even more acute, conditions which lead to increased deaths due to malnutrition and hunger. The underlying causes of such situations have to be addressed.

4.   Ladies and Gentlemen: the 50th anniversary celebrations furnish us with the opportunity to ask why international action, despite the existence of FAO, has been unable to alter this state of affairs. At the worldwide level sufficient food can be produced to satisfy everyone's needs. Why then are so many people threatened by starvation?

As you are well aware, there are many reasons for this paradoxical situation in which *abundance coexists with scarcity*, including policies which forcibly reduce agricultural production, widespread corruption in public life, and massive investment in sophisticated weapons systems to the detriment of people's primary needs. These and other reasons contribute to the creation of what you call "structures of famine." Here we are speaking of the mechanisms of international business by which the less favoured countries, those most in need of food, are excluded in one way or another from the market, thus preventing a just and effective distribution of agricultural products. Yet another reason is that certain forms of assistance for development are made conditional on the implementation by poorer countries of policies of structural adjustment, policies which drastically limit those countries' ability to acquire needed foodstuffs. Nor can a serious analysis of the underlying causes of hunger overlook that attitude found in the more developed countries, where a consumerist culture tends to exalt artificial needs over real ones. This has direct consequences for the structure of the world economy, and for agriculture and food production in particular.

FAO is essential to fostering international cooperation

These many reasons have their source not only in a false sense of the values which should sustain international relations, but also in a widespread attitude which emphasizes *having* over *being*. The result is a real inability on the part of many to appreciate the needs of the poor and the starving; indeed, to appreciate the poor themselves in their inalienable human dignity. An effective campaign against hunger thus calls for more than merely indicating the proper functioning of market mechanisms or attaining higher levels of food production. It is necessary, first and foremost, *to recover a sense of the human person*. In my *Address* to the General Assembly of the United Nations on 5 October last, I pointed to the need to build relationships between peoples on the basis of a constant "exchange of gifts," a real "culture of giving" which should make every country prepared to meet the needs of the less fortunate (n.14).

5. In this perspective, FAO and other bodies have an essential role to play in fostering a new sense of international cooperation. During the last 50 years it has been the merit of FAO to promote people's access to land, thus favouring agricultural workers and fostering their rights as a condition for raising production levels. Food assistance, often exploited as a way of exerting political pressure, has been modified by means of a new concept: *food security*, which considers the availability of food not only in relation to the needs of a country's population, but also in relation to the productive capacity of neighbouring areas, precisely with a view to the rapid transfer or exchange of foodstuffs.

In addition, the concern which the international community shows for environmental issues is reflected in FAO's involvement in activities aimed at limiting damage to the ecosystem and safeguarding food production from phenomena such as desertification and erosion. The promotion of effective social justice in relations between peoples entails the awareness that the goods of Creation are meant for all people, and that the economic life of the world community should be oriented to sharing those goods, their use and their benefits.

Today it is more necessary than ever for the international community to recommit itself to fulfilling the primary purpose for which FAO was established. Daily bread for every person on earth — that "Fiat panis" which FAO refers to in its motto — is an essential condition of the world's peace and security. Courageous choices must be made, choices made in the light of a correct ethical vision of political and economic activity. Modifications and reforms of the international system, and of FAO in particular, need to be rooted in an *ethic of solidarity* and a *culture of sharing*. To direct the labours of this Conference to this end can be a most fruitful way of preparing for the important meeting of the World Summit on Nutrition which FAO has scheduled for November 1996.

Struggle against hunger must be a priority

6.   In all these efforts the Catholic Church is close to you, as attested to by the attention with which the Holy See has followed the activity of FAO since 1948. In celebrating this 50th Anniversary with you, the Holy See wishes to demonstrate its continuing support for your endeavours. A symbolic sign of this support and encouragement will be the bell to be placed in the FAO headquarters as a remembrance of the establishment, 50 years ago, of the Family of the United Nations. Bells symbolize joy; they announce an event. But bells also ring out a call to action. On this occasion, and in the context of FAO's activity, this bell is meant to call everyone — countries, different international organizations, all men and women of goodwill — to even greater efforts to free the world from famine and malnutrition.

The words inscribed on the base of the bell evoke the very purpose of the United Nations system: "Nation shall not lift up sword against nation, neither shall they learn war any more" (*Is* 2:4). These are the words of the Prophet Isaiah, who proclaimed the dawn of universal peace. But, according to the Prophet, this peace will come about — and this has great meaning for FAO — only when "they shall beat their swords into ploughshares, and their spears into pruning hooks" (*ibid*). For only when people consider the struggle against hunger as a priority, and are committed to providing everyone with the means of gaining their daily bread instead of amassing weapons, will conflicts and wars come to an end and humanity be able to set forth on a lasting journey of peace.

This is the sublime task to which you, the representatives of the nations and the leaders of FAO, are called.

Upon your work and upon FAO, I invoke the abundant blessings of almighty God, ever rich in mercy.

MESSAGE OF
HIS HOLINESS POPE JOHN PAUL II
TO MR. JACQUES DIOUF
DIRECTOR-GENERAL OF FOOD AND AGRICULTURE ORGANIZATION
FOR THE ANNUAL OBSERVANCE OF WORLD FOOD DAY

CONVEYED BY
HIS EMINENCE ANGELO CARDINAL SODANO
SECRETARY OF STATE OF HIS HOLINESS
12 OCTOBER 1996

"Mr. Director-General,

The annual observance of World Food Day provides His Holiness Pope John Paul II with an opportunity to express once more his appreciation to you, Mr. Director-General, to the representatives of the member States of FAO and to all those who with different tasks and responsibilities are involved in the effort to alleviate malnutrition and hunger.

The anniversary of the establishment of FAO invites us to reflect together on one of the most striking paradoxes of our time. While the goals which the human family has achieved encourage us to hope for a future ever more responsive to human needs, the world remains divided between those who live in abundance and those who lack the necessary daily bread. This division has been accentuated by recent events, natural disasters and situations caused by deliberate human action.

There is an increased need for more effective action by the international community and its institutions on behalf of all — men, women, families, communities — who live in the poorest areas of the world. In fact, attention to the causes and effects of malnutrition and hunger must never lead us to neglect the necessity of practical action on behalf of those unable to share in the resources and fruits of creation. The response therefore cannot be a continued disregard of the attitude of solidarity required for a more effective intervention.

Recent experience has also heightened humanity's awareness that technical solutions, however elaborate, are not effective if they lack the necessary reference to the central importance of the human person — the beginning and end of the inalienable rights of every individual, community and people. Among these rights there emerges the fundamental right to nutrition, but the actual putting into practice of this right cannot be seen merely as a goal to be striven for. This right, in fact, must inspire action aimed at promoting a life consistent with the demands of human dignity and free from those external constraints which, under any form, can limit freedom of choice and even compromise the survival of individuals, families and civil communities.

It is the hope of His Holiness Pope John Paul II that these brief reflections will help to foster in everyone the conviction that material aid, the modification of habits linked to affluent lifestyle, and attention to preserving resources and the environment are not enough in the fight against hunger and malnutrition. Also needed is a "choice of life" which, by rediscovering a sense of sharing and by realizing the human dimension of the tragedy of hunger and malnutrition, will be able to overcome special interests, also in the area of international activity. This could be the right direction for efforts aimed at enabling every people and nation to achieve an adequate level of food security.

With these sentiments, the Holy Father invokes upon FAO and its work abundant heavenly blessings, and he renews to you, Mr. Director-General, his cordial best wishes."

PONTIFICAL COUNCIL "COR UNUM"

WORLD HUNGER

*A Challenge For All:
Development In Solidarity*

*

Preface by
Secretary of State of His Holiness
His Eminence Cardinal Angelo Sodano

VATICAN CITY
1996

TABLE OF CONTENTS

PREFACE 875
INTRODUCTION 877

I

THE REALITY OF HUNGER

The challenge of hunger 881
A scandal that has lasted too long: hunger destroys life 881
Malnutrition jeopardizes the present and future of a population 881
Chief victims: the most vulnerable populations 882
Hunger generates hunger 883
Causes that may be remedied 883

    A) Economic causes 884
        Root causes 884
        Debt of the mis-developing countries 885
        Structural adjustment programmes 887

    B) Socio-cultural causes 889
        The social situation 889
        Demography 889
        The implications 890

    C) Political causes 891
        The influence of politics 891
        Concentration of resources 893
        Economic and social de-structuring 893

    D) The earth can feed all its inhabitants 894
        The great progress made by humanity 894
        Agri-food markets 895
        Modern agriculture 896

II

ETHICAL CHALLENGES TO BE TAKEN UP BY ALL

Ethical dimension of the problem 897
Love of our neighbour in order to achieve development 899
Social justice and the universal destination of goods 899

Costly abuse of the common good: the "structures of sin" 900
Giving preference to listening to the poor and serving them: sharing . . . 902
An integrated society 904
Peace, a balance of rights 904
Disarmament, an urgent need to be met 905
Respect for the environment 906
Ecology and equitable development 906
Taking up the challenge together 907
Acknowledging the contribution of the poor to democracy 907
Community initiatives 908
Access to credit 909
Paramount role of women 909
Integrity and a social sense 910

III

TOWARDS AN ECONOMY BASED ON GREATER SOLIDARITY

To better serve humanity and all human beings 912
Channeling the work of all to the same end 913
Political will of industrial countries 914
Establishing fair terms of trade 915
Overcoming the debt problem 916
Increasing overseas development assistance 917
Rethinking aid 918
Emergency aid: a temporary solution 918
Coordinated aid 919
Food security: a permanent solution 919
Giving priority to local production 920
Importance of agrarian reform 920
Role of research and education 921
International organizations: Catholic International Associations
    Catholic International Organizations (CIO's), Non-Governmental
    Organizations (NGO's) and their networks 922
The twofold mission of international organizations 923
Partnership in solidarity 923

IV

THE JUBILEE OF THE YEAR 2000
A STAGE IN THE BATTLE AGAINST HUNGER

The Jubilees: rendering to God what is God's 924
Becoming "providence" for our fellow human beings 925

The dignity of the human being and the fruitfulness of labour 925
The economy degraded by a lack of justice 927
Fairness and justice in the economy 928
An appeal for Jubilee proposals 929

V

HUNGER: A CALL TO LOVE

The poor are calling us to love 932
The poverty of God 932
The Church is with the poor 933
Poor and rich alike are called to freedom 934
Necessary reform of the human heart 935
"Place not your trust in idols!" 936
Listening to the poor 937
Listening to God 938
Changing our lives 938
. . . to change life 938
Supporting initiatives 939
Every Christian is on a mission in all activities 941

PREFACE

I am very pleased to present the document *"WORLD HUNGER - A Challenge For All: Development in Solidarity."* It has been prepared with great care by the Pontifical Council "Cor Unum," upon the request of His Holiness Pope John Paul II. In addition this year in his Lenten Message, the Successor to St. Peter, has given voice to those who lack the vital minimum: "The crowds of starving people — children, women, the elderly, immigrants, refugees, the unemployed — raise to us their cry of suffering. They implore us, hoping to be heard."

The document follows the path laid down by Christ to his disciples. The person and message of Jesus Christ are, in fact, centered on the manifestation that "God is love" (1 *Jn* 4:8), a love which redeems humanity and saves it from a manifold misery in order to restore all men and women to their full dignity. Throughout the centuries, the Church has given many concrete expressions of this divine care. The history of the Church can be written as a history of love and charity towards the poorest of the poor. This is thanks to the many Christians who have given witness to their needy brothers and sisters, thus showing Christ's love in laying down his life for all.

The study now published intends to give a further contribution to the commitment of Christians, that of sharing in the needs of all. The themes dealt with are very much of the present day, not only in describing the present situation in the world as far as hunger is concerned, but also the ethical implications of this problem which concerns all who are of goodwill. This publication is also important in view of the Jubilee of the year 2000, which the Church is preparing to celebrate. The spirit of this document is not based on any particular ideology; it is lead by the logic of the Gospel and extends an invitation to follow Jesus Christ in daily life.

It is my hope that this document will reach a large audience so that the conscience of many persons will become more sensitive to the exercise of distributive justice and human solidarity.

Vatican City, 4 October 1996, Feast of Saint Francis of Assisi.

✠ ANGELO Card. SODANO
Secretary of State

WORLD HUNGER

A CHALLENGE FOR ALL: DEVELOPMENT IN SOLIDARITY

"So widespread is the phenomenon that it brings into question the financial, monetary, production and commercial mechanisms that, resting on various political pressures, support the world economy. These are proving incapable either of remedying the unjust social situations inherited from the past or of dealing with the urgent challenges and ethical demands of the present. By submitting man to tensions created by himself, dilapidating at an accelerated pace material and energy resources, and compromising the geophysical environment, these structures unceasingly make the areas of misery spread, accompanied by anguish, frustration and bitterness...." "This difficult road of the indispensable transformation of the structures of economic life is one on which it will not be easy to go forward without the intervention of a true conversion of mind, will and heart. The task requires resolute commitment by individuals and peoples that are free and linked in solidarity."

(POPE JOHN PAUL II, Encyclical Letter *Redemptor hominis*, 1979, No. 16)

INTRODUCTION *

The right to food is one of the principles enshrined in the 1948 *Universal Declaration of Human Rights*.[1]

The 1969 *Declaration on Social Progress and Development* declared the need for "the elimination of hunger and malnutrition and the guarantee of the right to proper nutrition."[2] Likewise, the *Universal Declaration on the Eradication of Hunger and Malnutrition*, adopted in 1974, declared that every person has the inalienable right to be free from hunger and malnutrition for their full development and to preserve their physical and mental capacities.[3] In 1992 the *World Declaration on Nutrition* recognized that access to suitable, wholesome and safe food is a universal right.[4]

These words leave no room for doubt. The public conscience has spoken out unambiguously. Yet, millions of people are still marked by the ravages of hunger and malnutrition or the consequences of food insecurity. Is this due to a lack of food? Not at all! It is generally acknowledged that the resources of the planet, taken as a whole, are sufficient to feed everyone

---

[1] Cf. UNITED NATIONS (U.N.), *Universal Declaration of Human Rights*, adopted and proclaimed by the U.N. General Assembly in Resolution 217 A (III) on 10 December 1948, art 25 § 1.

[2] UNITED NATIONS, *Declaration on Social Progress and Development*, proclaimed by the U.N. General Assembly in Resolution 2542 (XXIV) on 11 December 1969, Part II, art. 10b.

[3] UNITED NATIONS, *World Food Conference*, Rome, 16 November 1974, No. 1.

[4] FOOD AND AGRICULTURE ORGANIZATION OF THE UNITED NATIONS (FAO) AND WORLD HEALTH ORGANIZATION (WHO), *Final Report of the International Conference on Nutrition, World Declaration on Nutrition*, Rome 1992, No. 1.

---

* When drafting this document, particular care has been taken to draw on a wide range of recent studies and research. However, the fact that they are cited in this document does not imply unreserved and full approval by the Holy See.

living on it.[5] Indeed, the per capita availability of food worldwide has even increased by about 18% over the past few years.[6]

The challenge facing the whole of humanity today is certainly economic and technological in character, but it is more specifically an ethical, spiritual and political challenge. The challenge is as much a matter of practical solidarity and authentic development as it is of material advancement.

1. The Church holds that economic, social and political issues cannot be properly approached unless the transcendental dimension of the human being is taken into account. Greek philosophy, which has so thoroughly permeated the western world, took this view: the human being can only discover or pursue truth, goodness and justice using his own faculties if his awareness is enlightened by the Divine. It is precisely the Divine that enables human nature to consider disinterested duty towards others. Christians believe that it is Divine grace which gives human beings the strength needed to act according to their own discernment.[7] Nevertheless, the Church appeals to all men and women of goodwill to accomplish this gigantic task. The Second Vatican Council stated that: "Since there are so many people prostrate with hunger in the world, this sacred Council urges all, both individuals and governments, to remember the aphorism of the Fathers, 'Feed the man dying of hunger, because if you have not fed him, you have killed him.'"[8] Such a solemn warning urges everyone to be firmly committed to combating hunger.

---

[5] Cf. *ibid.*, No. 1 Cf. *also* FAO, *Dimensions of Need: An Atlas of Food and Agriculture*, Rome 1995, p. 16: "In the world as a whole, an average of about 2700 calories of food is available per person per day, enough to meet everyone's energy requirements. But food is neither produced nor distributed equally. Some countries produce more food than others, while distribution systems and family incomes determine access to food."

[6] Cf. FAO, *World Agriculture: Towards 2010*, Rome 1993, p. 1.

[7] Cf. SECOND VATICAN ECUMENICAL COUNCIL, Pastoral Constitution *Gaudium et spes* (1965), No. 40: "...the Church...goes forward together with humanity and experiences the same earthly lot which the world does. She serves as a leaven and as a kind of soul for human society as it is to be renewed in Christ and transformed into God's family. That the earthly and the heavenly city penetrate each other is a fact accessible to faith alone... ."

[8] SECOND VATICAN ECUMENICAL COUNCIL, Pastoral Constitution *Gaudium et spes* (1965), No. 69.

2.   The urgent nature of this problem has prompted the Pontifical Council "Cor Unum" to offer some findings of its own research. It is duty-bound to appeal to individual and collective responsibility for ensuring that more effective solutions are adopted. The Council supports all those who are already earnestly dedicated to this noble pursuit.

This document attempts to provide a global, but not exhaustive, analysis and description of the causes and consequences of world hunger. It is specifically based on the Gospel and the Church's social teaching. It does not set out primarily to take stock of the present economic situation. The document, therefore, will not concentrate on the statistics relevant to the present situation, nor the numbers of people threatened with death by starvation, nor the percentage of the under-nourished, nor the most at-risk regions, nor the economic measures needed to stave off the threat. Drawing its inspiration from the Church's pastoral mission, the purpose of this document is to send out a pressing appeal to her members and to all humanity. "The Church is an 'expert in humanity,' and this leads her necessarily to extend her religious mission to the various fields in which men and women expend their efforts in search of the always relative happiness which is possible in this world."[9] Today, the Church again takes up the provocative appeal that God made to Cain, asking him to account for the life of his brother Abel: "What have you done? The voice of your brother's blood is crying to me from the ground..." (*Gen* 4:10). It is certainly not an unfair or aggressive exaggeration to apply these forbidding, almost unbearable, words to the plight of our contemporaries who today are starving to death. These words spell out a priority and are intended to touch our consciences.

It would be an illusion to expect any ready-made solutions. The issue which needs to be faced depends on economic policies of those who lead and manage, but also of producers and consumers. Further, it is deeply rooted in our own lifestyles. Thus, this appeal makes demands upon everyone, and we are hopeful that a decisive improvement can be brought about as a result of human relations that are increasingly based on solidarity.

3.   This document is addressed to Catholics throughout the world, and to national and international leaders who have the power and the responsibility to take action in this sphere. But, it is also addressed to all humanitarian organizations and to all men and women of goodwill. Its specific purpose is to give encouragement to the thousands of people, in all

---

[9] JOHN PAUL II, Encyclical Letter *Sollicitudo rei socialis* (1987), No. 41: *AAS* 80 (1988), p. 570.

walks of life and occupations, who daily strive to ensure that all peoples are given the same right "to be seated at the table of the common banquet."[10]

---

[10] JOHN PAUL II, Encyclical Letter *Sollicitudo rei socialis* (1987): *AAS* 80 (1988), p. 558. Cf. *also* PAUL VI, Encyclical Letter *Populorum progressio* (1967), No. 47: *AAS* 59 (1967), p. 280.

I

THE REALITY OF HUNGER

The challenge of hunger

4. Our planet should be able to feed everyone adequately.[11] Before taking up the challenge of hunger, the many facets and the real causes of hunger must be examined. However, there is no exact understanding of all the situations of hunger and malnutrition that exist in the world. Several major causes have nevertheless been identified. We shall begin by setting out the reasons for this approach, before moving on to examine the main causes of this scourge.

A scandal that has lasted too long: hunger destroys life

5. Hunger must not be confused with malnutrition. Hunger threatens not only people's lives but also their dignity. A serious and protracted lack of food breaks down the organism, generating apathy, a loss of a social sense, and indifference or even cruelty towards those who are weaker — particularly children and the elderly. Whole groups of people are then condemned to waste away to death. Throughout history this tragedy has been played out over and over again. But, today people are more scandalised by starvation than was the case in the past.

Until the nineteenth century, famines which decimated whole populations were more often the work of nature. Today they may be not so vast, but in most cases are man-made. One need only cite a few regions or countries to be convinced: Ethiopia, Cambodia, the former Yugoslavia, Rwanda, Haiti, etc. At a time when humanity is better equipped than ever before to deal with hunger, such situations are a veritable dishonour to humanity.

Malnutrition jeopardises the present and the future of a population

6. The great efforts that are now being deployed have brought some benefits, but the fact remains that malnutrition is more widespread than

---

[11] Cf. FAO, *Dimensions of Need: An Atlas of Food and Agriculture*, Rome 1995, p. 16. Cf. *also* Footnote No. 4.

hunger, and takes widely different forms. A person can be malnourished without being hungry. Yet the organism's physical, intellectual and social potential is impaired just the same.[12] Malnutrition may be due to food quality, or a poorly balanced diet (by excess or lack of). Often it is also due to not having enough to eat and becomes acute when there is a shortage of available food. Some call this de-nutrition or under-nutrition.[13] Malnutrition encourages the dissemination of some infectious and endemic diseases and aggravates their consequences. Further, it increases mortality rates, particularly among children under five years of age.

Chief victims: the most vulnerable populations

7. The poor are the chief victims of malnutrition and hunger in the world. The fact of being poor almost invariably means falling more easily prey to the many hazards that threaten survival, and being less resistant to physical sickness. Since the Eighties poverty has grown increasingly more serious and is threatening ever larger numbers of people in most parts of the world. Within a poor population, the first victims are always the weakest individuals: children, pregnant women, nursing mothers, the sick and the elderly. There are also other vulnerable groups that run a very high risk of malnutrition: refugees and displaced persons, as well as victims of political turmoil.

But it is in the 42 Least Developed Countries (LDCs) — of which 28

---

[12] Cf. A. BERG, *Malnutrition: What can be done? Lesson from World Bank Experience*, The John Hopkins University Press for the World Bank, Baltimore, Maryland 1987.

[13] According to FAO and WHO surveys, the minimum daily calorie intake should be about 2,100, while daily food availability should be 1.55 times the basic metabolism rate. Below these levels, a person may be considered to be suffering from chronic under-nutrition (cf. FAO and WHO, *International Conference on Nutrition, Nutrition and Development: A Global Assessment*, Rome 1992). There are still about 800 million people in the world who are under-fed. An adult requires an average daily intake of about 2,500 calories. However, people living in industrial countries have about 800 calories a day in excess of their requirements, while the developing countries have to be content with only two-thirds of this ration (cf. *Le Sud dans votre assiette. L'interdépendance alimentaire mondiale*, CRDI, Ottawa 1992, p. 26).

are in Africa alone — that hunger is most severe.[14] "About 700 million people in developing countries — 20% of their population — still do not have access to enough food to meet their basic daily needs for nutritional well-being."[15]

Hunger generates hunger

8. In the developing countries, it is commonplace for populations whose livelihood depends on low-yielding subsistence agriculture, to suffer from hunger during the interval between two harvests. When earlier harvests have also been insufficient, food shortages can occur and give rise to an acute phase of malnutrition. This weakens the population physically, placing them at risk just when all their energy is required to prepare for the next harvest. Food shortages place the future of these people in jeopardy since they eat crop seeds, plunder natural resources, and accelerate soil erosion, degradation or desertification on their lands.

In addition to the distinction between hunger (or famine) and malnutrition, there is a third type of situation — food insecurity — which leads to famine or malnutrition by making it impossible to plan and implement any long-term measures to foster and attain sustainable development.[16]

Causes that may be remedied

9. Climatic factors and disasters of all kinds, however consequential, are

---

[14] Cf. UNITED NATIONS CONFERENCE ON TRADE AND DEVELOPMENT (UNCTAD), Preparatory document for the *Second United Nations Conference on the Less Developed Countries*, Paris 1990.

[15] FAO and WHO, *Final Report of the International Nutrition Conference, World Declaration on Nutrition*, Rome 1992, No. 2.

[16] Cf. WORLD BANK, *Poverty and Hunger*, 1986. This document describes the degrees of food insecurity (transitory or chronic), as well as the underlying economic causes of such situations and the means of remedying them in the medium and longer term. It is a useful distinction to draw, but its weakness is that it does not immediately reflect correlations between different causes, which could more clearly bring out their comparative importance, for some causes are themselves the effects of more deep-seated causes. Sustainability originally meant development that was compatible with respect for the physical environment. Today the concept also implies the permanency of development.

far from being the sole causes of hunger and malnutrition. In order to deal effectively with the problem of hunger and all its causes, whether contingent or permanent, the linkages between them should be considered. We will now examine the main causes, grouping them into the usual categories: economic, socio-cultural and political.

A) ECONOMIC CAUSES

Root causes

10. The primary cause of hunger is poverty. Food security essentially depends upon an individual's purchasing power and not the physical availability of food.[17] Hunger exists in every country. It has resurfaced in European countries, west and east alike, and is very widespread in countries that are insufficiently and incorrectly developed. However, the history of the 20th century shows that economic poverty is not an inevitability. Many countries have taken off economically and are continuing to do so at this very moment. At the same time still others are foundering after falling prey to national or international policies based on false premisses.

Hunger stems simultaneously from *inter alia*:

a) non-optimum economic policies in every country since unsound policies implemented in the developed countries indirectly, but strongly, affect all the economically poor people in every country;

b) structures and customs that are ineffective or which are tantly destructive of national wealth:
— at the domestic level in mis-developing countries[18] — the large public or private organisations enjoying monopoly status (which is sometimes inevitable) often hamper development instead of fostering it as demonstrated by the adjustments undertaken in many countries over the past ten years;
— at the domestic level in developed countries —

---

[17] Cf. WORLD BANK, *Poverty and Hunger*, 1986.

[18] The term "mis-developing countries," which covers a wider sphere than the economy alone, is applied to countries whose economic and social development exacts an excessively high toll in terms of human suffering and financial resources, as well as the destruction of the expertise, well-tried practices and assets acquired throughout the centuries.

shortcomings are less noticeable at the international level, but are no less damaging, directly or indirectly, to all the world's deprived;
— at the international level — constraints on trade and economic incentives are often ill-conceived;

c) morally reprehensible conduct such as the craving for money, power and a public image, as ends in themselves, is evidenced by a diminished sense of public service for the sole benefit of individuals or worthy groups; this is accompanied by a high level of corruption in a variety of different forms, from which no country may fairly claim to be exempt.

All this reveals the contingent nature of human activities. For despite the best intentions, mistakes are often committed, creating unstable situations. Pointing them out is one means of setting about to resolve them. Economic development has to be cultivated with institutions and individuals sharing in the responsibility for this. The most effective role that the State can play is the one set out in the Church's social teaching and found in the analyses of the Church's social encyclicals.

The root cause of non-development or mis-development is the lack of will and ability to freely serve humanity, by and for each human being, which is a fruit of love. This is something that runs throughout this entire complex situation: at every level of technology in the broad sense of the term, in structures, legislation and in moral conduct. It is manifested in the design and performance of acts and instruments whose economic scope may be either broad or narrow.

The lack of skills, structures which are no longer capable of serving cost-effectively, individual moral deviance and the absence of love are the causes of hunger. Shortcomings in terms of any one of these points, anywhere in the world, inevitably lead to a further reduction in the share rightfully due to the hungry.

Recent economic and financial developments throughout the world are an illustration of these complex phenomena. Technology and morality are closely implicated in them and determine economic performance. This leads us to the question of the debt crisis in the majority of the mis-developing countries along with the adjustment measures that have been, or are about to be, implemented.

Debt of the mis-developing countries

11. The unilateral massive rise in oil prices that occurred in 1973 and

1979 had far-reaching percussions on the non-oil producing countries. The releasing of massive volumes of liquid funds, that the banking system endeavoured to recycle, caused a general economic slow-down, as a result of which the poor countries suffered considerably. For a variety of reasons, during the Seventies and Eighties most countries were able to borrow heavily at variable rates of interest and the countries of Latin America and Africa were able to develop their public sector to an exceptional degree. This period of easy money led to many excesses: unnecessary projects which were poorly designed or badly implemented, the wholesale destruction of traditional economies, and the spread of corruption in every country. Some countries in Asia managed to avoid these mistakes and were able to develop very rapidly.

Soaring interest rates — caused by the mere interplay of unbridled and probably uncontrollable market forces — placed most of Latin America and Africa in a position of having to withhold debt repayments. This caused a flight of capital abroad, which in the short-term, posed a threat to the local social fabric, in many cases already mediocre and vulnerable, and also threatened the very existence of the banking system. That made it possible to gauge the extent of the damage caused in every sphere: economic, structural and moral. Purely technical and organizational solutions were initially sought. But such measures, which are necessary when sound, need to be supported by a thorough overhaul of behaviour on the part of everyone, particularly people who, in every country and at all levels, are able to evade the enormous constraints which poverty imposes on decisions regarding their lives.

At the beginning of the adjustment period, transfers became negative: loans were blocked; oil prices were artificially pegged at unsustainable levels for developing countries; raw material prices slumped as a result of the economic slow-down due to the high price of oil compounded by the debt crisis itself. Added to this was the excessively slow reaction evidenced on the part of international organizations, except for the International Monetary Fund, to re-inject liquidity into the system. During all this time, living standards in the over-indebted countries began to fall.

This demonstrates the knowledge required to manage money, and not merely technical and economic know-how. The release of such huge volumes of liquid funds created considerable structural and personal damage instead of leading to any spectacular worldwide improvement in the plight of the most deprived.

There is a conclusion to be drawn from this: human advancement depends on the human being's capacity to practice altruism, love in other words, which has extremely important practical implications. In succinct and realistic terms, love is not a luxury. It is a condition for the survival of a very large number of human beings.

Structural adjustment programmes

12.   The violence of the monetary phenomena has forced many countries to adopt very stringent measures to tackle the crises and restore the balance in key areas. By their very nature, these measures considerably reduce a country's average purchasing power.

Enormous difficulties and sufferings are caused by these economic crises, even though once they are resolved they eventually make it possible to rebuild a better life.

The crises highlight the country's weaknesses which may be inherent or acquired, including those originating from the development errors committed by successive governments, their partners or even by the international community. These weaknesses are manifold, and sometimes only become evident *a posteriori*. Others are the result of a country's independence policies, because what constituted the strength of the former colonial power may constitute the weakness of the independent country, without the emergence of any means of compensation for them. Then there is the major role played by large-scale projects. These mark out moments of truth, where the need for solidarity is strongly felt in every country. But in reality, the prime effect of these readjustment policies is a reduction in overall expenditure, and hence a decline in incomes. The economically poor in the country are faced with a single alternative: either to place their trust in successive governments, or seek to get rid of them. They themselves often fall victim to ambitious groups seeking power through ideology or out of greed, ignoring all the rules of democracy, and where necessary calling on support from outside forces.

Economic reforms demand great political decision-making skills on the part of governments. This is one of the criteria by which to gauge the quality of their work. Not only must the stabilisation plan be technically successful, it must be able to keep the support of the majority of the people, including the most deprived. This demands the ability to convince the other sectors of society to bear a real part of the burden. These constitute only a small circle of persons and are made-up of those with incomes of international standards and civil servants, who in the past enjoyed standards that were enviable in their country and who could find themselves with severely reduced resources, or even poverty-stricken, from one day to the next. It is here that traditional solidarity comes into play, with the poor always willing to support the members of their family who have fallen back into a state of want from which they believed they had emerged forever.

Concern to protect the very poorest people in these readjustment processes has only been gradually taken on board by national and international agencies. It took several years for the concept of concomitant operations, targeted at the most vulnerable groups, to become widely accepted. Furthermore, here as in emergency situations, there is always a risk of applying the brakes too late and too suddenly, with a whiplash effect that might considerably increase the sufferings of those standing at the back of the queue.

Vast projects have been implemented in Africa and in Latin America[19] involving:

— structural adjustment programmes, requiring stringent macro-economic measures;
— substantial new borrowing;
— far-reaching structural reforms to overcome local inadequacies partly due to the existence of State monopolies which consume a substantial share of national income without providing an adequate quality of service for the benefit of everyone. In many of these countries all the public services have suffered, and with weeds often growing among the good wheat, even efficient sectors have been adversely affected as well.[20]

Some governments, which are often little known on the international scene, have acted admirably. They have found the political courage to adopt unavoidable measures, while at the same time taking into account external pressure and opinion, setting a fine example to increase cooperation and solidarity in their countries, and avoiding any backlash. It should be noted that the influence that the example of a leader has depends not only on his know-how and governance skills, but also his capacity to curtail social

---

[19] As a general result of better policies and better implementation, Asia's performance has been more effective overall even though the quality of interpersonal relations cannot be said to have improved, or corruption reduced.

[20] Cutbacks have had to be made in education in some countries. It should be remembered that in many of the countries struggling for development, one of the recurrent problems that international institutions must address in their dialogue with the leadership, is the leaders' tendency to favour higher education at the expense of primary education.

injustice, which is always present in such situations.

The developed countries must seriously ask themselves the following question: is their attitude, and even their preferences regarding the mis-developing countries, based on the social, technical and political performance of their leadership, or is their support determined by other standards?

B) SOCIO-CULTURAL CAUSES

The social situation

13. Certain socio-cultural factors have been shown to increase the risks of famine and chronic malnutrition. Food taboos, the social and family status of women — their real influence within the family, the lack of training for mothers in feeding and nutrition techniques, widespread illiteracy, and insecurity regarding work and unemployment are some of the factors that can accumulate and cause malnutrition as well as dire poverty. Let us keep in mind that not even the developed countries themselves are immune to this scourge. The same factors create occasional or chronic malnutrition on the part of many of the "new poor" just as they are beginning to catch up with the others who live in affluence and over-consumption.

Demography

14. Ten thousand years ago, the world probably had a population of five million. In the 17th century, with the dawning of the modern age, it had reached five hundred million. Then the demographic growth rate began to rise more steeply: to one billion by the beginning of the 19th century, 1.65 billion at the beginning of the 20th, 3 billion in 1964, 4 billion in 1975, 5.2 billion in 1990, 5.5 billion in 1993, and 5.6 billion in 1994.[21] For a time, the demographic situation developed differently between the "affluent" and the "developing" countries.[22] This situation is still evolving. Let us not forget

---

[21] Cf. UNITED NATIONS POPULATION FUND (UNFPA), *The State of World Population 1993*, New York 1993. Cf. *also* UNITED NATIONS, *World Population Prospects: the 1992 Revision*, New York 1993. Cf. *also* UNFPA, *The State of World Population 1994, Choices and Responsibilities*, New York 1994.

[22] UNITED NATIONS DEVELOPMENT PROGRAMME (UNDP), *World Human Development Report 1990*, Oxford University Press, New York 1990. Cf. *ibid*, p.

that proliferation is a reaction by nature — and consequently by the human being — to threats to the survival of the species.

Research has shown that as peoples and nations become more affluent, high birth rates and high death rates are reversed to low birth rates and low death rates.[23] The transition period may be critical in terms of food resources, because the death rate falls before the birth rate. Technological changes must accompany population growth, otherwise the regular agricultural production cycle is broken due to the depletion of the soils, the reduction of fallow periods and the lack of crop rotation.

The implications

15. Is rapid population growth a cause or a consequence of under-development? Except in extreme cases, population density cannot account for hunger. Let us look first at the following facts. It was in the over-populated deltas and valleys of Asia that the "green revolution" agricultural innovations were first applied. Yet, countries with small populations, like Zaire or Zambia which could have fed a population 20 times the size of their own without requiring any major irrigation schemes, are still short of food. The reason lies in the skewed measures imposed by governments and in economic management and policies, not in any objective causes or economic poverty. Today it is said that there is a greater chance of reducing excessive demographic growth by trying to reduce mass poverty than there is of combating poverty merely by reducing the population growth rate.[24]

The demographic situation will only evolve slowly so long as families

---

94. In the developing countries, where the majority of people suffering from hunger live, the rural population has more than doubled and the urban population has tripled or even quadrupled in the space of thirty years (between 1950 and 1980).

[23] Cf. F. BÖCKLE, et al., *Armut and Bevolkerungs-entwicklung in der Dritten Welt*, Herausgegeben von der Wissenschaftlichen Arbeitsgruppe für weltkirchliche Aufgaben der Deutschen Bischofskonferenz, Bonn 1991. Cf. also *Poverty and Demographic Growth in the Third World*, published by the Scientific Working Party for Universal Church Issues of the German Bishops' Conference, Bonn 1991.

[24] Cf. PONTIFICAL ACADEMY OF SCIENCES, *Population and Resources. Report*, Vatican City 1993 (The Statistics given in this report have since changed).

in the developing countries believe that their production capacity and their security can only be guaranteed by having a large number of children. It should once again be reiterated that it is generally economic and social changes[25] that enable parents to accept the gift of a child. In this area, developments depend to a very large extent on the parents' socio-cultural background. Thought should therefore be given to educating couples in responsible planning of family size and the spacing of births in full respect for moral and ethical principles and in harmony with the true nature of the human being.[26]

C) POLITICAL CAUSES

The influence of politics

16. Depriving people of food has been used throughout history, and is still used today, as a political or military weapon. In some cases this is a veritable crime against humanity.

Yet there have been many such cases in the 20th century, such as:

---

[25] Cf. PONTIFICAL COUNCIL FOR THE FAMILY, *Ethical and Pastoral Dimensions of Population Trends*, Vatican City 1994. Cf. *Le contrôle des naissances dans les pays du Sud: promotion des droits des femmes ou des intérêts du Nord*, "Inter-Mondes," vol. 7, October 1991, No. 1, p. 7: In many areas of the world, research has shown, that in addition to birth control there are three other factors which also contribute to reducing world population growth. One is economic and social development, another is improving the living conditions of women and, paradoxically, reducing infant mortality. Cf. also UNITED NATIONS CHILDREN'S FUND (UNICEF), *The Situation of Children in the World*, Geneva 1991.

[26] JOHN PAUL II, *Address* to the delegates attending the Week of Study on "Population and Resources" organised by the Pontifical Academy of Sciences, 22 November 1991, Nos 4 and 6: "The Church is aware of the complexity of the problem... The urgency of the situation must not lead into error in proposing ways of intervening. To apply methods which are not in accord with the true nature of man actually ends up by causing tragic harm... and can risk placing the heaviest burden on the poorest and weakest sectors of society, thus adding injustice to injustice": *AAS* 84 (1992), pp. 1120-1122. Cf. also ANGELO CARDINAL SODANO, *Address* to the United Nations Conference on Environment and Development (UNCED), Rio de Janeiro, 3-14 June 1992, *L'Osservatore Romano*, 15-16 June 1992.

a) Stalin's systematic withholding of food from the Ukrainian peasants around 1930, causing the deaths of some 8 million people. This crime, which remained unknown, or almost, for a long time, was confirmed with the opening up of the Kremlin archives.

b) The recent sieges in Bosnia, particularly of Sarajevo, when even humanitarian aid itself was held hostage.

c) The resettlement of whole populations in Ethiopia to enable the one-party government to gain political control. Hundreds of thousands of people died as a result of the famine caused by forced migration and by abandoning the crops.

d) The cutting off of food to Biafra in the Seventies was used as a weapon against political secession.

The collapse of the Soviet Union has helped to remove one of the causes of civil wars, the provocation by direct Soviet intervention, or reaction to its intervention including: revolutions resolving nothing, displaced populations, the breakdown of organised agriculture, tribal strife and genocide. However many situations still remain, or have re-emerged, which could give rise to the same phenomena once again. Even though possibly not on the same scale, these are no less damaging to the people. Today's situations are mainly a matter of resurgent nationalism being fostered by a few ideologically driven regimes, local repercussions of struggles for influence between the developed countries, and power struggles in certain countries, especially in Africa.

Also noteworthy are the embargoes, imposed for political reasons, against countries such as Cuba or Iraq. These are regimes, deemed to be a threat to international security, which keep their own people hostage. Indeed, it is the people themselves who are the first to fall victim to such acts of force. This is why the costs, in humanitarian terms, of such decisions must be carefully taken into account. Furthermore, some leaders play on the misery of their people, brought about by their actions, in order to force the international community to resume supplies. These are situations that have to be dealt with on a case-by-case basis in the spirit of the *World Declaration on Nutrition* which states that "Food aid must not be denied because of political affiliation, geographic location, gender, age, ethnic, tribal or religious identity."[27]

---

[27] Cf. FAO and WHO, *Final Report of the International Conference on Nutrition, World Declaration on Nutrition*, Rome 1992, No. 15.

Lastly, political actions can also have repercussions in terms of hunger. On a number of occasions we have seen developed countries, with agricultural surpluses, exporting these surpluses (for example wheat) free of cost to mis-developing countries whose staple diet is rice. The purpose is to underpin domestic commodity prices. These free exports have had very negative effects, altering the people's eating habits and discouraging the local farmers, who need to be strongly encouraged to produce more.

Concentration of resources

17. Economic disparities within the mis-developing countries are greater than those that exist in developed countries, or even between the countries themselves. Wealth and power are highly concentrated in a restricted but complex section of society that is in contact with the international arena and is able to control the State apparatus, which is itself full of shortcomings. This holds up all chance of improvement, and even causes economic and social decline. Differences in living standards not only give rise to conflict which can lead to a spiral of violence, but these differences further encourage patronage as the only means of achieving personal self-fulfillment. As a result, all purely economic initiatives are paralysed, while the altruism that exists in all traditional societies is seriously jeopardised. In such situations, the State often has a major part to play, enabling it to encourage the export sector — which is good in itself — but leaving little profit for the local people as a whole.

In other cases, as a result of weakness or political ambition, the authorities set agricultural commodity prices at such low levels that the small farmers actually subsidise the town-dwellers, which encourages rural exodus. The mass media, electronics and advertising also contribute to the population drain from the countryside. Development aid to such countries then becomes a more or less indirect source of encouragement to the governments that pursue these dangerous policies, benefiting as they do from this financial support which is totally illegitimate, because these are policies that fly in the face of the real interests of their people. The industrial countries should ask themselves whether they may unfortunately have been sending out negative signals in this regard over so many years.

Economic and social de-structuring

18. Economic and social de-structuring stems both from bad economic policies as well as national and international political pressure (cf. § Nos. 11-13 and 17). Here are a few of the most frequently found and most

harmful examples of this:

a) National policies, which artificially lower agricultural commodity prices to the detriment of local food producers, under pressure from the deprived town dwellers who are seen as a potential threat to the political stability of the country. This situation became widespread in Africa during 1975-85 and caused local output to slump. Many countries with a substantial agricultural potential, such as Zaire and Zambia, became net food importers for the first time.

b) Most industrial countries pursue a policy which widely protects their own agriculture and encourages overproduction which is exported at prices lower than the domestic level (the price of dumping). Without such protection world prices would be higher, benefiting other producing countries. The beneficiaries of such protection in Europe are currently enjoying an unfair advantage after years of receiving production incentives which have led to serious de-structuring of the whole agricultural system. Although this policy is supported by local public opinion at large, it may be basically contrary to the general interest of world consumers, privileged and poorest alike. In protected countries, this is the expense of protection. In countries without such protection it is the local farmers who, as an essential component of the well-being of any country, are penalised by importation at reduced prices thus lowering the domestic agriculture prices and speeding the demise of the local farmers and their migration to cities.

c) Traditional food crops are often threatened by poorly targeted economic development. For example, traditional commodities are being replaced by industrial agriculture for both export (large volumes of agricultural commodities are earmarked for export and are dependent upon international agricultural markets) and local substitute commodities (for example, sugar-cane in Brazil to produce alcohol for vehicle fuel, in order to reduce oil imports, has caused the migration of large numbers of uprooted peasants).

D) THE EARTH CAN FEED ALL ITS INHABITANTS

The great progress made by humanity

19. Despite the enormous errors mentioned above, it should not be forgotten that no less spectacular progress has been responsible for increasing

the world population from 3 to 5.3 billion over 30 years (1960-1990).[28] In the developing countries, "... life expectancy at birth [has risen] from 46 years in 1960 to 62 years in 1987. They halved the mortality rates for children under five and immunised two-thirds of all one-year-olds against major childhood diseases... The per capita average calorie supply increased by 20 per cent between 1965 and 1985."[29]

Between 1950 and 1980 total world food production doubled and, at the present time, "globally there is enough food for all."[30] The fact that people continue to starve despite this shows that the problem is structural, and that "inequitable access is the main problem."[31] It is a mistake to gauge the actual food consumption of households merely by the statistical parameter of per capita cereals availability. Hunger is not a problem of availability, but of meeting demand. It is an issue of poverty. It should also be noted that the survival of a multitude of individuals is guaranteed by the informal economy; by definition this is undeclared, difficult to quantify and unreliable.

Agri-food markets

20. The world agri-food markets trade in a certain number of commodities which are not always the ones consumed in most of the mis-developing countries.[32] Excessive price fluctuations are against the interests of both producers and consumers. These fluctuations are caused by spontaneous adjustment mechanisms and amplified by specific features of the relevant markets. Attempts to stabilise them have all proven fairly

---

[28] Cf. FAO, *World Agriculture: Towards 2010*, Rome 1993, No. 2 § 13.

[29] UNDP, *World Human Development Report 1990*, Oxford University Press, New York 1990, p. 18.

[30] FAO and WHO, *Final Report of the International Conference on Nutrition, World Declaration on Nutrition*, Rome 1992, No. 1.

[31] *Ibid*.

[32] Argentina is one of the leading wheat and beef exporting countries. It is, therefore, not a mis-developing country. It is an industrialised country whose long-term economic performance used to be disappointing for reasons that were mainly to do with weaknesses in its political system. This situation has improved considerably in recent years, and the economic effects are already evident.

unsatisfactory, if not to say harmful, to producers. Furthermore, the raising of prices is made impossible by the way the markets themselves operate. The small number of international trading corporations prevents price manipulation, and constitutes an impenetrable barrier to any new market entrants. This is always unhealthy. Developing production capacities has much more to do with disseminating advances in production techniques (progress in genetics and implementation). We note that Indonesia's average rice output has risen from 4 to 15 tons per hectare in the space of one generation, far outstripping its already record population growth rate. In most countries where agriculture is making progress, yields are improving to such an extent that output is increasing, sometimes very steeply, despite the sharp decline in the number of farmers.

Modern agriculture

21. Intensive farming is increasingly being accused of damaging the environment and threatening such natural resources as water and land, particularly because of the ill-advised use of fertilisers and plant health products. A preliminary definition of agricultural intensification is the increase in the ratio of intermediate consumption — mainly by industry — to agricultural acreage employed. Agricultural technologies are now becoming independent of the land, which is their natural medium. The reciprocity which formerly linked them is being reduced and replaced by a more hazardous duality between agricultural technology and the economic environment. Agricultural intensification generally requires substantial capital investment. But most of the developing countries still practice subsistence farming, based mainly on human "capital," with limited technical resources and difficulties in finding adequate water supplies. Even though the "green revolution" has been fairly successful, it has not managed to solve the food production problems for a large number of developing countries.

It is certainly possible to predict progress to improve intensive farming, and to limit damage to the environment. But as in the developed countries, other production systems should be used which will better conserve natural resources and ensure widespread ownership of productive land. Crop and livestock farmers' associations, joint management of water supplies, and the creation of cooperatives should be encouraged to move in this direction.

II

ETHICAL CHALLENGES TO BE TAKEN UP BY ALL

Ethical dimension of the problem

22.   In order to make progress with solving the problem of hunger and malnutrition throughout the world, it is indispensable to grasp the ethical nature of the whole issue.

If the cause of hunger is a moral evil, above and beyond all the physical, structural and cultural causes, the challenges are also of a moral nature. This is capable of motivating all men and women of goodwill who believe in the universal values of every culture, particularly Christians who experience the preferential relationship which the Almighty Lord wishes to establish with all men and women without distinction.

This challenge involves acquiring a better understanding of the phenomena, people's capacity for mutual service — which may be done merely through the interplay of well-understood economic forces, and also doing away with corruption of every kind. Apart from all this, the challenge lies above all at the level of freedom for every person to cooperate in the advancement of all human beings and the integral human being in their daily work, namely, by working together to foster the development of the common good.[33] This kind of development involves social justice and the universal destination of the goods of the earth, the practice of solidarity and subsidiarity, peace, and respect for the physical environment. This is the direction that must be taken in order to restore hope and build up a world that is more welcoming to future generations.

In order to make this progress possible, the organic pursuit of the common good must be protected, promoted, and where necessary, reactivated as a central component of the basic motivations in the thinking and work of everyone engaged in politics and the economy, at all levels and in every country.

Personal and institutional motivations are necessary to ensure the

---

[33] Cf. CATECHISM OF THE CATHOLIC CHURCH, Geoffrey Chapman, 1994, § 1906 in which the definition of "common good," based on *Gaudium et spes* (1965), No. 26 § 1, reads "the sum total of social conditions which allow people, either as groups or as individuals, to reach their fulfillment more fully and more easily."

sound operation of society, which includes families. But all people must accept this conversion personally and collectively, so that striving for the common good is not sacrificed to serving their own strictly personal interests, or the interests of their kinsmen, employers, clans or countries, however legitimate all these may be.

The principles which the Church has gradually emphasised in her social teaching, therefore, provide valuable guidance for combating hunger. The pursuit of the common good combines the following:

— the quest for greater efficiency in the management of earthly goods;
— greater respect for social justice, which is possible through the universal destination of goods;
— the skillful and constant practice of subsidiarity, which assures those in power against having the power taken from them, which in reality is a power to serve others;
— the practice of solidarity, which prevents the appropriation of financial resources by the affluent and protects all people from being excluded from social and economic life and deprived of their fundamental dignity.

It is, therefore, the whole of the social teaching of the Church which must imbue the thinking of our leaders in all that is done, whether consciously or otherwise.

This statement might well be greeted with scepticism or even cynicism. Many leaders operate in a harsh, sometimes cruel environment, which gives rise to distress and causes them to proudly seek power for the sake of power and to retain it. Such individuals might perhaps be inclined to consider ethical considerations as handicaps. Yet, our frequent daily experience, in a wide variety of different environments, shows this not to be the case. Only balanced development for the common good will prove authentic and contribute in the long-term to social stability. At every level and in every country, many people are working constantly and discreetly, respectful of the legitimate interests of their fellow beings.

The huge task facing Christians everywhere is to foster conduct of this kind. Like a small amount of yeast in very hard dough, they are called by a close adhesion to the love which Our Lord has for all people: a love experienced in the very depths of one's being.

This exciting task is to set an example at every level: technical, organizational, moral and spiritual. It involves mutual assistance at every level of responsibility, which includes all those who are not "excluded" by their own social conditions.

Love of our neighbour in order to achieve development

23. Striving in this way for the common good must necessarily be underpinned by concern for and love of humanity. In the most varied situations, people are faced daily with the alternative between personal and collective self-destruction or love for our neighbour. Love for our neighbour therefore demonstrates our awareness that there is a responsibility from which one cannot shrink when faced with our own limitations, or with the enormous magnitude of the duties to be performed out of love for all men and women. "How would history judge a generation which had all the means to feed the population of the planet, and yet with fratricidal indifference refused to do so?... Would a world in which poverty fails to encounter lifegiving love not be a desert?"[34]

Love is far more than mere giving. Development is cultivated through the work of those who have the greatest courage, the greatest competence and honesty. These leaders feel solidarity with all humanity and humanity is affected, to a greater or lesser degree, whether near or far, by what these individuals do or should be doing. This concrete universal responsibility is an essential manifestation of altruism.

Solidarity is obviously a demand that is placed on all. Fortunately, it is not necessary to wait for the majority of humanity to be converted to love of their neighbour in order to gather the fruits of the work of those acting in their own particular situation without waiting. Hope must be drawn from the results of the work of such persons who, in their daily work at all levels, act in the service of the integral human being and of all humanity.

Social justice and the universal destination of goods

24. At the very heart of social justice lies the principle of the universal and common destination of the goods of the earth. Pope John Paul II has expressed it in the following words: "God gave the earth to the whole human race for the sustenance of all its members, without excluding or favouring

---

[34] JOHN PAUL II, *Address* at the Headquarters of West African Economic Community (CEAO), Ouagadougou, 29 January 1990: *AAS* 82 (1990), p. 818.

anyone."[35]   This constant affirmation in the Christian tradition is not sufficiently reiterated, even though it is evidently of relevance to the whole of humanity, irrespective of creed. This axiom is a necessary foundation on which to build a society based on justice, peace and solidarity.   For, generation after generation, we must see ourselves as the temporary stewards of the resources of the earth and the production system. In consideration of the purposes of creation, the right to property is not absolute. It is one of the expressions of the dignity of each person. However, only if it is ordered to the common good and when it assists the advancement of all is it just. This is exercised and recognised in different ways in different cultures.

Costly abuse of the common good: the "structures of sin"

25.   Ignorance of the common good goes hand in hand with the exclusive and sometimes excessive pursuit of particular goods such as money, power or reputation, when viewed as absolutes to be sought for their own sakes: namely as idols. This is what created the "structures of sin,"[36] all those places and circumstances in which habits are perverse and which demand proof of heroism on the part of all new arrivals if one is to avoid acquiring such habits.

The "structures of sin" are numerous and vary in scope. Some are worldwide, for example the mechanisms and the conduct which creates hunger. Others are on a much smaller scale but equally capable of creating imbalances thus making it more difficult to do good to the people affected by them. These "structures" always generate high costs in human terms and are the places in which the common good is destroyed.

Their costly and degrading effects in economic terms, are less often

---

[35] JOHN PAUL II, Encyclical Letter *Centesimus annus* (1991), No. 31: *AAS* 83 (1991), p. 831.

[36] Cf. JOHN PAUL II, Apostolic Exhortation *Reconciliatio et paenitentia* (1984), No. 16: *AAS* 77 (1985), pp. 213-217 (referring to social sin producing social evils), the Encyclical Letter *Sollicitudo rei socialis* (1987), Nos. 36-37: *AAS* 80 (1988), pp. 561-564, and the Encyclical Letter *Centesimus annus* (1991), No. 38: *AAS* 83 (1991), p. 841. These documents also use expressions such as "situations of sin" or "social sins" but always giving the cause of these sins as egotism, the search for profit or the lust for power.

commented upon. One could cite a number of striking examples of this.[37] Development is not only hampered by ignorance and incompetence. There are also many large-scale "structures of sin" which deliberately steer the goods of the earth away from their true purpose, that of serving the good of all, toward private and sterile ends in a process which spreads contagiously.

It is obvious that the human being cannot subject and dominate the earth effectively while adoring the false gods of money, power and reputation considered to be ends in themselves and not means for serving each man and women and all humanity. Greed, pride and vanity blind those who fall prey to them, eventually preventing them from realising the limitations of their perceptions and the self-destructive nature of their actions.

In view of the universal destination of goods, money, power and reputation must be sought so as to:

a) create the means of production of goods and services which will have a truly useful social purpose and promote the common good;

b) share with the deprived, who embody the need for the common good in the eyes of all men and women of goodwill. The deprived are the living witnesses of the lack of this common good. For Christians, the deprived are indeed the cherished children of God, who comes to visit us through them and in them.

Pursuing these riches as an absolute good in themselves, robs them wholly or partially of utility for the common good. The world economic system is: globally mediocre (in comparison with the peak performances achieved in some countries for quite considerable periods of time) so costly in human terms (when it functions properly and where it does not function at all), paying dearly for bad habits and imposing a veritable moral yoke on people.

---

[37] The manufacture of chemical weapons, which have no positive fallout and are only used to attack or for self-defence, is one example. To appreciate the scale of the problem, 500,000 tons of deadly chemical products, sufficient to wipe out 60 billion men and women, are still stockpiled in the former Soviet Union. The cost of production for these weapons was about US $200 billion, and their cost to destroy will be the same. These are real resources, and are therefore a net loss to the planet. This perverse adventure lowers living standards (mainly, but not solely, in the former USSR) and can even cause hunger in families that would otherwise never have experienced it.

Conversely, as soon as groups of men and women begin working together in order to take due account of the need to serve the whole community, and each individual member of it, remarkable developments can be achieved. People previously deemed rather useless become outstanding for the quality of their services, and a positive effect gradually improves the material, psychological and moral conditions of their lives. This is really the "obverse" of the "structures of sin." One might call them the "structures of the common good" which pave the way to the "civilisation of man."[38] Our experience in such situations gives some idea of what the world might be like if people were more concerned about the common interests and the fate of each man and woman, in all they do and in the exercise of all their responsibilities.

**Giving preference to listening
to the poor and serving them: sharing**

26. If the poor, in the economic sense of the term, bear witness to the lack of concern for the common good, they have something specific to tell us. They have their own opinions and experiences with regard to real daily life about which the better-off know nothing. As John Paul II said in his Encyclical Letter *Centesimus annus* "... it will be necessary above all to abandon a mentality in which the poor — as individuals and as peoples — are considered a burden, as irksome intruders trying to consume what others have produced ... the advancement of the poor constitutes a great opportunity for the moral, cultural and even economic growth of all humanity."[39]

The views of those living in poverty — which are no more accurate or complete than those of the leaders — are though, however, essential to leaders if they desire to ensure long-term work which does not lead to self-destruction. Embarking upon difficult and costly social and economic policies, without taking account of the perception of reality by the most humble members of society, can eventually lead to extremely costly dead-ends for the whole world. This is what has happened in the case of Third World debt. If the lenders and the borrowers had heeded the personal opinions of the poorest people, as one of the essential elements of reality, greater wisdom would have meant greater caution, and in very many

---

[38] Cf. PAUL VI, 1975 Christmas *Homily* for the end of the Holy Year: *AAS* 68 (1976), p. 145. This concept was used for the first time by Pope Paul VI.

[39] JOHN PAUL II, Encyclical Letter *Centesimus annus* (1991), No. 28: *AAS* 83 (1991), p. 828.

countries the adventure would not have turned out so badly, or it may have turned out well.

Considering the complexity of the problems to be solved, or rather the complexity of living conditions to be improved, giving preference to heeding the poor will prevent us from falling into the slavery of short-term perspective, technocracy, bureaucracy, ideology, or idolatry regarding the role of the State or the role of the market. Each of these has its essential usefulness, but only as a means and never as an absolute end.

Intermediate entities have the main function of ensuring that the voices of those living in poverty are heard and of collecting their views, needs and desires. But these entities are often quite inadequate for the task, suffering either from the fact of occupying a monopolistic position which leads them to cultivate their own power, or competing with others who seek to use the poor as a means of acquiring power. The work of the trade unions is therefore particularly necessary, verging on heroism when they strive to perform such an essential function without being destroyed or taken over.[40]

---

[40] Cf. L. SALMEN, *Listen to the People, Participant-Observer Evaluation of Development Projects*, The World Bank and Oxford University Press, 1987. In this connection, one might recall the participating observer method used by one World Bank consultant. Driven on by a deep love for humanity, he did not hesitate to spend periods of between three and six months living in the shanty-towns in South America (in Quito and La Paz in particular) to lead the same life as the local people. This enabled him to routinely advise architects working on urban renewal to ensure that the new constructions were not systematically turned into slums by the new occupiers who had previously lived in hovels. This is what is meant by giving preference to listening to the poor, who in this case are also customers, and it is also sound common sense. But it demands heroism. This method subsequently spread in Thailand, drawing on the world-wide authority of the World Bank to convince the officials in Bangkok to go and spend time living with their own deprived fellow citizens in order to ensure the success of their urban resettlement programmes.

Also noteworthy is the extraordinary work of an English Protestant Minister, Stephen Carr, who spent 20 years living in two African villages, using traditional resources and techniques alone. He acquired a powerful influence in these two places, and on an unscheduled visit to Washington in 1985/86 he was interviewed by the World Bank. What he had to tell them enlightened the World Bank specialists who had come up against one failure after another in the Bank's agricultural projects in Africa. There is a symbiosis between the peasant and his land. The land of Africa is beautiful and rich, but it is also very fragile. New farming practices by the peasants brought about by the contemporary economy and the loss of ancestral beliefs has led to the destruction of the land. Catholic

Under these conditions, sharing becomes genuine cooperation and collaboration in which every person contributes to all what the human community needs. The poorest play their role, which is essential, particularly in view of the fact that in reality they are excluded.[41] This is a paradoxical situation which should not surprise the Christian.

The duty to give every person the same right of access to the indispensable minimum to live on does not stem merely from a moral imperative to share with the poor, which is already a major obligation. The duty is also to reincorporate those living in poverty into the community as a whole, which without them, tends to wither and can eventually be destroyed. People living in poverty do not belong on the sidelines, in a marginalised position. Everything must be done to prevent this. They must be placed at the very centre of our concerns, at the centre of the human family. It is there that the poor can play a unique role within the community.

It is in this perspective that social justice, which is also commutative justice, acquires its full significance. As the basis of every action in the defence of rights, it guarantees social cohesion, peaceful co-existence between nations, but also their common development.

An integrated society

27. The concept of justice rooted in human solidarity, and by that very characteristic requiring the strongest to come to the aid of the weakest, should guide our steps wherever the voice of the poor is heard, working to create a world in which justice, peace and charity are jointly guaranteed.

Societies cannot be properly built up by excluding some of their members. To be consistent, this evidently means that people living in poverty are also entitled to organise themselves so as to better obtain assistance for enabling them to free themselves from poverty.

Peace, a balance of rights

---

missionaries — and perhaps others too — have realised this. The old missions respected the talents and above all the traditional experience of the local people. This has now been rediscovered by a number of NGOs, including the FIDESCO which is based in France and several other European countries.

[41] Cf. the work of FR. JOSEPH WREJINSKY and ATD Fourth World.

28. Lasting peace is not the result of a balance of forces, but of a balance of rights. Peace is not the fruit of the victory of the strongest over the weakest, but fruit of the victory of justice over unjust privileges, of freedom over tyranny, of truth over falsehood within and among peoples,[42] of development over hunger, poverty or humiliation. In order to establish true peace and real international security, it is not sufficient to prevent war and conflict. Development must also be fostered, creating the right conditions to fully guarantee fundamental human rights.[43] In this context, democracy and disarmament become two of the requirements of peace, which is indispensable for all genuine development.

Disarmament, an urgent need to be met

29. Regional conflicts have cost the lives of about seventeen million people in under fifty years. "In the 1980's, world military expenditures grew to unprecedented peacetime level; at an estimated [annual] $1 trillion [one million million], they accounted for roughly 5 per cent of total world income."[44] This demonstrates the importance and the urgent need for all political and economic leaders to ensure that the vast amounts of money earmarked for death, in the northern hemisphere as in the southern hemisphere, should henceforth be earmarked for life. Such an attitude would be the practical implementation of the moral grounds militating in favour of progressive disarmament. Such a course would also provide the opportunity to release substantial financial resources, for the benefit of developing countries, and vital for their authentic progress.[45] One particularly resilient "structure of sin" is the export of weapons. This occurs in quantities which far exceed the lawful self-defence needs of the purchasing countries, or even the use by international traffickers, whose catalogues, produced for the benefit of those who can afford to pay, contain the most highly sophisticated

---

[42] Cf. JOHN XXIII, Encyclical Letter *Pacem in terris* (1963), Chapter III: *AAS* 55 (1963), pp. 279-291.

[43] JOHN PAUL II, *Address* to the FAO Conference to celebrate the 50th Anniversary of the Organisation, 23 October 1995, No. 2; *L'Osservatore Romano*, 23-24 October 1995.

[44] WORLD BANK, *World Development Report 1990*, Washington 1990, p. 19.

[45] Cf. PONTIFICAL COUNCIL "JUSTICE AND PEACE", *The International Arms Trade: An Ethical Reflection,* Vatican City 1994.

weapons. In this field, corruption is rife; but the evil caused is even more deep-seated. Congratulations are due to those governments which, on coming to power after regimes that had formerly committed their countries to purchasing weapons far in excess of their needs, have found the courage to terminate such agreements with the risk of losing goodwill and the support of arms exporting countries.

Respect for the environment

30. At present, nature is teaching all a lesson in solidarity that could easily be forgotten. In the very act of producing food, everyone discovers that they are either active or passive component parts of an ecosystem. A new sphere of responsibility is opening up to people's consciences.

The pretense of pretending to want to provide more food to more people and at the same time weaken agriculture cannot continue. Agriculture seems to be contributing more pollution (with the wholesale use of fertiliser, pesticides and machines) as it reaches the industrial stage, before having developed the capacity to work without polluting. In addition to the other elements necessary in life, the atmosphere, water, soil and the woodlands are all threatened by pollution, over-consumption, man-made desertification and deforestation. In the space of fifty years, half the tropical forests have been cleared, more often than not in the quest for more land or because of short-term policies to intensify farming in order to offset the debt burden. In the poorest regions, desertification is being caused by survival practices that actually are increasing poverty. These include over-grazing as well as felling trees and shrubs for cooking and heating.[46]

Ecology and equitable development

31. It is urgently necessary to manage this planet in an ecologically sustainable manner. From the viewpoint of agri-food production, which is already substantial, there are two elements to be considered. First of all, this sort of environmentally-friendly management will have a cost which will need to be incorporated into economic activity.[47] We should be asking ourselves

---

[46] Cf. FAO, *Sustainable Development and the Environment, FAO Policies and Actions*, Rome 1992.

[47] Cf. JOHN PAUL II, *Address* to the 25th Session of the FAO Conference, 16 November 1989, No. 8: *AAS* 82 (1990), pp. 672-673.

whether it will always be those living in poverty who have to bear this burden to the detriment of their nutrition. Secondly, of concern is the gaining of a better understanding of linkage of ecology and the economy within the current notion of sustainable development. But this objective must not distract from the need to put even greater effort into promoting equitable development. In the end, development cannot be sustainable unless equitable. Otherwise it is likely that the present distortions will be compounded by new ones.

Taking up the challenge together

32. Hunger and malnutrition require specific actions which cannot be separated from that of striving to achieve the integral development and advancement of all human beings and peoples. Faced with the magnitude of this phenomenon, the Catholic Church must increasingly contribute to improving the situation. She is therefore appealing to everyone for their participation, concerted effort and perseverance.

Fortunately, much has already been done by individuals, non-governmental organizations, government authorities and international organizations to combat hunger. We would merely recall the Freedom From Hunger campaign and other initiatives in which Christians readily take part.

Acknowledging the contribution of the poor to democracy

33. There is little appreciation of how dynamic the poor really are. To remedy this, a great many attitudes and practices — economic, social, cultural and political — have to be changed. When people living in poverty are excluded from taking part in drafting projects of relevance to them, history has demonstrated that, overall, little benefit is derived from such projects. The solidarity of the human community must be built up. It will not be possible to learn to share our daily bread unless it is agreed to re-direct our consciences and work throughout the whole of society.[48] Such attitudes lead

---

[48] Cf. *The Papal Writs (Chirographs)* establishing the two Pontifical Foundations, "John Paul II for the Sahel" on 22 February 1984, and the "Populorum Progressio" Foundation on 13 February 1992. Both foundations have their headquarters at the Pontifical Council "Cor Unum," Vatican City State. The headquarters of the Board of Directors of the "John Paul II for the Sahel" Foundation is in Ouagadougou (Burkina Faso) and the "Populorum Progressio" Foundation has its headquarters in Santafé de Bogotá (Colombia).

to genuine democracy.

Democracy is generally acknowledged to be essential to human development because it enables everyone to play a responsible part in the governance of society. Moreover, the two go together and the weakness of one can jeopardise the other. If the principle of equality yields to force, the place of the poor in society may be reduced to the bare minimum. A democracy is judged in terms of the way it manages to dovetail freedom and solidarity, radically distancing itself from absolute liberalism or other doctrines that deny the sense of freedom or which act as stumbling blocks to genuine solidarity.[49]

Community initiatives

34. Faced with misery and poverty, more people and groups are increasingly choosing to take part in community action everywhere. These initiatives must be strongly encouraged. At the present time, more countries are increasingly supporting people's participation. But, in some places attempts are still being made to thwart these initiatives, where they are a source of irritation — sometimes with very dire consequences — even though they are the indispensable foundations of genuine development.

The Non-Governmental Organisations (NGOs) set up locally to undertake development work have encouraged the constitution of a new people-based civil society in many developing countries. These NGOs have devised a wide range of different ways to work together and provide support. Thanks to the impetus given by the people who have paved the way, many of the very poorest people are now able to break free of poverty and improve their plight in terms of hunger and malnutrition.

Over the last few years, Catholic International Associations and New Ecclesial Communities have embarked on initiatives in the socio-economic field. In combating hunger and poverty those groups have been basing their work on the medieval guilds, and above all, the cooperative unions in the 19th century when advocates of the common good created institutions according to the spirit of the Gospel or based on social solidarity. The first person to emphasise the need to create organizations for social advancement was the Quaker P. C. Plockboy († 1695). Other pioneers of notoriety are:

---

[49] Cf. JOHN PAUL II, *Address* to the United Nations General Assembly for the celebration of its 50th Anniversary, 5 October 1995, Nos. 12 and 13; *L'Osservatore Romano*, 6 October 1995.

Félicité Robert de Lamennais (1782-1854), Adolf Kolping († 1856), Robert Owen (1771-1858) and Baron Wilhelm Emmanuel von Ketteler (1811-1877). Today, associations are coming into being to advance the common good of society, and to stave off selfishness, pride and greed which are often the laws that govern community life. These experiences throughout history and the achievements of these new initiatives bode well for the future.[50]

Access to credit

35. "One of the great successes of the NGOs has been to give the poor access to credit."[51] This access by people living in poverty has become a defining practice today, thus enabling an informal subsistence economy to make progress towards the formation of a real grassroots economic fabric. Perhaps it is not yet possible to be able to calculate the Gross National Product (GNP) accurately, but its importance also lies in that which it signifies and heralds. Supporting community initiatives and relying on local partners prevents the persistence of an aid-driven approach, making it possible to gradually lay the foundations for integral development.[52]

Paramount role of women

36. Women play a primary role in combating hunger and fostering development, but their role is not always adequately acknowledged and appreciated. It is important to emphasise the essential role that women play in the survival of whole populations, especially in Africa. Often it is the women who produce the bulk of food for their family. Particularly in the developing countries, they are responsible for providing their family members with a wholesome and balanced diet. However, women become the first victims of decisions taken without their knowledge, such as decisions to abandon particular food crops and local markets of which they are the main operators. Such treatment shows a failure to respect women and hampers

---

[50] To mention some by name: Economia di Comunione/Opera di Maria, the Focolare Movement (Grottaferrata), AVSI/Communion and Liberation (Milan), Fidesco/Emmanuel Community (Paris), "Famille en Mission"/Neocatechumenal Path (Rome), and "Kolping International" (Cologne).

[51] UNDP, *op. cit.*, p. 31. Cf. also Footnote No. 29.

[52] Cf. INTERNATIONAL FUND FOR AGRICULTURAL DEVELOPMENT (IFAD), *The Role of Rural Credit Projects in Reaching the Poor*, Rome-Oxford 1985.

development. Under these conditions, the transition to the market economy and the introduction of technologies can, despite the best intentions, make the drudgery of women even worse.

Malnutrition particularly affects women who are the first to suffer. This has further repercussions on their childbearing and affects the health and education prospects of their young children.

But the purpose of this effort, to highlight the role of women in the fight against hunger and malnutrition and in favour of development, must form part of a more ambitious framework. It should be one designed to enhance the social status of women in the poor countries, by providing them with greater access to health care, vocational training and credit. This will enable women to make their full contribution in increasing production, fostering development, and in the economic and political evolution of their countries.[53]

Progress must, however, ensure that the roles of men and women are preserved, without driving a wedge between them and without feminising men or masculinising women.[54] As the status of women improves, as is hoped, sight should not be lost of the attention women must provide to newly-created and developing life. Some developing countries are setting a positive example by curbing excesses that now occur in the West with regard to altering the sensitivity of women, without shutting women up in their traditional role. In this sphere, the mistakes made in the past must not be repeated by playing down traditional structures to boost western models, which are particularly unsuitable for local situations if adopted without adjustment.

Integrity and a social sense

37.   Lastly, it is absolutely essential to motivate all the parties acting in society and in the economy to favour development policies whose priority objective is to give all people an equal chance to live with dignity, making all the necessary effort and sacrifices to achieve this. However, this is

---

[53] Cf. JOHN PAUL II, *Letter to Women*, 29 June 1995, No. 4: *AAS* 87 (1995), pp. 805-806.

[54] Cf. JOHN PAUL II, Apostolic Exhortation *Mulieris dignitatem* (1988), Nos. 6-7: *AAS* 80 (1988), pp. 1662-1667. Cf. also the Post-Synodal Apostolic Exhortation *Christifideles laici* (1988), No. 50: *AAS* 81 (1989), pp. 489-492.

impossible if those who occupy posts of responsibility fail to give unambiguous signs of their integrity and to demonstrate their sense of the common good. The flight of capital, wasting or misappropriating resources for the benefit of a minority based on kinship, social and ethnic ties or political affiliations are widespread and well-known to the public. Such errant behaviour is frequently denounced. But this does not really encourage those responsible to refrain from these activities, which are damaging to those living in poverty particularly when done on a large scale.[55]

It is often corruption[56] that hampers the reforms needed to pursue the common good and ensure justice, which go hand in hand. Corruption has many causes. Yet, it is always a very serious abuse of the trust placed by society, in those appointed to represent that society, and who exploit this social authority for personal gain. Corruption is one of the constituent elements of many "structures of sin," and the cost to the planet is far superior to the sum total of all the funds embezzled.

---

[55] The magnitude of corruption can be gauged from the amount of "laundered" money as estimated by the authorities responsible for preventing fraud.

[56] Cf. JOHN PAUL II, Encyclical Letter *Sollicitudo rei socialis* (1987), No. 44: *AAS* 80 (1988), pp. 576-577.

III

TOWARDS AN ECONOMY BASED ON GREATER SOLIDARITY

To better serve humanity and all human beings

38. Increased wealth is necessary for development. However, major macroeconomic reforms — which always hold down incomes — can fail when the structural reforms are not undertaken with the necessary political courage and energy. This is true particularly in the public sector when reforming the role of the State, as well as political and social obstacles. These reforms cause suffering which is to no avail, and precipitate yet another reversal. These stringent and sometimes excessively harsh reforms are always accompanied by aid from the international community. But the international community also brings pressure to bear in the political sphere, often at the request of politicians, in order to force the country to face its choices and help the politicians take decisions which the developed countries adopted at the time of post-war reconstruction.

Part of the duty of international institutions is, after consultations with governments, to incorporate into the plans drawn up by governments targeted provisions to relieve the suffering of those who will be most seriously impacted by these necessary measures. It is the duty of international institutions to foster trust and confidence in the national leaders so as to enable the country to qualify for financial support from public and private lenders. International institutions must also bring pressure to bear on the government so that every sector of society can play a part in the joint effort. Otherwise, the government will not be able to move in the direction of the common good and social justice, which are so difficult to safeguard even to a minor degree, under these circumstances.

In order to achieve this, the personnel of international institutions need to work, as they are fortunately accustomed to doing, with technical rigour. But they must also show concern for the people. This concern is something that cannot be inculcated by bureaucratic instructions or by a purely economics-oriented background. This is precisely where giving preference to listening to those living in poverty must be particularly carefully practiced. Specific provisions must be envisaged for this, by joint agreement with the NGOs and Catholic Associations, both of which are in contact with and at the service of the most vulnerable people. One can never emphasise enough the importance of this point. It is essential. Yet national and international leaders easily neglect it because the technical work already gives rise to considerable difficulties.

Generally speaking, all international and national organizations having permanent and on-going contacts with each mis-developing country, must establish personal and unofficial lines of communication between the people in the field serving the population and the technical personnel defining the reform plans. This has to be done in a spirit of mutual trust between people sharing a common service to all humanity and each man and woman, so as to avoid falling prey to economism and ideology.

Channelling the work of all to the same end

39.   The richest countries have a major responsibility in the process of reforming the world economy. In recent times, at least, they have given priority to relations with countries undergoing economic takeoff — that is to say, the true developing countries — and also with countries in Eastern Europe whose development can pose a geographically close threat.

The rich countries have their own economically poor and need to embark on difficult reforms in their own territories. They are, therefore, tempted to relegate the economically poor in the mis-developing countries to a secondary plane. "We are not responsible for the world's poverty," is something that one hears frequently in the globally rich countries.

If such an attitude were to become common, it would be both unworthy and short-sighted. All people, regardless of location, but particularly those who possess economic resources and wield political authority, must constantly allow themselves to be challenged by the poverty of the most deprived so that the interests of those living in poverty are taken into account in decision-making and action. This is an appeal addressed to everyone responsible for decisions affecting the developing countries.

It is also addressed to all, in every country and at the international level, who are *de facto* holding up the possibility of pursuing the common good in order to protect interests which, in themselves, may be wholly legitimate. Protecting these vested interests in such countries may cause hunger to persist in some parts of the world without being able to accurately identify a causal link or even victims. That makes it easy to deny their existence. Other forms of conservatism, at other levels and in other places, can also contribute to these same bottlenecks.

The reform of international trade continues apace and continues to be advocated. It concerns, above all, the poor people in the affluent countries.

This is why it is vital for these priorities not to conceal the plight of people living in poverty in the poor countries, who have virtually no one to speak out for them internationally. They must be given back their central place in international concerns, in common with the other priorities. However, the "poverty eradication" priorities that the World Bank laid down several years ago are extremely welcome.

The leaders of developing countries should not rely on some hypothetical international reform before embarking on reforms in their own countries. Such reforms are often needed, evidently, to foster some degree of economic take-off. This take-off does not depend on any specific recipes, but its requirements demand a bold and unflagging implementation of simple rules. Rules which make it possible for those who are able to take sound initiatives to do so and to retain part of the rewards of the efforts. Further, they prevent persons incapable of drawing on national resources from being rewarded without regard for their own contribution. Nations must realise that they "are primarily responsible, and that they are the principal artisans in the promotion of their own economic development and social progress."[57] As identified earlier, it is the responsibility of governments and institutions dealing with the developing countries, to clearly spell out their preference for responsible and fearless attitudes in the service of the national communities.

Political will of the industrial countries

40. Authorities of globally rich countries must influence public opinion to become sensitive to the plight of the poor, whether near or far. It is also their responsibility to strongly support the work being done by international organizations to deal with these sufferings, helping them to adopt immediate and enduring measures to root out hunger worldwide. This is what the Church has been demanding of everyone with such determination for over a hundred years, insisting that, among other things, the rights of the weakest are protected by the authorities themselves.[58]

In order to sensitise and mobilise the international community, particularly with regard to the ethical dimension of these issues, outspoken references are made in many texts published by such bodies as the Economic

---

[57] JOHN XXIII, Encyclical Letter *Pacem in terris* (1963), Chapter III: *AAS* 55 (1963), p. 290.

[58] Cf. LEO XIII, Encyclical Letter *Rerum novarum* (15 May 1891): *Leonis XIII P.M. Acta*, XI, Romae 1892, pp. 97-114.

and Social Council (particularly the Commission on Human Rights) and UNICEF. Restricting our references to the works published by FAO, which is well-known in this connection, there is striking evidence of the convergence just mentioned between the teaching of the Church and the increasing efforts deployed by the international community in a number of instruments such as: the Peasants' Charter set out in the *World Declaration on Agrarian Reform and Rural Development* (1979),[59] the *World Food Security Compact* (1985),[60] *The World Declaration on Nutrition* and the *Plan of Action* adopted by the World Nutrition Conference (1992).[61] These are included without overlooking the various politically and morally mandatory codes of best practice or international undertakings on pesticides, plant genetic resources, etc. It is important to note that this ethical point of view was recently adopted by the World Bank.[62]

Human development will not come about as a result of economic mechanisms operating alone; a belief that all that is necessary is to encourage them. The economy will only become more human and humane if a whole range of reforms are carried out at every level. Designed to provide the best possible service for the genuine common good, these reforms must take an ethical approach based on the infinite value of each man and woman and of all humanity. That is an economy which allows itself to be inspired by "the need to build relationships between peoples on the basis of a constant 'exchange of gifts,' a real 'culture of giving' which should make every country prepared to meet the needs of the less fortunate."[63]

Establishing fair terms of trade

---

[59] Cf. FAO, *The Report of the World Conference on Agrarian Reform and Rural Development: Declaration of Principles and Programme of Action and The Peasants' Charter*, Rome 1979.

[60] Cf. FAO, *Final Report of the 23rd Session of the FAO Conference*, No. C85/REO, Rome 9-28 November 1985, p. 46.

[61] Cf. Footnote No. 4.

[62] WORLD BANK, *World Development Report 1990, Introduction*, Washington 1990.

[63] JOHN PAUL II, *Address* for the 50th Anniversary of FAO, No. 4; *L'Osservatore Romano*, 23-24 October, 1995.

41. If the markets are to operate in a way that fosters development, sound regulation is needed. The market has its own laws which range beyond the decision-making capacity of those involved, however numerous and sufficiently independent they may be. This is the case for raw materials markets, despite the great efforts undertaken by governments — also a number of international institutions, particularly UNCTAD (United Nations Conference on Trade and Development) — as well as by the private sector. For political and humanitarian reasons it is not possible to ignore the price levels resulting from the blind operation of the markets. However, it is essential to prevent any attempts to manipulate them.

It is the responsibility of the importing countries to remove barriers and to refrain from raising new ones to selectively keep out exports from countries where a major proportion of the population is suffering from hunger. Importing countries must also ensure that the profits from such commercial operations largely benefit the most deprived. This is a very sensitive issue which requires a fearless and unambiguous attitude.

Overcoming the debt problem

42. As indicated earlier, since 1985 the international community has been managing the debt burden. Its prime concern is to avoid the destruction of the financial system which holds together the financial institutions in every country. It is thanks to this system that, in different countries, and from one crisis to another, the debts have been consolidated and all the debtors of one and the same country placed on an equal level. This is neither legal nor socially just. Conversely, all the lenders have been led to waive a proportion of their debt claims, varying in each case. This demands a great deal of fair-mindedness and vigilance so that the brave and reform-minded countries are not penalised more than others.

It is evident that the debt needs to be substantially reduced still further. But it is right that this reduction should be accompanied by reforms — in every country — to ensure that the circumstances that originally gave rise to the debt situation are not forgotten, and there is no repetition of the same mistakes including: excessive and poorly-targeted public expenditure, local private development without relevance to the national economy, excessive competition between lending and exporting countries, and encouraging unnecessary and even detrimental sales. In any case, it must be acknowledged that conditions in the mis-developing countries cannot be improved unless there is greater stability in the social and political/institutional framework.

Increasing overseas development assistance

43. For the second development decade, UNCTAD set the target for aid to the developing countries at 0.7% of GNP of the industrialized countries. This target has only been achieved by a few countries[64] but it was recently redefined at the Copenhagen summit.[65] On average, aid to developing countries currently stands at 0.33%, which is not even one-half of the target!

The fact that some countries achieve the target and others do not clearly shows that solidarity depends upon the determination of peoples and governments, and not on any automatic technical mechanisms. A greater share of this aid should also be set aside to finance projects in which the poor themselves have a role in the design. Since political leaders of democratic countries depend on public opinion at home, they must seek to broadly enlist public support to make it more clearly aware of the issues and stakes involved in the development assistance budget. "We all share responsibility for the fact that populations are undernourished. [Therefore], it is necessary to arouse a sense of responsibility in individuals and generally, especially among those more blessed with this world's goods."[66]

Government aid raises many ethical problems, both to the donor countries and the beneficiaries. The moralisation of fresh money circuits is a difficult problem everywhere, and the ethical shortcomings may benefit interest groups or lobbies, official or otherwise, in exporting countries. In this way, situations of power which could be described in terms of "structures of sin" become firmly "locked in," fostering patronage on all sides. Powerful mechanisms hold back genuine reform and the development of the common

---

[64] Cf. UNDP, *World Human Development Report 1992.* Cf. also UNITED NATIONS, *Report of the United Nations Conference on Environment and Development* (UNCED), Rio de Janeiro, 3-14 June 1992, No. 33.13: "Developed countries reaffirm their commitments to reach the accepted United Nations target of 0.7 percent of GNP for ODA and, to the extent that they have not yet achieved that target, agree to augment their aid programmes in order to reach that target as soon as possible ... Some countries who have already reached the target are to be commended and encouraged to continue to contribute to the common effort to make available the substantial additional resources that have to be mobilised."

[65] Cf. *Report of the World Summit for Social Development*, Copenhagen, 6-12 March 1995, *Declaration and Programme of Action*, No. 88b.

[66] JOHN XXIII, Encyclical Letter *Mater et magistra* (1961), Chapter III: *AAS* 53 (1961), p. 440.

good. These can have formidable consequences, such as local unrest and inter-tribal strife in countries that are vulnerable in this respect.

Combating these "structures of sin" is a source of great hope for the most deprived countries.

Rethinking aid

44. It is the responsibility of the industrialized countries not only to increase their aid to the developing countries but also to reappraise the way in which it is distributed. Conditional aid is to be criticised when considered in terms of the lending or donor country, and when it is tied or linked to conditionalities that bind the recipient country to: purchasing goods manufactured in the donor state, using specialized expatriate labour to the detriment of local labour, complying with structural adjustment programmes, etc. Conversely, unconditioned aid may be considered to truly produce the best results, as evidenced in multiple cases. However, this does not mean that conditional aid should be discarded out of hand, provided that it is designed in such a way that it fairly distributes the benefits to all the parties concerned and makes it possible to manage soundly the resources provided.

Emergency aid: a temporary solution

45. Emergency food aid deserves comment, since it is sometimes criticised for not tackling the root causes of hunger. Some view it as a humanitarian activity. Still others perceive it as a development lever, while some even consider it as a trade weapon. It is faulted for: discouraging local farmers; changing feeding habits; being a tool for bringing political pressure to bear by creating dependency; arriving too late; fostering a free hand-out mentality; profiting ultimately only the middlemen; encouraging corruption and not getting through to the poorest people. In some countries food aid is extended endlessly, not without reason, and eventually becomes established as a structural fact. It then becomes a form of permanent balance of payments aid by reducing the national deficit. This aid can also be provided at a difficult period of structural adjustment, as an accompanying measure, after consumption subsidies for basic commodities have been abolished.

Emergency food aid must remain a temporary solution and its purpose is strictly that of enabling people to survive through a crisis. As a humanitarian measure, it cannot in principle be challenged. It is only deviations in food aid that give rise to criticism. Among these criticisms are: it often arrives late or does not meet the real needs; its distribution is poorly organised or misdirected by political or ethnic factors or patronage; because of theft and corruption, the food does not always reach the poorest people. Other criticisms note that emergency food aid is sustainable structural aid, that some consider to be a development lever, while others view it as a trade weapon, a factor which destabilizes production and feeding habits causing dependency. In reality, its effects can be both beneficial and harmful. Apart from the fact that it enables whole populations to survive, all its positive aspects — such as the infrastructure work that it makes possible, tripartite transactions, and the build-up of reserves in the developing countries — should not be forgotten. Even if it is a weapon that can be used for good or ill, it cannot be ignored.

Coordinated aid

46. Despite the criticisms leveled against it, emergency food aid could be improved by concerted action between all the partners in the chain: governments, local authorities, NGOs and Church associations. Aid could be limited in time and be much better targeted for the people who are really suffering from food shortages. Local products should be used whenever possible. Above all, emergency aid must help to free populations from their dependency. In order to do this, in addition to having adequate infrastructure and local distribution capacities, aid must always be accompanied by projects to enable the affected populations to take precautionary measures enabling them to guard against future food shortages. In this way, emergency or relief aid, under certain conditions, may be considered as an outstanding act of international solidarity. For "this kind of assistance does not bring a satisfactory solution as long as conditions of extreme poverty are allowed to continue and become even more acute, conditions which lead to increased deaths due to malnutrition and hunger."[67]

Food security: a permanent solution

47. The problem of hunger cannot be resolved without an improvement in local food security.[68] "Food security exists when all people at all times

---

[67] JOHN PAUL II, *Address* to FAO on its 50th Anniversary, No. 3; *L'Osservatore Romano*, 23-24 October 1995.

[68] Cf. UNDP, op. cit., pp. 164-165. Cf. Footnote No. 64.

have access to the food they need for a healthy active life."[69] It is therefore important to develop programmes to exploit local production, while having at the same time effective legislation to protect croplands and guaranteeing access to them by the peasant population. One of the reasons why this has not yet been done in the developing countries is that so many obstacles have been raised. It is becoming increasingly more difficult and complicated for economic and business leaders in the developing countries to even define an agricultural policy. Of the many reasons for this situation, the main ones are price and currency fluctuations, both effects of the over-production of agricultural commodities. In order to guarantee food security, the stability and equity of international trade will also have to be facilitated.[70]

Giving priority to local production

48. It is now acknowledged that in every development process agriculture is of paramount importance. Whatever the state of international trade or the economic and political independence, the nutritional status of people in developing countries would be improved if agricultural systems were established, giving pride of place to their internal development while remaining open to the exterior. For this to be done, an economic and social environment must be created based on a better understanding and a better management of the following: local agricultural markets, rural credit development and vocational training, guarantee of remunerative local prices, improvement of the processing and marketing circuits for local products, genuine consultation between the developing countries, possibility for small farmers to organise themselves and to collectively defend their own interests. All of these are tasks that depend on human skill and will.

Importance of agrarian reform

49. Local food production is often hampered by poor land distribution and irrational land use. Over half the population in developing countries is

---

[69] FAO, *Dimensions of Needs*, p. 35. Cf. Footnote No. 11, Food security depends generally on four elements: food *availability*; *access* to sufficient food; *stability* of supplies; *cultural acceptance* of the food or certain combinations of foods.

[70] Cf. also the *World Food Security Compact*, 1985, mentioned earlier in text in No. 40.

landless and this proportion is continually growing.[71] Even though virtually all the developing countries have agrarian reform policies, few of them have actually implemented them. Moreover, the agricultural land used by the multinational food corporations are almost solely used to feed the populations of the North. The exploitation of these lands is causing their depletion and exhaustion. It is urgently necessary to embark upon a "bold reform of the structures and new models of relations between governments and peoples."[72]

Role of research and education

50. The duties expected of political and financial leaders are of primary importance. However, in order to be able to tackle such huge challenges as hunger, malnutrition and poverty, everyone is called to ask themselves what they are doing and what more they might still do. This will require:

— the contribution of science — Intellectual élites are invited to marshall their knowledge and influence in order to try to solve this problem. Biotechnology research, for example, can help to improve world food security, health care, and energy supplies, both in the North and the South. The human sciences can provide a more accurate reading and a more just interpretation of social organisation in order to reveal more clearly the discrepancies in existing systems and the evil effects engendered, in order to help redress them. They can also contribute towards defining and implementing new ways of establishing solidarity between peoples.

— the sensitisation of individuals and whole peoples — Love of our neighbour is the duty of parents, educators, political leaders of all levels, and media specialists. The latter have a major part to play in bringing about progress in the conscience of humanity.

— authentic development in every country — Maximum importance must be given to the kind of education which is not merely a matter of handing on the knowledge needed for communication or for work of personal or public benefit. It must also lay the foundations for the human being's moral conscience. Any dichotomy between education and development must

---

[71] Cf. FAO, *Landlessness: a Growing Problem*, "Economic and Social Development Series," Rome 1984, No. 28.

[72] JOHN PAUL II, *Message for World Peace Day of 1 January 1990*, "Peace with God the Creator, Peace with All Creation," (1990), No. 11: *AAS* 82 (1990), p. 153.

be removed. These are such inter-dependent objectives and are so strictly linked to one another that, both of them must be pursued together if sustainable results are to be forthcoming. It is a duty in solidarity to enable everyone to benefit from "an education ... suitable to the particular destiny of all."[73]

International organisations:
Catholic International Associations,
Catholic International Organisations (CIOs),
Non-Governmental Organisations (NGOs) and their networks

51. Over the past few decades a number of organisations founded by volunteers have come into being, joining others already in existence, to serve individuals and populations in difficulty. These international organizations are often known as Catholic International Associations, Catholic International Organisations (CIOs), and Non-Governmental Organisations (NGOs). They are held in high repute thanks to their dynamism. These organizations have shown their courage in promoting the integral development of people living in poverty and in responding to emergency situations (famine and drought in this particular instance). They have experience in drawing attention to desperate situations, marshalling private and public resources and organising relief in the field. Most of them have supplemented their battle against hunger over the years by embarking on a more forward-looking, longer-term activity to foster development. Their most evident successes include projects for new initiatives implemented locally and autonomously, and projects designed to strengthen local communities and institutions.

The Catholic Church has always (even long before NGOs first came into existence as such) encouraged, inspired and coordinated these efforts and resources through countless parish, diocesan, national and international associations, and through large networks.[74]

---

[73] SECOND VATICAN ECUMENICAL COUNCIL, *Declaration Gravissimum educationis*, No. 1, referring to PIUS XI, Encyclical Letter *Divini illus magistri* (1929), No. 1: *AAS* 22 (1930), p. 50 ff.

[74] Cf. also PONTIFICAL COUNCIL "COR UNUM," *Catholic Aid Directory*, 4th Edition, Vatican City, 1988 (the 5th Edition is being prepared). Let us take, by way of example, the member organisations of "Cor Unum": the International Association of St. Vincent de Paul, Caritas Internationalis, the International Union of Superiors General, the Union of Superiors General, Australian Catholic Relief, Caritas Italiana, Caritas Lebanon, Catholic Relief Services (United States Catholic

We wish to pay tribute here to the work of all the International Organisations, whether they are directly Christian-inspired[75] or whether they are religious or secular in inspiration.

The twofold mission of international organizations

52. The international organizations have a twofold mission: awareness-building and action. While the second of these is obvious, the first is often unknown. Yet, the two are inseparable. Prime importance must be given to sensitising people to the reality and causes of mis-development wherever they are. Attracting private resources and making more people aware of the issues are crucial. It is necessary to build up this grassroots base in order to increase Official Development Assistance and change the "structures of sin."

Partnership in solidarity

53. The international organisations must work as real partners with the groups they assist. This produces a form of solidarity, with a brotherly and sisterly face, in dialogue and mutual trust while respectfully listening to one another.

John Paul II has given a sign of his particular interest in this very sensitive area of partnership by instituting the "John Paul II for the Sahel" Foundation to help combat desertification in the countries south of the Sahara, and the "Populorum Progressio" Foundation to help the poorest people of Latin America, both of which are managed by the local churches themselves in their respective regions.[76]

Conference), Deutscher Caritasverband, Manos Unidas, Organisation Catholique Canadienne pour le Développement et la Paix, Secours Catholique, Kirche in Not, the Society of St. Vincent de Paul, the Secretariat of Caritas in French-speaking Africa, Caritas Aotearoa (New Zealand), Caritas Bolivia, Caritas Spain, Caritas Mozambique, Misereor, Österreichische Caritaszentrale, the Knights of Malta.

[75] Unit IV of the World Council of Churches in Geneva is of great importance here, as is the worldwide work of the Red Cross.

[76] Cf. Footnote No. 48.

IV

THE JUBILEE OF THE YEAR 2000
A STAGE IN THE BATTLE AGAINST HUNGER

The Jubilees: rendering to God what is God's

54. In his Apostolic Letter *Tertio millennio adveniente,* Pope John Paul II, in looking forward to the celebration of the 2000th anniversary of the birth of Christ, recalls the very ancient practice of Jubilees in the Old Testament, rooted in the concept of the sabbatical year. The sabbatical year was a time dedicated in a special way to God and it occurred every seventh year according to the law of Moses. During this year the earth was left fallow, slaves were set free and all debts were cancelled. The Jubilee Year fell every 50 years, during which the customs of the sabbatical year were broadened still further. Israelite slaves were not only freed, but they were also given back their ancestral land. "You shall hallow the 50th year, and proclaim liberty throughout the land to all its inhabitants; it shall be a Jubilee for you, and each of you shall return to his property and each of you shall return to his family" (*Lev* 25:10).

The theological basis of this redistribution was the following: "(Israelites) could never be completely deprived of the land because it belonged to God; nor could the Israelites remain forever in a state of slavery since God had 'redeemed' them for himself as his exclusive possession by freeing them from slavery in Egypt."[77]

Here also we find once more the demand for the universal destination of goods. The social lien on the right to private property was thereby regularly expressed in public law in order to make up for the individual failures to comply with this demand. These failures include: the excessive desire for wealth, ill-gotten profits and so many other ways of exercising ownership, possession, and knowledge, along with the denial of the fact that created goods must always serve everyone equitably.

This legal framework associated with the Jubilee and the Jubilee Year formed the general blueprint for the Church's social teaching which was fashioned around the New Testament. Unfortunately, few concrete achievements accompanied the social ideal attached to the Jubilee. What was

---

[77] Cf. JOHN PAUL II, Apostolic Letter *Tertio millennio adveniente* (1994), No. 12: *AAS* 87 (1995), p. 13.

needed was a just government, capable of imposing earlier precepts with the purpose of re-establishing a degree of social justice. The social teaching of the Church, which has mainly developed since the 19th century, has partly transformed these precepts into a exceptional principle, essentially relating to the duty of the State and designed to restore to everyone their right to enjoy part of the goods of creation. This principle is regularly recalled and proposed to those who wish to heed it.

Becoming "providence" for our fellow human beings

55. The practice of the Jubilees refers fundamentally to Divine Providence and to the history of salvation.[78] On the basis of this relationship, hunger and malnutrition may be considered to be a consequence of human sin, revealed in the very first verses of the book of Genesis: "The Lord said to Cain: 'Where is Abel your brother?' He said, 'I do not know; am I my brother's keeper?' And the Lord said, 'What have you done? The voice of your brother's blood is crying to me from the ground. And now you are cursed from the ground which has opened its mouth to receive your brother's blood from your hand. When you till the ground, it shall no longer yield to you its strength; you shall be a fugitive and a wanderer on the earth'" (*Gen* 4:9-12).

The image given here expresses with perfect clarity the relationship between respect for the dignity of the human person and the fertility of the ecological receptacle — the earth — that had now been sullied and broken. This relationship resounds like an echo throughout the whole of human history and probably formed the theological background of the relations of causality examined earlier when discussing hunger and malnutrition. Everything happens as if the unpredictabilities of nature, often so unfavourable to the human being, are amplified by the consequences of an inordinate thirst for power and profit and by the "structures of sin" from which they stem. By turning away from God's creative plan, the human being has only a shortsighted view of self, one's brothers and sisters and the future. This condemns the human being to the experience of the wanderer, and thus affecting the human race: "... what have you done to your brother?"

The dignity of the human being and the fruitfulness of labour

56. God does not cease wishing to restore creation to humanity and,

---

[78] Cf. *ibid*. No. 13: *AAS* 87 (1995), pp. 13-14.

thanks to Christ the Redeemer, to help all to till and care for the garden (cf. *Gen* 2:15-17) and avoid spoiling it or excluding anyone from it. In this situation every effort made to restore the dignity of the human person and the harmony between the human being and the whole of creation forms, for the Church, part of the mystery of the Redemption wrought by Christ, symbolically represented by the tree of life in the original garden (cf. *Gen* 2:9). When the human being enters freely into communion with this mystery, the person transforms the wandering into a pilgrimage, visiting places and performing actions of faith, learning once again to create a just relationship with God, with one's brothers and sisters and with the whole of creation. The person then knows that this justification comes about and is nourished by faith and by trust in God, and that it is often illustrated in the poor in spirit. This person then becomes once again a full participant in the completion of creation, that had fallen as a result of original sin: "... for the creation waits with eager longing for the revealing of the sons of God... (to) obtain the glorious liberty of the children of God" (*Rom* 8:19, 21).

The sense of the human economy is thus revealed in its fullness. Each person and all of humanity can now cultivate the earth, and live from "the earth ... [where] the body of a new human family grows, foreshadowing in some way the age which is to come."[79] The dynamic of this economy on the move comes from our acceptance of this pilgrimage, so that it can "become flesh" in our own person. Surrendering to it, gradually shedding all our reservations, brings us back to the Church, this people of pilgrims on the move, and leads her forward together towards the Kingdom of God. It is therefore the responsibility of each person, each man and woman baptised in Christ, to reveal this fruitfulness of which the Church is the custodian, with the mission to restore fertility to the whole of creation. When faced with the rationales of the "structures of sin" which weaken the human economy, we are called to be men and women who allow themselves to be intimately examined by God and who thus take up a critical attitude regarding the dominant models.

In this perspective, the Church invites all people to develop their knowledge, skills and experience, each according to the gifts received and according to their own vocation. These gifts and these vocations, that are proper to each person, are admirably expressed in the three parables (the Servant, the Ten Bridesmaids and the Talents) which quite rightly precede the parable of the Last Judgment (cf. *Mt* 24:45-51 and 25:1-46) mentioned earlier. The complementarity and diversity of vocations and charisms direct

---

[79] SECOND VATICAN ECUMENICAL COUNCIL, Pastoral Constitution *Gaudium et spes* (1965), No. 39.

the human being's response of love, called as one is to become "providence" for all men and women: "a wise and intelligent providence, guiding human development of the world along the path of harmony with the Creator's will for the well-being of the human family and the fulfillment of each individual's transcendent calling."[80]

The economy degraded by a lack of justice

57. The Apostolic Letter *Tertio millennio adveniente* proposes very specific initiatives to actively pursue social justice.[81] It thereby encourages us to discover other ways of responding to the problem of hunger and malnutrition which this Jubilee of the Year 2000 might adopt.

The Jubilee is a particularly necessary practice in the field of the economy, for if left to itself, the economy becomes drained of its life-blood because it no longer does justice. Every economic crisis, the extreme effects of which are food shortages, essentially appears as a crisis of justice which is no longer being carried out.[82] The chosen people of the Old Testament had already sensed this, and today it must be made a reality. This crisis must be analysed today within the framework of the free market. In each country, as in international relations, the free market may be an appropriate instrument for sharing resources and responding effectively to people's needs.[83] Social justice makes trade permanent. Every human being has the right to accede to it, at the risk of foundering in an economic neo-Malthusianism based upon a stereotyped vision of solvency and efficiency.

---

[80] JOHN PAUL II, *Meditation* at the Prayer Vigil at Cherry Creek State Park as part of the celebrations of the 8th World Youth Day, 14 August 1993: *AAS* 86 (1994), p. 416.

[81] JOHN PAUL II, Apostolic Letter *Tertio millennio adveniente* (1994), No. 51: "...proposing the Jubilee as an appropriate time to give thought, among other things, to reducing substantially, if not cancelling outright, the international debt which seriously threatens the future of many nations": *AAS* 87 (1995), p. 36.

[82] Cf. HUDE, H., *Éthique et Politique*, Chapter XIII "La justice sur le marché," Ed. Universitaires, Paris 1992.

[83] Cf. JOHN PAUL II, Encyclical Letter *Centesimus annus* (1991), No. 34: *AAS* 83 (1991), pp. 835-836.

However, it must be noted that justice and the market are often analysed as two contradictory realities, which relieves the human person of any responsibility for social justice. The need for equity is then no longer the responsibility of the individual, who is resigned to succumbing to the market, but is transferred to the State and more specifically to the Welfare State.

In general terms, prevailing moral philosophies are largely responsible for a shift in thinking in this area. This shift has moved away from the field of just behaviour to the field of just structures and procedures, a theoretical construction that is now out of our reach. Furthermore, this State-provided welfare, *ad intra* and *ad extra,* now seems to be running out of steam and to be increasingly less able to guarantee any genuine distributive justice, to the point of threatening the efficiency of the national economy. Should this not be cause to reflect on the relationship between the lack of an individual contribution to the establishment of social justice and of moderation in our own economic behaviour; on the other hand, the increasing ineffectiveness of existing re-distribution mechanisms that eventually diminishes the overall efficiency of our economy?

Fairness and justice in the economy

58. To respond to this opposition between the market and justice, the Church's social teaching works on the basis of the notion of just price, derived from Scholasticism. This refers not only to the criterion of commutative justice, but more broadly to the criterion of social justice, namely, all the rights and duties of the human person. This realisation of social justice, thanks to a just price, is based on a twofold conformity: the conformity of the legal environment of the market to the moral law and the conformity of multiple individual economic acts which set market prices to the moral law.

It is insufficient to consider personal responsibility as being restricted solely to civil law, because in many cases this involves "renouncing personal conscience."[84] Just as the market price is based on a variety of customary values agreed upon by consumers, so it is our moral conduct, as the arbiter of agreed customary values, that will cause the market price to converge or not to converge with the just price. When market agents fail to incorporate their duty to ensure social justice into their economic decisions, the market mechanism itself will dissociate the competitive price from the just price.

---

[84] JOHN PAUL II, Encyclical Letter *Evangelium vitae* (1995), No. 69: *AAS* 87 (1995), p. 481.

As we prepare for the Jubilee of the Year 2000, we are all invited to embody the moral law in our daily economic activities.[85] From this stems the concept that the just or unjust character of the price is to a certain extent "in our own hands", the hands of the producer and the investor, the hands of the consumer and of the public policy-makers.

All this does not dispense the State, nor the community of States, from the duty to exercise protection that is capable, among other things, of imperfectly making up for the lack of the individual duty to ensure social justice. This lack is the absence of conformity to the moral law, a duty incumbent on each one of us. The common good is a political object which has primacy over the mere commutative justice in trade.

An appeal for Jubilee proposals

59. God's call, handed on by his Church, is evidently a call to share in active and practical charity. It is a call addressed not only to Christians but to all men and women of goodwill, and to all those who are capable of goodwill, namely to the whole of humanity without exception. The Church, out of concern for the human person in general and of each person in particular, is therefore at the head of the movements that promote love in solidarity. Being present and active by the side of all those who are carrying out humanitarian work to meet the needs, and to assure the most fundamental

---

[85] The Encyclical Letter *Centesimus annus* (1991) by Pope John Paul II gives a number of indications in this connection in para. No. 36: "In singling out new needs and new means to meet them, one must be guided by a comprehensive picture of man which respects all the dimensions of his being and which subordinates his material and instinctive dimensions to his interior and spiritual ones. If, on the contrary, a direct appeal is made to human instincts — while ignoring in various ways the reality of the person as intelligent and free — then consumer attitudes and lifestyles can be created which are objectively improper and often damaging to the person's physical and spiritual health. Of itself, an economic system does not possess criteria for correctly distinguishing new and higher forms of satisfying human needs from artificial new needs which hinder the formation of a mature personality. Thus a great deal of educational and cultural work is urgently needed, including the education of consumers in the responsible use of their power of choice, the formation of a strong sense of responsibility among producers and among people in the mass media in particular, as well as the necessary intervention by public authorities... I am referring to the fact that even the decision to invest in one place rather than another, in one productive sector rather than another, is always a moral and cultural choice.": *AAS* 83 (1991), pp. 838-840.

rights of their fellow human beings, the Church regularly recalls that the "solution" to the social issue demands the effort of all.[86]

All men and women of goodwill can perceive the ethical issues that are at stake and are linked to the future of the world economy: combating hunger and malnutrition, contributing to food security and the endogenous agricultural development of the developing countries, developing these countries' export potential and preserving the natural resources of planet-wide relevance. The Church's social teaching views all these as constituent components of the universal common good which must be identified and fostered by the developed countries. These components must also stand as the essential objective of international economic organisations and as the challenge facing the globalisation of trade. This universal common good, once it has been recognised, should be the inspiration for strengthening the legal, institutional and political framework governing international trade and new proposals for the Jubilee Year. This will demand courage on the part of the leaders of social, governmental and trade union institutions, since it is today so difficult to set the interests of each individual within a consistent vision of the common good.

The Church is not responsible for proposing technical solutions in this regard, but she does wish to seize on this occasion of preparation for the Great Jubilee to launch a wide-ranging appeal for suggestions and proposals, which may hasten the eradication of hunger and malnutrition.

Among these proposals, there are two areas to which particular attention should be given.

— Food buffer stocks, following the example of Joseph in Egypt (cf. *Gen* 41:35), make it possible to provide concrete aid when there is a temporary crisis threatening populations with disaster. The procedures for building up and managing these stocks must be designed in such a way as to stave off any temptation to create a bureaucracy which opens the gates to struggles for political or economic influence on the one hand, and corruption on the other, as well as to prevent any direct or indirect market manipulation.

Promotion of family vegetable gardens, especially in regions where poverty deprives the people, particularly heads of families and their loved ones, from gaining access to land-use and from staple foods. This is similar to what Pope Leo XIII demanded for workers in the 19th century, and for the

---

[86] JOHN PAUL II, Encyclical Letter *Centesimus annus* (1991), No. 60: *AAS* 83 (1991), pp. 865-866.

same reasons: "Men learn to love the very soil that yields in response to the labour of their hands, not only food to eat, but an abundance of good things for themselves and those that are dear to them."[87] In most parts of the world schemes must be designed and implemented to make available to the poorest people some corner of the earth, and the necessary knowledge and minimum of tools, which will enable them to make great progress and break out of their state of grave distress.

— Lastly, and taking a broader perspective, it is necessary to collect information and surveys based on experience and observation, in specific situations, in order to build up a data bank containing practical descriptions of real-life situations, of "structures of sin" and of "structures of the common good" from every point of view.[88]

---

[87] LEO XIII, Encyclical Letter *Rerum novarum* (1891), No. 35.

[88] "Cor Unum" will be asking specific questions in this connection.

V

HUNGER: A CALL TO LOVE

The poor are calling us to love

60. The experience of daily life in every country of the world calls us, if we do not close our eyes, to look the hungry in the eye. In this look is the blood of our brothers and sisters crying out (cf. *Gen* 4:10). We know that it is God calling out to us through the hungry. The sentence of the universal Judge condemns without compassion: "Depart from me, you cursed, into the eternal fire prepared for the devil and his angels. For I was hungry and you gave me no food ..." (*Mt* 25:41 95).

These words, which spring from the heart of God-made-man, enable an understanding of the deep significance of meeting the fundamental needs of every man and woman in the eyes of their Creator. Do not allow the person, who is made in the image of God, to fall down for that would be letting the Lord fall! In the groaning of the hungry, it is God who is hungry and who is calling. Being a disciple of God, who is self revealing, the Christian is urged to heed the cries of the poor. It is a call to love.

The poverty of God

61. According to the writers of the psalms, those songs of the Old Testament, "the poor" are identified with "the just," "the righteous," those who "seek God," "fear God," "trust in God," those who "are blessed," "his servants" and who "know his name."

The whole of the light of the "ANAWIM," the poor under the first Covenant, converges toward the woman who forms the hinge between the two Testaments, as if reflected in a concave mirror. In Mary, all the devotion to Yahweh and all the experience which guided the people of Israel shone forth and took flesh in the person of Jesus Christ. Her "Magnificat" is the hymn of praise which bears witness to Christ: the hymn of the poor whose wealth is God alone (cf. *Lk* 1:46 95).

This hymn opens with an explosion of joy, expressing immense gratitude: "My soul magnifies the Lord and my spirit rejoices in God my saviour." But it is not for riches or power that Mary rejoiced. She saw herself as small, lowly and humble. This basic idea runs throughout her hymn of praise, in total contrast to anything dealing with pride, or the thirst for power and wealth. Those who desire these things are "scattered," "put down from their thrones" and "sent empty away."

Jesus himself took up this teaching of his mother in his Gospel discourse on the Beatitudes. They open — and it is no coincidence — with the words, "Blessed are the poor." His words show what this new person is in opposition to the "wealth" which he criticizes.

It is to the poor that Jesus addresses his Good News (cf. *Lk* 4:18). The "allurement of wealth," conversely, prevents people from following Christ (cf. *Mk* 4:19). We cannot serve two masters, God and mammon (cf. *Mt* 6:24). Concern for the morrow is the sign of a pagan mentality (cf. *Mt* 6:32). For Jesus, these are not just fine words. Indeed, he bore witness to them in his own life: "The Son of Man has nowhere to lay his head" (*Mt* 8:20).

The Church is with the poor

62. The Biblical precept must not be distorted nor disguised. It runs counter to the spirit of the world and to our natural sensitivity. Our nature and our culture are repelled by poverty.

People living in poverty and wealth alike sometimes refer to the poverty of the Gospel in cynical terms. Christians are then accused of wishing to perpetuate poverty. But to scorn poverty in this way would be the work of the devil. The mark of Satan (cf. *Mt* 4) is refusing to do the will of God by quoting his own Words.

An address delivered by Pope John Paul II helps us to avoid this conclusion, which is a trap that could justify our selfishness. During his visit to the Lixão de São Pedro shantytown in Brazil on 19 October 1991, the Holy Father reflected on the first Beatitude of the Gospel of St. Matthew. He explained the link between poverty and trust in God, between happiness and total surrender to the Creator. He then continued, "But there also exists another poverty, which is quite different from the poverty that Christ declared to be blessed, and which affects a multitude of our brethren, hampering their integral development as persons. Faced with this kind of poverty, which is the lack and deprivation of the material things they need, the Church speaks out ... This is why the Church knows that all social changes must necessarily come about through a conversion of hearts, and she prays for this. That is the first and the main mission of the Church."[89]

As we have already said, the call of God handed on through the Church is evidently an appeal to share in active and practical charity, addressed not only to Christians but to everyone. As in the past, and more than ever today, the Church is present to all those who are performing humanitarian work to serve other human beings, working for their needs and their most basic rights.

The Church's contribution to the development of each human being and whole peoples is not restricted to combating poverty and underdevelopment. There also exists a form of poverty caused by the conviction that the pursuit of technical and economic progress is enough to make each person more worthy to be called a human being. But soulless development cannot suffice for the human being, and an excess of wealth and affluence is as harmful to the person as an excess of poverty. It is in the "development model" created by the northern hemisphere and spreading throughout the southern hemisphere, that the sense of religion and the human values stand the risk of being overwhelmed by a mentality of consumption, sought after for its own sake.

Poor and rich alike are called to freedom

63. God does not want people — namely, all men and women — to be poor, since Our Creator cries out to all through each one of the poor. God tells us quite simply that the poor, like the rich who are blinded by their wealth, are mutilated beings. The poor are mutilated by circumstances which lie far from their control, while the rich are mutilated by their handfuls and with their collusion. Both are thereby prevented from finding that interior freedom to which God unceasingly calls all humanity.

By being "filled with good things," the poor are not given some selfish revenge against their ill fate, but are placed in a situation that ensures that their most fundamental capacities are not diminished. The rich who are "sent empty away" are not being punished for being rich, but they are relieved of the burden and the blindness caused by being too exclusively attached to goods of all kinds. The hymn of the Magnificat is not a condemnation, but a call to freedom and to love.

---

[89] JOHN PAUL II, 2nd visit to Brazil, 12-21 October 1991, *Address* at the Lixão de São Pedro shantytown, *Insegnamenti di Giovanni Paolo II*, XIV/2 (1991), p. 941.

In this two-fold healing process, the poor are called to heal their hearts wounded by injustice, which can lead them to hate themselves and others. The rich are called to cast off their shoddy burden. Instead they cover their ears, close their eyes and stifle their hearts, submerged under their worthless riches of money, power, image and pleasures of every kind. This gives them a narrow view of themselves and of others, and as they increase their possessions, their appetites continue to grow.

Necessary reform of the human heart

64. World hunger makes us identify the weaknesses of the human being at every level. The rationale of sin shows how sin — that evil lurking in the heart of every person — lies at the root of the miseries in society as a result of what might be called the "structures of sin." For the Church, this is culpable egoism, the pursuit of wealth, power and glory regardless of the cost, challenging the very value of progress as such. "For when the order of values is jumbled and bad is mixed with the good, individuals and groups pay heed solely to their own interests, and not to those of others. Thus it happens that the world ceases to be a place of true brotherhood and sisterhood. In our own day, the magnified power of humanity threatens to destroy the race itself...."[90] Conversely, the love which comes to dwell in the human heart enables men and women to overcome their limitations and to act in the world by creating "structures of the common good." This encourages people around them to move towards a "civilisation of love"[91] and to attract others.

Thus the human being is called to reform his or her actions. This issue is of vital importance to the world. The person is led to this reformation of the heart by a movement of self toward the unification of the self and of the human community in love. This reform of the human being, the whole person, is radical in its depth and in what it entails, for the very

---

[90] SECOND VATICAN ECUMENICAL COUNCIL, Pastoral Constitution *Gaudium et spes* (1965), No. 37. Cf. also JOHN PAUL II, Encyclical Letter *Sollicitudo rei socialis* (1987), Nos. 27-28: "Such an idea [of development], linked to a notion of 'progress' with philosophical connotations deriving from the Enlightenment... A naïve mechanistic optimism has been replaced by a well-founded anxiety for the fate of humanity... There is a better understanding today that the mere accumulation of goods and services, even for the benefit of the majority, is not enough for the realization of human happiness.": *AAS* 80 (1988), pp. 547-550.

[91] Cf. Footnote No. 38.

essence of love is radical. Love does not suffer from division, it encompasses all the prompting of the person — acts and prayers, material goods and spiritual riches.

The conversion of the heart of everyone, of each and every human being, is God's proposal which can profoundly change the face of the earth, wiping away the hideous marks of hunger which disfigure part of its face. "Repent and believe in the Gospel" (*Mk* 1:15) is the imperative which accompanies the proclamation of the Kingdom of God and which brings about its coming. The Church knows that this deep-seated and intimate change in people will encourage, in daily life, a look beyond immediate interests, to gradually change the way of thinking, working and living, in order to learn to love in daily life, fully exercising faculties in the world as it is.

Whatever little we do, God will watch over us.

"Place not your trust in idols!"

65. Here is the promise which Our Lord makes us: "You shall be clean from all your uncleannesses and from all your idols I will cleanse you. A new heart I will give you, and a new spirit I will put within you; and I will take out of your flesh the heart of stone and give you a heart of flesh. And I will put my spirit within you, and cause you to walk in my statutes and be careful to observe my ordinances" (*Ezek* 36:25-27).

Let us not be misled by this magnificent biblical language. It is not an appeal to fine sentiments, to bring about a mere material sharing, however worthwhile and effective that might be. It is the most far-reaching proposal that could ever be put to us. It is the proposal of God, who comes to offer each one of us liberation from our idols and to teach us to love. This commits our whole being, reunified in this way. Then we can overcome our fears and our selfishness in order to be attentive to our brothers and sisters and to serve them.

Our idols are all near us. They are our longings as individuals and as communities, whether we are rich or poor, for material goods, power, reputation and pleasure, viewed as ends in themselves. By serving these idols, the human being is enslaved and the planet impoverished (cf. § No. 25). The profound injustice suffered, by those who cannot meet the bare necessities of life, is precisely the fact that they are forced, by necessity, to seek material goods above all else.

The heart of the poor Lazarus was freer than the heart of the evil rich man, and through the voice of Abraham, God not only asks the unrighteous rich man to share his feast with Lazarus, but demands a change of heart and acceptance of the law of love, in order that he become a brother to Lazarus (cf. *Lk* 16:19 ff).

It is by freeing us from our idols that God will enable us to set about transforming the world, not only by increasing riches of all kinds, but above all by directing the work of humanity towards the service of all. The world can then rediscover its original beauty which is not only the beauty of nature on the day of Creation, but the beauty of the garden that was perfectly tended, tilled and rendered fertile by the human being, at the service of one's brothers and sisters, in the loving presence of God and out of love for God.

"Fight hunger by changing your lifestyle" is the motto which has emerged in Church circles and which shows the people in the affluent country how to become the brothers and sisters of those living in poverty.[92]

Listening to the poor

66. Wherever in the world God has placed them, Christians must respond to the call of those who are hungry by personally questioning their own lives. The call of the hungry urges one to question the meaning and the value of daily actions, to seek out the immediate and sometimes more remote consequences of professional and voluntary work, handicrafts and domestic work. Further, one must gauge the magnitude, which is much more concrete and wide-ranging than could be imagined, of the consequences of all one does, even the most ordinary things, and hence appraise real responsibility. Christians must question the way time is managed, which in the modern world often suffers by default or by excess because of unemployment, causing such destruction. The eyes of the spirits and hearts of Christians will be opened if they know how to accept this invitation from God, extended to all men and women, to go out as a matter of routine, discreetly and humbly to listen to and serve anyone in need. This is a very particular appeal to all known in current parlance as leaders or officials.

St. Paul states unequivocally that: "Jesus Christ ... though rich ... for your sake he became poor" (2 *Cor* 8:16). Christ wished to make us rich through his poverty and through the love we must always show to those living in poverty.

---

[92] JOHN PAUL II, Encyclical Letter *Redemptoris missio* (1990), No. 59: *AAS* 83 (1991), pp. 307-308.

Listening to God

67. Listening to God, in the presence of the poor, will open up the human heart and lead it to seek an ever-new personal encounter with God. This encounter, which God is seeking, in a ceaseless search for all humanity and the whole human being, will continue along the daily path which gradually transforms the lives of those who agree to "open the door" to God who humbly knocks (cf. *Rev* 3:20).

Listening to God demands time with and for God. It is personal prayer. This alone enables the human being to have a change of heart and hence of deeds. The time taken up by God is not taken away from the poor. A strong and balanced spiritual life has never removed anyone from the service of their brothers and sisters. If St. Vincent de Paul († 1660) — who was so well known for his commitment to the poorest of the poor — was able to say: "Leave off your prayer if your brother asks you for a cup of tea." Let us not forget that he prayed for seven hours a day, and it was on this that he built up everything he did.

Changing our lives ...

68. Those who listen to their brothers and sisters and open up to God's presence and action will begin, little by little, to question their own habits of life. The race for affluence — which more and more people are joining in, often in a world of increasing poverty — will gradually give way to a greater simplicity of life which is already a distant memory in so many countries. This becomes possible once again, and even desirable, as soon as concern for appearances is no longer a consumer's choice.

Lastly, those who thus agree to change their views in order to adopt the view that God has shown us in the words of Christ, and to reflect on the consequences of our actions, whether apparently important or insignificant, will be enabled to place themselves at the service of the common good and of the integral advancement of all humanity and each and every human being.

... to change life

69. Gradually freed of fears and purely material ambitions and enlightened as to the possible consequences of their own actions, wherever they may be, those welcoming the presence of God in every aspect of life will become artisans of the civilisation of love. Working discreetly and in depth,

their work will take on the character of a mission in which their talents must be exercised and developed. A mission where they are called to contribute towards reforming structures and institutions. This exemplary behaviour will then encourage their neighbours to do likewise and to be essentially devoted to serving the dignity of all men and women and their common good.

The circumstances of life are such that some consider this attitude toward work to be impossible. But experience has shown that even in situations of apparent stalemate, people always have a tiny margin to maneuver, and their choices have a real significance for those working near them and for the common good. To a certain extent one might say that every man and woman is responsible for everyone else.[93] This is one of the aspects of God's call to love, which never ceases to resound. It is the responsibility of everyone, under what are often difficult circumstances and may even cause suffering to the point of martyrdom, to draw on the strength of God who promises us help if we place him at the very centre of our lives, including our active lives.

"Take courage, all you people of the land, says the Lord; work, for I am with you" (*Hag* 2:4-5). The Christian then becomes a combatant against the "structures of sin" and even their agent of destruction. This will ensure that anything that hampers social and economic development will be less widespread. In regions where Christians lead men and women of goodwill with courage and determination, poverty can be halted in its tracks, consumption habits can be changed, reforms implemented, solidarity can flourish and hunger recede.

Supporting initiatives

70. These Christians are led, first and foremost, by Religious and ordained pastors, who are called to give their lives to God and to their fellow men and women.

Throughout the history of the Church, since the time of the deacons in the Acts of the Apostles (cf. *Acts* 6:1 ff) until today, there have been

---

[93] This conviction is not only common amongst Christians. It lies at the basis of a movement that was recently instituted in the United States, "Communitarianism." The sociologist, A. Etzioni, has set out the tenets of the movement which works for the promotion of the common good of all men and women in his study entitled *The Spirit of Community: Rights, Responsibilities and the Communitarian Agenda*, Crown Publishers, Inc., New York 1993.

extraordinary men and women,[94] Religious Orders and Missionary Orders, associations of the Christian laity and Church institutions and initiatives that have set out to assist those living in poverty and the hungry. They have fought against suffering and misery in all its forms, in obedience to Christ.

The Church is thankful to all those who are presently performing these services by undertaking specific activities for the good of their neighbour, in dioceses, parishes, missionary organizations, charity organizations and other NGOs. They are handing on the love of God and demonstrating the authenticity of the Gospel.

The Catholic Church is present in every continent. She has almost 2,700 dioceses or circumscriptions with widely differing features,[95] many of which have long been occupied with combating hunger and poverty. Dioceses and parishes are the special places for discerning what Christians are able to achieve. In these situations they encourage the organization of grassroots groups, local groups and whole communities. Welcoming communities, composed with a strong human dimension, can restore people's confidence, help organise better living, and draw people out of resignation and subjugation. The Gospel once again becomes a hope for those living in poverty, in a crucible in which the strength of Christ and the strength of the disinherited join forces.

Each one is called to take part in this work. The call to love, which God sends out through the presence of our fellow humans who are suffering from hunger, must become a reality for each of us, whatever our state of life, place in the world and our most immediate surrounding. The wonderful variety of humanity, in the diversity of cultures, leads to an array of different commitments and missions.

Every Christian must, therefore, encourage local initiatives of all kinds. The Catholic Church knows that she can share this commitment with the other Christian Churches and religious communities, and with all men and women of goodwill. Humanitarian work is an important sphere of action for Christians. But, they must then make a particular contribution to ensuring that the purposes pursued by their association and in their own work are for the integral service of humanity, without excluding the spiritual dimension.

---

[94] JOHN PAUL II, Encyclical Letter *Sollicitudo rei socialis* (1987), No. 40: *AAS* 80 (1988), p. 569.

[95] Cf. SECRETARIA STATUS RATIONARIUM GENERALE ECCLESIAE, *Annuarium Statisticum Ecclesiae*, Typis Vaticanis 1994, p. 41.

In this way, they will be a bulwark against all those who might seek to deflect the dynamism of these associations to serve political ends inspired by materialism and by ideologies which ultimately always destroy the human being.

Every Christian is on a mission in all activities

71. Christians are at the service of their brothers and sisters in every aspect of their work and their lives. Love put into practice appeals to all Christians in their daily work and in their personal initiatives. The commitment of Christians, like their humanitarian and charitable work, stems from the same call to mission.

In their paid work and in their unpaid voluntary work, or working at home, which is often heavy, men and women are called to live the same mission, to manifest the Good News and serve it through their daily sufferings and joys and in every situation. The quality of their work, participation in just reforms, humble behaviour, concern for others, which is always present regardless of personal and lawful institutional objectives — all this is the daily lot of men and women seeking an opportunity, in every aspect of their lives, to allow God to draw close to them and to make the world grow in Divine love. They will then be increasingly better able to combat confusion and injustice, and offer up their sufferings and their joys to Christ the Saviour who gives them his spirit in their daily lives.

Christians will seek to link their work, whatever it may be, to the One who speaks directly to our hearts through the mouths of all the poor. Christians, who are leaders of all men and women of goodwill, with whom they share fundamental human values, must ensure that their personal work and that of their fellow Christians is inspired by the Word of God and anchored in the Divine Life, in union with the Church and her pastors. The community in action must be a community working with the Lord, who will ensure that this work is planned and implemented in the Holy Spirit, and thereby ensure that it preserves its quality as a mission of divine essence in which the Servant of Man is sought personally as the source, the strength and the end of the work itself.

Christians will find support at all times in the prayer of our Blessed Lady, praying and acting in one and the same movement of unreserved service to God and to humanity. The Mother of God will intercede with the Holy Spirit to flood the minds and hearts of all Christians, thereby making them responsible and trusting, cooperating freely in an undertaking that will bear witness by itself to the Love of God, and which will have the weight of eternity.

Vatican City, Palazzo San Calisto, 4 October 1996,
Feast of St. Francis of Assisi.

✠ ARCHBISHOP PAUL JOSEF CORDES
President, Pontifical Council "Cor Unum"

MSGR. IVÁN MARÍN
Secretary, Pontifical Council "Cor Unum"

STATEMENT BY
HIS EXCELLENCY ARCHBISHOP RENATO R. MARTINO
APOSTOLIC NUNCIO, PERMANENT OBSERVER OF THE HOLY SEE
TO THE UNITED NATIONS
BEFORE THE SECOND COMMITTEE
OF THE 51ST SESSION OF THE GENERAL ASSEMBLY ON ITEM 97:
"SECTORAL POLICY QUESTIONS, FOOD
AND SUSTAINABLE AGRICULTURAL DEVELOPMENT"
NEW YORK, 25 OCTOBER 1996

Mr. Chairman,

The topic of our consideration, "Food and Sustainable Agricultural Development" is obviously of primary importance. It is literally a matter of life and death. For this reason, during his *Address* to the United Nations General Assembly in 1979, His Holiness Pope John Paul II stated: "Permit me to enumerate some of the most important human rights that are universally recognized: the right to life, liberty and security of person; the right to food, clothing, housing, sufficient health care, rest and leisure; the right to freedom of expression, education and culture . . . " The fundamental importance of food as an essential component of the human right to an adequate standard of living has also been unequivocally asserted by the international community, most notably in the *Universal Declaration of Human Rights*, (N. 25), the *Universal Declaration on the Eradication of Hunger and Malnutrition* of 1974 (N. 1), and the *World Declaration on Nutrition* of 1992. My Delegation strongly hopes that the right to food will be enshrined once more in the Document to be approved by the coming World Food Summit to be held in Rome in mid-November.

As the right to have enough to eat is fundamental and inalienable for every person and for their family, the international community and national governments have the obligation to see that everyone does indeed have sufficient food. For this reason, solutions which bring only temporary or occasional relief to the hunger suffered by our fellow human beings — especially by women and by girl children — are not satisfactory for the human family. Moreover, no one is exempt from the duty of providing such immediate aid, especially when food producing countries have at their disposal an abundance of goods.

In order to respond to this pressing need, there is much talk and reflection about how to achieve "food security" for all. Such a concept must be based in a desire for deeper solutions which flow from a profound solidarity among all people, rich and poor; citizens of countries which are developed and of those which are on their way to development. Food security must stress components such as: the production of a sufficient amount of food, a stable supply throughout the year, access to food for all, a proper and equitable distribution, and a commitment to producing the components of a balanced and healthy diet in keeping with the local nutritional practices.

Concrete efforts must be made to bring about true agrarian reform. In some countries, for example, 1% of the population controls 50% of the land. A more equitable distribution of land, with the consequent increase in participation in food production, especially by the poor, is an important component of any such solution. In this regard the right of women to have access to land must also be strongly reaffirmed.

Accompanying such a change must be a commitment to offer proper training and education, especially to small farmers, so that they can learn to maximize the results of their labors. Such training should stress sustainable agricultural practices which are suited to local realities and cultures.

On a global scale, sustainable agricultural development must be fostered by encouraging study and development of crops which produce a high yield. It is particularly important that, wherever possible, results of such development be made available to parts of the world where agricultural production is deficient. In addition, economic policies which result in an inadequate distribution of the already existing food which is sufficient to feed the world's population cannot be allowed to continue.

If the world is to have sustainable agriculture, the international community must acknowledge that peace is a prior and fundamental condition. Wars not only bring about poverty, they also breed famine by forcing massive displacements of peoples and render land either unsafe or unsuitable for growing food. Once again, the Holy See wishes to stress the urgent need for the cessation of the production, sale, stockpiling, export and use of land mines. How many people throughout the world are hungry precisely because they fear to use the land at their disposition, or because land mines have killed or maimed for life those who were being counted on to be the breadwinner of a family?

As we consider the conditions for food security and sustainable agriculture, we must admit that in our day there exist what Pope John Paul has called "structures of famine" (*Address to the Participants in the 28th Conference of the FAO*, 23 October 1995). These can be overcome only with an attitude of solidarity touching on every aspect of development: formation and use of capital, investments, surpluses, production, and distribution systems. Each phase has an underlying moral and ethical dimension. Indeed economic policies themselves cannot be separated from ethical considerations. As His Holiness has stated, "Individuals and whole peoples will be finally judged by history in relation to how they actually fulfill their obligation to contribute to the good of their fellow human beings. ... It is to be hoped that everyone — individuals, groups, private undertakings and public bodies — will take proper care of the most needy, beginning with the basic right to satisfy one's own hunger." (*Homily* during the Mass at St. Peter's Basilica to commemorate the fortieth anniversary of the FAO, 10 November 1985).

I would like to inform this Committee that just yesterday, the Holy See published a Document entitled, *"World Hunger, A Challenge for All: Development in Solidarity."* This serves as a more complete and articulated contribution of the Holy See to the discussion surrounding the scandal of hunger in a world which has the means to feed every person.

I would conclude by citing the *Message* of Pope John Paul to the Director-General of the FAO on the occasion of World Food Day 1996. He stated, "Recent experience has also heightened humanity's awareness that technical solutions, however elaborate, are not effective if they lack the necessary reference to the central importance of the human person — the beginning and end of the inalienable rights of every individual, community and people. Among these rights there emerges the fundamental right to nutrition, but the actual putting into practice of this right cannot be seen merely as a goal to be striven for. This right, in fact, must inspire action aimed at promoting a life consistent with the demands of human dignity and free from those external constraints which, under any form can limit freedom of choice and even compromise the survival of individuals, families and civil communities."

Statement by
His Excellency Archbishop Renato R. Martino
Apostolic Nuncio, Permanent Observer of the Holy See
to the United Nations
at the UN/FAO Pledging Conference for the
World Food Programme
New York, 4 November 1996

Mr. President,

The Delegation of the Holy See is pleased to participate in this Pledging Conference for the World Food Programme.

As I mentioned this morning when announcing the contributions of the Holy See for Development Activities, my Delegation is keenly aware that this year of 1996 is the International Year for the Eradication of Poverty. One of the most devastating results of poverty and the lack of development is hunger and malnutrition.

The Catholic Church throughout the world, by means of the efforts of its various members, organizations and Church-related Agencies, is deeply involved in the effort to alleviate hunger, especially in its work among women and young children, as well as with refugees. For this reason, I wish to announce this afternoon that the Holy See will offer a symbolic contribution of $10,000.00 to the World Food Program. This offering is intended to serve as an expression of recognition and encouragement on the part of the Holy See for the activities of the United Nations, especially those of the World Food Program, toward feeding the hungry and poor people of the world.

At the same time, the Holy See is very hopeful that the coming World Food Summit, to be held in Rome this November, will reinforce the commitment to caring for those who are malnourished by clearly reaffirming the "right to food" for all people, and by adopting concrete programs and strategies to eradicate hunger from our world.

Thank you, Mr. President.

INDEX

A

Abortion, 65, 79, 84, 96, 113-114, 189, 194, 196, 200, 204, 213, 215, 226, 229, 231-232, 233-235, 255-256, 259, 261-262, 266, 285, 290, 293-294, 303-309, 315-316, 319-320, 325, 328-329, 333, 337-338, 342-344, 347, 349, 374, 422-423, 462, 473, 477-478, 491, 498, 501, 508-509, 515, 518, 520-521, 528, 532-534, 543, 548, 576, 577, 650, 703-704, 713, 727-735, 739, 746-747, 750, 752, 755, 760-761, 774-775, 777-778, 786, 788-794, 798-819, 849-851

- "safe/unsafe" abortion, 774, 778

- (abortion) not to be used as a method of family planning, 114, 190, 194, 196, 215, 226, 232, 255, 276, 290, 305, 319, 338, 342, 528, 792, 806, 812, 816

- (abortion) not to be used as a component of reproductive health care, 325, 533, 576

- reawakening of conscience regarding respect for life, 681

- science offers confirmation of the embryo's human nature, 215

Adolescents/youth, 49, 52, 63, 66, 78, 88, 90, 91, 95, 197, 201, 219, 221, 228, 232-233, 236, 256-257, 259, 266, 271, 282, 288, 294-295, 299, 303, 305, 308-309, 316-317, 320, 324, 326, 338, 342-344, 354, 356, 448, 498, 503, 506-07, 511, 521, 546-547, 557, 622, 626, 661, 690, 727, 737, 767, 776, 781, 786, 788, 792, 804, 812, 816, 851, 927

Aged persons *(See "Elderly")*

AIDS *(See "HIV/AIDS")*

Appendix, 603

B

Beijing Conference *(See "Women, Fourth World Conference on Women")*

Birgitta of Sweden (Saint), 430-431, 504

Birth Rates *(See "Population Growth")*

Bodet, Monsignor Henri, 58

Boutros-Ghali, Secretary-General Boutros, 771, 785

C

Cabrini, Saint Frances Xavier, 433-444, 504

Cairo Conference *(See "ICPD, International Conference on Population and Development")*

Casaroli, Cardinal Agostino, 46, 52, 56, 72, 85, 97, 101-103

Catherine of Siena (Saint), 432-33, 504, 837

"Catholics for a Free Choice" *(See also "Pro-Choice")*, 491, 607-608, 849, 850, 851-852, 853, 854

CELAM (Latin American Episcopal Council), 87, 98, 769, 780, 795-796

Charter of the Rights of the Family, 697

Children, *(See also "Women, status of women"; "Human Generation, technologies of")*

- (children) and war, 92

- child prostitution/trafficking in children, 91, 529

- children forced to work, 91

- church structures dealing with

children, 86

- education of children, 90, 313, 355, 500, 639, 663, 772

- sex education, 81, 96, 705, 727, 781, 794, 807

- sexual exploitation of children, 90, 91, 93-94, 99

- special measures to protect children, 90

- street children, 60, 91, 98, 564, 570

Children's Summit *(See "World Summit for Children")*

Clinton, President William *(Letter from U.S. Cardinals and Conference President)*, 770, 787, 812

Coercion *(See "Family Planning, freedom from coercion")*

Cohabitation, forms other than marriage - same sex unions - consensual unions - "other unions", 225, 243, 254, 703, 776, 789, 803, 813

Complementarity and reciprocity of woman and man *(See "Women, complementarity and reciprocity of woman and man)*

Consumption patterns
- impact of consumption patterns on the environment, 125, 134, 195, 248, 263, 284, 388, 527, 618-619, 725, 739, 812, 814, 889, 906, 934, 939

Contraception, 84, 95-96, 113-114, 209, 212, 213, 233, 261, 271, 285, 290, 309, 320-321, 328-329, 333, 337-338, 342, 344, 349, 374, 501, 508, 515-516, 518, 533, 543, 547, 703, 728, 735-737, 750, 752, 755, 759, 760-762, 788, 792, 798, 800, 801, 814

- hormonal contraception, 508, 543, 728

- sterilization *(See "Sterilization")*

- the two dimensions (unitive and procreative) of conjugal union cannot be artificially separated without damaging the deepest truth of the conjugal act itself, 645

Convention on the Rights of the Child, 44-45, 48-49, 56, 58-59, 61, 64-65, 67, 69, 71-72, 73, 77, 82-83, 85, 87, 92-93, 96, 101, 142, 245, 342, 503, 511, 521, 538, 546, 858

"Couples and individuals," 231-232, 308, 321, 533

Cordes, Archbishop Paul Josef, 479, 559, 942

"Cor Unum" *(See "Pontifical Council 'Cor Unum'")*

Chrétien, Prime Minister Jean *(Letter from Canadian Bishops' Conference)*, 805

D
DeAndrea, Monsignor Joseph A., 284

Debt Relief *(See "External Debt")*

Development
- environment and development (interrelation of), 129, 131

- human beings are at the center of development, 122, 129-130, 133, 189, 287, 311, 337, 369, 379-380, 391, 408, 523, 563, 569, 572

- human development and the family *(See "Family, human development and the family")*

- human security (concept of), 386-387

- "overdevelopment," 806

- overseas development assistance *(See "Overseas Development Assistance")*

- population and development (relationship between), 200, 235, 252, 269, 273, 309, 312, 324, 331-332

- relation of development and the environment to population growth, 263

- right to development, 125, 129, 141, 145, 149, 170, 282, 324, 815

- sustainable development, 123, 125-126, 131, 133, 169, 248, 273, 274-275, 279, 284, 337, 352, 371, 389, 398, 405-406, 499, 516, 523, 562, 569, 572, 582, 621, 726, 781, 791, 814-815, 883, 907

Dewane, Monsignor Frank, 279, 390, 391, 471

Disabled persons/chronically ill persons, 59, 78, 80, 88-89, 221, 284, 395, 398, 402, 484, 564, 570, 637, 658-659, 692, 704, 707, 847, 898

Divorce, 210-211, 242-243, 667-668, 676, 705

Donahoe, Mrs. Patricia, 402

Domestic violence/family violence, 468, 471-472, 477, 488, 495, 510, 542

E
ECOSOC (Economic and Social Council of the United Nations), 87, 375, 377, 405-407

Elderly/aged persons, 195-196, 219, 221-222, 225-226, 244, 266, 275, 277, 282, 312, 395, 400, 443, 444, 446, 477, 529, 556, 560, 567, 577, 591, 707, 719, 767, 804, 812, 827, 857, 875, 881-882

- changing age structure/aging of the population, 56, 103, 221, 227, 263-264, 719, 738

Environment *(See also "Consumption patterns")*
- technology's effect on the environment, 619

- centrality of the human person regarding environment and development *(See also "Development, human beings are at the center of development" and "Development, sustainable development")*, 122, 129-130, 311, 379, 380, 391, 408

- (need for) education in international solidarity and respect for the environment, 554, 564

- impact of consumption patterns on the environment *(See "Consumption patterns, impact of consumption patterns on the environment")*

- interrelation of environment and development, 129, 131

- moral dimension, 123

- relation of population and environment *(See also "Environment, technology's effect on the environment")*, 617

- stewardship and solidarity, 124

Environment and Development, Conference on *(See "UNCED"; See also "Rio+5")*

Etchegaray, Cardinal Roger, 92, 147, 234, 246, 252, 375

Ethical and Pastoral Dimensions of Population Trends, 297, 299, 301,

711, 779, 891

European Union, 304, 537, 776, 816

Euthanasia, 142, 719, 736, 755-756, 808, 819, 832

External debt/foreign debt, 145, 270, 274, 312, 324, 384-285, 396, 399, 410, 483, 592-593, 620, 723, 902

F

Family *(See also "John Paul II, Letter to Families")*
- (the family is) based on marriage, 208, 242, 324, 701, 796

- breakdown of the family, 481, 629

- complementarity of woman and man *(See "Women, complementarity of woman and man")*

- Charter of the Rights of the Family, 697

- (the family) constitutes the fundamental educating community, 467

- "domestic church," 627-629, 658, 661, 662, 672, 687-688, 796

- family is entitled to protection by society and the State, 113, 253, 274, 286, 500, 517, 537

- (the family is) fundamental to the life of every society, 663

- (the family) exists prior to the State or any other community, 79, 204, 218, 234, 240, 242, 701, 765

- family size *(See "Family Planning")*

- first and vital cell of society; fundamental unit of society, 48, 113, 193, 200, 203, 206, 218, 229, 235, 238, 253, 274, 286, 292, 314, 500, 510, 517, 537, 632, 785

- (the) first school of how to be human, 657

- (the) first and most important way of the Church, 689

- human development and the family, 192

- (an) indispensable and essential value of the civil community, 238, 690

- "in its many forms," 286, 537, 543, 576, 789, 817

- men, role of men, 309, 421, 439, 494, 520, 524, 528, 536, 647, 659-660, 670, 672, 673

- (the family) originates in a marital communion *(See also "Marriage")*, 632

- rights of the family/family rights, 92, 238, 239-240, 243-244, 261, 446, 663-665, 697, 700, 732, 736, 746, 752, 753, 764, 767, 769, 774, 797, 832, 846, 858

- (the family possesses a) unique role in the transmission of values, 271, 481

Family Planning *(See also "Natural Family Planning")*, 45, 65, 69, 74, 83, 113, 126, 155, 225, 227-228, 232, 238, 266, 271, 275, 277, 281, 290, 292, 305, 308, 314-315, 321, 339, 342, 353, 357, 374, 474, 528, 533, 540, 576, 598, 621, 703, 729, 737, 746, 756, 757, 760, 762-763, 774, 776, 777, 794, 799, 816, 858, 891

- freedom from coercion/enforced plans of population control; economic aid must not be conditioned on acceptance of programmes of contraception, sterilization or abortion, 113, 116, 278, 281-282, 324, 501, 518, 703, 726, 738, 741, 745, 746, 747, 788

- morally unacceptable methods of family planning, 232, 314

FAO (U.N. Food and Agriculture Organization), 330, 593, 595-596, 600-601, 735, 855, 861-865, 867-868, 877-878, 881-883, 892, 895, 905-906, 915, 919-921, 944-945, 946

Food *(See "Hunger")*

Food Summit *(See "World Food Summit")*

Foreign debt *(See "External Debt")*

Freedom
- authentic freedom, 650, 653, 797

- antithesis between individualism and personalism, 653

- individualistic understanding of freedom, 654

G

"Gender", 508, 512, 532, 534, 536, 576, 598

- gender equality/gender equity, 285, 295, 319, 354-355, 475, 545

Girl child, 275, 473, 484, 494, 526, 532, 534, 541, 546, 599, 943

Glendon, Professor MaryAnn, 523, 531, 539, 544

Global warming, 120

Goods, Principle of the universal and common destination of the goods of the earth/universal destination of goods, 744, 871, 898-899, 901, 924

Gore, Mr. Al, 307

H
Habitat II Conference *(See "Human Settlements, Second World Conference on Human Settlements")*

Health
- environmental degradation (and its effects on health), 126, 130, 226-227

- maternal health/safe motherhood, 74, 304, 473, 803

- maternal mortality, 74, 195, 227, 325, 333, 339-340, 473, 534, 717, 808, 818

- mortality and health, 226

- "sexual and reproductive health" *(See also "Rights, sexual and reproductive")*, 190, 254, 258, 281-282, 289, 293-294, 303-307, 309, 315-316, 320-321, 325, 329, 338-339, 353-357, 374, 401, 478, 501, 503, 508, 520, 532-534, 543, 547-548, 576, 598, 621, 750, 774, 792, 799-800, 803, 808, 812, 816

High Commissioner for Human Rights (UNHCR), 145

HIV/AIDS, 54, 89, 91, 102, 299, 320, 338, 374, 501, 508, 533, 547, 720, 792

- AIDS/HIV (use of condoms in prevention programmes), 320, 338, 374

Holy See
- Diplomatic Service of the Holy See (origins of), *(See Forewords, pgs 7-13)*

- seeks to be the voice of human conscience, 693

- voice for those without a voice, 189

Homosexual and Lesbian Unions *(See*

"Cohabitation, forms other than marriage")

Housing (See *"Human Settlements"*)

Human Generation, technologies of, 214, 761

Human life
- begins at the moment of conception, 48, 62, 78-79, 88, 93, 189, 215-217, 319, 326, 473, 637-638, 680-681, 704, 758, 782, 798

Human person
- centrality of the human person (See also *"Environment, centrality of the human person"*; *"Development, human beings are at the center of development"* and *"Development, sustainable development"*), 122, 129-130, 189, 311, 379-380, 391, 408

Human rights
- collective dimension of human rights, 141

- democracy and human rights, 148

- development and human rights, 149

- family rights (See *"Family, rights of the family"*)

- human rights exist prior to the formation of the State, 140

- indivisibility and universality of human rights, 153

- obligations and duties, 154

- right to development (See *"Development, right to development"*)

- right to education, 80, 338, 525-526, 354, 526, 545

- right to food (See *"Hunger, right to food"*)

- right to freedom of religion and conscience, 59, 82, 142, 152, 157-158, 164, 216, 367, 482, 496, 498, 511, 706, 733, 756

- right to housing (See *"Human Settlements, right to housing"*)

- right to life (See also *"Human life"*), 48, 53, 62, 64, 66-67, 79, 85, 88, 93, 127, 140, 142, 145-146, 161, 206, 216, 227, 275-276, 325, 329, 342, 379, 473, 520, 568, 599, 622, 680, 746, 755, 774, 781-784, 808, 813, 815, 826-827, 858, 943

- universality of human rights (See *"Human Rights, indivisibility and universality of human rights"*)

- violations of human rights, 142-143, 782, 826

Human Rights Conference (See *"World Conference on Human Rights"*)

Human Settlements, Second World Conference on Human Settlements, 549-586

- (human settlements are) a means of expression of the human soul, 570

- human beings are deeply affected by their habitat, 544, 555

- importance of the family in addressing problems related to shelter, 562-583

- lack of decent housing threatens the dignity and rights of the poor, 563

- mega-cities, phenomenon of, 568

- parents have the primary responsibility for housing, 569

- places of worship, 554, 564-565, 570, 571

- right to housing, 557-558, 563, 568, 583, 707

- rural-urban balance *(See also "Human Settlements, urbanization")*, 565

- spiritual, moral and ethical vision (regarding housing), 564, 569

- urbanization, 118, 389, 617, 718, 721, 735

Hunger
- causes of hunger, 883

- emergency food aid, 918-919

- ethical dimension of the problem (of hunger), 897

- famine (in recent times) in most cases is man-made, 881

- food resources and population *(See "Population Growth, food resources and population")*

- food security, 312, 593, 595, 599, 600, 857, 862-863, 868, 884, 915, 919-921, 930, 943-944

- (food security) not only an economic and technical challenge, but in the first place an ethical and spiritual one, 596

- importance of food as an essential component of the human right to an adequate standard of living, 599, 943

- lack of uniformity in food production or distribution, 595

- malnutrition *(See "Malnutrition")*

- need for true agrarian reform, 600, 920-921, 944

- peace is a prior and fundamental condition for eliminating poverty and hunger, 596, 600, 944

- planet's resources are sufficient to feed everyone, 877

- right to food, 568, 599, 877, 943, 946

- role of women in combating hunger, 909

- "structures of famine", 600, 863, 944

I
IAEA (International Atomic Energy Agency), 9

ICCB (International Catholic Child Bureau), 87, 91, 94, 98

ICO (International Catholic Organizations), 86

ICPD (International Conference on Population and Development), 179-358

- Bucharest Population Conference (1974), 199-200, 230-232, 234, 249, 252, 269, 273, 318, 319, 331, 617, 724, 750, 777, 816

- Mexico City Population Conference (1984), 114, 194, 196, 199-200, 215, 230-232, 235, 249, 251-252, 255, 259, 269, 273, 275, 292, 305, 312, 318-319, 331-332, 497, 505, 508, 617, 724, 729, 737, 777, 812, 816

-selected statements by bishops' conferences, pro-life leaders and other organizations regarding the ICPD, 780-809

- UNICEF Follow-up to the ICPD, 352, 356

ILO (International Labour

Organization), 9-10, 87, 94

Individualism *(See also "Freedom, individualistic understanding of freedom"; "Sexuality, individualistic view of sexuality")*, 266, 292, 294-295, 423, 455, 531, 534, 563, 653-654, 719, 794, 804, 807

Infanticide, 730, 732

J

John Paul II, Pope
- Children, Letter to, 609

- Families, Letter to, 623

- Heads of State, Letter to (Cairo Conference), 199

- Nafis Sadik, Message to Mrs., 191

- Women, Letter to, 829

- World Day of Peace Message, 1995 (Women), 821

- World Migration Day Message, 1995 (Migrant Women), 839

- World Communications Day Message, 1996 (Media/Women), 845

K

Keeler, Cardinal William, 787, 789, 849, 850, 854

Klink, Mr. John M., 73, 100, 281, 352, 356, 417, 545, 607, 811

Knights of Columbus, 809

L

Land Mines, 403, 484, 584, 600, 944

Life, Right to *(See "Human Rights, right to life")*

M

Malnutrition *(See also "Hunger")*, 101, 171, 591, 595, 599, 611, 856, 858, 862, 864, 867-868, 877, 881, 889, 897, 907-908, 910, 919, 921, 925, 927, 930, 943, 946

- malnutrition is more widespread than hunger, 881

Marín, Monsignor Iván, 177

Marriage *(See also "Family, based on marriage")*, 193, 196, 200, 207-211, 218-219, 225, 235, 238-244, 249, 253-254, 287, 293, 295, 297, 301, 308, 313, 318, 322, 324, 332, 338, 344, 371, 374, 455, 480, 533, 537, 569, 576, 615, 627-628, 630, 632-636, 638-639, 641, 645, 647-648, 650, 656, 663, 667-672, 678, 690, 701-705, 733-734, 742, 746, 758, 764, 766-767, 769-773, 787, 790, 796, 803, 813, 817

- "great mystery", 211, 637, 639, 670-678, 687

- indissoluble character of marriage, 210-211, 242, 386, 388, 397, 402, 405, 572, 768, 775

Martin, Monsignor Diarmuid, 236, 269, 287, 291, 378, 383, 386, 388, 397, 402, 405, 572, 768, 775

Martino, Archbishop Renato Raffaele, 11, 43, 61, 64, 67, 71, 82, 85, 93, 97, 103, 118, 122, 129, 133, 169, 189, 236, 273, 311, 318, 323, 328, 331, 333, 335, 337, 408, 487, 493, 541, 567, 575, 579, 581, 582, 599, 775, 816, 943, 946

Marucci, Monsignor Carl J., 13, 15

McHugh, Bishop James T., 263, 617

Men *(See "Family, men")*

Migrants/migrant families/immigration *(See also "Refugees," "Women refugees")*, 196, 221-224, 267, 275, 279-280, 284, 297, 318-319, 326, 335-336, 338, 341, 354-355, 372, 387, 396, 403, 422, 433-434, 446, 458, 459-460, 472, 477, 481, 499,

510, 518, 521, 539, 557, 564, 567, 569, 579, 618, 708, 718-721, 812, 815, 832, 839-843, 875, 892, 894

- "push factor", 223

- temporary migrations, 224, 280

Mongella, Mrs. Gertrude, 419, 441, 497, 829

Moral Poverty, 743

Mother Teresa, Missionaries of Charity, 345, 350, 468, 473, 577

Motherhood, *(See also "Parenthood, responsible parenthood")*, 195, 212, 217, 330, 420, 439, 440-441, 443, 451, 455, 458, 480, 500, 508, 510, 517-518, 521, 524-525, 531, 537-538, 543, 631, 633-634, 636, 639, 644-648, 659-660, 661, 665, 672, 678, 683, 691, 742, 831, 845

- breast-feeding, 95, 195

- maternal mortality, 74, 195, 227, 325, 333, 339-340, 473, 534, 717, 808

- motherhood must be protected, 480

- "safe motherhood" *(See "Health, maternal health/safe motherhood")*

- social role of mothers, 195

N
Natural Disaster Reduction Conference *(See "World Conference on Natural Disaster Reduction")*

Natural Family Planning/Natural Methods of Regulating Fertility, 69, 83-84, 95, 213, 226, 261, 271, 285, 290, 301, 315, 349, 508, 747, 757, 758-762, 763, 787, 799

Natural Law, 178, 206-208, 211, 237, 733, 764, 813

Navarro-Valls, Dr. Joaquín, 302, 306, 341, 393, 401, 402, 505, 511-514

NCCB/USCC (National Conference of Catholic Bishops/United States Catholic Conference - USA), 491, 789, 790, 849, 850, 851, 854

O
O'Connor, Cardinal John, 261

Overseas Development Assistance (ODA), 917

P
Parents *(See also "Family")*
- first and most important educators of children, 660

- (parents) are partners with the Creator in transmitting the sacred gift of human life, 746

- responsible parenthood, 193, 212, 214, 225, 266, 300-301, 314, 330, 344, 464, 528, 644-646, , 648, 690, 732, 734-735, 737, 739-740, 746, 783, 798-799, 804, 807, 859

- rights and responsibilities of parents, 249, 294, 324, 338, 511, 520-521, 789

Paul VI, Pope, 7, 61, 115, 121, 139, 149, 216, 230, 247, 251, 301, 365, 370, 375, 378, 442, 594, 645-646, 648, 684, 689, 694, 732-735, 739, 753-754, 822, 837, 880, 902

Pérez de Cuéllar, Secretary-General Javier, 44-46, 47, 71-72, 101-102

Places of Worship *(See "Human Settlements, places of worship")*

Pontifical Academy for Life, 755

Pontifical Academy of Sciences, 115-117, 268, 297-298, 300-301, 622, 739-741, 890-891

Pontifical Council "Cor Unum," 177,

409-410, 593, 718, 869

Pontifical Council for the Family *(See also "Trujillo, Cardinal Alfonso López"; "Sgreccia, Bishop Elio")*, 85-86, 91, 92-93, 95, 297, 299, 690, 711, 757, 795, 802, 807, 891

Pontifical Council for Justice and Peace *(See also "Etchegaray, Cardinal Roger"; "Martin, Monsignor Diarmuid")*, 411-412, 593

Population and Development, relationship between, 200, 235, 252, 269, 273, 309, 312, 324, 331-332

Population Conference *(See "ICPD, International Conference on Population and Development")*

Population growth/decline; global population situation *(See also "ICPD, Bucharest Population Conference" and "ICPD, Mexico City Population Conference")*, 191, 195, 213, 218, 221, 227, 249, 256, 263, 274, 277, 292, 301, 308, 312, 329, 341, 617-620, 711-754, 755, 760, 782, 794, 890-891

- birth rate does not create greatest drain on resources, 617

- demographic growth and standards of living, 722

- economic aid and the imposition of targets for demographic growth/conditioning of aid on acceptance of specific family planning programmes *(See also "Family Planning, freedom from coercion")*, 228

- environment and population; environmental implications of population growth *(See "Environment, environment and population")*

- food, resources and population, 723

- impact of consumption patterns on the environment is far more disastrous on the ecological balance than population growth alone *(See "Consumption patterns, impact of consumption patterns on the environment")*

- population control methods must respect the person and the person's inalienable rights *(See also "Abortion," "Contraception, hormonal contraception," "Infanticide," "Sterilization")*, 739

- population control and development *(See also "Development, relation between population and development")*, 739

- population growth and age structure/changing age structure *(See also "Elderly")*, 221

- population growth and population geography, 717

- population growth rates and trends differ considerably between the more developed and less developed regions, 617

- public authorities' intervention in demographic realities, 733

- technology's effect on the environment is significantly greater than the influence of population size or of affluence *(See "Environment, technology's effect on the environment")*

Pornography, 93-94, 461, 469, 477, 481, 489, 494, 496, 506, 677, 749

Poverty
- "feminization of poverty," 518, 521, 527

- can still prevent women from attaining their basic needs, 472,

475
- moral poverty *(See "Moral Poverty")*
- reduction and elimination of widespread poverty, 388
- (poverty as) primary cause of hunger, 884
- structural forms of poverty, 116, 127
- underlying causes of poverty must be addressed, 861

"Pro-Choice" *(See also "Abortion")*, 774
- pro-abortion tendencies which vainly try to hide behind the so-called "right to choose," 650

Procreation *(See "Parenthood, responsible parenthood")*

Prostitution, 91, 93-94, 461-462, 472, 477, 494, 500, 506, 509, 518, 529, 840-841

Q

R

Rape, 462, 477, 518, 832

Refugees *(See also "Women, refugee women")*, 91-92, 222, 267, 272, 275, 335-336, 355, 469-470, 481, 484, 495, 539, 557, 564, 567, 569, 574, 579, 592, 708, 718, 862, 875, 882, 946

Religious Freedom *(See "Human rights, right to freedom of religion and conscience")*

"Reproductive Rights" *(See "Rights, Sexual and Reproductive")*

"Reproductive Health" *(See "Health, Sexual and Reproductive")*

"Reproductive Services" *(See "Rights, Sexual and Reproductive")*

Responsible Parenthood *(See "Parenthood, responsible parenthood")*

Rickert, Ms. Sheri, 467, 483, 491

Right to Development *(See "Development, right to development")*

"Rights, Sexual and Reproductive," 190, 193, 254-255, 258, 281-282, 285, 289-290, 293, 295, 303-305, 307-309, 320-321, 329, 338-339, 353-357, 374, 401, 473-474, 478, 501, 503, 508, 520, 532-534, 543, 547-548, 576, 598, 621, 750, 774, 778-779, 799-800, 803, 805, 808, 816

Rio Conference *(See "UNCED, U.N. Conference on Environment and Development")*

Rio+5 (19th Special Session of the United Nations General Assembly), 621

Rubiolo, Monsignor Candido, 475

S

Sadik, Dr. Nafis, 190, 191, 213, 234, 249, 260, 287, 297, 305, 332, 774, 780, 811

Science and technology
- are at the service of the human person, 112, 122, 125, 835

"Sexual Orientation" (and "lifestyle"), 502, 508

Sexual and Reproductive Health *(See "Health, sexual and reproductive")*

Sexuality, 204-209, 271, 312-313, 314-316, 321, 325-326, 423, 438, 501, 508, 527, 533-534, 674, 729, 731, 757-761, 784, 798-800

- individualistic view of sexuality, 196, 200, 218, 233, 235, 257, 288, 308, 316, 321, 326

Sgreccia, Bishop Elio, 254, 265, 297, 802

Small Island Development States *(See "World Conference on the Sustainable Development of Small Island Developing States")*

Social Development Summit *(See "World Summit for Social Development")*

Social Integration, 365-367, 381, 390, 394, 397, 402, 475, 560

Sodano, Cardinal Angelo, 7, 89, 98, 103, 115, 229, 369, 595, 741, 768, 867, 869, 875, 891

Solidarity, 112, 115-116, 120-121, 124-125, 130-131, 149, 153-154, 170, 191, 265-267, 269, 284, 336-337, 371, 380-381, 387, 391, 409-410, 554-558, 563, 567-568, 596, 620, 724, 745, 864, 869, 912-923

Squicciarini, Archbishop Donato, 161, 163

Stein, Edith, 434-435, 504

Sterilization, 84, 113-114, 194, 228, 231, 257-258, 315, 320, 357, 374, 462, 703, 727-729, 736-737, 746-747, 749, 755, 760, 788, 799-801, 807

- forced sterilization, 462, 477, 501, 509, 516, 518, 703, 752

Stewardship, 111, 118, 121, 124-125, 130, 170, 287, 331

Subsidiarity, Principle of, 242, 423, 660, 665, 738, 744-745, 897-898

T

Tauran, Archbishop Jean-Louis, 9, 151, 156, 234, 251, 497, 621

Technology *(See "Environment, technology's effect on the environment")*

Teheran Human Rights Conference, 151, 157, 249, 254, 278, 288, 474

Trujillo, Cardinal Alfonso López, 85-86, 92-94, 234, 238, 253, 688, 757, 764, 768, 802

U

Unemployment, 134, 156, 366, 393-394, 402, 460, 464, 495, 707, 718, 889, 937

- one of the most serious threats to family life, 665

UNCED (United Nations Conference on Environment and Development); *(See also "Rio+5")*, 105-134

UNDP (United Nations Development Programme), 74, 150, 247, 889, 895, 909, 917, 919

UNFP/UNFPA (United Nations Population Fund), 74, 126, 190-191, 230, 231, 234, 269, 297, 328, 353, 354, 781, 889

UNESCO (United Nations Educational, Scientific and Cultural Organization), 10, 87, 90, 559, 561, 664

UNICEF (United Nations Children's Fund) *(See also "ICPD, UNICEF Follow-up to the ICPD"; Women, Fourth World Conference on Women, UNICEF Follow up to the Fourth World Conference on Women")*, 52-54, 57, 61, 64-65, 73-75, 86-87, 93-94, 100, 103, 339, 353-354, 545-548, 891, 915

UNHCR (United Nations High Commissioner for Refugees) *(See also "Refugees"; "Women, refugee women")*, 9

Urbanization *(See "Human Settlements, urbanization")*

V

Violence, Domestic *(See "Domestic*

Violence"; See also "Women, violence towards women")

W

WFP (World Food Programme), 946

WHO (World Health Organization), 10, 303-304, 307, 329, 501, 506, 595, 724, 757, 816, 855-856, 859, 867

Women *(See also "Women, Fourth World Conference on Women"; See also "John Paul II: Letter to Women, Messages for World Day of Peace 1995, World Migration Day 1995, World Communications Day 1996; "Motherhood"; "Poverty")*
- commercialization of the woman's body, 760

- (women) and peace/women as educators of peace, 518

- complementarity and reciprocity of woman and man *(See also "Women, diversity of roles [between women and men]")*, 195, 242, 420, 438, 442-443, 447, 454, 463, 476, 480, 504, 516, 517, 536, 632, 638, 701, 703, 796, 823, 834, 836-837, 861

- diversity of roles [between women and men] *(See also "Women, complementarity and reciprocity of woman and man")*, 536, 836

- (and) education; urgent need for basic education/women and education, 541

- eliminating every form of discrimination, 456

- empowerment of women, 319, 475

- equal in dignity to men, 7, 195, 334, 420, 457, 533, 632, 732, 751

- "feminine genius", 217, 440-441, 443, 446, 449, 459, 835, 837, 845, 847

- (women's) freedom of conscience and religion/spiritual dimensions of a woman's life, 482, 496, 498, 511

- genital mutilation, 509, 516

- Holy See endeavours in favour of women, 464

- (women and) illiteracy, 332-333, 402, 426, 458, 464, 484, 494, 506, 526

irreplaceable role of women in the family *(See also "Motherhood")*, 16, 333, 420, 423, 458, 471, 500

- manipulation of women's image in industry and in the advertising 489, 496, 1, 469, 477, 481,

- media: mod promoting the r forum for society *(See: "Jf women in Pope: World Con Paul II, Day, 1996") cations*

- participation in public (economic, social, political);

- (women as) participants in the life of the Church, 449

- pornography *(See "Pornography"; See also "Women, manipulation of women's image in the media and in the advertising industry")*

- prenatal sex selection/abortion of the unborn girl child/infanticide, 473, 509

- prostitution *(See "Prostitution")*

- refugee women, 469, 452

- right of women to have access to land, 600, 944

Index 959

- role of women in combating hunger and fostering development *(See "Hunger: role of women in combating hunger")*

- rural women, 472, 484, 488

- status of women and children/Commission on the Status of Women, 74, 194, 255, 333-334, 435, 463, 467, 471, 484, 491, 493, 497, 849-850, 853-854, 889, 910

- (women as) "teachers of peace" *(See also "John Paul II, World Day of Peace Message, 1995",* 365, 421, 430, 432, 433, 499, 821-828

- trafficking of women and girls, 372, 472, 529

- violence toward women *(See also "Domestic Violence,")*, 461-462, 457-458, 476, 529, 453, 498, 500, 505-506, 481, 485, 528-529, 531, 534, 509, 542

- effects of persecution and armed conflicts on women/in civil and international conflicts *(See also "Rape")*, 499, 542

- women's liberation, 531, 536, 539, 833

World Conference on Human Rights, 135-164

World Conference on Human Settlements, Second *(See "Human Settlements, Second World Conference on Human Settlements")*

World Conference on Natural Disaster Reduction, 173-178

World Conference on the Sustainable Development of Small Island Developing States, 165-172

World Food Programme, 946

World Food Summit *(See also "Hunger")* 587-602

Women, Fourth World Conference on Women, 413-548

UNICEF Follow-up to the Fourth World Conference on Women, 545-548

- UNICEF Follow-up to the ICPD, 352, 356

World Summit for Children, 39-104

World Summit for Social Development *(See also "Poverty"; "Unemployment"; "Social Integration")*, 359-412

X

Y
Youth/young people *(See "Adolescents")*

Z